FIFTH EDITION

Criminal LAW in Canada

Cases, Questions & the Code

SIMON N. VERDUN-JONES

School of Criminology
Simon Fraser University

NELSON EDUCAT

NELSON / EDUCATION

Criminal Law in Canada: Cases,
Questions, and the Code, Fifth Edition
by Simon N. Verdun-Jones

Vice President,
Editorial Director:
Evelyn Veitch

Editor-in-Chief,
Higher Education:
Anne Williams

Senior Acquisitions Editor:
Lenore Taylor-Atkins

Senior Marketing Manager:
David Tonen

Developmental Editor:
Caroline Winter

Production Service:
KnowledgeWorks Global Ltd.

Copy Editor:
Elizabeth Phinney

Proofreader:
Monikandan

Indexer:
Diane Witt

Manufacturing Manager:
Joanne McNeil

Design Director:
Ken Phipps

Managing Designer:
Franca Amore

Interior Design:
Tammy Gay

Cover Design:
Carianne Sheriff

Cover Image:
Jacinthe Tétrault, Open Studio

Compositor:
KnowledgeWorks Global Ltd.

Printer:
Edwards Brothers

Library and Archives Canada
Cataloguing in Publication

Verdun-Jones, Simon N. (Simon
Nicholas), 1947-
    Criminal law in Canada : cases,
questions, and the code / Simon
Verdun-Jones. — 5th ed.

Includes bibliographical references
and indexes.
ISBN 978-0-17-650172-3

1. Criminal law—Canada—
Textbooks. 2. Criminal
law—Canada—Cases. I. Title.

KE8809.V47 2010   345.71
C2009-906232-1
KF9220.ZA2V47 2010

ISBN-13: 978-0-17-650172-3
ISBN-10: 0-17-650172-X

All legal cases quoted in this textbook except for *Tesar* can be found in *Canadian Criminal Cases* (Canada Law Book), *Supreme Court Reports* (Canadian Government Publishing), and/or on www.CANLII.org. The *Tesar* case can be accessed through QuickLaw at http://www.lexisnexis.ca/en/quicklaw/ (LexisNexis Canada Inc.).

In Memoriam, Richard V. Ericson (1948–2007)
"But if the while I think on thee, dear friend,
All losses are restored, and sorrows end."
William Shakespeare, *Sonnet 30*

BRIEF CONTENTS

CONTENTS

CHAPTER 11
Necessity and Duress: Two Excuses
Recognized by the Courts as Defences to
a Criminal Charge   272

CHAPTER 12
Self-Defence and Defence of Property   290

APPENDIX I
A Brief Note on the Canadian Criminal Court
System   309

APPENDIX II
A Brief Guide to Law Reports   311

APPENDIX III
Using the Internet to Expand Your Knowledge
of the Criminal Law and to Conduct Basic
Legal Research   313

PREFACE FOR INSTRUCTORS

The previous editions of this book owed a great deal to the author's extensive experience in the challenging task of teaching criminal law to students who, for the most part, did not intend to enter the legal profession. This book is designed to meet the very specific needs of these particular students. Law school textbooks were not appropriate because the depth of their coverage went far beyond the requirements of such students. Paradoxically, other criminal law textbooks in Canada, although specifically written for non-lawyers, were far too general in their approach and did not provide enough details about the law for these particular students. Indeed, many of these students will be required to acquire a broad understanding of criminal law in order to carry out their future duties in various professions related to the criminal justice system (probation, police, and parole officers, court workers, forensic mental health professionals, etc.). As a consequence, it was felt that a different kind of criminal law textbook was needed for non-law students in Canada. It is hoped that *Criminal Law in Canada* successfully meets the requirements of these students.

One of the most effective methods of teaching criminal law to criminology, criminal justice, or law and security students is the *case-oriented approach*, in which the student is encouraged to study not only the general principles of criminal law but also the specific details of decided cases. By combining the study of general principles with a close analysis of specific cases, students learn to apply these principles of criminal law to concrete, factual situations that arise in everyday life or to situations that they may encounter in their professional lives. This book unequivocally adopts the case-oriented approach to the study of criminal law. Individual decided cases are discussed in considerable detail, and there are numerous extracts from the opinions of judges. It is hoped that this approach will more adequately meet the needs of students who seek to acquire a working knowledge of Canadian criminal law and render the study of law somewhat more palatable. Indeed, reading real-life "stories" should be an inherently appealing task for those students who are seeking

employment in the criminal justice system, or in closely related areas (such as forensic mental health).

As part of the case-oriented approach, a number of study questions have been included at the end of each chapter. These are specifically designed to encourage students to test the extent to which they have absorbed the major principles of law covered in each substantive chapter. However, it is important to recognize that the questions are not intended to be particularly complex or difficult; if they were, they would not serve the function of permitting the average student to test his or her understanding of the major principles covered in the chapter. In the author's experience, answering the study questions is a necessary first step in the student's assimilation of the principles of criminal law and should be followed by more complex problem-solving exercises that draw together a number of different topics and encourage the student to see the criminal law as a whole rather than as a series of separate compartments. It usually takes a few weeks before students are ready to tackle these more complex exercises; instructors might wish to delay their use until students have completed at least the first three chapters of the book.

The fourth edition of *Criminal Law in Canada* contained a number of significant changes to the basic structure of the textbook. The current (fifth) edition has left this revised structure in place; the major goal of this latest edition has been to ensure that the most recent case law and legislative changes have been incorporated into the text. It is noteworthy that, prior to the preparation of earlier editions, the author was faced with a steady stream of major decisions by the Supreme Court of Canada in the field of Criminal Law. However, since the fourth edition was published in 2007, the strength of that stream has been somewhat reduced. Among the recent Supreme Court decisions that have been added to the fifth addition are *Ontario (Attorney General) v. Chatterjee* (2009) and *Ferguson* (2008), which perhaps reflect an increasing reluctance to set aside legislation on constitutional grounds; *Turningrobe* (2008), which examines the extent to which the impact of alcohol should be considered when an individual is charged with first degree murder; *Beatty* (2008), which includes a definitive review of the *actus reus* and *mens rea* elements of the offence of dangerous driving; *Lévis (Ville) v. Tétreault* (2006), which definitively recognizes the validity of the defence of officially induced error; *Déry* (2006), which conclusively rejects the possibility of an offence of attempting to conspire; *Daley* (2007), which furnishes an authoritative overview of the status of intoxication as a defence to a criminal charge; and *McKay* (2007), which offers some important observations on the power of householders to use force to remove trespassers from their premises. In order to provide readers with a more profound understanding of the manner in which the criminal law deals with contemporary situations that occur within Canada, a significant number of recent decisions by provincial and territorial courts of appeal have also been included in the fifth edition.

Student should be encouraged to take full advantage of the various additional features contained in the textbook. The extensive glossary should prove to be of great assistance to beginning students who are struggling to come to grips with new terms in a completely new area of academic inquiry. The brief guide to law reports and the very concise overview of Canadian criminal courts assist students to understand the context in which criminal law is developed, without encumbering them with excessive details. Appendix III, which provides a very comprehensive introduction to the use of the Internet and commercial electronic legal data bases, should prove to be a valuable aid to students who wish to develop some basic skills in legal research.

The author would be most interested to hear from instructors how their students react to this book and how it may be improved as a teaching instrument. It is hoped that instructors will consider using the companion volume to this textbook—Simon Verdun-Jones's *Canadian Criminal Cases: Selected Highlights*, 2nd ed. (2007). The author has found that students' comprehension of the principles discussed in the textbook is greatly enhanced when they read a limited number of edited cases. This casebook contains 43 edited decisions of the Supreme Court of Canada, strictly limited in length in order to maintain student interest and facilitate the process of learning Canadian criminal law.

The revised *Instructor's Manual*, which accompanies the fifth edition of *Criminal Law in Canada*, contains a number of features that should prove to be of considerable assistance to instructors. In addition to summaries of the textbook chapters, the *Manual* includes banks of multiple-choice, short-answer, and essay questions. It also includes class assignments, role-playing games, Internet exercises, and discussion questions.

PREFACE FOR STUDENTS

At the beginning of the classic movie *The Paper Chase* (1973), Professor Kingsfield (portrayed by Oscar-winning actor John Houseman) addresses the first-year class at a distinguished American law school. The imposing professor says something along the following lines: "The study of law is a subject that is new and unfamiliar to most of you. You enter law school with a skull full of mush, and you leave thinking like a lawyer." No doubt, Professor Kingsfield's speech captures the popular view that studying law is something completely different from anything the average citizen has ever done before and that only dedicated law students can possibly unravel its dark mysteries. The layperson tends to be somewhat intimidated by the abstruse language used by lawyers, and therefore the study of law often assumes Herculean proportions for those who have no ambitions to enter the legal profession. It is hoped that this book will satisfy the reader that such perceptions of the nature of legal studies are greatly exaggerated. There is no reason why the study of law should not be straightforward, rewarding, and even enjoyable.

The book makes considerable use of the *case method* of studying law. In other words, it seeks to discuss the general principles underlying Canadian criminal law in the context of specific cases decided by the courts. Each chapter contains not only a statement of the relevant principles of law but also a discussion of the facts of decided cases and numerous extracts from the judgments of the courts. This case-oriented approach is intended to equip the reader to apply the general principles of Canadian criminal law to the kinds of concrete factual situations one may encounter in everyday life or read about in the newspaper.

Provided the reader progresses, step by step, through the book, there should be no difficulty in understanding the basic concepts that underlie Canadian criminal law. It is hoped that each chapter of the book will gradually increase the reader's knowledge of the basic principles of Canadian criminal law so that, by the end of the book, all the "pieces of the puzzle" will fit neatly together in the reader's mind. Provided the reader is patient and thorough, the study of criminal law should prove to be a rewarding challenge that need arouse none of the fears so frequently associated with it.

The book includes a number of devices to assist the reader in the "digestion" of the material presented. At the end of each chapter, there is a series of study questions that have been designed to ensure that the reader has absorbed the major points in the author's presentation of the relevant legal principles. It is strongly recommended that the reader attempt to answer these questions before proceeding to a new chapter. There is also an extensive glossary that will facilitate the reader's understanding of the major technical terms used in the book. Furthermore, there are three appendixes that provide valuable background information. Appendix I presents a brief overview of the Canadian criminal court system; Appendix II contains a concise introduction to the use of law reports; and Appendix III identifies and describes a number of key websites as well as commercial electronic legal data bases that readers should find of great value in pursuit of their own independent legal research. The instantaneous availability of legal resources on the Internet and through access to commercial electronic data bases provides every student with remarkable opportunities to explore important cases decided by the courts, significant legislation enacted by Parliament and other legislative bodies, as well as academic analysis of many issues relating to criminal law.

Finally, readers are strongly urged to supplement their study of this book with an in-depth exploration of some of the leading criminal cases that have been decided by Canadian courts. A closer study of some of the critical cases that have helped to shape the contemporary body of Canadian criminal law will certainly add new—and valuable—dimensions to the task of understanding the vital issues that confront Canadian courts on an ongoing basis. To this end, readers might wish to consider obtaining the companion volume to this book: Simon Verdun-Jones, *Canadian Criminal Cases: Selected Highlights*, 2nd ed. (2007). This casebook contains 43 key decisions of the Supreme Court of Canada in the field of criminal law. These cases have been extensively edited so that the reader will be able to grasp the essential elements of each of the Supreme Court's judgments within just a few pages of text.

ACKNOWLEDGMENTS

The first edition of this book was the offspring of a distance education course that I prepared for Simon Fraser University in the mid-1980s. At that time, my colleague and friend, Karlene Faith, strongly encouraged me to write a textbook based on some of the course materials. Karlene kindly gave me the benefit of her invaluable expertise as an effective communicator with students as I attempted to render the criminal law accessible to readers who, for the most part, found law to be a daunting area of study. I gratefully acknowledge her salient role in the genesis of this book.

I owe a tremendous debt to the many students at Simon Fraser University who have studied criminal law with me and have exchanged their views on practically every aspect of the book. Their enthusiasm and support have made my role thoroughly worthwhile, and their constructive criticisms have greatly assisted me in the preparation of the various editions of this book. In addition, I am most grateful to my colleagues at the School of Criminology who have contributed directly or indirectly to so many aspects of the fifth edition of this book—particularly, Vanessa Andreatti, Neil Boyd, Johann Brink, Ray Corrado, Liz Elliott, Lauren Freedman, Margaret Jackson, Richard Konarski, Jaclyn Knox, Michelle Lawrence, Jamie Livingston, John Lowman, Patrick Lussier, David MacAlister, Neil Madu, Tamara O'Doherty, Rick Parent, Danijel Ristic; Kate Rossiter, Ron Roesch, Petra Vidovic, John Whatley, and Vladimir Zaychenko. I also wish to acknowledge the valuable technical assistance and support provided so generously by Roxanne Jantzi, Donna Robertson, and Malcolm Toms.

A very special debt of gratitude is owed to Elizabeth Carefoot and Greg Holoboff, who created the book's imaginative cartoons. Their remarkable ability to highlight important issues in a perceptive and humorous manner is a source of real amazement to me.

Finally, I wish to express my profound thanks to the accomplished and highly supportive editorial team at Nelson Education. Particular recognition is owing to Lenore Taylor-Atkins, senior acquisitions editor; Caroline Winter, developmental editor; and David Tonen, senior marketing manager. The expert advice and patient assistance of these members of the team are deeply appreciated. A special debt of gratitude is also owed to Elizabeth Phinney, the copy editor, whose great diligence and expertise rendered the rigorous editing process a remarkably painless and rewarding experience. I would like as well to recognize the important contributions made by Rose James, the proofreader.

CHAPTER ONE

INTRODUCTION TO CANADIAN CRIMINAL LAW

OVERVIEW

This chapter examines the following:

1. the definition of a crime in Canada;
2. the classification of crimes in Canada into three categories: indictable, summary conviction, or "hybrid" (dual) offences;
3. the difference between "true crimes" and "regulatory offences";
4. the distinction between private law and public law;
5. the categorization of criminal law as a form of public law;
6. the sources of criminal law: legislation and judicial decisions;
7. the exclusive authority of Parliament to enact legislation concerning "criminal law and the procedures relating to criminal matters";
8. the major criminal law *statutes*: the Criminal Code, the Controlled Drugs and Substances Act, and the Youth Criminal Justice Act;
9. the nature and scope of the federal criminal law power;
10. the nature of quasi-criminal law (regulatory offences) and the ability of provinces/territories to enforce their regulatory legislation by means of penalties;
11. the invalidity of provincial/territorial legislation that impinges on Parliament's exclusive jurisdiction to enact criminal law;
12. the extent to which judicial decisions constitute a source of criminal law;
13. the impact of the *Canadian Charter of Rights and Freedoms* on the field of criminal law;
14. the circumstances in which the courts may strike down legislation as being invalid under the *Charter*;
15. the importance of section 1 of the *Charter* as a means of justifying an infringement of a *Charter* right or freedom as being a "reasonable limit in a free and democratic society";
16. the so-called *Oakes* test devised by the Supreme Court of Canada as a means of giving guidance to the courts when they are called upon, under section 1 of the *Charter*, to balance the rights of the individual against those of society as a whole; and
17. the extent to which the courts consider striking down legislation to be a measure of last resort in their application of section 1 of the *Charter*.

WHAT IS CRIMINAL LAW?

THE DEFINITION OF CRIME IN CANADA

Before embarking on an analysis of criminal law, it is necessary to define the legal concept of a crime and to explain how crimes are classified within the Canadian criminal justice system. It is essential to recognize the importance of legal definitions and categories because they have enormously practical consequences. For example, the legal definition of a crime is a matter of critical significance because only the Parliament of Canada has the jurisdiction under the *Constitution Act, 1867* to enact **criminal law** and thereby create crimes; this jurisdiction is known as the **federal criminal law power**. Similarly, the manner in which individual crimes are categorized determines how they are tried and the penalties that may be imposed on conviction.

In Canada, a **crime** consists of two major elements:

1. conduct that is prohibited because it is considered to have an "evil or injurious or undesirable effect upon the public"[1]; and
2. a penalty that may be imposed when the prohibition is violated.

The conduct that is prohibited may include not only actions but also a failure to act when there is a legally imposed duty to take action. The penalty may range from a fine to a sentence of imprisonment.

In Canada, crimes are classified into three categories:

1. summary conviction offences;
2. indictable offences; and
3. hybrid (or dual) offences, which, at the discretion of the Crown prosecutor, may be tried either by indictment or by summary conviction procedures.

Summary conviction offences may be tried only before a provincial/territorial court judge, and the maximum penalty is normally a fine of $2000 or a sentence of six months in prison or both. "Summary" refers to the fact that these offences are tried rapidly within the provincial/territorial court and without any complex procedures. Examples of summary conviction offences are falsifying an employment record,

wilfully doing an indecent act in public, being nude in a public place without lawful excuse, causing a disturbance in a public place, soliciting in a public place, and taking a motor vehicle without consent.

Indictable offences are more serious in nature and are punishable by more severe sentences (in some cases, life imprisonment). The indictment is the formal document that sets out the charge(s) against the **accused** person and is signed by the attorney general or his or her agent. Unlike summary conviction offences, indictable offences may be tried by more than one court procedure, depending on the seriousness of the offence concerned. Some serious indictable offences, such as murder, may be tried only by a superior court judge sitting with a jury, while some less serious indictable offences may be tried only by a provincial/territorial court judge without a jury. However, in most cases, a person charged with an indictable offence may elect to be tried by a provincial/territorial court judge, a superior court judge sitting alone, or a superior court judge sitting with a jury. In most cases, individuals charged with an indictable offence have the right to a preliminary inquiry before a provincial/territorial court judge, who will decide whether there is "sufficient evidence" to put the accused person on trial. Examples of indictable offences are murder, manslaughter, sexual assault with a weapon, aggravated sexual assault, robbery, theft over $5000, and breaking and entering.

Most offences in Canada's *Criminal Code* are **hybrid (or dual) offences**. There are very few *Criminal Code* offences that may be tried only by summary conviction procedures, although most hybrid (or dual) offences are, in practice, tried by summary conviction procedures. Examples of hybrid (or dual) offences are assault, assaulting a peace officer, sexual assault, unlawful imprisonment, theft under $5000, fraud under $5000, and failing to comply with a probation order.

TRUE CRIMES AND REGULATORY OFFENCES

A noteworthy distinction that must be drawn before one embarks on a study of criminal law is the distinction between **true crimes** and **regulatory offences**. The courts treat these two types of offence in a significantly different manner, and the consequences for a person convicted of one of the two types of offence differ significantly in terms of the severity of the penalties that may be imposed

---

[1] The phrase "evil or injurious or undesirable effect upon the public" was coined by Justice Rand in the *Margarine Reference* case (1949), which is discussed later in this chapter.

and the degree of stigma associated with a finding of guilt. Justice Cory of the Supreme Court articulated the nature of the distinction between true crimes and regulatory offences in his judgment in *Wholesale Travel Group Inc.* (1991):

> Acts or actions are criminal when they constitute conduct that is, in itself, so abhorrent to the basic values of society that it ought to be prohibited completely. Murder, sexual assault, fraud, robbery and theft are all so repugnant to society that they are universally recognized as crimes. At the same time, some conduct is prohibited, not because it is inherently wrongful, but because unregulated activity would result in dangerous conditions being imposed upon members of society, especially those who are particularly vulnerable.

> The objective of regulatory legislation is to protect the public or broad segments of the public (such as employees, consumers and motorists, to name but a few) from the potentially adverse effects of otherwise lawful activity. Regulatory legislation involves a shift of emphasis from the protection of individual interests and the deterrence and punishment of acts involving moral fault to the protection of public and societal interests. While criminal offences are usually designed to condemn and punish past, inherently wrongful conduct, regulatory measures are generally directed to the prevention of future harm through the enforcement of minimum standards of conduct and care.

Regulatory offences arise under both federal and provincial/territorial legislation and deal with such diverse matters as the maintenance of the quality of meat sold to the public, the regulation of the packaging of food products, the establishment of rigorous standards concerning the weights and measures used by retailers, the regulation and control of pollution, the control of misleading advertising, and the establishment and maintenance of a regime of traffic regulation. Indeed, as Justice Cory stated in *Wholesale Travel Group Inc.* (1991), "Regulatory measures are the primary mechanisms employed by governments in Canada to implement public policy objectives," and "it is through regulatory legislation that the community seeks to implement its larger objectives and to govern itself and the conduct of its members." He went on to say that

> [i]t is difficult to think of an aspect of our lives that is not regulated for our benefit and for the protection of society as a whole. From cradle to grave, we are protected by regulations; they apply to the doctors attending our entry into this world and to the morticians present at our departure. Every day, from waking to sleeping, we profit from regulatory measures which we often take for granted. On rising, we use various forms of energy whose safe distribution and use are governed by regulation. The trains, buses and other vehicles that get us to work are regulated for our safety. The food we eat and the beverages we drink are subject to regulation for the protection of our health.

> In short, regulation is absolutely essential for our protection and well being as individuals, and for the effective functioning of society. It is properly present throughout our lives. The more complex the activity, the greater the need for and the greater our reliance upon regulation and its enforcement.... Of necessity, society relies on government regulation for its safety.

One of the most significant aspects of the distinction between true crimes and regulatory offences is to be found in the differing concepts of fault that underlie the two categories of prohibited conduct. Conviction of a true crime (such as murder or robbery) necessarily involves a judgment that the offender has seriously infringed basic community values and is, therefore, considered to be morally culpable for his or her actions. In contrast, conviction of a regulatory offence (such as accidentally mislabelling a food item) may involve very little (if any) moral culpability on the part of the offender. Similarly, the penalties that may be imposed following conviction of a true crime are generally far more severe than those that may imposed when a person has been found guilty of a regulatory offence.

In brief, true crimes are acts that are generally considered to be inherently wrong by the majority of Canadians (e.g., murder, burglary, and sexual assault). On the other hand, regulatory offences are directed toward the control of activities that are considered by the majority of Canadians to be inherently lawful (selling food, driving a motor vehicle, or placing an advertisement in the local newspaper). Business, trade, and industry need to be regulated for the benefit of society as a whole, and penalties may be imposed for breach of the requirements of the regulatory regime. For example, whether Canadians should drive on the left or right side of the road does not raise a question of fundamental values. However, in order to avoid chaos, each country has to make a choice as to which side of the road its motorists should use: it would be absurd to permit individual motorists to make that choice for themselves.

In other words, although driving is an inherently legitimate activity, there has to be a regulatory regime in order to protect the interests of all those individuals who use the highways. The penalties associated with regulatory offences are directed not at the underlying activities themselves but rather at breaches of the regulatory regime that ensures the orderly and safe conduct of those activities.

In Chapter 6, we shall examine regulatory offences in more depth and demonstrate that the prosecution (the Crown) has been granted the benefit of certain advantages that render it easier to obtain a conviction in relation to a regulatory offence than in relation to a true crime. Most significantly, when an accused person is charged with a true crime, the general rule is that the Crown must prove all the elements of the offence beyond a reasonable doubt. However, when the charge in question concerns a regulatory offence, the Crown merely has to prove that the accused person committed the act prohibited by the legislation in question: once the commission of the prohibited act has been established, then the accused person must prove, on the balance of probabilities, that he or she was not negligent.

Since regulatory offences differ significantly from true crimes, they are frequently characterized as constituting a body of **quasi-criminal law.** This term means that the body of regulatory offences closely resembles criminal law but nevertheless lacks two key characteristics of criminal law—namely, the prohibition of conduct that is regarded as inherently wrong and the potential severity of the sentences that may be imposed.[2] Later in this chapter, we shall explore the implications of the concept of quasi-criminal law for the field of constitutional law in Canada.

CRIMINAL LAW AS A FORM OF PUBLIC LAW

Law may generally be defined as the collection of rules and principles that govern the affairs of a particular society and that are enforced by a formal system of control (courts, police, etc.). It is usual to divide law into two parts: public law and private law.

Public law is concerned with issues that affect the interests of the entire society. Constitutional law deals with the allocation of powers between the various

provinces/territories of Canada and the various levels of government (legislature, courts, and executive). It also deals with the relationship between the state and individual citizens. Administrative law defines the powers, and regulates the activities, of government agencies, such as the Immigration and Refugee Board and the Canadian Radio-Television and Telecommunications Commission. Criminal law is also considered to be part of public law because the commission of a crime is treated as a wrong against society as a whole and it is the Crown that prosecutes criminal cases on behalf of all Canadians; indeed, all criminal cases are catalogued as "Regina" (the Queen) versus the accused person concerned.

Private law is concerned with the regulation of the relationships that exist among individual members of society. It includes the legal rules and principles that apply to the ownership of property, contracts, torts (injuries inflicted on another individual's person or damage caused to the individual's property), and the duties of spouses and other family members toward one another. The resolution of private disputes may be sought through the commencement of a "civil suit" in the appropriate court.

THE SOURCES OF CRIMINAL LAW IN CANADA

Perhaps the most basic question we can raise in relation to the Canadian criminal law is, "Where does it come from?" The answer is that there are two **primary sources of law** (or main **sources of criminal law**): (i) legislation and (ii) judicial decisions that either interpret such legislation or state the "common law."

FEDERAL LEGISLATION

Since Canada is a federal state, legislation may be enacted by both the Parliament of Canada and the provincial or territorial legislatures. However, under the Canadian *Constitution*, there is a distribution of legislative powers between the federal and provincial or territorial levels of government. Which level of government has the power to enact criminal law? It is clear that criminal law is a subject that falls within the exclusive jurisdiction of the Parliament of Canada. Indeed, by virtue of section 91(27) of the *British North America Act, 1867* (renamed the *Constitution Act, 1867* in 1982), the federal Parliament has exclusive jurisdiction in the field of "criminal law and the procedures relating to criminal matters."

---

[2] The word "**quasi**" means "seeming," "not real," or "halfway."

Just how extensive is the scope of the criminal law power under section 91(27) of the *Constitution Act*? As we have seen, two essential characteristics of a crime are a *prohibition* of certain conduct and an accompanying *penalty* for violating that prohibition. Does that mean that the Canadian Parliament can pass legislation on any issue that it chooses and justify it on the basis that, because it contains both a prohibition and penalty, it must be criminal law? If this were the case, there would be absolutely no limits on the scope of the criminal law power. In fact, the Supreme Court of Canada has stated clearly that there must be a third factor, in addition to a prohibition and a penalty, in order for legislation to be recognized as being a genuine exercise of the criminal law power. What is this third factor?

In the famous *Margarine Reference* case (1949), Justice Rand, of the Supreme Court of Canada, argued that the additional factor is the requirement that the prohibition and penalty contained in the legislation are directed toward a "public evil" or some behaviour that is having an injurious effect upon the Canadian public:

> A crime is an act which the law, with appropriate penal sanctions, forbids; but as prohibitions are not enacted in a vacuum, we can properly look for some evil or injurious or undesirable effect upon the public against which the law is directed. That effect may be in relation to social, economic or political interests; and the legislature has had in mind to suppress the evil or to safeguard the interest threatened.

Justice Rand asserted that, if the Parliament of Canada chooses to prohibit certain conduct under the criminal law power, then this prohibition must be enacted "with a view to *a public purpose which can support it as being in relation to criminal law....*" The public purposes that would be included in this category are "public peace, order, security, health, [and] morality," although Justice Rand acknowledged that this is not an exclusive list.

For example, in *Hydro-Québec* (1997), the Supreme Court of Canada considered the significant question of whether the federal criminal law power could be used to punish those who engage in serious acts of environmental pollution. The case involved the alleged dumping of highly toxic polychlorinated biphenyls (PCBs) into a Quebec river. Charges were laid under the authority of the *Canadian Environmental Protection Act*, R.S.C. 1985, c. 16. However, it was contended by the accused that the relevant provisions of the Act were unconstitutional because they did not

Regulation of firearms falls within the federal criminal law power.

represent a valid exercise of the federal criminal law power. It is noteworthy that the Supreme Court held that the offences created by the legislation did fall within the scope of that power. Indeed, Justice La Forest stated—in dramatic terms—that

> ... pollution is an "evil" that Parliament can legitimately seek to suppress. Indeed ... it is a public purpose of superordinate importance; it constitutes one of the major challenges of our time. It would be surprising indeed if Parliament could not exercise its plenary power over criminal law to protect this interest and to suppress the evils associated with it by way of appropriate penal prohibitions.

It is clear that this legislation was deemed to be criminal law because Parliament was unequivocally concerned with the need to safeguard public health from the devastating consequences of toxic pollution.

In this context, it is noteworthy that the Supreme Court of Canada upheld the validity of amendments made to the *Criminal Code* by the *Firearms Act*, S.C. 1995, c. 39. This legislation required all gun owners to obtain licences and to register all firearms. There are approximately 2 million gun owners and some 7 million guns in Canada; hence, this legislation has far-reaching effects. The Government of Alberta launched a constitutional challenge, claiming that the new firearms legislation represented an intrusion into the provinces' jurisdiction to regulate private property and that it could not be considered a legitimate exercise of Parliament's criminal law power under the *Constitution Act, 1867*. However, a unanimous Supreme Court of Canada rejected this contention in *Reference re Firearms Act (Canada)* (2000). The Court stated that

> [w]e conclude that the gun control law comes within Parliament's jurisdiction over criminal law. The law in "pith and substance" is directed to enhancing

public safety by controlling access to firearms through prohibitions and regulations. This brings it under the federal criminal law power. While the law has regulatory aspects, they are secondary to its primary criminal law purpose. The intrusion of the law into the provincial jurisdiction over property and civil rights is not so excessive as to upset the balance of federalism.

The Supreme Court emphasized that the evil or harm that Parliament was seeking to suppress or reduce consisted of both the potential misuse of firearms by all those who have them in their possession and the ability of criminals to acquire firearms and to use them in the commission of violent crimes:

> By requiring everyone to register their guns, Parliament seeks to reduce misuse by everyone and curtail the ability of criminals to acquire firearms. Where criminals have acquired guns and used them in the commission of offences, the registration system seeks to make those guns more traceable.

Similarly, in *R. v. Malmo-Levine; R. v. Caine* (2003), the Supreme Court of Canada ruled that Parliament had the authority, by virtue of its criminal law power, to prohibit the simple possession of marijuana. Even though simple possession may be viewed as a "victimless crime," the criminal law power may nevertheless be used to protect the users of marijuana from self-inflicted harm. Indeed, Justices Gonthier and Binnie stated that the "evil or injurious or undesirable effect" that Parliament sought to address is "the harm attributed to the non-medical use of marihuana." The Court, therefore, upheld the constitutional validity of the relevant provisions of the *Narcotic Control Act*, R.S.C. 1985, c. N-1.[3] According to Justices Gonthier and Binnie,

> The purpose of the NCA fits within the criminal law power, which includes the protection of vulnerable groups....
> ... The protection of the chronic users identified by the trial judge, and adolescents who may not yet have become chronic users, but who have the potential to do so, is a valid criminal law objective.... In our view, the control of a "psychoactive drug" that "causes alteration of mental function" clearly raises issues of public health and safety, both for the user as well as for those in the broader society affected by his or her conduct.

... The use of marihuana is therefore a proper subject matter for the exercise of the criminal law power.... [I]f there is a reasoned apprehension of harm Parliament is entitled to act, and in our view Parliament is also entitled to act on reasoned apprehension of harm even if on some points "the jury is still out". In light of the concurrent findings of "harm" in the courts below, we therefore confirm that the *Narcotic Control Act* in general, and the scheduling of marihuana in particular, properly fall within Parliament's legislative competence under s. 91(27) of the *Constitution Act, 1867*.

What important pieces of legislation (or statutes) has the Canadian Parliament enacted in the field of criminal law? Undoubtedly, the most significant federal statute, dealing with both the substantive criminal law and the procedural law relating to criminal matters, is the *Criminal Code*, R.S.C. 1985, c. C-46 (first enacted in 1892). **Substantive criminal law** refers to legislation that defines the nature of various criminal offences (such as murder, manslaughter, and theft) and specifies the various legal elements that must be present before a conviction can be entered against an accused person. Similarly, in this context, the term refers to legislation that defines the nature and scope of various defences (such as provocation, duress, and self-defence).

The term **criminal procedure** refers to legislation that specifies the procedures to be followed in the prosecution of a criminal case and defines the nature and scope of the powers of criminal justice officials. For example, as we have already noted, the procedural provisions of the *Criminal Code* classify offences into three categories: indictable offences, offences punishable on summary conviction, and dual (or hybrid) offences. These provisions then specify the manner in which these categories of offences may be tried in court. For example, they specify whether these offences may be tried by a judge sitting alone or by a judge and jury, and indicate whether they may be tried before a judge of the superior court or a judge of the provincial (or territorial) court.

The procedural provisions of the *Criminal Code* are also concerned with the powers that are exercised by criminal justice officials. For example, the *Code* clearly specifies the nature and scope of the powers of the police in relation to the arrest and detention of suspects. Similarly, it also specifies the powers of the courts in relation to such matters as sentencing. In addition to the *Criminal Code*, there are a number of other federal statutes that undoubtedly create "criminal law." These include the *Controlled Drugs*

---

[3] This Act was repealed in 1996. Possession of marijuana is now prohibited by section 4 of the *Controlled Drugs and Substances Act*, S.C. 1996, c. 19 (which came into force on May 14, 1997).

and Substances Act, S.C. 1996, c. 19, the *Crimes against Humanity and War Crimes Act*, S.C. 2000, c. 24, and the *Youth Criminal Justice Act*, S.C. 2002, c. 1.

It should be noted that there are two other significant federal statutes that have an indirect impact upon the criminal law. These are the *Canada Evidence Act*, R.S.C. 1985, c. C-5, and the *Constitution Act, 1982*, as enacted by the *Canada Act 1982* (U.K.), c. 11. The *Canada Evidence Act*, as its name would suggest, is concerned with establishing various rules concerning the introduction of evidence before criminal courts. For example, the Act indicates when a wife or husband may be compelled to give evidence against her or his spouse and indicates in what circumstances the evidence of a child under 14 years of age may be admissible in a criminal trial. The *Constitution Act* is of great significance to both the substantive criminal law and the law of criminal procedure, since Part I of the Act contains the *Canadian Charter of Rights and Freedoms*. The *Charter* is of immense importance since, as we shall shortly see, it permits courts to strike down, and declare invalid, any legislative provisions that infringe upon the fundamental rights and freedoms of Canadians.

QUASI-CRIMINAL LAW: REGULATORY OFFENCES AND THE *CONSTITUTION*

In the preceding section, it was established that the *Constitution Act, 1867* granted the federal Parliament exclusive jurisdiction in the field of criminal law and the procedures relating to criminal matters. At this point, the reader no doubt feels that he or she has a clear grasp of the principle involved. Unfortunately, the situation is rendered considerably more complex by the existence of the body of regulatory offences that we have described as "quasi-criminal law." Under the *Constitution Act, 1867*, the provincial/ territorial legislatures have been granted the power to enact laws in relation to a number of specific matters. For example, section 92 of the Act indicates, *inter alia,* that "property and civil rights in the province" and "generally all matters of a merely local or private nature in the province" fall within the exclusive jurisdiction of the provincial/territorial legislatures. By virtue of judicial interpretation of the various provisions of section 92, it is clear that a number of other critical matters fall within the legislative jurisdiction of the provinces/territories, such as municipal institutions, health, education, highways, liquor control, and hunting and fishing.

Significantly, section 92(15) of the *Constitution Act, 1867* provides that the provincial/territorial legislatures may enforce their laws by "the imposition of punishment by fine, penalty or imprisonment." At this point, the reader will immediately exclaim that the imposition of fines, penalties, or imprisonment looks suspiciously like the apparatus of criminal law. One is compelled to ask whether this means that the *Constitution Act, 1867* is contradicting itself, since criminal law is a matter reserved to the exclusive jurisdiction of the federal Parliament. However, the answer is in the negative because such provincial/territorial legislation is not considered to be "real" criminal law. Instead, lawyers have termed it "quasi-criminal law." Since this type of provincial/territorial legislation is considered to be "quasi" rather than "real" criminal law, it is possible to argue that it does not impinge upon the federal Parliament's exclusive jurisdiction in the field of (real) criminal law.

Cynics will, no doubt, point to the semantic acrobatics involved in the categorization of the provincial/territorial offences as quasi-criminal laws. However, the designation of quasi-criminal law can be very well justified on a pragmatic basis. As mentioned earlier in this chapter, regulatory offences are generally far less serious in nature than the "true crimes" that may be committed against the *Criminal Code* or other federal legislation, such as the *Controlled Drugs and Substances Act*.

Provincial/territorial legislatures may delegate authority to municipalities to enact municipal ordinances or **bylaws**. This municipal "legislation" may also be enforced by the "big stick" of fines or other penalties. Municipal bylaws or ordinances may be considered to fall within the category of quasi-criminal law.

It should be added that regulatory offences may also be found in a broad range of federal statutes (for example, the *Competition Act*, R.S.C. 1985, c. C-34; the *Food and Drugs Act*, R.S.C. 1985, c. F-27; the *Fisheries Act*, R.S.C. 1985, c. F-14; the *Migratory Birds Convention Act*, S.C. 1994, c. 22; the *Motor Vehicle Safety Act*, S.C. 1993, c. 16; the *Nuclear Safety and Control Act*, S.C. 1997, c. 9; the *Plant Protection Act*, S.C. 1990, c. 22; the *Quarantine Act*, S.C. 2005, c. 20; the *Species at Risk Act*, S.C. 2002, c. 29; the *Tobacco Act*, S.C. 1997, c. 13; and the *Trade-Marks Act*, R.S.C. 1985, c. T-13).

Taken together with quasi-criminal offences generated under provincial/territorial and municipal legislation, these federal offences contribute to a vast pool of regulatory law that has become increasingly complex as modern society has developed. Some idea of the vast number of regulatory offences that currently exist in Canada, and are technically considered to be crimes, may be gleaned from a report issued by the Federal Law Reform Commission in 1976. The commission estimated that each Canadian faced some 20 000 offences under federal statutes and a further 20 000 arising under the legislation of each province/ territory; significantly, this estimate does not even attempt to include the large number of municipal offences. However, it is noteworthy that, in *Wholesale Travel Group Inc.* (1991), Justice Cory of the Supreme Court noted that the Law Reform Commission of Canada had estimated that by 1983 the number of regulatory offences, *at the federal level alone*, had climbed to some 97 000! As Justice Cory remarked, "There is every reason to believe that the number of public welfare [or regulatory] offences at both levels of government has continued to increase."

This vast body of regulatory criminal law does not make good bedtime reading for the average citizen. Indeed, even the average lawyer is acquainted with only a fraction of the regulatory offences that currently exist. Nevertheless, as we shall see later in Chapter 9, it is a firm principle of criminal law that "ignorance of the law is no excuse."

PROBLEMS OF JURISDICTION IN THE ENACTMENT OF LEGISLATION

Before leaving the complex area of quasi-criminal law, it is important to remember that the provincial/ territorial legislatures are restricted to the enactment of legislation genuinely falling within the jurisdiction assigned to them under the *Constitution Act, 1867*. More specifically, it is clear that provincial/ territorial legislatures may not encroach upon the exclusive federal jurisdiction to legislate "real" criminal law. Unfortunately, it is often difficult for the courts to determine whether provincial/territorial legislation has strayed beyond the boundaries of the jurisdiction assigned to the provinces/ territories under the *Constitution Act* and whether such legislation is invalid because it has infringed upon the federal Parliament's exclusive criminal law domain. The formidable challenge posed by this task can best be demonstrated through some illustrative cases.

In the *Morgentaler* case (1993), the Supreme Court of Canada was called upon to consider whether the Nova Scotia legislature had encroached upon the federal criminal law power when it enacted legislation that permitted the provincial/territorial government to prohibit the provision of certain medical services, including abortion, in premises other than hospitals. As we shall see later in this chapter, the Supreme Court of Canada ruled, in the *Morgentaler, Smolig and Scott* case (1988), that the abortion provisions of the *Criminal Code* were invalid under the *Charter* and, as a consequence, abortion was no longer prohibited by the criminal law. Dr. Morgentaler subsequently indicated that he intended to establish a free-standing abortion clinic in Halifax. The provincial legislature responded by enacting the *Medical Services Act*, R.S.N.S. 1989, c. 281, which provided that the government could designate certain medical services that must be performed in a hospital and imposed a penalty of a fine between $10 000 and $50 000 on those individuals who performed such services outside a hospital. The provincial government designated nine services under this legislation; one of the services was abortion. Dr. Morgentaler was charged, under the *Medical Services Act*, with performing 14 abortions outside a hospital. The Supreme Court of Canada ultimately accepted Dr. Morgentaler's contention that the legislation was invalid because it encroached upon Parliament's exclusive jurisdiction over criminal law.

Justice Sopinka noted that "it cannot be denied that interdiction of conduct in the interest of public morals was and remains one of the classic ends of our criminal law," and that "it seems clear to me that the present legislation, whose primary purpose is to prohibit abortions except in certain circumstances, treats of a moral issue." He went on to say that the legislation was "in pith and substance" criminal law:

> This legislation deals, by its terms, with a subject historically considered to be part of the criminal law—the prohibition of the performance of abortions with penal consequences. It is thus suspect on its face. Its legal effect partially reproduces that of the now defunct [s. 287] of the *Criminal Code* in so far as both precluded the establishment and operation of free-standing abortion clinics. The primary objective of the legislation was to prohibit abortions outside hospitals as socially undesirable conduct, and any concern with the safety and security of pregnant women or with health care policy, hospitals or the regulation of the medical profession was merely ancillary. This legislation involves the regulation of the place where an abortion may be obtained, not from the viewpoint of health care policy, but from the viewpoint of public wrongs or crimes....

On the other hand, in the case of *Ontario (Attorney General) v. Chatterjee* (2009), the Supreme Court of Canada ruled that the Ontario *Remedies for Organized Crime and Other Unlawful Activities Act, 2001*, S.O. 2001, c. 28 (also known as the *Civil Remedies Act, 2001)*, which authorizes the forfeiture of the proceeds of "unlawful activity," did not encroach on the federal criminal law power and is, therefore, not *ultra vires* (or outside the jurisdiction of) the Ontario legislature.

Robin Chatterjee was stopped by the York Regional Police because his vehicle did not have a front licence plate. A computer search revealed that Chatterjee was in breach of a recognizance (a promise) to reside in Ottawa: therefore, the police officers arrested him and conducted a search of his car. They found about $29 000 in cash as well as an exhaust fan and other objects. The police officers asserted that these items smelled of marijuana, even though no marijuana was actually found. Chatterjee was not charged with any offence in relation to the cash or the other objects but the Attorney General of Ontario applied, under the *Civil Remedies Act*, for the forfeiture of the money which had been seized on the basis that it constituted the "proceeds of unlawful activity" and of the other items because they constituted "instruments of unlawful activity." Chatterjee challenged the constitutionality of the *Civil Remedies Act*, claiming that it infringed upon the federal criminal law power. However, ultimately, the Supreme Court of Canada unanimously upheld the constitutionality of the Ontario legislation.

The Supreme Court rejected Chatterjee's assertion that the forfeiture provisions of the *Civil Remedies Act* were, in reality, criminal law. Instead, the court accepted the argument of the Ontario Attorney General to the effect that the *Civil Remedies Act* constitutes legislation concerning "property and civil rights," which are matters that fall within provincial jurisdiction under section 92(13) of the *Constitution Act*.

In delivering the judgment of the Supreme Court, Justice Binnie noted that the *Civil Remedies Act* had been enacted in order to "deter crime and compensate its victims." He stated:

> The former purpose is broad enough that both the federal government (in relation to criminal law) and the provincial governments (in relation to property and civil rights) can validly pursue it. The latter purpose falls squarely within provincial competence. Crime imposes substantial costs on provincial treasuries. Those costs impact many provincial interests, including health, policing resources, community stability and family welfare. It would be out of step with modern realities to conclude that a province must shoulder the costs to the community of criminal behaviour but cannot use deterrence to suppress it.

Furthermore, the forfeiture proceedings were brought against the seized items, rather than Chatterjee himself. This procedure clearly differs from the quintessential approach of the criminal law, which combines a prohibition with a penalty levied against an individual person. Justice Binnie agreed that

> … forfeiture may have *de facto* punitive effects in some cases, but its dominant purpose is to make crime in general unprofitable, to capture resources tainted by crime so as to make them unavailable to fund future crime and to help compensate private individuals and public institutions for the costs of past crime. These are valid provincial objects.

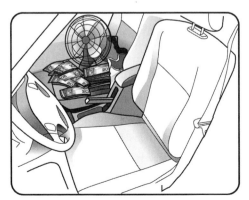

Ontario legislation authorizing the seizure of the "proceeds of unlawful activity" does not encroach on the federal criminal law power.

Deciding whether provincial/territorial legislation should be struck down on the basis that it infringes on the federal criminal law power clearly involves a considerable degree of judicial discretion, and the outcome may be almost impossible to predict with any degree of certainty. Indeed, there may well be some justification for the view that criminal law, like beauty, lies in the eye of the beholder.

JUDICIAL DECISIONS AS A SOURCE OF CRIMINAL LAW

In addition to legislation, such as the *Criminal Code*, a major source of criminal law is the numerous judicial decisions that either interpret criminal legislation or expound the "common law." A significant proportion of this book is concerned with the interpretation of the provisions of the *Criminal Code* by Canadian courts. However, the common law still plays an important role in Canadian criminal jurisprudence. Essentially, **common law** refers to that body of judge-made law that evolved in areas that were not covered by legislation.

Historically, a considerable proportion of English criminal law was developed by judges, who were required to deal with a variety of situations that were not governed by any legislation. Indeed, until relatively recently, much of the English law concerning theft and fraud was developed by judges in this way. One common law offence, which is of particular relevance to present day criminal law in Canada, is **contempt of court**. However, the common law not only expanded the number of offences in the criminal law but also developed special defences that were not covered by any legislation. For example, the Canadian courts have single-handedly developed the law relating to the defence of necessity (a defence that does not appear in the *Criminal Code*); hence, necessity is known as a common law defence.

It should be noted that, since 1954, *with the single exception of the offence of contempt of court*, it has not been possible for a Canadian to be convicted of a common law offence (see section 9 of the *Criminal Code*). However, section 8(3) of the *Criminal Code* preserves any common law "justification," "excuse," or "defence" to a criminal charge "except in so far as they are altered by or are inconsistent with this Act or any other Act of the Parliament of Canada." This provision is particularly significant since it means that common law defences, such as necessity, are still applicable in a Canadian criminal trial. In short, although Canadian judges cannot create any new offences at common law, they may still apply the common law principles relating to certain defences, provided, of course, that these principles are not inconsistent with legislation enacted by the Canadian Parliament.

THE IMPACT OF THE *CANADIAN CHARTER OF RIGHTS AND FREEDOMS* ON THE CRIMINAL LAW IN CANADA

The enactment of the *Canadian Charter of Rights and Freedoms* as part of the *Constitution Act, 1982* heralded a dramatic new era in the relationship between the members of Canada's judiciary, on the one hand, and the elected representatives of Canada's federal Parliament and provincial/territorial legislatures, on the other. As an entrenched bill of rights, the *Charter* empowers judges, in certain circumstances, to declare any piece of legislation to be invalid—and of no force or effect—if the latter infringes upon an individual's protected rights. Canadian judges have demonstrated their willingness to use this awesome power where they believe that it is necessary to do so. Indeed, since 1982, there have been numerous court decisions that have resulted in the judicial nullification of various statutory provisions concerning criminal law.

Perhaps the case that has been most decisive in underlining the potential impact of the *Charter* upon Canadian criminal law is *Morgentaler, Smolig and Scott* (1988), in which the Supreme Court of Canada struck down section 287 of the *Criminal Code*, which regulated the performance of abortions in Canada. Section 287 made abortion a criminal offence unless it was carried out in an accredited hospital after being approved by a therapeutic abortion committee, which had certified that the continuation of the pregnancy "would or would be likely to endanger" the woman's "life or health." Dr. Morgentaler and his associates were charged with conspiracy to procure the miscarriage of female persons contrary to the provisions of section 287. The charges stemmed from their establishment of a free-standing clinic in Toronto to perform abortions on women who had not obtained a certificate from a therapeutic abortion committee.

The Supreme Court ultimately ruled that section 287 of the *Criminal Code* infringed section 7 of the *Charter*, which guarantees the "right to life, liberty and security of the person and the right not to be deprived thereof except in accordance with the principles of fundamental justice." Chief Justice Dickson ruled that section 287 clearly violated the security of the person:

> Forcing a woman, by threat of criminal sanction, to carry a fetus to term unless she meets certain criteria unrelated to her own priorities and aspirations, is a profound interference with a woman's body and thus a violation of security of the person.

Such a violation of personal security cannot be permitted under the provisions of the *Charter* unless it is undertaken in accordance with the principles of fundamental justice. The Supreme Court held that the violation of personal security, imposed by section 287, did not meet these critical requirements of the *Charter*. In the view of the Court, the system of therapeutic abortion committees was "manifestly unfair" because many Canadian women did not have access to such a committee unless they were willing to travel great distances at substantial expense and considerable personal inconvenience. It was also pointed out that the delays caused by the committee system actually put women's physical and mental health at greater risk.

The Court also ruled that section 287 of the *Code* could not be salvaged by section 1 of the *Charter*, which states that the rights and freedoms set out in the *Charter* are guaranteed "subject only to such reasonable limits prescribed by law as can be demonstrably justified in a free and democratic society." Section 287 was not a reasonable limitation on the right to personal security because the administrative structure of the therapeutic abortion committees was both arbitrary and unfair, and certain of the rules governing the access to these committees were unnecessary in light of Parliament's objectives of protecting the fetus and protecting the pregnant woman's life or health. The Supreme Court did not rule that the criminal law cannot be used against the performance of abortions in any circumstances. It merely stated that, if Parliament wishes to infringe upon the right to security of pregnant women, it must do so according to the principles of fundamental justice guaranteed by section 7 of the *Charter*.

In 1992, the government of Canada did attempt to replace section 287 with new *Criminal Code* provisions dealing with abortion, but this amendment was never enacted. Although the new provisions passed the House of Commons, they failed to gain approval in the Senate, and there has been no subsequent attempt to bring abortions under the purview of the

Criminal Code. As a consequence, abortions are no longer subject to the criminal law and are treated in the same manner as any other medical procedure in Canada.

The *Morgentaler* case illustrates, in dramatic fashion, the scope of the wide-ranging powers that the *Charter* has placed in the hands of Canadian judges. Indeed, as Chief Justice Dickson pointed out, in the Morgentaler case,

> Although it is still fair to say that courts are not the appropriate forum for articulating complex and controversial programmes of public policy, Canadian courts are now charged with the crucial obligation of ensuring that the legislative initiatives pursued by our Parliament and legislatures conform to the democratic values expressed in the *Canadian Charter of Rights and Freedoms*.

However, it is important to recognize that the *Charter* does not require that the courts strike down every legislative provision that is considered to be in violation of an accused person's constitutional rights. Indeed, as we have already seen, section 1 of the *Charter* states that

> [t]he Canadian Charter of Rights and Freedoms guarantees the rights and freedoms set out in it subject only to such reasonable limits prescribed by law as can be demonstrably justified in a free and democratic society. [emphasis added]

As Chief Justice McLachlin said in delivering the judgment of the Supreme Court of Canada in *Canada (Attorney General) v. JTI-Macdonald Corp.* (2007), "Most modern constitutions recognize that rights are not absolute and can be limited if this is necessary to achieve an important objective and if the limit is appropriately tailored, or proportionate."

Section 1, in effect, requires the courts to engage in an elaborate balancing act in which they must decide whether the infringement of an individual's rights can be justified in the name of some "higher good." In the *Oakes* case (1986), the Supreme Court of Canada devised a specific test for the purpose of identifying the factors that should be considered when the courts attempt to decide whether the violation of a *Charter* right is justifiable as a "reasonable limit" in a "free and democratic society." This test has since become known as the *Oakes* test.

In delivering the judgment of the majority of the justices of the Supreme Court of Canada in the *Oakes* case (1986), Chief Justice Dickson prefaced his remarks concerning section 1 of the *Charter* by emphasizing that the burden of establishing that an infringement of a *Charter* right is justified as a reasonable limit is on the "party seeking to uphold the limitation": in a criminal case, this will nearly always be the Crown. In other words, there will have to be very strong grounds for overriding individual rights guaranteed by the *Charter*. However, the chief justice recognized that rights and freedoms guaranteed by the *Charter* "are not absolute" and that "it may become necessary to limit rights and freedoms in circumstances where their exercise would be inimical to the realization of collective goals of fundamental importance."

What issues should a court address when attempting to decide whether a *Charter* violation is justified under section 1? In the *Oakes* case, Chief Justice Dickson stated that this process should be divided into two separate questions:

> To establish that a limit is reasonable and demonstrably justified in a free and democratic society, two central criteria must be satisfied. First, the objective, which the measures responsible for a limit on a *Charter* right or freedom are designed to serve, must be "of sufficient importance to warrant overriding a constitutionally protected right or freedom." … It is necessary, at a minimum, that an objective relate to concerns which are pressing and substantial in a free and democratic society before it can be characterized as sufficiently important.
>
> Secondly, once a sufficiently significant objective is recognized, then the party invoking s. 1 must show that the means chosen are reasonable and demonstrably justified. This involves "a form of proportionality test." … Although the nature of the proportionality test will vary depending on the circumstances, in each case courts will be required to balance the interests of society with those of individuals and groups. There are, in my view, three important components of a proportionality test. First, the measures adopted must be carefully designed to achieve the objective in question. They must not be arbitrary, unfair or based on irrational considerations. In short, they must be rationally connected to the objective. Secondly, the means, even if rationally connected to the objective in the first sense, should impair "as little as possible" the right or freedom in question…. Thirdly, there must be a proportionality between the *effects* of the measures which are responsible for limiting the *Charter* right or freedom, and the objective which has been identified as of "sufficient importance."
>
> With respect to the third component, it is clear that the general effect of any measure impugned under s. 1 will be the infringement of a right or freedom guaranteed by the *Charter*; that is the

reason why resort to s. 1 is necessary…. Even if an objective is of sufficient importance, and the first two elements of the proportionality test are satisfied, it is still possible that, because of the deleterious effects of a measure on individuals or groups, the measure will not be justified by the purposes it intends to serve. The more severe the deleterious effects of a measure, the more important the objective must be if the measure is to be reasonable and demonstrably justified in a free and democratic society.

In the *Oakes* case itself, the Supreme Court of Canada had been faced with the question of whether or not to rule that section 8 of the (now repealed) *Narcotic Control Act*, R.S.C. 1985, c. N-1, was invalid in light of the *Charter*. Section 8 placed a peculiar burden upon the shoulders of an accused person charged with trafficking in narcotics (contrary to section 4(1) of the Act): specifically, the provision stated that, once the Crown had proved that the accused was in possession of a narcotic, then the **burden of proof** automatically fell on the accused to establish that he or she was *not* in possession for the purpose of trafficking.

The Supreme Court briskly found that section 8 infringed an accused person's right—enshrined in section 11(d) of the *Charter*—"to be presumed innocent until proven guilty." Undoubtedly, section 8 of the *Narcotic Control Act* forced accused persons into the position of having to prove their innocence and, in so doing, constituted a clear breach of section 11(d) of the *Charter*. However, the critical issue in *Oakes* was whether section 8 of the *Narcotic Control Act* could be "saved," under the terms of section 1 of the *Charter*, as a "reasonable limit" on the presumption of innocence. Ultimately, the Supreme Court took the view that section 8 did not constitute a reasonable limit that could be "demonstrably justified in a free and democratic society" and declared it to be invalid and "of no force and effect."

In applying (what is now known as) the *Oakes* test, Chief Justice Dickson first inquired whether Parliament's objective in enacting section 8 of the *Narcotic Control Act* was sufficiently important to justify overriding a *Charter* right. The chief justice noted that Parliament's objective was manifestly that of "curbing drug trafficking" by rendering it easier for the Crown to obtain convictions of those who engaged in such harmful conduct. There was absolutely no doubt that Parliament's objective of reducing the extent of drug trafficking in Canada could be characterized as being "pressing and substantial" in nature and Chief Justice Dickson was clearly convinced that there was a need to protect society "from the grave ills associated with drug trafficking."

Having determined that Parliament's objective in enacting section 8 of the *Narcotic Control Act* was sufficiently important to warrant overriding a *Charter* right, Chief Justice Dickson turned to the second part of the test that he articulated in the *Oakes* case. More specifically, were the means used by Parliament (placing the onus of proof on the shoulders of an accused person found in possession of narcotics to establish that he or she was not in such possession for the purpose of trafficking) *proportional to Parliament's objective?* As we noted, Chief Justice Dickson referred to three different components of the proportionality test. However, in the *Oakes* case itself, he stated that it was necessary to refer only to the first of these components; namely, was there a rational connection between section 8 and Parliament's objective of reducing drug trafficking? Chief Justice Dickson concluded that there was no such rational connection. Possession of a minute amount of narcotics does not automatically warrant drawing the inference that the accused intended to traffic in such drugs. Indeed, he said that it "would be irrational to infer that a person had an intent to traffic on the basis of his or her possession of a very small quantity of narcotics." Although section 8 might ensure that more accused persons will be convicted of drug trafficking, a conviction of a person found in possession of only a minimal amount of drugs does nothing to reduce the actual incidence of trafficking in narcotics because such an individual is clearly not involved in such activity in the first place! As the chief justice remarked,

> The presumption required under s. 8 of the *Narcotic Control Act* is overinclusive and could lead to results in certain cases which would defy both rationality and fairness.

It should be noted that the nature of the third step in the proportionality test articulated in *Oakes* was subsequently clarified by the Supreme Court of Canada in the *Dagenais* case (1994), in which Chief Justice Lamer suggested that it is important for the courts to examine *both the salutary and deleterious effects* of an impugned legislative provision on both individuals and groups in Canadian society. He, therefore, stipulated that the third step in the Oakes test should be re-phrased in the following manner:

> … there must be a proportionality between the deleterious effects of the measures which are responsible

for limiting the rights or freedoms in question and the objective, and *there must be a proportionality between the deleterious and the salutary effects of the measures.*

It is possible that a court might find that a particular legislative provision—adopted by Parliament in order to achieve a "pressing and substantial" objective—creates relatively few deleterious effects. However, in Chief Justice Lamer's view, that should not mean that the provision automatically meets the requirements of the third component of the proportionality test. Indeed, it may well be the case that the legislative provision in question, although it does not have any significantly harmful effects, does not produce any significantly salutary effects either! If a court should come to this conclusion, then it should rule that the legislative provision has failed the third component of the proportionality test; after all, any infringement of *Charter* rights is a serious matter and certainly cannot be justified if it does not have any significantly positive effects. Section 1 of the *Charter* should not be used to "save" legislation from invalidation unless the positive benefits of the legislation substantially outweigh any of its potentially negative impacts upon both individual Canadians and Canadian society as a whole.

The *Oakes* test has been routinely applied by Canadian courts whenever they have been confronted with the arduous, but nevertheless delicate, task of balancing the individual rights of Canadians against the collective rights of society under section 1 of the *Charter*. Therefore, in applying the *Oakes* test, the courts are required to pay very close attention to the broader social context within which a particular case may be located. As Justice Bastarache stated, in delivering the majority opinion of the Supreme Court of Canada in *Thomson Newspapers Co. v. Canada (Attorney General)* (1998):

> The analysis under s. 1 of the *Charter* must be undertaken with a close attention to context. This is inevitable as the test devised in *R. v. Oakes …* requires a court to establish the objective of the impugned provision, which can only be accomplished by canvassing the nature of the social problem which it addresses. Similarly, the proportionality of the means used to fulfil the pressing and substantial objective can only be evaluated through a close attention to detail and factual setting. In essence, context is the indispensable handmaiden to the proper characterization of the objective of the impugned provision, to determining whether that objective is justified, and to weighing whether the

means used are sufficiently closely related to the valid objective so as to justify an infringement of a *Charter* right.

(For a detailed example of the application of the Oakes test in a case where the Supreme Court of Canada ruled that a violation of a *Charter* right was justified under section 1 of the *Charter*, the reader may wish to turn to Chapter 6 and peruse the discussion of the *Wholesale Travel Group Inc.* case (1991).)

Before leaving this discussion of the impact of the *Charter* on the fabric of the criminal law in Canada, it should be emphasized that there may well be a tendency to exaggerate the extent to which the courts may use their *Charter* powers to override the will of democratically elected legislators. Indeed, it is highly significant that the Supreme Court of Canada stated in the *Mills* case (1999) that, in the context of the application of the *Charter*, it is more useful to view the relationship between Parliament and the courts as being one of *constructive "dialogue."* For example, Justices McLachlin and Iacobucci emphasized the view that the courts must always presume that Parliament intends to enact legislation that meets the requirements of the *Charter* and, therefore, must do all they can to give effect to that intention. What the Supreme Court appears to be suggesting is that the invalidation of legislation enacted by democratically elected representatives is a step that should be undertaken only very reluctantly on the part of the courts. Furthermore, even when legislation is struck down as being of no force or effect, it is always possible for Parliament or the provincial or territorial legislature to enact new statutory provisions that respond to the *Charter* concerns expressed by the courts. The *Mills* case suggests that, ultimately, these new provisions will be upheld if the legislators have "listened" to what has been said by the judges in their ongoing dialogue with Parliament and the provincial/territorial legislatures. In essence, according to the Supreme Court in the *Mills* case, the appropriate role of the courts is to assist legislators to implement the will of the people in a manner that is consistent with the Canadian values expressed in the *Charter*. In this view, legislators and courts are working in a partnership and it would be wrong to suggest that the *Charter* is being used to frustrate decisions made in a democratic manner.

In *Mills* (1999), the Supreme Court rejected a *Charter* challenge to provisions of the *Criminal Code* that were enacted in 1997 with the objective of restricting the use that may be made by lawyers for

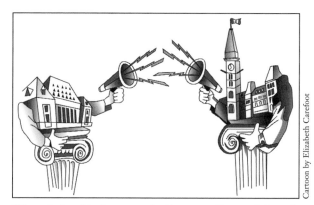

The relationship between the Supreme Court of Canada and Parliament is one of constructive "dialogue."

the accused of the confidential therapeutic records of complainants in trials involving charges of sexual assault. Such records may have been made by psychiatrists, psychologists, or counsellors when a victim of sexual assault has sought assistance and may give intimate information that the victim has every reason to believe will be kept in confidence. In Mills, **counsel** for the defence had claimed that, by restricting access to such records and by limiting the circumstances in which they could be used in evidence, the new provisions of the *Criminal Code* seriously infringed the accused's right to make "full answer and defence"—a right that is enshrined in sections 7 and 11(d) of the *Charter*. However, the Supreme Court firmly rejected this argument and declined to invalidate provisions that represented the will of elected members of Parliament to protect the victims of sexual assault from unconscionable attacks by defence counsel. Justices McLachlin and Iacobucci advanced the view that "constitutionalism can facilitate democracy rather than undermine it" and that "one way in which it does this is by ensuring that fundamental human rights and individual freedoms are given due regard and protection." It is noteworthy that the two justices admitted that "[c]ourts do not hold a monopoly on the protection and promotion of rights and freedoms; Parliament also plays a role in this regard and is often able to act as a significant ally for vulnerable groups." In their view, this principle is of particular importance in the context of sexual violence and they conclude that

> [i]f constitutional democracy is meant to ensure that due regard is given to the voices of those vulnerable to being overlooked by the majority, then this court has an obligation to consider respectfully Parliament's attempt to respond to such voices.

It is significant that the Supreme Court of Canada more recently dismissed a *Charter* challenge against those provisions of the (now repealed) *Narcotic Control Act*, R.S.C. 1985, c. N-1, which made simple possession of marijuana a criminal offence. As noted previously, in *R. v. Malmo-Levine; R. v. Caine* (2003), the Supreme Court held that Parliament was entitled to use its criminal law power to prohibit possession of a drug that was harmful or potentially harmful to those who use it. The Court also ruled, however, that Parliament's decision to criminalize the simple possession of marijuana did not infringe the fundamental principles of justice that are guaranteed by section 7 of the *Charter*. The Court took the view that, although the possibility of a prison sentence upon conviction of the offence of simple possession did indeed place limitations on the autonomy of those who used marijuana, this did not mean that section 7 protected their right to engage in a lifestyle that centred on the recreational use of the drug. As Justices Gonthier and Binnie noted,

> … While we accept Malmo-Levine's statement that smoking marihuana is central to his lifestyle, the Constitution cannot be stretched to afford protection to whatever activity an individual chooses to define as central to his or her lifestyle. One individual chooses to smoke marihuana; another has an obsessive interest in golf; a third is addicted to gambling. The appellant Caine invokes a taste for fatty foods. A society that extended constitutional protection to any and all such lifestyles would be ungovernable. Lifestyle choices of this order are not, we think, "basic choices going to the core of what it means to enjoy individual dignity and independence." …

According to the Supreme Court, Parliament had a legitimate interest in seeking to prevent the harm that marijuana may cause to those who use it. Provided Parliament's response to the threat posed by the use of marijuana was not "grossly disproportionate," there was no infringement of the fundamental principles of justice enshrined in section 7 of the *Charter*. In the words of Justices Gonthier and Binnie,

> The criminalization of possession is a statement of society's collective disapproval of the use of a psychoactive drug such as marihuana … and, through Parliament, the continuing view that its use should be deterred. The prohibition is not arbitrary but is rationally connected to a reasonable apprehension of harm. In particular, criminalization seeks to take marihuana out of the hands of users and potential users, so as to prevent the associated harm and to eliminate the market for traffickers. In light of these findings of

fact it cannot be said that the prohibition on marihuana possession is arbitrary or irrational, although the wisdom of the prohibition and its related penalties is always open to reconsideration by Parliament itself.

The Court also emphasized that the offence of simple possession of marijuana did not attract a minimum sentence and that, in fact, imprisonment was imposed only in exceptional circumstances.

The *Mills* and the *Malmo-Levine* and *Caine* cases demonstrate that the Supreme Court of Canada is far from being overzealous in its application of the *Canadian Charter of Rights and Freedoms* to legislation enacted by the Parliament of Canada under the authority of its criminal law power. The fear expressed by some politicians and commentators that the democratic will of Canadians may be thwarted by unelected judges using the *Charter* to strike down criminal legislation is not based on a sound analysis of the manner in which the Supreme Court of Canada has actually interpreted and applied the *Charter*. Although the Court has indeed declared certain legislation to be invalid, it has generally expressed its reluctance to do so. Following the Mills case, it would appear that the Supreme Court of Canada will view its role as being that of assisting the Parliament of Canada and the various provincial and territorial legislatures to implement the will of Canadians in legislation that is consistent with the basic principles expressed in the *Charter*.

Finally, it is important to recognize that declaring a statutory provision to be invalid in light of the *Charter* is considered to be a measure of last resort. For example, a court may decide that the provision may be found valid if just one offending phrase is "severed" or removed from it (a process also known as "reading down"). Furthermore, a court may rule that the constitutional validity of a statutory provision may be affirmed by "reading in" (or adding) words that would safeguard the individual's *Charter* rights. As Chief Justice McLachlin stated, in delivering the judgment of the Supreme Court of Canada in *Ferguson* (2008):

> Section 52(1) [of the *Constitution Act, 1982*] grants courts the jurisdiction to declare laws of no force and effect only "to the extent of the inconsistency" with the Constitution. It follows that if the constitutional defect of a law can be remedied without striking down the law as a whole, then a court must consider alternatives to striking down. Examples of alternative remedies under s. 52 include severance, reading in and reading down.…

However, the courts cannot "read in" or "read down" words in a statutory provision if to do so would clearly contravene the intention of the Parliament of Canada or of the relevant provincial or territorial legislature. Chief Justice McLachlin also addressed this issue in *Ferguson* (2008):

> … [I]t has long been recognized that in applying alternative remedies such as severance and reading in, courts are at risk of making inappropriate intrusions into the legislative sphere. An alternative to striking down that initially appears to be less intrusive on the legislative role may in fact represent an inappropriate intrusion on the legislature's role. This Court has thus emphasized that in considering alternatives to striking down, courts must carefully consider whether the alternative being considered represents a lesser intrusion on Parliament's legislative role than striking down. Courts must thus be guided by respect for the role of Parliament, as well as respect for the purposes of the *Charter* ….

STUDY QUESTIONS

1. How does criminal law differ from private law?

2. What are the main branches of public law?

3. Do you think that the Parliament of Canada may use its criminal law power under the *Constitution Act, 1867* to prohibit any conduct that it considers to be harmful to Canadians?

4. May a provincial legislature prohibit any conduct it considers to be harmful and impose a fine if the prohibition is violated?

5. Why are judicial decisions considered to be one of the sources of criminal law in Canada?

6. Do you think that the so-called *Oakes* test is an appropriate mechanism for determining whether a particular legislative provision should be considered valid even though it infringes one or more of the rights guaranteed by the *Canadian Charter of Rights and Freedoms*?

7. Should the Parliament of Canada have the power to criminalize conduct that does not harm other persons (e.g., personal use of marijuana)?

8. How do the courts distinguish between true crimes and regulatory offences?

FURTHER READING

Baar, C. 2003. Trial Court Reorganization in Canada: Alternative Futures for Criminal Courts. 48 *Criminal Law Quarterly*: 110–125.

Barnard, C. 2001. The Changing Scope of the Fundamental Principle of Equality? 46 *McGill Law Journal*: 955–978.

Benedet, J. 2004. Hierarchies of Harm in Canadian Criminal Law: The Marijuana Trilogy and the Forcible "Correction" of Children. 24 *Supreme Court Law Review*: 217–241.

Billingsley, B. 2006. *Oakes* at 100: A Snapshot of the Supreme Court's Application of the *Oakes* Test in Social Policy v. Criminal Policy Cases. 35 *Supreme Court Law Review (2nd Series)*: 347–411.

Boyd, N. 2007. *Canadian Law: An Introduction*. 4th ed. Toronto: Thomson Nelson.

Brown, D.H. 1989. The Genesis of the Canadian *Criminal Code* of 1892. Toronto: *University of Toronto Press*.

Brudner, A. 1997. Guilt under the *Charter*: The Lure of Parliamentary Supremacy. 40 *Criminal Law Quarterly*: 287–325.

Burstein, P. 2003. What's the Harm in Having a "Harm Principle" Enshrined in Section 7 of the *Charter*? 24 *Supreme Court Law Review (2nd Series)*: 159–194.

Calarco, P. 2008. *R. v. Ferguson*: An Opportunity for the Defence. 54 *Criminal Reports (6th Series)*: 223–227.

Campbell, M.E. 2000. Politics and Public Servants: Observations on the Current State of Criminal Law Reform. 42 *Canadian Journal of Criminology*: 342–354.

Carter, M. 2006. Recognizing Original (Non-delegated) Provincial Jurisdiction to Prosecute Criminal Offences. 38 *Ottawa Law Review*: 163–189.

Carter, M. 2008. The Rule of Law, Legal Rights in the Charter, and the Supreme Court's New Positivism. 33 *Queen's Law Journal*: 453–486.

Choudry. S. 2006. So What Is the Real Legacy of *Oakes*? Two Decades of Proportionality Analysis under the Canadian *Charter's* Section 1. 34 *Supreme Court Law Review (2nd Series)*: 501–535.

Choudry, S., and C. Hunter. 2003. Measuring Judicial Activism on the Supreme Court of Canada: A Comment on *Newfoundland (Treasury Board) v. NAPE*. 48 *McGill Law Journal*: 535–564.

_____. 2004. Continuing the Conversation: A Reply to Manfredi and Kelly. 49 *McGill Law Journal*: 765–778.

Colvin, E., and S. Anand. 2007. *Principles of Criminal Law*. 3rd ed. Toronto: Thomson Carswell. Ch. 1.

Cossman, B. 2003. Disciplining the Unruly: Sexual Outlaws, Little Sisters and the Legacy of Butler. 36 *University of British Columbia Law Review*: 77–99.

Cox, H.J., G. Lafontaine, and V. Rondinelli. 2009. *Criminal Evidence Handbook*, 2009–2010. Aurora, ON: Canada Law Book.

Currie, R.J. 2004. *Charter* without Borders? The Supreme Court of Canada, Transnational Crime and Constitutional Rights and Freedoms. 27 *Dalhousie Law Journal*: 235–284.

Deimann, S. 1998. *R. v. Hydro-Québec*: Federal Environmental Regulation as Criminal Law. 43 *McGill Law Journal*: 923–954.

Downie, J., & C. Nassar. 2007. Barriers to Access to Abortion through a Legal Lens. 15 *Health Law Journal*: 143–173.

Elliot, R. 2002. The *Charter* Revolution and the Court Party: Sound Critical Analysis or Blinkered Political Polemic? 35 *University of British Columbia Law Review*: 271–328.

Esmonde, J. 2002. Criminalizing Poverty: The Criminal Law Power and the *Safe Streets Act*. 17 *Journal of Law & Social Policy*: 63–68.

Farmer, L. 2000. Reconstructing the English Codification Debate: The Criminal Law Commissioners, 1833–45. 18 *Law & History Review*: 397–426.

Friedland, M.L. 1993. Canadian Criminal Justice, 1892–1992. 42 *University of New Brunswick Law Journal*: 175–188.

_____. 2004. Criminal Justice in Canada Revisited. 48 *Criminal Law Quarterly*: 419–473.

Gotell., L. 2008. Tracking Decisions on Access to Sexual Assault Complainants' Confidential Records: The Continued Permeability of Subsections 278.1–278.9 of the *Criminal Code*. 20 *Canadian Journal of Women and the Law*: 111–154.

Grant, I. 2008. The Boundaries of the Criminal Law: The Criminalization of the Non-Disclosure of HIV. 31 *Dalhousie Law Journal*: 123–180.

Griffiths, C.T., and S.N. Verdun-Jones. 1994. *Canadian Criminal Justice*. 2nd ed. Toronto: Harcourt Brace. 209–277.

Guidice, M. 2002. Unconstitutionality, Invalidity, and *Charter* Challenges. 15 *Canadian Journal of Law & Jurisprudence*: 69–83.

Haigh, R., and M. Sobkin. 2007. Does the Observer Have an Effect? An Analysis of the Use of the Dialogue Metaphor in Canada's Courts. 45 *Osgoode Hall Law Journal*: 67–90.

Harris, P.J. 2009. *Youth Criminal Justice Act Manual*. Aurora, ON: Canada Law Book.

Harris, P.J., and M.H. Bloomenfeld. 2009. *Weapons Offences Manual*. Aurora, ON: Canada Law Book.

Hiebert, J.L. 2002. *Charter Conflicts: What Is Parliament's Role?* Montreal & Kingston: McGill-Queen's University Press.

Hill, C., D.M. Tanovich, L.P. Strezos, and S.C. Hutchison. 2009. *McWilliams' Canadian Criminal Evidence*. 4th ed. Aurora, ON: Canada Law Book.

Hogg, P.W. 2001. The *Charter* Revolution: Is It Undemocratic? 12 *Constitutional Forum*: 1–8.

Hogg, P.W. 2008. *Constitutional Law of Canada*. Student ed. Toronto: Thomson Carswell.

Hogg, P.W., and A.A. Bushell. 1997. The *Charter* Dialogue between Courts and Legislatures (Or Perhaps the *Charter of Rights* Isn't Such a Bad Thing after All). 35 *Osgoode Hall Law Journal*: 75–124.

Hogg, P.W., A.A. Bushell Thornton, and W.K. Wright,. 2007. *Charter* Dialogue Revisited— or "Much Ado About Metaphors." 45 *Osgoode Hall Law Journal*: 1–65.

Hogg, P.W., and C.F. Zwibel. 2005. The Rule of Law in the Supreme Court of Canada. 55 *University of Toronto Law Journal*: 715–732.

Iacobucci, F. 2002. The *Charter*: Twenty Years Later. 21 *Windsor Yearbook of Access to Justice*: 3–32.

James, P., D.E. Abelson, and M. Lusztig. 2003. *The Myth of the Sacred: The Charter, the Courts, and the Politics of the Constitution in Canada*. Montreal & Kingston: McGill-Queen's University Press.

Kahana, T. 2005. Constitutional Cosiness and Legislative Activism. 55 *University of Toronto Law Journal*: 129–154.

Kaposy, C., & J. Downie. 2008. Judicial Reasoning about Pregnancy and Choice. 16 *Health Law Journal*: 281–304.

Kelly, J.B. 2005. *Governing with the Charter: Legislative and Judicial Activism and Framers' Intent*. Vancouver: University of British Columbia Press.

Koshan, J. 1998. Aboriginal Women, Justice and the *Charter*: Bridging the Divide? 32 U.B.C. *Law Review*: 23–54.

Kramer, M.H. 2004. On the Separability of Law and Morality. 17 *Canadian Journal of Law & Jurisprudence*: 315–335.

Law Commission of Canada. 2004. *What Is a Crime? Defining Criminal Conduct in Contemporary Society*. Vancouver: U.B.C. Press.

Levine, R.J. 2004. In Harm's Way: The Limits to Legislating Criminal Law. 24 *Supreme Court Law Review (2nd Series)*: 195–216.

L'Heureux-Dubé, C. 2000. The Search for Equality: A Human Rights Issue. 25 *Queen's Law Journal*: 401–415.

Linden, A.M. 1989. Recodifying Criminal Law. 14 *Queen's Law Journal*: 3–30.

Liu, M. 2000. A "Prophet with Honour": An Examination of the Equality Jurisprudence of Madam Justice Claire L'Heureux-Dubé of the Supreme Court of Canada. 25 *Queen's Law Journal*: 417–478.

Luther, G. 2006. Of Standing and Factual Foundations: Understanding How an Accused Challenges the Constitutionality of Criminal Legislation. 51 *Criminal Law Quarterly*: 360–388.

MacFarlane, B.A., R.J. Frater, and C. Proulx. 2009. *Drug Offences in Canada*. 3rd ed. Aurora, ON: Canada Law Book.

Magnet, J.E. 2004. *Modern Constitutionalism: Equality, Identity and Democracy*. 2nd ed. Markham, ON: Butterworths.

Majury, D. 2002. The *Charter*, Equality Rights and Women: Equivocation and Celebration. 40 *Osgoode Hall Law Journal*: 297–336.

Manfredi, C.P. 2001. Judicial Power and the *Charter*: Three Myths and a Political Analysis. 14 *Supreme Court Law Review*: 331–340.

———. 2002. *Judicial Power and the Charter: Canada and the Paradox of Liberal Constitutionalism*. 2nd ed. Toronto: Oxford University Press.

Manfredi, C.P., and J.B. Kelley. 2001. Dialogue, Deference and Restraint: Judicial Independence and Trial Procedures. 64 *Saskatchewan Law Review*: 323–346.

———. 2004. Misrepresenting the Supreme Court's Record? A Comment on Sujit Choudhry and Claire E. Hunter, "Measuring Judicial Activism on the Supreme Court of Canada." 49 *McGill Law Journal*: 741–764.

Manning, M. 2003. Rethinking Criminal Law in the Age of the *Charter of Rights*. 47 *Criminal Law Quarterly*: 405–406.

Manson, A. 2001. *The Law of Sentencing*. Toronto: Irwin Law.

Manson, A., P. Healy, G. Trotter, J. Roberts, and D. Ives. 2008. *Sentencing and Penal Policy in Canada: Cases, Materials and Commentary*. 2nd ed. Toronto: Emond Montgomery.

Martin, R. 2001. Case Comment: *R. v. Sharpe*. 39 *Alberta Law Review*: 585–596.

Mathen, C. 2007. Dialogue Theory, Judicial Review, and Judicial Supremacy: A Comment on "Charter Dialogue Revisited." 45 *Osgoode Hall Law Journal*: 125–146.

McLachlin, B. 1999. *Charter* Myths. 33 U.B.C. *Law Review*: 23–46.

———. 2007. The *Charter* 25 Years Later: The Good, the Bad, and the Challenges. 45 *Osgoode Hall Law Journal*: 365–368.

McLeod, R.M., J.D. Takach, M.D. Segal, and H.F. Morton. 2008. *Canadian Charter of Rights: The Prosecution and Defence of Criminal and Other Statutory Offences*. Scarborough, ON: Carswell.

Mellon, H. 2002. Meeting the Public: The *Charter*, Public Debate, and the Judiciary. 21 *Windsor Yearbook of Access to Justice*: 33–45.

Mewett, A.W. 1967. The Criminal Law, 1867–1967. 45 *Canadian Bar Review*: 726–772.

———. 1993. The Canadian *Criminal Code*, 1892–1992. 72 *Canadian Bar Review*: 1–27.

Monahan, P. 2006. *Constitutional Law*. 3rd ed. Toronto: Irwin Law. Ch. 11.

Moon, R. 2002. Justified Limits on Free Expression: The Collapse of the General Approach to Limits on *Charter* Rights. 40 *Osgoode Hall Law Journal*: 338–368.

Muttart, D.M. 2005. Dodging the Issue: Activism in the Supreme Court of Canada. 54 *University of New Brunswick Law Journal*: 101–113.

Nolin, P.C., and C. Kenny. 2003. *Cannabis: Report of the Senate Special Committee on Illegal Drugs*. Toronto: University of Toronto Press.

Paciocco, D.M. 2003. Pragmatism, Legal Culture, and the Protection of Rights and Freedoms. 8 *Canadian Criminal Law Review*: 5–32.

Paciocco, D., and L. Stuesser. 2005. *The Law of Evidence*. 4th ed. Toronto: Irwin Law Inc.

Pink, J.E., and D. Perrier. 2007. *From Crime to Punishment: An Introduction to the Criminal Law System*. 6th ed. Toronto: Carswell.

Pue, W.W. 2003. The War on Terror: Constitutional Governance in a State of Permanent Warfare? 41 *Osgoode Hall Law Journal*: 267–292.

Roach, K. 1999. *Due Process and Victims' Rights: The New Law and Politics of Criminal Justice*. Toronto: University of Toronto Press.

_____. 2001. *Constitutional Remedies in Canada*. Aurora, ON: Canada Law Book.

_____. 2001. *The Supreme Court on Trial: Judicial Activism or Democratic Dialogue*. Toronto: Irwin Law.

_____. 2002. Twenty Years of the *Charter* and Criminal Justice. 46 *Criminal Law Quarterly*: 1–3.

_____. 2005. Common Law Bills of Rights as Dialogue between Courts and Legislatures. 55 *University of Toronto Law Journal*: 733–766.

_____. 2007. Sharpening the Dialogue Debate: The Next Decade of Scholarship. 45 *Osgoode Hall Law Journal*: 169–191.

_____. 2009. *Criminal Law*. 4th ed. Toronto: Irwin Law. Ch. 1.

Rothstein, M. 2000. Section 1: Justifying Breaches of *Charter* Rights and Freedoms. 27 *Manitoba Law Journal*: 171–183.

Ryder, B. 2003. The Harms of Child Pornography Law. 36 U.B.C. *Law Review*: 101–135.

Salhany, R.E. 2009. *Canadian Criminal Procedure*. 6th ed. Aurora, ON: Canada Law Book.

Saunders, R.P. 2002. *Criminal Law in Canada: An Introduction to the Theoretical, Social and Legal Contexts*. 4th ed. Toronto: Carswell.

Sharpe, R.J., K.E. Swinton, and K. Roach. 2005. *The Charter of Rights and Freedoms*. 3rd ed. Toronto: Irwin Law.

Stuart, D. 2002. Time to Recodify Criminal Law and Rise above Law and Order Expediency. 28 *Manitoba Law Journal*: 89–112.

_____. 2004. A Less Activist Supreme Court: Gross Disproportionality. 16 *Criminal Reports (6th Series)*: 112–116.

_____. 2005 *Charter Justice in Canadian Criminal Law*. 4th ed. Toronto: Thomson Carswell

_____. 2007. *Canadian Criminal Law: A Treatise*. 5th ed. Toronto: Thomson Carswell. Chap. 1.

Stuart, D., R.J. Delisle, and S. Coughlan. 2009. *Learning Canadian Criminal Law*. 11th ed. Toronto: Thomson Carswell. Ch. 1.

Sunter, A.F. 2007. The Harm of Drug Trafficking: Is There Room for Serious Debate? 32 *Manitoba Law Journal*: 174–212.

Van Dieen, J. 2002. The 20th Anniversary of the *Charter*: Developments in Criminal Law under Section 7 of the *Charter*. 21 *Windsor Yearbook of Access to Justice*: 129–151.

Verdun-Jones, S.N. 2007. *Canadian Criminal Cases: Selected Highlights*. 2nd ed. Toronto: Thomson-Nelson. Ch. 1.

Waddams, S.M. 2004. *Introduction to the Study of Law*. 6th ed. Toronto: Carswell.

CHAPTER TWO

THE *ACTUS REUS* ELEMENTS OF A CRIMINAL OFFENCE

OVERVIEW

This chapter examines the following:

1. the essential nature of the legal concept of *actus reus*;
2. the three major elements associated with the *actus reus*: conduct, circumstances, and consequences;
3. the exceptions to the general rule that these three elements must be proved before there can be a conviction of a criminal offence;
4. the situations in which omissions (failures to act) can give rise to criminal responsibility;
5. the question of whether there should be a legislated duty to rescue those in urgent need of assistance;
6. the requirement that the *actus reus* and *mens rea* elements of an offence coincide; and
7. the element of voluntariness that must exist before an individual may be convicted of a criminal offence.

INTRODUCTION

In general, an accused person may not be convicted of a criminal offence unless the prosecution can prove *beyond a reasonable doubt*

1. that a particular event or state of affairs was "caused" by the accused's conduct (*actus reus*); and
2. that this conduct was accompanied by a certain state of mind (*mens rea*).

With their ingrained love of mystification, lawyers have traditionally referred to a famous Latin maxim in order to summarize this critical legal principle: "*Actus non facit reum nisi mens sit rea.*" Translated literally, this means that an act does not render a person guilty of a criminal offence unless his or her mind is also guilty. In legal parlance, the concept of *mens rea* refers to the mental elements of an offence, while the term *actus reus* refers to all the other elements of the offence that must be proved by the Crown beyond a reasonable doubt. As Justice Cory pointed out in delivering the judgment of the majority of the justices of the Supreme Court of Canada in the case of *Daviault* (1994),

> Originally a crime was considered to be the commission of a physical act which was specifically prohibited by law. It was the act itself which was the sole element of the crime. If it was established that the act was committed by the accused then a finding of guilt would ensue. However, as early as the 12th century, in large part through the influence of canon law, it was established that there must also be a mental element combined with the prohibited act to constitute a crime. That is to say that the accused must have meant or intended to commit the prohibited act. The physical act and the mental element which together constitute a crime came to be known as the *actus reus* denoting the act, and the *mens rea* for the mental element. Like so many maxims they are imprecise and in many instances misleading.

In practice, the courts do not draw a sharp line between the physical and mental elements of an offence. Indeed, there is an increasing degree of acceptance by Canadian courts of the view that the *actus reus* of a criminal offence includes the element of voluntariness (discussed later in this chapter). As Justice McLachlin said in delivering the judgment of the majority of the justices of the Supreme Court of Canada in the case of *Théroux* (1993),

> The term *mens rea*, properly understood, does not encompass all of the mental elements of crime. The

actus reus has its own mental element; the act must be the voluntary act of the accused for the *actus reus* to exist.

Leaving aside the issue of voluntariness for the moment, why is it important to focus on the *actus reus* elements of criminal offences? In response to this question, Gold, in *Lessons about* Mens Rea (1994, p. 157), for example, has suggested that it is necessary to undertake this task because the *actus reus* elements "identify a human oriented act that merits designation as a crime by society and merits society's undertaking to locate and deal with those human actors responsible." In other words, it is the existence of the *actus reus* elements of an offence that justifies the intervention of the criminal justice system. It is not enough that an individual may be considered dangerous and that he or she *might* commit a crime in the future. On the contrary, before an accused person may be held criminally responsible, the Crown must establish that he or she has engaged in *conduct that is defined as criminal in the sense that all the necessary actus reus elements can be proved beyond a reasonable doubt.*

One important legal principle that inevitably flows from the maxim *actus non facit reum nisi mens sit rea* is that, even in situations where the accused person has the necessary *mens rea* for a particular offence, he or she nevertheless may not be convicted of that offence unless the *mens rea* coincides with the commission of the *actus reus* of the offence. For example, let us suppose that Casanova becomes disillusioned with his marriage to Emma and commences an affair with Lisa. Casanova then decides to leave his wife and persuades Lisa (who is unaware of Emma's existence) to marry him. Casanova and Lisa subsequently participate in a marriage ceremony. Casanova derives some perverse pleasure from his belief that the marriage to Lisa is bigamous. However, Casanova subsequently receives a telephone call and he is informed that Emma was struck by a car and expired 20 minutes before the marriage ceremony with Lisa. It is clear that Casanova had the necessary *mens rea* for the offence of bigamy (section 290 of the *Criminal Code*). However, he cannot be convicted of the offence of **bigamy** because he did not commit the *actus reus* of the offence. Section 290(1)(a)(i) indicates that the offence of bigamy is committed where, *inter alia*, an accused person "*being married*, goes through a form of marriage with another person." Although Casanova fully *intended* to enter into a bigamous union with Lisa, he was (as a consequence of the fatal mishap that befell Emma) no longer a married person at the time of the wedding ceremony.

This tale represents a clear illustration of an underlying principle of criminal law—namely, that the state should punish citizens for *overt actions* rather than for their "wicked" **intentions**. Canadian criminal law generally requires that, before an individual may be convicted of an offence, the Crown must prove both an element of conduct and an accompanying mental element. As Herbert Packer (1968) said, "The limitation of criminal punishment to conduct constitutes the first and most important line of defense against erosion of the idea of culpability, for it keeps the criminal law from becoming purely the servant of the utilitarian ideal of prevention."

THE *ACTUS REUS* AS A COMBINATION OF CONDUCT, CIRCUMSTANCES, AND CONSEQUENCES

In general, it is possible to identify three separate elements of the *actus reus* of a criminal offence:

1. **conduct** (a *voluntary* act or omission constituting the central feature of the crime);
2. the surrounding and "material" **circumstances**; and
3. the **consequences** of the voluntary conduct.

As an illustration of the application of this analytical framework, we may turn to the offence of assault causing bodily harm. In order to define the elements of the *actus reus* of this offence, it is necessary to refer to three different sections of the *Criminal Code*. First, section 265 defines the nature of an **assault**: in particular, section 265(1)(a) states that

A person commits an assault when

    (a)   without the consent of another person, he applies force intentionally to that other person, directly or indirectly....

Second, we must turn to section 267 of the *Code* in order to find the provision that establishes the offence of assault causing bodily harm. This section proclaims that

    (1)   Every one who, in committing an assault,

    (a)   carries, uses or threatens to use a weapon or an imitation thereof, or

    (b)   *causes bodily harm to the complainant*, is guilty of an indictable offence.... [emphasis added]

The third, and final, piece of the definitional jigsaw puzzle is to be found in section 2 of the *Code*, which stipulates that

… "bodily harm" means any hurt or injury to a person that interferes with the health or comfort of the person and that is more than merely transient or trifling in nature....

How can we analyze the offence of assault causing bodily harm in terms of the three elements of conduct, circumstances, and consequences? The element of conduct is represented by the application of force to the person of the victim. The most critical of the material *circumstances* is that such force was applied without the consent of the victim. Finally, the *consequence*, which must be proved, is that the victim sustained actual bodily harm. As to this final requirement, it may be noted that in the case of *Robinson* (2001), the Ontario Court of Appeal agreed with the trial judge's ruling that the accused had caused bodily harm when he rubbed his beard against the victim's chin with such an excessive degree of vigour that the skin was rubbed off, leaving an oozing sore. Such an injury clearly interfered with the health or comfort of the victim and could not be considered as being merely transient or trifling in nature. However, in *Taylor* (1991), the Appellate Division of the Nova Scotia Supreme Court held that, although throwing beer over someone may amount to an assault under section 265 of the *Code*, it could not be considered an assault causing bodily harm within the meaning of the definition in section 2. Does the term "bodily harm" include *psychological* harm? In the case of *McCraw* (1991)—a case involving threats of sexual assault—the Supreme Court of Canada answered this question in the affirmative: "there can be no doubt that psychological harm may often be more pervasive and permanent in its effect than any physical harm."

This method of analyzing the basic elements of the *actus reus* may also be profitably applied to the offence of sexual assault. Section 271 of the *Criminal Code* indicates that "[e]very one who commits a sexual assault is guilty of" either an indictable or summary conviction offence. The section does not, however, define what a sexual assault is. In order to formulate such a definition, it is necessary to look first at section 265, which defines assault in general:

(1) A person commits an assault when

    (a) without the consent of another person, he applies force intentionally to that other person, directly or indirectly;

    (b) he attempts or threatens, by an act or gesture, to apply force to another person, if he has, or causes that other person to believe upon reasonable grounds that he has, present ability to effect his purpose; or

    (c) while openly wearing or carrying a weapon or an imitation thereof, he accosts or impedes another person or begs.

(2) This section applies to all forms of assault, including sexual assault....

Since Parliament has not defined the word "sexual" in the context of the offence of "sexual assault," this task has been left to the courts.

How can the basic elements of sexual assault be identified in terms of the requirements of conduct, circumstances, and consequences? In essence, the element of *conduct* generally consists of the intentional application of force (or the threat of the application of force) to the person of the victim. The *consequences* that must be established are either that the accused actually applied force to the victim or that the accused caused the victim to believe on reasonable grounds that the accused had "the present ability" to apply such force (section 265(1)(b)). The relevant *circumstances* that must be proved are that the application of force or the threat of such force took place without the consent of the victim and that the assault is of a "sexual nature."

The requirement that the assault be of a "sexual nature" was considered by the Supreme Court of Canada in *Chase* (1987). In this case, Chase took hold of a 15-year-old girl around her shoulders and arms and grabbed her breasts. When the girl struggled, Chase said, "Come on dear, don't hit me. I know you want it." According to the victim, he also tried to grab her "private" but she prevented him from doing so. Chase was convicted of sexual assault, but he appealed to the New Brunswick Court of Appeal, which substituted a verdict of guilty of common assault. The Court of Appeal held that, in order for an accused person to be convicted of *sexual* assault, there must be contact with the genitals. The Crown appealed against this decision on the basis that the Court of Appeal's definition of

sexual assault was too narrow. The Supreme Court of Canada agreed with the Crown and restored Chase's conviction for sexual assault. In delivering the judgment of the Supreme Court, Justice McIntyre asserted that

> [s]exual assault is an assault within any one of the definitions of that concept in s. [265(1)] of the *Criminal Code* which is committed in circumstances of a sexual nature, such that the sexual integrity of the victim is violated. The test to be applied in determining whether the impugned conduct has the requisite sexual nature is an objective one: "Viewed in the light of all the circumstances, is the sexual or carnal context of the assault visible to a reasonable observer." ... The part of the body touched, the nature of the contact, the situation in which it occurred, the words and gestures accompanying the act, and all other circumstances surrounding the conduct, including threats which may or may not be accompanied by force, will be relevant....

In this particular case, the Supreme Court found no difficulty in deciding that a reasonable observer, in light of all the circumstances, would have concluded that Chase's grabbing of the victim's breasts was of a sexual nature. Similarly, in the case of *Larue* (2003), the complainant was naked from the waist down and the accused was on top of her with a knife. In the circumstances, the Supreme Court of Canada held that any reasonable observer would, on this evidence alone, conclude that the assault was sexual in nature.

It is possible for a court to hold that an assault was sexual in nature even if the accused person establishes that his or her intent was not to obtain sexual gratification. The subjective intent of the accused person is only one among a number of factors that must be considered in making the determination that the assault was sexual in nature. The application of the objective test is perhaps best illustrated by the case of *V. (K.B.)* (1993), in which the accused had, on several occasions, violently grabbed his three-year-old son's genitals in order to deter him from grasping the genital region of adults. The accused was charged with *sexual* assault even though he claimed that his actions were motivated solely by considerations of discipline. Despite this argument, the accused was convicted at trial and his conviction was ultimately upheld by the Supreme Court of Canada. The majority of the justices ruled that a reasonable observer would have concluded that the "sexual integrity" of the victim had been violated even if the father had not engaged in this conduct for any sexual purpose. As Justice Iacobucci said,

> Among other things, [the father], on three occasions, violently clutched the little boy's scrotum and there was evidence of bruising and severe pain. In my view, it was clearly open to the trial judge to conclude from all the circumstances that the assault was one of a sexual nature and that the assault was such that the sexual integrity of the ... son was violated.

Similarly, in the *Bernier* case (1998), the Supreme Court of Canada ruled that the accused, who worked in a facility providing care for people with developmental disabilities, was guilty of sexual assault when he touched the breasts of female residents and testicles of male residents—even though the accused claimed that he had no hostile intent, sought no sexual gratification, and was only "joking." The Supreme Court agreed with the Quebec Court of Appeal that any reasonable person would have "perceived the sexual context of the touchings": indeed, the sexual integrity of the victims had been seriously violated by the accused and it was irrelevant that he claimed that he was just "having fun" by "bugging" and "kidding" them.

In the *Ewanchuk* case (1999), the Supreme Court of Canada made an important point about the circumstances that the Crown has to prove as a critical component of the *actus reus* of sexual assault. Specifically, the Supreme Court noted that, whereas the issue of whether an assault is "sexual" in nature is decided on an objective basis, the decision as to whether there was a lack of consent to sexual touching must be decided on a purely subjective basis. Of course, in determining whether there was a lack of consent, the court is concerned with the *subjective intent of the* **complainant** rather than the accused. As Justice Major noted,

> The *actus reus* of sexual assault is established by the proof of three elements: (i) touching, (ii) the sexual nature of the contact, and (iii) the absence of consent. The first of these two elements are objective. It is sufficient for the Crown to prove that the accused's actions were voluntary. The sexual nature of the assault is determined objectively; the Crown need not prove that the accused had any *mens rea* with respect to the sexual nature of his or her behaviour....
>
> The absence of consent, however, is subjective and determined by reference to the complainant's subjective internal state of mind towards the touching, at the time it occurred....

EXCEPTIONS TO THE GENERAL RULE REQUIRING CONDUCT, CIRCUMSTANCES, AND CONSEQUENCES

OFFENCES WHERE CONSEQUENCES ARE NOT A REQUIRED ELEMENT OF THE *ACTUS REUS*

Although the three elements of conduct, circumstances, and consequences are usually present in the *actus reus* of a criminal offence, there are, nevertheless, certain exceptions to the general rule. For example, there is a significant number of offences in relation to which the Crown is not required to prove that the accused's conduct caused any particular consequences. Illustrative of such offences is the crime of perjury. Section 131(1) of the *Code* states that

> ... every one commits perjury who, with intent to mislead, makes before a person who is authorized by law to permit it to be made before him a false statement under oath or solemn affirmation, by affidavit, solemn declaration or deposition or orally, knowing that the statement is false.

It is clear that the offence is complete just as soon as the accused has intentionally uttered the false statement; it is not necessary for the Crown to prove that anyone either believed or was influenced by the false statement. As Justice Lyon stated, in delivering the judgment of the Manitoba Court of Appeal in *Evans* (1995), "[I]t is not necessary that the false statement actually misled the court, but only that the accused intended to mislead the court." In other words, the *actus reus* of perjury lacks the element of consequences since the accused may be convicted of the offence regardless of whether his or her false statement influenced anyone.

However, as one might expect, the element of consequences does constitute an essential feature of the *actus reus* of most criminal offences. Take, for example, the case of *V.B. (J.G.)* (2002), in which the accused had been charged with causing a disturbance by fighting contrary to section 175(1)(a) of the *Criminal Code*. This section provides, in part, that "every one who not being in a dwelling-house, causes a disturbance in or near a public place, by fighting" is guilty of an offence punishable on summary conviction. The accused and another person were preparing to fight each other just outside a shopping mall. However, an employee of the mall told them not to fight there. The accused and his antagonist then engaged in a fight in an open area called "Liquor Lane," which was some 100 metres from the street. Five or six of their friends followed them to Liquor Lane but there was no evidence that anyone else saw or heard the fight. The Nova Scotia Court of Appeal held that the accused must be acquitted of the charge under section 175(1)(a) because the Crown had not proved that he had caused the consequence that is an essential element of the *actus reus* of the offence—namely, that someone was disturbed. As Justice Hamilton stated,

> To constitute a disturbance for the purpose of s. 175(1)(a) in this case, there must be someone whose use of Liquor Lane was disturbed. Here there was no one whose use of Liquor Lane was interfered with. The friends' use of Liquor Lane was not interfered with. The only reason they went there was because of the pending fight. They would not have been there otherwise. There is no evidence that anyone other than the friends saw or heard the fight.

OFFENCES WHERE CONDUCT IS NOT A REQUIRED ELEMENT OF THE *ACTUS REUS*

Although *conduct* constitutes a vital element of the *actus reus* of the great majority of criminal offences, there is an exceptional group of offences that do not require the proof of any conduct on the part of the **defendant**. In order to obtain a conviction in relation to such an offence, the Crown is merely required to prove that *the accused was discovered in a particular "condition" or "state."* Examples of such offences are being in possession of housebreaking instruments; being an occupant of a motor vehicle knowing that it was taken without the consent of the owner; and being in "care or control" of a motor vehicle while impaired or "above 80."

Being in Possession of Housebreaking Instruments

Section 351(1) of the *Code* provides that

> [e]very one who, without lawful excuse, the proof of which lies on him, has in his possession any instrument suitable for the purpose of breaking into any place, motor vehicle, vault or safe under circumstances that give rise to a reasonable inference that the instrument has been used or is or was intended to be used for any such purpose, is guilty of an indictable offence....

A classic example of an individual who would be "caught" by this section is the masked man who is discovered lurking around a house at 2:00 a.m. with a large crowbar in his hand. However, a legitimate tradesperson with a set of professional tools would not be caught under this provision if he or she was arriving at the house in order to carry out repairs at the request of the owner. Clearly, the tradesperson would have a "lawful excuse" for being in possession of the tools concerned whereas the masked man would manifestly not have any such justification.

An instructive application of section 351 occurred in *K. (S.)* (1995): in this case, the accused was charged with possession of instruments suitable for breaking into a motor vehicle. He had been discovered with a knapsack, out of the top of which was sticking an "ignition punch." The arresting police officer searched the knapsack and found "vice grips, gloves, seven assorted screws of different sizes and a slot-head screwdriver." The accused was convicted at his trial and his appeal to the British Columbia Court of Appeal was dismissed. In delivering the judgment of the Court of Appeal, Justice Prowse noted that, although the instruments found in the possession of the accused "can be used for legitimate automotive purposes, they are also well known to police for their use in the breaking into, and theft of, automobiles" and that this "is particularly true of the ignition punch." There was no doubt, therefore, that the tools discovered in the knapsack were suitable for breaking into motor vehicles, and it was perfectly clear that the accused had no legitimate reason for possessing them. However, the accused asserted that the Crown must prove that he had "targeted" a particular motor vehicle before it could be established that it was reasonable to draw the inference that the tools were intended to be used for the purpose of break-ins. In dismissing this argument, Justice Prowse stated that

> [w]hile a nexus in time and place between an accused's possession of the instruments and a particular automobile would be a significant factor in determining whether it was appropriate to draw an inference that the accused intended to use the instruments for the prohibited purpose, the absence of such a nexus would not be fatal to a conviction if the other surrounding circumstances were sufficiently compelling to permit the inference to be drawn.

In other words, accused persons can be convicted of possession under section 351 even if they have not given any thought to the question of which particular house, car, and so forth, will be the target of their break-in activities. All that the Crown must establish is that the instruments in the accused's possession are suitable for the purpose of breaking into houses or cars in general. Evidently, the offence of unlawful possession of housebreaking instruments does not involve any act on the part of the accused; instead, he or she must merely "be found" in possession of the illicit instruments. Of course, the rationale supporting this offence is one of crime prevention. It is better to intervene and arrest aspiring burglars before they actually use the housebreaking instruments to enter someone's house or business premises and commit theft or other crimes therein.

Being the Occupant of a Motor Vehicle Knowing That It Was Taken without the Owner's Consent

Section 335(1) of the *Criminal Code* makes it an offence to be "the occupant of a motor vehicle knowing that it was taken without the consent of the owner." It is not necessary that the Crown establish that a person accused of this offence was involved in the *taking* of the vehicle without the owner's consent: indeed, all that has to be proved is that he or she was *found in the vehicle* with the necessary guilty knowledge. Significantly, section 335(1.1) does provide the accused with a defence—namely the accused will be acquitted if it can be shown that "on becoming aware that [the vehicle] was taken without the consent of the owner, [he or she] attempted to leave the motor vehicle, to the extent that it was feasible to do so, or actually left the motor vehicle."

In the case of *H. (P.)* (2000), it is noteworthy that the Ontario Court of Appeal soundly rejected the view that section 335(1) imposed liability upon individuals for "morally blameless conduct" and, therefore, refused to find that it violated sections 7 and 11(d) of the *Charter*. Indeed, the court clearly stated that, "by its terms, s. 335 plainly requires the Crown to establish beyond a reasonable doubt that the occupant of the motor vehicle knows that the vehicle was taken without the consent of the owner" and this does not constitute a "morally blameless state of mind."

Being in Care or Control of a Motor Vehicle While Impaired or "Above 80"

Perhaps the best known example of an offence that does not require proof of any conduct on the part of the accused is having the "**care or control**" of a motor vehicle either while one's ability to drive a motor vehicle has been impaired by "alcohol or a drug" or while one's blood alcohol level is above that of 80 milligrams of alcohol in 100 millilitres of blood (section 253(1) of the *Criminal Code*).[1]

Once again, this offence does not require that the Crown prove that the accused was engaged in any act (such as driving); instead, it must merely be established that the *accused was found to be in the condition of having care or control of a vehicle while his or her ability to drive was impaired or while his or her blood level* was above the prescribed level (often referred to as being "above 80").

The first element of the *actus reus* that the Crown must prove under section 253 is that the accused was "impaired" or "above 80." The latter condition must be proved by submitting the results of tests conducted on samples of the accused's breath or blood (see sections 254 to 258.1 of the *Code*). However, the *Criminal Code* does not stipulate any specific test for determining whether the accused was "impaired." Indeed, in *Stellato* (1993), Justice Labrosse, speaking on behalf of the Alberta Court of Appeal, unequivocally rejected the suggestion that the Crown must prove that the accused's conduct "demonstrated a marked departure from that of a normal person." On the contrary, Justice Labrosse held that "impairment is an issue of fact which the trial judge must decide on the evidence," and that

> ... before convicting an accused of impaired driving, the trial judge must be satisfied that the accused's ability to operate a motor vehicle was impaired by alcohol or a drug. If the evidence of impairment is so frail as to leave the trial judge with a reasonable doubt as to impairment, the accused must be acquitted. If the evidence establishes *any degree of impairment ranging from slight to great*, the offence has been made out. [emphasis added]

The Supreme Court of Canada later indicated its total agreement with Justice Labrosse's ruling on this issue (see *Stellato* (1994)). However, it is important to emphasize that the critical issue under section 253 is not whether the accused's *general abilities* are impaired by alcohol or other drugs but rather whether his or her *ability to drive* is impaired. As Justice Conrad said,

---

[1] In 2008, the *Criminal Code* was amended and section 253(2) was added. It reads: "For greater certainty, the reference to impairment by alcohol or drug ... includes impairment by a combination of alcohol and a drug."

in delivering the majority judgment of the Alberta Court of Appeal in *Andrews* (1996),

> [t]he courts must not fail to recognize the fine but crucial distinction between "slight impairment" generally, and "slight impairment of one's ability to operate a motor vehicle." Every time a person has a drink, his or her ability to drive is not necessarily impaired. It may well be that one drink would impair one's ability to do brain surgery, or one's ability to thread a needle. *The question is not whether the individual's functional ability is impaired to any degree. The question is whether the person's ability to drive is impaired to any degree by alcohol or a drug.* [emphasis added]

Similarly, in *Tran* (2001), the Ontario Court of Appeal ruled that it is not enough for the trial judge to find that alcohol or another drug merely had "some effect" on the accused person's driving: rather, there must be a finding that the accused person's "ability to drive his motor vehicle at the time of the accident was impaired."

The next element of the *actus reus* that must be established under section 253 of the *Code*, assuming that the accused was not driving the vehicle concerned, is that he or she was "in care or control" of the vehicle. It is important to recognize that the courts have interpreted the concept of being in care or control of a motor vehicle in an extremely expansive manner. For example, in the case of *Ford* (1982), the defendant had been present at a party. As the night proceeded, he entered his vehicle on a number of occasions and started the engine in order to keep it warm. Ford had made arrangements with another person to drive him home because he was impaired. However, the police found Ford behind the steering wheel of the car, with the engine running. It was accepted that Ford was later going to trade places with his friend and that, therefore, he had *no intention to drive the car himself*. He was acquitted at his trial, but the **acquittal** was set aside by the Prince Edward Island Court of Appeal and the case was sent back to the magistrate on the basis that an intention to drive was **not** an essential element of the offence of being in care or control of a motor vehicle. The Supreme Court of Canada dismissed Ford's appeal against this ruling. Justice Ritchie, speaking for the majority of the Court, said:

> Nor, in my opinion, is it necessary for the Crown to prove an intent to set the vehicle in motion in order to prove a conviction.... Care or control may be exercised without such intent where an accused performs some act or series of acts involving the use of the car, its fittings or equipment, such as occurred in this case, *whereby the vehicle may unintentionally be set in motion creating the danger the section is designed to prevent.* [emphasis added]

A similar approach was adopted in the case of *Buckingham* (2007), where the accused had driven a truck to a bar and, as was his usual practice, he decided to take a taxi to his home because he did not want to risk a charge of impaired driving— particularly since his employment depended on his maintaining his driving licence. However, he had to wait for a taxi to arrive and, since it was cold and he was lightly dressed, Buckingham decided to enter the truck in order to keep warm. He started the engine and depressed the accelerator so that the heater would function as swiftly as possible. However, he fell asleep over the wheel and the police found Buckingham with his foot "hard down on the gas pedal," although the gear lever was in the "park" position. At his trial, Buckingham was acquitted of a charge of being in care or control while "over 80" but the Saskatchewan Court of Appeal ultimately entered a conviction on the basis that his conduct had created a clear risk that the vehicle might be set in motion. In delivering the judgment of the Court of Appeal, Justice Smith stated that

> ... it is my respectful view that the trial judge paid too little attention to the fact that the respondent had started the engine and, indeed, was exerting pressure on the accelerator to rev it when he was discovered. This was a significant use of the vehicle's fittings and equipment by an individual in a highly intoxicated state, and one that necessarily enhanced both the risk that the vehicle could inadvertently be set in motion, and the risk that if he awoke, he might intentionally set the vehicle in motion, given his intoxicated state. However small those risks were, they were not negligible, and the realization of those risks was considerably more likely as a result of the motor being activated than it would otherwise have been. It is just this creation of risk that s. 253 of the *Code* is intended to address.

On the other hand, in the case of *Toews* (1985), the Supreme Court of Canada ruled that the accused could not be considered to be in care or control of a vehicle where he was merely using his truck as a bedroom. The police had found Toews's truck on private property at 5:15 a.m. He was lying on the front seat, wrapped up in a sleeping bag. The key was in the

Cartoon by Greg Holoboff

"Care or Control": the Buckingham case. Realizing he is impaired, the driver calls for a taxi and then turns on the engine to keep warm. Good intentions are not relevant.

ignition but the engine was not running. Speaking for the Court, Justice McIntyre stated that

> ... *acts of care or control, short of driving, are acts which involve some use of the car or its fittings and equipment, or some course of conduct associated with the vehicle which would involve a risk of putting the vehicle in motion so that it could become dangerous.* Each case will depend on its own facts and the circumstances in which acts of care or control may be found will vary widely.... In the case at bar the car was on private property and the respondent was not in occupation of the driver's seat. He was unconscious and clearly not in *de facto* control. The fact of his use of a sleeping bag would support his statement that he was merely using the vehicle as a place to sleep.... It has not been shown then that the respondent performed any acts of care or control and he has therefore not performed the *actus reus.* [emphasis added]

It appears that the critical facts in this case were that Toews's vehicle was on private property and that he was lying on the front seat wrapped up in a sleeping bag. Although the key was in the ignition, it was there for the purpose of playing the stereo system and not for starting the motor. Furthermore, Toews had been driven to the party by a friend and was waiting for that friend in his truck. The verdict might have been very different if Toews had driven himself to the party in his truck and parked it in the street, returning to the truck some time later and placing the key in the ignition: in these circumstances, the Court might well have concluded that the accused was in a position to set the vehicle in motion, thereby constituting a danger to the public.

A similar conclusion was reached in the case of *Burbella* (2002), in which the accused had driven his vehicle into a snow-filled ditch. The vehicle was severely damaged and it was necessary to summon a tow truck in order to remove it from the ditch. The tow truck operator requested that the accused turn on the engine so that the steering mechanism would be disengaged—a necessary step in the process of extracting the vehicle from the ditch. The accused was arrested at the scene and later charged with being in care or control of the vehicle while impaired. The accused stated that he had been drinking alcohol in the period between the accident and the arrival of the tow truck. At trial, the Crown conceded that the vehicle was "wholly inoperable" and did not pose a danger to the public. Burbella was convicted but the Manitoba Court of Appeal set aside his conviction and entered an acquittal. In the words of Chief Justice Scott, "[T]he Supreme Court in its decisions has been consistent that danger is an essential element of care or control" and he ruled that the absence of any possibility that the accused could set the vehicle in motion meant that Burbella was not in care or control of it.

More recently, in the case of *Pike* (2004), the Ontario Court of Appeal emphasized the need to focus on the question of whether the accused was in a situation that created a real danger to the safety of the public. Pike's car was in the parking lot of a shopping mall when a police officer saw Pike approach the car with the keys in his hand, open the passenger's door, and deposit a package of liquor inside. At that point, the police officer administered a breath test, which Pike failed. At trial, Pike was convicted of being in care or control of his motor vehicle while "above 80." The trial judge held that the act of opening the passenger door was an act that involved some use of the car, "so that it could become dangerous, or its fittings and equipment so that it could become dangerous." However, the Court of Appeal set aside the conviction and ordered a new trial because it considered the trial judge's ruling to be unreasonable. In the words of the Court,

> The trial judge's conclusion that there was a risk of danger from the act of opening the passenger door in the parking lot and placing a package inside and contact with the knobs of the car was unreasonable. If there was any danger from the appellant depositing the package of liquor in the car, that danger did not exist at the time the appellant was arrested. The trial judge did not analyze or address what may have occurred in the not too distant future having regard to the appellant's earlier course of conduct. There was no indication from the appellant that he intended to resume driving. The trial judge had earlier found that there was a break in the care and control of the vehicle when the appellant parked the car and went to the liquor store. Having regard to the central part the opening of the passenger door played in the trial judge's reasons we cannot sustain the conviction.

Although it may seem somewhat strange to convict someone of an offence in the absence of any conduct on his or her part, it cannot generally be called unjust since the condition or state in which the accused is found is invariably *preceded* by voluntary conduct that is accompanied by *mens rea* (guilty mind). Would-be housebreakers deliberately arm themselves with the tools of their trade and they do so with the manifest purpose of engaging in nefarious criminal activities. Similarly, impaired drivers drink voluntarily, with the knowledge that drinking may impair their ability to drive, before they ever enter a motor vehicle. As Chief Justice Lamer, of the Supreme Court of Canada, said in the *Penno* case (1990),

> Such persons can reasonably be held responsible when they voluntarily consume intoxicating substances and risk putting the public safety in danger by assuming care or control of a motor vehicle, whether they intended to assume care or control or whether intoxication did not allow them to realize what they were doing. By voluntarily taking the first drink, an individual can reasonably be held to have assumed the risk that intoxication would make him or her do what he or she otherwise would not normally do with a clear mind.

In the cases of both the housebreaker and the impaired driver, it is clear that voluntary (and culpable) conduct precedes the discovery of the accused in the prohibited state or condition. On the other hand, where the accused's condition or state has not been voluntarily induced, then it would be unreasonable to convict him or her of such an offence. For example, in *Butler* (1939), it was suggested in the Alberta Court of Appeal that a highly intoxicated person, who (without his knowledge or consent) is placed in a motor vehicle by his "friends," may not be convicted of having care or control of a vehicle while impaired. Clearly, in this situation, the accused would not have entered the vehicle voluntarily and, since he would not have foreseen that his friends would place his insensible body in the vehicle, it would be patently unjust to convict him of an offence.

Nevertheless, it is significant that it has been suggested that there are certain elements of the offence of "being in care or control" of a motor vehicle while "impaired" or "above 80" that may subject an accused person to the very real threat of unjust treatment. Those who consider the offence created by section 253 to be problematic, in terms of its basic fairness, point to section 258(1)(a) of the *Code*, which must be read in conjunction with section 253. Section 258(1)(a) provides that

> [w]here it is proved that the accused occupied the seat or position ordinarily occupied by a person who operates a motor vehicle, ... the accused shall be deemed to have had the care or control of the vehicle ... *unless the accused establishes that the accused did not occupy that seat or position for the purpose of setting the vehicle ... in motion....* [emphasis added]

What this section does is to require trial courts to make the finding that accused persons, discovered sitting in the driver's seat of a motor vehicle, were in care or control of that vehicle for the purposes of section 253 of the *Code* unless they can establish that they did not occupy the driver's seat for the purpose of setting the vehicle in motion. Obviously, this places an extremely valuable weapon in the arsenal of the prosecution, because the Crown does not have to prove the *actus reus* element of being in care or control once it can demonstrate that the accused was sitting in the driver's seat: he or she will automatically be *deemed* to have been in care or control. Where the Crown relies on the "presumption of care or control" articulated in section 258(1)(a), the onus shifts to the accused to prove that, although sitting in the driver's seat, he or she did not have any intention of driving the vehicle in question.

The operation of section 258(1)(a) is well illustrated by the case of *Hatfield* (1997), in which the accused was *sleeping* on the *fully reclined* driver's seat of his car, which had been parked in an industrial parking lot. He was discovered by the police in this position and was charged with being in care or control of a motor vehicle while impaired or "above 80." Hatfield's defence was that he had been drinking at a restaurant, had driven a short distance, and immediately decided that he was not fit to drive; therefore, he proceeded to the parking lot in order to "sleep it off." The Ontario Court of Appeal was required to determine whether the presumption encapsulated in section 258(1)(a) applied to the particular circumstances of Hatfield's case: it answered this question in the affirmative and upheld Hatfield's conviction of being in care or control while impaired. Speaking for the court, Justice Goudge emphasized that it was irrelevant that the driver's seat was in a fully reclined position at the time of the police intervention. It was indisputable that Hatfield was occupying the seat ordinarily occupied by the operator of the motor vehicle. Therefore, the "plain language of the section" dictated that the presumption of care or control should be triggered in the Crown's favour: "where all that is necessary is for the occupant to bring the driver's seat up to its vertical position, the presumption must apply unless rebutted." The next issue that arose was whether Hatfield could successfully rebut the presumption by claiming that, *at the time that the police officers found him in the parking lot*, his intention was merely to sleep—not to put the vehicle in motion. The Court of Appeal strongly rejected Hatfield's argument:

> ... [T]o rebut the presumption of care or control the appellant must show that his occupancy began without the purpose of setting the vehicle in motion. The evidence here was entirely to the opposite effect. The appellant occupied the driver's seat in order to drive the vehicle away from the restaurant where he had been drinking. He intended to continue driving when he decided that he was no longer impaired.

However, in the case of *Shuparski* (2003), the Saskatchewan Court of Appeal adopted a sharply different approach to the interpretation of section 258(1)(a)—even though the facts in *Shuparski* were remarkably similar to those in the *Hatfield* case. By a majority vote of 2–1, the Court of Appeal in *Shuparski* took the view that an accused person's purpose in occupying the driver's seat may change: indeed, in the view of the majority of the Court, it would be absurd to require the accused person first to exit and then to re-enter the vehicle after that purpose has changed in order to rebut the presumption

of care or control imposed by section 258(1)(a). According to Chief Justice Bayda,

> The evidence is that before 12:10 the defendant's purpose for occupying the driver's seat was to set or keep the vehicle in motion. At 12:10 the purpose changed. It was a rational, deliberate decision on the part of the defendant to change purposes. He was tired and he needed to sleep. He testified that he often pulled over to sleep when he was tired....
>
> To accomplish that changed purpose he stopped the vehicle, that is, he ceased "the motion" of the vehicle. He then put the vehicle in "park", turned off the engine, took the keys out of the ignition, reclined the seat and fell asleep. All of these steps are totally inconsistent with "the purpose of setting the vehicle in motion." ... It is incongruous to suggest that ... when the defendant was asleep ... he acquired another purpose, the purpose of driving, that is of setting the vehicle in motion, after he awakened. A sleeping person is unconscious and cannot perform the mental act of acquiring a new purpose. Even if he had a broad general intention before he fell asleep to drive home after he was awake and refreshed, and even if that broad general intention may be construed and narrowed to a particular purpose for occupying the driver's seat, then at that critical point it was not the controlling or dominant purpose for occupying the driver's seat. At most, it was a contingent, inchoate or incidental purpose, but not "the" purpose.

The Court of Appeal affirmed Shuparski's acquittal and the Supreme Court of Canada later refused (without giving any reasons) to hear an appeal by the Crown against this decision (September 18, 2003). It remains to be seen whether the *Shuparski* case will be followed by other appellate courts but it is significant that trial courts in Alberta, Nova Scotia, and Ontario have already questioned its authority as a **precedent**. In terms of public policy, it may well be the case that the *Hatfield* decision better serves the public interest in ensuring public safety and that an impaired driver who decides to pull off the road in order to "sleep it off" should be rewarded with a reduced sentence rather than an acquittal.[2]

---

[2] In *Shuparski*, the Court held that section 258(1)(a) did not apply in the circumstances and then acquitted the accused because it did not consider that he was in care or control of the vehicle.

Other appellate courts have emphasized that the decision in *Shuparski* must be confined to its particular facts. For example, in *Armstrong* (2005), the accused was convicted in circumstances that were very similar to those which occurred in *Shuparksi*: however, the Alberta Court of Appeal held that *Shuparski* had not changed the generally accepted interpretation of the concept of "care or control" and held that it would not consider it to be a precedent-setting case.

Does section 258(1)(a) infringe section 11(d) of the *Charter*, which enshrines the presumption of innocence? Under this provision of the *Charter*, if legislation stipulates that an accused person can be convicted of an offence even though there is a reasonable doubt as to his or her guilt or innocence, it will be held to be in violation of section 11(d). The question then becomes one of whether it can be saved under section 1 of the *Charter* as a "reasonable limit" on a *Charter* right. When Parliament uses phrases such as "unless the accused establishes," the courts usually interpret this as meaning that the accused must prove the issue (e.g., the absence of an intent to drive a vehicle) "on the balance of probabilities." In this light, it is clear that, under the terms of section 258(1)(a), accused persons can only escape conviction under section 253 by proving that it is more probable than not that they occupied the driver's seat *without entertaining any intention to drive the vehicle in question*. It is not enough for them to raise a reasonable doubt as to their intentions in this respect.

On the face of it, therefore, it would appear that section 258(1)(a) infringes section 11(d) of the *Charter* because an accused person may be convicted of the offence of being in care or control under section 253 even if, at the end of the trial, there is a reasonable doubt as to whether he or she occupied the driver's seat with the intention of setting the vehicle in motion. In the case of *Whyte* (1988), the Supreme Court of Canada held that section 258(1)(a) did indeed infringe section 11(d) of the *Charter*. However, the Court refused to declare section 258(1)(a) invalid because it considered it to be a reasonable limit under section 1 of the *Charter*.

Chief Justice Dickson, in delivering the judgment of the Supreme Court, pointed out that it does not follow, as a matter of inexorable logic, that everyone who is found sitting in the driver's seat of a vehicle has care or control of that vehicle for the purposes of the offences under section 253 of the *Code*. For example, a taxi driver may enter his or her vehicle and occupy the driver's seat merely in order to use the radio to report an accident; clearly, the taxi driver has no intention, in these circumstances, of doing anything to the vehicle that might set it in motion. As Chief Justice Dickson stated,

> A person can be seated in the driver's seat without an intention to assume care or control of the vehicle within the meaning of [s. 253] ... reasonable

explanations for sitting in the driver's seat can readily be imagined. It cannot be said that proof of occupancy of the driver's seat leads inexorably to the conclusion that the essential element of care or control exists....

The Chief Justice went on to say that

> [section 258(1)(a)] requires the trier of fact to accept as proven that an accused had care or control of a vehicle, an essential element of the offence, *in spite of a reasonable doubt about the existence of that element*. The section therefore breaches the presumption of innocence guaranteed by s. 11(d) of the *Charter*. [emphasis added]

In ruling that section 258(1)(a) was "saved" by section 1 of the *Charter*, the Supreme Court noted that it would be impractical to require the Crown to prove that the accused intended to drive the vehicle of which he or she is found to be in care or control. If proof of such an intention were required in order to convict an accused person under section 253 of the *Code*, it might be possible for extremely intoxicated persons to claim that they were "too drunk" to form the intent to drive, even though their advanced state of intoxication rendered them a serious danger to the public. According to Chief Justice Dickson, the "presumption of care or control" contained in section 258(1)(a) represents a reasonable compromise in attempting to deal with the manifest dangers posed by drunk drivers. On the one hand, the Crown does not have to shoulder the impossible burden of proving that the accused intended to drive his or her vehicle; indeed, the Crown only has to establish that the accused became intoxicated voluntarily. On the other hand, an accused person will not be convicted *automatically* merely because he or she was found sitting in the driver's seat while impaired or "over 80." Section 258(1)(a) does permit such a person to escape conviction by showing that there was some reason (other than driving) for entering the vehicle and occupying the driver's seat. The Supreme Court, therefore, found section 258(1)(a) to be a "restrained parliamentary response to a pressing social problem" and, accordingly, ruled that it was a "reasonable limitation" on the presumption of innocence.

Having examined the difficult exceptions to the general rule that the *actus reus* of an offence consists of conduct, circumstances, and consequences, we now turn our attention to the problems that arise when the Crown claims that the accused's conduct consisted of a "failure to act."

CAN A FAILURE TO ACT CONSTITUTE A CRIMINAL OFFENCE?

THE GENERAL PRINCIPLE: NO LIABILITY FOR OMISSIONS UNLESS THERE IS A PREEXISTING DUTY TO ACT

In the preceding discussion of the essential elements of the *actus reus*, it was pointed out that some conduct on the part of the accused is, generally, a prerequisite for conviction of a criminal offence. In what circumstances may a mere failure to act (or an **omission**) render an accused person liable to conviction of a criminal offence?

Let us suppose that Desmond is walking past a lake. As he walks along, he hears pitiful screams emanating from Jeremy, a four-year-old boy who is drowning in the lake. Desmond, who is quite capable of rescuing Jeremy from the relatively shallow water, callously ignores the pleas for help and walks directly to his place of business. Can Desmond be convicted of the offence of manslaughter for failing to rescue Jeremy? The simple answer to this blunt question is "no" (except, perhaps, in the province of Quebec, where there is a statutory duty to rescue those in danger where this may be done without undue risk to the rescuer). The principle of law applicable to this situation is that *an accused person may not be convicted on the basis of a mere omission unless he or she is under a prior (legal) duty to act.* For example, if Jeremy had been Desmond's son, the outcome would have been very different because a parent is under a legal duty to preserve the life of his or her child when it is reasonably possible for him or her to do so (see section 215(1)(a) of the *Code*, which places a parent or guardian under a duty to provide the "necessaries of life" to a child under the age of 16 years).

A valuable illustration of the application by the courts of the general principle just outlined is furnished by the case of *Browne* (1997). Here, Browne (aged 22) and his female friend, Greiner (aged 19), were dealers in crack cocaine. The trial judge noted that they were "at the very least close friends, probably boyfriend–girlfriend," although they did not live with each other. Both Browne and Greiner had been searched by the police in a drug "crackdown" and subsequently released. However, in order to avoid detection, Greiner had swallowed a plastic bag containing crack cocaine. Tragically, she could not subsequently throw up the bag and the

drug entered her system, causing a highly toxic reaction. By the time Greiner reached the hospital, she had died. Browne was charged with criminal negligence causing death on the basis that he had "failed to render assistance to Audrey Greiner by failing to take her immediately to the hospital." The Ontario Court of Appeal noted that the relationship between Greiner and Browne did *not* fall into any of the categories of relationship (such as husband–wife, parent–child or caregiver–dependant) that impose an automatic legal duty to provide care and assistance. Therefore, Browne was under no duty to take care of Greiner: the existence of a "boyfriend–girlfriend" relationship does not *per se* render either of the parties criminally liable for a failure to act.

VOLUNTARILY ASSUMING A LEGAL DUTY UNDER SECTION 217 OF THE *CRIMINAL CODE*

Even though individual citizens in Canada are under no general legal duty to act, it is possible that they may voluntarily assume responsibility for undertaking a particular service and, in certain circumstances, they will be required to fulfill that commitment if a failure to do so would be dangerous. This legal principle is enshrined in section 217 of the *Criminal Code*, which states that "[e]very one who undertakes to do an act is under a legal duty to do it if an omission to do the act is or may be dangerous to life." The courts have emphasized that section 217 only applies where the accused makes a serious, conscious undertaking to carry out a certain task and where reliance by another person on this undertaking would be considered reasonable in all of the circumstances. Take, for example, the case of *Browne* (1997), discussed above. The trial judge had found that Browne had given an undertaking to Greiner to render assistance to her and to take her to the hospital as rapidly as possible. This undertaking, which the trial judge ruled fell within the scope of section 217, was made when Browne "took charge" of Greiner, "after he knew that she had ingested crack." The accused was convicted of criminal negligence causing death because, according to the trial judge, his failure to call 911 instead of taking her to hospital in a taxi constituted "wanton and reckless disregard" for Greiner's life. However, the Ontario Court of Appeal unanimously set aside the conviction and acquitted Browne. Justice Abella pointed out that the word "undertaking" in section 217 must be interpreted in light of the fact that an accused person, such as Browne, could be liable to a maximum sentence of life imprisonment if there is a conviction for criminal negligence causing death that is based on a failure to perform such an undertaking:

> The threshold definition must be sufficiently high to justify such serious penal consequences. The mere expression of words indicating a willingness to do an act cannot trigger the legal duty. There must be something in the nature of the commitment, generally, though not necessarily, upon which reliance can reasonably be said to have been placed.

Essentially, the trial judge had found that, because Browne and Greiner were partners in drug dealing, Browne had made an implicit undertaking that he would take Greiner to hospital if she were ever to swallow cocaine. However, the Court of Appeal took the view that there was absolutely no undertaking "in the nature of a binding commitment." As Justice Abella stated, Browne's words to Greiner when he knew she was in a life-threatening situation, "I'll take you to the hospital," "hardly constitute a legal undertaking creating a legal duty under s. 217" and, in the absence of such an undertaking, "there can be no finding of a legal duty."

Of course, one can readily think of situations in which courts would almost certainly find that a binding commitment has been made. For example, a mountain guide is not forced to take a group of climbers into dangerous terrain that is unknown to them. However, once the expedition is underway, the guide cannot suddenly flee the scene if it would create a situation that would be dangerous to the climbers' lives. Under these circumstances, the guide would be considered to have made a solemn undertaking that clearly falls within the purview of section 217. If, as a direct consequence of the guide's abandonment of his or her duty, one of the climbers fell down a precipice and died, then the guide would be liable to conviction for criminal negligence causing death or manslaughter.

SPECIFIC LEGAL DUTIES IMPOSED BY THE *CRIMINAL CODE*

There are a number of statutory provisions that impose a legal duty to act in a variety of situations in Canada; for example, section 129(b) (duty to assist a police officer), sections 215–218 of the *Code* (various

"duties tending to the preservation of the lives of children and others who are in a position of dependence on others"),[3] and section 263 (duty to safeguard an opening in ice or an excavation on land so that people do not fall in).

THE DUTY TO PROVIDE THE NECESSARIES OF LIFE TO DEPENDENT PERSONS

Section 215 is a very significant provision that imposes a duty to act on persons who are, in one way or another, responsible for the welfare of others. Section 215 states that

(1)   Every one is under a legal duty

    (a)   as a parent, foster parent, guardian or head of a family, to provide necessaries of life for a child under the age of sixteen years;

    (b)   to provide necessaries of life to their spouse or common-law partner; and

    (c)   to provide necessaries of life to a person under his charge if that person

       (i)   is unable, by reason of detention, age, illness, mental disorder or other cause, to withdraw himself from that charge, and

       (ii)   is unable to provide himself with necessaries of life.

(2)   Every one commits an offence who, being under a legal duty within the meaning of subsection (1), fails without lawful excuse, the proof of which lies on him, to perform that duty, if

    (a)   with respect to a duty imposed by paragraph (1)(a) or (b),

       (i)   the person to whom the duty is owed is in destitute or necessitous circumstances, or

       (ii)   the failure to perform the duty endangers the life of the person to whom the duty is owed, or causes or is likely to cause the health of

---

[3] Section 217.1, for example, imposes a duty on everyone who has the authority to dictate how another person undertakes their work to take reasonable steps to prevent bodily harm from occurring either to that person or to a third party as a consequence of performing tasks related to that work. This duty would be imposed on the manager of a construction site, by way of illustration.

that person to be endangered permanently; or

(b) with respect to a duty imposed by paragraph (1)(c), the failure to perform the duty endangers the life of the person to whom the duty is owed or causes or is likely to cause the health of that person to be injured permanently....

By "necessaries of life," Parliament meant to include not only food and drink but also medical care and any other goods or services that preserve life. For example, a parent is under a duty to rescue a child from perishing in a fire or drowning in a swimming pool if it is reasonably possible for him or her to do so in all of the particular circumstances of the case.

An important question that arises under section 215 is whether the accused was aware of the fact that a person to whom he or she owed a duty to provide the necessaries of life was actually in need of the accused's assistance. For example, parents may not be convicted of an offence under section 215 for failing to provide medical services to a child if they had no reason to know that their child was suffering from a medical problem. However, does this mean that a parent who has an *unreasonable* belief that a child is not sick is entitled to an acquittal on this basis? An example of an unreasonable belief arises in the situation where a parent knows that a child needs a certain medical treatment to maintain life (e.g., insulin injections for a diabetic child) but withdraws all treatment because an "angel" told the parent that the child was cured. Although the parent in this example may be totally sincere in his or her religious belief, there is no doubt that most people would regard the withdrawal of treatment from a sick child in these circumstances as being unreasonable. Parents do have the absolute right to refuse treatment for themselves, but there is no right to withhold treatment from their children who are too young to make such important decisions for themselves. If the test of criminal responsibility under section 215 is purely *subjective* (based on what the particular accused believed, regardless of the reasonableness of that belief), the accused must be acquitted. However, if the test is *objective* in nature (based on what the *reasonable* parent would have appreciated in the circumstances), the accused must be convicted. What test should be applied by the courts?

In the case of *Naglik* (1993), the Supreme Court of Canada held that the standard to be applied under section 215 of the *Code* is an *objective* one. *Naglik* involved a situation in which the accused and her common-law husband had been charged with aggravated assault and failing to provide the necessaries of life to their son, aged 11 weeks. The charge of failing to provide necessaries related to a failure to take the infant for urgent medical treatment. Chief Justice Lamer stated that

[s]ection 215 is aimed at establishing a uniform minimum level of care to be provided for those to whom it applies, and this can only be achieved if those under the duty are held to a societal, rather than a personal, standard of conduct. While the section does not purport to prescribe parenting or caregiving techniques, it does serve to set the floor for the provision of necessaries, at the level indicated by, for example, the circumstances described in subs. (2)(a)(ii). The effects of a negligent failure to perform the duty will be as serious as an intentional refusal to perform the duty....

... s. 215(2)(a)(ii) punishes a marked departure from the conduct of a reasonably prudent parent in circumstances where it is objectively foreseeable that the failure to provide the necessaries of life would lead to a danger to the life, or a risk of permanent endangerment to the health, of the child.

A recent application of section 215 occurred in the case of *Barry* (2004). Ms. Barry was charged with failing to provide the necessaries of life to her infant daughter, who was less than one month old. The basis of the charge was Barry's failure to seek prompt medical attention for her baby, who had fractures in both of her arms. Before leaving hospital following the baby's birth, Barry was warned by a childcare worker that Barry's boyfriend, Shawn Sheppard, had been charged with assaulting a child. Barry made an agreement with the childcare worker to the effect that Sheppard would not be present in her home with the children unless she or her grandmother were present and would not be permitted there overnight. This agreement was not honoured by Barry. The Crown alleged that Barry's failure to perform her duty to provide the necessaries of life to her baby met the criteria specified in section 215(2)(a)(ii)—namely, that "the failure to perform the duty endangers the life of the person to whom the duty is owed, or causes or is likely to cause the health of that person to be endangered permanently." In delivering the judgment of the

Newfoundland and Labrador Court of Appeal, Justice Welsh stated that

> [t]here was ample evidence on which to conclude that it was objectively foreseeable in the circumstances that Ms. Barry's failure to obtain prompt medical attention for the baby was likely to put the infant at risk of permanent harm to her health....
>
> The uncontradicted evidence of the physicians is that the injury would have been painful. If Ms. Barry was present when the injury occurred, acting as a reasonably prudent parent, she would have sought medical assistance without delay. If she was not present, a reasonably prudent parent in her position would have soon recognized the likelihood the baby had been injured, given the baby's crying, the lack of mobility in the arm, the clammy condition of her skin, and the presence of Shawn Sheppard whom child care workers had advised her could not be left alone with the baby. In the circumstances, a heightened level of awareness and vigilance was appropriate and, indeed, required.
>
> ... Ms. Barry failed to obtain prompt medical attention for her baby. It was objectively foreseeable in the circumstances that this failure was likely to put the infant at risk of permanent harm to her health. Ms. Barry's conduct was a marked departure from the standard of a reasonably prudent parent in the circumstances.

On the other hand, in the more recent case of *P. (K.)* (2007), the Ontario Court of Appeal ruled that the Crown had not proved that an infant boy's health had been "permanently endangered" when his mother had delayed seeking medical treatment for injuries to her son's leg. The Court reached that conclusion because the delay had lasted for only one weekend.

It is important to recognize that section 215(2) of the *Criminal Code* makes a specific defence available to those individuals who have been charged with failing to provide the necessaries of life: namely, the defence of "lawful excuse." However, section 215(2) states that the burden of proving this defence lies on the shoulders of the accused. In *Curtis* (1998), the Ontario Court of Appeal ruled that placing the onus of proof on the accused in this manner infringed the presumption of innocence that is enshrined in section 11(d) of the *Charter* and could not be justified under section 1. Instead of declaring the whole of section 215 of the *Criminal Code* to be invalid, however, the court held that only the words "the proof of which lies on him" should be struck down under the Charter. Therefore, as a consequence of the Curtis decision, the defence of "lawful excuse" continues to exist, under section 215(2); however, at the end of a criminal trial, the Crown will now be required to prove—beyond a reasonable doubt—that the accused did not have a "lawful excuse" for the failure to provide necessaries. *Curtis* is a decision of the Ontario Court of Appeal, and it remains to be seen whether the appellate courts in other provinces and territories—and, ultimately, the Supreme Court of Canada—will adopt the same approach. As far as the substance of the "lawful excuse" defence is concerned, one can well imagine circumstances in which parents, for example, might not be aware that their child is in necessitous circumstances: if such parents have acted reasonably, then the absence of any knowledge of the danger threatening their child would constitute a "lawful excuse." Similarly, an individual who sees his or her spouse drowning in a swollen, fast-running, and deep river would be considered to have a "lawful excuse" not to jump in to the rescue if he or she is unable to swim (of course, one would expect the individual concerned, at least, to seek help from other parties and there would generally be no "lawful excuse" for failing to do so).

CRIMINAL NEGLIGENCE, MANSLAUGHTER, AND FAILURE TO ACT

If a failure to perform a legal duty results in death or bodily harm to the person to whom the duty is owed, the accused may be liable to conviction for the more serious offences of *causing death by criminal negligence* (section 220 of the *Code*) or *causing bodily harm by criminal negligence* (section 221 of the *Code*). According to section 219(1)(b) of the *Code*, if an accused person fails to perform a legally imposed duty and, by this failure, "shows wanton or reckless disregard for the lives or safety of other persons," he or she is guilty of **criminal negligence** causing bodily harm or death (as the case may be). It is also important to bear in mind that the offence of **manslaughter** may be committed where the accused causes the death of his or her victim as a consequence of criminal negligence on the part of the accused (see sections 222(5)(b) and 234 of the *Code*). The elements that the Crown must prove in order to obtain a conviction for both the offences of criminal negligence causing death and manslaughter (by means of criminal negligence) are identical in each case. Which charge the Crown ultimately chooses to pursue is primarily a matter of prosecutorial tactics.

One possible explanation for the existence of these twin charges is that, historically, Canadian juries were reluctant to convict motorists charged with manslaughter as a consequence of criminally negligent driving conduct. On the other hand, it is contended that juries were more willing to convict the accused for engaging in such conduct where the charge was that of criminal negligence causing death (despite the fact that conviction of the charge carries exactly the same maximum penalty of life imprisonment), which was generally perceived to bear a lesser degree of stigma than the crime of manslaughter. Apparently for this reason, the offence of criminal negligence causing death was added to the provisions of the *Criminal Code*. However, it seems that even this change did not bring about a satisfactory rate of conviction of motorists who caused death on the roads and, in 1985, Parliament created the offences of dangerous driving causing death (section 249(4)) and impaired driving causing death (section 255(3)). The offence of dangerous driving causing death imposes a maximum penalty of 14 years' imprisonment, whereas the offence of causing death while impaired or "above 80" carries a maximum penalty of life imprisonment.[4]

IS THERE A DUTY TO ACT WHEN A PERSON CREATES A DANGEROUS SITUATION BY ACCIDENT?

Should the criminal law impose a duty to act upon an individual who creates a dangerous situation by accident? Needless to say, the nature of the duty would be to take steps to combat the dangerous situation created by the accused's own act. Apparently, there is no authoritative Canadian precedent on this point; however, this issue was considered by the House of Lords in the English case of *Miller* (1983), in which the accused had been drinking and had subsequently stretched himself out on his mattress and lit a cigarette. He fell asleep while smoking and awoke to find the mattress on fire. However, instead of dealing with the fire, he just went into another room and went to sleep. He was charged with arson.

---

[4] In 2008, Parliament added the new driving offences of causing death while fleeing from a peace officer (s. 249.1) and causing death by criminal negligence while street racing (s. 249.2): the maximum penalty for each offence is life imprisonment.

It was clear that the fire had started through the **negligence**, rather than the deliberate conduct, of the accused.

In his judgment, Lord Diplock stated that

> I see no rational ground for excluding from conduct capable of giving rise to criminal liability conduct which consists of *failing to take measures that lie within one's power to counteract a danger that one has oneself created, if at the time of the conduct one's state of mind is such as constitutes a necessary ingredient of the offence.* I venture to think that the habit of lawyers to talk of "*actus reus*," suggestive as it is of action rather than inaction, is responsible for any erroneous notion that failure to act cannot give rise to criminal liability in English law. [emphasis added]

In this particular case, the accused should have taken reasonable steps to prevent or minimize the damage to the property at risk. The House of Lords, therefore, upheld his conviction of arson.

The *Miller* case opens the door to a potentially significant expansion of criminal liability in relation to omissions. To date, the principle that one may be held criminally responsible for failing to act when one has created a dangerous situation has not been embraced by any appellate court in Canada. However, it was applied by Judge Bourassa of the Territorial Court of the Northwest Territories in the case of *Tesar* (1992). The accused was charged under section 140(1)(b) of the *Criminal Code*, which provides that

> [e]very one commits public mischief who, with intent to mislead, causes a peace officer to enter on or continue an investigation by … doing anything intended to cause some other person to be suspected of having committed an offence that the other person has not committed, or to divert suspicion from himself....

On March 6, 1991, Tesar had informed the police that someone had forged her signature in order to gain credit for the purchase of groceries and she named a particular suspect—a woman called Arsenault. However, on March 13, Tesar's sister telephoned her to let the accused know that it was she (the sister) who had actually forged the accused's signature. Tesar did not provide the police with the information about her sister's confession, and Arsenault was arrested at her home on March 19 and released the following day. However, Arsenault later confronted Tesar's sister, who admitted that she had forged the signature and this information was relayed to the

RCMP. Two days before Arsenault's arrest, Tesar had been in contact with the investigating officer and had failed to provide him with the information about her sister's confession—even though that information would have entirely absolved Arsenault of any responsibility for the forgery. The issue before Judge Bourassa was whether Tesar could be convicted of public mischief because she failed to provide the information about her sister's confession to the police. Judge Bourassa referred to the judgment of Lord Diplock in the *Miller* case (1983) and found that Tesar had created a dangerous situation by contacting the police and casting suspicion on Arsenault. After Tesar became aware that her accusation was unjustified, she developed the *mens rea* for the offence of public mischief. Here, Tesar had the power to prevent the police from pursuing an innocent woman but she deliberately refrained from doing so. The situation was parallel to what occurred in the *Miller* case, and Tesar was convicted of public mischief. In the circumstances, her failure to take action after creating a dangerous situation constituted the *actus reus* of the offence. In the words of Judge Bourassa:

> Again, going back to March 13th, which in my view is the pivotal turning point in the case. Bryony Tesar knew her sister had forged her signature. She did absolutely nothing about it. She was in contact with the Police before an innocent person was arrested, and did not inform them of the facts.
>
> In my view, the mental element crystallized on the 13th, and it operated in conjunction with the danger that she created. I have both the mental elements and the factual elements necessary for criminal liability.

SHOULD THERE BE A DUTY TO RESCUE?

There has been a good deal of heated controversy concerning the approach of the criminal law in the area of omissions. More specifically, it has been contended that every citizen should be under a duty to rescue a fellow citizen whose life or safety is in peril, provided, of course, that it is reasonably safe and practical to undertake such a rescue. Proponents of this viewpoint would urge that criminal liability should be imposed on such a person as Desmond who, in the example outlined previously, declined to assist a drowning child.

Indeed, the Law Reform Commission of Canada has recommended that the *Criminal Code* impose a general duty on all citizens to render aid in an

Is there a duty to rescue?

emergency. The commission points to the single exception to the general legal rule in Canada as a concrete demonstration that the proposal is certainly within the realm of practicality. This exception is contained in legislation passed by the province of Quebec. Section 2 of the *Quebec Charter of Human Rights and Freedoms* (R.S.Q., c. C-12) provides that

> [e]very human being whose life is in peril has a right to assistance. Every person must come to the aid of anyone whose life is in peril, either personally or calling for aid, by giving him the necessary and immediate physical assistance, unless it involves danger to himself or a third person, or he has another valid reason.

The Quebec provision does not create a criminal offence *per se*; in other words, there is no offence of failing to rescue a person in danger. However, the provision may nevertheless play a significant role in leading to the conviction of an accused person under the *Criminal Code* because the *Code* imposes criminal liability, in certain circumstances, for failure to perform a duty imposed by law. The Quebec provision imposes just such a duty. For example, a failure to provide assistance to a victim who subsequently dies, in circumstances indicating a wanton and reckless disregard for the life or safety of the victim, could possibly result in a conviction of manslaughter by criminal negligence or criminal negligence causing death.[5]

---

[5] In *Maltais v. Simard* (2006), the Quebec Court of Appeal rejected the argument that other people had a duty, under section 2 of the *Charter*, to intervene and prevent a heavily intoxicated Maltais from diving into shallow water.

However, the present approach of Canadian criminal law is, as we have seen, to impose criminal liability for a failure to act only when such an omission occurs in the context of a prior legal duty to act. Among the arguments in support of the *status quo* is the contention that it would be difficult to enforce a "duty to rescue." Just how far are individual citizens expected to go in attempting to save their fellows from danger? This question is almost impossible to answer in the abstract and it has always been felt that the criminal law should set clear standards of liability, so that every citizen knows, ahead of time, exactly what he or she must do to avoid criminal liability. Furthermore, it is suggested that the criminal law should abstain from trying to force people to live up to a higher standard of morality; this should be a job for organized religion or the schools rather than the blunt instrument of the criminal sanction.

WHEN A FAILURE TO ACT MAY RENDER AN ACCUSED PERSON LIABLE AS A PARTY TO AN OFFENCE COMMITTED BY ANOTHER PERSON

To this point, we have been discussing the circumstances in which an accused person may be convicted of an offence in which the *actus reus* element of conduct may consist of a failure to act on his or her part. However, there are some situations in which a failure to act may lead to an accused person becoming a party to an offence that is *actually committed by someone else*. This might occur where the accused fails to perform a legal duty and this failure to act is considered to amount to aiding and/or abetting (assisting or encouraging) an offence committed by another party. Paragraphs (b) and (c) of section 21(1) provide that an accused person is a "party to an offence" if he or she "does or omits to do anything for the purpose of aiding any person to commit it" or "abets any person in committing it."

For example, in the case of *Nixon* (1990), the accused was the officer in charge of the lock-up or jail where a prisoner was assaulted. The accused was charged with aggravated assault, but the trial judge was not satisfied that he had actually committed the assault himself. However, the Court of Appeal ruled that the trial judge was correct in convicting the accused on the basis that he aided or abetted the officers who did commit the assault. The accused was unquestionably under a duty to protect the prisoner under both British Columbia's *Police Act* and the

Criminal Code. Nixon's failure to protect the prisoner, when he was under a clear legal duty to do so, therefore constituted aiding or abetting of the assault committed by his fellow officers (assuming that this failure to act was prompted by the intention to assist or encourage the other officers in their criminal activities). As Justice Legg stated, in delivering the judgment of the Court of Appeal,

> A person becomes a party under s. 21(1)(b) if he fails to act for the purpose of aiding in the commission of the offence. Where there is a duty to act, and the accused does not act, it is open to the court to infer that the purpose of the failure to act was to aid in the commission of the offence.
>
> Similarly, under s. 21(1)(c), a person who "abets" the offence becomes a party. The cases show that in some circumstances a failure on the part of the accused to act to prevent the offence may constitute positive encouragement. One situation in which this will be the case is where the accused had a duty to prevent the offence and failed to act. Thus, s. 21(1)(c) also punishes omissions in the sense that it punishes the encouragement of an offence that is provided by the omission.
>
> ... [I] t is clear from [the trial judge's] judgment that she inferred that [Nixon] had encouraged the commission of the offence by finding that [he] was at the scene when the vicious act occurred and failed to perform his duty as a police officer to protect [the prisoner].

THE NEED FOR THE *ACTUS REUS* AND *MENS REA* TO COINCIDE

The phrase *actus non facit reum nisi mens sit rea* necessarily implies that, before an accused person may be convicted of a crime, the Crown must prove that there was a moment when both the *actus reus* and *mens rea* elements of the offence coincided. In other words, there is a requirement of simultaneity between the *actus reus* and *mens rea* elements of an offence.

This requirement is well illustrated by the case of *Newell* (2007), in which the accused entered a supermarket and placed some meat in a basket. However, Newell left the store without paying for the meat. As Newell was entering the parking lot, a security officer tapped him on the shoulder and told him that he would have to return to the store. Newell spun around, dropping the basket in the process. There was a scuffle with the security officer. However, Newell had a knife in one hand and he swung it at the officer, who immediately backed off. Newell fled the scene, leaving the meat on the ground. Newell was charged with robbery, under section 343(a) of the *Criminal Code*, which states that everyone commits robbery who "steals, and for the purpose of extorting whatever is stolen or to prevent or overcome resistance to the stealing, uses violence or threats of violence to a person or property." The trial judge found Newell guilty of robbery and Newell appealed against the conviction to the Newfoundland and Labrador Court of Appeal. Newell admitted the theft but asserted that he could not be properly convicted of robbery because the violence that he perpetrated against the security officer took place after the theft had been completed.

The Court of Appeal granted Newell's appeal and substituted a conviction for theft. The Court stated that, under section 343(a), it was clear that Parliament intended that the violence must precede—or be contemporaneous with—the theft in order for the crime of robbery to be proved. Clearly, in this case, the *actus reus* and *mens rea* elements for the offence of robbery did not coincide. When Newell took the meat, he did not use violence or the threat of force. After he left the store, the theft was complete. When he assaulted the security officer and threatened him with a knife, Newell had the intent to use force but his purpose was simply to escape from the scene rather than to facilitate a theft. If he had used violence at the time of, or immediately before, the theft, Newell would have been guilty of robbery because the *actus reus* and *mens rea* elements of robbery would have coincided.

The requirement of simultaneity clearly makes excellent sense when applied to the great majority of situations in which it is alleged that the accused has committed a crime. However, there are certain circumstances in which the application of this principle becomes problematic. In a case of homicide, for example, it may well happen that the victim dies as a consequence of a series of violent acts committed by the accused over an extended period of time. In such circumstances, the Crown may not be able to prove that the accused had the necessary *mens rea* for murder or manslaughter at the exact moment that the fatal blow was delivered, even though it is clear that the accused did have such *mens rea* at some stage during the series of acts that resulted in the victim's death. Does this mean that the accused must be acquitted of murder or manslaughter because the Crown cannot prove the simultaneity of *actus reus*

The actus reus and mens rea of robbery do not coincide: the theft was complete before the violence occurred.

Cartoon by Greg Holoboff

and *mens rea*? In the case of *Cooper* (1993), the Supreme Court of Canada answered this question in the negative.

Cooper was charged with murder after fatally strangling a young woman. He stated that he became angry with the victim, hit her, grabbed her by the throat, and shook her. He claimed that he could not remember anything else until he woke up and discovered the victim's body next to him. Expert evidence established that the victim had died of manual strangulation and that death had occurred between 30 seconds and two minutes after pressure was applied to her neck. Under section 229(a) of the *Criminal Code*, culpable homicide is murder where the accused either intends to kill the victim or "means to cause" the victim "bodily harm that he knows is likely to cause his death, and is reckless whether death ensues or not." Cooper asserted that he did not have the necessary *mens rea* for murder at the time that the victim was actually killed because he had "blacked out" before her death occurred. Nevertheless, he was convicted at trial and the Supreme Court of Canada ultimately ruled that his conviction was justified.

Justice Cory pointed out that, where an accused person has committed a series of acts that result in the death of the victim, these acts should be considered as being "all part of the *same transaction*," and that, if the necessary *mens rea* for murder coincides *at any time* with one or more of these separate acts, the accused may be convicted. For example, let us suppose that an individual repeatedly beats a victim about the head with a baseball bat. It is clear that this individual could be convicted of murder if, at any time, the necessary *mens rea* for murder coincided with one or more of the blows administered by the accused.

In *Cooper*, the Crown took the view that the accused did, at some point, have the intention to inflict bodily harm that he knew was likely to cause death and was reckless whether death ensued or not (see section 229(a)(ii)). After all, the accused must have been aware that "breathing is essential to life" and that strangulation was likely to cause the victim's death. Justice Cory held that the jury had acted reasonably in concluding that the necessary *mens rea* did exist at some stage, even though it might not have lasted during the whole episode of strangulation. In his view,

> ... I do not think that it is always necessary that the requisite *mens rea* (the guilty mind, intent or awareness) should continue throughout the commission of the wrongful act.
>
> There is no question that in order to obtain a conviction the Crown must demonstrate that the accused intended to cause bodily harm that he knew was ultimately so dangerous and serious that it was likely to result in the death of a victim. But that intent need not persist through the entire act of strangulation....
>
> Here the death occurred between 30 seconds and two minutes after he grabbed her by the neck. It could be reasonably inferred by the jury, that when the accused grabbed the victim by the neck and shook her that there was, at that moment, the necessary coincidence of the wrongful act of strangulation and the requisite intent to do bodily harm that the accused knew was likely to cause death.... *It was sufficient that the intent and the act of strangulation coincided at some point. It was not necessary that the requisite intent continue throughout the entire two minutes required to cause the death of the victim.* [emphasis added]

Another problem arises with the application of the principle of simultaneity of *actus reus* and *mens rea* when the accused commits an initially innocent act but subsequently forms the *mens rea* necessary for conviction of a criminal offence. The courts have taken the view that, if the *actus reus* committed by the accused was fully completed before the moment that the necessary *mens rea* was formed in the accused's mind, then there is no criminal offence. However, the courts have also held that *mens rea* can be "superimposed" on an initially innocent act so as to justify convicting the accused of a crime. This situation would arise where the accused has been found to have committed a "continuing *actus reus*" (such as repeating a false statement) and to have subsequently developed the necessary *mens rea*. Here, the courts would rule that the *actus reus* and *mens rea* elements of the offence did coincide, at some point, and that, therefore, a crime has been committed.

The notion of a continuing *actus reus* was utilized by the Supreme Court of Canada in *Detering* (1982), in which the accused was charged with fraud, contrary to section 380 of the *Criminal Code*. An employee of the Ontario Ministry of Consumer and Commercial Relations had been involved in the monitoring of garage repair businesses. She had taken a "well-used car" to Detering's repair shop. She knew that the transmission had been "slightly tampered with and could be rectified with a few minutes work." She informed Detering that she had transmission trouble. After road-testing the vehicle, Detering informed her that the transmission needed to be rebuilt and that the repair costs would be $189 plus tax. When the ministry employee reclaimed the car, she paid this sum. The bill indicated that the transmission had been rebuilt; however, it was established that this was not true. Detering was convicted, at his trial, and appealed to the Ontario Court of Appeal, which dismissed his appeal but substituted a conviction for *attempt* to commit fraud since the ministry employee had not, in fact, been deceived by Detering's representation. Detering then appealed to the Supreme Court of Canada.

One of the arguments advanced by his counsel was that there was no concurrence between the *actus reus* of the offence (namely, the representation as to the need for the transmission to be rebuilt) and the requisite *mens rea* (namely, the intent to defraud). In effect, Detering claimed that he made the representation as to the need for the rebuilding of the transmission *before* he knew that it was untrue. Therefore, he asserted that the *actus reus* of the offence was completed before the necessary *mens rea* came into existence. However, the Supreme Court of Canada soundly rejected this contention. In delivering the judgment of the Court, Chief Justice Laskin stated that the accused "renewed" or "continued" his original representation, that the transmission required fixing, after he became aware that it was untrue. In this particular case, therefore, there was a concurrence between the *actus reus* (the representation) and the *mens rea* (knowledge that the representation was false).

In light of cases such as *Cooper* and *Detering*, it is clear that the courts may manifest considerable ingenuity in "bending the rules" concerning the requirement of simultaneity in relation to the *actus reus* and *mens rea* elements of criminal offences in order to achieve what they perceive to be a just result.

THE ELEMENT OF VOLUNTARINESS IN THE *ACTUS REUS*

It is a fundamental principle of criminal law that a defendant's conduct cannot render him or her criminally responsible unless it is proved that such conduct was "voluntary." **Voluntariness** refers to the conduct being of the accused's own free will. If the accused's conduct is involuntary, he or she cannot be held criminally responsible because the consequences of such conduct did not flow from the exercise of his or her "free will."

As Justice Cory stated, in delivering the judgment of the majority of the justices of the Supreme Court of Canada in *Daviault* (1994),

> ... [U]nless the legislator provides otherwise, a crime must consist of the following elements. First, a physical element which consists of committing a prohibited act, creating a prohibited state of affairs, or omitting to do that which is required by the law. Secondly, *the conduct must be willed; this is usually referred to as voluntariness.* Some writers classify this as part of the *actus reus*, others prefer to associate it with *mens rea*; however, all seem to agree that it is required.... If persons other than lawyers were asked what constituted willed or voluntary conduct they would respond that such an act or conduct must involve a mental element. *It is the mental element, that is the act of will, which makes the act or conduct willed or voluntary.* [emphasis added]

For example, take the case of (the perhaps inappropriately named) *Lucki* (1955), who negotiated a right-hand turn on an icy street. *Through no fault of his own*, his car skidded on a sheet of ice and came to rest on the wrong side of the street. He was charged with being on the wrong side of the dividing line but was acquitted on the basis that he had arrived at this position through no voluntary act of his own. Similarly, if an extremely intoxicated person is placed by his or her friends in a motor vehicle in a state of unconsciousness, he or she would not be convicted of being in "care or control" of the vehicle because the entry into the vehicle was not voluntary.

When an accused person acted involuntarily because he or she was in a seriously impaired state of consciousness at the time of the alleged offence, it may be possible to raise the defence of automatism. Since the courts have experienced considerable difficulty in drawing a line between the defence of automatism and the defence of not criminally responsible on account of mental disorder, these two defences will be discussed together in Chapter 8.

STUDY QUESTIONS

1. Jim is a youth worker who is employed by the provincial government. While he was one of the staff members at a custodial institution, some youths complained that he touched them on the arms and legs. Jim is surprised that there have been such complaints, and he says that he only touched the youths as a means of demonstrating his genuine concern for their welfare. Crown counsel is considering laying charges of sexual assault against Jim. Do you think such charges would be likely to succeed at a trial?

2. David lives with his five-year-old son, Nemo, and his wife, Mary, in a third-floor apartment. Since she was severely injured in a motor vehicle accident some time ago, Mary has been confined to a wheelchair and requires constant attention. One night, David goes out to a bar where he indulges in some drinking with a friend. When he is walking up the street toward his home, he sees both flames and smoke coming out of the apartment building. There are a number of people outside the building but there is no sign of the fire department. David refuses to enter the building because, he says, he is "frightened of fires." A few minutes later, two neighbours emerge from the building and bring out Nemo and Mary, who have been burned and are suffering from smoke inhalation. They subsequently recover in hospital. However, a neighbour reports David's failure to go into the building and the police decide to lay charges against him. What charge(s) (if any) could reasonably be laid against David?

3. Quilp is the owner of a clothing store. The central heating system breaks down and, since it is the middle of winter, Quilp makes temporary use of an old-fashioned oil heater. As he is leaving the store, he accidentally knocks the heater over and leaking oil is ignited, causing a fire to ignite and

spread. Quilp does nothing to extinguish the fire because he suddenly decides that it would be to his financial advantage to let the store burn down and claim the insurance money. He waits near the store to watch the progress of the fire. Quilp was unaware that Rudge, a burglar, had hidden in the store with the intention of removing the stock in the middle of the night. Rudge is trapped inside the store because, owing to the intensity of the fire, he is unable to reach the exit. Rudge screams for help but Quilp ignores his pleas because he has a deep hatred for burglars. Quilp does not even call 911. In fact, a passerby sees the fire and calls the fire department on his cell phone. When the fire fighters arrive on the scene, it is too late to save Rudge, who has died in the conflagration. Quilp is charged with arson [section 433] and manslaughter [section 236]. He claims that he did not start the fire intentionally and that he was under no duty to rescue Rudge. Does he have any defences that are likely to succeed at his trial for arson and manslaughter?

4. Daniel is driving, within the speed limit, on a country road. He suddenly skids on some ice and his car slides into a ditch. He leaves the car, with the keys still in the ignition, and asks for help at a nearby farmhouse. The farmer calls for a tow truck and he gives Daniel a few whiskeys since Daniel looks as though he is in a state of shock. Daniel returns to the car to wait for the tow truck. However, a police car arrives and Daniel is asked to take a breath test. Daniel is subsequently charged with being in care or control of a motor vehicle while impaired by alcohol (contrary to section 253 of the *Code*). Is he likely to be found guilty of this offence?

5. Codlin has been drinking alcohol at a party. He leaves his friend's house and drives his car in the direction of his home. However, he realizes that he is quite intoxicated and decides to pull off the road and park his car in the parking lot of a shopping mall. He gets out of his car in order to make a call on his cellular phone because the signal is not very strong in that particular location. He calls a taxi to pick him up and take him home. He then re-enters the car and sits in the driver's seat. He removes the key from the ignition and puts it in his pocket. A passing police officer notices Codlin sitting in his vehicle and demands that he undergo a breathalyzer test.

Codlin's blood-alcohol level is 150 milligrams of alcohol per 100 millilitres of blood. Codlin is charged with being in care or control of a motor vehicle while being "over 80" (contrary to s. 253(1)(b) of the *Criminal Code*). Does Codlin have any defence(s) to this charge?

6. Joyce is a single mother who is trying to raise her young daughter, Melody, as best she can. Melody has diabetes and Joyce's physician has told her that Melody will die if she does not have regular injections of insulin. One day, Joyce believes that she has experienced a vision and that an angel has told her that Melody has been cured and no longer needs her injections. Joyce stops giving her daughter the insulin and Melody eventually goes into a coma. By the time Melody is taken to hospital, it is too late to save her and she dies. Joyce claims that she honestly believed that her daughter was cured and that she did not need any treatment. The police are convinced that Joyce's religious beliefs are sincerely held. Nevertheless, Crown counsel is considering laying criminal charges against Joyce. What charges (if any) would be likely to succeed at trial?

7. Fred is climbing a mountain with his friend, Barney. They enter into a ferocious conflict and Fred knocks Barney unconscious by hitting him on the head with an ice pick. Fred comes to believe that Barney is dead and, four hours later, he throws Barney over a cliff. The body is later recovered by the police. Forensic experts are prepared to testify that Barney was still alive when he was thrown over the cliff and that he would most probably have survived had he not been so gravely wounded by the fall from the top of the cliff. Fred's lawyer claims that her client cannot be convicted of a homicide offence, because when he threw his friend off the cliff, he honestly believed the latter was dead. What charge(s) would you bring (if any) against Fred and what degree of success would the charge(s) be likely to have at trial?

FURTHER READING

Boyle, C. 1984. *Sexual Assault*. Toronto: Carswell.

———. 1994. The Judicial Construction of Sexual Assault Offences. In J.V. Roberts and R.M. Mohr, eds., *Confronting Sexual Assault: A Decade of Legal and Social Change*. Toronto: University of Toronto Press. 136–156.

Buxton, R. 1984. Circumstances, Consequences and Attempted Rape. [1984] *Criminal Law Review* 25–34.

Colvin, E., and S. Anand. 2007. *Principles of Criminal Law*. 3rd ed. Toronto: Thomson Carswell. Ch. 1.

Dagan, H. 1999. In Defense of the Good Samaritan. 97 *Michigan Law Review*: 1152–1200.

Gold, A.D. 1993. Case Comment: *R. v. Cooper* (1993). 35 *Criminal Law Quarterly*: 299– 304.

———. 1994. Lessons about *Mens Rea*: Three Recent Cases. 36 *Criminal Law Quarterly*: 157–167.

Grant, I. 2008. The Boundaries of the Criminal Law: The Criminalization of the Non-disclosure of HIV. 31 *Dalhousie Law Journal*: 123–180.

Kelley, D.N. 2000. A Psychological Approach to Understanding the Legal Basis of the No Duty to Rescue Rule. 14 *Brigham Young University Education & Law Journal*: 271–293.

Law Reform Commission of Canada. 1987. Report No. 31: *Recodifying Criminal Law*. Rev. ed. Ottawa: L.R.C.C.

Levit, N. 2001. The Kindness of Strangers: Interdisciplinary Foundations of a Duty to Act. 40 *Washburn Law Journal:* 463–479.

Libman, R. 1991. The Defence of Drinking and Driving Offences: Too Drunk to Drive; Too Drunk for a Defence? 3 *Journal of Motor Vehicle Law*: 15–33.

Mandhane, R. 2000. Duty to Rescue through the Lens of Multiple-Party Sexual Assault. 9 *Dalhousie Journal of Legal Studies*: 1–35.

McInnes, M. 1991. Psychological Perspectives on Rescue: The Behavioral Implications of Using the Law to Increase the Incidence of Emergency Intervention. 20 *Manitoba Law Journal*: 656–697.

———. 1994. Protecting the Good Samaritan: Defences for the Rescuer in Anglo-Canadian Criminal Law. 36 *Criminal Law Quarterly*: 331–371.

———. 1994. Restitution and the Rescue of Life. 32 *Alberta Law Review*: 37–70.

Mewett, A.W., and M. Manning. 1994. *Mewett & Manning on Criminal Law*. 3rd ed. Toronto: Butterworths. Ch. 5.

Packer, H.L. 1968. *The Limits of the Criminal Sanction*. Palo Alto: Stanford University Press.

Quigley, T. 2003. Annotation: *R. v. Shuparski* (2003). 9 *Criminal Reports (6th Series)*: 272–273.

Roach, K. 2009. *Criminal Law*. 4th ed. Toronto: Irwin Law. Ch. 2.

Solomon, R., and E. Chamberlain. 2003. Calculating BACs for Dummies: The Real-World Significance of Canada's 0.08% Criminal BAC Limit for Driving. 8 *Canadian Criminal Law Review*: 219–235.

Stewart, H. 2009. Sexual Offences in Canadian Law. Aurora, ON: Canada Law Book.

Stuart, D. 2007. *Canadian Criminal Law: A Treatise*. 5th ed. Toronto: Thomson Carswell. Ch. 2.

Stuart, D., R.J. Delisle, and S. Coughlan. 2009. *Learning Canadian Criminal Law*. 11th ed. Toronto: Thomson Carswell. Ch. 2.

Trotter, G.T. 2003. Annotation: *R. v. Shuparski* (2003). 9 *Criminal Reports (6th Series)*: 273–274.

Usprich, S.J. 1987. A New Crime in Old Battles: Definitional Problems with Sexual Assault. 29 *Criminal Law Quarterly*: 200–221.

Verdun-Jones, S.N. 2007. *Canadian Criminal Cases: Selected Highlights*. 2nd ed. Toronto: Thomson Nelson. Ch. 2.

Wilson, L.C. 1988. The Defence of Others: Criminal Law and the Good Samaritan. 33 *McGill Law Journal*: 756–814.

Ziegler, M. 2000. Nonfeasance and the Duty to Assist: The American Seinfeld Syndrome. 104 *Dickson Law Review*: 525–560.

Ziff, B. 1984. A Comment on *R. v. Miller*. 22 *Alberta Law Review*: 281–290.

CHAPTER THREE

CAUSATION IN THE CRIMINAL LAW

OVERVIEW

This chapter examines the following:

1. the fundamental principles of causation that apply in the criminal law, with specific reference to the law of homicide;
2. the requirement that there be a causal connection between the accused's conduct and the consequences prohibited by the criminal law (the "but for" test);
3. the requirement of *foreseeability* as a vital element in determining whether an accused should be held accountable for his or her conduct;
4. the legal definition of death and its impact on the situation where the victim is maintained on life-support machinery;
5. the principle that a defendant can be considered to have caused the death of a person, even if the effect of the defendant's actions is only to accelerate the victim's death from some other disease or disorder, and the implications of this principle for the medical treatment of terminally ill patients;
6. the criminal responsibility of those individuals who are involved in acts of euthanasia and assisted suicide;
7. the principle that there can be more than one cause of death;
8. the approach adopted by the courts when there is an *intervening act* between the defendant's wounding of a victim and the latter's ultimate demise;
9. the requirement that the defendant's act be a "significant contributing cause" to the victim's death, a requirement articulated by the Supreme Court of Canada in the *Nette* case (2001);
10. the special rule of causation that applies in relation to first degree murder under section 231(5) & (6) of the *Criminal Code* (the *Harbottle* test);
11. the legal principles that are applicable in the situation where a wounded victim is given improper medical treatment and subsequently dies;
12. the problem of determining the cause of death where the victim refuses life-saving medical treatment; and
13. the special rules that apply where death has been caused by the impact of the accused's actions upon the mind of the victim.

CAUSATION IN CRIMINAL LAW

Where an essential element of the *actus reus* of an offence is the occurrence of certain specified consequences, it must be proved that the defendant's conduct actually caused those consequences. For example, in the *Trotta* case (2004), a husband and wife were charged with various offences following the death of their eight-month-old son. The evidence was to the effect that the husband had assaulted the baby, and that the wife, who knew of the physical abuse, did nothing to prevent it. The trial judge instructed the jury that

> ... the Crown must prove that Marco Trotta caused the death of Paolo Trotta. Perhaps the best way to approach this third ingredient, the ingredient of causation, is to ask yourselves the following question. Would Paolo Trotta have died if Marco had not committed assaultive behaviour toward him? In other words, would Paolo's death have occurred anyway even if Marco had not been assaultive towards him?

The husband was convicted of second degree murder and the wife of criminal negligence causing death. Their appeals were dismissed by the Ontario Court of Appeal. One of the grounds of the appeal concerned the trial judge's instruction to the jury on the matter of causation. Justice Doherty, in delivering the judgment of the Court of Appeal, stated that he read the trial judge's instruction "as an indication to the jury that it must find a 'but for' causal link between an assault on Paolo by Marco and Paolo's death" and held that this was "a correct instruction in the circumstances of this case." In all cases where consequences are an essential element of the *actus reus*, it is clear that the Crown must prove that, "but for" the actions of the accused, the prohibited consequences would not have occurred.

In the *Nette* case (2001), the Supreme Court ruled that there are two—quite distinct—issues that must be considered in determining whether or not the accused's conduct caused a certain prohibited consequence: namely, **factual causation** (or **causation in fact**) and **legal causation** (or **causation in law**). In the words of Justice Arbour,

> In determining whether a person can be held responsible for causing a particular result, in this case death, it must be determined whether the person caused that result both in fact and in law. Factual causation, as the term implies, is concerned with an inquiry about how the victim came to his or her death, in a medical, mechanical, or physical sense, and with the contribution of the accused to that result. Where factual causation is established, the remaining issue is legal causation.
>
> Legal causation, which is also referred to as imputable causation, is concerned with the question of whether the accused person should be held responsible in law for the death that occurred. It is informed by legal considerations such as the wording of the section creating the offence and principles of interpretation. These legal considerations, in turn, reflect fundamental principles of criminal justice such as the principle that the morally innocent should not be punished.... In determining whether legal causation is established, the inquiry is directed at the question of whether the accused person should be held criminally responsible for the consequences that occurred.

In order to establish factual causation, the Crown must prove that, *"but for" the accused's conduct, the prohibited consequences would never have occurred.* This is generally a simple task, which can often be determined by scientific or other expert evidence. However, merely because there is a causal link between the accused person's conduct and the prohibited consequence does not necessarily mean that he or she should be held criminally responsible. For example, a careful motorist may briefly pull out of his lane to see if he may pass the vehicle in front of him. However, he notices that another car is coming toward him from some considerable distance away and he quite properly pulls back into his original lane. Let us suppose that the oncoming driver inexplicably panics and brakes sharply. Her vehicle skids on some ice on the roadway and there is a terrible accident, which kills her passenger. Of course, there is a causal link between the motorist pulling out of his lane and the accident that claimed the life of the passenger in the oncoming vehicle: "but for" his action in pulling out of his lane, the fatal accident would never have occurred. However, a court would conclude that, in law, the accident was caused by the negligence of the oncoming driver: the prudent motorist who pulled out of his lane cannot be held responsible for the unforeseeable misconduct of another driver. This was essentially the situation that was found to exist in the case of *Ewart* (1990), in which Justice McClung of the Alberta Court of Appeal said that

> I can agree ... that on the evidence the operation of the Ewart vehicle was the traceable origin of Mrs. Rossman's reaction and the ensuing collision.

But that does not cast Ewart's attempt to pass as criminal.... In a court applying criminal sanction it is doubtful whether any driver can become, by operation of law alone, an insurer against extreme and unforeseeable responses of other users of the road.

Once factual causation has been established, the next issue to be decided is whether there is legal causation. In other words, even if there is a link in fact between the accused person's conduct and the prohibited consequence, it must still be decided whether the conduct should be considered sufficiently blameworthy to warrant criminal punishment. In general, the courts consider prohibited consequences to be imputable to the accused person only if they were foreseeable. As we shall discover in the next two chapters, **foreseeability**—or whether or not a consequence was foreseeable—is also a central issue in deciding whether the *mens rea* elements of the offence in question have been proved. In this respect, Justice Arbour stated in the *Nette* case (2001):

> While causation is a distinct issue from *mens rea*, the proper standard of causation expresses an element of fault that is in law sufficient, in addition to the requisite mental element, to base criminal responsibility. The starting point in the chain of causation which seeks to attribute the prohibited consequences to an act of the accused is usually an unlawful act in itself. When that unlawful act is combined with the requisite mental element for the offence charged, causation is generally not an issue. For example, in the case of murder, where an accused intends to kill a person and performs an act which causes or contributes to that person's death, it is rare for an issue to arise as to whether the accused caused the victim's death.

If the consequences of one's actions are foreseeable, it is relatively simple to conclude that there is a causal link between those actions and their consequences. From another point of view, it might also be pointed out that the requirement of foreseeability ensures that an accused person's criminal responsibility for his or her actions is not unlimited; he or she can be punished only for prohibited consequences that could be foreseen.

The distinction between factual and legal causation was dramatically illustrated by the tragic case of *Trakas* (2008). Trakas planned to sell a motorcycle. An individual came to Trakas's house and took the machine for a test drive, leaving his pickup truck in the driveway. However, another man who had been hidden drove the pickup truck away, and Trakas realized that he had been duped. Trakas decided to follow the pickup truck in his SUV. The wild chase lasted for more than 25 minutes. The two vehicles reached speeds ranging between 110 and 180 km/h. They were also observed running stop signs, tailgating, passing dangerously, making sudden lane changes and, generally, driving "erratically." During the pursuit, Trakas repeatedly contacted the police by means of his cellular phone and requested their intervention. A police officer who was intending to deploy a spike belt suddenly entered the roadway on foot and was struck by Trakas's vehicle. The officer was thrown about 88 metres and died from extremely severe injuries.

Trakas was charged with criminal negligence causing death. However, he contended that the officer's decision to suddenly jump into the roadway constituted an intervening act that severed the chain of causation between Trakas's conduct and the police officer's death. There was no doubt that Trakas caused the death of the police officer insofar as *factual causation* was concerned. After all, it was Trakas's vehicle that struck and killed the officer. However, the Crown also had to prove *legal causation* before Trakas could be convicted of the offence with which he had been charged. In order to do so, the Crown would have to establish that, at the time of the accident, Trakas was driving in a criminally negligent manner, showing wanton and reckless disregard for the lives and safety of other persons. However, Trakas had no reason to believe that a police officer would be on this particular stretch of the highway. In addition, the evidence was that Trakas was not exceeding the speed limit and was driving normally in a lane of traffic when the fatal accident occurred. The jury concluded that the Crown had failed to prove legal causation and acquitted Trakas of criminal negligence causing death. However, Trakas was convicted of dangerous driving in light of the evidence of his undoubtedly hazardous driving prior to the accident.

The Crown appealed against Trakas' acquittal on the charge of criminal negligence causing death. However, the Ontario Court of Appeal rejected the Crown's appeal.[1] In delivering the judgment of the Court, Justice Lang noted that the trial judge had correctly instructed the jury about the need for the Crown to prove both factual and legal causation, in

---

[1] The Court also rejected Trakas's appeal against his conviction of dangerous driving.

accordance with Justice Arbour's judgment in the *Nette* case. According to Justice Lang:

> First, the trial judge's instructions clearly put before the jury the question of whether the officer's presence on the road was in some way a response to the actions of the respondent in initiating and pursuing the chase or whether it was an independent intervening act. The trial judge specifically instructed the jury to consider whether the collision was "within the scope of the risk created by James Trakas when he was involved in a high-speed pursuit of Mr. Shilon over this great distance." He also put forward the Crown's position that the officer's action in stepping on the road was not an independent intervening cause because he attended at the scene only in response to the dangerous situation created by the respondent. Second, the instruction on legal causation was correctly based on *Nette*.... Among other instructions, the trial judge instructed the jury that a legally blameworthy cause must be "at least a significant" cause and "more than one that is trifling or minor."
>
> Factual causation was simply not an issue; the respondent hit the officer with his Durango and caused the officer's death. The issue, as the jury was told and would have appreciated, was whether there was any independent intervening act by the officer that severed the link of causation to the respondent's conduct.

Clearly, the jury rejected the contention that Trakas could have foreseen the officer's presence on the road and, since he was driving normally at the time of the accident, he should not be held responsible for the officer's death.

The significance of foreseeability in establishing legal causation was also demonstrated in the case of *Shilon* (2006). Shilon was the driver of the pickup truck that Trakas had been pursuing, and he had also been charged with criminal negligence causing death. The *Shilon* case turned on the issue of whether the accused should be committed for trial on this charge. The Ontario Court of Appeal ruled that Shilon should indeed be tried for criminal negligence causing death. In delivering the judgment of the Court, Justice Gillese stated that

> [r]easonable foreseeability of harm, it seems to me, is relevant in the analysis of legal causation in negligence based offences. On this view, the fact that Trakas actually caused the police officer's death does not preclude an inquiry as to whether the driver of the pickup truck ought also to be held criminally responsible for the death. There is nothing in the wording of the offence that constrains the concept of causation to preclude such an inquiry.

> In my view, where conduct is inherently dangerous and carries with it a reasonably foreseeable risk of immediate and substantial harm, the test for legal causation will have been met. On the facts of this case, there is some evidence of both criteria.
>
> ... [T]he driver of the pick-up truck drove in a criminally negligent fashion. Not only was the driving inherently dangerous, it clearly carried with it the reasonably foreseeable consequence of immediate and substantial harm. Trakas' actions were reasonably foreseeable—they were a predictable consequence of the actions of the driver of the pick-up truck. Indeed, the preliminary inquiry judge stated that the officer's death was an entirely foreseeable consequence of the conduct of the driver of the pick-up truck.
>
> Accordingly, it was an available inference that the police officer's death occurred in the ambit of the risk created by the actions of the driver of the pick-up truck and that the driver ought reasonably to have foreseen such harm.

SPECIFIC RULES CONCERNING CAUSATION IN HOMICIDE CASES

Perhaps because of the severe nature of the crimes concerned, there are a number of special rules concerning the issue of causation in relation to such offences as murder, manslaughter, infanticide, criminal negligence causing death, dangerous driving causing death, and impaired driving causing death.

The Definition of Death for the Purposes of Criminal Law

It almost goes without saying that, in order to convict an accused person of murder, manslaughter, infanticide, criminal negligence causing death, or impaired/dangerous driving causing death, the Crown must prove that the victim was, in fact, *dead* after the accused inflicted injuries on him or her. In the vast majority of cases, criminal courts have no difficulty deciding when a human being has died. If an individual has ceased breathing and the heart has stopped beating (and normal resuscitation procedures, if appropriate, fail to work), then it is clear that he or she is dead. However, in today's hospitals, it is possible to use life-support machines that artificially maintain heart and circulatory functions, and the application of this medical technology can potentially create some difficulties for criminal courts that are faced with the problem of pinpointing the moment when a patient can legitimately be considered dead.

Suppose, for example, that Brutus inflicts a severe head injury on Julius in the course of a robbery. When Julius is taken to hospital, the doctors immediately conclude that, without the use of life-support machinery, he will not be able to breathe or maintain the circulation of blood in his body. After Julius is hooked up to a life-support machine, the attending medical practitioners decide that he has suffered such a massive brain injury that he is "clinically dead." Julius's next of kin is consulted and the life-support machine is switched off by his physician. Could Brutus turn around at his trial and claim that, since the life-support machine could have maintained Julius's respiratory and circulatory functions on an indefinite basis, there is no evidence that he killed Julius and that, in fact, it was the physician's act of flicking the switch that really precipitated death? The answer to Brutus's argument would be that, if the doctors' diagnosis was that Julius had suffered *total, irreversible brain death*, then he was *dead* from the point of view of modern medical science and switching off the life-support machine was merely a recognition of that tragic reality; hence, Brutus could not claim that Julius was still alive when the artificial life support was withdrawn.

Unfortunately, to date, Parliament has not kept pace with modern medical technology and has not defined "death" for the purposes of criminal law. However, the Law Reform Commission of Canada recommended, some two decades ago, that death should be defined in legislation in a manner that is consistent with modern medical developments. More precisely, the commission advocated the adoption of the following definition: "a person is dead when an irreversible cessation of all that person's brain functions has occurred." In its 1981 report, *Criteria for the Determination of Death*, the commission recommended that the Canadian Parliament amend the *Interpretation Act*, R.S.C. 1985, c. I-21, so as to contain the following provision:

For all purposes within the jurisdiction of the Parliament of Canada,

(1) a person is dead when an irreversible cessation of all that person's brain functions has occurred.

(2) the irreversible cessation of brain functions can be determined by the prolonged absence of spontaneous circulatory and respiratory functions.

(3) when the determination of the prolonged absence of spontaneous circulatory and

respiratory functions is made impossible by the use of artificial means of support, the irreversible cessation of brain functions can be determined by any means recognized by the ordinary standards of medical practice.

Where an individual is *not* connected to a life-support machine, death will be determined on the basis of whether breathing or blood circulation is still taking place. For example, if Boris and Ivan both shoot Vladimir within seconds of each other, there may be a question as to whether Vladimir was still alive between the shot by Boris and the shot by Ivan. If there is some bleeding from the gunshot wound inflicted by Boris, then it is clear that Vladimir was still alive at the moment that Ivan pulled the trigger.

Various medical protocols have been developed to provide guidance to physicians who are called upon to determine whether an individual who is on life support has suffered total brain death. However, these protocols usually require that the same medical tests be repeated at an interval of 24 hours or so in order to ensure that the patient really has suffered total brain death rather than, for example, a temporary reaction to a drug that causes a major depression of the nervous system. This means that it takes considerable time before it can be determined beyond question that total brain death has occurred when the patient is being kept artificially alive by life-support machines. Adoption of the Law Reform Commission's definition of death would clearly resolve any uncertainty that currently exists in Canada.

Until 1999, the *Criminal Code* (section 227) maintained the archaic rule that an accused person could not be convicted of an offence of homicide unless the death of the victim occurred "within one year and

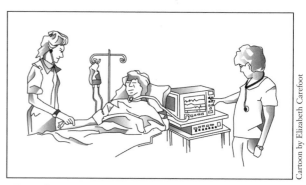

The definition of death is the irreversible cessation of all brain functions.

one day from the time of the occurrence of the last event by means of which [he/she] caused or contributed to the cause of death." Centuries ago, this old common law rule made some sense insofar as the relatively primitive state of medical science rendered it very difficult for the Crown to prove that there was the necessary causal link if a victim were to linger for a long period. However, today, modern medicine is much better equipped to establish such a link and, for this reason, Parliament repealed section 227 in 1999 (S.C., c. 5, s. 9(1)). Furthermore, it may be noted that the repeal of section 227 has the effect of forestalling the creation of a situation in which a court may be compelled to acquit an accused person of a homicide offence simply because the victim had been on life-support machinery for a period that is greater than one year and a day. Under the current law, this issue now becomes utterly irrelevant.

Acceleration of Death

A most significant legal principle relating to causation is enshrined in section 226 of the *Code*:

> Where a person causes to a human being a bodily injury that results in death, he causes the death of that human being notwithstanding that the effect of the bodily injury is only to accelerate his death from a disease or disorder arising from some other cause.

It is clear that a murderer should not be excused from punishment for a heinous act merely because the victim was, for example, a terminally ill patient who had only a few more weeks to live. However, the application of section 226 becomes more problematic when it is considered in the context of the treatment of the terminally ill by legitimate medical practitioners. If a physician administers a lethal dose of a drug with the clear intention of carrying out a so-called "mercy killing," he or she is guilty of murder; **active euthanasia** (deliberately taking steps to terminate the life of another person) is certainly not permitted under Canadian law (see section 14 of the *Criminal Code*, which clearly states that "no person is entitled to consent to have death inflicted upon him" and that the criminal liability of the person who inflicts death, in such circumstances, is not affected by the giving of such consent). However, what is the situation where the physician administers a drug with the explicit intention of reducing the agony suffered by a terminal patient but, nevertheless, realizes that this treatment may have the incidental effect of hastening death? This issue was considered in the English case of

Bodkin Adams (1957). In his summing-up to the jury, Justice Devlin said,

> ... [M]urder was an act or series of acts, done by the prisoner, which were intended to kill, and did in fact kill. It did not matter whether Mrs. Morrell's death was inevitable and that her days were numbered. If her life were cut short by weeks or months it was just as much murder as if it was cut short by years. There had been a good deal of discussion as to the circumstances in which doctors might be justified in administering drugs which would shorten life. Cases of severe pain were suggested and also cases of helpless misery. The law knew of no special defence in this category, but that did not mean that a doctor who was aiding the sick and dying had to calculate in minutes or even hours, perhaps not in days or weeks, the effect on a patient's life of the medicines which he would administer. If the first purpose of medicine— the restoration of health—could no longer be achieved, there was still much for the doctor to do, and he was entitled to do all that was proper and necessary to relieve pain and suffering even if the measures he took might incidentally shorten life by hours or perhaps even longer. The doctor who decided whether or not to administer the drug could not do this job if he were thinking in terms of hours or months of life. The defence in the present case was that the treatment given by Dr. Adams was designed to promote comfort, and if it was the right and proper treatment, the fact that it shortened life did not convict him of murder.

Dr. Adams was subsequently acquitted. It is most likely that a Canadian court, faced with the same circumstances, would adopt the approach taken by Justice Devlin in the *Bodkin Adams* case. It is particularly noteworthy that Justice Sopinka explicitly approved the principle contained in *Bodkin Adams* when he delivered the majority judgment of the Supreme Court of Canada in the *Rodriguez* case (1993):

> The administration of drugs designed for pain control in dosages which the physician knows will hasten death constitutes active contribution to death by any standard. However, the distinction here is one based on intention—in the case of palliative care the intention is to ease pain, which has the effect of hastening death, while in the case of assisted suicide, the intention is undeniably to cause death.... In my view, distinctions based on intent are important, and in fact form the basis of our criminal law.

It is important to emphasize that a physician does not commit murder where he or she acts on a request by a competent adult patient to withdraw treatment and death ensues as a consequence. In fact, the physician is required to withdraw treatment in these circumstances since every competent adult has the right to refuse treatment even if such a refusal results in death. For example, in the case of *Nancy B. v. Hôtel-Dieu de Québec* (1992), Nancy B. was a 25-year-old woman who had suffered for two and a half years from an incurable neurological disorder known as Guillain-Barré syndrome. She was paralyzed and depended on a respirator to keep her alive. She knew that her condition could not be reversed and decided that she would rather die than continue her life "literally tied to her hospital bed." She sought a court order directing the hospital and her physician to disconnect the respirator.

Justice Dufour of the Quebec Superior Court determined that Nancy B. was competent to make decisions for herself and that she, therefore, had a right to refuse treatment. The physician was given permission to disconnect the respirator. Nancy B. later died after the physician carried out her request. This is an example of so-called **passive euthanasia** (withdrawing medical treatment with the clear understanding that death will ensue).[2] While **active euthanasia** constitutes murder, **passive euthanasia** is not considered to be a crime.

However, a physician may not give assistance to a patient who wishes to commit suicide. Indeed, section 241(b) of the *Criminal Code* states that it is an indictable offence to aid or abet a person to commit suicide. Is section 241(b) valid under the *Charter*? The Supreme Court has answered this question in the affirmative. In the *Rodriguez* case (1993), Sue Rodriguez, a 42-year-old woman who was dying from amyotrophic lateral sclerosis (a degenerative disease of the muscles), sought a declaration that she had a right, under the *Charter*, to have assistance from a physician in committing suicide when her life became no longer bearable. Her condition was deteriorating rapidly and, at some point, she would be completely unable to move. Her life expectancy was between 2 and 14 months. The Supreme Court ultimately rejected the assertion that, under the terms of the *Charter*, a terminally ill person has the right to an **assisted suicide** and upheld the validity of section 241(b).

In the *Rodriguez* case (1993), the Supreme Court recognized that section 241(b) effectively deprived Sue Rodriguez of her autonomy and caused her both physical pain and psychological distress. However, a bare majority of the justices (five to four) held that section 241(b) was nevertheless valid because it reflected the principle of the sanctity of life. More specifically, it did not infringe the rights of Sue Rodriguez under section 7 (right to security of the person), section 12 (right to be free from cruel and unusual punishment), or section 15 (right to equality) of the *Charter*. According to Justice Sopinka, speaking for the majority of the justices,

> Section 241(b) has as its purpose the protection of the vulnerable who might be induced in moments of weakness to commit suicide. This purpose is grounded in the state interest in protecting life and reflects a policy of the state that human life should not be depreciated by allowing life to be taken. This policy finds expression not only in the provisions of our *Criminal Code* which prohibit murder and other violent acts against others notwithstanding the consent of the victim but also in the policy against capital punishment and, until its repeal, attempted suicide. This is not only a policy of the state, however, but is part of our fundamental conception of the sanctity of human life.

According to Justice Sopinka, a blanket prohibition of suicide (such as that contained in section 241(b)) "is the norm among western democracies, and such a prohibition has never been adjudged to be unconstitutional or contrary to fundamental human rights." In his view, "to permit a physician to lawfully participate in taking life would send a signal that there are circumstances in which the state approves of suicide."[3]

It is not entirely clear that the strong legal distinction that Justice Sopinka draws between the situations that pertained in the cases of *Nancy B.* (1992) and *Rodriguez* (1993) is quite as logically compelling as he suggests. Nancy B. could die only *with the assistance of her physician*, who ultimately turned off the respirator because her patient was *physically* incapable of doing it herself. Was this not a case of physician-assisted suicide? It is no doubt true that, in Nancy B.'s case, one can argue that it was her terrible disease that killed her through suffocation, whereas in Sue Rodriguez's case, it would have been

---

[2] Withholding food and nutrition from an individual in a "persistent vegetative state" may also be a form of passive euthanasia.

[3] In *Wakeford v. Canada* (2001), the Ontario Court of Appeal refused to support an attempt to persuade the Supreme Court of Canada to reconsider the *Rodriguez* decision. In 2002, the Supreme Court of Canada refused to hear an appeal from the Court of Appeal's decision.

the overdose of drugs that would have brought about her death. However, let us suppose entirely by way of hypothesis that another physician switched off the respirator *without Nancy B.'s consent*. Would we not say, in these circumstances, that it was the physician who caused the patient's death? After all, Nancy B. would have survived indefinitely if the machine had continued to operate. Most of us would have little difficulty in determining that the hypothetical rogue physician committed murder by switching off the machine against the patient's will. In this sense, it was the physician's act that was the immediate cause of death. However, in the real-life case of Nancy B. (1992), can one deny that the physician's conduct in turning off the switch was a cause of the patient's death (it, at least, *accelerated* Nancy B.'s death)? If the act of switching off the machine is a contributing cause of death, then one could make the argument that Nancy B. was granted a right to a physician-assisted suicide. However, Sue Rodriguez was denied the right to a physician-assisted suicide because she was seeking the right to die by means of an overdose of drugs rather than by switching off a respirator. There is clearly a difference between the facts in *Nancy B.* (1992) and *Rodriguez* (1993), but does this difference justify granting one patient a right to commit suicide with the assistance of her physician but denying it to another? Ironically, Nancy B. might have survived for many years on the respirator but Sue Rodriguez's days were very limited. This is not to argue that Nancy B. should have been forced to live on, contrary to her wishes. Indeed, it is a fundamental principle of Canadian law that no doctor can continue to administer any form of treatment if a mentally competent patient refuses to give consent. What is being suggested is that Sue Rodriguez should have been granted the same option as Nancy B. and that, perhaps, the justifications for upholding section 241(b) of the *Code* are not quite as overwhelming as the majority judgment of the Supreme Court would appear to suggest.[4] Undoubtedly, this whole issue is complex and will remain a source of profound disagreement among many Canadians.

---

[4] Belgium and the Netherlands have enacted legislation that permits both euthanasia and physician-assisted suicide under strictly regulated conditions. In the U.S.A., the State of Oregon permits physicians to prescribe a lethal drug to terminally ill patients who wish to commit suicide: *Death with Dignity Act*, 1994. In 2008, the voters of the state of Washington approved Initiative 1000, which is based on the Oregon *Death with Dignity Act*.

Liability of the Accused Where There Is More Than One Cause of Death

One principle of causation that is frequently misunderstood concerns the proposition that the defendant's act does not have to be the "sole" cause of the victim's death in order to convict him or her of culpable homicide. For example, let us suppose that Desmond strikes and wounds Vincent, who subsequently dies from massive internal hemorrhaging. Medical evidence establishes that Vincent was a hemophiliac and that the wound inflicted by Desmond would not have caused the death of a person who was not suffering from this medical condition. Desmond cannot claim that, because hemophilia was a significant "cause" of death, he should be excused from liability for culpable homicide. In other words, while both Desmond's wounding of Vincent and the latter's hemophilia each contributed to his demise, Desmond is still liable to punishment. Depending on his intention at the time of the wounding, Desmond will be convicted of murder or manslaughter. This example also illustrates the principle that aggressors must "take their victims as they find them." They cannot point to their victims' physical weaknesses as an excuse for their homicidal acts.

The application of this principle was dramatically illustrated in the tragic case of *Smithers* (1977). In this case, the accused was charged with manslaughter. He was a member of a "midget hockey" team. The deceased, Cobby, had been a member of an opposing team that had been playing Smithers' team on the day of the incident in question. Smithers had been subjected to racial insults by Cobby and others. Smithers and Cobby were later given game misconducts following a "heated and abusive exchange of profanities." Smithers threatened to "get" Cobby, who was very apprehensive as a consequence. When the latter tried to leave the arena, Smithers pursued him. Cobby hurried toward a waiting car but Smithers caught up with him and "directed one or two punches" to his head. Smithers' teammates intervened and grabbed him. However, he managed to deliver a hard, fast kick to Cobby's stomach (the latter had been making no effort to defend himself). Seconds after this kick, Cobby collapsed, gasping for air. He stopped breathing and was dead upon his arrival in hospital. It was found that Cobby had died as a result of the "aspiration of foreign materials present from vomiting." Normally, when a human being vomits, the epiglottis comes into operation and covers the windpipe. The folded epiglottis thereby prevents the stomach contents from entering the air passage. For some reason, this mechanism failed in Cobby's case.

Smithers was convicted of manslaughter and ultimately his appeal went to the Supreme Court, where the central issue was that of causation. Smithers' counsel argued that there was insufficient evidence that the accused's kick caused the vomiting. On this issue, Justice Dickson made the observation that

> ... it may be shortly said that there was a very substantial body of evidence, both expert and lay, before the jury indicating that the kick was at least a contributing cause, outside the *de minimis* range, and that is all that the Crown was required to establish. It is immaterial that the death was in part caused by a malfunctioning epiglottis to which malfunction the appellant may, or may not, have contributed.

Later in his judgment, Justice Dickson stated that it is a "well-recognized principle that one who assaults another must take his victim as he finds him." Ultimately, Smithers' appeal was dismissed. Of course, while the accused's conduct does not have to be the "sole" cause of death, it must nevertheless constitute a "significant" cause. In the *Smithers* case (1977), Justice Dickson expressed this principle by stipulating that the accused person's act must be a "contributing cause, outside the *de minimis* range" (i.e., it must be shown to have had more than a minimal impact on the events leading to the victim's death). However, this manner of articulating an important principle may well be confusing to jurors and, subsequently, the Supreme Court of Canada ruled that it would be preferable to instruct juries that the accused person's conduct should constitute a *"significant contributing cause."* As Justice Arbour stated in the *Nette* case (2001),

> The only potential shortcoming with the Smithers test is not in its substance, but in its articulation. Even though it causes little difficulty for lawyers and judges, the use of Latin expressions and the formulation of the test in the negative are not particularly useful means of conveying an abstract idea to a jury. In order to explain the standard as clearly as possible to the jury, it may be preferable to phrase the standard of causation in positive terms using a phrase such as "significant contributing cause" rather than using expressions phrased in the negative such as "not a trivial cause" or "not insignificant." Latin terms such as *"de minimis"* are rarely helpful.

In the *Nette* case (2001), the facts were that the victim, who was a 95-year-old widow living on her own, was discovered dead in her own bedroom. Her house had been robbed and she had been "hog-tied" with electrical wire. The victim's hands had been bound behind her back and her legs had been forced upward behind her back and attached to her hands. An item of clothing had been tied around the victim's head and neck and covered her chin. This "garment formed a moderately tight ligature around her neck, but did not obstruct her nose or mouth." The victim was left alone in this condition and, at some point, she fell off the bed onto the floor. During the period of 24 to 48 hours that followed the robbery, the victim died of asphyxiation. The forensic pathologist, who testified for the Crown, stated that the victim "died as a result of asphyxiation due to an upper airway obstruction." According to this expert, there was no single factor that could be said to have caused death. In his view, there were a number of different factors that contributed to the asphyxiation of the victim—"in particular, her hogtied position, the ligature around her neck, as well as her age and corresponding lack of muscle tone." In addition, the expert agreed that the victim's "congestive heart failure and asthma may possibly have speeded up the process of asphyxiation."

The accused persons argued that this was a case in which there were multiple causes of death and that their own conduct was not a significant contributing factor to the victim's death. However, the Supreme Court rejected this line of argument. Indeed, Justice Arbour said,

> ... [I]t is only in cases involving multiple causes that the jury need be charged on the applicable standard of causation. In my view, this is not such a case. The fact that the appellant's actions might not have caused death in a different person, or that death might have taken longer to occur in the case of a younger victim, does not transform this case into one involving multiple causes. Clearly, where an accused person hog ties an elderly woman, places a ligature of clothing around her neck and abandons her, in the knowledge that she lives alone, without notifying anyone of her plight, it is not unexpected that death will result if no one rescues the victim in time.
>
> ... There was no evidence that anything other than the actions of the appellant and his accomplice caused Mrs. Loski's death.

Similarly, in the later case of *Younger* (2004), the accused was charged with the murder of a two-and-a-half-year-old boy, whom he had kidnapped or unlawfully confined. The child was left in a van in a vacant lot in Winnipeg at a time when the outside temperature was around minus 2 degrees Celsius. Tragically, he died of hypothermia. Younger was convicted of murder at his trial. The Manitoba Court of Appeal dismissed Younger's appeal against his conviction. In delivering the judgment of the Court, Justice Twaddle stated that

> [t]he means by which the death is caused are irrelevant as long as the death is caused in some way by the offender. The abandonment of a scantily clad young child is certainly an act which, in my opinion, can be accepted by a jury as the cause of the child's death.
>
> Causation is a question of fact for the jury to decide subject to this: the offender's conduct need not be the sole cause of death as long as it was a significant contributing cause; a cause that is not trivial or insignificant.

The Special Test of Causation That Applies to First Degree Murder Under Section 231(5) & (6) of the *Criminal Code*

Normally, the Crown must prove that a murder was "planned and deliberate" if the accused is to be convicted of **first degree murder** (see section 231(2) of the *Criminal Code*). However, there are a number of significant exceptions to this general rule (for example, murder of a peace officer or a prison guard). Among these exceptions is section 231(5) of the *Code*, which stipulates that murder will automatically be treated as first degree murder where death occurs in the course of the commission (or attempted commission) of certain (very serious) offences, which may best be characterized as crimes of unlawful domination:

> Irrespective of whether a murder is planned and deliberate on the part of any person, murder is first degree murder in respect of a person when the death is caused by that person while committing or attempting to commit an offence under one of the following sections:
>
> (a) section 76 (hijacking an aircraft);
>
> (b) section 271 (sexual assault);
>
> (c) section 272 (sexual assault with a weapon, threats to a third party, or causing bodily harm);
>
> (d) section 273 (aggravated sexual assault);
>
> (e) section 279 (kidnapping and forcible confinement);
>
> (f) section 279.1 (hostage taking).

In the case of *Harbottle* (1993), the accused and another man had participated in a sexual assault of a 17-year-old girl and then discussed how they could kill her. The other man eventually strangled the victim with her bra while Harbottle held her legs in order to prevent her from resisting the deadly attack. The victim died and Harbottle was charged with first degree murder. The Crown relied on section 231(5) of the *Code* in light of the fact that the victim had died in the course of a sexual assault. The question arose as to whether the *Smithers* test of causation was adequate in the context of a first degree murder charge. The Supreme Court of Canada ruled that, although the *Smithers* test was adequate for a charge of manslaughter, it was not strict enough for a charge of first degree murder under section 231(5). However, the Court did not rely on the Charter in arriving at this conclusion. Rather, it referred to the seriousness of the consequences of a conviction of first degree murder and to the specific wording of section 231(5). In delivering the judgment of the Court, Justice Cory noted that

> [t]he consequences of a conviction for first degree murder and the wording of the section are such that the test of causation for [s. 231(5)] must be a strict one. In my view, an accused may only be convicted under the subsection if the Crown establishes that the accused has committed an act or series of acts which are of such a nature that they must be regarded as a substantial and integral cause of the death....
>
> The substantial causation test requires that the accused play a very active role—usually a physical role—in the killing. Under [s. 231(5)], the actions of the accused must form an essential, substantial and integral part of the killing of the victim....

According to Justice Cory, the evidence in the *Harbottle* case (1993) clearly established that the accused's conduct "was a substantial and an integral cause of the death" of the victim:

> There is every reason to believe that, had it not been for Harbottle's holding of her legs, she would have been able to resist the attempts to strangle her. In those circumstances, it is difficult to believe that Ross could have strangled her in the absence of the assistance of Harbottle.

In the subsequent case of *Nette* (2001), the Supreme Court of Canada ruled that the *Harbottle* case (1993) had not changed the factual test of causation in homicide—the *Smithers* (1977) test still applies to all cases of homicide (although, as we have seen, the Supreme Court held that the test should be rephrased so as to require that the accused person's conduct constitute a "significant contributing cause"). However, according to Justice Arbour, *Harbottle* (1993) decided that, in order to reflect the increased sentence and greater degree of stigma associated with first degree murder, Parliament has imposed an additional "causation" requirement in section 231(5):

> ... The additional "causation" requirement under s. 231(5) does not refer to factual causation but rather to an increased degree of legal causation. In other words, once the jury has determined that the accused committed murder, which entails a finding that the accused caused the victim's death in both factual and legal terms, it is then necessary to consider whether the moral culpability of the accused, as evidenced by his role in the killing, justifies a verdict of first degree murder. As [Justice] Cory ... states in *Harbottle*, "The gravity of the crime and the severity of the sentence both indicate that a substantial and high degree of blameworthiness, above and beyond that of murder, must be established in order to convict an accused of first degree murder."... Such a high degree of blameworthiness would only be established where the actions of the accused were found to be "an essential, substantial and integral part of the killing of the victim."... The terminology of "substantial cause" is used to indicate a higher degree of legal causation but it is a standard that only comes into play at the stage of deciding whether the accused's degree of blameworthiness warrants the increased penalty and stigma of first degree murder.

Significantly, Justice Arbour pointed out that the wording of section 231(6) is very similar to that of section 231(5) and that, therefore, the "**substantial-and-integral-cause**" test that was articulated in *Harbottle* (1993) should also be applied to section 231(6), which deals with murder committed while the accused person is committing or attempting to commit an offence of criminal harassment contrary to section 264 of the *Criminal Code*.[5]

The Problem of Intervening Acts

Some of the most challenging issues of causation in the criminal law relating to homicide undoubtedly arise when there is an **intervening act** or event that occurs between the defendant's original wounding

of the victim and the latter's subsequent death. Suppose that Adonis stabs Jason with a pocket knife and that, three minutes later, Hercules arrives on the scene and strangles Jason to death. In terms of the criminal responsibility of Adonis, there is a very real issue of causation: namely, did the intervening act of Hercules sever the chain of causation between the original stab wound inflicted by Adonis and Jason's subsequent death? What principles do the courts turn to when confronted by such difficult questions?

We have seen that the *Smithers* case (1977) established that an accused person generally cannot be convicted of a homicide offence unless his or her conduct made a significant contribution to the victim's death. However, in the context of a case involving an intervening act or event, the Crown must also show that the original wound inflicted by the accused person was "operative" (or continuing to have some impact) at the time of the victim's death.

Kitching and Adams (1976) provides an excellent illustration of a case in which it was determined that an intervening act had not severed the chain of causation. In this case, the defendants were charged with the manslaughter of a man called Junor. The defendants inflicted severe brain injuries upon the victim by dropping him on the sidewalk while he was in a state of extreme intoxication. Junor was taken to hospital and attached to a respirator. A neurologist determined that Junor, who was unable to breathe on his own, had suffered complete brain death. However, the respirator continued to maintain the victim's bodily functions until his kidneys could be removed for transplant purposes. After removal of the kidneys, the respirator was switched off.

At their trial, the defendants were convicted. They then appealed to the Manitoba Court of Appeal. Upon their appeal, Kitching and Adams contended that the removal of the kidneys caused Junor's death and that the conduct of the doctors, in effecting this removal, broke the chain of causation between their conduct and Junor's tragic death. However, this contention was rejected by the Court of Appeal. For example, Justice O'Sullivan said,

> The assumption underlying counsel's conduct in this case is that there can be only one cause of death. I think the law is that the conduct of a defendant in a criminal trial need not be shown to be the sole or "the effective" cause of a crime. It is sufficient if it is a cause.... I think the authorities are clear that there may be two or more independent operative causes of death.

---

[5] Parliament later added subsections (6.01), (6.1), & (6.2) to section 231. These subsections contain similar wording to subsections (5) and (6) and, therefore, it would appear that the *Harbottle* test should also be applied to these new provisions.

Without in this case criticizing the doctors of Health Sciences Centre or suggesting that they were guilty of any improper conduct, I am of the opinion that their conduct was irrelevant to the questions before the jury. Even if it could be shown that the actions of the doctors constituted an operative cause of Mr. Junor's death—and I emphasize that I do not suggest that the evidence would support such a conclusion—still that would not exonerate the accused unless the evidence left a reasonable doubt that the accused's actions also constituted an operative cause of the deceased's death.

On that question, the evidence was overwhelming. Whether or not the kidneys had been removed, the deceased could not have lasted more than a short period of time even with artificial assistance.

In effect, the court held that, even if the removal of the kidneys did constitute an operative cause of death, *the actions of the doctors had not broken the chain of causation* between the defendants' conduct and Junor's death: beyond any reasonable doubt the massive brain injury significantly contributed to Junor's death. It was irrelevant that the doctors' conduct might also have contributed to Junor's death, since there can be more than one legal cause of death.

Of course, there may be situations in which an intervening act does operate to sever the causal chain between the conduct of the accused and the ultimate death of the victim. For example, suppose that Villain poisons his elderly uncle, Moneybags, in order to gain the latter's fortune prematurely. However, before the poison has any serious effect, Moneybags is attacked by his demented butler, Grovel. In the attack, Grovel cuts Moneybags's throat with a sword taken from Moneybags's collection of weapons. Moneybags dies within five minutes of the attack. In these circumstances, it is clear that the intervening act (the attack by Grovel) was so overwhelming in its impact that it broke the causal chain between Villain's poisoning of Moneybags and the latter's untimely demise. Of course, Villain would be guilty instead of attempted murder.

The case of *Reid* (2003) highlighted a situation in which there was a very real question as to whether an intervening act had severed the chain of causation. Reid and another man, Stratton, had both kicked and punched the victim (MacKay), following an altercation. After MacKay ceased resisting, another individual clumsily administered CPR and MacKay was transported to hospital. At the trial of Reid and Stratton, the medical evidence unequivocally stated that the cause of death was asphyxiation of vomit that

had been forced into the MacKay's lungs during the "botched" attempt to administer CPR. Reid and Stratton were convicted of manslaughter. However, the Nova Scotia Court of Appeal ordered a new trial because the trial judge's instruction to the jury on the issue of causation had been inadequate. Justice Saunders indicated that the trial judge should have provided some examples of situations in which an intervening act severs the chain of causation:

> … [C]onsider the situation where A strikes B and leaves him unconscious under a tree where later a branch falls, killing the man by its own weight. Or A strikes B and the blow renders B unconscious. Other people carry B to a nearby clinic but en route they tumble down an open well where B drowns; or they are waylaid by a gang of thieves and in the ensuing robbery B is stabbed to death; or upon arrival at the hospital for treatment B contracts streptococcus, flesh eating disease from which he dies within days. These are all examples where the law would recognize a supervening cause, an interrupting exculpatory event. The intervening acts break the chain of causation. They interrupt the original infliction of injury. Some other act or event has intervened before death. The question for the jury is whether the initial injury can still be viewed as a significant contributing cause of the victim's death. Such situations ought to have been mentioned to illustrate for the jury the notion of intervening cause in law so that the jury might then go on to decide as a matter of fact whether such had occurred in this case.

Justice Saunders then suggested that the trial judge should have instructed the jury in the following terms:

> In order to be satisfied beyond a reasonable doubt that Stratton or Reid caused the death of MacKay, you are required to consider the whole of the evidence and decide: 1. Whether the accused's unlawful acts (specifically, as I have reviewed with you, in the case of Stratton the so-called headlock and in the case of Reid the alleged kicks) in fact amounted to a significant contributing cause of MacKay's death? If you are satisfied as to the first question, you should then go on to ask yourselves: 2. Whether any intervening cause which resulted in MacKay's death occurred between the accused's acts and the victim's death? Put another way, are you satisfied beyond a reasonable doubt that the actions of either Stratton or Reid are so connected to the death of MacKay that they can be said to have had a significant causal effect which continued up to the time of his death, without having been interrupted by some other act or event, in this case the failed attempts at CPR?

Similar considerations apply when the victim dies as a result of some external event or act of nature that would not have killed the victim if the accused had not wounded the victim and left him or her exposed to the elements. In these circumstances, the liability of the accused will depend upon *whether the victim's death from the external event or act of nature can be viewed as a "natural consequence" of the accused person's conduct*. In other words, the question is, would a reasonable person have foreseen the likelihood of the victim's death from the external event or act of nature? For example, in *Bradley* (1956), the accused attacked his victim, who fell unconscious to the pavement of a city street. Unfortunately for the victim, it was a January night in Winnipeg and the temperature was a bitterly cold minus 20 degrees Celsius. Furthermore, the victim was severely intoxicated. It did not appear that Bradley realized that the victim had suffered a severe head injury, but the Supreme Court assumed that, given the circumstances, it was a "natural consequence" of the accused person's conduct that the victim would die from exposure if left unconscious in such freezing weather. In this situation, therefore, it was foreseeable that death would ensue from Bradley's attack and subsequent abandonment of the unconscious victim.

A somewhat similar situation arose in the *Younger* case (2004). Here, the accused had left a two-and-a-half-year-old boy in a van in a parking lot in Winnipeg at a time when the outside temperature was around minus 2 degrees Celsius. The boy died of hypothermia. The accused was convicted of murder and his appeal was rejected by the Manitoba Court of Appeal. In delivering the judgment of the Court, Justice Twaddle ruled that the verdict of the jury at Younger's trial was not unreasonable:

> ... [T]he jury was entitled to infer that someone living in Winnipeg in the winter months would know that continued exposure to a sub-zero Celsius temperature for even an hour or so would likely cause the death of a scantily clad young child.

On the other hand, suppose that Feste stabs Toby, who is taken to hospital for treatment. After two weeks, Toby has made a good recovery, and a decision is made to transport him to another medical facility for a special diagnostic test. However, en route, Malvolio, the ambulance driver, has a massive heart attack and the ambulance goes over a cliff. Toby dies in the crash. In these circumstances, it is likely that a court would hold that Toby's death in the wreck of the ambulance is not a natural consequence of Feste's original stab wound: *this is not an outcome that can reasonably be foreseen* and, therefore, Feste would not be convicted of murder or manslaughter (of course, he could be found guilty of an offence such as aggravated assault or attempted murder).

The Impact of Improper Medical Treatment upon the Chain of Causation

A fascinating area of the law concerns the question of whether **improper medical treatment** administered to the victim may be considered to have broken the chain of causation between the accused's original wounding of the victim and the latter's death. The two leading cases in this area are English, but the principles expressed in them have certainly been approved by Canadian courts. In *Jordan* (1956), the accused had been convicted of the murder of a man called Beaumont and had been sentenced to death. Jordan had stabbed Beaumont in the abdomen in the course of a disturbance at a café. However, upon his appeal to the English Court of Criminal Appeal, new medical evidence was introduced. The evidence tended to establish that Beaumont had been subjected to improper medical treatment. First, he had been administered an antibiotic drug to which he proved to be intolerant. After severe diarrhea developed, the administration of the drug was discontinued. However, the next day, a different physician recommenced therapy with the same drug. Second, in the words of the court,

> Other steps were taken which were also regarded by the doctors as wrong—namely, the intravenous introduction of wholly abnormal quantities of liquid far exceeding the output. As a result the lungs became water-logged and pulmonary oedema was discovered. Mr. Blackburn said that he was not surprised to see that condition after the introduction of so much liquid, and that pulmonary oedema leads to broncho-pneumonia as an inevitable sequel, and it was from broncho-pneumonia that Beaumont died.

Another critical element of the medical evidence was the assertion that, although the original stab wound had penetrated the intestine of the victim, it had "mainly healed at the time of death." In these circumstances, the court quashed Jordan's conviction. Clearly, the improper (and grossly negligent) treatment had *broken the chain of causation between the original wounding and Beaumont's tragic death*. Indeed, since the wound was mainly healed, it could not be said that it was an operative cause of death at the time that Beaumont expired. In effect, it was the physicians who effectively killed Beaumont, not the accused.

In stark contrast to Jordan is the English case of *Smith* (1959), in which the accused was convicted by a general court-martial of the murder of Private Creed (a soldier in a "rival" regiment). Smith had stabbed Creed with a bayonet in the course of a confrontation between men of two British regiments stationed in Germany. Creed was dropped twice on his way to the first aid station, where the attending medical officer was so busy dealing with other victims of the disturbance that he did not have time to appreciate the seriousness of Creed's medical condition. He was given artificial respiration (which was an inappropriate treatment given the fact that his lung had been punctured) and a transfusion of saline solution, since no facilities for a blood transfusion were available. The unfortunate Private Creed died approximately two hours after the stabbing had occurred. Medical evidence for the defence contended that, had Creed not received such inappropriate treatment and had he been given a blood transfusion, the chances for his recovery would have been "as high as 75 percent."

Defence counsel relied on the *Jordan* case in pressing the Courts-Martial Appeal Court to quash Smith's conviction. Nevertheless, the conviction was upheld. Lord Chief Justice Parker stated that

> [i]t seems to the court that if at the time of death the original wound is still an operating cause and a substantial cause, then the death can properly be said to be the result of the wound, albeit that some other cause of death is also operating. Only if it can be said that the original wounding is merely the setting in which another cause operates can it be said that the death does not result from the wound. Putting it another way, only if the second cause is so overwhelming as to make the original wound merely part of the history can it be said that the death does not flow from the wound.

Since Private Creed died so quickly after the original stab wounds, it was clear that Smith's conduct was "an operating and substantial cause" of death at the time Creed expired. In the *Jordan* case, the victim died a number of days after the original wounding and, furthermore, the stab wounds had mainly healed when the improper treatments were administered. In this sense, the original wound was "merely part of the history" that led to the victim being in the hospital. In the *Smith* case, Lord Chief Justice Parker concluded the judgment of the Court by saying,

> A man is stabbed in the back, his lung is pierced and haemorrhage results; two hours later he dies of haemorrhage from that wound; in the interval there is no time for a careful examination and the treatment given turns out in the light of subsequent knowledge to have been inappropriate and, indeed, harmful. In those circumstances no reasonable jury or court could, properly directed, in our view possibly come to any other conclusion than that the death resulted from the original wound.

The *Smith* case was decided in England, but the legal principle applied is also enshrined in section 225 of the Canadian *Criminal Code*:

> Where a person causes to a human being a bodily injury that is of itself of a dangerous nature and from which death results, he causes the death of that human being notwithstanding that the immediate cause of death is proper or improper treatment that is applied in good faith.

It will be noted that section 225 refers only to treatment "that is applied in good faith." Presumably, improper medical treatment that is administered, for example, by a grossly intoxicated surgeon, would not be considered to have been applied in good faith; therefore, in such a case, the accused might well argue that the chain of causation has been broken by the improper treatment and that, owing to its specific wording, section 225 is not applicable.

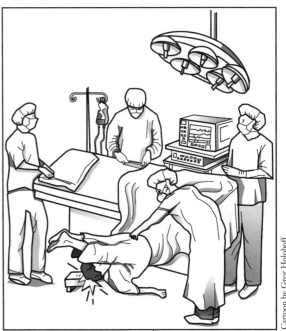

A seriously wounded patient crashes to the floor. Is the chain of causation broken?

Refusal of Treatment by the Victim of an Assault

Another provision of the *Criminal Code* that raises important issues concerning causation in homicide cases is section 224:

> Where a person, by an act or omission, does anything that results in the death of a human being, he causes the death of that human being notwithstanding that death from that cause might have been prevented by resorting to proper means.

One potential application of this section of the *Code* is to the situation where the victim of an assault refuses to take medical treatment. For example, in the old English case of *Holland* (1841), the accused was charged with the murder of a man called Garland. He had severely cut him across one of his fingers with an iron instrument during the course of an ambush. Despite medical advice concerning the very real dangers of infection, Garland refused to have his finger amputated. Two weeks later, Garland contracted lockjaw (tetanus) from the wound and, although the finger was then amputated, it was too late to save his life. Holland was, nevertheless, convicted of murder. Justice Maule said,

> ... [I]t made no difference whether the wound was in its own nature instantly mortal, or whether it became the cause of death by reason of the deceased not having adopted the best mode of treatment, the real question is, whether in the end the wound inflicted by the prisoner was the cause of death?

It might well be contended that the victim did not behave unreasonably in this case since the standards of surgical amputation in 1841 might well have given cause for second thoughts even to the bravest of men or women. Today, it is likely that the victim in the *Holland* case would be advised to have an anti-tetanus injection in order to prevent a catastrophic infection of his wound. One wonders if a modern court should convict an accused person of murder if the victim of a finger injury chooses to ignore this medical counsel and subsequently succumbs to a tetanus infection. After all, if the defendant can show that a simple injection could have prevented death from a relatively minor wound, should he or she be convicted of manslaughter if the victim resolutely refused a treatment that would have been highly effective and would have been both safe and relatively painless? Unfortunately, section 224 would appear to require that the accused be convicted in spite of these considerations because it does not require that the original wound be serious in nature.

Traditionally, criminal law has taken the view that violent persons must take their victims as they find them. It is no defence for an accused person to claim that the victim had a "thin skull" or an exceedingly weak heart. Equally, it is no defence to claim the victim brought about his or her own death by refusing treatment. Quite simply, the problem is that it is difficult to decide whether a victim's refusal of treatment is *reasonable or unreasonable*. There may be many other reasons why an accused person might refuse treatment. For example, what is the situation where a victim refuses a potentially life-saving treatment because it offends his or her religious beliefs? Who is to say whether another person's sincerely held religious beliefs are reasonable or unreasonable?

In the case of *Tower* (2008), the accused had struck his neighbour, Grismajer, across the back with some long-handled pruning shears. Grismajer suffered serious injuries, including fractured ribs and a ruptured spleen. Unfortunately, he stubbornly refused all offers of medical treatment and died in police custody two days later. Tower was charged with manslaughter and, at his trial, one of his defences was that the victim's refusal to accept treatment constituted an intervening act that broke the chain of causation. Tower was nevertheless convicted of manslaughter and his appeal against conviction was dismissed by the Nova Scotia Court of Appeal.

Justice Cromwell of the Court of Appeal noted that "the common law of causation in criminal law has generally held that failing to obtain medical treatment, or receiving inadequate treatment, could not break the chain of causation between an injury and death" and he pointed out that section 224 of the *Criminal Code* "may well reinforce this view." Justice Cromwell also emphasized that, "even with the appropriate care," the victim had suffered "a very serious injury" at Towers' hands and would have required major surgery "with all its inherent risks."

Given the undoubted severity of the injuries inflicted by Tower, few would dispute the justice of his conviction of manslaughter. However, it might well be argued that the *Criminal Code* should be amended so that section 224 only applies to those cases *where the initial injury is serious in nature*. This would mean that Tower would not be able to contend that the chain of causation was broken by his victim's failure to accept treatment, because the wound undoubtedly amounted to a life-threatening injury. On the other hand, Holland (if tried today) would be acquitted under such an amended provision, because the initial injury to the victim's finger was relatively minor and the latter's refusal to take an injection could be considered to have broken the chain of causation. In the *Holland* case, a relatively minor injury led to an infection that killed the victim. In today's setting, he could have avoided this infection very easily by accepting a simple, effective, and (almost) painless injection. To date, no such amendment to the *Criminal Code* has been proposed and, for the present, the courts must continue to convict such defendants as Holland.

Causing Death by Acting on the Victim's Mind

Sections 222(5)(c) and (d) and 228 of the *Criminal Code* establish a number of important principles concerning the causation of death by acting on the victim's mind. Section 225(5)(c) states that a person commits culpable homicide when he or she causes the death of another person "by causing that human being, by threats of fear or violence or by deception, to do anything that causes his death." This section applies in the following situation, for example. David threatens to assault Goliath, who has no route of escape. Goliath is so terrified by David's extraordinarily violent threats to disfigure him that he jumps to his death from the window of his 10th-storey apartment. In these circumstances, David would be held to have caused Goliath's death and would be criminally liable for the culpable homicide.

However, section 228 of the *Criminal Code* indicates that there are strict limitations upon the criminal law's power to punish individuals for homicides caused by an "influence on the mind." This section provides that

> No person commits culpable homicide where he causes the death of a human being
>
> (a) by any influence on the mind alone, or
>
> (b) by any disorder or disease resulting from influence on the mind alone, but this section does not apply where a person causes the death of a child or sick person by wilfully frightening him.

Essentially, this provision states that an accused person cannot be convicted of homicide if he or she causes death solely by psychological means—except where he or she deliberately frightens a child or sick victim. Section 225(5)(d) explicitly recognizes the exception to the general rule since it provides that culpable homicide is committed when an accused person causes the death of another "by wilfully frightening that human being, in the case of a child or sick person."

Section 228 was relied upon by the Alberta Court of Appeal when it quashed a verdict of manslaughter in the case of *Powder* (1981). It appears that the accused was involved in a break-in when he was confronted by the deceased. There was a struggle and the deceased died as a result of acute heart failure that had been caused by the "fear and emotional stress" generated by the break-in and subsequent conflict. There was no evidence that the physical strain involved in the struggle or any blow struck by the accused contributed in any way to the victim's death. The deceased had a pre-existing heart condition that was precipitated by the fear and emotional stress that engulfed him. In other words, the deceased had died as a consequence of an "influence on his mind alone"; therefore, section 228 was applicable and the accused could not be convicted of homicide.

Wilfully frightening a sick person to death is culpable homicide.

The *Powder* case (1981) should be compared with that of *Rusland* (1992). Here, the accused had physically assaulted a 66-year-old man who had suffered a heart attack a few months prior to the assault and was waiting for bypass surgery. The victim died as a consequence of the fracas. The trial judge acquitted Rusland and purported to follow the *Powder* (1981) decision insofar as he concluded that "the death of the deceased, by reason of his medical history, was not culpable homicide, being caused by stress only in an emotional situation." However, the Crown's appeal against this acquittal was allowed by the Ontario Court of Appeal, which ordered a new trial. The Court of Appeal pointed out that there was evidence that Rusland *actually knew about the dangerous health condition* suffered by the victim:

> Despite that knowledge, there is evidence that [Rusland] placed his hands on the deceased's shoulders and pushed or chucked the deceased who had come to intervene after the respondent had struck his own mother in the face.

If the new trial established that Rusland knew about the victim's perilous state of health and *wilfully frightened him to death*, section 228 would not save him from a conviction of manslaughter—even though the deceased died as a consequence of an "influence on the mind alone."

What is the difference between the *Powder* (1981) and *Rusland* (1992) cases? In the *Powder* case (1981), the accused did not know of his victim's heart disease and thus could not have wilfully (deliberately) frightened him to death. In *Rusland* (1992), there was evidence to suggest that the accused knew about the deceased's cardiac condition and deliberately frightened him to death by pushing him around.

STUDY QUESTIONS

1. Krook's driving licence has been suspended following a conviction for impaired driving. However, Krook, who has an extensive criminal record, continues to drive a pickup truck even though he has been banned from operating a motor vehicle and has no insurance. While driving in a mainly rural area, Krook is recognized by Boffin, a police officer who is patrolling in a cruiser. Boffin turns on his flashing lights and uses a loudspeaker to order Krook to pull over and stop. Krook deliberately ignores Boffin's command and flees the scene at very high speed. Boffin pursues Krook and turns on his siren. Krook and Boffin reach speeds of 160 km/h, drive through a red light, and ignore at least one stop sign. Sadly, Boffin's vehicle strikes and kills Pip, a young child who is crossing the road in a small rural town. Krook is charged with the offence of causing death by operating a motor vehicle while fleeing from a police officer (contrary to section 249.1 of the *Criminal Code*). Krook's lawyer contends that his client cannot be convicted of this offence since Krook was not operating the vehicle that actually struck and killed Pip. What arguments do you think the Crown could advance in order to obtain a conviction of the offence under section 249.1?

2. Grimwig attacks Dora with a knife and gravely injures her. He steals her handbag and runs away into the bush. Dora is taken to hospital where she is told that she must have a blood transfusion. She refuses this treatment on religious grounds. Dora dies a day later, and Grimwig is charged with murder. A doctor says Dora would have had a 95 percent chance of survival if she had taken the transfusion. Is Grimwig guilty of murder?

3. Bill is late for a critical business appointment and he is desperately searching for a taxi to provide him with swift transportation to his destination. He notices that Mike is just about to enter a taxi, so he violently pushes Mike away and jumps into the back seat of the vehicle. Tragically, Mike falls and his head hits the sidewalk. Mike later dies from his head injuries. The neurological specialist is prepared to testify that Mike had an "eggshell-thin" skull and that, although the fall would not have killed an ordinary person, the combination of the fall and the structural weakness of the skull was the sole cause of death in this particular case. Bill is charged with manslaughter. His counsel argues that Bill did not cause Mike's death; in fact, she argues, it was caused by what amounts to an "act of God." Does Bill have a valid defence?

4. Arthur shoots Cecil in the abdomen and the latter is immediately taken to hospital. An emergency operation is undertaken and the bullet is removed from Cecil's body. At first, Cecil appears to be making excellent progress, but after about a week, he develops some internal bleeding. Cecil is operated on by Dr. Death, who

has taken a large dose of amphetamines. Dr. Death fails to stop the bleeding and Cecil dies the next day. An independent medical specialist states that "any competent surgeon" would have saved Cecil's life. Would Arthur be considered criminally responsible for Cecil's death?

5. Duncan attacks Macbeth, who is strolling through a wheat field on the Canadian prairies. Duncan knocks Macbeth unconscious and then leaves him lying on the ground. An hour later, a combine harvester passes over the spot where Macbeth is lying and he is killed. Is Duncan criminally responsible for Macbeth's death?

6. Clara knows that her husband, Sampson, has a very serious heart condition. Indeed, his physician has made it clear to Clara that excessive exertion and/or fright could kill Sampson. One night, Clara turns off all the electrical power in their house and puts on a terrifying mask. She then goes into the room where Sampson is resting on his bed and jumps on him. Sampson believes that Clara is an intruder who is trying to kill him. Suddenly, he loses consciousness and expires then and there. A medical expert concludes that Sampson died of a catastrophic heart attack that had probably been caused by fright. Clara says that she was only indulging in some fun and that she and Sampson frequently played such games with each other. If Clara were to be charged with murder or manslaughter, would she have a defence?

7. Lillyvick, Magwitch, and Nubbles are drinking heavily in a bar. They enter into a heated argument with Orlick, who is also very intoxicated. Lillyvick, Magwitch, and Nubbles attack Orlick, who falls to the ground. Each of Orlick's assailants kicks Orlick in the head and upper body. Orlick lapses into a state of unconsciousness. Orlick is taken to the hospital where he is diagnosed as suffering from a brain injury, and it is decided that he requires immediate surgery to stop the bleeding within his skull. While Orlick is being transported to the operating room, he falls off the trolley and suffers a further injury to his head. This accident occurs because the hospital staff did not follow the recognized procedures for securing an unconscious patient and did not maintain a proper lookout while transporting him. Orlick undergoes surgery and, after two days, he appears to have a chance of recovery. However, he then succumbs to a virulent bacterial infection and dies within a week of the original assault upon him in the bar. There is evidence that the infection was almost certainly caused by negligent sterilization procedures that were followed in the operating room. A neurologist will testify that the assault on Orlick in the bar caused serious injury to the brain and that it is impossible to determine whether he would have recovered from this injury if he had not been the object of poor treatment in the hospital. The neurologist also states that the head trauma suffered by Orlick when he fell off the trolley probably aggravated his preexisting injury. Lillyvick, Magwitch, and Nubbles are charged with manslaughter but they contend that, in light of what transpired in the hospital, they did not cause Orlick's death. Is it likely that they would be acquitted of manslaughter?

8. In light of the *Nancy B.* (1992) and *Rodriguez* (1993) cases, do you think that it is fair to grant a patient in Nancy B.'s situation the right to die with the assistance of her physician but to deny the same right to a patient in the situation facing Sue Rodriguez?

9. In 2001, the Netherlands legalized—and strictly regulated—euthanasia and assisted suicide, provided they are carried out by medical practitioners. Belgium later enacted similar legislation. Using the Internet and other library-based methods of research, examine the experience with euthanasia and assisted suicide in the Netherlands and Belgium. You might also wish to examine the experience of Oregon, which has legalized physician-assisted suicide in certain circumstances (in 2008, the voters of Washington State voted in favour of a proposition for a law based on Oregon's legislation). In light of your research, do you agree or disagree with the decision of the Supreme Court in *Rodriguez* (1993)?

10. Flintwich follows his enemy, Gargery, to a deserted beach. Flintwich hits Gargery repeatedly on the head with a baseball bat. Gargery is quickly rendered unconscious, and Flintwich leaves him crumpled up on the sand. Flintwich knows that there is a tide that will cause the seawater to advance up the beach where Gargery is lying unconscious. Subsequently, the tide comes in and Gargery is drowned. A postmortem

reveals that Gargery died from drowning and that, since no major brain damage could be identified, he would most probably have recovered from his head wounds. Flintwich is charged with manslaughter. His defence is that he did not cause Gargery's death: as the medical evidence demonstrates, Gargery died as a result of drowning and not as a consequence of his head wounds. Do you think that Flintwich's defence would be successful at trial?

FURTHER READING

Anand, S. 2002. Determining Causal Standards for First Degree Murder in the Wake of *Nette*: When Does the Substantial Cause Test Apply? 46 *Criminal Law Quarterly*: 282–292.

Batavia, A.I. 2000. So Far So Good: Observations on the First Year of Oregon's *Death with Dignity Act*. 6 *Psychology, Public Policy, & Law*: 291–304.

———. 2000. The Relevance of Data on Physicians and Disability on the Right to Assisted Suicide: Can Empirical Evidence Resolve the Issue? 6 *Psychology, Public Policy*, & Law: 546–558.

Beever, A. 2001. Cause-in-Fact: Two Steps out of the Mire. 51 *University of Toronto Law Journal*: 327–366.

Brock, D.W. 2000. Misconceived Sources of Opposition to Physician-Assisted Suicide. 6 *Psychology, Public Policy, & Law*: 305–313.

Cerminara, K.L., and A. Perez. 2000. Therapeutic Death: A Look at Oregon's Law. 6 *Psychology, Public Policy, & Law*: 503–525.

Colvin, E., and S. Anand. 2007. *Principles of Criminal Law*. 3rd ed. Toronto: Carswell.

Cormack, M. 2000. Euthanasia and Assisted Suicide in the Post-*Rodriguez* Era: Lessons from Foreign Jurisdictions. 38 *Osgoode Hall Law Journal*: 591–641.

Culver, K.C., and B. Cupples. 1999. Why Withholding Treatment Is Not Assisted Suicide. 20 *Health Law Canada*: 12–16.

De Haan, J. 2002. The New Dutch Law on Euthanasia. 10 *Medical Law Review*: 57–75.

Dickens, B.M. 1993. Medically Assisted Death: *Nancy B. v. Hôtel-Dieu de Québec*. 38 *McGill Law Journal*: 1053–1070.

Downie, J. 2004. *Dying Justice: A Case for Decriminalizing Euthanasia and Assisted Suicide in Canada*. Toronto: University of Toronto Press.

Downie, J., & S. Bern. 2008. *Rodriguez* Redux. 16 *Health Law Journal*: 27–54.

DuVal, G. 1995. Assisted Suicide and the Notion of Autonomy. 27 *Ottawa Law Review*: 1–31.

Galloway, D. 1989. Causation in Criminal Law: Interventions, Thin Skulls and Lost Chances. 14 *Queen's Law Journal*: 71–83.

Gorsuch, N.M. 2000. The Right to Assisted Suicide and Euthanasia. 23 *Harvard Journal of Law & Public Policy*: 599–710.

Grant, I. 2008. The Boundaries of the Criminal Law: The Criminalization of the Non-disclosure of HIV. 31 *Dalhousie Law Journal*: 123–180.

Grant, I., D. Chunn, and C.L.M. Boyle. 1994. *The Law of Homicide*. Toronto: Carswell. Ch. 3.

Hall, M.I. 2005. Case Comment: Duty, Causation, and Third-Party Perpetrators. 50 *McGill Law Journal*: 597–616.

Healy, P. 1994. Suicide and Solitude. 24 *Criminal Reports (4th Series)*: 389–394.

Hoffmaster, B. 1994. Dragons in the Sunset: The Allure of Assisted Death. 14 *Windsor Yearbook of Access to Justice*: 269–299.

Horder, J. 2005. Can the Law Do Without the Reasonable Person? 55 *University of Toronto Law Journal*: 253–269.

Hwang, K. Attitudes of Persons With Physical Disabilities Toward Physician-Assisted Death. 16 *Journal of Disability Policy Studies*: 16–21.

Jones, D.J. 1993. Retrospective on the Future: Brain Death and Evolving Legal Regimes for Tissue Replacement Technology. 38 *McGill Law Journal*: 394–415.

Kelly, B. 2006. Physician-Assisted Suicide and Psychiatry. 5 *Psychiatry*: 289–291.

Kerkhof, A.J.F.M. 2000. How to Deal with Requests for Assisted Suicide: Some Experiences and Practical Guidelines from the Netherlands. 6 *Psychology, Public Policy, & Law*: 452–466.

Law Reform Commission of Canada. 1981. Report No. 15: *Criteria for the Determination of Death*. Ottawa: Ministry of Supply and Services Canada.

———. 1983. Report No. 20: *Euthanasia, Aiding Suicide and Cessation of Treatment*. Ottawa: Ministry of Supply and Services Canada.

———. 1984. Working Paper No. 33: *Homicide*. Ottawa: Ministry of Supply and Services Canada.

———. 1987. Report No. 31: *Recodifying Criminal Law*. Rev. ed. Ottawa: L.R.C.C.

Lee, B.C., and J.L. Werth, Jr. 2000. Observations on the First Year of Oregon's *Death with Dignity Act*. 6 *Psychology, Public Policy, & Law*: 268–290.

Libman, R. 1990. The Requirement of Causation in the New Offences of Impaired Driving Causing Bodily Harm or Death and Dangerous Driving Causing Bodily Harm or Death; An Update. 17 *Motor Vehicle Reports (2nd Series)*: 227–255.

MacIntyre, D. 1989. Impaired Driving Causing Death or Bodily Harm: The Causality Issue. 1 *Journal of Motor Vehicle Law*: 125–130.

Manga, P. 2001. Euthanasia and Medically Assisted Suicide—The Case for Legalizing Physician Assisted Suicide. 20 *Medicine and the Law*: 451–462.

Manson, A. 1993. Rethinking Causation: Implications of *Harbottle*. 24 *Criminal Reports (4th Series)*: 153–165.

Marlyn, S., and H.J. Bourguignon. 2000. Physicians' Decisions about Patient Capacity: The Trojan Horse of Physician-Assisted Suicide. 6 *Psychology, Public Policy, & Law*: 388–401.

Martel, J. 2001. Examining the Foreseeable: Assisted Suicide as a Herald of Changing Moralities. 10 *Social & Legal Studies*: 147–170.

Mewett, A.W. 1994. Editorial: Causation and the *Charter*. 37 *Criminal Law Quarterly*: 1–3.

Mewett, A.W., and M. Manning. 1994. *Mewett & Manning on Criminal Law*. 3rd ed. Toronto: Butterworths. 145–154.

Meyers, D.W., and J.K. Mason. 1999. Physician-Assisted Suicide: A Second View from Mid-Atlantic. 28(3) *Anglo-American Law Review*: 265–286.

Moore, M.S. 2000. The Metaphysics of Causal Intervention. 88 *California Law Review*: 827–878.

Morse, S.J. 2000. The Moral Metaphysics of Causation and Results. 88 *California Law Review*: 879–894.

Nuccetelli, S., and G. Seay. 2000. Relieving Pain and Foreseeing Death: A Paradox about Accountability and Blame. 28 *The Journal of Law, Medicine & Ethics*: 19–25.

Ogden, R. 1994. *Euthanasia and Assisted Suicide in Persons with Acquired Immunodeficiency Syndrome (AIDS) or Human Immunodeficiency Virus (HIV)*. New Westminster, BC: Peroglyphics Publishing.

Orentlicher, D. 2000. The Implementation of *Oregon's Death with Dignity Act*: Reassuring, but More Data Are Needed. 6 *Psychology, Public Policy, & Law*: 489–502.

Parks, R.C. 2000. A Right to Die with Dignity: Using International Perspectives to Formulate a Workable U.S. Policy. 8 *Tulane Journal of International & Comparative Law*: 447–482.

———. 2001. On Scarlet Fever and Falling Trees: Blamable Causation and *Mens rea*. 25 *Criminal Law Journal*: 59–63.

Plaxton, M. 2000. Imputable Causation as *Mens rea*: A Reply to Professor Yeo. 33 *Criminal Reports (5th Series)*: 78–82.

Presser, J. 1994. All for a Good Cause: The Need for Overhaul of the *Smithers* Test of Causation. 28 *Criminal Reports (4th Series)*: 178–193.

Reik, J. 2000. Physician-Assisted Suicide: Is There a Right to Die? *4 Journal of Medicine & Law*: 237–253.

Roach, K. 2009. *Criminal Law*. 4th ed. Toronto: Irwin Law.

Rodgers, G. 1991. The Test of Causation in Criminal Driving Cases. 3 *Journal of Motor Vehicle Law*: 137–144.

Rosenefeld, B. 2000. Assisted Suicide, Depression, and the Right to Die. 6 *Psychology, Public Policy, & Law*: 467–488.

Rozovsky, L.E., and F.A. Rozovsky. 1997. *The Canadian Law of Consent to Treatment*. 2nd ed. Toronto: Butterworths.

Ryan, H.R.S. 1994. Leaving Euthanasia for Parliament. 24 *Criminal Reports (4th Series)*: 366–368.

Searles, N. 1996. Silence Doesn't Obliterate the Assisted Truth: A Manitoba Survey on Physician Assisted Suicide and Euthanasia. 4 *Health Law Review*: 9–16.

Sheehy, A. 2005. Causation, Common Sense, and the Common Law: Replacing Unexamined Assumptions with What We Know About Male Violence. 17 *Canadian Journal of Women and the Law*: 87–116.

Sneiderman, B. 1985. Why Not a Limited Defence? A Comment on the Proposals of the Law Reform Commission of Canada on Mercy-Killing. 15 *Manitoba Law Journal*: 85–96.

———. 1993. The Case of Nancy B.: A Criminal Law and Social Policing Perspective. 1 *Health Law Journal*: 25–38.

———. 1997. A Winnipeg Inquest: A Case of Natural Death or Physician-Assisted Suicide? 24 *Manitoba Law Journal*: 365–380.

———. 1999. *Latimer, Davis,* and *Doerksen*: Mercy Killing and Assisted Suicide on the Op. Ed. Page. 25 *Manitoba Law Journal*: 449–466.

Sneiderman, B., and R. Deutscher. 2002. Dr. Nancy Morrison and Her Dying Patient: A Case of Medical Necessity. 10 *Health Law Journal*: 1–30.

Sneiderman, B., and M. Verhoef. 1995. Patient Autonomy and the Defence of Medical Necessity: Five Dutch Euthanasia Cases. 34 *Alberta Law Review*: 374–415.

Somerville, M. 2001. *Death Talk: The Case against Euthanasia and Physician-Assisted Suicide*. Montreal & Kingston: McGill-Queen's University Press.

Stuart, D. 2007. *Canadian Criminal Law: A Treatise*. 5th ed. Toronto: Thomson Carswell. 136–160.

Stuart, D., R.J. Delisle, and S. Coughlan. 2009. *Learning Canadian Criminal Law*. 11th ed. Toronto: Thomson Carswell. Ch. 2.

Tanovich, D.M., and J. Lockyer. 1996. Revisiting *Harbottle*: Does the "Substantial Cause" Test Apply to All Murder Offences? 38 *Criminal Law Quarterly*: 322–332.

Trotter, G.T. 2002. Developments in Criminal Law and Procedure: The 2001–2002 Term. 18 *Supreme Court Law Review*: 203–270.

Van Bruchem-van de Scheur, G.G. et al. 2007. Euthanasia and Physician-Assisted Suicide in the Dutch Homecare Sector: The Role of the District Nurse. 58 *Journal of Advanced Nursing*: 44–52.

Verdun-Jones, S.N. 2007. *Canadian Criminal Cases: Selected Highlights*. 2nd ed. Toronto: Thomson Nelson. Chap. 3.

Werth, J.L. Jr., G.A.H. Benjamin, and T. Farrenkopf. 2000. Requests for Physician-Assisted Death: Guidelines for Assessing Mental Capacity and Impaired Judgment. 6 *Psychology, Public Policy, & Law:* 348–372.

Werth, J.L., & H. Wineberg. 2004. A Critical Analysis of the Oregon *Death with Dignity Act*. 29 *Death Studies*: 1–27.

White, M., and D. Callahan. 2000. Oregon's First Year: The Medicalization of Control. 6 *Psychology, Public Policy, & Law*: 331–341.

Wineberg, H., & J.L. Werth. 2003. Physician-Assisted Suicide in Oregon: What Are the Key Factors? 27 *Death Studies*: 501–518.

Wright, W. 2000. Historical Analogies, Slippery Slopes, and the Question of Euthanasia. 28 *The Journal of Law, Medicine & Ethics*: 176–186.

Yeo, S. 2000. Blamable Causation. 24 *Criminal Law Journal*: 144–163.

———. 2000. Giving Substance to Legal Causation. 29 *Criminal Reports (5th Series)*: 215–224.

———. 2002. Causation, Fault and the Concurrence Principle. 10 *Otago Law Review*: 213–228.

Youngner, S.J. 2000. Bureaucratizing Suicide. 6 *Psychology, Public Policy, & Law*: 402–407.

CHAPTER FOUR

THE MENTAL ELEMENT IN THE CRIMINAL LAW: SUBJECTIVE LIABILITY

OVERVIEW

This chapter examines the following:

1. the definition of *mens rea:* namely, all of the mental elements (other than voluntariness) that the Crown must prove in order to obtain a conviction of a criminal offence;

2. the paramount importance in criminal law of the *mens rea* elements of an offence because they operate to ensure that only those who are *morally blameworthy* are convicted of "true crimes";

3. the fact that subjective *mens rea* is based on the notion that accused persons may not be convicted of a criminal offence unless (1) they *deliberately intended* to bring about the consequences prohibited by law or (2) *subjectively realized* that their conduct might produce such prohibited consequences and proceeded with that conduct regardless of their actual knowledge of that risk;

4. the principle that subjective *mens rea* requires that the Crown prove that the accused *deliberately chose* to do something wrong;

5. the basic forms of subjective *mens rea* that the Crown may be required to prove: *intention, knowledge, recklessness,* and *wilful blindness*;

6. the certain technical terms in the *Criminal Code* that require the Crown to prove a particular mental state in addition to intention or knowledge—for example, "fraudulently" (in relation to theft, under section 322), "fraudulent" (in relation to the offence of fraud under section 380), and "planned and deliberate" (in relation to the distinction between first and second degree murder, under section 231);

7. the explanation that direct intention refers to intention in the popular sense of an individual acting with the desire, purpose, aim, objective, or design to achieve a certain consequence;

8. the principle that indirect intention exists where an accused person does not desire that his or her conduct produce a prohibited consequence but nevertheless knows that this consequence is a necessary step on the way to accomplishing the objective that he or she really does wish to achieve;

9. the fact that indirect intention also exists where an accused person does not desire to bring about a prohibited consequence but knows that it is "substantially certain" to result from his or her conduct, which is designed to accomplish some other objective;

10. the sharp distinction in criminal law between intent and motive and the fact that, in most criminal trials, the Crown must prove intent rather than motive;

11. the explanation that intent refers to the accused person's deliberate choice to use particular means to bring about a consequence that is prohibited by criminal law;

12. the principle that motive is the mental condition that precedes, and induces, the accused person's deliberate choice to do something wrong;

13. the fact that, for most crimes, the requisite *mens rea* elements contain no reference to motive;

14. the principle that, under the doctrine of transferred intent, if an accused person means to kill or assault A but unexpectedly kills or assaults B, then he or she will be convicted of murder or assault respectively;

15. the common law doctrine of transferred intent that applies to many crimes but that is operative only where the accused person intended to

commit the *actus reus* of the same offence with which he or she is charged;

16. The form of *mens rea*, known as recklessness, which exists where the accused person subjectively realizes that his or her conduct creates a risk of bringing about a prohibited consequence but, nevertheless, unjustifiably assumes that risk;

17. the principle that recklessness involves both a subjective and an objective component; the accused must subjectively appreciate the risk and the Crown must prove that a reasonable person acting prudently would not have assumed that risk;

18. the principle that wilful blindness arises where an accused person is virtually certain that illicit circumstances exist (for example, that goods have been stolen) but deliberately shuts his or her eyes to these circumstances in order to avoid acquiring actual knowledge of those circumstances;

19. the fact that wilful blindness is treated as being equivalent to actual knowledge.

MENS REA: AN INTRODUCTION

In Chapter 2, we saw how the terms *actus reus* and *mens rea* were derived from the Latin maxim "*actus non facit reum nisi mens sit rea,*" or "an act does not render a person guilty of a criminal offence unless his or her mind is also guilty." Chapters 4 and 5 turn the spotlight on the principles that apply when a court is required to determine whether an accused person's "mind is guilty." In short, these two chapters will identify the various *mens rea* elements of a criminal offence that must be established before an individual may be held criminally responsible for his or her conduct.

In Chapter 2, it was also pointed out that it would be a mistake to assume that there is a clear-cut distinction between the physical and mental elements of a criminal offence. Indeed, since an accused person's act must be voluntary in order for a court to find that the *actus reus* elements are present, the *actus reus* in essence contains its own mental element. So what is meant by the term *mens rea*? Simply put, *mens rea* refers to all of the mental elements (other than voluntariness) that the Crown must prove in order to obtain a conviction of a criminal offence. These mental elements inevitably vary from crime to crime. The *mens rea* for murder is obviously very different from the *mens rea* required for theft or arson. In order to ascertain the necessary *mens rea* elements that must be established by the Crown, it is therefore vital to analyze the mental element(s) that are required in relation to each component of the *actus reus* of the specific offence concerned (that is, conduct, circumstances, and consequences). For example, the Crown may be required to prove that the accused acted intentionally, with full knowledge of the relevant circumstances and of the probable consequences of his or her actions.

The *mens rea* elements of an offence are of paramount importance in criminal law because they operate to ensure that only those who are *morally blameworthy* are convicted of "true crimes" under the *Criminal Code.* As Justice McLachlin of the Supreme Court of Canada said in the case of *Théroux* (1993),

> *Mens rea* ... refers to the guilty mind, the wrongful intention, of the accused. Its function in the criminal law is to prevent the conviction of the morally innocent—those who do not understand or intend the consequences of their acts.

Similarly, Justice Lamer of the Supreme Court of Canada said in the *Reference Re Section 94(2) of the Motor Vehicle Act* case (1985),

It has from time immemorial been part of our system of laws that the innocent not be punished. This principle has long been recognized as an essential element of a system of justice which is founded upon a belief in the dignity and worth of the human person and on the rule of law.

Significantly, Justice Lamer went on to assert that this principle is one of the "fundamental principles of justice" enshrined in section 7 of the *Charter*.

In essence, the *mens rea* requirements of criminal law operate to excuse from criminal liability all those accused persons who cannot be considered to be blameworthy for their conduct. For example, accused persons who act under a fundamental mistake of fact as to an essential element of the *actus reus* of an offence must be acquitted of a true crime because they would lack the necessary *mens rea* for that offence. Consider the situation in which an accused person takes another individual's cellular phone, mistakenly believing that it belongs to him or her. There would be no question of convicting the accused of theft because he or she would lack knowledge of an essential element of the *actus reus* of that crime—namely, that the cellular phone was the property of another person. On the facts as the accused honestly believed them to be, he or she was not committing any crime and, therefore, lacked one of the necessary elements of the *mens rea* for theft.

An accused person may also lack the necessary *mens rea* elements for conviction of an offence where he or she does not understand or intend the consequences of his or her actions. Indeed, this proposition was underscored by Justice McLachlin of the Supreme Court of Canada in the case of *Théroux* (1993):

> Typically, *mens rea* is concerned with the consequences of the prohibited *actus reus*. Thus in the crimes of homicide, we speak of the consequence of the voluntary act—intention to cause death, or reckless and wilfully blind persistence in conduct which one knows is likely to cause death. In other offences, such as dangerous driving, the *mens rea* may relate to the failure to consider the consequences of inadvertence.

Clearly, an accused person who does not foresee the consequences of his or her actions cannot be convicted of murder because it is an essential element of the *mens rea* of murder that the accused person foresees the likelihood that death will ensue. Similarly, section 16 of the *Criminal Code* provides that those individuals who are so mentally disordered that they do not appreciate what they are doing should be found not criminally responsible: these individuals would not understand the consequences of their actions and are, therefore, lacking in *mens rea*. Likewise, section 13 of the *Criminal Code* stipulates that children who are under the age of 12 years cannot be held criminally responsible for their actions. Parliament enacted this provision in recognition of the view that young children are not capable of fully understanding the consequences of their conduct, and, in this sense, they do not have the necessary *mens rea* for conviction of a criminal offence.

SUBJECTIVE AND OBJECTIVE *MENS REA*

Although it is clear that an individual who lacks the necessary *mens rea* for an offence cannot be held criminally responsible because he or she is morally innocent, it is important to recognize that there are two distinct types of *mens rea* requirements in Canadian criminal law. Supreme Court of Canada Justice McLachlin stated in the case of *Creighton* (1993),

> The *mens rea* of a criminal offence may be either subjective or objective, subject to the principle of fundamental justice that the moral fault of the offence must be proportionate to its gravity and penalty. Subjective *mens rea* requires that the accused have intended the consequences of his or her acts, or that, knowing of the probable consequences of those acts, the accused have proceeded recklessly in the face of the risk. The requisite intention or knowledge may be inferred directly from the act and its circumstances. Even in the latter case, however, it is concerned with "what was actually going on in the mind of this particular accused at the time in question."...
>
> Objective *mens rea*, on the other hand, is not concerned with what the accused intended or knew. Rather the mental fault lies in failure to direct the mind to a risk which the reasonable person would have appreciated. Objective *mens rea* is not concerned with what was actually in the accused's mind, but with what should have been there, had the accused proceeded reasonably.

Subjective *mens rea* is based on the notion that accused persons may not be convicted of a criminal offence unless they (1) *deliberately intended* to bring about the consequences prohibited by law or (2) *subjectively realized* that their conduct might produce such prohibited consequences and proceeded with that conduct regardless of their actual knowledge of that risk. Subjective *mens rea*, therefore, requires that the Crown prove that the accused *deliberately chose* to do something wrong.

Objective *mens rea*, in contrast, does not require proof that accused persons deliberately intended to bring about a prohibited consequence or even that they subjectively appreciated the risk that their conduct might produce such a result. Objective *mens rea* is predicated on the principle that reasonable persons, in the same circumstances as the accused, would have appreciated that their conduct was creating a risk of producing prohibited consequences and would have taken action to avoid doing so. Here the fault of the accused does not lie in deliberately choosing to do something wrong; instead, the fault is to be found in the fact that the accused had the capacity to live up to the standard of care expected of a reasonable person and failed to do so. As Justice McLachlin said, in the passage quoted above from the *Creighton* case (1993), "[T]he mental fault lies in failure to direct the mind to a risk which the reasonable person would have appreciated."

It is important to acknowledge that those accused persons who have subjective *mens rea* will generally be treated as being more culpable than those who are convicted on the basis of objective *mens rea*: after all, the former have deliberately chosen to do something wrong, whereas the latter were not even aware of the risk that their conduct was creating (although a reasonable person would have been). The Supreme Court has, therefore, ruled that, in order to ensure that the degree of punishment imposed on offenders is commensurate with the extent of their fault, the most serious punishments should be reserved for those who are proved to have possessed subjective *mens rea*. As we shall see, the most important example of the application of this principle is in relation to the offence of murder. The Supreme Court of Canada has ruled that, since murder carries the most severe penalty in the *Criminal Code* as well as the greatest degree of associated stigma, accused persons may not be convicted of this offence unless they subjectively foresaw the risk that their conduct would bring about someone's death (see the *Martineau* case (1990) discussed later in this chapter).

PARTICULAR FORMS OF SUBJECTIVE *MENS REA*

The basic forms of subjective *mens rea* that the Crown may be required to prove are *intention, knowledge, recklessness,* and *wilful blindness*. However, as we shall see later, over and above these basic forms of *mens rea*, there are certain situations in which the Crown must also prove some special mental element that is required by the definition of the particular offence in question (such as "fraud" in the case of a charge of theft under section 322).

THE CONCEPTS OF INTENTION AND KNOWLEDGE

Many of the definitions of criminal offences contained in the *Criminal Code* explicitly require the proof of *mens rea* in the form of an *"intended" consequence or actual "knowledge" of particular circumstances.* For example, section 265(1) of the *Criminal Code* provides that

[a] person commits an assault when

(a) without the consent of another person, he applies force *intentionally* to that other person, directly or indirectly.... [emphasis added]

Similarly, section 155(1) of the *Code* provides that

[e]very one commits incest who, *knowing* that another person is by blood relationship his or her parent, child, brother, sister, grandparent or grandchild, as the case may be, has sexual intercourse with that person. [emphasis added]

In other circumstances, the requirement that the accused intended to bring about a certain consequence, or that he or she engaged in conduct with knowledge of particular circumstances, may not be expressly stated in the *Code*: nevertheless, the courts may well hold that such a requirement is "implied" by the language used by Parliament. For example, in the case of *Lecompte* (2000), the accused had been charged (under section 66 of the *Criminal Code*) with being a member of an unlawful assembly. Section 63 of the *Code* states that

[a]n unlawful assembly is an assembly of three or more persons who, with intent to carry out any common purpose, assemble in such a manner or so conduct themselves when they are assembled as to cause persons in the neighbourhood of the assembly to fear, on reasonable grounds, that they

(a) will disturb the peace tumultuously; or
(b) will by that assembly, needlessly and without reasonable cause provoke other persons to disturb the peace tumultuously.

Section 63 does not state explicitly that an accused person must have knowledge of the likelihood that the assembly of which he or she is a member will disturb the peace or provoke other individuals to disturb

the peace tumultuously. Nevertheless, the Quebec Court of Appeal ruled that such knowledge is an implied element of the *mens rea* requirements for this offence. As Justice Beauregard stated,

I am of the view that, even before the *Charter*, s. 66 had to be interpreted so as not to render culpable a member of an assembly who did not have knowledge of a fact which gave rise to the fear that the peace would be disturbed tumultuously. The criminal law has never intended to punish a person who is unaware of a relevant fact situation.

Sometimes the *Criminal Code* employs other terms to indicate a requirement of intent. For example, section 139(1) states that "everyone who wilfully attempts in any manner to obstruct, pervert or defeat the course of justice in a judicial proceeding," in the specified circumstances, is guilty of an offence. Similarly, section 229 of the *Code* provides that

[c]ulpable homicide is murder

(a) where the person who causes the death of a human being

(i) *means to* cause his death, or
(ii) *means to* cause him bodily harm that he knows is likely to cause his death, and is reckless whether death ensues or not.... [emphasis added]

Not surprisingly, Canadian courts have ruled that such terms as "wilfully" and "means to" are merely synonymous with the requirement of "intent."

One final point should be made about the *mens rea* requirement of "knowledge." Where the Crown is required to prove *knowledge* of a particular circumstance, or set of circumstances, it must also prove that this particular circumstance or set of circumstances did, in fact, exist. As Supreme Court of Canada Justices Cory and Iacobucci stated in the *Dynar* case (1997), *it is not possible to know something that is false.* Put another way, "knowledge implies truth." In *Dynar*, the Supreme Court ruled that an individual may not be convicted of the crime of laundering money "knowing" that the funds in question are the "proceeds of crime," if the funds have not, in fact, been obtained or derived as a consequence of criminal activity. This reasoning applies even if the accused mistakenly *believed* that the money in question constituted the proceeds of crime. It is significant that, in 1997, after the *Dynar* case went to trial, section 462.31 of the *Criminal Code* was amended so that the relevant offence is now one of laundering money "*knowing or believing* that all or a part of that property or of those proceeds was obtained or derived directly or indirectly" from the commission of a crime.

SPECIAL MENTAL ELEMENTS THAT MUST BE PROVED IN ADDITION TO INTENTION AND KNOWLEDGE

Canadian courts have ruled that certain terms in the *Criminal Code* have special, technical meanings. When such technical terms are employed in the *Code*, the Crown is required to prove a particular mental state in addition to intention or knowledge. Conspicuous examples of such special, technical terms are "**fraudulently**" (in relation to theft, under section 322), "**fraudulent**" (in relation to the offence of fraud under section 380), and "**planned and deliberate**" (in relation to the distinction between first and second degree murder, under section 231).

The Meaning of "Fraudulent" in Section 380

As Justice Cory pointed out, on behalf of the majority of the Supreme Court of Canada in *Cuerrier* (1998), "[T]he essential elements of fraud are *dishonesty ... and deprivation or risk of deprivation.*" Therefore, in their interpretation of the term "fraudulent" in the specific context of section 380(1) of the *Criminal Code*, the courts have insisted that the Crown prove that the accused acted *dishonestly*. This element of dishonesty is required in addition to proof that the accused acted intentionally or with knowledge of the particular circumstances. The judicial interpretation of the concept of **fraud** has clearly emerged in relation to charges laid under section 380 of the *Criminal Code*. Section 380(1) states that

> [e]very one who, by *deceit, falsehood or other fraudulent means*, whether or not it is a false pretence within the meaning of this Act, defrauds the public or any person, whether ascertained or not, of any property, money or valuable security or any service ... [is guilty of an offence]. [emphasis added]

It is clear that fraud is not confined to the obtaining of property and so forth by deceit or falsehood—forms of behaviour that essentially involve lying on the part of the defendant. After all, section 380(1) specifically refers to "other fraudulent means," which means that the concept of fraud in the *Code* extends beyond situations where the defendant deliberately tells a lie. In the case of *Olan, Hudson and Hartnett* (1978), the Supreme Court of Canada ruled

that "the words 'other fraudulent means' in s. [380(1)] include means which are not in the nature of a falsehood or a deceit; they encompass all other means which can properly be stigmatized as dishonest."

The facts in the *Olan* case are undoubtedly complex. However, a somewhat simplified version will suffice for our purposes. The accused were charged with defrauding a dry cleaning company, Langley's Limited, of money and valuable securities worth some $1 million. Beauport Holdings Limited, a company controlled by one of the accused, took over Langley's Limited by purchasing a controlling block of its shares; however, it needed a substantial bank loan to do so. Representatives of Beauport Holdings Limited were then placed in control of the board of directors of Langley's Limited. The new directors caused Langley's Limited to divest itself of its holdings in "blue chip" securities (that is, valuable and secure investments) and to purchase shares in another company, Beauport Financial Corporation Limited, which was controlled by two of the accused. Some $790 000, which was acquired by Beauport Financial as a result of the share purchase, was then loaned to Beauport Holdings. This money was used to pay off part of the bank loan that Beauport Holdings had used to purchase the controlling block of Langley's shares. In essence, Langley's had exchanged its secure and valuable investment portfolio for shares in Beauport Financial, whose principal asset was the debt owed to it by Beauport Holdings. In the previous year, Beauport Holdings sustained a net operating loss and its current liabilities exceeded its assets by more than $1 million. Clearly, the value and security of the shares in Beauport Financial were somewhat shaky at best. On these facts, it was contended by the Crown that the sale of Langley's shares had been carried out for the personal interests of the new directors rather than for the ***bona fide*** business interests of Langley's Limited.

It was clear that the accused had not been deceitful or uttered any falsehood. Indeed, the accused vigorously claimed that their activities had all been "above board." However, the question arose as to whether their conduct nevertheless constituted fraud within the meaning of section 380 of the *Code*. The Court emphasized that the prosecution was not required to prove any deception on the part of the accused. Indeed, Justice Dickson, in delivering the judgment of the Court, stated that the words "other fraudulent means" in section 380(1) "encompass all other meanings which can properly be stigmatized as dishonest." In the view of the Supreme Court of Canada, the prosecution must establish two separate elements in order to prove fraud, namely *dishonesty* (the *mens rea*) and *deprivation* (the *actus reus*). Insofar as this particular case was concerned, Justice Dickson said that

> [u]sing the assets of the corporation for personal purposes rather than *bona fide* for the benefit of the corporation can constitute dishonesty in a case of alleged fraud by directors of a corporation....
>
> The element of deprivation is satisfied on proof of detriment, prejudice, or risk of prejudice to the economic interest of the victim. *It is not essential that there be actual economic loss as the outcome of the fraud.* [emphasis added]

The Supreme Court of Canada ruled that, although the accused may well have intended to have Beauport Holdings repay the loan to Beauport Financial, this would not prevent them from being found fraudulent if their conduct was otherwise shown to involve dishonest deprivation for their own personal ends. In this particular case, the Court ordered a new trial, which was to be conducted in accordance with the principles enunciated by Justice Dickson.

The *Olan* case clearly defined fraud as dishonest deprivation. However, Justice Dickson did not provide any detailed guidance as to the necessary *mens rea* that the Crown must prove in a case of fraud. He merely agreed with the trial judge that it must be established that the accused's "conduct must be deliberately dishonest." It was left to the later case of *Théroux* (1993) for the Supreme Court of Canada to clarify the *mens rea* requirements of fraud. Indeed, Justice McLachlin stated that, in order to establish the *mens rea* elements of fraud, the Crown has to prove only "that the accused knowingly undertook the acts which constitute the falsehood, deceit or other fraudulent means, and that the accused was aware that deprivation could result from such conduct." Most significantly, the Supreme Court ruled that, where fraud is charged under section 380 of the *Code*, it is not necessary for the Crown to prove that the accused subjectively appreciated that his or her act was dishonest. If the *mens rea* elements defined by Justice McLachlin are proved, then it does not matter if the accused believes that he or she was acting in a perfectly legitimate manner.

In *Théroux* (1993), the accused was a businessman who was involved with a company that was constructing two residential housing projects. Théroux falsely represented to potential buyers that their deposits would be insured by the *Fédération de Construction du Québec*. The construction company became insolvent and the projects were not finished. As a consequence, most of the potential buyers lost the entire amount of their deposits. At the accused's trial for fraud, the trial judge found that Théroux honestly believed that the housing projects would succeed and that the buyers would not lose their deposits. However, the trial judge stated that this was not a defence to a charge of fraud and convicted Théroux. The accused's appeals to both the Quebec Court of Appeal and the Supreme Court of Canada were dismissed.

According to Justice McLachlin, the accused's belief that the projects would succeed and that the buyers would not lose any money was irrelevant. In defining the offence of fraud under section 380, she stated that

> [t]he prohibited act is deceit, falsehood, or some other dishonest act. The prohibited consequence is depriving another of what is or should be his, which may, as we have seen, consist in merely placing another's property at risk. The *mens rea* would then consist in the subjective awareness that one was undertaking a prohibited act (the deceit, falsehood or other dishonest act) which could cause deprivation in the sense of depriving another of property or putting that property at risk. If this is shown, the crime is complete. The fact that the accused may have hoped the deprivation would not take place, or may have felt there was nothing wrong with what he or she was doing, provides no defence.... The personal feeling of the accused about the morality or honesty of the act or its consequences is no more relevant to the analysis than is the accused's awareness that the particular acts constitute a criminal offence.
>
> ... The "dishonesty" of the means is relevant to the determination whether the conduct falls within the type of conduct caught by the offence of fraud; what reasonable people consider dishonest assists in the determination whether the *actus reus* of the offence can be made out on particular facts. That established, it need only be determined that an accused knowingly undertook the acts in question, aware that deprivation, or risk of deprivation, could follow as a likely consequence.

As far as the facts in *Théroux* (1993) were concerned, it was clear that the accused had committed the *actus reus* of fraud. He had deliberately told falsehoods to the potential buyers and those lies caused deprivation in two respects: first, the depositors failed to obtain the insurance that they were promised, and second, their money was placed at risk (a risk that ultimately did materialize since the majority of them lost the entire amount of their deposits). The critical question, therefore, was whether the *mens rea* elements of fraud had been proved. Justice McLachlin answered this question affirmatively:

> [Théroux] told the depositors they had insurance protection when he knew that they did not have that protection. He knew this to be false. He knew that by this act he was depriving the depositors of something they thought they had, insurance protection. It may also be inferred from his possession of this knowledge that [he] knew that he was placing the depositors' money at risk. That established, his *mens rea* is proved. The fact that he sincerely believed that in the end the houses would be built and that the risk would not materialize cannot save him.

The Meaning of "Fraudulently" in Section 322 of the *Code* (Theft)

Another example of a special mental element that must be established as part of the *mens rea* of an offence is the requirement that the accused person act "fraudulently" in the context of a charge of theft under section 322 of the *Criminal Code*. The implications of this requirement are well illustrated by the application of the legal principle that an accused person may not be convicted of theft if he or she has engaged in conduct that the court considers to have been merely a "prank" or a "well-intentioned blunder." It has been ruled, in such circumstances, that the accused person did not act *fraudulently* and, therefore, lacked the necessary *mens rea* for conviction of theft. Section 322 of the *Criminal Code* provides that

(1) Every one commits theft who fraudulently and without colour of right takes, or fraudulently and without colour of right converts to his use or to the use of another person, anything whether animate or inanimate, with intent,

  (a) to deprive, temporarily or absolutely, the owner of it, or a person who has a special property or interest in it, of the thing or of his property or interest in it....

In the case of *Wilkins* (1965), the accused was charged with the theft of a police officer's motorcycle. Nichol, the police officer, was engaged in the act of writing out a parking ticket to place on the windshield of a motorcar, owned by Wilkins's friend. At this point, Wilkins told Nichol that he would ride the officer's vehicle around the parking lot if Nichol did not cease ticketing the friend's car. The officer did not hear what was being said to him and Wilkins drove the motorcycle down the street, where he was intercepted by a police cruiser. He was, subsequently, charged with theft. Wilkins stated, most forcefully, that he had no intention of stealing the motorcycle and was merely playing a joke on Nichol. The accused was ultimately acquitted by the Ontario Court of Appeal. In ordering the accused's acquittal, Justice Roach stated that

> [i]n the instant case the facts could not possibly justify a conviction of theft. The accused did not intend to steal the vehicle, that is, to convert the property in it to his own use but only to drive it ... his intention was merely to play a joke on Nichol and the Judge so found. The intention to perpetrate this joke, stupid though it was, is incompatible with the evil intent which is inherent in the crime of theft.

However, the courts have emphasized that the so-called "prank" defence is one that has a very narrow scope. For example, in the case of *Neve* (1999), the accused was convicted of robbery (an offence that generally requires the Crown to prove *both* an *assault* and a *theft*). Neve believed that the complainant in this case had beaten one of her pregnant friends, causing a miscarriage. Neve and an associate took the complainant to a field located near a major highway just outside Edmonton. Neve and the associate tore off the complainant's clothes with a knife and left her standing naked in the field, in a temperature of about 5 degrees Celsius. The police found one item of the complainant's clothing at the scene of the incident but, owing to the extreme darkness, did not find any of her other clothes in the immediate vicinity. Neve claimed that her sole objective had been to humiliate the complainant to "get even" for what Neve believed the latter had done to a friend. She emphatically denied that she had taken any of the complainant's clothes for the purpose of sale and so forth. Indeed, the defence suggested that the missing items of clothing had been thrown out of Neve's car when she was leaving the field.

In order to establish that a theft (and, hence a robbery), had occurred, the Crown was required, under section 322(1), to prove that Neve had acted "fraudulently." However, Neve said that she had not acted dishonestly. Her counsel contended that dishonesty necessarily involves "swindling or trickery" and that, in this case, Neve's actions had taken place without any "deceit, falsehood, or trickery." Indeed, when the complainant had refused to disrobe herself, then Neve and her friend had "simply removed the complainant's clothes in a straightforward and open manner." Both the trial court and the Alberta Court of Appeal soundly rejected this line of argument and Neve's robbery conviction was ultimately upheld. The Court of Appeal noted that it is irrelevant that the complainant's clothes had been removed in an "open manner":

> The reality is that many thefts and robberies are committed openly, without deception or trickery. The fact that an offender openly and blatantly takes property from a victim makes little difference to the victim. The result is the same; the victim's property has been wrongly taken.
>
> ... [F]or property to be taken "fraudulently," it is enough that the taking be done intentionally, under no mistake, and with knowledge that the thing taken is the property of another person. This will suffice to characterize the taking as fraudulent.

Defence counsel also advanced the argument that Neve had been engaging in a "prank" and, therefore, could not be considered to have acted "fraudulently." Although the Court of Appeal apparently recognized that certain types of pranks may not amount to theft, it emphatically took the view that, in Neve's case, there was absolutely no basis for characterizing her violent act as a "prank":

> A prank is a practical joke. What happened here does not fit that description. It was a taking for the purpose of depriving the victim, albeit not for the benefit of the taker. It was not a joke and motive does not change the character of the act if the property was taken for the purpose of depriving the owner. Accordingly, the defence thesis that Neve did not take the complainant's clothing "fraudulently" must fail.

Incidentally, it is important to remember that section 322(1)(a) of the *Code* provides that, in relation to a charge of theft, the Crown must prove that the accused intended to deprive the victim of his or her property "*temporarily or absolutely*." Therefore, it is of no importance that Neve only intended to keep the complainant's clothes for a short period; as the Court of Appeal noted, "the obvious intent was to deprive the complainant of [her clothes] for a period of time, however brief."

In this context, it is noteworthy that the Supreme Court of Canada has emphasized that an accused person can be considered to have acted "fraudulently" even if he or she claims that there was never any intention to cause loss to the victim. For example, in *Skalbania* (1997), the accused had been charged with theft of $100 000. The Crown relied on section 332 of the *Criminal Code*, which specifies that the crime of theft has been committed if the accused, having received money for a specific purpose, "*fraudulently*" applies that money to some other, unauthorized purpose. Skalbania had approached a man called Gooch and encouraged him to participate in a real estate deal that the accused was seeking to make with a third party. Gooch gave Skalbania a cheque for $100 000, with an explicit direction that it was to be kept in a trust account pending the outcome of the business negotiations. Skalbania instructed his bookkeeper to transfer the $100 000 from his company's trust account to the company's current account, and all of the money was spent on matters entirely unrelated to the business deal in which Gooch was planning to participate. The business deal never came off and, more than two months later, Skalbania repaid Gooch his $100 000 together with "a sum by way of compensation for delay and inconvenience."

Had Skalbania committed theft when he deliberately misappropriated money that had been given to him for one specific purpose—namely, the proposed joint business venture between Skalbania and Gooch? It was clear that Skalbania had used the funds in the trust account for unauthorized purposes but had he acted "*fraudulently*"? The accused claimed that he always intended to reimburse Gooch in full, should the business deal fall through, and that he had demonstrated his good faith by returning the money with interest. The Supreme Court of Canada held that Skalbania had, in fact, acted "fraudulently," even though the accused was adamant that he had not intended to *steal* Gooch's money. As Justice McLachlin said, in delivering the judgment of the Court,

> ... [A]n intentional misappropriation, without mistake, suffices to establish the *mens rea* under s. 332(1).... The word "fraudulently," as used in this section, connotes no more than this. *The dishonesty inherent in the offence lies in the intentional and unmistaken application of funds to an improper purpose....*
>
> In short, the trial judge found: that the appellant knew that the money belonged to Mr. Gooch; that the appellant knew the purpose to which the money was supposed to be applied; and that the appellant knowingly, without mistake, applied the money to different purposes. [emphasis added]

However, in the case of *He* (2008), the accused was charged with the theft of electricity, contrary to section 326 of the *Criminal Code*. She was found to be the temporary caretaker of a marihuana grow-operation in the basement of a residence. A hydroelectric-bypass was found in the adjoining garage: this device permitted the illegal extraction of free electricity. A wire that passed through a hole in the wall of the garage was visible but there was no evidence that the accused understood the purpose of this device. Section 326 provides that theft is committed when a person takes electricity "fraudulently, maliciously, or without colour of right." The question in this case was whether the accused acted "fraudulently." She was merely the caretaker of the grow-operation and, therefore, it could not be assumed that she knew that electricity was being stolen. In order to prove the fraud that is a necessary component of the crime of theft, the Crown would have to establish that the accused intentionally and deliberately participated in the scheme to take electricity without paying for it.

Although He was convicted at her trial of the theft of electricity, the B.C. Court of Appeal set aside the conviction and entered an acquittal on this charge because it had not been proved that she had the necessary *mens rea* for theft. In delivering the judgment of the Court of Appeal, Justice Bauman stated that

[w]ith respect, I think it difficult to infer, from the appellant's knowledge and control of the grow-op, the *mens rea* necessary to support the finding of fraud in the offence created by s. 326(1)(a) of the *Code*. Nor is the appearance of the bypass in the garage, as depicted in the photographic exhibit, so obviously a device for stealing electricity that any non-expert would have appreciated what it was. The opening in the wall does not provide a reasonable basis for the judge's finding that the appellant was aware of the bypass.

"Fraudulently" in section 326 connotes an intentional and deliberate taking of service that was not the accused's to obtain....

Knowledge and control of the grow-op by an accused who acts in the role of a caretaker ... does not necessarily support, to the criminal law standard, the inference that she is intentionally and deliberately taking the electrical service that was not hers to obtain in order to power the operation.

The Meaning of "Planned and Deliberate" in Section 231(2) (First Degree Murder)

A final example of a special mental element that the Crown must establish in order to achieve a conviction is contained in section 231(2) of the *Criminal Code*. This provision states that "murder is first degree murder when it is planned and deliberate." In order to convict an accused person of the crime of murder, the Crown is normally required to prove that the accused intended to kill his or her victim or meant to cause bodily harm that is likely to cause death and is reckless whether death ensues or not (section 229(a) of the *Code*). Once the Crown has established that the accused acted intentionally, the issue then arises as to whether he or she should be found guilty of first or second degree murder. Section 235 of the *Code* provides that, in either case, the accused will be sentenced to life imprisonment. However, Parliament has drawn a clear distinction between first and second degree murder in relation to the time that individuals must serve before they may be eligible for parole. Section 745(a) provides that persons convicted of first degree murder will automatically be ineligible for parole until they have served 25 years of their sentence. However, when an individual is convicted of second degree murder, there is more flexibility in the sentence. The period of ineligibility for parole may range from a minimum of 10 years to a maximum of 25 years: the trial judge makes this decision, after seeking advice from the jury [sections 745(c), 745.2, and 745.4, of the *Criminal Code*]. Under the existing *Code* provisions, those individuals who have been convicted of murder and whose parole ineligibility exceeds 15 years may seek a review of their ineligibility period after they have served 15 years of their life sentence—the so-called "faint hope clause" [section 745.6]. However, in June 2009, the Government of Canada introduced legislation that would abolish the "faint hope clause" for those who are convicted of murder after its implementation and render it more difficult for those who are currently serving life sentences to apply for "early parole."

In order to establish first degree murder, the Crown must normally prove not only that the accused intended to kill his or her victim but also that he or she did so in a "planned and deliberate manner."[1]

---

[1] Section 231 also specifies certain circumstances in which an accused person may be found guilty of first degree murder, *even though the homicide was not "planned and deliberate"*: namely, murder of a police officer, sheriff, prison warden, prison guard, and so forth, if the killing occurs while the victim is acting in the course of his or her duties; and murder committed in the course of hijacking, sexual assault, kidnapping or hostage taking, criminal harassment, terrorist activity, using explosives in connection with the activities of a criminal organization, or intimidation.

What do these words mean? The current judicial interpretation of "planned and deliberate" was succinctly summarized by Justice Hunt of the Alberta Court of Appeal in the case of *K. (M.M.)* (2006):

A planned murder is one that was conceived and carefully thought out prior to being committed.... It requires that a design or scheme be arranged beforehand....

A deliberate murder is one that is considered, not impulsive.... A person commits deliberate murder when he thinks about the consequences and carefully thinks out the act, rather than proceeding hastily, rashly or impulsively....

An instructive example of the judicial interpretation of the words, "planned and deliberate," is furnished by the case of *Smith* (1980), in which the accused was charged with first degree murder following the death of a man named Skwarchuk. It appears that Smith and Skwarchuk had been on a hunting trip together. After stopping at an abandoned farmhouse, a vigorous argument erupted and Smith shot Skwarchuk in the left elbow. Skwarchuk, who was screaming and yelling, ran away from Smith. Skwarchuk's arm was hanging down and blood was squirting on the ground. However, Smith reloaded his shotgun and shot Skwarchuk, at least twice, from long range. It appeared that some pellets from Smith's gun hit Skwarchuk in the back. Skwarchuk continued to run, but Smith shot Skwarchuk again and the latter fell down. Smith then approached Skwarchuk, who was sitting on the ground, and shot him in the back of the head. At this point, Skwarchuk died. Smith was subsequently arrested by the police and charged. At his trial, he was convicted of first degree murder; however, on appeal, the Saskatchewan Court of Appeal substituted a conviction for second degree murder. The Court of Appeal was not satisfied that the killing was both "planned and deliberate." Chief Justice Culliton stated that

[t]here must be some evidence the killing was the result of a scheme or design previously formulated or designed by the accused and the killing was the implementation of that scheme or design. It is obvious a murder committed on a sudden impulse and without prior consideration, even though the intent to kill is clearly proven, would not constitute a planned murder.

In the present case, there is not the slightest evidence the appellant (Smith) had given any consideration to the murder of Skwarchuk until after he and Skwarchuk had left the house....

I am satisfied that there was no evidence whatever to support the conclusion that the actions of the appellant, cruel and sadistic as they were, in killing Skwarchuk was the implementation of a previously determined design or scheme. I think it is obvious his actions were the result of a sudden impulse. It would be pure speculation to try and determine what triggered that impulse.

The courts have often recognized that an important factor to consider in determining whether the accused acted in a "planned and deliberate" manner is whether the accused acted in a state of intoxication. As we shall see in Chapter 10, if intoxication prevents the accused person from forming the specific intent to kill, it serves as a partial defence and reduces the severity of the charge from murder to manslaughter. However, it may well be that the accused's state of intoxication was not so serious as to prevent him or her from forming the specific intent to kill. Nevertheless, his or her state of intoxication may still be particularly relevant to the issue of whether the accused acted in a planned and deliberate manner when he or she killed the victim. Indeed, intoxication may well prevent the accused person from formulating a plan or from acting in a deliberate manner. In the words of Justice Gale in the *Widdifield* case (1961),

The capacity to form the essential intent to kill or to do harm and the capacity to plan and deliberate are not the same. A greater mental capacity is surely required to formulate a plan, even a simple one, and to deliberate upon that plan than is required to form the intent to kill or to do harm. *The Code does not envisage the deliberation, as it seems to me, of a mind which is substantially impaired by alcohol. Conversely, a lesser degree of intoxication will surely interfere with and render impossible a plan or deliberation such as is envisaged by the Code....* [emphasis added]

In the case of *Wallen* (1990), the Supreme Court of Canada ruled that a trial judge must always direct the jury to consider the issue of intoxication and its effect on whether the accused acted in a planned and deliberate manner quite separately from the issue of intoxication and its effect on whether the accused formed the intent to kill. Furthermore, in *Turningrobe* (2008), the Supreme Court ordered a new trial for the accused because the trial judge had instructed the jury in such a manner that they may well have concluded that the central issue for them to decide was whether alcohol had affected Turningrobe's *capacity* to act in a planned and deliberate manner. The central issue, however, was whether, in all the circumstances—including her heavy drinking—she did, in fact, carry out the killing of the victim in a planned and deliberate manner. Merely possessing the capacity to formulate a plan or to act deliberately does not mean that one actually did so at the time that the victim was killed.

Similarly, the Supreme Court of Canada has clearly acknowledged that mental illness may also have the effect of negativing the element of *planning and deliberation* required for conviction of first degree murder. As Chief Justice Lamer stated in the *Jacquard* case (1997),

> It is true that some factor, such as a mental disorder, that is insufficient to negative the charge that the accused *intended* to kill, may nevertheless be sufficient to negative the elements of *planning and deliberation*. This is because one can intend to kill and yet be impulsive rather than considered in doing so. It requires less mental capacity simply to intend than it does to plan and deliberate.

Of course, it must be emphasized that, if an accused person suffered from a particularly severe form of *mental disorder* at the time that the alleged offence was committed, then it is possible that the accused might be able to prove that he or she should be found "not criminally responsible on account of mental disorder" (NCRMD) under the terms of section 16 of the *Criminal Code* (a special defence that is discussed in Chapter 8). However, an accused person who is not successful in raising this defence and is convicted of murder may still point to the mental disorder at the time of the killing and claim that it prevented him or her from acting *with planning and deliberation*. If the accused manages to raise a reasonable doubt on this issue, then there must be a conviction of *second degree*, rather than first degree, murder.

The *Allard* case (1990) demonstrates the various stages that must be followed when the issue of mental disorder is raised in relation to a charge of first degree murder. The accused was charged with this offence after she administered a vitamin capsule, laced with a fatal dose of strychnine, to her husband. The accused's defence was that she was not criminally responsible on account of mental disorder and that, in any event, she did not kill her husband intentionally or in a planned and deliberate manner. The trial judge instructed the jury that, if the accused failed to prove that she was not criminally responsible under section 16 of the *Code*, they must "disregard [the mental disorder] defence completely." Allard was subsequently convicted of first degree murder. However, the Quebec Court of Appeal allowed her appeal and ordered a new trial. The court found that the original trial judge should have pointed out to the jury that, even if the accused had not proved that she was not criminally responsible under the terms of section 16 of the *Code*, she might be able to raise a reasonable doubt as to whether her mental disorder prevented her from forming the intent to kill; if she did raise such a doubt, she would have to be acquitted and convicted of manslaughter instead. However, if the jury were satisfied beyond a reasonable doubt that the accused did form the intent to kill her husband, it would still have to consider the totally separate question of whether her mental disorder prevented her from acting in a planned and deliberate manner; if she could raise a reasonable doubt on this score, she would be acquitted of first degree murder and convicted of second degree murder.

THE DISTINCTION BETWEEN DIRECT AND INDIRECT INTENTION

For the purpose of legal analysis, it is possible to draw a distinction between *direct* and *indirect intention*. The term **direct intention** refers to intention in the popular sense of an individual acting with the desire, purpose, aim, objective, or design to achieve a certain consequence. In this sense, it clearly reflects the average citizen's comprehension of the word "intention." Furthermore, if an accused person deliberately sets out to bring about a certain consequence, he or she will be considered to have intended that consequence even if there is only a slim chance that the accused person will be successful. For example, if Pumblechook points a rifle at Jaggers and pulls the trigger with the intention of killing him, then it is irrelevant that Pumblechook is not likely to be successful because Jaggers is located at a considerable distance from Pumblechook. If Jaggers is indeed fatally shot, then it is beyond doubt that Pumblechook would be considered to have intended Jaggers's death and is, therefore, guilty of murder. If Pumblechook misses, then he would be guilty of attempted murder.

What is meant by **indirect intention**? Let us suppose that Marley does not desire that his conduct produce a certain consequence B but nevertheless knows that consequence B is a necessary step on the way to accomplishing the objective that he really does wish to achieve (consequence A). Can we say that Marley "intends" the undesired consequence B?

The answer is yes. Imagine that Cratchitt wishes to wound Scrooge by hurling a rock at him. Scrooge unfortunately happens to be visiting Fred's house. Cratchitt is a close friend of Fred and would certainly not intend to cause him any trouble. Nevertheless, the only way in which Cratchitt can accomplish his objective of wounding Scrooge is by hurling the rock through the closed window. There is no doubt that Cratchitt does not desire to break the window but, on the other hand, he realizes that he must do so in order to attain his objective of wounding Scrooge. Let us suppose that Cratchitt throws the rock at Scrooge, knowing the window is closed. There is no difficulty in determining that Cratchitt intends to wound Scrooge. However, does he "intend" to break Fred's window? For the purpose of the criminal law, Cratchitt will be held to have *indirectly* intended to break the window and is liable to conviction of mischief (wilful damage of property, contrary to section 430(1)(a) of the *Criminal Code*). Putting it in legal terms, Cratchitt is deemed to have intended to break the window because he knew this *undesired* consequence was a condition precedent to the attainment of his *desired* objective of wounding Scrooge.

There is another situation in which the concept of indirect intention becomes of critical importance. Consider the following hypothetical example. Murdstone joins a gang of terrorists and is ordered to destroy a shipment of arms destined for the military. To this end, he buries a land mine under the road. The land mine is designed to detonate by remote control, and Murdstone's plan is to explode the bomb as the truck, carrying the shipment, passes over it. Murdstone does not wish to kill the driver of the truck but he necessarily knows that the explosion is "virtually certain" to cause the driver's death. It is just possible that the driver may escape alive but Murdstone knows that this is highly unlikely. When the truck passes over the land mine, Murdstone detonates it and, in the ensuing explosion, the driver (Noggs) is killed instantaneously. Did Murdstone "intend" to kill Noggs, even though he did not wish to cause this consequence? The answer must be in the affirmative. Murdstone realized that the death of the driver of the truck was virtually certain to happen, even though he hoped that the driver would not be killed and thought there was a remote possibility that the driver might miraculously escape death. In these circumstances, Murdstone would be deemed to have *indirectly* intended the death of Noggs and, therefore, would be guilty of murder.

An interesting example of this type of indirect intention is provided by the case of *Buzzanga and Durocher* (1979), in which the two defendants were charged with wilfully promoting hatred against an identifiable group, contrary to section 319(2) of the *Criminal Code*. More specifically, they were charged with promoting hatred against members of the francophone community in Essex County (Ontario), by communicating statements contained in copies of a handbill entitled "Wake up Canadians Your Future is at Stake!" The prosecution of Buzzanga and Durocher was steeped in irony since they both identified themselves strongly with French-speaking Canadians. The prosecution arose as a consequence of the attempt of the defendants to secure the construction of a French-language high school in Essex County, which the local board of education had decided not to build. The accused had disseminated a handbill that contained the following inflammatory statements:

> Did you know that those of the French minority who support the building of the French-language high school are in fact a subversive group and that most French Canadians of Essex County are opposed to the building of that school?
>
> Who will rid us of this subversive group if not ourselves?
>
> If we give them a school, what will they demand next ... independent city states? Consider the ethnic problem of the United States, and take heed.
>
> We must stamp out the subversive element which uses history to justify its freeloading on the taxpayers of Canada, now.
>
> The British solved this problem once before with the Acadians, what are we waiting for...?

Durocher testified that his purpose was to demonstrate the prejudice against French Canadians and to "expose the truth" about the problem with the French-language school, while Buzzanga stated that he intended the pamphlet to be considered merely as a "satire." They both appeared to have believed that the pamphlet would create a "furor" that would provoke a reaction on the part of the Ontario government, which would then put pressure on the school board to build the French-language school. Their evidence, if believed, suggested that neither of them actually wished to promote hatred against French-speaking people; indeed, as they pointed out, if they *had* nursed such an intention, they would have been promoting hatred against themselves. Nevertheless, at their trial, the defendants were convicted and they appealed to the Ontario Court of Appeal. Their appeal was allowed and a new trial ordered.

The judgment of the Ontario Court of Appeal was delivered by Justice Martin, who held that the word "wilfully," in the context of section 319(2), means "with the intention of promoting hatred." Therefore, the critical issue was clearly whether the defendants could be deemed to have intended to promote hatred, when their long-term objective was to obtain what they considered to be a benefit to the French-speaking community—namely, a French-language high school. Justice Martin agreed that

[a]s a general rule, a person who foresees that a consequence is certain or substantially certain to result from an act which he does in order to achieve some other purposes, intends that consequence. The actor's foresight of the certainty or moral certainty of the consequence resulting from his conduct compels a conclusion that if he, none the less, acted so as to produce it, then he decided to bring it about (albeit regretfully), in order to achieve his ultimate purpose. His intention encompasses the means as well as his ultimate objective.

I conclude, therefore, that the appellants "wilfully" (intentionally) promoted hatred against the French Canadian community of Essex County only if: (a) Their conscious purpose in distributing the document was to promote hatred within that group, or (b) They foresaw that the promotion of hatred against that group was certain or morally certain to result from the distribution of the pamphlet, but distributed it as a means of achieving their purpose of obtaining the French-language high school.

Alternative (b) identified by Justice Martin represents a conspicuous example of the application of the concept of indirect intention. Having established the appropriate principles that should be applied in cases of this nature, the Ontario Court of Appeal ordered a new trial for Buzzanga and Durocher. Significantly, Justice Martin's interpretation of section 319(2) was subsequently affirmed by the Supreme Court of Canada in the cases of *Keegstra* (1990) and *Andrews* (1990).

Another example of indirect intention is furnished by the case of *Guess* (2000). The accused was charged, under section 139(2) of the *Criminal Code*, with attempting to obstruct, pervert, or defeat the course of justice by engaging in a "personal relationship" with a defendant (Gill) who was being tried on a charge of homicide. The charge arose from the fact that Guess was a juror in the trial of Gill. Although Guess's main objective was to engage in a romantic

relationship with Gill, she nevertheless knew that an inevitable consequence of this relationship would be to obstruct or pervert the trial process. Guess was convicted at her trial and her subsequent appeal was dismissed by the B.C. Court of Appeal. In the words of Justice Hall of the Court of Appeal,

That the appellant [Guess] well knew what she was doing in carrying on an affair with an accused was not in accord with her duties as a juror is clear from the evidence. She was secretive about the matter and in discussions with her sister and friends she acknowledged that what was occurring was wrong. She observed that she felt "conflicted". That, of course, precisely identifies the difficulty—she was in a position of impossible conflict. Would this conduct have a tendency to pervert or obstruct the course of justice? The answer to this question is obviously in the affirmative. The juror would be privy knowingly or unknowingly to information not possessed by other jurors and because of the emotional ties between her and the accused would be hampered in properly performing the impartial functions of a judicial officer. In the context of this offence, the term "wilfully" may be taken to connote the concept that the offence could not be made out of the basis of accidental or unknowing conduct. But as the conversations of the appellant that were placed before the jury indicated, she was keenly aware that she was doing what she ought not to do during the course of the trial when she was serving as a juror. These words of Martin J.A. in the case of *R. v. Buzzanga and Durocher* ... are apposite here: ... as a general rule, a person who foresees that a consequence is certain or substantially certain to result from an act which he does in order to achieve some other purpose, intends that consequence. The actor's foresight of the certainty or moral certainty of the consequence resulting from his conduct compels a conclusion that if he, none the less, acted so as to produce it, then he decided to bring it about (albeit regretfully), in order to achieve his ultimate purpose. His intention encompasses the means as well as to [*sic*] his ultimate objective.

INTENTION AND MOTIVE DISTINGUISHED

It is important to draw a clear distinction between intention and motive. Indeed, in the *Lewis* case (1979), Justice Dickson, of the Supreme Court of Canada, stated that

[i]n ordinary parlance, the words "intent" and "motive" are frequently used interchangeably, but in the criminal law they are distinct. In most criminal trials, the mental element, the *mens rea* with which

the Court is concerned, relates to "intent," i.e., the exercise of a free will to use particular means to produce a particular result, rather than with "motive," i.e., that which precedes and induces the exercise of the will. The mental element of a crime ordinarily involves no reference to motive....

In the decision of the Supreme Court of Canada in the *United States v. Dynar* case (1997), Justices Cory and Iacobucci articulated a clear rationale for drawing this distinction between intention and motive:

> Society imposes criminal sanctions in order to punish and deter undesirable conduct. It does not matter to society, in its efforts to secure social peace and order, what an accused's motive was, but only what the accused intended to do. It is no consolation to one whose car has been stolen that the thief stole the car intending to sell it to purchase food for a food bank.

The case of *Buzzanga and Durocher* (1979), discussed in the previous section, is an excellent illustration of the need to distinguish between intention and motive. The defendants' motive for issuing the handbill was laudable (namely, the construction of a French-language high school); however, it is quite possible that, in accordance with the second alternative principle identified by Justice Martin, they could be found guilty of intentionally promoting hatred against the very group whose interests they wished to advance.

In a similar vein, Justice McLachlin of the Supreme Court of Canada said in the case of *Théroux* (1993) that an accused person's personal system of values is not a relevant consideration in determining whether he or she has the necessary *mens rea* for conviction of an offence:

> A person is not saved from conviction because he or she believes that there is nothing wrong with what he or she is doing. The question is whether the accused subjectively appreciated that certain consequences would follow from his or her acts, not whether the accused believed the acts or their consequences to be moral. Just as the pathological killer would not be acquitted on the mere ground that he failed to see his act as morally reprehensible, so the defrauder will not be acquitted because he believed that what he was doing was honest.

As we noted in Chapter 3, a physician who deliberately injects a massive overdose of drugs in order to terminate the painful existence of a slowly dying patient may be convicted of murder on the basis that he or she *intended* to cause death, despite the fact that his or her **motive** was to bring an end to extreme suffering. In short, if defendants cause the *actus reus* of a crime with the necessary *mens rea*, it is entirely irrelevant that they claim to be acting out of what some may consider to be laudable motives. In the example of the doctor who carries out euthanasia, we can see that the *mens rea* for murder is, normally, an intention to kill or an intention to inflict bodily harm that is likely to cause death and recklessness as to whether or not death ensues. The doctor clearly intends to bring about the death of the patient and, if the patient does in fact die, the doctor has committed the *actus reus* of murder together with the requisite *mens rea*. The doctor's motive is absolutely irrelevant because it is not part of the definition of the crime of murder. In this particular case, if the doctor was convicted of first degree murder, the judge could not take the motive into account because there is a fixed sentence (life sentence with a minimum non-eligibility-for-parole period of 25 years). However, for most other offences, trial judges have considerable discretion in setting the appropriate sentence, and it is highly likely that noble (albeit misguided) motives will result in a more lenient sentence being imposed.

The *Latimer* case (2001) illustrates the immense difficulty that may arise when an accused person's motives may not be taken into account because of a mandatory sentence that is prescribed in the *Criminal Code*. Robert Latimer asphyxiated his severely disabled 12-year-old daughter with carbon monoxide and claimed that he had killed her out of compassion— his motive had been to end (what he perceived to be) his daughter's intolerable suffering. Since it was clear that Latimer carried this act out *intentionally*, he was convicted of second degree murder. Both the trial judge and jury appeared to accept that Latimer was telling the truth when he stated that he had engaged in a so-called "mercy killing." However, section 745 of the *Code* imposes a mandatory sentence for second degree murder. That sentence is one of life imprisonment, with no eligibility for parole for a period of between 10 and 25 years (this period is to be set by the trial judge, who is required to consult with the jury on the issue). When consulted in relation to the appropriate non-parole eligibility period, the jury in the *Latimer* case (2001) recommended that the accused be eligible for parole after only one year in custody (a sentence that is not permitted, in light of the *mandatory minimum* period of 10 years that is imposed by section 745). In a highly unusual move, the trial judge ruled that, in light of the fact that Latimer acted out of compassionate (albeit profoundly misguided) motives, it would constitute cruel and unusual punishment under section 12 of the *Charter* to sentence him to life imprisonment with no eligibility for parole for 10 years. Consequently, Justice Noble granted Latimer a **constitutional exemption** from the provisions of section 745 and sentenced him to one year in prison and one year on probation. However, the Crown appealed this sentence and the Saskatchewan Court of Appeal set it aside, substituting a sentence of life imprisonment with no eligibility for parole for 10 years. The Court of Appeal rejected the notion that Latimer was entitled to a constitutional exemption and stated that it is up to Parliament to deal with the question of whether there should be special sentencing provisions to deal with the issue of so-called "mercy killing."

The Supreme Court of Canada later affirmed the decision of the Court of Appeal. In the words of the Court,

> On the one hand, we must give due consideration to Mr. Latimer's initial attempts to conceal his actions, his lack of remorse, his position of trust, the significant degree of planning and premeditation, and Tracy's extreme vulnerability. On the other hand, we are mindful of Mr. Latimer's good character and standing in the community, his tortured anxiety about Tracy's well-being, and his laudable perseverance as a caring and involved parent. Considered together we cannot find that the personal characteristics and particular circumstances of this case displace the serious gravity of this offence.

The Court concluded that "the minimum mandatory sentence is not grossly disproportionate in this case" and that "we cannot find that any aspect of the particular circumstances of the case or the offender diminishes the degree of criminal responsibility borne by Mr. Latimer." However, the Supreme Court of Canada did emphasize the fact that the Government of Canada has the power to grant clemency in cases such as that of *Latimer* (2001). This power is known as the "royal prerogative of mercy" and is found in section 749 of the *Criminal Code*. Significantly, the Supreme Court emphasized that "the prerogative is a matter for the executive, not the courts."

The question of whether those who commit murder from compassionate motives should be treated more leniently than other individuals who perpetrate this crime is highly controversial and has deeply divided Canadians. Some would argue that the justice system is functioning in a profoundly unjust manner if "mercy killers," such as Latimer, are treated in the same manner as those who kill for motives of which we profoundly disapprove. On the other hand, some would contend that the life of Latimer's daughter was taken *without her consent* and that she was killed because she was severely disabled; therefore, it may be argued, if we grant more lenient sentences to those who kill in such circumstances, we are effectively devaluing the lives of all persons with a disability.

Although the accused's motive is not one of the mental elements that must be established by the Crown in order to establish criminal responsibility, it may, nevertheless, be very relevant to the trial process. More specifically, the presence of motive(s) may well be a critical part of the Crown's case in establishing the guilt of the accused. As Justice Dickson asserted, in delivering the Supreme Court's judgment in the case of *Lewis* (1979), the prosecution can always introduce evidence that an accused person had a motive for committing the offence because, if it can prove the existence of such a motive, it is more likely that the accused did commit the offence. As Justice Dickson pointed out, "[M]en do not usually act without a motive." Conversely, if the accused can establish that he or she had no motive for committing the crime, then this is an important fact in his or her favour when the **trier of fact** comes to consider the question of innocence or guilt. For example, in the *Stone* case (1999), Justice Bastarache, on behalf of the majority of the Supreme Court of Canada, emphasized that the credibility of a defence of *automatism* (see Chapter 8) is considerably enhanced if there is no apparent motive for the alleged crime:

> ... [T]he plausibility of a claim of automatism will be reduced if the accused had a motive to commit the crime in question.... On the other hand, if the involuntary act is random and lacks motive, the plausibility of the claim of automatism will be increased.

The practical importance of motive in a criminal trial is illustrated by the decision of the Supreme Court in *Charemski* (1998). In this case, the accused had been charged with the murder of his estranged wife, whose dead body had been found in her bathtub. There had been evidence concerning Charemski's "*animus*" (hatred) toward his wife (allegedly arising from his anger concerning her relationships with other men) and a financial motive for killing her. The Supreme Court of Canada ruled that this was the kind of case in which evidence of motive should be considered by the jury. Justice Bastarache stated that

> [t]he Crown also led evidence suggesting the appellant may have had a financial motive to kill his wife. The appellant, who receives social assistance, held a life insurance policy on the deceased in the amount of $50 000. The Crown adduced evidence to establish that this represents a great deal of money in Poland, where the appellant (who is Polish) has been living on and off for the past five years. On the basis of these facts, the Crown, in my opinion, adduced sufficient evidence from which a jury, properly instructed, could have inferred the requisite mental state for homicide. That is, the jury could have inferred from the evidence of the animus and financial motive that the accused intended to kill his wife.

Conversely, if the accused can establish that he or she had no motive for committing the crime, then this is an important fact in his or her favour when the trier of fact (judge or jury) is called upon to consider the question of innocence or guilt. However, as the Manitoba Court of Appeal stated in the *Ilina* case (2003), it is important to bear in mind that there is a difference between the "absence of a proved motive" to commit a crime and the "proved absence of motive." It is only where there is a "proved absence of motive" that a trial judge is required to instruct the jury about the significance of the absence of motive.

PROVING INTENTION: USING THE TEST OF THE "REASONABLE PERSON" AS A MEANS OF DETERMINING SUBJECTIVE INTENT

One of the more difficult tasks confronting the prosecution in a criminal trial is proving that the defendant had the requisite intention or knowledge. How can these elements be proved? Sometimes, "the facts may speak for themselves." It will be obvious that the accused must have had the necessary intention or knowledge and, unless he or she comes up with an explanation that casts doubt on that conclusion, a judge or jury will have no difficulty in finding the accused guilty. As Justice McLachlin, speaking on behalf of the majority of the Supreme Court of Canada, asserted in the *Théroux* case (1993),

> ... [T]he Crown need not, in every case, show precisely what thought was in the accused's mind at the time of

the criminal act. In certain cases, subjective awareness of the consequences can be inferred from the act itself, barring some explanation casting doubt on such inference. The fact that such an inference is made does not detract from the subjectivity of the test.

However, the facts will not always speak for themselves, and other methods must be used in order to determine the accused's subjective intent or knowledge at the time of the incident in question. Of course, either at the time that the alleged offence was committed or at their trial, accused persons may volunteer a statement as to what their intention or knowledge was at the critical time. Such statements or "confessions" may well be sufficient to ensure a conviction. On the other hand, accused persons may state that they did not possess the requisite intention or knowledge and, therefore, ought to be acquitted. In these circumstances, the judge or jury, as the case may be, could well choose to believe such a statement and acquit them. However, since accused persons have a vested interest in exculpating themselves, there may be a real question as to their credibility.

How can an accused person's credibility be determined? One way in which his or her credibility may be tested is to ask the question, "What would a *reasonable* person have intended or known in the particular circumstances in which the accused found him or herself?" In answering this question, the judge or jury will, no doubt, apply their own experience of everyday life. If there is a great divergence between what the reasonable person would have intended or known and what the accused person states that he or she intended or knew, it is quite likely that the accused person's version of events will not be believed. Conversely, if there is a close similarity between the accused person's statement of what they intended or knew and what the judge or jury feels an reasonable person would have intended or known in the same circumstances, it is most likely that the judge or jury will consider that the accused person is actually telling the truth.

The willingness of the courts to employ the "common sense" standard of the reasonable person is reflected in the ancient common law maxim that people must generally be taken to have "intended" the natural and probable consequences of their acts. As Justice Gillese of the Ontario Court of Appeal remarked in *Magno* (2006):

> A person's state of mind may be determined by what a person says and does. It may be deduced also by considering what the natural consequences of

someone's actions are and whether the person, by acting in the manner for which there would be natural consequences, foresaw that those natural consequences would occur. While there is no legal presumption that a person foresees or intends the natural consequences of his or her acts, it is a common sense proposition.

Suppose, for example, that Pecksniff places the barrel of a revolver against Jonas's head and pulls the trigger, knowing that the gun is loaded. What are the natural and probable consequences of pulling the trigger of a revolver in these circumstances? The obvious answer is the death of Jonas. Since it is clear that a reasonable person would have appreciated what the natural and probable consequences of his or her act would be, in these circumstances, it is certainly makes good sense to assume that Pecksniff intended to kill Jonas.

However, the courts have emphasized that the "natural and probable consequences" inference only serves as a useful yardstick that may—or may not—be appropriate to use in all the circumstances of an individual case. Certainly, the trier of fact is not bound to draw the inference that a particular accused person had the necessary *mens rea* simply because a reasonable person would have done so. As Justice Cory of the Supreme Court of Canada noted in *Seymour* (1996), the "common sense inference that people are usually able to foresee the consequences of their actions" should be considered "a reasonable inference which *may* be drawn but is not required to be drawn by juries." If, in light of all of the circumstances of the particular case, it is not an appropriate inference, then it should not be drawn.

Putting this another way, whenever a criminal offence is defined in terms of subjective *mens rea* requirements, then it is critical to ensure that the "natural and probable consequences test" is only used in a genuine effort to establish what the particular accused person in the case *subjectively knew and intended*. As Justice Cory stated in the *Seymour* case (1996), "[T]he common sense inference as to intention, which may be drawn from the actions of the accused, is simply a method to determine the accused's *actual* intent."

In the majority of cases, no doubt, the judge or jury will tend to disbelieve accused persons who claim that they did not possess the requisite knowledge or intention when the reasonable person, in the same circumstances as the accused, would have possessed such knowledge or intention. However, it is very important to bear in mind that people do not always act reasonably, nor do they always have the same capacities as the hypothetical reasonable person. For example, certain individuals may be so mentally impaired that they are incapable of foreseeing the consequences of their actions even though a reasonable person, in exactly the same circumstances, would have done so. Similarly, even an average person, under stress, may well panic and fail to act as the hypothetical reasonable person would have done in the same circumstances.

If there is a reasonable doubt that the accused possessed the requisite intention or knowledge, he or she must be acquitted despite the fact that the "reasonable" person would have possessed the necessary *mens rea* in the same circumstances. For example, in *Beyo* (2000), the accused had visited the home of relatives of his estranged wife. Among other acts, he broke the window in a door and he was charged, *inter alia*, with the offence of mischief (wilfully destroying or damaging property, contrary to the provisions of section 430(1)(a) of the *Criminal Code*). The critical issue on this charge was whether Beyo "wilfully" broke the window. There was Crown evidence to the effect that the accused had pounded on the glass with a closed fist in "what seemed to be an attempt to break the glass to gain entry into the house." However, Beyo himself testified that he was merely "banging on the glass to make noise to attract attention": he claimed that he had done this because he believed that his son had been kidnapped and was in the house. Therefore, the accused person's version of events was that he had struck the window repeatedly in the hope that the noise would cause the police to intervene and he stated that "*he did not intend to break the glass* and as soon as it broke he immediately offered to pay for the damage."

The trial judge brought to the jury's attention the "old common law rule" that "every man's intention must be presumed from the manner in which he behaves" and stated that

> [t]here is a glass door and Mr. Beyo is an educated man.... He must know that continued hitting of that glass is likely to break it. Any reasonable person must know that and he would therefore be found guilty of the mischief with regard to the offence of breaking the window. [emphasis added]

The accused was convicted and he appealed to the Ontario Court of Appeal, which set aside the finding of guilt of mischief. On behalf of the court, Justice Rosenberg noted that the trial judge did not bring to the jury's attention the accused's own evidence as to the state of his mind at the time of the alleged offence. Indeed,

> ... if the appellant's version of events were accepted, a finding of guilt, while possible, was not inevitable. His state of mind had to be determined by a consideration of the evidence including the appellant's testimony, the evidence of others that he was obviously in an agitated state and concerned for the welfare of his son. *It could not be determined by application of any legal presumption nor solely from a comparison with what a reasonable person would know.* [emphasis added]

Clearly, in *Beyo*, it was not appropriate to draw the "common sense inference" as to intention because there was some credible evidence that was capable of raising a reasonable doubt as to whether the accused did in fact intend to break the window. Similarly, if an accused person is intoxicated, the trial judge must make it crystal clear that, if the members of the jury harbour any doubts about that person's *actual* intention or knowledge in relation to a crime requiring proof of subjective *mens rea*, then the "common sense inference" may not be applied at all (see the Supreme Court of Canada decisions in *Robinson* (1996) , *Seymour* (1996) and *Daley* (2007), which are discussed in Chapter 10, under the heading of "Intoxication").

THE CONCEPT OF TRANSFERRED INTENT

Let us suppose that Guppy throws a rock with the intention of hitting Skimpole. However, the rock misses its mark and instead hits and wounds Arabella. It is clear that Guppy "intended" to hit Skimpole. However, can he be convicted of an assault causing bodily harm to Arabella? The answer is that Guppy could, indeed, be convicted under section 267 of the *Code* because of the operation of the ancient common law principle of **transferred intent**. As the Ontario Court of Appeal stated in *Gordon* (2009):

> The common law doctrine of transferred intent takes the *mens rea* of an offence in relation to an intended victim and transfers it to the *actus reus* of the same offence committed upon another victim. Considered separately, each prospective crime lacks an essential part. The *mens rea* (intended victim) lacks an *actus reus*. And the *actus reus* (actual victim) lacks *mens rea*. In combination, however, they amount to a whole crime through the application of a legal fiction.

In essence, the principle of transferred intent provides that Guppy's intention to hit Skimpole can be *transferred* to the assault actually committed against Arabella. Guppy intended to commit the *actus reus* of

an assault (albeit the victim was supposed to be Skimpole) and actually committed the *actus reus* of assault when he hit Arabella. Therefore, it seems to be both just and reasonable to convict him of assault causing bodily harm.

A specific example of the general principle of transferred intent may be found in section 229(b) of the *Criminal Code*:

> Where a person, meaning to cause death to a human being or meaning to cause him bodily harm that he knows is likely to cause death, and being reckless whether death ensues or not, by accident or mistake causes death to another human being, notwithstanding that he does not mean to cause death or bodily harm to that human being ... [is guilty of murder].

A rather bizarre set of circumstances led to the application of this section by the Supreme Court of Canada in *Droste* (1984). In this case, the defendant was charged with first degree murder. The Crown introduced evidence to the effect that Droste had told his co-workers that he intended to kill his wife. It appeared that he was sexually involved with another woman, and that he wished to recover the proceeds of an insurance policy that had recently been placed on Mrs. Droste's life. He told one of his co-workers that he planned to crash his car, set it on fire, and leave his spouse to perish in the conflagration. On the day of the incident in question, Droste was seen to be applying gasoline to the inside of his car. He later entered the car with his wife and their two small children and left for a birthday party. On the way, a fire broke out. His wife stated that Mr. Droste then tried to hit her on the head with a screwdriver and yelled at her to release her grip on the steering wheel. Tragically, the car struck the abutment of a bridge. The parents managed to extricate themselves from the blazing wreck, but they were unable to save the children, who were asphyxiated by the smoke. There was no evidence whatsoever that Mr. Droste harboured any ill will toward his children.

The trial judge instructed the jury that, if they were satisfied beyond a reasonable doubt that Droste's intention to kill his wife was planned and deliberate and that in the course of carrying out that intention he caused the death of his children by accident or mistake, the resulting homicide constituted first degree murder. The jury convicted, and both the Ontario Court of Appeal and the Supreme Court ultimately upheld the conviction. Justice Dickson noted, in the Supreme Court, that

[t]he jury found that Mr. Droste, meaning to cause the death of a human being (Mrs. Droste), by accident caused the death of another human being (each of the children). He is therefore guilty of murder pursuant to [s. 229(b)]....

However, in the case of *Fontaine* (2002), the Manitoba Court of Appeal held that the doctrine of transferred intent, which is embodied in section 229(b), does not apply to the situation where the accused attempts to commit suicide and accidentally kills another person. In this case, the accused had attempted to commit suicide by driving his vehicle into a parked semitrailer. Instead, he caused the death of one of the passengers in his car. In the view of the Court of Appeal, there was a marked difference between the intent to commit suicide and the intent to kill another person:

> First degree murder is perhaps the most stigmatizing offence known to law. It carries with it the most draconian minimum sentence of life imprisonment with no parole for 25 years. It is normally associated with the act of one who plans and deliberates to take the life of another person. Society as a whole condemns this crime.
>
> Suicide on the other hand is normally seen as an act of desperation, often impulsive, and the act of a person who is ill and in need of treatment. By removing the crime of attempted suicide from the *Criminal Code*, Parliament recognized society's desire to see individuals who attempt suicide treated instead of criminalized.

Similarly, in the case of *Gordon* (2009), the Ontario Court of Appeal ruled that the doctrine of transferred intent does not apply to the offence of attempted murder (a so-called "inchoate crime"

because the accused person fails to commit the *actus reus* of the intended crime—in this case, the death of a human being). Gordon had fired a shotgun at a drug dealer with whom he had been in conflict. None of the shotgun pellets struck their intended target but three bystanders were hit by pellets and suffered serious injuries. The trial judge instructed the jury that Gordon could be guilty of attempted murder of the three bystanders through the application of the doctrine of transferred intent, provided, of course, that the Crown proved beyond a reasonable doubt that Gordon had intended to kill the drug dealer when he pulled the trigger of the shotgun. Gordon was convicted of the attempted murder of the bystanders but the Ontario Court of Appeal set aside these convictions and substituted convictions of aggravated assault.

In delivering the judgment of the Court of Appeal, Justice Watt stated that

> [f]irst, every crime, inchoate or substantive, involves both *mens rea* and an *actus reus*. The *actus reus* of many but not all crimes may include an element of harm, as for example the crimes of unlawful homicide. In most cases, including offences against the person, the *mens rea* and *actus reus* relate to the same victim. When transferred intent principles are in play, however, the *mens rea* relates to an intended victim and the *actus reus* relates to the actual victim. The principles connect a culpable mental state in relation to one with a result or harm visited upon another.
>
> The principles underlying transferred intent apply to crimes that require a result as part of the *actus reus*, for example, death of a human being in cases of unlawful homicide. But inchoate crimes in general, and attempted murder in particular, do *not*

In this case, the doctrine of transferred intent would apply.

Cartoon by Elizabeth Carefoot

require a result or harm as part of their *actus reus*. The *actus reus* is complete upon the first act beyond preparation.

As noted by the Manitoba Court of Appeal in *Vandergraaf* (1994), a critical component of the doctrine of transferred intent is the requirement that the accused's intent may be transferred only where the *actus reus* and *mens rea* of the same offence coincide. In this case, the accused had intended to throw a small jar of peanut butter onto the ice at a hockey arena. As was the case for many other fans, he was upset that the team he supported had lost a game in overtime. Tragically, his aim was erratic, and the jar hit a woman who was standing in the front row at ice level, causing an injury to her. The accused was charged with assault with a weapon (section 267). The trial judge convicted the accused because he had the "intention to apply force in a general sense." However, the Manitoba Court of Appeal allowed Vandergraaf's appeal and entered an acquittal. As Justice Philp said, "[W]ithout proof of an intention to apply force to the complainant, or to another person, there cannot be a conviction of assault." Vandergraaf never intended to apply force to a human being and he, therefore, lacked the *mens rea* for assault even though he accidentally committed the *actus reus* of this offence. Therefore, the doctrine of transferred intent could not apply.

The limitations upon the doctrine of transferred intent may be illustrated by considering the following hypothetical examples:

1. Let us suppose that Sinbad, the knife thrower at the local circus, has a burning desire to kill Hercules (the circus strong man). One evening, as dusk falls, he sees what he thinks is the silhouette of Hercules against the evening sky. He throws a knife at the figure and his aim is true. However, when Sinbad goes to inspect the corpse, he discovers that he has killed Leo (the lion tamer) by mistake. In these circumstances, it is clear that Sinbad is guilty of murder. After all, he killed the person at whom he was aiming his knife, and it is irrelevant that he was mistaken as to the person's identity.

2. Sinbad is walking in the local park when he sees Hercules coming toward him. He decides to seize his chance to kill Hercules and takes aim with one of his knives. Just as he is throwing the knife, he trips and the knife deviates from its course, killing Chuckles, the clown, who was walking unseen in the long grass. Once again, it is clear that Sinbad is guilty of murder under section 229(b). He intended to kill one human being and actually killed another.

3. Sinbad is still desperate to kill Hercules. He sees him walking side by side with Jumbo, the circus elephant, in a parade. Once again, he decides to strike while the iron is hot and aims his knife at Hercules. However, the knife misses its mark and instead kills Jumbo. Unlike examples 1 and 2, the doctrine of transferred intent may not be applied since the *actus reus* and *mens rea* of the same crime do not coincide. Although Sinbad committed the *actus reus* of killing an animal, contrary to section 445 of the *Code*, he did not intend to commit this offence and his intention to commit murder (in relation to Hercules) cannot be transferred from one type of offence to another. In brief, intention can only be transferred within the limits of the same offence.

4. A dispirited Sinbad decides to kill Bruin, the circus bear. He takes aim with his knife and throws it toward the bear. However, at the last minute the knife deviates from its course and kills Hercules. Sinbad's intent to kill an animal (contrary to section 445 of the *Code*) cannot be transferred so as to convict him of murder—even though he has committed the *actus reus* of homicide by killing Hercules. Of course, it is probable that Sinbad would be convicted of causing death by criminal negligence, contrary to section 220 of the *Code*. It is also probable that Sinbad could be convicted of an attempt to kill an animal, just as he could have been convicted of attempted murder in example 3. However, liability for these attempted offences would clearly not be based upon the doctrine of transferred intent, but rather on general principles of criminal law.

The doctrine of transferred intent has been criticized because it might lead to a situation in which an individual is punished for what is, at best, an *accident*. The Ontario Court of Appeal expressed some sympathy for this view in *Irwin* (1998). In this case, the accused was fighting a man called Graham on the outdoor patio of a restaurant. As the two men grappled with each other, they fell over the victim, causing him serious injuries. The Crown laid a charge of assault causing bodily harm and relied on the principle of transferred intent. The accused was convicted and appealed to the Ontario Court of

Appeal. This court took the view that the doctrine of transferred intent, in the specific context of an *assault* charge, "raises difficult problems." Justice Doherty stated that "these problems could have been avoided had the appellant been charged with unlawfully causing bodily harm to [the victim]" (see section 269 of the *Criminal Code*). The court amended the indictment so as to charge Irwin with unlawfully causing bodily harm and then affirmed his conviction. What the Court of Appeal did in *Irwin* is to signal to Crown counsel that, wherever possible, they should try to avoid using the theory of transferred intent in cases of this type. The offence of unlawfully causing bodily harm was an appropriate charge to lay in the *Irwin* case because the accused's unlawful behaviour had caused injury to the victim, and it was only necessary for the Crown to prove that any reasonable person engaged in fighting in a public place would have foreseen the risk that someone in the vicinity of the fight might be physically injured. This approach neatly avoids the need to rely on the doctrine of transferred intent. Whether *Irwin* heralds a general move away from judicial reliance on the doctrine of transferred intent in cases of this type remains to be seen.

SPECIFIC OR ULTERIOR INTENT

The concept of *specific intent* or *ulterior intent* is somewhat difficult to understand in the abstract. However, it is important to bear in mind that the concept is primarily relevant to the defence of intoxication, which will be discussed in considerable detail in Chapter 10. Basically, it will be seen that intoxication may be a **partial defence** to a charge of a crime requiring proof of specific or ulterior intent. In sharp contrast, under section 33.1 of the *Criminal Code*, intoxication can never be a defence to a charge of a so-called **general (or basic) intent offence** if it involves "an element of assault or any other interference or threat of interference by a person with the bodily integrity of another person."

For most criminal offences, the Crown need only prove that the accused committed the prohibited act intentionally and with the necessary knowledge of the material circumstances. For example, in relation to a charge of assault, the Crown need only prove that the defendant intended to bring about the *actus reus* of assault (either the application of force without the consent of the victim or a threat to use force in the situation where the victim reasonably believes that the

accused has the present ability to carry out the threat). Similarly, in relation to a charge of wilful damage to property (section 430(1)), the Crown need only prove that the accused intentionally caused the *actus reus* of the offence (namely, the infliction of actual damage to the property in question). These two offences are called basic or general intent crimes. In each case, the Crown need only prove that the accused intended to commit the *actus reus* of the offence in question. Other examples of basic or general intent offences are manslaughter, sexual assault, impaired driving, forcible confinement, pointing a firearm, and unlawfully causing bodily harm.

However, there are a number of offences in relation to which the Crown must prove a further mental element in order to obtain a conviction. In relation to these offences, the Crown must prove not only an intention to commit the *actus reus* of the crime in question, but also the intention to produce some further consequence beyond the *actus reus*. This additional mental element places such offences within the category of **specific intent offences** contained in the *Criminal Code*. The following are considered to be examples of specific intent offences:

1. Murder—this crime can be defined, in most cases, as an assault committed with the specific (or ulterior) intent to kill (section 229(a)).
2. Assault with intent to resist or prevent the lawful arrest or detention of the accused or another person (section 270(1)(b)).
3. Possessing a weapon for a purpose dangerous to the public or for the purpose of committing an offence (section 88).
4. Theft—for example, taking something fraudulently and without colour of right with intent to deprive (either temporarily or absolutely) the owner of it or a person who has a special property or interest in it of the thing or of his or her property or interest in it (section 322(1)(a)).
5. Robbery—for example, assaulting a person with intent to steal from her or him (section 343(c)).
6. Breaking and entering with intent to commit an indictable offence (section 348(1)(a)).
7. Discharging a firearm with intent to wound, maim, or disfigure a person, to endanger the life of any person, or to prevent the arrest or detention of any person (section 244).

There have been various attempts to define the elements that separate specific or ulterior intent crimes from basic intent crimes. In Canada, one of the most authoritative attempts to offer such a definition was made in the case of *George* (1960), in which the accused was charged with the offence of robbery. The evidence indicated that the accused had visited the home of an 84-year-old man called Averis, and demanded money from him. He then beat Averis severely with his bare fists, broke his nose, and caused numerous other serious bodily injuries to the victim. He then stole the sum of $22. The victim indicated that George had threatened to kill him unless he gave him money.

George's main defence was that he was in a severe state of intoxication at the time of the alleged offence. At his trial, the County Court judge acquitted the accused on the following basis:

> You are being acquitted not because you didn't do it—there is no doubt in my mind that you did do it—you are being acquitted because I have found that you were so drunk on the night in question that you were unable to form an intent to do it.

The Crown appealed the accused's acquittal. The appeal was unsuccessful in the British Columbia Court of Appeal but was ultimately successful before the Supreme Court of Canada. Essentially, the Supreme Court affirmed the accused's acquittal on the charge of robbery. Since robbery is a specific or ulterior intent offence, drunkenness may be a partial defence. Therefore, the Court judged that the accused had been rightly acquitted. However, every charge of robbery necessarily includes a charge of assault (in essence, a robbery normally involves both an assault and a theft), and an accused person may always be convicted of any lesser offence that is considered to be included in the charge upon which he or she is tried. The Court pointed out that a simple assault is a **crime of general (or basic) intent,** and drunkenness cannot be a valid defence to such a charge. Therefore, the Supreme Court of Canada entered a verdict of guilty of common assault against George. The case is important since at least two justices of the Supreme Court of Canada endeavoured to define the concept of specific or ulterior intent. Justice Fauteux provided the following definition:

> In considering the question of *mens rea* a distinction is to be made between (1) intention as applied to acts considered in relation to their purposes and (2) intention as applied to acts considered apart from their purposes. A general intent attending the commission of an act is, in some cases, the only intent required to constitute the crime while, in others,

there must be, in addition to that general intent, a specific intent attending the purpose for the commission of the act. [emphasis added]

Justice Ritchie furnished an alternative explanation for the distinction between basic (or general) and specific (or ulterior) intent offences:

> In considering the question of *mens rea, a distinction is to be drawn between "intention" as applied to acts done to achieve an immediate end on the one hand and acts done with a specific and ulterior motive and intention of furthering or achieving an illegal object on the other hand. Illegal acts of the former kind are done "intentionally" in the sense that they are not done by accident or through honest mistake, but acts of the latter kind are the product of preconception and are deliberate steps taken towards an illegal goal. The former acts may be purely physical products of momentary passion, whereas the latter involve the mental process of formulating a specific intent. A man, far advanced in drink, may intentionally strike his fellow in the former sense at a time when his mind is so befogged with liquor as to be unable to formulate a specific intent in the latter sense.... [emphasis added]*

In his dissenting judgment in the *Bernard* case (1988), Chief Justice Dickson strongly—albeit unsuccessfully—contended that the distinction between specific and general intent was "artificial" and should be eliminated. However, it is significant that, in the later case of *Daviault* (1994), the Supreme Court of Canada unequivocally reaffirmed the existence of this distinction as a fundamental element of Canadian criminal law. As Justice Cory stated, in *Daviault,*

> The distinction between crimes of specific and general intent has been acknowledged and approved by this court on numerous occasions.... The categorization of crimes as being either specific or general intent offences and the consequences that flow from that categorization are now well established in this court.

RECKLESSNESS AS A FORM OF SUBJECTIVE *MENS REA*

DEFINITION OF RECKLESSNESS

One form of subjective *mens rea* that may be sufficient for conviction of a criminal offence is recklessness. In some instances, Canadian courts have expanded the *mens rea* elements required in relation to true crimes to include **recklessness** as an alternative to intention or knowledge. For example, when considering the offence of sexual assault in the *Sansregret* case (1985), the Supreme Court of Canada accepted the view that recklessness as to the victim's consent was sufficient *mens rea* to sustain a conviction. In other words, the Court indicated that either actual knowledge that the victim did not consent or recklessness as to this matter are both states of mind that will justify conviction of sexual assault (Parliament later amended the *Criminal Code* in order to reflect the Supreme Court's ruling in this respect: see section 273.2, enacted in 1992).

In addition, the *Criminal Code* specifically states that recklessness is a form of *mens rea* sufficient to justify conviction of the accused in relation to a number of categories of criminal offences. Before discussing these categories of offences, however, it is necessary to define the concept of recklessness. People are reckless, with respect to a consequence of their actions, when they foresee that it may occur but do not desire it or foresee it as certain. For example, Dogberry fires a gun into a crowded lecture hall in order to "scare people." Dogberry does not wish to kill anyone, but he necessarily realizes that someone may be killed. He decides to proceed with his irresponsible conduct regardless of this risk. In these circumstances, we would clearly say that Dogberry is reckless as to the consequence that someone may be killed by his actions. People are reckless with respect to a circumstance when they realize that it may exist but neither know, nor desire, that it exists. For example, suppose that Caliban points a revolver at Prospero. Caliban does not know whether the gun is loaded. He hopes that the gun is not loaded but decides to pull the trigger regardless. We would have little difficulty in branding Caliban as reckless. It will be noted that, in both the above examples, the accused undoubtedly foresee the risk that their conduct creates. They then decide to proceed with their course of conduct regardless of their appreciation of the inherent risk of so doing.

Recklessness contains both a subjective element and an objective element. The subjective element consists of subjective foresight of the risk(s) created by the conduct of the accused person. The objective element consists of an unreasonable assumption of that risk—in the sense that a reasonable person acting prudently would not have assumed the risk that the accused foresaw. Clearly, it would be absurd to penalize everyone who foresees that his or her conduct creates a risk: therefore, the objective element of recklessness is a vital component of this particular form of *mens rea*. The subjective element of recklessness requires that the accused person actually foresee the risk created by his or her conduct and, for this reason, recklessness is sometimes referred to as "advertent negligence": a reckless person "adverts" or directs his or her mind to the risk in question. As Justice McIntyre said in the decision of the Supreme Court in the *Sansregret* case (1985),

> In accordance with well established principles for the determination of criminal liability, recklessness, to form a part of the criminal *mens rea*, must have an element of the subjective. It is found in the attitude of one who, aware that there is danger that his conduct could bring about the result prohibited by the criminal law, nevertheless persists, despite the risk. It is, in other words, the conduct of one who sees the risk and takes the chance.

The objective element of recklessness is based on the recognition that the criminal law should only punish individuals who assume *unreasonable* risks. If a reasonable person, acting prudently and facing the same circumstances as the accused, would have assumed the risk in question, then the accused person's conduct may not be branded as reckless. For example, a surgeon may assume a high degree of risk in carrying out a particular surgical procedure if this is the only way in which he or she may save the life of a patient. If the procedure has a 60 percent chance of failure, the surgeon may still be justified in proceeding with the surgery if the only alternative (a failure to intervene) is certain death. Conversely, a surgeon would not be justified in carrying out a high-risk procedure if there are alternative procedures that are less perilous and offer the patient equal, if not better, chances for recovery.

By way of summary, therefore, it can be stated that reckless people subjectively appreciate the risk that their conduct creates; however, criminal responsibility

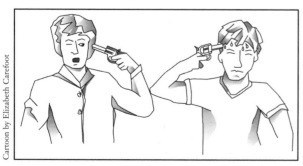

Cartoon by Elizabeth Carefoot

Recklessness is knowingly taking an unjustified risk.

is imposed only if reasonable persons would not have assumed such a risk in the same circumstances. Since reckless people fully appreciate that their conduct creates a substantial risk and proceed regardless, we may say that they deliberately choose to do something wrong. Liability for recklessness, therefore, is clearly based upon the moral blameworthiness of the individual defendant.

EXAMPLES OF *CRIMINAL CODE* OFFENCES REQUIRING PROOF OF RECKLESSNESS

Although the courts have themselves expanded the concept of *mens rea* to include recklessness in relation to a number of criminal offences, the *Criminal Code* expressly states that recklessness is a sufficient form of *mens rea* for conviction in relation to the four following categories of offences.

1. Murder

Section 229 of the *Criminal Code* provides that

[c]ulpable homicide is murder

    (a)   Where the person who causes the death of a human being

        (i)   means to cause his death, or

        (ii) means to cause him bodily harm that he knows is likely to cause his death, and is reckless whether death ensues or not.

Section 229(a)(ii) deals with the situation where the accused person has killed someone and the Crown can prove that he or she intentionally inflicted bodily harm that he or she subjectively realized would be likely to cause death. If the Crown can also establish that the accused continued with the assault on the victim, regardless of his or her knowledge of that deadly risk, there will be a conviction of **murder**. This would be a classic example of recklessness as a form of subjective *mens rea*, because the accused clearly chooses to inflict a degree of injury that he or she subjectively realizes is likely to cause the death of the victim. As Chief Justice Finch, of the Court of Appeal of the Yukon Territory remarked in *Rodrigue* (2007):

... [W]ithin the meaning of s. 229(a)(ii), reckless refers to the foreseeability of a likely, as opposed to simply a possible, consequence flowing from the bodily harm that he is occasioning the victim.... In other words, within the legal definition of the

mental element for murder, reckless is synonymous with a substantially subjective state of mind, and not with imprudence or carelessness.

Although recklessness is a sufficient basis for establishing murder under section 229(a)(ii), it is important to recognize that the Crown nevertheless has to establish some onerous *mens rea* requirements in order to obtain a conviction. For example, in the *Cooper* case (1993), Justice Cory of the Supreme Court of Canada emphasized that "it is not sufficient that the accused foresee simply a danger of death; the accused must foresee a likelihood of death flowing from the bodily harm that he is occasioning the victim." This principle was applied in the later case of *Czibulka* (2004), when the Ontario Court of Appeal held that the trial judge had made an error in his instructions to the jury when he defined recklessness in the context of section 229(a)(ii) as being aware that there is a "danger that the conduct could bring about death." The Court ruled that the trial judge should not have used the word "danger" in this particular context. Under section 229(a)(ii), the accused must foresee the "likelihood" of death and not merely a "danger" of death. As Justice Rosenberg pointed out, in delivering the judgment of the Court of Appeal, "[T]he risk of death embodied in the terms 'danger' and 'likelihood' are not of the same magnitude."

2. Damage to Property, Etc.

Section 429(1) of the *Criminal Code* provides that

[e]very one who causes the occurrence of an event by doing an act or by omitting to do an act that is his duty to do, knowing that the act or omission will probably cause the occurrence of the event and being reckless whether the event occurs or not, shall be deemed, for the purposes of this Part, wilfully to have caused the occurrence of the event.

Parliament has unequivocally chosen to treat reckless defendants in exactly the same manner as those who have acted wilfully (or intentionally) in relation to the various property offences set out in Part XI of the *Code*. These offences include mischief in the sense of damage to property, data, religious property, and so forth (section 430); injuring or endangering cattle (section 444); injuring or endangering other animals (section 445); causing unnecessary suffering to animals or birds (s. 445.1); and wilful neglect causing damage or injury to animals or birds for which one has a legal responsibility (s. 446).

3. Arson

Sections 433 and 434 of the *Criminal Code* impose criminal liability for both intentional and reckless damage to property that is caused by fire or explosion. Section 433 states that

[e]very person who intentionally or recklessly causes damage by fire or explosion to property, whether or not that person owns the property, is guilty of an indictable offence and liable to imprisonment for life where

> (a) the person knows that or is reckless with respect to whether the property is inhabited or occupied; or
>
> (b) the fire or explosion causes bodily harm to another person.

Section 434 provides that

[e]very person who intentionally or recklessly causes damage by fire or explosion to property that is not wholly owned by that person is guilty of an indictable offence and liable to imprisonment for a term not exceeding fourteen years.

Take, for example, the case of *Brain* (2003). The accused in this case was charged with "intentionally or recklessly" committing arson contrary to section 434. He had set fire to a storage hut and denied that he had done so intentionally. However, he admitted that he had been smoking cigarettes in the hut and that the fire might have started as a consequence of his having accidentally discarded or flipped a cigarette butt into a cardboard container. The trial judge convicted Brain on the basis that Brain had started the fire "recklessly." He held that

... the defendant must have known that his conduct, the reckless flipping of a live cigarette [butt] into flammable material, would cause the event, namely a fire, and that he was reckless as to whether or not the fire occurred. In other words, he just did not care one way or the other, and that moves the conduct into the realm of the criminal.

The British Columbia Court of Appeal unanimously rejected an appeal by Brain against his conviction.

4. Criminal Harassment

Section 264(1) of the *Criminal Code* clearly specifies that the necessary *mens rea* for the offence of criminal harassment is either actual knowledge that the victim is being harassed or recklessness as to this circumstance:

No person shall, without lawful authority and knowing that another person is harassed or *recklessly* as to whether the other person is harassed, engage in conduct referred to in subsection (2) that causes that other person reasonably, in all the circumstances, to fear for their safety or the safety of anyone known to them. [emphasis added]

Section 264(2) sets out four types of conduct that may constitute the *actus reus* of criminal harassment: (a) "repeatedly following" someone; (b) "repeatedly communicating" with someone; (c) "besetting or watching the dwelling house" or workplace of someone; and (d) "engaging in threatening conduct" directed at someone.

As Justice Berger noted, on behalf of the Alberta Court of Appeal in the case of *Sillipp* (1997),

A conviction under s. 264 requires the accused have "known" that his subsection (2) conduct was causing the complainant to be harassed, or that he was aware of such risk and was reckless or wilfully blind as to whether or not the person was harassed.

Since criminal harassment is an offence that requires proof of subjective *mens rea*, the accused can successfully raise the defence of honest mistake of fact by raising a reasonable doubt as to whether he or she subjectively realized there was a risk that the complainant was aware of being harassed. For example, if an accused person indicates that he or she honestly believed that, although the accused was frequently standing outside of the complainant's residence, the latter was completely unaware of his or her presence, then the accused must be acquitted of the charge. As Justice Berger noted, a "'morally innocent accused' who honestly believed that his subsection (2) behaviour was not known to the complainant, and who was not reckless or wilfully blind, would escape criminal liability." It is noteworthy that, in the case of *Krushel* (2000), the Ontario Court of Appeal explicitly approved Justice Berger's analysis of the *mens rea* elements of criminal harassment.

WILFUL BLINDNESS AS A FORM OF SUBJECTIVE *MENS REA*

Canadian courts have expanded the *mens rea* requirement of certain offences to include **wilful blindness**. This form of *mens rea* exists when accused persons are virtually certain that particular circumstances exist (for example, that goods are stolen) but deliberately "shut their eyes" to these circumstances. It does seem reasonable that accused persons, who suspect that they are involved in criminal activities but deliberately refrain from "asking the final question" that will reveal all, should be treated as though they actually knew the circumstances that rendered conduct criminal. If the law did not adopt this policy, unscrupulous defendants would be permitted to cheat justice with impunity. In the *Harding* case (2001), the Ontario Court of Appeal summarized the requirements for establishing wilful blindness in the following manner: "the actor must first have (1) a subjective realization (2) of the likely result of his actions and (3) deliberately avoid actual knowledge while engaging in or pursuing the activity."

Although wilful blindness may appear to be a close relative of recklessness, the Supreme Court of Canada has emphasized that the two concepts should be sharply distinguished from each other. Indeed, in the case of *Sansregret* (1985), Justice McIntyre asserted that

> [w]ilful blindness is distinct from recklessness because, while recklessness involves knowledge of a danger or risk and persistence in a course of conduct which creates a risk that the prohibited result will occur, wilful blindness arises where a person who has become aware of the need for some inquiry declines to make the inquiry because he does not wish to know the truth. He would prefer to remain ignorant. The culpability in recklessness is justified by consciousness of the risk and by proceeding in the face of it, while in wilful blindness it is justified by the accused's fault in deliberately failing to inquire when he knows there is reason for inquiry.

It is significant that Canadian courts have routinely expanded the scope of subjective *mens rea* to include wilful blindness, even when Parliament has not referred to it in its definition of an offence in the *Criminal Code*. The reason for this approach lies in the judicial view that wilful blindness is "the equivalent of actual knowledge." This point was made by the Alberta Court of Appeal in *Vinokurov* (2001). In this case, the accused was the manager of a pawnshop and had received stolen goods from a customer. He was charged with several counts of possession of stolen property. Section 354(1) of the *Criminal Code* provides that

> [e]very one commits an offence who has in his possession any property or thing or any proceeds of any property or thing or of the proceeds was obtained by or derived directly or indirectly from (a) the commission in Canada of an offence punishable by indictment; or (b) an act or omission anywhere that,

if it had occurred in Canada, would have constituted an offence punishable by indictment.

Section 354(1) clearly requires that the accused person know that the property was stolen. The Alberta Court of Appeal ruled that wilful blindness is equivalent to actual knowledge and that it is, therefore, sufficient *mens rea* for conviction of the offence. However, the Court also ruled that recklessness would not be sufficient. As Justice Berger stated, "[W]ilful blindness is imputed knowledge while recklessness is 'something less than that.'" Vinokurov's convictions were set aside and a new trial was ordered because the trial judge had erroneously taken the view that recklessness was sufficient *mens rea* for conviction of the offence of possessing stolen property.

EXAMPLES OF WILFUL BLINDNESS

The doctrine of wilful blindness was applied in the case of *Oluwa* (1996), in which the accused had been charged with importing heroin and possession of heroin for the purpose of trafficking. The circumstances were somewhat bizarre. The accused had been travelling by air from Tokyo to Mexico City. The accused's flight had a short stopover at Vancouver International Airport. He was required to wait in the "Transit Departure Facility," while the plane was being cleaned and refuelled. Oluwa's behaviour aroused suspicion and it was discovered that he was carrying heroin packages in his intestinal tract. The accused's defence was that he lacked the *mens rea* for the charge of importing a narcotic because there was no evidence to prove that he actually knew his plane would be stopping in Canada and, therefore, he could not be said to have intended to come to this country. In support of this position, he pointed out that his ticket did not indicate that there would be a stopover. However, this argument was rejected at his trial, and his conviction was subsequently upheld by the B.C. Court of Appeal. On behalf of the majority of the court, Chief Justice McEachern indicated that, even if the Crown could not prove actual knowledge on the part of the accused, proof of recklessness or *wilful blindness* as to the risk that the plane would land in a country, such as Canada, would suffice for a conviction of importing a narcotic. The chief justice noted that Oluwa was an experienced international traveller and that "it is common for long-distance flights to make scheduled stops." Insofar as the issue of wilful blindness was concerned, Chief Justice McEachern concluded that

[i]n this case, with respect, I cannot conclude other than that the appellant, if he did not know his flight would stop in Canada, which seems inconceivable, was *wilfully blind to that fact. His lack of knowledge, if any, resulted from his wilful failure to obtain information which was readily available and which was of significant importance to him. Because of his wilful blindness, the law attributes such knowledge to him.* [emphasis added]

Similarly, in the *Tejani* case (1999), the accused, a Toronto currency exchange dealer, had been charged with attempted money laundering, contrary to the provisions of section 19.2 of the (now repealed) *Narcotic Control Act*, R.S.C. 1985, c. N-1.[2] A critical element in the *mens rea* for this offence was the accused's *belief* that the funds in question constituted the "proceeds of drug trafficking, importing or exporting." The Ontario Court of Appeal, in upholding the accused's conviction, stated unequivocally that the offence could be proved on the basis of the accused's *wilful blindness* as to the source of the money that was intended to be laundered. Indeed, Justice Laskin stated that, on a charge of attempting to launder money, the necessary *mens rea* requirements "can be satisfied not only by a finding of belief but also by a finding of wilful blindness." In the view of the Court of Appeal, the trial judge had not erred in finding that Tejani was wilfully blind:

> [The trial judge] … could reasonably conclude that the appellant shut his eyes to the source of Debellis' money because the appellant knew or strongly suspected that inquiring would fix him with the knowledge the funds were the proceeds of illicit dealing in drugs.

The courts have emphasized, however, that wilful blindness exists only when accused persons have every reason to suspect the existence of circumstances that would render their actions criminal but deliberately shut their eyes because they think it will serve their purposes to plead ignorance to the authorities. It is not enough for the Crown to contend that the accused was negligent in the sense of failing to make the inquiries that a reasonable person would have made in the circumstances. Merely neglecting to make inquiries (even those that a "reasonable person" might make) does not *per se* constitute wilful blindness—a considerably more culpable state of mind must be proved by the Crown.

However, the courts may find that there is wilful blindness even in those situations where an accused person, whose suspicions have been aroused, actually

does make an inquiry. It would be ridiculous if that person were to be acquitted merely because he or she made a half-hearted inquiry that resulted in a denial of criminality by another party. For example, in the case of *Lagace* (2003), the accused had been charged with both fraud and possession of property worth over $5000. Lagace was a dealer in used motor vehicles. He had entered into an arrangement with two car dealers in Quebec who purchased wrecked vehicles from the United States, removed their vehicle identification numbers, and then placed these numbers on stolen cars. These dealers then sold the stolen cars to Lagace, who then sold them as repaired vehicles to members of the public. The accused denied any awareness of the fact that the cars were stolen and claimed that he had contacted one of the Quebec dealers, who had assured him that "the cars were not stolen, that he had no criminal record, and that the police had been harassing him since 1992." Lagace contended that he had been satisfied with this explanation. However, the accused was convicted at his trial and, although the Ontario Court of Appeal granted Lagace a new trial, the appellate court made some important observations concerning the nature of wilful blindness and the significance of the fact that the accused had made some kind of inquiry that resulted in a denial of criminality by the individual with whom the accused was dealing:

> Culpability on the basis of wilful blindness rests on a finding of deliberate ignorance. An accused who suspects that property is stolen but declines to make the inquiries that will confirm that suspicion, preferring instead to remain ignorant, is culpable. Where an accused makes some inquiry, the question remains whether that accused harboured real suspicions after that inquiry and refrained from making further inquiries because she preferred to remain ignorant of the truth. Where some inquiry is made, the nature of that inquiry will be an important consideration in determining whether the accused remained suspicious and chose to refrain from further inquiry because she preferred to remain deliberately ignorant of the truth.

SUBJECTIVE *MENS REA* AS A *CHARTER* REQUIREMENT: THE CASE OF MURDER

IMPACT OF THE *CHARTER* ON THE DOCTRINE OF *MENS REA*

We have seen that the *mens rea* elements of a criminal offence may be based on subjective or objective liability. However, Parliament does not have a totally

---

[2] See what is now section 462.31 of the *Criminal Code*.

free hand in making this decision. Indeed, the Supreme Court of Canada has ruled that the *Charter* demands that there be a minimum requirement of subjective *mens rea* for "very few" offences, such as murder. In the case of *Martineau* (1990), the Supreme Court of Canada decided that, although Parliament may impose objective liability in relation to certain *Criminal Code* offences, such as dangerous driving or manslaughter, the crime of murder is so serious that the *Charter* requires that the Crown prove that the accused either deliberately intended to kill or, at the very least, subjectively foresaw the risk that his or her conduct was likely to cause death. To convict an accused person, in the absence of these subjective elements, would amount to depriving him or her of "the right to life, liberty and security of the person" in a manner that contravenes the "fundamental principles of justice" enshrined in section 7 of the *Canadian Charter of Rights and Freedoms*. As Chief Justice Lamer stated,

> In my view, in a free and democratic society that values the autonomy and free will of the individual, the stigma and punishment attaching to the most serious of crimes, murder, should be reserved for those who choose to intentionally cause death or who choose to inflict bodily harm that they know is likely to cause death. The essential role of requiring subjective foresight of death in the context of murder is to maintain a proportionality between the stigma and punishment attached to a murder conviction and the moral blameworthiness of the offender. Murder has long been recognized as the "worst" and most heinous of peace-time crimes. It is, therefore, essential that to satisfy the principles of fundamental justice, the stigma and punishment attaching to a murder conviction must be reserved for those who either intend to cause death or to cause bodily harm that they know will likely cause death.

In *Vaillancourt* (1987), *Martineau* (1990), and *Sit* (1991), the Supreme Court of Canada declared the various parts of section 230 of the *Criminal Code* invalid under the *Charter*. Section 230 had made it possible to convict accused persons of murder even though they did not subjectively foresee the likelihood that their conduct would cause death. Since this section is now invalid, it will not be discussed further. However, the constitutional requirement—that *subjective foresight must be proved before an individual may be convicted of murder*—is clearly of vital significance to the development of Canadian criminal law. What remains to be seen is the extent (if any) to which the Supreme Court may be willing to expand the category of offences for which proof of subjective *mens rea* is a *Charter* requirement.

THE *CHARTER* REQUIREMENT OF SUBJECTIVE *MENS REA* AND SECTION 229(C) OF THE *CRIMINAL CODE*

Section 229 of the *Criminal Code* defines the circumstances in which culpable homicide will be categorized as murder. Section 229(a) states that

[c]ulpable homicide is murder

    (a) where the person who causes the death of a human being

        (i) means to cause his death, or

        (ii) means to cause him bodily harm that he knows is likely to cause his death, and is reckless whether death ensues or not.

The vast majority of murder charges fall within the scope of section 229(a) of the *Code*, and it is clear that both of the *mens rea* requirements under subsections (i) and (ii) are based on the accused's *subjective foresight of the likelihood of death*. Therefore, section 229(a) clearly meets the constitutional standard prescribed by the Supreme Court in the *Martineau* case (1990). However, section 229(c) of the *Code* expands the scope of the crime of murder to cover another set of circumstances: in so doing, it raises doubts concerning its constitutional validity. Section 229(c) states that murder has been committed

    (c) where a person, for an unlawful object, does anything that he knows or ought to know is likely to cause death, and thereby causes death to a human being, notwithstanding that he desires to effect his object without causing death or bodily harm to any human being.

In essence, section 229(c) states that accused persons may be convicted of murder provided that they caused the death of the victim with the purpose of carrying out an "unlawful object" and that they did so either

1. with actual knowledge that they were doing something that was "likely" to cause death to someone, or
2. in circumstances in which they "ought" to have known that the death of someone was a "likely" consequence of their conduct.

The use of the words "ought to know" clearly indicates that Parliament intended to impose an *objective* test of criminal responsibility in those situations where the Crown is unable to prove that the accused person had actual knowledge that death was a likely consequence of his or her conduct. In other words, the court is directed to consider what *reasonable* persons would have contemplated had they been confronted by exactly the same set of circumstances as the accused. This means that an accused person may be convicted of murder, under the provisions of section 229(c), even if he or she did not *subjectively* foresee the likelihood of death ensuing from his or her conduct: all that the Crown needs to prove is that a *reasonable person would have done so.* In this sense, the use of the words "ought to know" undoubtedly infringes the *Charter* requirement that an individual may be convicted of the extraordinarily serious crime of murder only where the Crown can prove subjective foresight of death.

In *Martineau* (1990) (a case that dealt with the constitutional validity of section 230 of the *Code*), Chief Justice Lamer expressed the view that the requirement of subjective foresight as a precondition for conviction of murder "casts serious if not fatal doubt on the constitutionality of part of [section 229(c)] of the *Code*, specifically the words 'ought to know is likely to cause death.'" He went on to state that

> [i]n my view, subjective foresight of death must be proven beyond a reasonable doubt before a conviction of murder can be sustained and, as a result, it is obvious the part of [s. 229(c)] of the *Code* allowing for a conviction upon proof that the accused ought to have known that death was likely to result violates ss. 7 and 11(d) of the *Charter*.

The chief justice also contended that section 229(c) could not be saved by section 1 of the *Charter* as a "reasonable limit in a free and democratic society."

Technically, Chief Justice Lamer's views on the validity of section 229(c) of the *Code* do not represent a definitive ruling by the Supreme Court on this question (*Martineau* (1990) was, after all, concerned with the validity of section 230, rather than section 229(c), of the *Code*). Nevertheless, there is little doubt that the chief justice's analysis of the application of the *Charter* to section 229(c) does constitute an accurate statement of the law. Therefore, the current situation is that the words "ought to know" in section 229(c) have no force and effect, and the courts must act as though these words have been expunged from this particular provision of the *Code*. Basically, section 229(c) now applies only where an accused person engages in a dangerous act that he or she subjectively foresees is likely to cause death, and does so for a *separate, unlawful object.*

What is meant by "unlawful object" in the specific context of section 229(c)? This aspect of the section was interpreted by the Supreme Court in the case of *Vasil* (1981), in which Justice Lamer (as he then was) stated that "unlawful object" in this particular context means "the object of conduct which, if prosecuted fully, would amount to a serious crime, that is an indictable offence requiring *mens rea*." In the *Vasil* case (1981), the Court stated that an intent to destroy property (which, if carried out, would constitute an indictable offence under section 430) constitutes an "unlawful object" under section 229(c) but an intent to seek revenge would not. Similarly, in *Magno* (2006), the unlawful object of a fatal incident of arson was alleged to be a conspiracy to commit arson for a fraudulent purpose (an indictable offence contrary to section 465 of the *Criminal Code*)— the object of the arson being the intention to submit a fraudulent claim to an insurance company.

An interesting application of Justice Lamer's definition of unlawful object occurred in the case of *Rabishaw* (1983). In the *Vasil* case (1981), the unlawful object required by section 229(c) was the accused's desire to damage property (which is an indictable offence under section 430 of the *Code*). In the *Rabishaw* case, the New Brunswick Court of Appeal faced a set of circumstances in which the accused was alleged to have set fire to property in a house; the dwelling burned down, with the tragic loss of a child's life. The Crown claimed that the unlawful objects, for the purposes of section 229(c), were the accused's desire to "embarrass someone" or his wish to "ingratiate himself with his girlfriend" by setting fire to the house and by subsequently rescuing his small son (presumably so as to appear as some sort of hero). The Court ruled that these were not unlawful objects, within the meaning of section 229(c); clearly, these goals, if achieved, would not amount to the commission of an indictable offence. On the other hand, if the Crown could establish an actual intent to burn, damage, or destroy the house, the unlawful object required by section 229(c) would be clearly established. In this particular case, a new trial was ordered in order to establish whether the accused's object really was unlawful according to the definition presented in the *Vasil* case.

A dramatic illustration of the application of section 229(c) occurred in the extraordinary case of *Meiler* (1999). The accused was convinced that his estranged wife was "seeing" a man called Roach. He later admitted that he decided to kill Roach and then commit suicide. He took a loaded shotgun, cocked it, and put his finger on the trigger with the intention of killing Roach. It appeared that Skrinjaric intercepted Meiler and jumped on his back. There was a struggle for the gun, which tragically discharged and killed Nick Biuk, who was standing close by. Meiler was charged with second degree murder. The Crown relied on the provisions of section 229(c) of the *Code* to establish the necessary *mens rea* for murder. The trial judge instructed the members of the jury that Meiler could be convicted of murder under section 229(c) if they found that, for the unlawful object of killing Roach, the accused had carried a loaded gun with his finger on the trigger and that he had known that what he was doing was *likely to cause the death of a human being*. The trial judge also stated that, if Meiler's conduct had caused the death of Biuk and if he had the necessary *mens rea* under section 229(c), then it was irrelevant that the gun discharged accidentally. Meiler was convicted of second degree murder and his subsequent appeal to the Ontario Court of Appeal was dismissed.

In delivering the judgment of the Court of Appeal in *Meiler* (1999), Justice O'Connor held that the Crown had established the necessary *mens rea* requirements for conviction of murder, under the provisions of section 229(c). Furthermore, the court rejected Meiler's argument that it would be unfair to convict him of murder when he did not foresee the *precise circumstances* in which a human being was likely to be killed (Meiler contended that he had intended to kill Roach, not Biuk, and the immediate cause of death had been the *accidental* discharge of the firearm during Meiler's tussle with Skrinjaric). Justice O'Connor stated that

> [i]n my view, s. 229(c) does not require that an offender foresee the precise situation or all of the events that result in the death. It is sufficient if the offender has the subjective foresight that the acts done for the unlawful object are likely to cause death and those acts are sufficiently linked to the death to have caused the death within the meaning of the section....
>
> The moral blameworthiness of an offender who does certain acts for an unlawful object knowing that those acts are likely to cause death to someone other than the subject of the unlawful object is no less

serious because the offender does not foresee the very situation or the precise circumstances that ultimately lead to that death.

STUDY QUESTIONS

1. Gride is a member of a violent gang that is involved in drug trafficking. Gride's gang is determined to eliminate the members of any other gang that attempts to deal drugs in what it considers to be its territory. Gride is given information that two members of a rival gang are sitting by the front window of a local restaurant. He drives to the restaurant and fires an automatic weapon at the two rival gang members. The bullets miss their intended targets and unfortunately ricochet off the walls of the restaurant. One bullet strikes and kills Dombey, a small boy who is standing outside the restaurant, and another bullet strikes and kills Bowser, a bulldog that is being exercised by a passerby. The Crown wishes to lay a charge of murder in relation to the death of Dombey (contrary to section 235 of the *Criminal Code*) and wilfully killing a dog (contrary to section 445 of the *Criminal Code*). Do you think that these charges would be likely to succeed at Gride's trial?

2. Nero sets fire to his pet food store at 2 a.m. on a Sunday in order to collect the insurance money. The store is located near a number of other business premises. There is a major fire and an alert passerby, seeing the flames, makes a"911" call. Owing to an unfortunate error on the part of the dispatcher, the fire department takes some time to arrive. In the meantime, the fire has spread to another building, a photography studio, owned by Claudius. Both Nero's store and Claudius's studio are reduced to mere burnt-out shells. Worse still, the firefighters discover the charred body of Vincent, a homeless person, who was using Claudius's studio as a place in which to sleep. There is some evidence that Nero knew that Vincent was present in Claudius's studio at night. Nero is charged with murder. Is he guilty of this offence?

3. Job Trotter is a young law and security student. On registration day, he goes to a crowded registrar's office and proceeds to a cashier's desk where he loudly demands "all the cash" and states that he has a gun in his pocket. When the

cashier dutifully produces the money, Trotter takes it but, seeing a security guard approaching in the distance, he suddenly scatters the money in the air and shakes the hand of the cashier, saying that, of course, he was "only joking." The police are immediately called to investigate this incident, and they ask Trotter to turn out the contents of his pockets. Among the contents is a screwdriver. Trotter claims that he has a reputation for being a practical joker. What charges could reasonably be laid against Trotter? Which (if any) would be most likely to result in conviction?

4. Bucket works for a government agency. His salary has been frozen for three years and he is becoming frustrated with his financial position. He complains to his immediate superior, who suggests that Bucket should "inflate" his expense accounts to compensate for his inadequate salary. Bucket follows this advice, but an auditor questions him and discovers that Bucket has submitted expense claims that exceed his actual expenditures by some $10 000. Bucket vociferously declares that he thought that he was not doing anything wrong because his superior had encouraged him to follow this course of action and because he had a moral right to rectify the injustice he had suffered as a consequence of the salary freeze maintained by the government. If you were Crown counsel in this case, what charge(s) (if any) would you lay against Bucket?

5. Bitzer is sitting at a bar, consuming a considerable quantity of alcohol. He is upset because he has been fired from his job as a security officer. He stands up and shouts, "I'm mad and I'm not going to take it anymore; I think I'm going to kill someone." He rushes out of the bar and makes his way up Main Street. He suddenly goes into a parking lot and decides to steal a car. He is just about to enter a car when he is challenged by Centurion, the night attendant. Without warning, Bitzer swings around and shoots Centurion in the chest. Centurion dies before the ambulance arrives. Bitzer is arrested and charged with first degree murder. Medical witnesses are agreed that Centurion was not so drunk as to prevent him from forming the intent to kill Centurion. Is he likely to be convicted of first degree murder? Would it make any difference to your answer if there is evidence that Bitzer was mentally disordered rather than intoxicated?

6. Snubbin goes into a bar where he meets Bumble, who claims that he is an artist. Bumble offers Snubbin a beautiful painting of a polar bear and says that he can have it for the sum of $100, provided that Snubbin gives him cash immediately. Snubbin purchases the painting and displays it in his office. Some days later, the police inform Snubbin that the painting was stolen from a famous art gallery and that it is actually worth $20 000. If you were Crown counsel, would you prosecute Snubbin even though he loudly proclaims that he did not know that the painting was stolen?

7. Steerforth is very angry with his friend Nadgett because the latter gave him a cheque that has been rejected by the bank on the basis of "insufficient funds." Steerforth decides to teach Nadgett a lesson by savagely beating him with a crowbar. Nadgett suffers such ghastly head injuries that he subsequently dies. Steerforth says that he realized that Nadgett was "hurting badly," but he claims that he never intended to kill him. Would it be possible to charge Steerforth with first or second degree murder?

8. Bill Sykes has recently separated from his spouse, Nancy. Sykes knows very well that Nancy does not want to have any form of communication with him and has told him that, if he does not leave her alone, she will summon the police. Sykes makes no effort to communicate with Nancy but he frequently parks his car a few hundred yards up the street from Nancy's house and keeps an eye on who is entering and leaving the residence. Nancy sees Sykes's car on a number of occasions and, fearing for her safety, calls the police. Sykes is arrested and subsequently charged with criminal harassment. Sykes indignantly claims that he had absolutely no intention of harassing Nancy and that he believed that she was entirely unaware of his presence in the street. Would Sykes have any defence against the charge laid against him?

9. Cloten decides to play a practical joke on his friend Pisanio. He takes a statue from Pisanio's garden and places it in front of the local police station. Cloten thinks that what he has done is very amusing but Pisanio is very angry and is pressing the police to lay a charge of theft. If you were Crown counsel, would you charge Cloten with theft?

10. Belarius steals Innogen's van from an underground parking lot. While Belarius is trying to exit the parking lot, he is confronted by Philario, who is the security guard. Belarius refuses to stop and deliberately drives the van toward Philario, who is killed in the ensuing collision. There is evidence that, on the previous day, Belarius told an acquaintance that he was intending to steal a van and that he would kill anyone who dared to stand in his way. A physician is also prepared to testify that Belarius had been drinking and that his blood alcohol level was "80 milligrams per 100 millilitres." Should Belarius be charged with first degree murder?

11. Durdles decides to kill Jasper, whom Durdles believes to be having an affair with Durdles's spouse. Durdles takes a loaded rifle and drives to Jasper's house. As Durdles is exiting his vehicle, he trips and the gun discharges. Tragically, the bullet kills Edwin, who happens to be walking along the sidewalk. If you were Crown counsel, would you charge Durdles with second degree murder? If Durdles is acquitted of a charge of murder, is it likely that he would be convicted instead of manslaughter?

FURTHER READING

Alexander, L. 2000. Insufficient Concern: A Unified Conception of Criminal Culpability. 88 *California Law Review*: 931–954.

Anand, S. 2001. Stopping Stalking: a Search for Solutions, a Blueprint for Effective Change. 64 *Saskatchewan Law Review*: 397–428.

Berman, M.N. 2005. Lesser Evils and Justification: A Less Close Look. 24 *Law and Philosophy*: 681–709.

Binder, G. 2000. Meaning and Motive in the Law of Homicide. 3 *Buffalo Criminal Law Review*: 755–774.

Brudner, A. 1996. Proportionality, Stigma and Discretion. 38 *Criminal Law Quarterly*: 301–321.

———. 2008. Subjective Fault for Crime: A Reinterpretation. 14 *Legal Theory*: 1–38.

Cairns-Way, R. 1990. Constitutionalizing Subjectivism: Another View. 79 *Criminal Reports (3rd Series)*: 260–264.

Campbell, K. L. 1993. Contract Killings. 35 *Criminal Law Quarterly*: 305–322.

Colvin, E., and S. Anand. 2007. *Principles of Criminal Law*. 3rd ed. Toronto: Carswell.

Coughlan, S. 2008. Reforming Homicide Law to Separate Guilt from Sentence: An International Gloss. 13 *Canadian Criminal Law Review*: 1–18.

Crocker, D. 2008. Criminalizing Harassment and the Transformative Potential of Law. 20 *Canadian Journal of Women and the Law*: 87–110.

Dressler, J. 2000. Does One *Mens Rea* Fit All? Thoughts on Alexander's Unified Conception of Criminal Culpability. 88 *California Law Review*: 955–964.

Enns, R. 1999. *A Voice Unheard: The Latimer Case and People with Disabilities*. Halifax: Fernwood Publishing.

Ferzan, K. K. 2007. Symposium: Mental States and Responsibility: Holistic Culpability. 28 *Carzozo Law Review*: 2523–2544.

Finkel, N. J. 2000. Commonsense Justice, Culpability, and Punishment. 28 *Hofstra Law Review*: 669-706.

Finkelstein, C. 2000. The Inefficiency of *Mens Rea*. 88 *California Law Review*: 895–920.

Fletcher, G. P. 1978. *Rethinking Criminal Law*. Boston: Little, Brown & Company.

———. 1998. The Meaning of Innocence. 48 *University of Toronto Law Journal*: 157-174.

———. 2000. The Nature and Function of Criminal Theory. 88 *California Law Review*: 687–704.

France, S. 1995. Gains and Lost Opportunities in Canadian Constitutional *Mens Rea*. 20 *Queen's Law Journal*: 533–555.

Galloway, D. 1992. Critical Note: Criminal Liability and the Centrality of Intention, Donald Galloway Writing on Duff. 5 *Canadian Journal of Law and Jurisprudence* 143–154.

Gold, A. D. 1994. Lessons about *Mens Rea*: Three Recent Cases. 36 *Criminal Law Quarterly*: 157–167.

Grant, I. 1990. The Impact of *Vaillancourt v. The Queen* on Canadian Criminal Law. 28 *Alberta Law Review*: 443–467.

Grant, I., N. Bone, and K. Grant. 2003. Canada's Criminal Harassment Provisions: A Review of the First Ten Years. 29 *Queen's Law Journal*: 175–241.

Hart, H. L. A. 1962. *Punishment and Responsibility*. Oxford: Clarendon Press.

Holland, W. H. 1998. *The Law of Theft and Related Offences*. Toronto: Carswell. 145–199.

Law Reform Commission of Canada. 1984. Working Paper No. 33: *Homicide*. Ottawa: Minister of Supply and Services Canada.

———. 1987. Report No. 31: *Recodifying Criminal Law*. Rev. ed. Ottawa: Law Reform Commission of Canada.

Lepofsky, M. D. 2001. The Latimer Case: Murder is Still Murder When the Victim is a Child with a Disability. 27 *Queen's Law Journal*: 319–359.

MacFarlane, B. A., R. J. Frater, and C. Proulx. 2005. *Drug Offences in Canada*. 3rd ed. Aurora, ON: Canada Law Book.

Manson, A. 2001. Motivation, the Supreme Court and Mandatory Sentencing for Murder. 39 *Criminal Reports (5th Series)*: 65–71.

McElman, M. 2000. A New Conception of Wilful Blindness: The Supreme Court of Canada's Decision in *R. v. Sansregret*. 9 *Dalhousie Journal of Legal Studies*: 324–343.

Nightingale, B. L. 2008. *The Law of Fraud and Related Offences*. Toronto: Carswell. Ch. 7–11.

Odujirin, A. 1998. *The Normative Basis of Fault in Criminal Law: History and Theory*. Toronto: University of Toronto Press.

Paciocco, D. M. 1995. Subjective and Objective Standards of Fault for Offences and Defences. 59 *Saskatchewan Law Review*: 271–309.

Packer, H. L. 1968. *The Limits of the Criminal Sanction*. Palo Alto: Stanford University Press.

Roach, K. 2009. *Criminal Law*. 4th ed. Toronto: Irwin Law. Ch. 4.

Sneiderman, B. 2001. The Case of Robert Latimer: A Commentary on Crime and Punishment. 37 *Alberta Law Review*: 1017–1044.

Stribopoulos, J. 1999. The Constitutionalization of "Fault" in Canada: A Normative Critique. 42 *Criminal Law Quarterly*: 227–285.

Stuart, D. 2001. A Hard Case Makes for Too Harsh Law. 39 *Criminal Reports (5th Series)*: 58–64.

_____. 2002. Confusing *Mens Rea* Principles in the Context of Wilful Promotion of Hatred. 48 *Criminal Reports (5th Series)*: 18–20.

_____. 2007. *Canadian Criminal Law: A Treatise*. 5th ed. Toronto: Thomson Carswell. Ch. 3.

Stuart, D., R.J. Delisle, and S. Coughlan. 2009. *Learning Canadian Criminal Law*. 11th ed. Toronto: Thomson Carswell. Ch. 3.

Thornton, M. 1992. Intention in Criminal Law. 5 *Canadian Journal of Law and Jurisprudence*: 177–194.

Verdun-Jones, S.N. 2007. *Canadian Criminal Cases: Selected Highlights*. 2nd ed. Toronto: Thomson Nelson. Chap. 4.

Yeo, S. "Murder" She Said: Canadian, Indian and Australian Formulations of the Fault Elements for Murder. 49 *University of New Brunswick Law Journal*: 21–32.

CHAPTER FIVE

THE MENTAL ELEMENT IN THE CRIMINAL LAW: OBJECTIVE LIABILITY

OVERVIEW

This chapter examines the following:

1. the nature of objective liability as a form of *mens rea* in Canadian criminal law;
2. the principle that it is only the most serious forms of negligence that render an individual guilty of an offence under the *Criminal Code*;
3. the requirement that the Crown must prove a marked departure from the standard of the reasonable person acting prudently in order to gain a conviction in offences that impose objective liability;
4. the principle articulated by the Supreme Court of Canada that a "modified test of objective liability" should be applied to criminal offences that impose objective *mens rea*. This test requires that, in determining whether there was a marked departure from the standard of the reasonable person, the courts should take into account the particular circumstances facing the accused and his or her perception of those circumstances;
5. the judicial view that objective *mens rea* is predicated on the principle that reasonable persons, in the same circumstances as the accused, would have appreciated that their conduct was creating a risk of producing prohibited consequences and would have taken action to avoid doing so;
6. the principle that the fault represented by objective *mens rea* lies in the fact that the accused had the capacity to live up to the standard of care expected of a reasonable person and failed to do so;

7. the principle that objective *mens rea* is not concerned with what went on in the accused person's mind but rather with what should have been there, if he or she had acted reasonably;
8. the difference between mere carelessness and criminal (or "penal") negligence;
9. the principle that objective liability does not take into account the peculiar personal characteristics of the accused except where he or she lacks the capacity to appreciate the nature of the risk that his or her conduct is creating;
10. the offences that impose objective liability, including dangerous driving, unlawful act manslaughter, criminal negligence causing death/bodily harm, manslaughter by criminal negligence, unlawfully causing bodily harm, assault causing bodily harm, and aggravated assault;
11. the nature and scope of the offence of dangerous driving and the modified objective test of liability;
12. the difference between dangerous driving and careless driving;
13. the nature and scope of the offence of unlawful act manslaughter and the critical impact of the decision of the Supreme Court of Canada in the *Creighton* case (1993);
14. the *mens rea* requirement for unlawful act manslaughter, unlawfully causing bodily harm, and assault causing bodily harm: namely, objective foreseeability of bodily harm;
15. the nature of offences based on criminal negligence, as defined in section 219 of the *Criminal Code*;

16. the failure of the Supreme Court of Canada to decide in the *Tutton and Tutton* (1989) and *Waite* cases (1989) whether the *mens rea* for criminal negligence is based on a subjective or an objective test;

17. the view that, in light of the Supreme Court of Canada decisions in *Hundal* (1993) and *Creighton* (1993), it may be expected that the Supreme Court will ultimately adopt an objective test of liability for criminal negligence;

18. the *Criminal Code* sections that impose an elevated standard of care for those individuals (such as surgeons) who engage in inherently dangerous activities that require a certain level of training and skill; and

19. the examples of situations in which the *Criminal Code* imposes an elevated standard of care: sections 79 (possession of explosives), 86(1) (use and storage of firearms), and 216 (administration of surgical and medical treatment).

WHAT IS OBJECTIVE LIABILITY?

In Chapter 4, we examined the *mens rea* elements of criminal offences that are based on the need for the Crown to prove intention, knowledge, recklessness, or wilful blindness. These *mens rea* elements are subjective in nature because they require that the particular accused be subjectively aware of the risk that his or her conduct will cause certain consequences that are prohibited by law. The present chapter explores the *mens rea* elements of criminal offences that are based on the need for the Crown to prove only that the accused person's conduct fell below the standard of the hypothetical reasonable person: it is irrelevant whether the accused person was subjectively aware of the risk that his or her conduct would cause consequences that are prohibited by the law. If the reasonable person, placed in the same circumstances as the accused, would have been aware of the risk and would have avoided taking it, the accused is guilty of the offence. This form of liability is objective in nature because it does not take into account what (if anything) actually went on in the accused's mind. As Justice McLachlin stated, in delivering the judgment of the majority of the justices of the Supreme Court of Canada in the *Creighton* case (1993),

> Objective *mens rea* ... is not concerned with what the accused intended or knew. Rather the mental fault lies in failure to direct the mind to a risk which the reasonable person would have appreciated. Objective *mens rea is not concerned with what was actually in the accused's mind, but with what should have been there, had the accused proceeded reasonably.* [emphasis added]

A person who falls below the standard of the reasonable person is considered to have acted *negligently*. However, it is only the more serious forms of negligence that will lead to an individual being convicted of a crime under the *Criminal Code*. Mere **carelessness** (that is, falling just a relatively small degree below the standard of the reasonable person) may render one liable, at **civil law**, to pay compensation, but it will not make one a criminal. As Justice Charron, of the Supreme Court of Canada, said in the case of *Beatty* (2008):

> Unquestionably, conduct which constitutes a departure from the norm expected of a reasonably prudent person forms the basis of both civil and penal negligence. However, it is important not to conflate the civil standard of negligence with the test for penal negligence. Unlike civil negligence, which is concerned

with the apportionment of loss, penal negligence is aimed at punishing *blameworthy* conduct.

What Justice Charron means is that, if someone carelessly causes injury to another person or damage to that person's property, it is fair to require that the individual who caused the injury or damage should compensate the victim of that carelessness. After all, the party who was careless should be made to shoulder the financial loss rather than the victim shouldering it. Suppose, for example, that I accidentally break my friend's antique porcelain figurine by knocking it off a table with my elbow. I am reading about the latest scandal involving a movie star and am so absorbed in this activity that I forget where I am. Suddenly, my cell phone chimes and I automatically get up from the table, not realizing that my elbow is next to the figurine. I am deeply shocked to find that I have knocked the figurine onto the floor, smashing it to pieces. I can honestly say that I caused this damage completely inadvertently (i.e., without being at all aware of the risk that my elbow might hit the figurine and cause it to fall on the floor).

However, my friend would justly say that I had been careless because a reasonable person would have been more careful in the circumstances. What I have done would not be considered a serious case of negligence. This is definitely not a situation where there has been a marked departure from the standard of the reasonable person: indeed, it is the kind of accident that could happen to anyone. Clearly, I should not be convicted of an offence under the *Criminal Code* for such simple carelessness. However, in all fairness, I should feel obligated to compensate my friend for the loss of the figurine since I was the one who was careless, and if I were to be so ungenerous as to refuse to pay up, my friend might be able to sue me for damages in a civil court.

However, although mere carelessness may render an individual liable to be sued in a civil court, it is not sufficient to render him or her liable for conviction of an offence under the *Criminal Code*. On the contrary, it is only where there is a marked departure from the standard of care expected of a reasonable person that the accused can be convicted of a *Criminal Code* offence. In other words, under this **marked departure test**, only the most serious forms of negligent behaviour can lead to a conviction of a true crime.

This principle is extremely important because the Supreme Court of Canada has recognized that section 7 of the *Charter*, which guarantees that no person may be deprived of life, liberty, or security of the person except in accordance with the fundamental principles of justice, dictates that an accused person may not be convicted of an offence under the *Criminal Code* unless he or she is morally blameworthy. Is a person whose behaviour constitutes a marked departure from the standard of the reasonable person morally blameworthy? In the *Creighton case* (1993), Justice McLachlin, speaking on behalf of the majority of the justices of the Supreme Court of Canada, answered this question in the affirmative:

> It is now established that a person may be held criminally responsible for negligent conduct on the objective test, and that this alone does not violate the principle of fundamental justice that the moral fault of the accused must be commensurate with the gravity of the offence and its penalty....
>
> Moreover, the constitutionality of crimes of negligence is also subject to the caveat that *acts of ordinary negligence may not suffice to justify imprisonment.*... The negligence must constitute a "marked departure" from the standard of the reasonable person. *The law does not lightly brand a person as criminal.* [emphasis added]

Justice McLachlin also made the important point that, in general, a person who commits an offence negligently should receive a less severe sentence than a person who acts with subjective awareness of the risk that his or her conduct creates. This merely reflects the principle that the punishment for an offence should be commensurate with the degree of fault manifested on the part of the offender.

A good example of the application of the principle that a high degree of negligence is required before an individual may be convicted of an offence under the *Criminal Code* is furnished by the case of *Finlay* (1993), in which the accused was charged with storing firearms and ammunition in a careless manner, contrary to the provisions of (what was then) section 86(2) of the *Criminal Code.* Section 86(2) stated that "every person who, without lawful excuse, uses, carries, handles, ships or stores any firearm or ammunition in a careless manner or without reasonable precautions for the safety of other persons" is guilty of an offence."[1]

---

[1] Section 86 of the *Code* was amended in 1995. The current provision, which replaced the subsection discussed in the text above, is section 86(1), which reads as follows: "Every person commits an offence who, without lawful excuse, uses, carries, handles, ships, transports or stores a firearm, a prohibited weapon, a restricted weapon, a prohibited device or any ammunition in a careless manner or without reasonable precautions for the safety of other persons."

On the face of it, section 86(2) undoubtedly imposed objective liability, but it also seemed to require the conviction of an accused person who has merely been careless in the storage of firearms and ammunition. However, the Supreme Court of Canada, while holding that section 86(2) did indeed impose objective liability, nevertheless stated that the fault requirement consisted of "conduct that is a marked departure from the standard of a reasonable person in the circumstances." If the Court had ruled that section 86(2) required the conviction of individuals who had merely acted carelessly, it would have been obliged to find that it was in violation of section 7 of the *Charter.* However, by interpreting the section as requiring a marked departure from the standard of the reasonable person, the Court was able to find that it met the requirement that a person may not be convicted of a *Criminal Code* offence unless he or she is morally blameworthy. Indeed, as Chief Justice Lamer noted in his judgment, section 86(2) of the *Code* clearly met the "minimal fault requirement" that is inherent in the principles of fundamental justice enshrined in section 7 of the *Charter:*

> By enacting s. 86(2), Parliament has seen fit to impose on all people owning firearms a specific and rigorous duty of care. It is a basic tenet of the principles of fundamental justice that the state not be permitted to punish and deprive of liberty the morally innocent. Those who have the capacity to live up to a standard of care and fail to do so, in circumstances involving inherently dangerous activities ... cannot be said to have done nothing wrong.

In the *Creighton* case (1993), Justice McLachlin emphasized that the objective test of liability does not take into account the peculiar personal characteristics of the accused person (such as background, education, or psychological disposition) except in the rare circumstance where the accused lacks the capacity to understand the nature and quality or the consequences of his or her acts or to appreciate the risk involved in his or her conduct. For example, a visually impaired person might not have the physical capacity to appreciate a risk that would be obvious to someone who had normal vision and, in this particular circumstance, a court would be obliged to enter an acquittal because it would be grossly unjust to hold an accused person to a standard of care that is physically impossible for him or her to meet. Another example was given by Justice McLachlin in the *Creighton* case. She hypothesized that an illiterate person who mishandles a bottle of nitroglycerin without realizing what it is would not be held to the standard of the reasonable and literate person who would, of course, be able to read the label on the bottle.

In essence, therefore, Justice McLachlin and the majority of the justices of the Supreme Court of Canada emphasized the need for the "maintenance of a single, uniform legal standard of care" for offences imposing objective liability "subject to one exception: incapacity to appreciate the nature of the risk the activity in question entails." She went on to state that

> I can find no support in criminal theory for the conclusion that protection of the morally innocent requires a general consideration of individual excusing conditions. The principle comes into play only at the point where the person is shown to lack the capacity to appreciate the nature and quality or the consequences of his or her acts. Apart from this, *we are all, rich and poor, wise and naïve, held to the minimum standards of conduct prescribed by criminal law.* This conclusion is dictated by a fundamental principle of social organization. As Justice Oliver Wendell Holmes wrote "... when men live in society, a certain average of conduct, a sacrifice of individual peculiarities going beyond a certain point, is necessary to the general welfare." [emphasis added]

Why is it necessary to maintain a uniform standard of conduct in the application of the test of objective liability? According to Justice McLachlin,

> The purpose of Parliament in creating an offence of objective foresight, as in manslaughter, is to stipulate a minimum standard which people engaged in the activity in question are expected to meet. If the standard is lowered by reason of the lack of experience, education, or the presence of some other "personal characteristic" of the accused, the minimum standard which the law imposes on those engaging in the activity in question will be eroded. The objective test inevitably is transformed into a subjective test, violating the wise admonition ... that there should be a clear distinction in the law between subjective and objective standards, and negating the legislative goal of a minimum standard of care for all those who choose to engage in criminally dangerous conduct.

The reasons why people fail to appreciate the risk inherent in their conduct are, according to Justice McLachlin, "legion":

> They range from simple absent-mindedness to attributes related to age, education and culture. To permit such a subjective assessment would be "coextensive

with the judgment of each individual, which would be as variable as the length of the foot of each individual" leaving "so vague a line as to afford no rule at all, the degree of judgment belonging to each individual being infinitely various."... *Provided the capacity to appreciate the risk is present, lack of education and psychological predispositions serve as no excuse for criminal conduct, although they may be important factors to consider in sentencing.* [emphasis added]

However, although the courts will not take account of personal characteristics of the accused when applying the objective test of liability, it is important to bear in mind that the test is not applied in a total vacuum. The court must take account of the nature of the particular activity in which the accused was engaged and the specific knowledge that he or she had of the relevant circumstances. The question for the court then becomes, "Would a reasonable person, having exactly the same knowledge of the relevant circumstances as the accused, realize that his or her conduct was creating a risk of bringing about consequences that are prohibited by the criminal law?" As Justice McLachlin asserted in the *Creighton* case (1993),

> ... [T]he answer to the question of whether the accused took reasonable care must be founded on a consideration of all the circumstances of the case. The question is what the reasonably prudent person would have done in all the circumstances. Thus a welder who lights a torch causing an explosion may be excused if he has made an inquiry and been given advice upon which he was reasonably entitled to rely, that there was no explosive gas in the area.

OFFENCES IMPOSING OBJECTIVE LIABILITY

DRIVING OFFENCES AND OBJECTIVE LIABILITY

There are two general offences that may arise from poor driving behaviour on the part of Canadian motorists: dangerous driving and careless driving.

Dangerous driving (or, more precisely, "dangerous operation of a motor vehicle") is an offence that arises under section 249(1) of the *Criminal Code*, which was, of course, enacted by the Parliament of Canada:

(1) Every one commits an offence who operates

    (a) a motor vehicle in a manner that is dangerous to the public, having regard to all the circumstances, including the nature, condition and use of the place at which the motor vehicle is being operated and the amount of traffic that at the time is or might reasonably be expected to be at that place;…

(2) Every one who commits an offence under subsection (1)

(a) is guilty of an indictable offence and liable to imprisonment for a term not exceeding five years; or

(b) is guilty of an offence punishable on summary conviction.

It should be noted that more severe penalties are applicable where the dangerous driving results in bodily harm (10 years) or death (14 years) (sections 249(3) & (4) respectively).

Careless driving is an offence that arises under the various provincial/territorial statutes that govern the operation of motor vehicles on the highways. For example, in Ontario, section 130 of the *Highway Traffic Act*, R.S.O. 1990, c. H.8 provides that

[e]very person is guilty of the offence of driving carelessly who drives a vehicle or street car on a highway without due care and attention or without reasonable consideration for other persons using the highway and on conviction is liable to a fine of not less than $200 and not more than $1000 or to imprisonment for a term of not more than six months, or to both, and in addition his or her licence or permit may be suspended for a period of not more than two years.

Similarly, in British Columbia, the offence is known as "driving without due care and attention,"

contrary to section 144 of the *Motor Vehicle Act*, R.S.B.C. 1996, c. 318.

Both of these driving offences involve the imposition of objective liability in the sense that the Crown does not have to prove that the accused was subjectively aware of the risk that his or her driving conduct created for other users of the highway. For each offence, the Crown has to establish negligence only in the sense that the accused's driving conduct fell below the standard of the reasonable driver acting prudently in all of the circumstances. The critical distinction between the two driving offences lies in the extent to which the Crown must prove that the accused departed from the standard of the reasonable driver. Conviction of dangerous driving can take place only where the accused's driving conduct constitutes a marked departure from the standard of care expected of the reasonable driver in the particular circumstances facing the accused.

For example, in *Brannan* (1999), Justice Donald of the British Columbia Court of Appeal stated that, although a driver's simple "failure to keep a proper lookout" might amount to "civil negligence," it nevertheless "falls short of the requirement for dangerous driving." Conviction of the offence of careless driving, in contrast, may occur whenever the accused falls below the standard of care expected of a reasonable driver. Indeed, any deviation from that standard of care (no matter how minor it might be) can lead to a conviction of careless driving.

Before embarking on a more detailed discussion of the offence of dangerous driving, it should be pointed out that it would be possible for motorists to be charged with the general offences of manslaughter,

Attending to a cellular phone may constitute carelessness on the road.

Cartoon by Greg Holoboff

criminal negligence causing bodily harm, or criminal negligence causing death as a consequence of their driving misconduct. However, it seems that it is now less likely that prosecutors will turn to these general charges when the specific offences of dangerous driving, dangerous driving causing death, and dangerous driving causing bodily harm are open to them. Indeed, the latter two offences carry maximum penalties of 14 and 10 years' imprisonment respectively. It is significant that an offence of "criminal negligence in the operation of a motor vehicle," which was contained in the *Criminal Code* for many years, was dropped in 1985.[2]

For many years, there was an ongoing controversy as to whether the offence of dangerous driving requires proof of subjective *mens rea* on the part of the accused or whether a conviction may be obtained on the basis of an objective standard of liability. The Supreme Court of Canada finally put this controversy to rest when, in the *Hundal* case (1993), it ruled that the appropriate test to apply in determining whether the accused had the necessary *mens rea* for dangerous driving is the **"modified objective test."** Justice Cory asserted that it would not be practical to require the Crown to prove that the accused subjectively appreciated the risk created by his or her driving conduct. Indeed, in his view,

> ... [T]o insist on a subjective mental element in connection with driving offences would be to deny reality. It cannot be forgotten that the operation of a motor vehicle is ... automatic and with little conscious thought....

Justice Cory, therefore, articulated an objective test in order to determine whether the accused had the necessary *mens rea* for dangerous driving. This test is as follows:

> ... [T]he trier of fact should be satisfied that the conduct amounted to a marked departure from the standard of care that a reasonable person would observe in the accused's situation.

However, Justice Cory also emphasized that the Court, in addressing this issue, must take into account the particular circumstances facing the accused and his or her perception of those circumstances. The question that should be asked is whether a reasonable person, with the same knowledge of the facts as the accused, would have appreciated the risk generated by the accused's driving conduct and would have refrained from taking such a risk. In this sense, said Justice Cory, the test can be considered a *modified objective test*:

> Although an objective test must be applied to the offence of dangerous driving, it will always remain open to the accused to raise a reasonable doubt that a reasonable person would have been aware of the risks in the accused's conduct. The test must be applied with some measure of flexibility. That is to say the objective test should not be applied in a vacuum but rather in the context of the events surrounding the incident.

For example, if the accused suffers a totally unexpected heart attack, epileptic seizure, or detached retina, he or she may engage in driving conduct that, from an objective point of view, represents a gross departure from the standard of the reasonable driver; indeed, the accused may, in such circumstances, become involved in a horrendous accident. However, the accused would be acquitted under the modified objective test because even a reasonable person, with the knowledge that the accused had, could not have foreseen that such a disastrous event might happen. On the other hand, if the accused knew that there was a chance, for example, that he or she was likely to have an epileptic seizure, there would be a conviction of dangerous driving because a reasonable person, armed with that knowledge, would have foreseen the risk created by continuing to drive and would have refrained from doing so. As Justice Cory put it,

> ... [I]f an explanation is offered by the accused, such as a sudden and unexpected onset of illness, then in order to convict, the trier of fact must be satisfied that a reasonable person in similar circumstances ought to have been aware of the risk and of the danger involved in the conduct manifested by the accused.

Justice Cory also stated that the modified objective test satisfied the minimal *mens rea* requirements dictated by the Charter. Indeed, he asserted the view that the *mens rea* requirement for dangerous driving that was articulated in the *Hundal* case (1993) was particularly appropriate for such an offence:

---

[2] In 2000, Parliament introduced a number of new—and very specific—driving offences: causing bodily harm or death while fleeing from a peace officer (s. 249.1); causing death by street racing (s. 249.2); and causing bodily harm by street racing (s. 249.3). In 2006, Parliament added the offences of dangerous driving while street racing; dangerous driving causing bodily harm while street racing; and dangerous driving causing death while street racing (s. 249.4). These new offences carry severe maximum penalties (for example, life imprisonment for any of the offences involving death of a victim).

... [T]he *mens rea* for the offence of dangerous driving should be assessed objectively but in the context of all the events surrounding the incident.... As a general rule, personal factors need not be taken into account. This flows from the licensing requirement for driving which assures that all who drive have a reasonable standard of physical health and capability, mental health, and a knowledge of the reasonable standard required of all licensed drivers.

In light of the licensing requirement and the nature of driving offences, a modified objective test satisfies the constitutional minimum fault requirement for [s. 249] of the *Criminal Code* and is eminently well suited to that offence.

In the *Hundal* case (1993) itself, the accused had driven his overloaded dump truck into an intersection in downtown Vancouver, where he collided with another vehicle, killing its driver. The evidence was that Hundal had entered the intersection after the relevant traffic light had turned red, while the deceased driver had proceeded into the intersection after receiving a green light. The accused claimed that the traffic light had just turned to amber and that, at this point, it was too late for him to try to stop his vehicle. However, several witnesses stated that the dump truck drove through the red light, and it was estimated that at least one second passed between the end of the amber light and the time when the accused's vehicle proceeded into the intersection. The trial judge, therefore, rejected Hundal's explanation for the accident and convicted him of dangerous driving. The Supreme Court of Canada ultimately upheld the conviction and ruled that the trial judge had been correct to apply a modified objective test in order to determine if Hundal had the necessary *mens rea* for dangerous driving. As Justice Cory noted,

> The trial judge carefully examined the circumstances of the accident. He took into account the busy downtown traffic, the weather conditions, and the mechanical conditions of the accused [*sic*] vehicle. He concluded, in my view very properly, that [Hundal's] manner of driving represented a gross departure from the standard of a reasonably prudent driver. No explanation was offered by the accused that could excuse his conduct....

If persons accused of dangerous driving have an excuse that might lead to their acquittal under the "modified objective test" articulated in the *Hundal* case (1993), then there is an onus on them to establish that there is some evidence that gives "an air of reality" to such a defence (this is the **"air-of-reality" test**). In other words, they must meet the **evidentiary burden of proof** before their excuse may be considered. In *Reed* (1997), for example, the accused had been charged with three counts of dangerous driving causing death. He had been driving his elevated truck at night and had taken a curve at a speed that was at least 20 km/h in excess of the posted speed limit. Reed lost control of the vehicle and crossed over into one of the oncoming lanes, where he collided with a vehicle carrying three young men, all of whom perished. The trial judge acquitted the accused but the B.C. Court of Appeal allowed the Crown's appeal and substituted verdicts of guilty. The Court of Appeal accepted the Crown's argument that, on its face, Reed's driving constituted *dangerous driving* and that he was, therefore, under an *evidentiary burden to establish an explanation for his conduct.* Beyond some reference to the claim that "almost all drivers" speed on the highway in question, there was no explanation on Reed's part that satisfied this evidentiary burden; therefore, the Court of Appeal held that he was guilty of the offence charged. As Justice Cumming noted,

> It cannot be said that the respondent's driving of the type of motor vehicle that he had, at night, at a speed more than 20 kilometers in excess of the speed limit, on a curve and totally on the wrong side of the road, is other than a "marked departure from the norm."

The Supreme Court of Canada subsequently upheld the judgment of the B.C. Court of Appeal (*Reed* (1998)).

On the other hand, in the *Stogdale* case (1995), the accused could offer an explanation for his conduct that led to his ultimate acquittal. The accused was the master of a Coast Guard vessel that was involved in a fatal collision with a fishing vessel on Lake Erie. The conditions were foggy, and Stogdale's vessel was operating at full speed without a foghorn. He was charged with dangerous operation or navigation of a vessel causing death. The trial judge convicted Stogdale, but the Ontario Court of Appeal set aside the conviction and entered an acquittal. Justice Austin stated that the trial judge had "*failed to consider all of the surrounding circumstances and the appellant's perception of those circumstances,*" as required by the "modified objective test." Even the expert testimony on behalf of the Crown had been to the effect that, if the visibility at the time of the accident had been "half a mile," then proceeding at full speed without a foghorn would have been "safe," since the vessel was using radar. The Court of Appeal noted that Stogdale had *mistakenly* believed that the visibility was, in fact, at least one-half mile and, therefore, had operated at full speed, *honestly* believing that it was safe to do so. Furthermore, the Court of Appeal considered that Stogdale's estimate of visibility, although it ultimately turned out to be inaccurate, was nevertheless a *reasonable* estimate (indeed, two other officers on his vessel agreed with it). Therefore, the Crown had not established the necessary *mens rea* for dangerous operation or navigation of the vessel. Stogdale had presented an excuse for what, on the face of it, might otherwise have been considered dangerous operation of his vessel. However, he was able to point to evidence that gave an air of reality to his defence that he had acted reasonably; in other words, he had satisfied the evidentiary burden of establishing a valid excuse. The Court of Appeal clearly believed that the Crown had not been able to prove beyond a reasonable doubt that a *reasonable person, on the basis of the facts as Stogdale honestly and reasonably believed them to be, would have appreciated the risk of danger and would have refrained from taking it.*

The authority of the modified objective test articulated in *Hundal* (1993) was strongly reaffirmed by the Supreme Court of Canada in *Beatty* (2008). In this tragic case, Beatty had been charged with three counts of dangerous driving causing death. For no apparent reason, his car had crossed the double solid centre line in the road and crashed into an oncoming vehicle, killing all three of its occupants. Beatty's driving was completely normal prior to the accident. There was no mechanical defect in his vehicle and there was no evidence of any intoxicants that may have affected his driving. Beatty could not remember what had happened, stating that he had lost consciousness—perhaps because of heat stroke (it was extremely hot on that day) or because he had fallen asleep. An expert witness indicated that it would have taken only 0.00268 seconds for Beatty's car to cross the centre line and make contact with the victims' car.

The trial judge acquitted Beatty of the charges because she believed that the momentary lapse of attention on Beatty's part did not constitute a marked departure from the standard of care expected of a reasonable person driving prudently. In her view, this was a case involving civil, but not criminal, negligence. The B.C. Court of Appeal allowed the Crown's appeal and ordered a new trial. However, the Supreme Court of Canada restored the acquittals, stating that the Crown had not proved the *mens rea* element of the offence of dangerous driving. Undoubtedly, the Crown had proved the *actus reus* element—suddenly crossing the centre line and crashing into an oncoming vehicle is definitely dangerous driving conduct. However, conviction of dangerous driving also requires proof of morally blameworthy behaviour (the *mens rea* element). While Beatty's driving conduct fell below the standard expected of the reasonable driver, a momentary lapse of attention could not be considered to constitute a *marked* departure from that standard of care. It could be certainly be regarded as an case of civil negligence, giving rise to a duty to provide compensation, but it was not sufficiently blameworthy to deserve punishment in the criminal justice system. For this reason, the Supreme Court agreed with the decision made by the trial judge.

The *Beatty* case is important because Justice Charron, writing on behalf of a majority of the Supreme Court of Canada, provided a very complete review of the nature of the modified objective test and clarified areas of difficulty that have arisen following the decision of the Court in *Hundal* (1993). She provided succinct summaries of both the *actus reus* and *mens rea* elements of the offence of dangerous operation of a motor vehicle. In articulating the *actus reus* element, Justice Charron took the view that it was not necessary to go beyond the actual wording of section 249(1)(a) of the *Criminal Code*:

> The trier of fact must be satisfied beyond a reasonable doubt that, viewed objectively, the accused was, in the words of the section, driving in a manner that was "dangerous to the public, having regard to all the circumstances, including the nature, condition and use of the place at which the motor vehicle is being operated and the amount of traffic that at the time is or might reasonably be expected to be at that place."

As far as the *mens rea* element, which is embedded in the modified objective test, is concerned, Justice Charron defined it in the following manner:

> The trier of fact must also be satisfied beyond a reasonable doubt that the accused's objectively dangerous conduct was accompanied by the required *mens rea*. In making the objective assessment, the trier of fact should be satisfied on the basis of all the evidence, including evidence about the accused's actual state of mind, if any, that the conduct amounted to a marked departure from the standard

of care that a reasonable person would observe in the accused's circumstances. Moreover, if an explanation is offered by the accused, then in order to convict, the trier of fact must be satisfied that a reasonable person in similar circumstances ought to have been aware of the risk and of the danger involved in the conduct manifested by the accused.

In *Beatty*'s case, the application of the modified objective test resulted in his acquittal because a reasonable person, armed with the knowledge of the circumstances that Beatty possessed, would not have foreseen that there might be a momentary loss of consciousness and a loss of control of the vehicle. However, if Beatty had previously experienced fainting attacks or sudden lapses in attention, his defence would have been rejected because a reasonable person, who was aware of these medical problems, would certainly have avoided driving and sought treatment. Driving while knowingly creating a risk of a serious accident would generally be regarded as a marked departure from the standard of care expected of the reasonable driver.

Similarly, in *Jiang* (2007), the accused was charged with dangerous driving causing death and bodily harm after she fell asleep while driving. Her car mounted the curb, crossed the sidewalk, and entered a parking lot where it struck two children, one of whom was killed and the other, injured. A psychiatrist testified that Jiang was suffering from undiagnosed chronic insomnia and had experienced "an intrusive sleep episode." The trial judge acquitted Jiang: there was no evidence of dangerous driving prior to the moment when Jiang's car left the roadway and, since she was not aware of her underlying medical condition, she had no reason to believe that she was likely to fall asleep at the wheel. The B.C. Court of Appeal affirmed Jiang's acquittal. On behalf of the Court, Justice Smith stated that

> ... the question was whether, during the period of time before she fell asleep, the respondent evinced the requisite want of due care to establish dangerous driving. In other words, whether she had the necessary *mens rea*. The burden is always on the Crown to establish the *mens rea* of the offence beyond a reasonable doubt. This burden never shifts to the accused. Thus, the Crown bore the burden of establishing beyond a reasonable doubt that the respondent should have appreciated the risk of falling asleep while she was driving and that, by driving in the circumstances, her conduct represented a marked departure from the standard of reasonable care.

Clearly, the Crown failed to prove beyond a reasonable doubt that a reasonable person, knowing what Jiang knew, would have realized that there was a risk that he or she would fall asleep at the wheel and create a danger to the public.

By way of contrast, in *Van Puyenbroek* (2007), the accused became intoxicated at a Christmas party and insisted on driving himself home. He struck two pedestrians who were walking on the shoulder of the highway. One of them was seriously injured. He was charged with, *inter alia*, impaired driving causing bodily harm and dangerous driving causing bodily harm. At his trial, the accused was convicted of these charges. The trial judge found that the accused enjoyed clear visibility and sufficient time in which to react. Even if there had been a "fleeting distraction," there was still ample time in which to avoid the two pedestrians. The trial judge, therefore, held that Van Puyenbroek's driving conduct constituted a marked departure from the standard of the reasonable person and "went well beyond a momentary lack of attention." Unlike the accused in the *Beatty* and *Jiang* cases, Van Puyenbroek did not have a plausible explanation that would raise a reasonable doubt as to whether he had the necessary *mens rea* for conviction of dangerous driving. The Ontario Court of Appeal agreed with the decision made by the trial judge and rejected Van Puyenbroek's appeal against his convictions.

DANGEROUS DRIVING AND CRIMINAL NEGLIGENCE

Sections 220 and 221 of the *Criminal Code* respectively provide for the offences of *criminal negligence causing death* and *criminal negligence causing bodily harm*. It is possible for the Crown to lay either of these charges in situations where an accused person's driving behaviour has caused death or bodily harm respectively. This immediately raises the question of how one is to distinguish between the offences of dangerous driving causing death or bodily harm (sections 249(3) and (4)) and the offences of criminal negligence causing death or bodily harm (sections 220 and 221). It appears that *both offences require proof of a "marked departure"* from the standard of the reasonable driver and that the *mens rea for both offences is objective in nature*. Therefore, the difference between the two sets of offences lies in *the degree to which the accused's behaviour departs from the standard of the reasonable*. The criminal negligence offences are considered to be more serious in nature and, therefore, a *more marked departure* from the standard of the reasonable driver must be established than is the case for the offences involving dangerous driving.

For example, in the *Palin* case (1999), Justice Deschamps, in delivering the judgment of the Quebec Court of Appeal, addressed the nature of the distinction between criminal negligence and dangerous driving in the following manner:

> [O]n a scale of seriousness which goes from civil liability to criminal negligence, criminal negligence is located higher up the scale than dangerous driving, that is that the departure must be more marked, this norm being present in both the physical and mental elements of the offence. [translation]

Similarly, in the case of *Willock* (2006), the Ontario Court of Appeal ruled that a higher degree of negligence must be proved to establish criminal negligence than that required to establish dangerous driving. Indeed, on behalf of the Court, Justice Doherty emphasized that the Crown must prove **both** a *marked* and *substantial* degree of departure from the norm in order to establish criminal negligence in the context of alleged driving misconduct:

> Criminal negligence in the context of driving-related allegations of criminal negligence requires proof that the accused's conduct constituted a marked and substantial departure from that expected of the reasonable driver and proof that the conduct demonstrated a wanton or reckless disregard for the lives or safety of other persons. The requisite wanton or reckless disregard may, but not must, be inferred from proof of conduct that constitutes a marked and substantial departure from that expected of the reasonable driver.

UNLAWFUL ACT MANSLAUGHTER

In a following section, we shall see that individuals may be convicted of manslaughter on the basis that they caused the death of a human being (*actus reus*) by criminal negligence (*mens rea*). However, this is not the only basis upon which individuals may be convicted of manslaughter under the *Criminal Code*. Indeed, there is another form of manslaughter that is known, by criminal law commentators, as **unlawful act manslaughter.** What is meant by this term? In order to explain the meaning of the term, it is first necessary to examine the *Code* provisions that deal with culpable homicide.

Section 222(4) of the *Criminal Code* identifies the various forms of culpable homicide: murder,

manslaughter, and infanticide. Subsection 222(5) indicates four means by which culpable homicide may be committed:

A person commits culpable homicide when he causes the death of a human being,

(a) by means of an unlawful act,
(b) by criminal negligence,
(c) by causing that human being, by threats of fear or violence or by deception, to do anything that causes his death, or
(d) by wilfully frightening that human being in the case of a child or sick person.

What are the distinctions between murder, infanticide, and manslaughter? Section 234 of the *Criminal Code* states that "culpable homicide that is not murder or infanticide is manslaughter." In other words, manslaughter is a *residual* category of culpable homicide because it is defined in terms of what it is not, rather than what it is. If culpable homicide is neither murder nor infanticide, then it must be categorized as manslaughter. Murder (according to section 229) is, in general terms, defined in terms of the accused's intent to kill, while **infanticide** (according to section 233) is committed where a woman kills her "newly-born child"[3] and her mind is "disturbed" because she has not fully recovered from the effects of giving birth or because of "the effect of lactation consequent on the birth." By a process of elimination, one may draw the conclusion that manslaughter must, generally, be defined as an unintentional form of killing that cannot be excused as an accident or justified in some other manner (such as self-defence). Section 222(5) indicates that, in general, there are two distinct forms of manslaughter: *unlawful act manslaughter* and *manslaughter by criminal negligence*.

As we shall see in the next section, manslaughter by criminal negligence is defined by referring to a combination of sections 222(5)(b) and 234 of the *Code*. However, another form of manslaughter may arise as a consequence of combining sections 222(5)(a) and 234; this is what has become known as "unlawful act" manslaughter. When the accused commits an unlawful act (usually an assault) that results in death, he or she will be convicted of murder if there is an intent to kill or if there is an

---

[3] Section 2 of the *Criminal Code* states that this term "means a person under the age of one year."

intent to inflict bodily harm that the accused knows is likely to cause death and is reckless as to whether death ensues or not (section 229(a)). Indeed, as the *Martineau* case (1990) established, an accused person cannot be convicted of murder in Canada unless he or she subjectively foresees the likelihood of death ensuing from his or her conduct.

However, let us suppose that an accused person causes the death of a victim as a consequence of an unlawful act (such as an assault) but does not possess the necessary *mens rea* for murder. In these circumstances, it is likely that the accused will be convicted of unlawful act manslaughter. Unfortunately, although section 222(5)(a) states that culpable homicide may be committed "by means of an unlawful act," it does not define the necessary *mens rea* for conviction of unlawful act manslaughter. As noted above, section 234 merely states that any culpable homicide that is neither murder nor infanticide is manslaughter. Since the *Code* provides no guidance in this respect, the Supreme Court of Canada has articulated the test that must be used by the courts when determining if the accused had the necessary *mens rea* for unlawful act manslaughter.

In the *Creighton* case (1993), the Supreme Court of Canada ruled that the *mens rea* for unlawful act manslaughter is the *objective foresight of the risk of bodily harm that is neither trivial nor transitory in nature*. In other words, in order to convict the accused of unlawful act manslaughter, the Crown must prove that the accused had the necessary *mens rea* for the commission of the unlawful act that resulted in death (e.g., an assault) and that a reasonable person, in the same circumstances as the accused, would have foreseen the risk of bodily harm, given the inherently dangerous nature of the unlawful act. In the *Creighton* case itself (1993), the accused had been charged with (unlawful act) manslaughter after he had injected a quantity of cocaine into the arm of the deceased. He had not sought to determine the quality or strength of the drug before doing so. After the injection, the deceased went into violent convulsions and appeared to stop breathing. The accused would not permit a friend to call 911 for emergency assistance, and the deceased was left on her bed for six to seven hours before such assistance was finally called. At this point, the deceased was pronounced dead.

What was the alleged "unlawful act" in *Creighton* (1993)? The Crown successfully argued that the accused had been trafficking in narcotics contrary to section 4 of the (now repealed) *Narcotic Control Act*, R.S.C. 1985, c. N-1.[4] Under that act, the word "traffic" included "giving" or "administering" a narcotic. Granted that Creighton had committed an unlawful act resulting in death (the *actus reus* of manslaughter), what *mens rea* elements must the Crown prove in order to obtain a conviction of manslaughter?

Justice McLachlin, speaking for a majority of the Supreme Court, stated that

... the test for the *mens rea* of unlawful act manslaughter in Canada ... is (in addition to the *mens rea* of the underlying offence) objective foreseeability of the risk of bodily harm which is neither trivial nor transitory, in the context of a dangerous act. Foreseeability of the death is not required.

Justice McLachlin also stated that the "question is what the reasonably prudent person would have done in all the circumstances" and that

... the *mens rea* for objective foresight of risking harm is normally inferred from the facts. The standard is that of the reasonable person in the circumstances of the accused. If a person has committed a manifestly dangerous act, it is reasonable, absent indications to the contrary, to infer that he or she failed to direct his or her mind to the risk and the need to take care. However, the normal inference may be negated by evidence raising a reasonable doubt as to lack of capacity to appreciate the risk. Thus, if a *prima facie* case for *actus reus* and *mens rea* is made out, it is necessary to ask a further question: did the accused possess the requisite capacity to appreciate the risk flowing from his conduct? If this further question is answered in the affirmative, the necessary moral fault is established and the accused is properly convicted. If not, the accused must be acquitted.

As far as the facts in the *Creighton* case (1993) were concerned, Justice McLachlin emphasized that the central issue was "whether the reasonable person in all the circumstances" facing the accused "would have foreseen the risk of bodily harm." To this question, Justice McLachlin believed there was a simple answer:

At the very least, a person administering a dangerous drug like cocaine to another has a duty to inform

---

[4] The equivalent offence is now contained in section 5 of the *Controlled Drugs and Substances Act*, S.C. 1996, c. 19. "Traffic" is defined in section 2 of the Act.

himself as to the precise risk the injection entails and to refrain from administering it unless reasonably satisfied that there is no risk of harm. That was not the case here....

A very straightforward example of unlawful act manslaughter occurred in the distressing case of *Sinclair* (2008). Sinclair's four-year-old daughter refused to go to bed. Sinclair picked her up, shook her, and threw her onto the bed. Unfortunately, the child bounced off the bed, hit the wall, and landed on the floor. She suffered a traumatic injury to the brain from which she later died. Sinclair was convicted by a jury of manslaughter, and his subsequent appeal to the Manitoba Court of Appeal was rejected. Chief Justice Scott, in delivering the judgment of the Court, stated that

> [h]ere, it cannot be doubted that the accused's con-duct caused the child's death, and that the risk of non-trivial bodily harm arising from the accused's actions was objectively foreseeable. All the required elements of unlawful act manslaughter were present.

The Court of Appeal also rejected the argument that Sinclair did not commit an assault on his daughter because, as a parent, he was using force by way of "rea-sonable correction" under section 43 of the *Criminal Code*.[5] On this issue, Chief Justice Scott ruled that

> [c]orporal punishment has always been and still is the prerogative of parents. It is unacceptable, how-ever, if it is administered arbitrarily, motivated by anger, and if it does not serve the purpose of edu-cating the child....
>
> ... The accused "snapped," as he said, and in anger and out of frustration threw his child onto the bed, thus depriving himself of the justification afforded by s. 43.

Not every unlawful act that results in death con-stitutes unlawful act manslaughter. This proposition is illustrated by the case of *Vaillancourt* (1995), in which the accused and his friend Palardy had gone to pick up a videocassette in Vaillancourt's apart-ment. Palardy noticed a .32 calibre revolver on the accused's night table and asked Vaillancourt how the firearm worked. The accused opened the magazine of the gun and let the bullets slide out into the palm of his hand. Vaillancourt closed the magazine without checking to see if any bullets remained inside it. He then pulled the trigger and, on four occasions, nothing happened. However, by the fifth try, Vaillancourt was pointing the gun at Palardy's head and, when the accused pulled on the trigger, a bullet, which had remained inside the magazine, was discharged and killed Palardy. Vaillancourt was charged with unlawful act manslaughter.

There was no doubt that Vaillancourt had engaged in an "unlawful act" because the *Criminal Code* (section 87) renders it an offence to point a firearm (*whether loaded or unloaded*) at another person if this is done "without lawful excuse." However, the critical issue in the case was whether Vaillancourt had the necessary *mens rea* for manslaughter. The evidence was to the effect that the accused honestly believed that the magazine had been fully emptied because it had an extractor, which was supposed to expel all of the bullets when it was opened. There was no evidence of any animosity between Vaillancourt and Palardy, and the latter showed no fear at the time of the shooting because he also believed that the gun was unloaded. Indeed, as the trial judge noted, Vaillancourt was, at Palardy's request, "simply demonstrating the operation of the gun." The trial judge emphasized that the accused had "taken the precaution of emptying the maga-zine, that he was familiar with the gun and that he had every reason to believe that all of the bullets had fallen out of it." The trial judge, therefore, acquitted the accused because there was *no evidence that a rea-sonable person, on the facts as the accused perceived them to be, would have foreseen the risk of nontrivial bodily harm* to Palardy. After all, in most circumstances, an unloaded firearm does not *per se* pose a threat of bodily harm, and Vaillancourt *honestly* (and *reason-ably*) believed that the gun did not contain any bul-lets. Put another way, the pointing of an unloaded firearm is not a "manifestly dangerous act" (a requirement identified by Justice McLachlin in the *Creighton* (1993) case as being an essential element in unlawful act manslaughter), and Vaillancourt believed that he was merely demonstrating the oper-ation of an unloaded revolver at the time of the fatal tragedy. The Quebec Court of Appeal upheld the acquittal of Vaillancourt. As Justice Brossard noted, on behalf of the Court, "in so far as the **respondent**

---

[5] Section 43: "Every schoolteacher, parent or person standing in the place of a parent is justified in using force by way of correction toward a pupil or child, as the case may be, who is under his care, if the force does not exceed what is reasonable under the circumstances."

is concerned, he pointed an unloaded gun, in the quite amicable context of demonstrating the handling of the gun, and without any malevolent intention of any nature whatsoever."

The Offences of Unlawfully Causing Bodily Harm and Assault Causing Bodily Harm

The offences of **unlawfully causing bodily harm** (section 269 of the *Code*) and *assault causing bodily harm* (section 267) also provide two significant examples of the imposition of objective *mens rea*. In the *DeSousa* case (1992), the Supreme Court of Canada held that the *mens rea* for unlawfully causing bodily harm is "*objective foresight of bodily harm*." If an accused person commits an "unlawful act" (an offence under federal or provincial/territorial legislation), which is *objectively dangerous*, then, if bodily harm is the consequence of that unlawful act, he or she will be convicted of unlawfully causing bodily harm. Put another way, if a reasonable person would have foreseen the risk of *non-trivial bodily harm*, then it is irrelevant whether this particular accused subjectively foresaw such a consequence. In the *DeSousa* case (1992), the accused was involved in a fight that resulted in a bystander being injured. The accused had allegedly thrown a bottle against a wall and a fragment of glass had struck the bystander, wounding her in the arm. The accused claimed that section 269 of the *Criminal Code* should be struck down under section 7 of the *Charter* because it contravened the "principles of fundamental justice" insofar as it "put an accused person at risk of imprisonment without the requirement of a blameworthy state of mind." The trial judge agreed with this argument and quashed the indictment against DeSousa. However, the trial judge's decision was later overturned by the Ontario Court of Appeal and the accused's appeal to the Supreme Court of Canada was firmly rejected.

Speaking on behalf of the Supreme Court, Justice Sopinka stated that the principles of fundamental justice, enshrined in section 7 of the *Charter*, were not infringed by the imposition of objective *mens rea* in relation to the offence of unlawfully causing bodily harm:

> One is not morally innocent simply because a particular consequence of an unlawful act was unforeseen by that actor. In punishing for unforeseen consequences the law is not punishing the morally innocent but those who cause injury through avoidable

unlawful action. Neither basic principles of criminal law, nor the dictates of fundamental justice require, by necessity, intention in relation to the consequences of an otherwise blameworthy act.

This *mens rea* requirement—of objective foresight of non-trivial bodily harm—also appears in the context of the offence of assault causing bodily harm (section 267). For example, in the case of *Dewey* (1999), the complainant had been fighting with another man when the accused came between them and "forcefully shoved the complainant," whose head then struck a jukebox or a corner of the wall as he was falling to the ground. The complainant suffered very serious injuries. At his trial, the accused was convicted of assault causing bodily harm. Dewey appealed to the Alberta Court of Appeal. He claimed that, although the offence did, indeed, impose objective liability, it was nevertheless necessary for the Crown to prove that a reasonable person would have foreseen *the particular type of bodily harm that ultimately occurred in this case* (namely, that the victim would fall and strike his head on the jukebox or the wall). In dismissing Dewey's appeal, the Alberta Court of Appeal stated that the Crown has satisfied the *mens rea* requirements for assault causing bodily harm if it proves that the reasonable person would have foreseen *any sort of non-trivial bodily harm whatsoever*. It is not necessary for the Crown to prove that the *specific type of bodily harm that was inflicted* could have been foreseen by a reasonable person placed in the same circumstances as the accused. As Justice McLung stated on behalf of the Court of Appeal,

> The trial judge found that Dewey pushed the complainant more forcefully than would cause a stumble. It is objectively foreseeable that this action would create a risk of bodily harm which is neither transitory nor trivial. [emphasis added]

The Offence of Aggravated Assault

Section 268(1) of the *Criminal Code* provides that

> [e]very one commits an aggravated assault who wounds, maims, disfigures or endangers the life of the complainant.

The courts have consistently held that this offence is one that imposes objective liability. For example, in the case of *MacKay* (2004), the accused, who was riding a motorcycle, ran down and seriously injured the victim, Drane, in the parking lot of a fast-food outlet. MacKay allegedly told a police officer at the scene of the incident that he had not intended to hurt

Drane but rather had intended just to "scare him." MacKay was acquitted at his trial but the New Brunswick Court of Appeal set aside the acquittal and ordered a new trial. The Court of Appeal held that the trial judge should have instructed the jury that they could also convict MacKay of aggravated assault—if MacKay had threatened to apply force to Drane and if a reasonable person would have "foreseen that in driving his motorcycle in the manner in which he did, a threatening act of force, it exposed Mr. Drane to the risk of serious injury." In delivering the judgment of the Court of Appeal, Justice Ryan said that

> ... it would not be necessary for the Crown to prove that Mr. MacKay intended to apply force. The crux of the matter is whether the threat to apply force and the ability to do so, in this case, carries with it the objective foresight of injury if the aggressor miscalculates. The Crown must prove its case, objective foreseeability of serious injury, beyond a reasonable doubt, the charge being that the act endangered the life of the victim.

The Supreme Court of Canada subsequently affirmed the Court of Appeal's decision to order a new trial (*MacKay* (2005)). The Supreme Court held that the jury should be instructed that MacKay could be convicted of aggravated assault, if either (i) he deliberately applied force to the victim or (ii) he intended to threaten the victim by riding his motorcycle close to him and (iii) a reasonable person would have foreseen the risk of serious injury from the application of force or from the threat, as the case may be.

OFFENCES INVOLVING CRIMINAL NEGLIGENCE

Section 219(1) of the *Code* provides that

> [e]very one is criminally negligent who
>
>> (a) in doing anything, or
>>
>> (b) in omitting to do anything that it is his duty to do,
>
> shows wanton or reckless disregard for the lives or safety of other persons.

This definition of criminal negligence is applicable to the following offences: causing death by criminal negligence (section 220), causing bodily harm by criminal negligence (section 221), and manslaughter by criminal negligence (section 222(5)(b) and section 234).

According to the provisions of section 219(1) of the *Criminal Code*, an accused person may be convicted of an offence involving criminal negligence in relation to both positive acts and omissions. Where the gist of the charges is that the accused failed to act, it must first be established that the accused was under a legal duty to act (section 219(2) indicates that "duty" means a "duty imposed by law"). It should also be pointed out that section 219 is concerned with the most culpable forms of negligence; indeed, it specifies that, in order to obtain a conviction, the Crown must establish that, in either doing something or failing to do something that it was his or her duty to do, the accused showed "wanton or reckless disregard for the lives or safety of other persons." As we shall see, this has been interpreted as meaning that the accused will be found guilty of criminal negligence where his or her conduct (whether it is an act or an omission) amounts to a *marked and substantial departure from the standard of the reasonable person* acting prudently in the circumstances facing the accused.

It would be easy to say, without qualification, that the *mens rea* elements of criminal negligence are based on objective liability. The Supreme Court of Canada had the opportunity to address this issue in 1989. However, in both the cases of *Tutton and Tutton* (1989) and *Waite* (1989), there was a three-to-three split between the justices as to whether the appropriate test was objective or whether it required a minimal degree of subjective awareness on the part of the accused of the risk created by his or her conduct. However, it is significant that, since the more recent cases of *Creighton* (1993) (unlawful act manslaughter) and *Hundal* (1993) (dangerous driving), the Supreme Court of Canada has unequivocally accepted the view that "penal negligence" is based on the modified objective test of liability, and most commentators on Canadian criminal law have assumed that, when the Court is called upon to revisit this issue, it will almost certainly rule that the *mens rea* for crimes involving proof of criminal negligence are also based on the modified objective test. Therefore, this chapter has included criminal negligence as a form of objective *mens rea*. Furthermore, it is significant that, in a series of cases decided after *Tutton and Tutton* (1989) and *Waite* (1989), the Ontario Court of Appeal took the view that, until the Supreme Court of Canada decides otherwise, it will continue to apply an objective test of criminal negligence (see, for example, *Nelson* (1990), *Cabral* (1990), and *Gingrich and McLean* (1991)). Other appellate courts have followed the lead of the Ontario Court of Appeal in this respect (see, for example, *Grimmer* (1998)).

The requirement that there be a "marked departure from the standard of the reasonable person" in a case of criminal negligence is well illustrated by the tragic case of *L. (J.)* (2006). In this case, the accused had been driving a van, which he had brought to a halt on the street. The victim, who was a friend of the accused, had jumped on to the hood of the stationary van. At this time, the victim was "smiling and laughing." The accused then set the van in motion but, after travelling a short distance, he realized that "what was going on was wrong" and stopped the vehicle. The victim slid off the hood and suffered a fatal head injury. The trial judge convicted L. (J.) of criminal negligence causing death (section 220). The trial judge placed great importance on the fact that the accused had admittedly foreseen the risk of injury to his friend as a consequence of driving the van with him on the hood. Therefore, the trial judge ruled that L. (J.)'s conduct showed wanton and reckless disregard for the life and safety of his friend and constituted criminal negligence, as defined by section 219 of the *Criminal Code*.

The Ontario Court of Appeal set aside the conviction of L. (J.) and ordered a new trial. The main reason for this decision was the failure of the trial judge to make a specific finding that the accused person's driving conduct amounted to a "marked departure from the norm." In delivering the judgment of the Court of Appeal, Justice Weiler remarked that "whether specific conduct should be categorized as criminal negligence is one of the most difficult and uncertain areas in the criminal law." Justice Weiler indicated that the Crown must prove a higher level of misconduct in relation to a charge of criminal negligence than is necessary to prove the lesser offence of dangerous driving:

> This higher standard has been described as a marked and *substantial* departure from the standard of care of a reasonable person ... It is not self-evident that [L. (J.)'s] act of putting the car in gear with a person on the hood satisfies this higher standard.

Justice Weiler concluded that

the trial judge committed a palpable and overriding error in finding that the appellant's conduct met the higher standard of criminal negligence without first making a finding regarding the appellant's driving.

The trial judge further erred in finding that the appellant was "wanton" or "reckless" without considering all of the circumstances surrounding the activity including the manner in which [L. (J.)] drove, his youthfulness, the instigation and encouragement of the activity he received from the deceased, and his conduct in trying to help his friend immediately after this tragic event.

This case is significant insofar as it emphasizes that, in order to establish criminal negligence, there must be both a *marked* and a *substantial* departure from the standard of care expected of the reasonable person.[6]

It will be remembered that section 219 of the *Criminal Code* indicates that criminal negligence occurs when an individual either does anything or omits to do "anything that it is his [or her] duty to do" and thereby shows "wanton or reckless disregard for the lives or safety of other persons." Clearly *criminal negligence includes acts of both commission and omission*. Should the required *mens rea* element that the Crown must prove in relation to a charge of criminal negligence be the same, or different, when the accused's conduct consists of an *omission* as opposed to an act of commission? In its decision in the *Tutton and Tutton* case (1985), the Ontario Court of Appeal had ruled that an objective test should be applied where the accused was charged on the basis of an act of commission but that a *subjective* test should be applied where the accused was charged on the basis of an *act of omission*. However, the majority of the justices of the Supreme Court of Canada appeared to reject the contention that the nature of the *mens rea* for criminal negligence may vary in the manner described by the Ontario Court of Appeal. Although the justices of the Supreme Court could not agree as to whether the *mens rea* for criminal negligence is subjective or objective in nature, they nevertheless appeared to be unanimous in holding the view that the same test (whether it be subjective or objective) applies to both positive acts and omissions. This principle was applied by the Ontario Court of Appeal in the more recent case of *Canhoto* (1999). Here, the accused had been convicted of manslaughter (by criminal negligence), following the death of her two-year-old daughter, Kira. A significant part of the

---

[6] Justice Weiler referred to the judgment of Justice McIntyre of the Supreme Court of Canada in the *Waite* case (1989) as authority for that proposition.

Crown's case against *Canhoto* was based on her *failure to intercede* when Kira's grandmother had forced water down the child's throat as part of a ritual to "expel evil spirits." As a consequence of this violent exorcism, Kira had died from asphyxiation. During her appeal to the Ontario Court of Appeal, Canhoto's counsel contended that "the fault component of crimes of criminal negligence must vary depending on whether liability arises out of conduct or an omission" and suggested that a more onerous standard should apply to omissions as opposed to acts of commission. Of course, counsel emphasized that Canhoto's conduct consisted of an omission (a failure to intervene during the fatal exorcism of her own daughter). However, the Court of Appeal decisively rejected Canhoto's appeal against her conviction and, in delivering the judgment of the Court, Justice Doherty held that the Supreme Court of Canada's decision in *Tutton and Tutton* (1989) had effectively rejected the line of argument advanced by her counsel:

> The determination of fault based on a failure to direct one's mind to a risk can be applied equally to acts and omissions. The need for a uniform standard for the determination of criminal culpability is as important where the law imposes a duty to act and no action is taken, as it is in cases where a person engages in conduct which creates that same risk. It would run contrary to the principle of uniformity and the values underlying that principle if the criminal law were to distinguish between a parent who chooses not to administer a life-saving drug to his child, thereby risking the life of that child, and a parent who actually removes the needle containing the drug from the arm of the child, thereby creating the very same risk.
>
> ... The fault element for crimes of criminal negligence should be the same, regardless of whether liability arises out of a failure to act where there was a duty to act or out of actions which create a risk.

CAUSING DEATH BY CRIMINAL NEGLIGENCE AND MANSLAUGHTER BY CRIMINAL NEGLIGENCE: IDENTICAL TWINS

The reader will, no doubt, have raised the following question while reading the preceding sections: what is the difference between the offences of causing death by criminal negligence (section 220 of the *Code*) and manslaughter by criminal negligence

(sections 222(5)(b) and 234)? The answer is that the elements of each offence are identical. Why, then, are there two separate offences? The answer appears to lie in historical considerations. The offence of causing death by criminal negligence was created in 1955 (at least in part) as a consequence of the notorious reluctance of juries to convict motorists who killed others while driving their vehicles of the offence of manslaughter. It was felt that juries would be more willing to convict motorists of an offence that did not bear the heavy stigma of manslaughter. The irony is that the critical elements of the two offences as well as the penalty are the same in all respects. Significantly, in 1985, Parliament later added two new offences that deal with vehicular homicide, namely, dangerous driving causing death (section 149(4)) and impaired driving causing death (section 255(3)). In 2000, Parliament introduced two new driving offences involving homicide: causing death while fleeing from a peace officer (s. 249.1) and causing death by street racing (s. 249.2). In 2006, Parliament added the offence of dangerous driving causing death while street racing (s. 249.4).

CRIMINAL CODE SECTIONS IMPOSING A SPECIAL STANDARD OF CARE

Where an individual is engaging in activities that are so inherently dangerous as to pose a serious risk to the safety of others, the *Criminal Code* may require him or her to meet an **elevated standard of care**: this is the standard of care expected of a reasonable person who has acquired the necessary expertise and training to engage in such activities. Examples of situations in which the *Criminal Code* imposes such an elevated standard of care are sections 79 (possession of explosives), 86(1) (use and storage of firearms), and 216 (administration of surgical and medical treatment). If there is a marked departure from the elevated standard of care, the accused's negligence will justify conviction of the relevant *Criminal Code* offence. Clearly, these sections all deal with situations in which one would expect the responsible citizen to acquire a reasonable degree of expertise before engaging in conduct that has the potential to be dangerous to the lives and safety of others. Undoubtedly, those who undertake to handle explosives, make use of firearms, or deliver medical care may all be said to be engaging in activities that are inherently fraught with many potential dangers. Therefore, a citizen who, for example, engages in medical treatment is judged by the standard of the reasonable medical practitioner rather than the reasonable person in the street who has no medical training. As Justice McLachlin stated in the *Creighton* case (1993),

> A person may fail to meet an elevated *de facto* standard of care in either of two ways. First, the person may undertake an activity requiring special care when he or she is not qualified to give that care. Absent special excuses like necessity, this may constitute culpable negligence. An untrained person undertaking brain surgery might violate the standard in this way. Secondly, a person who is qualified may negligently fail to exercise the special care required by the activity. A brain surgeon performing surgery in a grossly negligent way might violate the standard in this second way. The standard is the same, although the means by which it is breached may differ.

1. REASONABLE MEDICAL TREATMENT AND SECTION 216

Section 216 of the *Criminal Code* provides that

> [e]very one who undertakes to administer surgical or medical treatment to another person or to do any other lawful act that may endanger the life of another person is, except in cases of necessity, under a legal duty to have and to use reasonable knowledge, skill and care in so doing.

This section clearly imposes an elevated standard of liability on those who administer surgical or medical treatment or engage in other lawful activities that may endanger the lives of others. Such individuals are expected to possess the knowledge and skills of the average competent medical practitioner. This means that, although accused persons who administer such treatment may not subjectively appreciate the risk that their conduct is creating, they may still be convicted of an offence under the *Criminal Code* if the reasonable medical practitioner would have appreciated such a risk.

This principle is illustrated by the tragic case of *Rogers* (1968), in which the accused, a former doctor who had been struck from the rolls, was charged with causing death by criminal negligence. Although prohibited from engaging in medical practice, he continued to pose as a doctor and began to treat a little boy who suffered from a skin disorder. Rogers prescribed such an insufficient diet that the boy ultimately died of gross malnutrition. Rogers claimed that he honestly believed that his diet would be beneficial for the boy and that he did not foresee the risk that it might be dangerous. His counsel, therefore, argued that the Crown must prove that his client was reckless (or subjectively aware of the risk) before a conviction could be entered against him. Rogers was, nevertheless, convicted at trial and his appeal to the British Columbia Court of Appeal was dismissed. The Court of Appeal emphasized that section 216 of the *Criminal Code* prescribes an objective test of criminal responsibility and that the Crown was, therefore, not obliged to establish that the accused subjectively appreciated the risk that his conduct was creating. Since a reasonable doctor would have appreciated the risk created by the inadequate diet, Rogers was correctly convicted. As Justice Nemetz said in relation to this point,

> Once all of the medical witnesses had testified that the possessors of reasonable medical knowledge would foresee that the taking away of proteins and calories (as was in fact done by Rogers) would probably result in death, it became irrelevant for the trial judge to put Rogers' belief to the contrary to the jury. It was Rogers' duty to have the "reasonable knowledge" that was delineated and which represented the advances in scientific and medical knowledge to this day. If he persisted in this treatment notwithstanding that body of reasonable knowledge he ran the risk of bringing about the unwished result, namely, the death of the child.

In the case of *Sullivan and Lemay* (1986), Justice Godrey of the B.C. Supreme Court ruled that two midwives, who were serving as birth attendants at a home birth, were covered by the phrase "any other lawful act that may endanger the life of another person" that appears in section 216 of the *Code*. On this basis, they were considered to be under a "legal duty to have and to use reasonable knowledge, skill and care" in their activities. Therefore, they were required to meet the standard of "a competent childbirth attendant whether the title is midwife, general practitioner or obstetrician," notwithstanding the fact that they had no formal training as midwives. Similarly, in *Thornton* (1993), the Supreme Court of Canada ruled that a blood donor may be considered to be engaging in a "lawful act that may endanger the life of another person" and is, therefore placed under a legal duty by section 216 to take reasonable care. Indeed, Chief Justice Lamer stated, on behalf of the Court, that

[s]ection 216 imposed upon the appellant a duty of care in giving his blood to the Red Cross. This duty of care was breached by not disclosing that his blood contained HIV antibodies. This common nuisance obviously endangered the life, safety and health of the public.

2. The Duty to Take Reasonable Care in the Handling of Explosives and Firearms—Sections 79 and 86(1)

The *Criminal Code* imposes an elevated standard of care in relation to the handling of explosive substances. Section 79 states,

> Everyone who has an explosive substance in his possession or under his care or control is under a legal duty to use reasonable care to prevent bodily harm or death to persons or damage to property by that explosive substance.

A similar duty has been imposed on those who handle firearms. Section 86(1) of the *Code* provides that

> [e]very person commits an offence who, without lawful excuse, uses, carries, handles, ships, transports or stores a firearm, a prohibited weapon, a restricted weapon, a prohibited device or any ammunition or prohibited ammunition in a careless manner or without reasonable precautions for the safety of other persons.

In each case, these provisions would be interpreted by the courts as requiring that an accused person meet the standard of care expected of a reasonable person who has taken some training in the safe handling of explosives and firearms. The standard is not that of the "reasonable novice" who tries his or her best to cope with explosives or firearms with no knowledge of basic safety precautions. However, as the Supreme Court said in the *Finlay* case (1993), there can be a conviction of an offence under the *Criminal Code* only if the accused person's behaviour can be designated as a marked departure from the standard of care expected of a reasonable person who has the necessary training and skills to deal with explosives and firearms.

Significantly, the Supreme Court has ruled that the elevated standard of care imposed by provisions of the *Criminal Code*, such as section 86(1), is that of the reasonable person acting prudently. Naturally, the reasonable person will acquire sufficient knowledge about the use, storage, transportation, and so forth of firearms before undertaking such activity. As Justice McLachlin said in the *Creighton* case (1993),

Where individuals engage in activities for which they lack sufficient knowledge, experience, or physical ability, they may be properly found to be at fault, not so much for their inability to properly carry out the activity, but for their decision to attempt the activity without having accounted for their deficiencies. The law expects people embarking on hazardous activities to ask questions or seek help before they venture beyond their depth.

However, it is important to bear in mind that the criminal law requires the individual who uses firearms only to meet the standard of care expected of a reasonable person who is acting prudently and who has acquired the necessary knowledge to engage in this activity safely. *In other words, the law imposes a "single minimum standard" and does not raise it—or lower it—according to the particular expertise of the defendant in a specific case.* For example, in the *Gosset* case (1993), Chief Justice Lamer suggested that a "police officer trained and experienced in the use of

Handling explosives requires the need for an elevated standard of care.

Cartoon by Elizabeth Carefoot

firearms should be held to a higher standard of care in the handling of firearms than the non-police officer." However, the majority of the Supreme Court has rejected Chief Justice Lamer's approach. In *Creighton* (1993) Justice McLachlin clearly articulated the rationale for the position adopted by the majority of the justices of the Supreme Court:

> Just as the adoption of a uniform standard of care which is blind to personal characteristics of the accused short of incapacity precludes lowering the standard for deficiencies of experience and temperament, so it precludes raising the standard for special experience or training. Since the criminal law is concerned with setting minimum standards for human conduct, it would be inappropriate to hold accused persons to a higher standard of care by reason of the fact that they may be better informed or better qualified than the person of reasonable prudence. Some activities may impose a higher *de facto* standard than others; brain surgery requires more care than applying an antiseptic. But ... this flows from the circumstances of the activity, not from the expertise of the actor.

In other words, a police officer who is charged with an offence of criminal negligence as a consequence of his or her misuse of a firearm will be judged by the standard of the reasonable person who uses firearms prudently, and not by the standard of an expert in the use of firearms. The standard of care under section 86(1) is "elevated" in the sense that an individual must acquire a minimum level of knowledge and skill before embarking on such a manifestly dangerous enterprise as dealing with firearms. However, if that individual attains this minimum level of knowledge and skill and acts prudently, then he or she cannot be found to have been guilty of criminal negligence.

STUDY QUESTIONS

1. Crackit and Winkel are walking on the banks of a fast-flowing river. They are good friends and they are laughing and smiling. Crackit decides to "give Winkel a scare" and pushes him toward the river. Crackit believes that he will be able to hold on to Winkel so that he will not fall into the water. Unfortunately, as he pushes Winkel, Crackit slips on some slick grass and fails to maintain a hold on Winkel, who tumbles into the river. Winkel is unable to swim and is rapidly swept away by a strong current. Winkel drowns and his lifeless body is later found trapped under a rock. Do you think that Crackit would be convicted of a charge of manslaughter or criminal negligence causing death?

2. Nero has a personal grudge against Siegfried, a local farmer. In order to exact revenge, Nero decides to set fire to Siegfried's barn. The barn burns down before the firefighters can arrive to save it. Tragically, Crassus (a vagrant) had been sleeping in the barn at the time and was killed by the fire. Nero says that he honestly believed that there was no one in the barn when he set it alight. What charges might be laid (if any) against Nero?

3. Drummle and his sister, Polly, are looking through the vast quantity of items stored in their grandfather's basement. Polly finds an old-fashioned revolver, with a rotating cylinder, containing six bullet chambers. She quickly opens the gun and notices that the chamber opposite the firing pin is empty. She points the gun at Drummle, saying "Bang, bang, you're dead," and pulls the trigger. To her surprise, the gun discharges and Drummle is killed. A gun expert tells the police that, when the trigger is pulled on such a revolver, the cylinder containing the bullets rotates. The chamber opposite the firing pin was empty when Polly first looked at the gun but, when she pressed the trigger, an adjacent chamber containing a live bullet rotated into a firing position. Polly claims that she had no idea how revolvers operated and that she honestly believed the gun would not fire when she pulled the trigger; the expert says that this is just the sort of misconception that is quite common among those who are inexperienced with revolvers. The police are thinking of charging Polly with manslaughter. Would such a charge be likely to succeed in a criminal trial?

4. Tiny Tim, who is six years old, is taken for walk near a wading pool in Aquamarine Park by Fanny, his nanny. Tiny Tim splashes water on Creakle, a man of 28, who has never seen Tiny Tim before. Creakle has just been dismissed from his job without cause by his boss and is infuriated by Tiny Tim's behaviour. Creakle pushes the little boy into the pool. Tiny Tim screams and starts to flounder in the water. Creakle believes that Tiny Tim is "crying wolf"

because he assumes that the water in a wading pool must be very shallow. However, Flintwich (the municipal employee responsible for this part of the park) has failed to repair some deep holes that have developed at the bottom of the pool, and at the point where Tiny Tim falls in, the water is more than four feet deep. Tiny Tim cannot swim. Fanny is a former member of the Neptune University swimming team and can easily rescue Tiny Tim. However, Fanny is engaged in conversation with Swiveller, a good friend, and does nothing except wave to the struggling Tiny Tim and urge him to stop playing the fool. Swiveller is also an excellent swimmer. He goes over to the edge of the pond and reaches out for the boy, but Tiny Tim is too far from the edge and Swiveller returns to his intimate conversation with Fanny. Tiny Tim drowns. Creakle, who has already left the scene, does not learn that Tiny Tim drowned until he is visited by the police.

Consider:

a. The charges that might be laid in this case

b. The persons against whom the charges might be laid

c. The approach that might be taken by defence counsel

5. Barkis drives his truck straight through a stop sign and crashes into a lamppost. Fortunately, no one was injured. Barkis is charged with dangerous driving. He claims that he momentarily lost attention when he was changing the CD in his CD player, and when he realized that he was close to a stop sign, it was too late to bring his truck to a halt. He also claims that the truck was too heavy to bring to a halt within the few seconds during which he had become aware of the stop sign. Is he guilty of the charge laid against him? Would it make a difference if Barkis stated that he momentarily fell asleep because the driving conditions had been extremely treacherous (e.g., heavy snow or rain) and he was exhausted?

6. Forsyte is driving his car through a school zone when he suddenly experiences a massive heart attack and loses consciousness. Sadly, his car mounts the sidewalk and strikes a young child, who subsequently dies. Forsyte is charged with dangerous driving causing death. Is he likely to be convicted of this charge? Would it be a relevant consideration that Forsyte had already experienced two heart attacks?

7. Snubbin is driving his pickup truck on a highway. It is a fine, clear day and the driving conditions are excellent. Suddenly, Snubbin's truck crosses the median and collides head on with a car travelling in the opposite direction. The unfortunate driver of the car is Trotter, who is killed as a result of the collision. It appears that Snubbin fell asleep immediately before the accident. Pickwick, a physician who examines Snubbin after the accident, is prepared to testify that Snubbin suffers from narcolepsy (a condition that causes sudden and uncontrollable episodes of deep sleep). If you were Crown counsel, would you charge Snubbin with dangerous driving causing death?

8. Hamlet and Ophelia have a young daughter, Gertrude. They know that Gertrude, who has diabetes, requires regular insulin injections in order to stay alive. Hamlet and Ophelia are members of a society that organizes séances and both of them firmly believe in the existence of a "spirit world." Hamlet tells Ophelia that he has experienced a vision in which he saw his father's ghost, who told him that Gertrude was cured of her diabetes and there was no longer a need for any injections. Ophelia implicitly believes what Hamlet has told her and they cease giving Gertrude her insulin injections. Gertrude lapses into a coma and, by the time she is taken to hospital, it is too late to save her life. Crown counsel wishes to lay charges of manslaughter against Hamlet and Ophelia. Is it likely that such charges would be successful at a trial?

9. Magnus is an adult with a developmental disability who functions at the same level as an eight-year-old child. He finds a large rock and decides to go to a bridge that spans a highway. He then drops the rock on to a passing truck, killing its driver. The police wish to lay a charge of manslaughter or criminal negligence causing death against Magnus. What would you do if you were Crown counsel in this case?

10. Bagstock has three rifles and a large supply of ammunition in his residence. The guns are properly registered, as required by the *Criminal Code*. However, one day Bagstock leaves one of the rifles in the garage instead of locking it up in a

secure cabinet. His 10-year-old nephew, Jo, finds the gun and points it at his friend Oliver. Tragically, the gun is faulty and unexpectedly discharges, wounding Oliver in the leg. Could Bagstock be charged with criminal negligence causing bodily harm?

11. Hippocrates is a plastic surgeon who, for the past 30 years, has specialized in "face-lifts" and similar surgical procedures. One day, he is summoned to the emergency room of the hospital and is told that, since no other surgeon is available, he must operate on Traddles, a man who has suffered major internal injuries in a car accident. Hippocrates realizes that Traddles will die without immediate surgery, so he very reluctantly undertakes to perform the operation. Traddles subsequently dies, and it is suggested that Hippocrates was negligent because he did not know the latest surgical techniques that could have saved a patient who had suffered such devastating injuries as had Traddles. If you were Crown counsel, would you charge Hippocrates with manslaughter or criminal negligence causing death?

12. Rosalind is a single mother of very limited means. She lives in a tiny apartment. She has only a living room (where she and her son, Cupid, also sleep), a small kitchen, and a bathroom. Cupid, who is five years old, frequently plays in the bathroom, where he loves to float some plastic toys in the bathtub. One day, Verges, Rosalind's boyfriend, comes for a visit. Alcohol is consumed and the two adults decide to go to bed. Cupid is placed in the bathroom and told to play with his boats in the bathtub. Rosalind locks the bathroom door from the outside. She then engages in sexual relations with Verges. After about half an hour, the adults dress themselves and decide to play with Cupid. When they unlock and open the bathroom door, they discover Cupid floating face down in the water. Despite the application of mouth-to-mouth resuscitation techniques by Verges and the early arrival of the paramedics (summoned by a distraught Rosalind), Cupid cannot be revived. In light of this tragic drowning, Crown counsel is considering laying charges against Rosalind. What charges might reasonably be laid and what defences might be open to Rosalind in light of these charges?

13. Squeers and Snawley are fighting in a bar. Gride angrily throws a beer glass at them in order to bring the disturbance to an end. The glass unfortunately shatters as it strikes part of the sprinkler system. A large piece of glass is embedded in the arm of Smike, an innocent bystander. Smike is taken to hospital and 47 stitches are required to close his substantial wound. Gride tearfully tells the police that he never meant to harm anyone and appears to be genuinely contrite. What charge(s) might reasonably be laid against Gride?

14. Ledbrain has just purchased a quarry that produces limestone. Ledbrain has no prior experience with the extraction of minerals: indeed, his business experience has been limited to the operation of a large laundry. When Ledbrain takes over the quarry, he finds two large boxes containing explosives. He decides to transport the explosives to a hut on the other side of the quarry: his reason for this decision is that he believes that the explosives may be stolen from their existing location. After he has moved the boxes to the hut, Ledbrain drives home. Within minutes of his departure, there is a tremendous explosion in the hut. Tragically, two employees at the quarry are killed. A government inspector informs the police that the explosives were perilously unstable and should never have been moved in that condition. A distraught and repentant Ledbrain says that he is a complete newcomer to the field of explosives and that he had no idea that moving the boxes could trigger a deadly blast. The inspector states that anyone who had even the most elementary knowledge of dealing with explosive materials would never have moved these boxes in light of the dangerous instability of their contents. Is it likely that Ledbrain would be convicted of manslaughter or criminal negligence causing death?

FURTHER READING

Archibald, B.P. 1997. Fault, Penalty and Proportionality: Connecting Sentencing to Subjective and Objective Standards of Criminal Liability (with Ruminations on Restorative Justice). 40 *Criminal Law Quarterly*: 263–286.

Baker, B.M. 1987. *Mens Rea*, Negligence and Criminal Law Reform. 6 *Law and Philosophy*: 53–88.

Benedet, J. 2007. Annotation: *R. v. Jiang*, (2007) 48 C.R. (6th) 49 (B.C.C.A.). 48 *Criminal Reports (6th Series)*: 50–51.

Cairns, R. 1992. The *Charter*, the Supreme Court and the Invisible Politics of Fault. 12 *Windsor Yearbook of Access to Justice*: 128–178.

Carlton, T. 1992. A Principled Approach to the Constitutional Requirement of Fault. 24 *Ottawa Law Review*: 613–648.

Colvin, E., and S. Anand. 2007. *Principles of Criminal Law*. 3rd ed. Toronto: Carswell.

Connolly, R. 1994. Dangerous Operation of a Motor Vehicle: More Than Careless, but Less Than Criminally Negligent? 5 *Journal of Motor Vehicle Law*: 253–275.

Gold, A.D. 1993. Constructive Manslaughter Should Not Have Survived. 23 *Criminal Reports (4th Series)*: 262–264.

Grant, I., and C. Boyle. 1993. Equality, Harm and Vulnerability: Homicide and Sexual Assault Post-*Creighton*. 23 *Criminal Reports (4th Series)*: 252–262.

Hart, H.L.A. 1962. *Punishment and Responsibility*. Oxford: Clarendon Press.

Healy, P. 1990. *Anderson*: Marking Time or a Step back on Criminal Negligence? 75 *Criminal Reports (3rd Series)*: 58–63.

———. 1993. The *Creighton* Quartet: Enigma Variations in a Lower Key. 23 *Criminal Reports (4th Series)*: 265–279.

———. 1995. Repeal Criminal Negligence. 37 *Criminal Law Quarterly*: 205–219.

Horder, J. 1997. Gross Negligence and Criminal Culpability. 47 *University of Toronto Law Journal*: 495–521.

———. 2005. Can the Law Do without the Reasonable Person? 55 *University of Toronto Law Journal*: 253–269.

Klimchuk, D. 1996. Circumstances and Objectivity. 45 *Criminal Reports (4th Series)*: 24–32.

Law Reform Commission of Canada. 1985. Working Paper No. 46: *Omissions, Negligence and Endangering*. Ottawa: L.R.C.C.

———. 1987. Report No. 31: *Recodifying Criminal Law*. Rev. ed. Ottawa: L.R.C.C.

Marko, J.G., and S.C. Hutchinson. 1990. Ball of Confusion: Criminal Negligence after *Tutton*. 2 *Journal of Motor Vehicle Law*: 59–72.

McDonald, F. 2008. The Criminalisation of Medical Mistakes in Canada: A Review. 16 *Health Law Journal*: 1–25.

Mewett, A.W. 1992. The Enigma of Manslaughter. 34 *Criminal Law Quarterly*: 362.

Odujirin, A. 1998. *The Normative Basis of Fault in Criminal Law: History and Theory*. Toronto: University of Toronto Press.

Paciocco, D.M. 1995. Subjective and Objective Standards of Fault for Offences and Defences. 59 *Saskatchewan Law Review*: 271–309.

Roach, K. 2009. *Criminal Law*. 4th ed. Toronto: Irwin Law. Ch. 4.

Rosenberg, M. 1990. The *Mens Rea* Requirements of Criminal Negligence: *R. v. Waite* and *R. v. Tutton*. 2 *Journal of Motor Vehicle Law*: 243–259.

Stribopoulos, J. 1999. The Constitutionalization of "Fault" in Canada: A Normative Critique. 42 *Criminal Law Quarterly*: 227–285.

Stuart, D. 1989. Criminal Negligence: Deadlock and Confusion in the Supreme Court. 69 *Criminal Reports (3rd Series)*: 331–336.

———. 1993. Fault: Welcome New Directions from the Supreme Court. 19 *Criminal Reports (4th Series)*: 186–193.

———. 1993. The Implications of *De Sousa* for the Crimes of Aggravated Assault and Dangerous Driving. 16 *Criminal Reports (4th Series)*: 326–331.

———. 1998. Annotation: R. v. Reed. 15 Criminal Reports (5th Series): 29–30.

———. 2007. *Canadian Criminal Law: A Treatise*. 5th ed. Toronto: Thomson Carswell. Ch. 3.

Stuart, D., R.J. Delisle, and S. Coughlan. 2009. *Learning Canadian Criminal Law*. 11th ed. Toronto: Thomson Carswell. Ch. 3.

Tanovich, D.M. 2008. The Implications of *Beatty* for Criminal Negligence. 54 *Criminal Reports (6th Series)*: 38–44.

Verdun-Jones, S.N. 2007. *Canadian Criminal Cases: Selected Highlights*. 2nd ed. Toronto: Thomson Nelson. Ch. 5.

Westen, P. 2008. Individualizing the Reasonable Person in Criminal Law. 2 *Criminal Law and Philosophy*: 137–162.

Wilson, L.C. 2007. Too Many Manslaughters. 52 *Criminal Law Quarterly*: 433–469.

Yeo, S. 2000. The Fault Elements for Involuntary Manslaughter: Some Lessons from Down Under. 43 *Criminal Law Quarterly*: 291–304.

CHAPTER SIX

THE SPECIAL CASE OF REGULATORY OFFENCES: STRICT AND ABSOLUTE LIABILITY IN CANADA

OVERVIEW

This chapter examines the following:

1. the distinction between true crimes and regulatory offences;

2. the principle that the Crown is required to prove only the *actus reus* elements of a regulatory offence;

3. the distinction between absolute and strict liability in the context of regulatory offences;

4. how Canadian courts initially applied a rigid and universal regime of absolute liability for all regulatory offences;

5. how the imposition of absolute liability denies the accused person the opportunity to argue that he or she was not at fault;

6. how, in the case of *Sault Ste. Marie* (1978), the Supreme Court rejected the view that absolute liability should be imposed in relation to all regulatory offences and embraced instead a "halfway house" approach, which permitted the imposition of strict liability in relation to the majority of regulatory offences;

7. the principle that, in relation to strict liability offences, the accused person is granted a defence if he or she is able to prove on the balance of probabilities that he or she acted with "due diligence";

8. the threefold classification of criminal offences established in the *Sault Ste. Marie* case (1978): (1) offences that require the Crown to prove *mens rea*; (2) offences of strict liability, where in order to avoid conviction, the accused must prove "due diligence" on the balance of probabilities; and

(3) offences of absolute liability, where the accused may not raise any defence based on the absence of fault;

9. the basic principles that courts use to categorize regulatory offences and a recognition of the fact that the great majority of such offences are considered to fall within the category of strict liability;

10. the circumstances in which it is likely that a defence of "due diligence" will be successful when it is raised in response to a charge of an offence of strict liability;

11. why regulatory offences are so important to the process of implementing public objectives;

12. the ruling of the Supreme Court in the *Wholesale Travel Group* case (1991), which established that a regime of strict liability is not to be considered invalid under the *Charter*;

13. the fact that courts are generally reluctant to rule that a regulatory offence is one of absolute liability because of the likelihood that it will be declared invalid under the *Charter*;

14. the 1985 ruling of the Supreme Court in *Reference re Section 94(2) of the Motor Vehicle Act*, R.S.B.C. (1979) (1985), that established the principle that regulatory offences will generally be declared invalid under the *Charter* if they impose a regime of absolute liability coupled with the potential for imprisonment; and

15. the arguments for and against the imposition of strict and absolute liability in relation to regulatory offences.

INTRODUCTION

In Chapter 1, the distinction was drawn between true crimes and regulatory offences or quasi-criminal law. In this chapter, we examine the special principles and procedures that apply when an accused person is charged with a regulatory offence.

What are the practical consequences of drawing a distinction between true crimes and regulatory offences? Foremost among these consequences is the fact that, whereas the Crown must prove some form of *mens rea* in order to obtain the conviction of an offender for a true crime, it generally does not have to do so in the case of a regulatory offence. As we have seen in Chapters 3 and 4, when an accused person is charged with having committed a true crime, the Crown normally has to prove—in addition to the *actus reus* requirements—one or more of the following forms of *mens rea*: intention, knowledge, recklessness, wilful blindness, or criminal negligence (a marked departure from the standard of the ordinary person). However, in the case of a regulatory offence, all that the Crown normally has to prove are the *actus reus* elements.

REGULATORY OFFENCES AND ABSOLUTE LIABILITY

Historically, the courts took the view that those defendants who were charged with regulatory offences should not be given any opportunity to argue that they were not to blame for what had happened: indeed, if the Crown could prove the *actus reus* elements of the offence, then the issue of fault was considered to be completely irrelevant. For this reason, regulatory offences were described in the past as being offences of **"absolute liability."**

Ping Yuen (1921) is one of the most notorious cases in which a Canadian court imposed absolute liability on an accused person who had been charged with having committed a regulatory offence. In this case, the accused was a vendor of soft drinks in Moosomin, Saskatchewan. A police officer searched his business premises and removed five bottles of soft drinks from the accused's stock. When these bottles were analyzed, it was found that three of them contained a percentage of alcohol in excess of the amount allowed by the Saskatchewan *Temperance*

Act, 1917. The accused was charged with a violation of the Act. Under this statute, section 35(1) provided that "in case any person engaged in the business of selling soft drinks or non-intoxicating liquors keeps or has with his stocks of such drinks or liquors or on his business premises any liquor as defined by this Act, such person shall be guilty of an offence." At Ping Yuen's trial, the magistrate found that the accused did not know that any of the bottles contained more alcohol than the law permitted. Furthermore, even the prosecution admitted that it was not possible for the accused to test any of the bottles without destroying their contents for sale purposes; in other words, there was no practical way in which Ping Yuen could have avoided breaking the law! The accused was, nevertheless, convicted on the basis that since he was charged with a public welfare offence, the legislature must be taken to have intended to impose absolute liability in relation to the offence. The accused's conviction was subsequently upheld by the Saskatchewan Court of Appeal. In essence, the court ruled that Ping Yuen's offence was not a "true crime," to which any stigma attached. Instead, it was an act prohibited in the public interest under the threat of a financial penalty.

A critical point to bear in mind is the fact that, even though Ping Yuen had acted no differently than any "reasonable" retailer would have done in the circumstances, he was nevertheless convicted of the offence. In other words, Ping Yuen was not blameworthy in any sense whatsoever. Nevertheless, his lack of fault was considered to be irrelevant by the courts. Ping Yuen was fined $50. In the Court of Appeal, Justice Turgeon said:

> ... [I]n the case of beer in this province, it seems to me to be the true intent of the Act that persons who deal in the article are made responsible for it being of a certain quality, namely, not more than 1.13% of alcoholic content, and when they have a too strong alcoholic article in their possession they are liable to the penalty....

In essence, the court seemed to be saying that, in order to protect the public, the risk of possessing beer with an excessive alcoholic content was placed solely upon the retailer's shoulders. Since the accused was engaged in the retail business, he must accept such a risk as part and parcel of doing business.

Ping Yuen (1921): The vendor is absolutely liable for the contents of drinks sold in the store.

Cartoon by Elizabeth Carefoot

THE ARGUMENTS FOR AND AGAINST ABSOLUTE LIABILITY

Over the years, a number of arguments have been advanced in support of the concept of absolute liability. For example, it was asserted that those individuals who engage in activities that may harm the public welfare should be required to meet a high standard of care and attention. Many people believed that, by requiring the Crown to prove *mens rea* in relation to regulatory offences, too many legal loopholes would be created for individuals and corporations to evade their responsibilities to the public. It was argued that absolute liability would remove such loopholes and, thus, would act as an "incentive" for such persons to take precautionary measures, *over and above those that would normally be taken*, in order to ensure that mistakes and accidents did not occur. The theory was that, if an individual or a corporation realizes that there are no legal loopholes to slip through when they are charged with a regulatory offence, then they will take an extraordinary degree of care to avoid committing such an offence.

Another argument advanced in favour of absolute liability was that of administrative efficiency. It was alleged that it would be far too great a burden for the Crown to prove mental culpability in relation to the great number of petty regulatory offences that come before the courts. Since there is a need to process a large number of cases involving regulatory offences, it has been argued that the Crown must have access to a swift and administratively efficient system of law enforcement. It was contended that, if the Crown were required to establish *mens rea* in relation to regulatory offences, the whole system of justice would rapidly grind to a halt and, as a result, hundreds of thousands of violators would escape conviction. Therefore, it was contended that absolute liability was a pragmatic necessity if there was to be effective regulation of trade, commerce, and industry in the country.

There are, of course, numerous arguments that militate against the imposition of absolute liability. For example, one of the strongest arguments of this nature is that absolute liability contradicts a deeply ingrained sense of justice since it punishes those who lack any moral culpability. It is a basic notion in our society that an individual who lacks moral culpability should not be convicted of a criminal offence. As the great American Justice Oliver Wendell Holmes once said, "Even a dog distinguishes between being kicked and being stumbled over." Another argument against absolute liability is that it destroys the individual citizen's basic freedom of choice. Indeed, traditional legal theorists have persistently contended that the doctrine of *mens rea* is designed to maximize personal freedom because only the individual who deliberately chooses to break the law is subject to conviction. Absolute liability, of course, would destroy such freedom since it is not based on individual culpability.

In the *Sault Ste. Marie* case (1978), Justice Dickson of the Supreme Court of Canada presented a number of convincing arguments against the imposition of absolute liability:

> The most telling is that it violates fundamental principles of penal liability. It also rests upon assumptions which have not been, and cannot be, empirically established. There is no evidence that a higher standard of care results from absolute liability. If a person is already taking every reasonable precautionary measure, is he likely to take additional measures, knowing however much care he takes, it

will not serve as a defence in the event of breach? If he has exercised care and skill, will conviction have a deterrent effect upon him or others? Will the injustice of conviction lead to cynicism and disrespect for the law, on his part and on the part of others? These are among the questions asked. The argument that no stigma attaches does not withstand analysis, for the accused will have suffered loss of time, legal costs, exposure to the processes of criminal law at trial and, however one may downplay it, the opprobrium of conviction.

Similarly, in the decision of the Supreme Court of Canada in *Chapin* (1979), Justice Dickson pointed out that "the problems that may be encountered in the administration of a statute or regulation are a very unsure guide to its proper interpretation." Difficulty of enforcement is not *per se* a convincing reason for imposing absolute liability.

THE EMERGENCE OF A NEW APPROACH IN THE COURTS: THE "HALFWAY HOUSE" APPROACH

Whatever the arguments for and against absolute liability may be, there is little doubt that Canadian courts became increasingly uncomfortable with the rigid policy that they had embraced in relation to regulatory offences. Indeed, the courts had left themselves no room to manoeuvre: once they had decided that an offence was regulatory in nature, they would routinely impose absolute liability and thereby deprive the defendant of any defence based on his or her lack of fault.

Eventually, a more flexible judicial strategy began to emerge in relation to the disposition of cases involving regulatory offences. This strategy was based on the notion that it should be possible for defendants who are charged with regulatory offences to advance the defence that *they were not negligent*. Very quickly, this was dubbed the "**halfway house**" **approach** because it finds a middle ground between, on the one hand, requiring the Crown to prove all the *mens rea* elements of an offence beyond a reasonable doubt and, on the other, automatically convicting an accused person merely because he or she has committed the *actus reus* of a regulatory offence.

When the Crown charges an individual with a true crime, it must establish, beyond a reasonable doubt, all the elements of the *actus reus* and *mens rea* of the offence. In other words, the **primary or persuasional burden of proof** in relation to true crimes

is nearly always placed upon the shoulders of the Crown. Accused persons are under no obligation to prove their innocence, and it is enough for them to raise a reasonable doubt in order to escape conviction. However, the "halfway house" approach provides that the Crown merely has to prove that the accused committed the *actus reus* elements of the regulatory offence in question. At that point, the burden of proof shifts to the accused to establish his or her innocence by proving on the balance of probabilities that he or she was not negligent.

Placing the onus of establishing their innocence upon accused persons is clearly a fundamental departure from the normal rules of criminal law that apply in relation to real crimes. Indeed, the "halfway house" approach gives the Crown a significant advantage when prosecuting individuals for regulatory offences. This advantage is based on the fact that the Crown does not have to prove any mental element in relation to such offences. Unlike the doctrine of absolute liability, the "halfway house" approach *does* permit defendants to advance a defence: however, they must establish this "**due diligence**" defence on the balance of probabilities in order to escape conviction of a regulatory offence. It is not enough for the accused merely to raise a reasonable doubt as to whether he or she acted without negligence.

The term "**strict liability**" has been developed to distinguish those regulatory offences to which Canadian courts apply the "halfway house" approach from those regulatory offences to which the courts still apply the old regime of absolute liability.

THE SUPREME COURT ENDORSES THE "HALFWAY HOUSE" APPROACH: THE *SAULT STE. MARIE* CASE (1978)

In 1978, the Supreme Court of Canada strongly endorsed the "halfway house" approach in the seminal case of *Sault Ste. Marie* (1978). In his judgment, Justice Dickson delivered a strong critique of the various arguments that have been advanced in support of absolute liability. He noted that an increasing number of federal and provincial/territorial statutes were explicitly making provision for a defence of due diligence in the context of regulatory offences. Justice Dickson also pointed out that some Canadian courts were already attempting to apply the "halfway house" approach despite the fact that it had not yet been officially recognized by the Supreme Court of Canada. Justice Dickson then unequivocally expressed the view that the "halfway house" approach should be adopted as part of criminal law of Canada:

> The correct approach, in my opinion, is to relieve the Crown of the burden of proving *mens rea*, having regard to ... the virtual impossibility in most regulatory cases of proving wrongful intention. In a normal case, the accused alone will have knowledge of what he has done to avoid the breach and it is not improper to expect him to come forward with the evidence of due diligence. This is particularly so when it is alleged, for example, that pollution was caused by the activities of a large and complex corporation. Equally, there is nothing wrong with rejecting absolute liability and admitting the defence of reasonable care.
>
> In this doctrine it is not up to the prosecution to prove negligence. Instead, it is open to the defendant to prove that all due care has been taken. This burden falls upon the defendant as he is the only one who will generally have the means of proof. This would not seem unfair as the alternative is absolute liability which denies an accused any defence whatsoever. While the prosecution must prove beyond a reasonable doubt that the defendant committed the prohibited act, the defendant must only establish on the balance of probabilities that he has a defence of reasonable care.

THE THREE CATEGORIES OF OFFENCES SINCE THE *SAULT STE. MARIE* CASE (1978)

In delivering the judgment of the Supreme Court of Canada, Justice Dickson held that there are now three different categories of criminal offences in Canada:

1. Offences in which the existence of *mens rea* must be proved by the Crown beyond a reasonable doubt;
2. Strict liability offences, in which there is no necessity for the Crown to prove the existence of *mens rea* (however, defendants may avoid liability by proving that they acted with "due diligence");
3. Absolute liability offences, in which there is no necessity for the Crown to prove the existence of *mens rea* and in which it is not open to defendants to avoid liability by proving that they acted with "due diligence."

True crimes clearly fall within category 1. Nevertheless, some regulatory offences will also be included in category 1 if the legislature uses such words as "wilfully" or "knowingly," which indicate a clear intent to require proof of full *mens rea*. For example, in the case of *Stucky* (2009), the Ontario Court of Appeal ruled that the offence of making false or misleading representations to the public, contrary to s. 52(1) of the *Competition Act*, R.S.C. 1985, c. C-34, required proof of full *mens rea* because Parliament used the terms "knowingly or recklessly" in the definition of the offence.

However, *the vast majority of regulatory offences will fall within category 2 (strict liability).* Indeed, in *Kanda* (2008), the Ontario Court of Appeal took the view that, in the *Sault Ste. Marie* case, Justice Dickson had "articulated a presumption that public welfare offences are strict liability offences; accordingly, this presumption must be the starting point in an analysis of a regulatory provision." *Those regulatory offences that do not fall within categories 1 or 2 will be considered offences of "absolute liability" (category 3).* However, Justice Dickson stressed the point that regulatory offences will be placed in category 3 only where the legislature has made it perfectly clear that it intends to impose a regime of absolute liability. In this respect, Justice Dickson said that

> [t]he over-all regulatory pattern adopted by the Legislature, the subject-matter of the Legislation, the importance of the penalty, and the precision of the language used will be primary considerations in determining whether the offence falls into the third category.

It is significant that, almost 30 years later, in *Levis (Ville) v. Tétreault* (2006), the Supreme Court of Canada strongly reaffirmed the existence of the three categories of offences which were fashioned by Justice Dickson in the *Sault Ste. Marie* case. However, Justice LeBel, in delivering the judgment of the Supreme Court of Canada in *Levis*, noted that the three categories were "based on a presumption of statutory interpretation." It was not until 1982 (four years after the decision in *Sault Ste. Marie*), that the *Canadian Charter of Rights and Freedoms* was enacted and, since that time, the development of a body of *Charter* jurisprudence has undoubtedly had a far-reaching impact on the treatment of regulatory offences by the courts. In particular, as we shall see later in this chapter, the Supreme Court of Canada has ruled that imposing a regime of absolute liability, when conviction of the offence in question may result in the imprisonment of the offender, violates the fundamental principles of justice enshrined in section 7 of the *Charter*. Therefore, both statutory interpretation and Charter jurisprudence will have an impact on a court's decision whether to classify a regulatory offence as being one of strict or absolute liability. As Justice LeBel remarked in *Levis*, "[A]bsolute liability offences still exist, but they have become an exception requiring clear proof of legislative intent."

THE FACTS IN THE *SAULT STE. MARIE* CASE (1978)

In the *Sault Ste. Marie* case (1978), the facts were that the accused was a municipal corporation that had been charged with the offence of "discharging, causing to be discharged, or permitting to be discharged or deposited materials into a body of water or on the shore or bank thereof, or in such place that might impair the quality of the water," contrary to section 32(1) of the Ontario *Water Resources Act*, R.S.O. 1970, c. 332. The City of Sault Ste. Marie entered into an agreement with a private company for the disposal of all of the city's refuse. The company chose to dump garbage on a site that bordered a creek. Garbage was dumped over a number of freshwater springs that flowed into the creek. After a period, water pollution resulted from this method of garbage disposal. How did the Supreme Court determine into which category the offence charged fell? Was it a true crime requiring proof of full *mens rea* or was it a regulatory offence imposing either strict or absolute liability?

Justice Dickson indicated that "pollution offences are undoubtedly public welfare (regulatory) offences enacted in the interests of public health. There is thus no presumption of a full *mens rea*." Indeed, he said that such a presumption applies only in the case of offences that are "criminal in the true sense." Justice Dickson then decided that the offence charged fell within the second category of offences—namely, offences of strict liability. The major reason for this decision was that, in the legislation that created the offence with which the defendant was charged, the Ontario legislature had not used words that indicated unequivocally that it intended to impose absolute liability. By placing the offence charged within the category of strict liability offences, the Court, therefore, made available to the defendant a defence of acting with "due diligence." A new trial was ordered in which the City of Sault

Ste. Marie would have the opportunity to show that it had acted with such "due diligence."

THE CLASSIFICATION OF REGULATORY OFFENCES: STRICT OR ABSOLUTE LIABILITY?

How do the courts distinguish between those regulatory offences that impose strict liability and those regulatory offences that impose absolute liability? Fortunately, Parliament or the provincial/ territorial legislature concerned will often make explicit provision for a defence of due diligence in the legislation that creates the regulatory offence in question. Conversely, the relevant legislative body may explicitly state that a regulatory offence is one of absolute liability. However, there are many regulatory offences for which the legislators have made no explicit provision of this type: it is, therefore, left to the courts to decide whether these particular offences impose strict or absolute liability. It will be remembered that, in the *Sault Ste. Marie* case (1978), Justice Dickson referred to the following factors that should normally be considered by the courts when they are faced with the need to classify a regulatory offence as being one of strict or absolute liability: (1) the overall regulatory pattern adopted by the legislature, (2) the subject matter of the legislation, (3) the importance of the penalty, and (4) the precision of the language. These are, by no means, the only factors to be considered: indeed, *Charter* considerations may be a critical element in the decision-making process of the courts. Nevertheless, the four factors identified by Justice Dickson certainly constitute an important starting point.

1. THE IMPORTANCE OF EXAMINING THE OVERALL REGULATORY PATTERN IN A STATUTE

In his judgment in *Sault Ste. Marie* (1978), Justice Dickson referred to the "overall regulatory pattern" as being an important criterion in making the decision whether a particular regulatory offence should be considered as being one of strict or absolute liability. By this he meant that, if a legislature expressly included a defence of due diligence for some offences in a regulatory statute but failed to do so for other offences within the same statute, one may normally conclude that the legislature intended to impose absolute liability in relation to the second group of offences.

This principle is illustrated by the case of *Kurtzman* (1991), in which the Ontario Court of Appeal ruled that the offence of failing to stop at a red light, contrary to section 124(16) of the *Highway Traffic Act*, R.S.O. 1980, c. 198, was an offence of absolute, rather than strict, liability.[1] Justice Tarnopolsky stated that other provisions in the same part of the Act clearly envisaged that a defence of due diligence should be made available to the accused person and concluded that, "if the legislature had intended s. 124(16) to be construed in a similar manner, so as to exculpate an accused who has made reasonable and prudent efforts to stop his or her vehicle, it could have included similar language."

However, it does not necessarily follow that a court will always find a regulatory offence to be one of absolute liability in such circumstances (as we shall see in the *Rube* case (1992), which is discussed later in this chapter). Although the overall regulatory pattern of the statute is always a *relevant* factor, it is not always a *decisive* one.

2. THE IMPORTANCE OF EXAMINING THE SUBJECT MATTER OF THE REGULATORY OFFENCE

The "subject matter of the offence" is often an important consideration in determining whether a regulatory offence is one of absolute rather than strict liability. In general, it would appear that the greater the threat to the public that is posed by the commission of a regulatory offence, the more likely it is that this offence will be found to impose a regime of absolute liability.

For example, in Ontario, the Court of Appeal has indicated that, if public safety is the subject matter of regulatory legislation, then it is more likely that offences under that legislation will be considered as offences of absolute liability (if the legislature has not indicated otherwise by, for example, providing for a due diligence defence). In the *Kurtzman* case (1991), by way of example, the Court stated that the subject matter of the offence of failing to stop at a red light under the provisions of the *Highway Traffic Act* was indeed public safety:

> The apparent object of the *Highway Traffic Act* is the safe and orderly conduct of traffic on public highways. With respect to s. 124(16) specifically, users of the

highways obey traffic signals at intersections in reliance on similar obedience by other users of the highways. The need for strict regulation for the purposes of safety is thus apparent.

For similar reasons, the Ontario Court of Appeal has held that the offence of speeding, contrary to s. 128 of the *Highway Traffic Act*, R.S.O. 1990, c. H.8, is an offence of absolute liability.[2] For example, in *London (City) v. Polewsky* (2005), the Court stated that

> [s]peed is a factor in many collisions. The overall regulatory pattern adopted by the legislature, the subject matter of the legislation, and the language used suggest that speeding should continue to be interpreted as an offence of absolute liability.

By way of contrast, in *Kanda* (2008), the Ontario Court of Appeal ruled that the offence of driving a vehicle in which a passenger under the age of 16 is not wearing a seat belt is a strict, rather than an absolute, liability offence. The offence is defined by section 106(6) of the *Highway Traffic Act*, R.S.O. 1990, c. H.8.[3] Kanda had been charged with the offence after it was discovered by a police officer that Kanda's eight-year-old son was not wearing his seat belt. Kanda stated that he was unaware that his son had unfastened the belt after he had commenced his journey. The trial judge convicted Kanda, in spite of his explanation, because the offence was one of absolute liability. Upon appeal, however, it was decided that the offence was one of strict liability and that the case should be sent back to the trial judge in order to allow Kanda to raise a defence of having acted with due diligence. In delivering the judgment of the Ontario Court of Appeal, Justice MacPherson paid considerable attention to the subject matter of the offence:

> Section 106 of the *HTA* requires most people riding in motor vehicles to wear seat belts. The "important statutory purpose" of the seat belt law is "minimizing driver and passenger injuries resulting from car collisions."... Subsection 106(6) of the *HTA* advances this purpose by making drivers responsible

---

[1] See now section 144(18) of the *Highway Traffic Act*, R.S.O. 1990, c. H.8.

[2] Some appellate courts in other provinces/ territories have adopted the approach taken in Ontario and have also declared speeding to be an absolute liability offence: for example, the B.C. Court of Appeal did so in the case of *Harper* (1986). However, other appellate courts have refused to do so. For example, in *Williams* (1992), the Appeal Division of the Nova Scotia Supreme Court held that speeding was an offence of strict liability and that the accused, therefore, has the opportunity to advance a defence of due diligence.

[3] Now section 106(4).

for ensuring that all passengers under 16 years of age use seat belts. The provision is clearly intended to ensure the safety of vulnerable youthful passengers who cannot be relied upon to take responsibility for their own safety.

However, while the offence is concerned with public safety, this does not mean that it imposes absolute liability. Justice MacPherson asserted that the argument that absolute liability is necessary for effective enforcement does not hold water:

> … [T]o regard strict liability as a serious diminution of enforcement capacity is a misconception. Strict liability is what its name implies—a serious commitment to enforcement of the law. In most cases, if a person commits the act proscribed by the law a conviction will follow because establishing the defence of due diligence or reasonable care will not be easy.

Therefore, Justice MacPherson concluded that

> … the subject matter of s. 106(6) of the *HTA* supports a classification of the offence as strict liability. This classification strikes an appropriate balance between encouraging drivers to be vigilant about the safety of child passengers in their vehicles and not punishing those who exercise due diligence with respect to children's seat belts.

3. THE IMPORTANCE OF THE PENALTY IN DETERMINING WHETHER A REGULATORY OFFENCE IMPOSES STRICT OR ABSOLUTE LIABILITY

The Supreme Court of Canada's decision in *Chapin* (1979) illustrates the principle that, if a severe penalty may be imposed upon conviction of a regulatory offence, it is highly unlikely that the courts will

The Kanda case: strict liability and the duty to act with due diligence to buckle up children.

Cartoon by Greg Holoboff

consider such an offence to be one of absolute liability. Ms. Chapin was charged with an offence under section 14(1) of the *Migratory Bird Regulations*, which provided that "… no person shall hunt for migratory game birds within one-quarter mile of any place where bait has been deposited." There were a number of significant penalties that could be imposed following a conviction. Indeed, Section 12(1) of the *Migratory Birds Convention Act*, R.S.C. 1970, c. M-12, provided, "Every person who violates this Act or any regulation is, for each offence, liable upon summary conviction to a fine of not more than $300 and not less than $10, or to imprisonment for a term not exceeding six months, or to both fine and imprisonment." Section 22(1) of the Act also provided for a mandatory prohibition, upon conviction, of either holding or applying for a migratory game bird hunting permit for a period of one year from the date of conviction. Clearly, these were relatively severe penalties by any measure and it was this factor that persuaded the Supreme Court of Canada that the offence should be considered one of strict, rather than absolute, liability.

Justice Dickson pointed out that the normal presumption was that a regulatory offence imposes strict liability and that the Crown must, therefore, advance strong arguments as to why this presumption should be displaced in any given case. Justice Dickson, in delivering the judgment of the Supreme Court, rejected the argument that difficulties of enforcement justified the imposition of absolute liability and focused his attention on the relatively severe penalties that might be imposed upon conviction:

> Difficulty of enforcement is hardly enough to dislodge the offence from the category of strict liability, particularly when regard is had to the penalties that may ensue from conviction. I do not think that the public interest … requires that s. 14 of the Regulations be interpreted so that an innocent person should be convicted and fined and also suffer the mandatory loss of his hunting permit and the possible forfeiture of his hunting equipment, merely in order to facilitate prosecution.

In the *Chapin* case (1979), the perceived severity of the penalties that might have been imposed led the Supreme Court to conclude that the regulatory offence in question was one of strict, rather than absolute, liability. The *Kurtzman* case (1991) illustrates the converse proposition—namely, that the imposition of a light penalty may be one of the considerations that might persuade a court to rule that the legislature intended to render a regulatory offence one of absolute liability. In this case, the Ontario Court of Appeal ruled that the offence of failing to stop at a red light, in contravention of section 124(16) of the *Highway Traffic Act*, R.S.O. 1980, c. 198,[4] should be considered an absolute, rather than strict, liability offence because, among other reasons, the penalties were relatively trivial. Justice Tarnopolsky pointed out that the penalty for conviction of the offence was a minimum fine of $60 and a maximum of $500. He went on to state that

> [i]mprisonment is not a potential penalty except, perhaps, in default of payment. Also, I would agree ... that there is today little, if any, stigma attached to the violation of the *Highway Traffic Act* provisions concerning compliance with traffic signal indicators. I note, too, that suspension or revocation of one's driver's licence is not a penalty which may be imposed upon conviction under s. 124(16) alone.

4. The Importance of Examining the Precise Wording of Regulatory Legislation

The language used by the legislature has been considered an important yardstick in determining whether a regulatory offence is one of absolute, rather than strict, liability. For example, in the *Kurtzman* case (1991), the Ontario Court of Appeal paid close attention to the precise wording of the Ontario *Highway Traffic Act* in drawing the conclusion that failing to stop for a red light was an offence of absolute liability. In this respect, Justice Tarnopolsky noted that the "words used in s. 124(16) are mandatory and clearly do not anticipate a defence of due diligence or reasonable care being raised."[5] In his view, the language used in section 124(16) was "mandatory and absolute," and it made no sense to inquire into the "reasonableness of the driver's efforts":

> ... [T]he driver either stops or he does not. In this case, he did not and, therefore, in my view, he contravened the provision.

On the other hand, in the *Kanda* case (2008), the Ontario Court of Appeal held that the wording of another section of the Ontario *Highway Traffic Act*

imposes strict, rather than absolute, liability. In this case, the section in question was section 106:[6]

> 106(6) No person shall drive on a highway a motor vehicle in which there is a passenger who is under sixteen years of age and occupies a seating position for which a seat belt assembly has been provided unless that passenger is wearing the complete seat belt assembly and it is properly adjusted and securely fastened.

In delivering the judgment of the Court of Appeal, Justice MacPherson subjected the wording of this section to an extensive analysis before concluding that it created an offence of strict liability:

> ... [T]he *HTA* explicitly creates offences in all three categories of regulatory offences. Subsection 106(6) does not contain the triggering language that would make classification virtually automatic...
>
> First, the case law does not support the proposition that the language "no person shall" points to absolute liability....
>
> It is true that some offences employing the "no person shall" or "every driver shall" formulation have been interpreted as absolute liability offences.... However, in those cases the proscribed conduct resulted directly from the person's own action. Section 106(6) of the *HTA*, on the other hand, deals with a situation in which another person—the child passenger—is potentially involved in creating the violation.
>
> Second, s. 106(6) of the *HTA* does not expressly exclude the defence of due diligence. The language of absolute liability is well-known and has been used by the legislature in the *HTA* in s. 84.1. If the legislature wanted to impose the serious consequences that flow from the creation of an absolute liability offence, the means for so doing would have been known and available. Third,... where the section in essence creates an offence of failing to meet a standard or duty of care..., in respect of another person, it is counterintuitive to suggest that the defendant cannot raise a defence of due diligence or reasonable care.

Raising the Defence of Due Diligence

Once it has been established that the offence that has been charged is one of strict liability, the onus shifts to the accused person to prove that he or she acted with "due diligence." An excellent example of the application of the due diligence defence is furnished

---

[4] See now section 144(18) of the *Highway Traffic Act*, R.S.O. 1990, c. H. 8.
[5] See now section 144(18) &(20), *Highway Traffic Act*, R.S.O. 1990, c. H. 8.

[6] Now section 106(4).

by the case of *London Excavators & Trucking Ltd.* (1998). The accused company was an excavating subcontractor that had been hired to work on a large construction project at a hospital site. The general contractor told the accused company that the area to be excavated was "clear" of any "gas, electrical, and other services." The accused company had worked with the general contractor before and considered it to be "knowledgeable and reliable." During the course of the excavating operations, the accused company's backhoe operator struck some concrete and stopped his machine. The general contractor's assistant supervisor stated that the concrete was just "part of the footing of an old nursing station" and told the backhoe operator to remove it. In fact, the concrete encased a hydro duct and, when it was penetrated by the backhoe, there was an explosion. Neither the accused company's foreperson nor its backhoe operator had taken any steps to check the accuracy of the information that had been provided to them by the assistant supervisor of the general contractor. A plan of the construction site that was in the possession of the general contractor showed the existence and exact location of the hydro duct that was struck; however, it had never been shown to the accused company.

Fortunately, there were no injuries as a consequence of this excavating misadventure. However, the accused company was duly charged for having *failed to ensure that the required safety procedures were carried out* in accordance with the provisions of the Ontario *Occupational Health and Safety Act*, R.S.O. 1990, c. O.1. Under the relevant set of regulations, excavation work should not commence until the various services in the area have been "accurately located and marked." The accused company, as an employer, was placed under a statutory duty to "request the owner of the service to locate and mark the service." Section 25(1)(c) of the Act stated that the employer "shall ensure ... that the measures and procedures prescribed are carried out in the work." The Act made clear that a subcontractor will be considered an "employer" for the purposes of these safety provisions. Section 66(3) of the Act also established a due diligence defence: namely, "it shall be a defence for the accused to prove that every precaution reasonable in the circumstances was taken." In light of these statutory provisions, there was no doubt that the accused company had been charged with a strict liability offence and that it was required to prove the defence of due diligence on the balance of probabilities.

The accused company contended that it had honestly believed the information provided to it by the general contractor's supervisors to be accurate and had "faithfully passed it on" to the accused company's foreperson. However, the accused company was nevertheless convicted because it had not established that it had taken every reasonable precaution. It was not enough to claim that it had honestly relied on the word of the general contractor's supervisors. The Ontario Court of Appeal upheld the conviction of London Excavators & Trucking Ltd. Justice Catzman succinctly indicated why the accused company had failed to establish the due diligence defence:

> It was not objectively reasonable for the appellant to continue to rely, without further inquiry, upon the direction of the general contractor once an unexpected concrete obstacle had been encountered in a location the general contractor had pronounced safe to excavate. At that point, it was incumbent on the appellant, in the interest of the safety of its employees and others who might be exposed to the risk of harm, to ensure that the prescribed measures and procedures designed to protect their safety had been carried out in the workplace.... [T]he appellant could have done so in a number of ways: it could have insisted on seeing the site plan ... it could have insisted on seeing a locate certificate issued by the utility; if ... there was no such certificate, it could have halted work until the utility's representative had attended at the site and done the locates; or it could itself have ordered hydro locates for the area in which it was expected to excavate.

Similarly, in *Levis (Ville) v. Tétreault* (2006), a Quebec-based company (2629-4470 Québec Inc.) was charged, under s. 31.1. of the Quebec *Highway Safety Code*, R.S.Q., c. C-24.2, with operating a motor vehicle without the necessary registration fees. Tétreault (the driver) was charged with driving a vehicle without a valid driver's licence, contrary to s. 93.1 of the *Highway Safety Code*. It was established that both of these offences imposed strict liability, and both the company and Tétreault claimed that they had acted with due diligence. However, the company's defence was based merely on the fact that, while it had been informed that it would receive a renewal notice in relation to the registration fees, no such notice was ever delivered. Tétreault's defence turned on his assertion that he had also expected to receive a renewal notice in relation to his licence and that he had mixed up the expiry date for his licence with the due date for payment of the licence fees. The lower courts acquitted the company and Tétreault of the charges against them, accepting their defences of acting with due diligence. However, the Supreme Court of Canada set aside the acquittals and entered convictions because the accused had not proved that they had acted with due diligence. Indeed, the Court emphasized that "passive ignorance" does not constitute a valid defence to charges under regulatory legislation.

On behalf of the Supreme Court, Justice LeBel said:

> In Mr. Tétreault's case, the judgments of the courts below confused passivity with diligence. The accused did no more than state that he expected to receive a renewal notice for his licence and that he had confused the licence expiry date with the due date for paying the fees required to keep the licence valid. He proved no action or attempt to obtain information. The concept of diligence is based on the acceptance of a citizen's civic duty to take action to find out what his or her obligations are. Passive ignorance is not a valid defence in criminal law.

The Supreme Court took a similar approach in relation to the charge against the company. In Justice LeBel's words:

> In my view, the respondent's allegations of fact do not show conduct that meets the standard of due diligence. The respondent was aware of the date when the fees relating to the registration of its vehicle would be due and, accordingly, the date when the registration would cease to be valid. It could and should have been concerned when it failed to receive a notice. Instead, it did nothing. It had a duty to do more.

Employers are frequently made the target of prosecutions under regulatory legislation and, of course, they may raise the defence of due diligence if they are charged with an offence of strict liability. In this respect, it is important to remember that, although an *employee* is usually the individual who commits the act that effectively precipitates a prosecution for a regulatory offence, the trial court must nevertheless focus its attention upon the issue of whether the employer acted with due diligence. The court will generally ask whether the employer took *reasonable steps to ensure that his or her employees carried out their jobs in accordance with the standards set by the regulatory legislation concerned.* For example, did the employer institute an adequate training program for employees, and did the

employer maintain an adequate system for monitoring employee performance?

Take, by way of example, the Nova Scotia case of *Sobey's Inc.* (1998), where the employer, a corporation, had been charged with the sale of tobacco or a tobacco product to a person under the age of 19 years (contrary to section 5(1) of the *Tobacco Access Act*, S.N.S. 1993, c. 14). The Nova Scotia Court of Appeal emphasized that the central issue in the case was not whether the employee who allegedly sold the tobacco was "duly diligent," but rather whether Sobey's Inc. acted with due diligence in all of the circumstances. In delivering the judgment of the Court of Appeal, Justice Cromwell quoted the words of Justice Dickson in the *Sault Ste. Marie* case (1978):

> Where an employer is charged in respect of an act committed by an employee acting in the course of employment, the question will be whether the act took place without the accused's direction or approval ... and whether the accused exercised all reasonable care by taking reasonable steps to ensure the effective operation of the system.

IS STRICT LIABILITY A VALID DEVICE UNDER THE *CHARTER*?

The decision in the *Sault Ste. Marie* case (1978) is based on the recognition of a category of regulatory offences that impose strict liability. However, *Sault Ste. Marie* was decided before the enactment of the *Charter*, and a critical question that arises is whether strict liability is constitutionally valid. As we have noted, the very essence of strict liability is the requirement that the accused shoulder the responsibility of proving that he or she acted without negligence (the defence of due diligence). It might well be argued that requiring the accused to establish his or her innocence is an infringement of the presumption of innocence guaranteed by section 11(d) of the *Charter*, and that strict liability is, therefore, an invalid device that should be struck down. Precisely this argument was advanced in the case of *Wholesale Travel Group Inc.* (1991). However, a majority of the justices of the Supreme Court of Canada rejected this contention and upheld the constitutional validity of strict liability.

The *Wholesale Travel Group Inc.* case was concerned with the offence of false or misleading advertising under the provisions of the federal *Competition Act*, R.S.C. 1970, c. C-23. Under (what was then) s. 37.3(2) of the Act, Parliament made available a defence of due diligence to those charged with false or misleading advertising:

> No person shall be convicted of an offence under section 36 or 36.1, *if he establishes that,*
>
> > (a)   the act or omission giving rise to the offence with which he was charged was the result of error;
> >
> > (b)   he took reasonable precautions and exercised due diligence to prevent the occurrence of such error.... [emphasis added]

The majority of the justices of the Supreme Court of Canada took the view that placing the onus on the accused to prove the defence of due diligence was not invalid under the *Charter.* Three of the five justices in the majority took the view that strict liability did infringe section 11(d) of the *Charter* but that it was justified as a reasonable limitation under section 1. The other two justices in the majority contended that, if one looks at strict liability within the specific context of regulatory offences, it does not violate section 11(d) of the *Charter* and that, even if it did, it would be saved by section 1.

Speaking for those justices who believed that strict liability did infringe the *Charter* but was saved by section 1, Justice Iacobucci said that there was no doubt that "the reverse onus on the accused to establish due diligence on a balance of probabilities" violates section 11(d) of the *Charter.* However, the critical issue was whether this infringement of the accused's *Charter* right is "demonstrably justified in a free and democratic society." Justice Iacobucci applied the so-called *Oakes* test and concluded that the infringement was justified.

The first issue under the *Oakes* test is whether Parliament's objective was of "sufficient importance to warrant overriding a constitutionally protected right or freedom." In this particular case, Justice Iacobucci concluded that

> ... the specific objective of placing a persuasive burden on an accused to prove due diligence is to ensure that all those who are guilty of false or misleading advertising are convicted of these public welfare offences *and to avoid the loss of convictions because of evidentiary problems which arise because the relevant facts are peculiarly in the knowledge of the accused.* The legislative objective is of sufficient importance to warrant overriding the right guaranteed by s. 11(d) of the *Charter.* It relates to concerns which are "pressing and substantial" in Canadian

society; especially when one considers the over-all objective of the *Competition Act* which is to promote vigorous and fair competition throughout Canada. [emphasis in original]

The second issue under the *Oakes* test is whether there is an appropriate degree of proportionality between Parliament's legitimate objective and the means used to achieve that objective (namely, placing the onus on the accused to prove the defence of due diligence). Justice Iacobucci asserted that there clearly was a "rational connection between the desired objective and the means chosen to attain the objective." The device of strict liability and the undeniable advantages that it gives to the Crown in prosecuting an individual for having committed a regulatory offence undoubtedly advance the objective of ensuring that there is an increased likelihood of convicting those who have engaged in false or misleading advertising.

However, under the *Oakes* test, it must also be established that placing the onus on the accused to prove the due diligence offence impaired the presumption of innocence "as little as possible" in order to accomplish Parliament's objective. Justice Iacobucci concluded that there was no reasonable alternative device to which Parliament could have turned in order to pursue its objective of effective enforcement of regulatory legislation. In particular, he rejected the suggestion that Parliament could have adopted the alternative of imposing a "mandatory presumption of negligence" in regulatory offences. Adoption of this approach would mean that, once the Crown had proved the *actus reus* elements of the offence, there would be a presumption that the accused was negligent and, unless he or she introduced evidence that raised a reasonable doubt about this issue, the trial court must enter a conviction. The problem with this alternative, according to Justice Iacobucci, is that in practice the accused is the only person who is likely to have a detailed knowledge of the steps that he or she has taken to avoid committing a regulatory offence; in other words, the accused will usually be the only party who is in a position to bring forward evidence relating to due diligence. If an accused person could escape conviction of a regulatory offence merely by raising a reasonable doubt, it would place the Crown in a thoroughly disadvantageous position because, at the end of the trial, it would have to prove facts that were "largely within the peculiar knowledge of the accused." In the view of Justice Iacobucci, "[S]uch an alternative would in practice make it virtually impossible for the Crown to prove public welfare offences such as the one in question and would effectively prevent governments from seeking to implement public policy through prosecution."

Finally, under the *Oakes* test, it must be shown that "the means chosen must be such that their effects on the limitation of rights and freedoms are proportional to the objective." On this topic, Justice Iacobucci stated that

> ... regulated activity and public welfare offences are a fundamental part of Canadian society. Those who choose to participate in regulated activities must be taken to have accepted the consequential responsibilities and their penal enforcement. One of these consequences is that they should be held responsible for the harm that may result from their lack of due diligence. Unless they can prove on the balance of probabilities that they exercised due diligence, they shall be convicted and in some cases face a possible prison term. These participants are in the best position to prove due diligence since they possess in most cases the required information. Viewed in this context, and taking into account the fundamental importance of the legislative objective as stated and the fact that the means chosen impair the rights guaranteed by s. 11(d) as little as reasonably possible, the effects of the reverse onus on the presumption of innocence are proportional to the objective.

Justice Cory (with whom Justice L'Heureux-Dubé agreed) took the view that strict liability did not infringe section 11(d) of the *Charter* in the first place. In his view, in considering whether section 11(d) was infringed by placing the onus on the accused to prove the defence of due diligence, one must take account of the fact that the context is one of regulatory offences rather than true crimes:

> Criminal offences have always required proof of guilt beyond a reasonable doubt; the accused cannot, therefore, be convicted where there is a reasonable doubt as to guilt. This is not so with regulatory offences, where a conviction will lie if the accused has failed to meet the standard of care required. Thus, the question is not whether the accused exercised *some* care, but whether the degree of care exercised was sufficient to meet the standard imposed. If the false advertiser, the corporate polluter and the manufacturer of noxious goods are to be effectively controlled, it is necessary to require them to show on a balance of probabilities that they took reasonable precautions to avoid the harm which actually resulted. *In the regulatory context, there is nothing unfair about imposing that onus; indeed, it is essential for the protection of our vulnerable society.* [emphasis added]

Indubitably, the *Wholesale Travel Group Inc.* case (1991) has settled an extremely important question of principle under the *Charter* and has placed the "halfway house" approach, embodied in strict liability, on a firm constitutional basis. Unfortunately, many other questions still have to be answered in the area of regulatory offences in Canada, particularly insofar as absolute liability offences are concerned.

IS THERE ANY ROOM FOR STRICT LIABILITY IN THE *CRIMINAL CODE*?

In general, it appears to be well established that strict liability is a concept that is not applicable to the "real crimes" that are encapsulated in the *Criminal Code*. However, in the *Smillie* case (1998), the B.C. Court of Appeal suggested that there may well be exceptional circumstances in which it may be appropriate to characterize a *Criminal Code* offence as being one of strict liability. The accused had been charged with three counts of storing a firearm in a manner contrary to a regulation that had been issued under the authority of (what was then) section 116(1)(g) of the *Criminal Code*. At the time of the alleged offence, section 86(3) of the *Code* provided that[7]

> [e]very person who stores, displays, handles or transports a firearm in a manner contrary to a regulation made under paragraph 116(1)(g)(a) is guilty of an indictable offence and liable to imprisonment for a term not exceeding two years.

The trial judge ruled that the charges against the accused infringed the fundamental principles of justice protected by section 7 of the *Charter* and quashed all the counts in the indictment. However, the Crown appealed, and the B.C. Court of Appeal ruled that the offence charged did not, after all, violate the provisions of the *Charter*.

In delivering the judgment of the Court of Appeal, Justice Ryan noted that Parliament had

---

[7] The *Criminal Code* was amended in 1998. The equivalent provision is now s. 86(2), which provides: "Every person commits an offence who contravenes a regulation made under paragraph 117(h) of the Firearms Act respecting the storage, handling, transportation, shipping, display, advertising and mail-order sales of firearms and restricted weapons."

established a "strict regime with respect to the storage, display, handling, and transportation of firearms." In order to obtain a conviction under (what was then) section 86(3), the Crown was merely required to establish that the accused did not store firearms in accordance with the provisions of the regulations issued under the authority of the *Criminal Code*. In other words, Justice Ryan ruled that the offence under section 86(3) of the *Code* does not require the proof of any form of *mens rea* on the part of the accused. The Crown does not even have to establish that the accused acted negligently. It will suffice if it proves that the accused failed to abide by the terms of the relevant regulations. Justice Ryan held that the offence was, in reality, "quasi-regulatory" in nature: "although it is found in the *Criminal Code*, it is essentially a regulatory measure in the interest of public safety." Therefore, the Court of Appeal characterized the offence as being one of *strict liability* and noted that the accused could "defend the charge by raising a reasonable doubt with respect to a mistake of fact or by raising a doubt that he or she was duly diligent in his [*sic*] efforts to comply with the regulation in question."

In firmly rejecting the assertion of Smillie's counsel that section 86(3) infringed section 7 of the *Charter*, Justice Ryan ruled that the nature of the minimal fault requirements for conviction of an offence "are contextually flexible and will depend on a number of factors":

> "True" criminal offences are presumed to require full *mens rea*, but as the offence moves down the continuum to acquire a regulatory aspect, that is, to impose sanctions for the prevention of harm rather than to punish for past conduct, the requirement for full *mens rea* diminishes.

According to Justice Ryan, any person who enters a manifestly dangerous area of conduct, such as dealing with firearms, must fully expect that there will be government regulation of such activity, and it must be presumed that he or she will be aware of this regulatory regime:

> ... [W]here a person is voluntarily operating in a regulated area, and therefore deemed to have notice of the standard of care required of him or her, the *mens rea* requirement loses importance and, where the maximum punishment is not high, the necessity for full *mens rea* will not be as great.

The offence under (what was then) section 86(3) is, according to the B.C. Court of Appeal, a "quasi-regulatory" offence, which carries a maximum sentence of imprisonment of two years ("not insignificant, but not high for an indictable offence"). In this sense, Justice Ryan believed that the offence did not "give rise to a significant degree of stigma." Furthermore, the accused may rely on a defence of due diligence in relation to his or her efforts to meet the standards prescribed by the relevant regulation. In light of all these factors, Justice Ryan took the view that the offence under section 86(3) did not result in the punishment of individuals who are totally lacking in blameworthiness: "there is an element of mental fault or moral culpability present (that is) proportionate to the seriousness and consequences of the offence." That being the case, there was no infringement of section 7 of the *Charter*.

It is significant that Justice Ryan stated that the accused need only *raise a reasonable doubt* as to whether he or she acted with due diligence. This means that the type of strict liability referred to by the B.C. Court of Appeal in *Smillie* (1998) is significantly different from the type of strict liability with which we are all familiar in the context of federal and provincial/territorial regulatory legislation. Indeed, as we have seen, the "halfway house approach," which is the characteristic hallmark of strict liability in the context of federal and provincial/territorial regulatory legislation, is ultimately based on the requirement that the accused must prove the defence of due diligence *on the balance of probabilities*. Furthermore, it is noteworthy that, in 1998, Parliament amended section 86 of the *Criminal Code* so as to give the Crown the option of proceeding either by indictment or by the summary conviction procedure.[8]

THE *CHARTER* AND ABSOLUTE LIABILITY OFFENCES

The *Wholesale Travel Group Inc.* case (1991) unequivocally established that a regime of strict liability is not invalid under the *Charter*. However, the Supreme Court of Canada has adopted a fundamentally different approach vis-à-vis statutes that create offences of absolute liability. Indeed, the Court has held that, as a general rule, absolute liability offences are invalid under the *Charter*—if they may be punished by the imposition of a term of imprisonment.

---

[8] See s. 86(3), which came into effect on December 1, 1998.

The leading authority on this issue is the landmark decision of the Supreme Court of Canada in *Reference re Section 94(2) of the Motor Vehicle Act R.S.B.C. (1979)* (1985), which raised the issue of whether section 94(2) of the *Motor Vehicle Act*, R.S.B.C. 1979 was consistent with the requirements of the *Charter*. Section 94(1) of the *Motor Vehicle Act* stated that it was an offence for any person to drive a vehicle while he or she was prohibited or suspended from driving. The penalty for breaching the provisions of this section was, on first conviction, a fine and imprisonment for not less than seven days and not more than six months (in other words, a mandatory prison sentence). Section 94(2) explicitly stated that the offence created by section 94(1) "creates an absolute liability offence in which guilt is established by proof of driving, whether or not the defendant knew of the prohibition or suspension." Not surprisingly, the Supreme Court declared this draconian provision to be contrary to the provisions of the *Charter* and refused to "save" it under section 1. Justice Lamer stated the issue very simply:

> A law that has the potential to convict a person who has not really done anything wrong offends the principles of fundamental justice and, if imprisonment is available as a penalty, such a law then violates a person's right to liberty under s. 7 (of the *Charter*)....
>
> In other words, absolute liability and imprisonment cannot be combined. [emphasis added]

Significantly, Justice Lamer indicated that it makes no difference whether the imprisonment that may be imposed following a conviction of an absolute liability offence is *discretionary* or, as in the case of section 94(2), *mandatory*:

> Obviously, imprisonment (including probation orders) deprives persons of their liberty. An offence has that potential as of the moment it is open to the judge to impose imprisonment. There is no need that imprisonment, as in section 94(2), be made mandatory.

On the other hand, Justice Lamer did not address the critical issue of whether imprisonment, *as an alternative to the non-payment of a fine*, would contravene section 7 of the *Charter* when an absolute liability offence is concerned. In the later case of *Pontes* (1995), the majority of the Supreme Court of Canada expressly left this issue "up in the air." As Justice Cory stated,

> I would leave open for future consideration the situation presented by an absolute liability offence

punishable by fine with the possibility of imprisonment for its non-payment in those circumstances where the legislation provides that the imposition and collection of any fine is subject to a means test.

This issue has been addressed, however, by a few provincial/territorial courts of appeal. For example, the Saskatchewan Court of Appeal held, in *Burt* (1987), that section 7 of the *Charter* is infringed where conviction of an absolute liability offence could lead to imprisonment, if only as a consequence of non-payment of a fine. The Appeal Division of the Nova Scotia Supreme Court expressly adopted this approach in the case of *Williams* (1992). Furthermore, in *Nickel City Transport (Sudbury) Ltd.* (1993), one of the members of the Ontario Court of Appeal, Justice Arbour, expressed the view that "the combination of an absolute liability regime, *together with a scheme of imprisonment for default of payment of a fine that does not address ability to pay*," would infringe section 7 of the *Charter*. Significantly, Justice Arbour's analysis was subsequently endorsed by Justice Fish of the Quebec Court of Appeal in *Québec (Procureur Général) v. Enterprises M.G. de Guy Ltée* (1996). All of this would definitely appear to suggest that imprisonment for non-payment of a fine imposed upon conviction of an absolute liability offence will infringe section 7 only if there is no procedure in place that operates to ensure that the offender's ability to pay is taken into account. It is hoped that the Supreme Court of Canada will provide a definitive ruling on this important issue in the near future. Until it does so, the law relating to regulatory offences will continue to be cast in an aura of uncertainty.

The decision by the Supreme Court of Canada in *Reference re Section 94(2) of the Motor Vehicle Act R.S.B.C. (1979)* (1985) dramatically illustrates the profound impact that the *Charter* may have on the substantive criminal law. In the specific case of absolute liability offences, it is clear that the Supreme Court has greatly reduced the sting of such offences by severely circumscribing the range of punishments that may be imposed. Indeed, the Court has unequivocally stated that, if the legislature wishes to give the courts the option to impose a term of imprisonment upon conviction of a regulatory offence, it must ensure that it makes a due diligence defence available to those persons accused of such an offence.

The Supreme Court of Canada revisited this issue in the *Wholesale Travel Group Inc.* case (1991), in which the accused corporation had been charged with the offence of false or misleading advertising under the provisions of the *Competition Act*, R.S.C. 1970, c. C-23. We have already seen that, under (what was then) section 37.3(2) of the Act, Parliament made available a defence of due diligence to those persons who had been charged with false or misleading advertising. The relevant statutory provisions are as follows:

No person shall be convicted of an offence under section 36 or 36.1, if he establishes that,

(a) the act or omission giving rise to the offence with which he was charged was the result of error;

(b) he took reasonable precautions and exercised due diligence to prevent the occurrence of such error;

(c) he, or another person, took reasonable precautions to bring the error to the attention of the class of persons likely to have been reached by the representations or testimonial; and

(d) the measures referred to in paragraph (c), except where the representation or testimonial related to a security, were taken forthwith after the representation was made or the testimonial was published.

Paragraphs (c) and (d) of section 37.3(2) imposed a positive obligation on the accused to make an *immediate* retraction before he or she could claim the benefit of the defence of due diligence. This could lead to the result that an individual who did not make such an immediate retraction could be prevented from raising the defence—*even if he or she acted with due diligence*. For example, an accused person might not discover that he or she has made a false or misleading statement in an advertisement until sometime after it has been published. Even if the accused person issued a retraction as soon he or she became aware of the error, the defence of due diligence would not apply because the retraction had not taken place *immediately after the advertisement was originally published*. In effect, this means that absolute liability could be imposed on a blameless defendant who had, through no fault of his or her own, failed to make an immediate retraction and, since imprisonment was a potential penalty under the *Competition Act*, the Supreme Court of Canada ruled that paragraphs (c) and (d) of section 37.3(2) of the Act were invalid in light of section 7 of the *Charter*.

Chief Justice Lamer pointed out that the offence of false or misleading advertising carried a penalty of up to five years' imprisonment and that "it is clear from the developing jurisprudence of this court that the offence must not be one of absolute liability." On the contrary, there must be a "minimum fault requirement of negligence, in that at least a defence of due diligence must always be open to the accused to comply with the requirements of s. 7 of the *Charter*."

According to Chief Justice Lamer, paragraphs (a) and (b) of section 37.3(2) of the *Competition Act* unquestionably provide the accused with a defence of due diligence as that defence had been delineated in the *Sault Ste. Marie* case (1978):

... [P]aras. (a) and (b) operate so as to provide a defence to an accused who has taken reasonable precautions to prevent false/misleading advertising and who has been duly diligent in ensuring that advertising is not false or misleading in nature.

However, paragraphs (c) and (d) of section 37.3 (2) added an additional requirement to the defence: namely, that there must be a retraction "forthwith" after the false or misleading advertisement has been published. This requirement of "timely retraction" means, according to Chief Justice Lamer, that the defence embodied in section 37.3 of the *Competition Act* "is considerably more narrow than the common law defence of due diligence." He stated that he agreed with the majority of the Ontario Court of Appeal that

... paras. (c) and (d) of s. 37.3(2) could have the effect of depriving an accused of the defence of due diligence and could therefore require the conviction of an accused who was not negligent. Paragraphs (c) and (d) make the failure to undertake corrective advertising (a component of false/misleading advertising) an "offence" of absolute liability. Consequently, the constitutionally required fault level is not present in the false/misleading advertising provisions.

In addition to ruling that paragraphs (c) and (d) of section 37.3(2) of the *Competition Act* infringed an accused person's rights under section 7 of the *Charter* because they combined absolute liability with the possibility of imprisonment, Chief Justice Lamer also held that these paragraphs could not be justified under section 1 of the *Charter*. As a consequence, these two paragraphs were declared to be of "no force and effect."

However, it is important to bear in mind that the Supreme Court of Canada did not rule that all absolute liability offences are presumed to be invalid under the *Charter*. In fact, in the later case of *Pontes* (1995), the Supreme Court re-emphasized the point that absolute liability will infringe section 7 of the *Charter* only if it is coupled with the possibility of imprisonment. As was the case in *Reference re Section 94(2) of the Motor Vehicle Act R.S.B.C.* (1979) (1985), *Pontes* (1995) was concerned with the offence of driving while prohibited under the provisions of the B.C. *Motor Vehicle Act*, R.S.B.C. 1979, c. 288. Section 92 of the amended Act provided that a person who was convicted of one of a number of serious *Criminal Code* or provincial/territorial motoring offences "is automatically and without notice prohibited from driving a motor vehicle for 12 months from the date of sentencing." Section 94 of the Act made it an offence to drive while prohibited under section 92.

Having determined that the offence of prohibited driving under section 94 of the *Motor Vehicle Act* was an offence of absolute liability, the critical issue for the Supreme Court of Canada to decide was whether the offence was invalid under the *Charter*. The majority of the Court held that it was not invalid *because there was no potential for imprisonment upon conviction*. This situation was brought about by section 4.1 of the *Offence Act*, R.S.B.C. 1979, c. 305 (amended in 1990), which stated that "no person is liable to imprisonment with respect to an absolute liability offence" under any British Columbia legislation, and by section 72(1) of the *Offence Act*, which stipulated that no person shall be imprisoned for non-payment of a fine. As a consequence of these provisions of the *Offence Act*, Justice Cory stated that the absolute liability offence of prohibited driving did not infringe the *Charter*:

> An accused convicted under ss. 92 and 94 of the B.C. *Motor Vehicle Act* faces no risk of imprisonment and there is, accordingly, no violation of the right to life, liberty and security of the person under s. 7 of the *Charter*.

In the case of *R. v. 1260448 Ontario Inc.; R. v. Transport Robert* (1973) *Ltée* (2003), the Ontario Court of Appeal reached a similar decision in relation to section 84.1 of the *Highway Traffic Act*, R.S.O. 1990, c. H.8, which provided that the owner and operator of a commercial vehicle are guilty of an offence if a wheel separates from the vehicle while it is on a highway. However, section 84.1 also

stipulated that the defence of due diligence was not open to a person who is charged with this offence. The penalty to be imposed for this offence is a fine of not less than $2000 and not more than $50 000: however, there is no possibility of imprisonment—even in the event that the defendant should fail to pay the fine. Furthermore, there is no possibility that the defendant could be sentenced to probation. Although the Court of Appeal recognized that the offence was one of absolute liability, it ruled that section 7 of the *Charter* had not been infringed because, in the absence of any possibility that imprisonment or probation might be imposed, there was no threat to the accused person's right to liberty. The Court also rejected the argument that the accused person's *Charter* right to "security of the person" had been violated by section 84.1 of the *Highway Traffic Act*:

> ... [W]e are not convinced that a prosecution for the s. 84.1 offence engages the kind of exceptional state-induced psychological stress, even for an individual, that would trigger the security of the person guarantee in s. 7. The offence does not create a true crime, and like most regulatory offences, it focuses on the harmful consequences of otherwise lawful conduct rather than any moral turpitude.... The s. 84.1 offence focuses on the unintended but harmful consequences of the commercial trucking industry. We reject the proposition that a defendant charged with this offence is stigmatized as a person operating in a wanton manner, heedless of the extreme dangers to life and limb posed by his or her operation. Conviction for the offence at most implies negligence and like the misleading advertising offence considered in *Wholesale Travel*, any stigma is very considerably diminished.

The Court of Appeal also stated that it made no difference that the regulatory offence in question carried a penalty of a significant fine. The threat of a fine of this nature did not subject an accused person to the "kind of serious state-imposed psychological stress that is intended to be covered by security of the person." Indeed, in the view of the Court of Appeal, the right to security of the person, which is protected by section 7 of the *Charter*, "does not protect the individual operating in the highly regulated context of commercial trucking for profit from the ordinary stress and anxieties that a reasonable person would suffer as a result of government regulation of that industry."

Finally, it should be pointed out that the courts are generally somewhat loath to declare legislation invalid under the *Charter* if they can avoid doing so.

Since absolute liability offences that are coupled with the threat of imprisonment will almost always be struck down as being invalid under the *Charter*, there is a tendency on the part of the courts to designate a regulatory offence as being one of strict, rather than absolute, liability. The case of *Rube* (1992) neatly demonstrates this tendency. At the heart of this case was the allegation that the accused had mislabelled some sides of beef. The accused was, therefore, charged under section 5(1) of the (now repealed) *Food and Drugs Act*, R.S.C. 1970, c. F-27 with misleading labelling of food. The Act did not explicitly provide a defence of due diligence for those who, like the accused, packaged food items themselves and used a "false, misleading, or deceptive" label. However, section 29(1) of the *Food and Drugs Act* did provide such a defence, in the situation where the accused had purchased food items in prepackaged format from another person and sold them in their original packaging. The trial judge ruled that section 5(1) imposed a regime of absolute liability and that, since it was combined with the potential penalty of imprisonment, it was invalid under the *Charter*. However, the Crown appealed to the British Columbia Court of Appeal, which ruled that section 5(1) was an offence of strict, not absolute, liability and that it was, therefore, valid under the *Charter*.

Justice Toy held that, even though Parliament had not explicitly included a defence of due diligence when enacting section 5(1), there was no indication that it intended to impose absolute liability in relation to the offence of misleading labelling of food items. Justice Toy suggested that section 5(1) was directed at "saving the pocketbooks of members of the public" rather than at "the health, welfare or safety of the general public" and that the range of penalties under the Act could be "severe when viewed in the context of a lack of harm to the general public." In other words, the severity of the penalties prescribed by the Act suggested that the legislature did not intend to impose absolute liability.

The Supreme Court of Canada later affirmed the decision made by the British Columbia Court of Appeal. Chief Justice Lamer explicitly acknowledged the significance of *Charter* considerations in drawing the distinction between offences of strict and absolute liability:

> We agree that given the penalties, this is not an offence that could, without offending the *Canadian Charter of Rights and Freedoms*, be one of absolute liability.

On the presumption that Parliament intends its legislation to conform to the exigencies of the *Charter*, we are of the view that the section is one of strict liability and that a defence of due diligence is available to the accused.

STUDY QUESTIONS

1. Assume that a provincial legislature enacts the following provision in its *Retail Sales Act*:

   (1) No retailer shall sell packaged bread without indicating the date of baking on the package.

   (2) Every person who violates subsection (1) is guilty of an offence under this act and is liable to a maximum fine of five thousand dollars.

   The *Offence Act* of the province provides that a person may be imprisoned in default of payment of a fine but also stipulates that this penalty should only be used for a person who wilfully refuses to pay even though he or she has the means to do so.

   Merdle purchases a loaf of packaged bread from the corner grocery store, which is owned by Slackbridge. Merdle notices that the package does not bear a stamp indicating when the loaf was baked and he complains to the provincial authorities, who charge Slackbridge under the provisions set out above. Slackbridge claims that he purchased the loaf from the Crusty Bakery, which has always stamped its packaged loaves whenever he has obtained bread from it in the past. A spokesman from Crusty states that an inexperienced employee had forgotten to replenish the ink in the date stamp and had not noticed that the stamp was failing to make any impression on the packaging paper. What principles would the court apply in determining whether Slackbridge is guilty of the charge?

2. Imagine that you have been appointed the manager of a local hockey rink. You know that various safety regulations apply to the operation of a rink of this nature. What steps would you take to ensure that the other employees of the rink observe all of the safety regulations? If you were charged with a regulatory offence, would you be able to prove that you had acted with "due diligence"? On the basis of your thoughts about this hypothetical situation, do you believe that the "due diligence" standard is an appropriate one

for the courts to apply to most regulatory offences in Canada?

3. Ask your local supermarket manager if he or she knows the difference between strict and absolute liability offences. Also ask the manager what steps he or she takes to ensure that employees meet the requirements of the regulatory statutes that apply to the retail industry in your particular jurisdiction (e.g., hygiene regulations, packaging and labelling regulations, etc.).

4. Do you think that there is any justification for maintaining a category of absolute liability offences in Canada? Are there any circumstances in which absolute liability is more desirable—in terms of prudent social policy—than strict liability?

FURTHER READING

Archibald, B.P. 1991. Liability for Provincial Offences: Fault, Penalty and the Principles of Fundamental Justice in Canada (A Review of Law Reform Proposals from Ontario, Saskatchewan and Alberta). 14 *Dalhousie Law Journal*: 65–80.

Archibald, T., K. Jull, and K. Roach. 2004. The Changed Face of Corporate Liability. 48 *Criminal Law Quarterly*: 367–396.

Boyle, C., & S. de Groot. 2006. The Responsible Citizen in the City of *Lévis*: Due Diligence and Officially Induced Error. 36 *Criminal Reports (6th Series)*: 249–257.

Brudner, A. 1990. Imprisonment and Strict Liability. 40 *University of Toronto Law Journal*: 738–774.

Colvin, E., & S. Anand. 2007. *Principles of Criminal Law*. 3rd ed. Toronto: Carswell.

Edwards, C.A., and C.E. Humphrey. 2000. *Due Diligence under the Occupational Health and Safety Act: A Practical Guide*. Scarborough, ON: Carswell.

Forbes, M.G. 1993. Strict v. Absolute Liability: *R. v. Nickel City Transport (Sudbury) Ltd.* (1993). 47 Motor Vehicle Reports (2nd Series): 57–69.

Hughes, E.L. 1991. Environmental Prosecutions: Characterizing the Offence. 1 *Journal of Environmental Law and Practice*: 323–328.

Husak, D.N. 1995. Varieties of Strict Liability. 8 *Canadian Journal of Law & Jurisprudence*: 189–225.

Keefe, J. 1993. The Due Diligence Defence: A Wholesale Review. 35 *Criminal Law Quarterly*: 480–492.

Law Reform Commission of Canada. 1974. Working Paper No. 2: *The Meaning of Guilt: Strict Liability*. Ottawa: Information Canada.

———. 1974. *Studies in Strict Liability*. Ottawa: Information Canada.

Libman, R. 2002. *Libman on Regulatory Offences in Canada*. Saltspring Island, BC: Earlscourt Legal Press.

Mewett, A.W. 1992. Editorial: Regulatory Offences. 34 *Criminal Law Quarterly*: 257–258.

Ontario Law Reform Commission. 1990. *Report on the Basis of Liability for Provincial Offences*. Toronto: The Ontario Law Reform Commission.

Perry, S.R. 1988. The Impossibility of General Strict Liability. 1 *Canadian Journal of Law and Jurisprudence*: 147–171.

Presser, J.R. 1995. Absolute Liability and Mistakes of Law in the Regulatory Context: *Pontes* Disappoints and Confuses. 41 *Criminal Reports (4th Series)*: 249–260.

Requadt, S. 1993. Regulatory Offences since *Wholesale Travel*: The Need to Re-evaluate Sections 1, 7, and 11(d) of the *Charter*. 22 *Canadian Business Law Journal*: 407–465.

Roach, K. 2009. *Criminal Law*. 4th ed. Toronto: Irwin Law. Ch. 5.

Ruby, C., and K. Jull. 1992. The *Charter* and Regulatory Offences: A Wholesale Revision. 14 *Criminal Reports (4th Series)*: 226–244.

Simons, K.W. 1997. When Is Strict Liability Just? 87 *Journal of Criminal Law & Criminology*: 1075–1137.

Strantz, N.J. 1992. Beyond *Sault Ste. Marie*: The Creation and Expansion of Strict Liability and the "Due Diligence" Defence. 30 *Alberta Law Review*: 1233–1257.

Stuart, D. 1992. *Wholesale Travel*: Presuming Guilt for Regulatory Offences is Constitutional but Wrong. 8 *Criminal Reports (4th Series)*: 225–234.

———. 1999. Annotation: *R. v. Smillie*. 20 *Criminal Reports (5th Series)*: 180–181.

———. 2007. *Canadian Criminal Law: A Treatise*. 5th ed. Toronto: Thomson Carswell. 171–207.

Stuart, D., R.J. Delisle, and S. Coughlan. 2009. *Learning Canadian Criminal Law*. 11th ed. Toronto: Thomson Carswell. Ch. 3.

Stuesser, L. 1989. Convicting the Innocent Owner: Vicarious Liability under Highway Traffic Legislation. 67 *Criminal Reports (3rd Series)*: 316–329.

Swaigen, J. 1992. Negligence, Reverse Onuses and Environmental Offences: Some Practical Considerations. 2 *Journal of Environmental Law and Practice*: 149–188.

———. 1992. *Regulatory Offences in Canada: Liability and Defences*. Toronto: Carswell.

Tilleman, W.A. 1991. Due Diligence Defence in Canada for Hazardous Clean up and Related Problems: Comparison with the American Superfund Law. 1 *Journal of Environmental Law and Practice:* 179–198.

Tuck-Jackson, A. 1990. The Defence of Due Diligence and the Presumption of Innocence. 33 *Criminal Law Quarterly*: 11–42.

Verdun-Jones, S.N. 2007. *Canadian Criminal Cases: Selected Highlights*. 2nd ed. Toronto: Thomson Nelson. Ch. 6.

Wood, S., & L. Johannson. 2008. Six Principles for Integrating Non-Governmental Environmental Standards into Smart Regulation. 46 *Osgoode Hall Law Journal*: 345–395.

CHAPTER SEVEN

MODES OF PARTICIPATION IN CRIME AND INCHOATE OFFENCES

OVERVIEW

This chapter examines the following:

1. the various ways in which an accused person may become a party to a criminal offence;

2. the significance of section 21(1) of the *Criminal Code* and the essential differences that it establishes between the criminal liability of the person who "actually commits" a criminal offence (the principal) and the criminal liability of those individuals who become parties to criminal offences by aiding and/or abetting the offences committed by others;

3. the *actus reus* and *mens rea* elements of aiding and abetting and the general principle that mere passive acquiescence cannot found the basis for liability as an aider and/or abettor;

4. the manner in which accused persons may become parties to criminal offences that are committed by other persons whom they have "counselled" to do so (section 22);

5. the manner in which a person may become a party to a criminal offence by virtue of having shared a "common intent" to carry out an unlawful purpose with an individual who actually commits the offence (section 21(2)) and the circumstances in which that person may escape criminal liability by abandoning the common intent;

6. the nature and scope of the criminal liability that may arise where a party is considered to be an accessory after the fact (section 23(1));

7. the basic elements of the various *inchoate offences* defined in the *Criminal Code*—(a) counselling an offence that is not committed (section 464); (b) attempt (section 24); and (c) conspiracy (section 465);

8. the critical *mens rea* requirement that applies to all inchoate offences: namely, that the Crown must prove that the accused fully intended or was extremely reckless that the crime, which he or she counselled, attempted, or conspired to commit, would actually be committed;

9. the different *actus reus* requirements of the inchoate offences of counselling, attempt, and conspiracy;

10. the thorny problem of determining when an accused person has gone beyond mere preparation and has committed an act that is sufficiently "proximate" to the complete offence as to justify the imposition of liability for a criminal attempt; and

11. the three central elements of the offence of conspiracy:

    (a) an agreement for a common purpose;
    (b) an agreement between two or more parties; and
    (c) an agreement to commit a crime.

INTRODUCTION

This chapter examines two critical topics in the field of criminal law: (1) the various routes by which an individual may become a party to a criminal offence and (2) the inchoate (or uncompleted) offences of counselling, attempt, and conspiracy.

THE VARIOUS MODES OF PARTICIPATION IN A CRIMINAL OFFENCE

In Canada, an accused person may be convicted of a criminal offence on the basis that he or she

- actually committed the offence him- or herself;
- aided and/or abetted another person to commit the offence;
- counselled another person to commit an offence that was later perpetrated by that other person;
- became a **party to a criminal offence** committed by another person as a consequence of having formed a "common intention" with that other person; or
- acted as an accessory after the fact to a crime committed by another person.

ACTUALLY COMMITTING AN OFFENCE

The most obvious means by which an individual may become a party to an offence is by "actually committing" it. In this respect, section 21(1) of the *Criminal Code* provides:

> Every one is a party to an offence who
>
> > (a)   actually commits it ...

The **person who actually commits an offence** is sometimes referred to as the **principal** and is, for example, in the case of a murder by shooting, the individual who actually pulls the trigger. There may be more than one principal when an offence is committed: for example, two individuals could both commit the offence of robbery by simultaneously taking money from tellers in a bank.

Principals are, of course, always present when the crime is perpetrated. However, there are some rare situations in which their presence may be "constructive" (or "inferred") rather than "actual." In these situations, the courts may rule that an accused person has committed an offence through the innocent agency of another individual. For example, in the

case of *Berryman* (1990), the accused was working as a passport application officer in a passport office. On two occasions, she accepted passport applications knowing that the person from whom they were received was not, in fact, the applicant whose name appeared on the documents. Furthermore, she dishonestly stated, in writing, on the front of each application, that the applicant had produced evidence of citizenship and other identification. When the passport documents were completed, Berryman forged the signatures of the purported applicants so as to indicate that the documents had been picked up personally by the persons to whom they had seemingly been issued. She was charged with two counts of forgery of a passport (contrary to section 57(1)(a) of the *Criminal Code*).

However, the Crown was faced with the difficulty that Berryman did not "make" the passport documents herself; they were actually made by another employee who had no knowledge that the information contained in the applications was completely false. Could the accused be convicted of forgery in these circumstances? She was acquitted at trial, but the Crown appealed. The B.C. Court of Appeal ultimately allowed the appeal and entered convictions against the accused. The Court of Appeal basically held that the accused could be convicted of forgery under section 21(1)(a) even though the *actus reus* of the offence (the actual making of the passports) was carried out by an innocent agent. As Justice Wood pointed out in the judgment of the court, "[A] person who commits an offence by means of an instrument 'whose movements are regulated' by him, actually commits the offences himself."

However, the doctrine of *innocent agency* understandably has a somewhat limited scope. For example, in the case of *Verma* (1996), the accused, a physician, was charged with three counts of trafficking in a narcotic (namely, codeine), contrary to the provisions of section 4 of the (now repealed) *Narcotic Control Act*, R.S.C. 1985, c. N-1.[1] The allegation was that Verma had sold three prescriptions to an undercover police officer "for the use and in the name of the officer's fictitious girlfriend." In order to convict Verma of drug trafficking, the Crown would have to prove that any pharmacist who later filled Verma's prescriptions could legitimately be

---

[1] See now section 5 of the *Controlled Drugs and Substances Act*, S.C. 1996, c. 19.

considered to have acted as Verma's "innocent agent." Ultimately, the Crown could not establish this critical element of the *actus reus* of the crime of trafficking and Verma was acquitted at his trial. The Crown's subsequent appeal to the Ontario Court of Appeal was firmly rejected.

In delivering the judgment of the Court of Appeal, Justice Finlayson emphasized that "the actions of the innocent agent must be controlled by or directly attributable to the acts of the principal." However, in this particular case, Verma clearly had no control over the pharmacist. Indeed, it was the patient who would have to make the decision whether to present the prescriptions to a pharmacist and, if he did so, he would have to pay the pharmacist for the drugs concerned. In Justice Finlayson's words,

> The doctor does not "act through" the pharmacist; the doctor provides the means through which a purchaser may, in his or her discretion, obtain drugs from a pharmacist. *The doctor is not the "primary author" of the ultimate exchange of drugs for money between purchaser and pharmacist*; indeed, after writing the prescription the doctor has no control over whether such an exchange will even take place. [emphasis added]

Another reason for the Court of Appeal's refusal to apply the doctrine of innocent agency in the Verma case is that the pharmacist would not have committed the *actus reus* of any crime. Indeed, as Justice Finlayson noted, the doctrine of innocent agency only applies "where the *actus reus* of an offence is committed at the instigation of an accused by an innocent agent who has some exemption from liability that is personal to the agent." However, a pharmacist would not commit the *actus reus* of any crime when he or she merely supplies a narcotic pursuant to the presentation of a legitimate prescription. Compare the situation of the pharmacist in Verma with that of the person who actually made the passport documents in the Berryman case. The passport documents were forgeries in the sense that they were false documents: after all, the information contained in them was untrue in several material respects. The person who made the passports, therefore, committed the *actus reus* of the crime of forgery: of course, this person did not have the *mens rea* for the offence because there was no knowledge of the false statements that had been provided by Berryman.

AIDING AND ABETTING THE COMMISSION OF AN OFFENCE

The second route by which one may become a party to a criminal offence is by aiding and/or abetting another person to actually commit it. To this end, section 21(1) of the *Criminal Code* continues with the following provisions:

> Every one is a party to an offence who ...
>
> (a) does or omits to do anything for the purpose of aiding any person to commit it; or
>
> (b) abets any person in committing it.

What is meant by the use of the legal terms "aiding" and "abetting"? The word "**aiding**" simply means providing assistance or help to the person who actually commits an offence. "**Abetting**" means instigating, urging, or encouraging another person to commit an offence. Frequently, a person will both aid and abet another person. However, it is important to bear in mind that one may provide assistance to someone without necessarily encouraging that person to commit an offence: therefore, "aiding" and "abetting" are distinct concepts. For example, Gobler may sell an illegal firearm to Slout, knowing that Slout is a professional assassin. Gobler does not encourage Slout to commit an act of murder but he does know that Slout will use the firearm to kill another human being. By providing Slout with the firearm, Gobler "aids" Slout but does not "abet" him.

In order to gain a conviction on the basis of aiding under section 21(1)(b) the Crown must prove that the accused person actively rendered assistance to the person who actually committed the offence (*actus reus*) and did so with the intent to provide such assistance (*mens rea*). In order to obtain a conviction on the basis of abetting under section 21(1)(c), the Crown must prove that the accused person actively encouraged the person who actually committed the offence (*actus reus*) and did so with the intent to provide such encouragement (*mens rea*).

It is clear that, insofar as the matter of criminal responsibility is concerned, section 21(1) of the *Code* places the person who aids and/or abets an offence upon exactly the same footing as the person who actually commits it. For example, if the assassins Brutus and Cassius simultaneously inflict fatal stab wounds on the unfortunate Julius Caesar, they will both be considered to have "actually committed" the crime of murder. On the other hand, if Brutus merely supplies a knife to

Cartoon by Elizabeth Carefoot

The person who aids and/or abets another to commit an assault is also guilty of assault, according to section 21(1)(b) and (c) of the Code.

Cassius and maintains a "lookout" while Cassius stabs Caesar to death, then it is probable that Brutus will be considered to have been a party to the murder on the basis that he aided and/or abetted Cassius (assuming, of course that he knew that Cassius intended to kill Caesar). However, in both scenarios, Brutus would be convicted of the offence of either first or second degree murder. As the Ontario Court of Appeal stated in the *Suzack* case (2000), "[I]t is beyond question that where two persons, each with the requisite intent, act in concert in the commission of a crime, they are both guilty of that crime." However, whether they are principals or aiders and/or abettors depends on "what each did in the course of the common design."

The *Actus Reus* Elements of Aiding and Abetting

In general, mere passive acquiescence in the commission of an offence or mere presence at the scene of a crime is not a sufficient condition for the purpose of establishing that the accused aided and/or abetted the principal. However, in practice, it is often exceedingly difficult for the courts to draw a line between passive acquiescence or mere physical presence, on the one hand, and acts or omissions that actually assist or encourage the principal, on the other. This onerous task was attempted, however, by the Supreme Court of Canada in *Dunlop and Sylvester* (1979). In this case, the accused were charged with the offence of rape (today, the charge would be sexual assault). The evidence was that there had been a brutal "gang rape" in which some 18 members of a motorcycle club had forced sexual intercourse with a 16-year-old girl. *Dunlop and Sylvester*, along with other members of the club, had been present at a bar where the victim and a friend were drinking together; the latter were then taken to a dump site by two other gang members. The victim was, apparently, left alone for a few minutes. She was subsequently attacked and raped by other gang members. *Dunlop and Sylvester* testified that they had been requested to bring some beer to the dump site for a party and that they had done so. Although the victim claimed that the two accused had participated in the gang rape, Dunlop and Sylvester denied this. In fact, they claimed that, although they saw a woman having intercourse with gang members, they merely delivered the beer and left after a few minutes. At their trial, the accused were convicted and they launched an appeal.

The issue, which eventually came before the Supreme Court of Canada, concerned the liability of Dunlop and Sylvester as aiders and/or abettors under section 21(1)(b) and (c) of the *Criminal Code*—in other words, was their admitted presence at the scene of the crime sufficient to convict them of rape? In delivering the majority judgment of the Supreme Court, Justice Dickson said,

> Mere presence at the scene of a crime is not sufficient to ground culpability. Something more is needed: encouragement of the principal offender; an act which facilitates the commission of the offence, such as keeping watch or enticing the victim away, or an act which tends to prevent or hinder interference with accomplishment of the criminal act, such as preventing the intended victim from escaping or being ready to assist the prime culprit....

Justice Dickson then turned his attention to the particular set of circumstances that were alleged to exist in the *Dunlop and Sylvester* case (1979). He pointed out that there was no evidence that Dunlop and Sylvester provided any assistance or encouragement to the individuals who actually committed the rape of the victim. For example, the accused did not shout any encouragement to the principals nor did they prevent the victim from escaping or hinder any possible rescue. As Justice Dickson noted,

> A person is not guilty merely because he is present at the scene of a crime and does nothing to prevent it.... If there is no evidence of encouragement by him, a man's presence at the scene of the crime will not suffice to render him liable as aider and abettor. A person who, aware of a rape taking place in his presence, looks on and does nothing is not, as a matter of law, an accomplice. The classic case is the hardened urbanite who stands around in a subway station when an individual is murdered.

The Supreme Court of Canada ultimately allowed the appeals of both Dunlop and Sylvester and directed a verdict of acquittal in respect of each **appellant**.

As Justice Dickson emphasized, it would have been a very different outcome if Dunlop and Sylvester had knowingly provided assistance and/or encouragement to the individuals who committed the various crimes of rape against the victim. For example, in *Briscoe* (2008), the accused had driven a group of individuals to a golf course where a young woman, who had been lured into travelling with the group by the false promise of access to a party, was raped and then brutally killed by members of this group. "Throughout the rapes and the killing, Briscoe simply stood by and watched, offering no assistance to either Ms. C. or her assailants." Briscoe was charged with murder, kidnapping and aggravated assault (on the basis that he had provided assistance to those individuals who actually committed the crimes). The trial judge found that Briscoe had indeed facilitated the commission of these crimes by engaging in the following acts:

> (a) he drove the group to the deserted place where the crimes were committed; (b) he chose the place to stop, the characteristics of which facilitated the commission of the crimes; (c) he opened the trunk of his car and gave a pair of pliers to Laboucan, although they were apparently not used to commit the murder; and (d) he confronted the victim after she had been struck with the wrench and while holding her angrily told her to be quiet or "shut up."

Although the trial judge found that Briscoe had committed the *actus reus* of aiding the offences with which he was charged, Briscoe was acquitted because the trial judge was not satisfied that Briscoe had the necessary *mens rea*. Indeed, the trial judge ruled that it had not been proved that "Briscoe had actual knowledge that Ms. C. had been lured by fraud to accompany the group, that Laboucan intended to sexually assault her, or that Laboucan intended to kill or physically harm Ms. C." However, the Alberta Court of Appeal set aside the acquittals and ordered a new trial because there was evidence that Briscoe was, at the very least, *wilfully blind* as to the intentions of the group. Justice Martin, in delivering the judgment of the appellate court, stated:

> To create an air of reality, there must evidence [*sic*] that, if believed, would permit the trier of fact to find that Briscoe was wilfully blind....
>
> In this case, there was compelling evidence from Briscoe's statement that he had a strong, well-founded suspicion that someone would be killed at the golf course. Indeed, the evidence indicates that he was more than suspicious—he actually feared that he, or his girlfriend, S.B., would be targeted....
>
> There is also an air of reality to the position that Briscoe was a party to the offence of kidnapping.... In this case, the kidnapping and murder charges are, factually, closely related, such that if Briscoe "actually" knew or was wilfully blind to the prospect that the victim was to be taken from Edmonton to a remote place to be killed or seriously harmed, then it could easily be inferred that he must also have known or been wilfully blind to the fact that only a ruse could have induced her to agree to go along. In other words, that her consent was obtained by fraud....
>
> Further, the trial judge found that Briscoe knew "Mr. Laboucan anticipated to be sexually intimate with Ms. C." That finding, and the evidence that supported it, must be considered in context. Ms. C. was being taken to the golf course to be killed. If Briscoe is found to have been wilfully blind to that prospect, that is to say, he is found to have known that fact, then he may also be found to have been wilfully blind to the prospect that she would be sexually assaulted there.

However, where the accused person has not provided any prior assistance or encouragement, then he or she cannot be convicted as party to an offence that is committed while he or she stands passively by. Take, for example, the case of *Williams* (1998), in which the accused had been a passenger in a car that was driven by Snieg and that was owned by Snieg's girlfriend. When the car was searched as it crossed into Canada via Niagara Falls, New York, Canada Customs officers discovered seven bags of cocaine that had been hidden inside the vehicle. Williams was charged with, and subsequently convicted of, the serious offence of importing a narcotic, contrary to section 5(1) of the (now repealed) *Narcotic Control Act*, R.S.C. 1985, c. N-1.[2] However, the Ontario Court of Appeal later set aside the conviction and ordered a new trial on the basis that, *even if the Crown could prove that Williams knew of the presence of the drugs*, his "mere passive acquiescence" in their transportation by Snieg would not be sufficient to justify a conviction of importing a narcotic. In order to be successful, the Crown would have to prove that Williams actually provided some *assistance or encouragement* to Snieg (e.g., by helping Snieg to conceal the drugs in the car). Similarly, in the case of *Hofung* (2001), the Ontario Court of Appeal held that merely being present in one's apartment while heroin is traded does not *per se* render one liable to conviction as a party to trafficking in a narcotic.

However, there are certain exceptional circumstances in which a mere failure to act may well constitute aiding and/or abetting within the meaning of section 21(b) and (c) of the *Criminal Code*. If, for example, the accused is *under a legal duty to act and fails to do so*, then—*provided the failure to act is accompanied by the intent to provide assistance or encouragement* to the person(s) actually committing an offence—the accused will become a party to that offence as an aider and/or abettor. This was the principle that was articulated by the British Columbia Court of Appeal in the case of *Nixon* (1990). The accused was the officer in charge of the lock-up or jail where a citizen was brutally assaulted by one or more police officers. The victim's kneecap was completely broken as a consequence of the attack. Nixon was charged with aggravated assault, but the trial judge was not satisfied that he had actually committed the assault himself. However, the British Columbia Court of Appeal ruled that the trial judge had been correct to convict the accused on the basis that he aided or abetted the officers who did commit the assault. Under the provisions of the British Columbia *Police Act*,[3] the accused was clearly under a duty to enforce the criminal law (by, for example, preventing the commission of an assault). Furthermore, by virtue of the common law, Nixon was, as a person in charge of a jail, under a *clear duty to safeguard the lives and safety of his prisoners*. Nixon's

failure to perform these duties constituted aiding or abetting the assault, assuming, of course, that his failure to act was prompted by the intention to assist or encourage the other officers in their criminal activities. Speaking on behalf of the Court of Appeal, Justice Legg stated that:

> ... [T]he fact which is highly relevant to this case is that the accused has been found to have been present when the assault was committed and had a duty to prevent the offence and did not perform that duty. *Where an accused has such a duty and fails to act to discharge it, his failure to act may be held to have encouraged the offence.* [emphasis added]

The *Mens Rea* Elements of Aiding and Abetting

In order to establish the *mens rea* of aiding and/or abetting, the Crown must provide that the accused intended to render assistance and/or encouragement to the principal when the offence was actually committed. The vital importance of identifying the *mens rea* elements of aiding and abetting is particularly evident in those cases where the accused person is alleged to have assisted and/or encouraged another person to commit an act of culpable homicide. It is quite possible for the person who actually committed the homicide to be convicted of murder while other accused persons may be found guilty of the offence of manslaughter because they lacked the necessary *mens rea* for murder. This issue was addressed by the Supreme Court of Canada in the case of *Jackson and Davy* (1993). Jackson and Davy had both been charged with first degree murder following the death of Jackson's employer. On the night of the killing, Davy had driven Jackson to the victim's shop. Jackson admitted that he had killed the victim by striking him with a hammer. It appears that Davy remained near the door to the store and that he heard noises that would suggest that someone was being assaulted. When Davy tried to leave the scene, Jackson forced him to return to the shop and ordered Davy to collect the cash box. The trial judge did not adequately instruct the jury that it would be possible to convict Davy of manslaughter while simultaneously convicting Jackson of murder. Ultimately, Jackson was found guilty of first degree murder and Davy of second degree murder. The Ontario Court of Appeal overturned Davy's conviction of murder and ordered a new trial because the trial judge had failed to instruct the jury correctly on the question of

---

[2] See now section 6 of the *Controlled Drugs and Substances Act*, S.C. 1996, c. 19.

[3] See now *Police Act*, R.S.B.C. 1996, c. 367.

Davy's potential liability for the offence of manslaughter in accordance with the requirements of sections 21(1) and 21(2) of the *Criminal Code.*

The Supreme Court of Canada dismissed the Crown's appeal from the decision of the Court of Appeal. The Court noted that the necessary *mens rea*, which must be proved in relation to unlawful act manslaughter, is objective foreseeability of the risk of bodily harm that is neither trivial nor transitory (a rule laid down by the Supreme Court of Canada in the *Creighton* case (1993)). In the *Jackson and Davy* case (1993), the Supreme Court of Canada ruled that this objective test applies equally to a person charged with manslaughter on the basis of having aided and/or abetted someone to kill another person. In the words of Justice McLachlin,

> I conclude that a person may be convicted of manslaughter who aids and abets another person in the offence of murder, where a reasonable person in all the circumstances would have appreciated that bodily harm was the foreseeable consequence of the dangerous act which was being undertaken.

Davy had assisted someone who was ultimately convicted of murder. Nevertheless, the Supreme Court ruled that, if Davy lacked the necessary *mens rea* for conviction of murder (intent to kill or intent to inflict bodily harm that is likely to cause death and recklessness as to whether or not death ensues), he could still be convicted of manslaughter on the basis that he aided and/or abetted Jackson in the situation where a *reasonable person would have foreseen the risk of bodily harm to the victim.*

In the *Roach* case (2004), the Ontario Court of Appeal stated very clearly that, when an accused person is charged with an offence on the basis that he or she aided the person(s) who actually committed the offence, then the Crown must prove that the accused acted with intention or wilful blindness: mere recklessness will not be sufficient. Roach was charged with fraud over $5000 and conspiracy to commit fraud. Roach was alleged to have participated in a fraudulent telemarketing scheme, organized by a man called Dube. The victims of the fraudulent scheme were contacted by telemarketers who informed them that they had won valuable prizes in a legal contest. The victims were asked to pay taxes and handling and shipping charges up front in order to receive their prizes. These charges ranged from US$611 to US$9690. However, the victims were actually sent inexpensive watches and stereos.

Dube persuaded Roach to set up a business as a "shipper and receiver" in the telemarketing scheme. Although he testified that he did not know Dube's business was illegal, Roach was convicted of fraud and conspiracy at his trial. The trial judge told the jury that

> [t]he third element that the Crown must prove beyond a reasonable doubt is that the accused whom you are then considering intended to aid or abet Mr. Dube in committing the offence of defrauding the public. It is not enough that the accused's acts actually aided or abetted Mr. Dube. It must also be proven that the accused knew or intended that his acts would aid or abet Mr. Dube. If the accused knew that his acts were likely to assist or encourage Mr. Dube then you are entitled to conclude that such accused intended to aid and abet Mr. Dube in committing that offence.

The trial judge, when answering questions from the jury led them to believe that either recklessness or wilful blindness would be sufficient *mens rea* to convict Roach of fraud on the basis that he had aided Dube to actually commit this offence. Roach appealed to the Ontario Court of Appeal, which set aside his convictions and ordered a new trial. The Court emphasized that only an actual intention to assist the person who actually commits an offence or wilful blindness on the part of the accused will suffice for conviction as a party to that offence. As noted in Chapter 4, wilful blindness is treated as being equivalent to actual knowledge by the accused of the nature and consequence of his or her actions. The Court of Appeal referred to section 21(1)(b) of the *Criminal Code*, which provides that "every one is a party to an offence who ... does or omits to do anything for the purpose of aiding any person to commit it." The person's involvement in the crime in a secondary capacity makes him or her an accessory to the crime. In delivering the judgment of the Court, Justice Borins underscored the fact that Parliament had used the word "purpose" in section 21(1)(b) and held that "purpose is synonymous with intent and does not include recklessness." In summarizing the *mens rea* that must be established for liability as a party under section 21(1)(b), Justice Borins stated that

> ... the *mens rea* for party liability is contained in s. 21(1)(b) of the *Criminal Code* that requires that the aid given by the accessory to the principal be "for the purpose of aiding" the principal to commit the crime of which the accessory has been charged. To be convicted as an aider, the defendant must not only assist

the principal in the commission of the offence, but must intend to do so, although it is not necessary that the aider know all the details of the crime committed. It is sufficient that the aider was aware of the type of crime to be committed and knew the circumstances necessary to constitute the crime that he or she is accused of aiding.... [K]nowledge will include actual knowledge or wilful blindness, but will not include recklessness. This accords with Professor Roach's approach regarding the high level of *mens rea* required for party liability and with the opinions of the other legal scholars that I have reviewed.[4]

Aiding and Abetting in the Context of the Purchase of Illegal Drugs

A significant issue facing the courts is the extent to which those persons who provide incidental assistance to those who purchase illegal drugs should be held criminally responsible for their actions. This question was addressed by the Supreme Court of Canada in the case of *Greyeyes* (1997). The accused had been charged with the very serious offence of trafficking in cocaine, on the basis that he was a party to the crime by virtue of aiding and/or abetting. An undercover police officer, Morgan, had asked Greyeyes if he knew where he (Morgan) could obtain some cocaine. Greyeyes indicated that he knew where a source could be found, and he and Morgan went to an apartment building together. Greyeyes identified himself at the door of a particular apartment. An individual inside asked what Greyeyes and his companion wanted: Greyeyes responded with the word "cocaine." When asked how much cocaine was required, Greyeyes looked at Morgan, who indicated "one." Greyeyes relayed this information to the

supplier and told Morgan that he would have to pay $40. The person inside the apartment instructed Greyeyes to slide the money under the door. He did so and a small pink flap, containing two-tenths of a gram of cocaine, was passed under the door to him. Greyeyes then gave the drug to Morgan.

The trial judge acquitted Greyeyes on the basis that he had only acted as an agent for Morgan, who was the *purchaser*—not the *seller*—of the cocaine. In effect, the trial judge ruled that Greyeyes had only acted as the mouthpiece for the undercover police officer and had not done anything to assist the vendor in the making of the sale. However, the Saskatchewan Court of Appeal subsequently allowed an appeal by the Crown and convicted Greyeyes of trafficking in cocaine. The Supreme Court of Canada then rejected Greyeyes' ensuing appeal.

It is significant that Justice L'Heureux-Dubé, speaking on behalf of the majority of the Supreme Court, ruled that, in normal circumstances, the purchaser of an illegal drug is not found guilty of *trafficking*, but rather of *possession*. This is a critical difference because the severity of the penalty for trafficking is much greater than for mere possession (a maximum term of imprisonment of life as opposed to a term of seven years). Clearly, this logic should be extended to cover those individuals who have provided "no more than incidental assistance of the sale through rendering aid to the purchaser." Such individuals should be treated as parties to the offence of *possession*, rather than *trafficking*. As Justice L'Heureux-Dubé noted in her judgment, an individual whose conduct was primarily designed to assist a *purchaser* of illegal drugs should "share the culpability and stigma of the purchaser rather than that of the vendor."

In the particular circumstances of the *Greyeyes* case, however, the Supreme Court ruled that the accused had gone far beyond providing assistance to the purchaser, Morgan. Indeed, Justice L'Heureux-Dubé stated that the "facts demonstrate a concerted effort on his part to effect the transfer of narcotics." In her view,

> The appellant located the seller, brought the buyer to the site and introduced the parties. It is clear that without this assistance, the purchase would never have taken place. Moreover, he acted as a spokesperson, negotiated the price of the drugs, and passed the money over to the seller. He also accepted money for having facilitated the deal.... [W]ithout the appellant's assistance, the buyer would never have been able to enter the apartment building to contact the seller. *These are not the acts of a mere*

---

[4] A further example of the high level of *mens rea* required for proof of participation as a party to a crime committed by another person is the case of *Maciel* (2007), in which the Ontario Court of Appeal examined the *mens rea* requirements for conviction of being a party to first degree murder on the basis of aiding/abetting. The Court held that

> [t]he accused is liable as an aider only if the accused did something to assist the perpetrator in the planned and deliberate murder and if, when the aider rendered the assistance, he did so for the purpose of aiding the perpetrator in the commission of a planned and deliberate murder. Before the aider could be said to have the requisite purpose, the Crown must prove that the aider knew the murder was planned and deliberate. Whether the aider acquired that knowledge through actual involvement in the planning and deliberation or through some other means, is irrelevant to his or her culpability under s. 21(1).

purchaser, and as a result it is clear that the appellant aided the traffic of narcotics. [emphasis added]

Greyeyes, therefore, was found to be a party to the crime of *trafficking* (as an aider or abettor), because his actions were designed to provide a significant degree of assistance to the *seller* of the cocaine.

It is noteworthy that, in somewhat similar circumstances, the Alberta Court of Appeal ruled that an individual who plays an active role in transferring drugs from a seller to a buyer is actually committing the offence of trafficking and, therefore, it is irrelevant whether that individual was assisting the seller or the buyer.[5] In *Wood* (2007), the accused was charged with trafficking in crack cocaine, contrary to s. 5(1) of the *Controlled Drugs and Substances Act*. Undercover police officers requested Wood to obtain a small quantity of drugs for them. Wood used an officer's cellular phone to call a seller, who later drove to a rendezvous with Wood. Using an officer's money, Wood obtained crack cocaine from the seller and delivered it to the officers. The trial judge acquitted Wood because he had provided only incidental assistance, that he lacked the necessary *mens rea* for trafficking, and that his aid was not necessary to the consummation of the purchase. However, upon the Crown's appeal, the Alberta Court of Appeal set aside the acquittal and entered a conviction of trafficking. On behalf of the Court, Justice Côté emphasized that Wood's motive for transferring the drug was irrelevant and that Wood should be convicted on the basis that he had actually committed the offence of trafficking himself:

> … [K]nowingly and personally committing one of the elements of trafficking in the *Controlled Drugs and Substances Act*, means that one has committed the offence. No resort to s. 21 of the *Code* is then necessary.…
>
> To phrase that in more general terms, the law of accessories becomes relevant only if the accused has not personally committed the offence. That is elementary law.
>
> Here, [Wood] kept the seller and buyer separate, and shuttled between the two with the money. I will

assume that the accused was not himself a seller (and no one argued in the Court of Appeal that he was). However, it is at least arguable that he "gave" the cocaine to the buying undercover constables. He certainly "transferred" and "delivered" the cocaine. He carried it first across the parking lot, and then part of the distance up 109 Street to the park. And he certainly "offered to do" those things (before and at this time).

To What Extent Must the Aider or Abettor Know the Nature and Scope of the Principal's Plans?

One significant problem that arises in relation to the proof of the necessary *mens rea* for aiding and/or abetting an offence concerns the situation where the accused renders only *incidental assistance* to the principal (the person who actually commits the offence in question). The problem revolves around the issue of the precise extent to which the accused must have knowledge of the principal's plans at the time the accused provides such assistance. It is clear that the accused must know the principal's "general" purpose but, in many cases, the thorny issue arises as to exactly how far this knowledge must extend in order to render the accused liable to conviction as an aider and/or abettor.

The nature of the problem is well illustrated by the case of *Yanover and Gerol* (1985). Gerol was charged with the offence of placing dynamite with intent to cause an explosion at a restaurant and disco in Toronto (contrary to what is now section 81(1)(a) of the *Criminal Code*). Gerol had provided the dynamite that was ultimately used by a man called Moon in the creation of the explosion. Gerol asked Moon what the dynamite was for and was told that "my friend asked me to do the job." Apparently, Gerol did not ask Moon what the job was, nor did he inquire as to the identity of the friend. The accused was convicted at trial, but the Ontario Court of Appeal allowed his appeal and ordered a new trial.

The new trial was ordered because of matters relating to the admission of fresh evidence. However, the Ontario Court of Appeal did take the opportunity to articulate the general principles that should be applied when a trial court has to determine whether an individual in Gerol's circumstances possessed the requisite degree of *mens rea* for conviction of an offence on the basis of aiding or abetting. Clearly, Gerol himself had not been present at the time of the explosion. He was undoubtedly ignorant

---

[5] It is important to take into consideration the very broad definition of "traffic" in section 2 of the *Controlled Drugs and Substances Act*: "traffic" means, in respect of a substance included in any of Schedules I to IV, "(*a*) to sell, administer, give, transfer, transport, send or deliver the substance, (*b*) to sell an authorization to obtain the substance, or (*c*) to offer to do anything mentioned in paragraph (*a*) or (*b*), otherwise than under the authority of the regulations."

of the identity of the specific building that was going to be blown up and he did not know anything about its general location. Furthermore, he did not have any knowledge as to when the explosion would take place. However, it does appear that he was fully aware that the dynamite was to be used for the criminal purpose of causing an explosion. In these circumstances, the Ontario Court of Appeal ruled that it would be open to a jury to conclude that the accused was a party to the offence on the basis of aiding and/or abetting (under section 21(1)(b) or (c) of the *Criminal Code*). As Justice Martin stated, in delivering the judgment of the court,

> For liability to attach under s. 21(1)(b) or (c) it is unnecessary that the person supplying the instrument for the commission of the intended crime know the precise details of the crime intended to be committed such as the particular premises intended to be blown up or the precise time when the offence is intended to be committed, provided that the accused is aware of the type of crime intended to be committed.

Similarly, suppose that Badger assists and/or encourages Weasel to perpetrate an attack against Mole. As a consequence of the assault, Mole suffers bodily injuries that are primarily caused by a stab wound inflicted by Weasel. Is it open to Badger to deny that he was a party to the offence of assault causing bodily harm by claiming that he did not know that Weasel had a knife? The answer would be in the negative because Badger intended to assist or encourage Weasel in the commission of an act that clearly created a very real risk of non-trivial bodily injury. It does not matter exactly how the bodily harm was inflicted on Mole—whether by blows from the fists or by use of a weapon. Badger undoubtedly knew that Weasel intended to inflict bodily harm. He therefore knew the general nature of the offence that was to be committed and he would be convicted as a party to assault causing bodily harm, even though he might not have known exactly how Weasel would ultimately inflict the injuries in question.

This type of scenario actually unfolded in the *Cuadra* case (1998), in which the accused was charged with aggravated assault. Armed with a baseball bat, Cuadra had participated in an attack on a man called Hatchard. One of the other assailants, Arbuto, stabbed Hatchard, thereby inflicting serious injuries. There was no evidence to suggest that Cuadra had struck the victim with the baseball bat, and he claimed that he intended only to assist in a fist fight. At his trial, the accused was nevertheless convicted of aggravated assault (section 268 of the *Code*), and his subsequent appeal to the British Columbia Court of Appeal was dismissed. The Court of Appeal rejected the argument of Cuadra's counsel that the Crown had to establish that Cuadra was aware that Arbuto had a knife and that it was objectively foreseeable that the victim would be stabbed. As Justice Cumming said, in delivering the judgment of the Court of Appeal,

> ... [I]t is clear to me that an objective foresight of the specific wounds resulting from an assault is not the threshold test; the test is simply an objective foresight of bodily *harm*. Thus specific wounds do not have to be foreseeable....
>
> When Cuadra entered the fray he did so with a weapon, his weapon of choice was a baseball bat, he was assisting Arbuto in a fight that went beyond a mere "fist fight." The harm that resulted from the escalation of the fight may not have been specifically foreseeable but it is undeniable that bodily harm was objectively foreseeable and that ... is the *mens rea* requirement for the offence of aggravated assault.

However, it is important to bear in mind that the courts will not convict an accused person as a party to *murder* on the basis of aiding and/or abetting, unless he or she *intended to help or encourage the principal either to kill the victim or to inflict grievous bodily harm that the accused knows is likely to cause death.* This critical principle was applied, for example, in the case of *Hartford and Frigon* (1980), in which the accused were both charged with the murder of a man called Pollock, who had been drowned in a creek.

The evidence indicated that a third man, Rattray, had actually killed Pollock, perhaps with the assistance of one or both of the defendants. The latter claimed that Rattray "held the deceased underwater and pummelled him to get the air out of his lungs." It was clear that both Hartford and Frigon had "participated under Rattray's leadership in kicking the deceased and throwing him in the water from time to time." However, there was considerable dispute as to the precise nature of the accused's involvement in the act of drowning Pollock. The accused were convicted at trial, but their appeal to the British Columbia Court of Appeal was successful. A new trial was ordered because the trial judge, in his instruction to the jury, had left unclear the necessary *mens rea* for conviction as an aider and/or abettor. In delivering the judgment of the court, Justice Seaton said,

The jury was left with the impression that the intention to be found in an aider and abettor under s. 21(1)(b) and (c) was the intention to aid or abet, without the qualification that the aider know what he was aiding. That I think to be wrong. If one of the appellants aided Rattray, thinking that what they were going to do was rough the deceased up and not cause him any bodily harm that would be likely to cause death, then I think that that appellant might be guilty of manslaughter, notwithstanding that Rattray be guilty of murder.

The intention that the jury ought to have been directed to consider as an essential ingredient for a finding of murder on the basis of aiding and abetting would be the intention to help Rattray, knowing that he was going to kill or cause bodily harm that was likely to cause death, or the intention to help Rattray no matter which of a number of crimes he chose to commit....

COUNSELLING AN OFFENCE

An individual may also become a party to a criminal offence as a consequence of counselling a criminal act. Indeed, section 22 of the *Criminal Code* establishes a broad basis for the imposition of criminal liability:

22. (1) Where a person counsels another person to be a party to an offence and that other person is afterwards a party to that offence, the person who counselled is a party to that offence, notwithstanding that the offence was committed in a way different from that which was counselled.

   (2) Every one who counsels another person to be a party to an offence is a party to every offence that the other commits in consequence of the counselling that the person who counselled knew or ought to have known was likely to be committed in consequence of the counselling.

   (3) For the purposes of this Act, "counsel" includes procure, solicit or incite.

As a reading of section 22(1) readily indicates, if accused persons counsel an offence that is ultimately committed, they will be convicted of that offence in exactly the same manner as "aiders" and/or "abettors" may be convicted under section 21. Section 22(2) also saddles accused persons who counsel a crime with the responsibility for every other offence that the principal commits as a direct consequence of the counselling. The only limitation placed upon their liability is the requirement that the Crown establish that the accused knew, or *ought to have*

known, that such an offence was likely to be committed as a consequence of the counselling. The use of the words "ought to have known" clearly imposes an *objective standard of liability* based upon what the "reasonable" person would have known in the same circumstances as the accused. The only exception to this principle of objective liability would arise where the principal commits the offences of murder or attempted murder. In this situation, the Supreme Court's decision in *Martineau* (1990) (see Chapter 4) dictates that, in order to safeguard the rights of accused persons under sections 7 and 11(d) of the *Charter*, they cannot become parties to these criminal offences unless they had subjective foresight of the death of the victim.

Section 22(3) states that the word "counsel" includes "procure, solicit or incite." Therefore, the term "counselling" covers advising or recommending someone else to commit an offence as well as finding someone to commit an offence, persistently requesting someone to commit an offence, and provoking or instigating someone to commit an offence.

An interesting case involving the counselling of an offence is that of *Soloway* (1975). In this case, the accused was convicted by a provincial court judge of a charge that he "... did unlawfully steal a driver's licence, registration and Alberta Health Care Card of a value not exceeding $200...." It appears that the victim was invited to Soloway's home by a Mrs. Daniels, who was a friend of the accused. The victim felt tired and went to sleep, face-down, on a couch in Soloway's living room. The victim woke up when he felt Mrs. Daniels removing his wallet from his back pocket. He pretended he was still sleeping, because he feared that he might be attacked if he did not do so. There was no money in the wallet. In his evidence at trial, the victim said,

> When [Mrs. Daniels] ... decided that there was nothing in the wallet, she was going to return it ... like I figured common sense would tell them to; and Mr. Soloway says, "No, keep it,"... "It's worth good money, I can sell it at any bar." He says, "You know, there's good money in that sort of thing. You can take strangers around, bop them over the head, and get their wallets. If there is no money you can always make money on the other things that are in the wallets."

The trial judge convicted Soloway as a party to theft on the basis that he counselled Mrs. Daniels to steal the contents of the victim's wallet. Soloway appealed to the Appellate Division of the Alberta Supreme Court, but his conviction was affirmed. Justice Allen crystallized the central issue by stating that

> ... the whole point involved in this case is whether the appellant's presence when the wallet was extracted from [the victim's] ... hip pocket and the advice he gave to the woman with respect to keeping the credentials made him a party to the offence of stealing those credentials and thus guilty of the offence of theft....

Defence counsel had contended that Soloway could not be convicted of being a party to theft, because that crime was already complete when Mrs. Daniels removed the wallet from the victim's pocket. Justice Allen rejected this contention. Mrs. Daniels had intended to replace the wallet in the victim's pocket after she discovered that it contained no money. It was only Soloway's prompting that caused her to remove the credentials from the wallet. Viewed in this light, it was clear that the theft of the credentials was not completed until Mrs. Daniels appropriated them with the intention to deprive the victim of them. Therefore, Soloway was properly convicted as a party to a theft that he had counselled.

Becoming a Party to an Offence by Virtue of Common Intention
The Basic Principles of Liability under Section 21(2)

Section 21(2) of the *Criminal Code* provides:

> Where two or more persons form an intention in common to carry out an unlawful purpose and to assist each other therein and any one of them, in carrying out the common purpose, commits an offence, each of them who knew or *ought to have known* that the commission of the offence would be a probable consequence of carrying out the common purpose is a party to that offence. [emphasis added]

This provision basically codifies the ancient English common law doctrine of "**common intention**" whereby, if two or more persons set out to execute an unlawful purpose, each of them is equally liable for the consequences of the other's (or others') criminal acts that are committed in pursuit of that common objective. The *Code* imposes an objective test: once the Crown has established the "common purpose," accused persons are liable to conviction for any offence that they either knew or "ought to have known" would be a probable consequence of carrying it out.

Let us suppose by way of example that Kibble and Mudfog agree to rob Lumbey's corner store. Kibble hopes that Lumbey will hand over the cash from his till in response to threats rather than actual violence. However, Lumbey refuses to hand over the money and Mudfog strikes Lumbey on the head with a club. Mudfog and Kibble run off with the cash and are soon apprehended by members of the local constabulary. There is no doubt that Mudfog and Kibble are both guilty of *robbery*. However, Kibble claims that he is not guilty of the offence of *aggravated assault* (section 268 of the *Code*), because not only was it Mudfog who actually struck Lumbey, but it was also the case that he (Kibble) only intended to scare Lumbey by threats. In spite of his claims, Kibble would nevertheless be convicted of the crime of aggravated assault by virtue of the application of the principle of common intention, encapsulated in section 21(2) of the *Criminal Code*. Kibble and Mudfog formed a *common intention to commit the crime of robbery "and to assist each other therein."* The Crown would undoubtedly find it relatively easy to prove either that Kibble *actually knew*, or that he "*ought to have known*," that the infliction of non-trivial bodily harm would be a "probable consequence of carrying out the common purpose." After all, the very nature of a robbery is that the victim is exposed to the risk of non-trivial bodily harm.

In the case of *Vang* (1999), the accused had acted in concert with two other men to attack a man called Rampersaud. One of Vang's companions, Nguyen, stabbed Rampersaud in the back, puncturing his lung and lacerating his kidney—injuries that might have led to potentially fatal internal bleeding. Vang was charged with *aggravated assault* on the basis that he had formed a common intention with his companions to assault Rampersaud and that he either knew or ought to have known that a probable consequence of carrying out this common intention was the infliction of non-trivial bodily harm. There was no evidence that Vang knew that Nguyen had a knife, although it appeared that Vang had used a beer bottle as part of the assault on the victim. Vang was convicted of the charge and his subsequent appeal to the Ontario Court of Appeal was dismissed. Associate Chief Justice Morden stated that

> ... the question is whether the appellants, in engaging in the common unlawful purpose of assaulting Rampersaud, foresaw, or ought to have foreseen, that bodily harm was a probable consequence of carrying out the common purpose. If the answer is yes, then, provided Rampersaud's injuries did, in fact, endanger his life, the appellants are guilty of aggravated assault.

... The specific harm that resulted may not have been foreseeable, but it is clear that, as the trial judge found, bodily harm was objectively foreseeable as a probable consequence of engaging in the fight.

The application of section 21(2) was considered by the Supreme Court of Canada in the case of *Jackson and Davy* (1993). In this case (discussed above in the context of aiding and abetting), Jackson and Davy were charged with first degree murder. The theory of the Crown was that Davy drove Jackson to the house of the victim, where they both participated in the killing. The Crown also suggested that the motive for the killing was robbery and that both Davy and Jackson intended to kill the victim during the robbery. However, there was evidence that Davy did not actually participate in the slaughter of the victim, and he testified that he did not form any plan to rob and kill him. Jackson was convicted of first degree murder and the question arose as to whether Davy could be convicted of murder or manslaughter on the basis of having formed an intention in common to rob the victim. He was convicted of second degree murder, but the Ontario Court of Appeal granted him a new trial. This decision was later affirmed by the Supreme Court.

In her judgment, Justice McLachlin set out the circumstances in which Davy might be convicted of manslaughter by virtue of the operation of section 21(2):

On the evidence presented, one of the scenarios available to the jury was that Jackson and Davy had formed a common intention to rob Rae [the victim] and that, in the course of the robbery, Jackson murdered Rae. Even if he did not participate in the murder, Davy could be liable under s. 21(2) in this scenario. If he foresaw that murder was a probable consequence of carrying out the common purpose—in this case the robbery—he would be guilty of second degree murder. On the other hand, if Davy did not foresee the probability of murder but a reasonable person in the circumstances would have foreseen at least a risk of harm to another as a result of carrying out the common intention, Davy could be found guilty of manslaughter under s. 21(2).

The Requirement of Subjective Foreseeability of Death in Murder and Attempted Murder Cases

We have seen that section 21(2) imposes objective liability insofar as accused persons can be convicted of an offence that they "ought to have known" would be a probable consequence of carrying out the common unlawful purpose that they have formed with the principal offender(s). However, in the *Martineau* case (1990), the Supreme Court of Canada ruled that, in light of the guarantees provided by section 7 of the *Charter*, accused persons may not be convicted of murder unless they *subjectively* foresaw the likelihood of death ensuing from their conduct. What impact does this principle have in the context of section 21(2)?

In the cases of *Logan* (1990) and *Rodney* (1990), the Supreme Court of Canada ruled that section 7 of the *Charter* renders inoperative the words "ought to have known" in section 21(2), whenever the charge is murder or attempted murder. In other words, where the Crown seeks to obtain a murder (or attempted murder) conviction on the basis of common intention under section 21(2), it must be shown that the accused *actually foresaw* that the death of the victim was a probable consequence of carrying out the common purpose in question.

The Ontario Court of Appeal applied these principles in *Laliberty* (1997). In this case, three women had been charged with second degree murder. The theory of the Crown was that the accused had formed a plan to rob the victim and that one of them stabbed him with a butcher knife in the course of carrying out the robbery. All three of the accused were convicted at trial, but the Ontario Court of Appeal subsequently allowed their appeals and ordered a new trial because the trial judge had not given the jury a correct instruction concerning the application of section 21(2) of the *Criminal Code* to the facts of the specific case. Section 21(2) would, of course, apply to the two accused who did not actually stab the victim, and the Court of Appeal ruled, at a new trial, that the trial judge must make it clear to the jury that "guilt could only be found if each of the appellants, considered separately for the purposes of s. 21(2), had actual foresight or actual knowledge that another appellant would stab the deceased with the intent to kill him in carrying out the robbery of the deceased."

How Broad Is the Scope of the "Common Purpose" under Section 21(2)?

It will be remembered that section 21(2) refers to the "common purpose" of the accused and his or her accomplice(s). This phrase would appear to lay the basis for a potential defence based upon the contention that the accomplices committed an act that fell outside the scope of the so-called common purpose. However, the courts have emphasized that such a defence, if it is applicable, has a very limited scope.

For example, the issue was raised before the Manitoba Court of Appeal in the case of *Puffer, McFall and Kizyma* (1977). In this case, the co-accused were charged with murder. The body of the victim was discovered in a badly beaten state. However, it was established that the actual cause of death was asphyxiation because of a pillow being tied around his face. In the words of Chief Justice Freedman,

> So here is a man helplessly and hopelessly trussed up—his feet crossed and securely tied, his hands no less securely tied behind his back, and, covering his face, a pillow held firmly in place by a sweater, the arms of which were knotted at the back of his neck. Effectively immobilized as he was, he could not have survived very long.

The theory advanced by the Crown was that the accused had formed a plan to rob the deceased and that they killed him in order to facilitate the robbery or their subsequent escape. Statements given to the police by the accused indicated that they had indeed intended to rob the victim (or, as one accused put it, their plan was to "roll some fags"—meaning the robbery of some homosexuals). However, McFall and Puffer strenuously claimed that the tying of the pillow over the victim's face was perpetrated by Kizyma at a time when they were not present. However, evidence presented at the trial indicated that all three co-accused participated, to some extent, in beating the victim and tying his arms and legs. The co-accused were all convicted of non-capital murder, and they appealed to the Manitoba Court of Appeal.

Counsel for McFall and Puffer contended, in effect, that the tying of the pillow by Kizyma went beyond the scope of the common purpose formed among the three co-accused. Counsel, therefore, claimed that the trial judge should have instructed the jury that the bodily harm, which actually caused death, can only render the co-accused liable to conviction of murder if "it was of a nature or type falling within the scope of the plan or conspiracy." Since McFall and Puffer asserted that Kizyma's use of the pillow as a gag went beyond the scope of their plan, their counsel contended that they should not have been convicted of murder. This contention was firmly rejected by the Court of Appeal, which affirmed the convictions of all three co-accused.

In rejecting the point made by counsel for McFall and Puffer, Chief Justice Freedman said,

> In any event the present case is not one in which, either expressly or tacitly, the accused had agreed upon or defined just how far they would go or just what they would do. The enterprise was described merely as one to roll a fag. I find it completely unrealistic to say that blows to the face or body, the pinioning of hands, the tying of feet could be regarded as within the plan, but that the use of the pillow as a gag must be looked upon as falling outside the plan. Distinctions of this kind could lead to findings that a blow above the belt was within a scheme to rob, while a blow below the belt was not. The violence involved in the carrying out of a robbery ought not later to be measured or tested by Marquis of Queensbury rules or anything of that nature.

The facts in the *Puffer, McFall and Kizyma* case were such that it was highly unlikely that the defendants' arguments would be treated with even a scintilla of sympathy by the courts. However, there are no doubt other circumstances in which the defence of "going beyond the scope of the common intention" is much more likely to be successful. Suppose, for example, that Barbox and Gobler agree to break and enter Wisbottle's residence in order to steal a valuable painting. Barbox insists that they carry out their plan without any violence and expressly warns Gobler against bringing any sort of weapon with him. The two burglars break into Wisbottle's house and are about to remove the painting. However, at this point, Wisbottle disturbs them and says that he has called the police. Barbox wishes to surrender peacefully, but Gobler takes out a knife that he has concealed in his boot and stabs Wisbottle, causing him severe injuries. Here, Barbox could legitimately assert that Gobler's vicious assault on Wisbottle fell outside the scope of the common intent. Although Barbox would certainly be guilty of committing the offence of breaking and entering with intent to commit theft (section 348(1)(a) of the *Criminal Code*), it is highly unlikely that he would be convicted of aggravated assault under section 21(2) of the *Code*.

Withdrawal from the "Common Purpose"

In what circumstances may an accomplice withdraw from a common intention to carry out an unlawful purpose and thereby absolve himself or herself from liability for all acts subsequently committed by his or her co-conspirators? The courts have held that the accused person must demonstrate that he or she communicated the intent to abandon the common intention to the other person or persons involved and that he or she did so in an unequivocal and timely manner.

The case of *Kirkness* (1990) provides an illustration of circumstances in which the defence of "abandoning the common intent" was raised successfully. In this case, the accused had formed an intention in common with his co-accused to carry out the unlawful purpose of breaking and entering. The two men broke into the victim's house. The accused put a chair at the front door to prevent anyone from entering the premises and ransacked the house while the co-accused sexually assaulted and then killed the deceased by suffocation. There was no evidence to establish that the accused knew beforehand that the co-accused would commit sexual assault or kill the victim. Following the sexual assault and at the point when the co-accused was strangling the deceased, the accused told his co-accused not to do so because he might kill her. Was the accused a party to the killing by virtue of common intention under section 21(2)? Justice Cory, in delivering the majority judgment of the Supreme Court of Canada, dealt with the contention that the accused had abandoned the common intention prior to the killing and held that

> [t]here is no evidence that the appellant was a party to the suffocation of Elizabeth Johnson. Rather, he told Snowbird not to strangle the victim as he was going to kill her. His statement makes it clear that he was not aiding or abetting Snowbird in the strangulation or suffocation of Mrs. Johnson. These words of the appellant constituted "timely notice" to Snowbird that he was not a party to the strangulation and suffocation.... Thus in those misdeeds Snowbird was acting on his own. It is therefore apparent that even if the appellant could be considered a party to the sexual assault, by the time of the attempted strangulation he had clearly resiled from any agreement or arrangement with Snowbird and was not a party to the suffocation of the victim.

The *Kirkness* case stands in sharp contrast to *Forknall* (2003), in which the British Columbia Court of Appeal soundly rejected the contention that the accused had withdrawn from the common intention referred to in section 21(2) of the *Criminal Code*. Forknall and his co-accused, Copeland, were

charged with first degree murder. They had taken the victim to a remote place as part of a plan to kill her. Copeland struck the victim twice on the head, using a crowbar. Copeland turned over the crowbar to Forknall, who said that he could not hit the victim. Copeland told Forknall, "You're going to have to because I can't." Forknall then took the crowbar and hit the victim 12 times on the side of her head. Forknall and Copeland later hid the body in a hole that they had previously dug. Both Forknall and Copeland were convicted at their trial. Forknall appealed to the British Columbia Court of Appeal, which dismissed his appeal. One of the arguments advanced by Forknall was that he had effectively withdrawn from the common intention to kill the victim at the point when he initially refused to strike the victim. He further contended that the victim was already dead when he administered the 12 blows with the crowbar. In delivering the judgment of the Court of Appeal, Justice Ryan stated that the trial judge had not erred when he instructed the jury on the elements of Forknall's defence. Indeed, in the view of the Court of Appeal, there was "no air of reality" either to the defence of abandonment of common intention or to any defence based on causation:

> … Forknall said he told Copeland that he could not strike the first blow. Copeland took it upon himself to do that. When Copeland told Forknall that he could not strike the victim again, that Forknall would have to do it, Forknall picked up the crowbar and administered a flurry of blows. Forknall did not indicate his withdrawal from the plan. He merely said that he could not strike the first blow. This display of queasiness does not constitute evidence of an intention to abandon the enterprise, nor can it be said to be unequivocal notice of such an intention. In my view there was no air of reality to the defence of abandonment.
>
> Nor is there any air of reality to a defence based on causation. In this case no importance can be attached to the question [of] who struck the fatal blow. This murder was a joint enterprise. The blows of one were the blows of the other.

In the case of *B. (S.R.)* (2009), the Alberta Court of Appeal asserted that context is very important in determining whether the accused person has effectively abandoned a common intent. As Justice Berger noted, in delivering the majority judgment of the appellate court, the depth of the accused person's prior involvement in a criminal scheme with others may be an important factor in judging whether or not there was an unequivocal and timely communication of withdrawal from that scheme:

> By way of example, someone who was involved, but not deeply immersed in a joint enterprise, it might be thought, could demonstrate abandonment in a less definitive manner. Being within the circle, but on the periphery, might arguably require less in the way of express language or behaviour. On the other hand, someone who is deeply immersed in the joint scheme and, accordingly, closer to the centre of the circle, it might be thought, would be required to demonstrate in more certain terms that he or she has left the circle.
>
> In my opinion, context is critical. That is because it may equally be argued that the more deeply involved you are the more difficult it is to escape without incurring the wrath of your co-actors and that, accordingly, somewhat less of a demonstration of abandonment might for that reason suffice. It seems to me that these are the contextual factors that a trial judge properly takes into account in determining whether or not there is an air of reality to the defence.

In the *B. (S.R.)* case, the accused was one of a group of five individuals who lured a 13-year-old girl, N.C., and her friend, K.B., to a golf course, where N.C. was raped and killed. The accused hit N.C. on the head with a wrench, causing the victim to fall to the ground where she was sexually assaulted by two of the males in the group. Before the sexual assaults were completed, the accused left the scene with K.B., remarking that she was taking K.B. to the car because she was "cold and did not need to see this." There was evidence that, before proceeding to the golf course, the group of five had formed an intention in common to kill N.C. The accused was charged with first degree murder but raised the defence of abandonment and was convicted, instead, of manslaughter. The Crown appealed but the Alberta Court of Appeal dismissed the appeal, ruling that there was evidence at the trial that was capable of supporting a defence of abandonment.

What was the context in light of which the accused's action should be evaluated? There was evidence that at least one of the other members of the group was afraid and that K.B. was "terrified" and in a state of shock. The Court of Appeal, therefore, accepted that it was reasonable to assume that the accused was also afraid of the violent members in the group. Given the state of fear that had gripped the accused and the likelihood that she would have placed herself in danger if she openly confronted the violent members of the group, leaving the scene of the sexual assaults constituted a sufficiently unequivocal and timely communication of her wish to dissociate herself from the common intention to kill the victim. In the particular circumstances of this case, the accused's action clearly demonstrated that she wanted no further part in the deadly enterprise.*

LIABILITY AS AN ACCESSORY AFTER THE FACT

Section 23(1) of the *Criminal Code* provides that an **accessory after the fact**

> ... to an offence is one who, knowing that a person has been a party to the offence, receives, comforts or assists that person for the purpose of enabling that person to escape.

The *mens rea* and *actus reus* elements, defined by section 23(1), are relatively straightforward. For example, in the case of *Young* (1950), Justice Bissonnette said,

> This section obviously admits three constituent elements of the offence: knowledge that a crime had been committed, the desire to help the delinquent to escape and finally a positive act or omission intended to aid him in making his escape.

In the *Young* case (1950), it appears that a man named Douglas Perreault had killed a police constable in Montreal. Perreault's sister, Young, and two other men set out from Montreal to Sheenboro, Ontario, to inform Douglas Perreault's mother of the killing. Not long before reaching their destination, they met a car containing Douglas and Donald Perreault. Both cars stopped, and the Perreault brothers were informed that the police were looking for them in connection with the murder. They also learned that the police knew their names and the licence number of their car. Young offered to hide the Perreault brothers but his offer was refused. Young was convicted as an accessory after the fact to murder and appealed his conviction to the Quebec Court of Appeal. His appeal was dismissed. Justice Bissonnette addressed the critical issues in the following manner:

> In the present case, there is no doubt that Young knew that a crime had been committed by Douglas and Donald Perreault.... [T]he information that he furnished ... meant efficacious assistance to the delinquents' escape. To tell them that the police are on their trail is to tell them that they have been identified, when they were still able, at that moment, to entertain the hope that they were not suspected of being the authors of this crime. It was giving them, by this information, immediate and efficacious

---

* After going to press, the Supreme Court of Canada allowed an appeal by the Crown and substituted a verdict of first degree murder on the ground that there was no evidence to support a defence of abandonment: R .v Bird, 2009 SCC 60.

assistance. The fact that the accused chose, after this information, a method of escape different from that suggested by [the] appellant, does not dispel the efficacy of [the] appellant's intervention.

The requirement that the accused person "know" that an offence has been committed, by the individual to whom he or she gives assistance, is clearly of pivotal importance. However, the courts have emphasized that wilful blindness on the part of the accused will be treated as being equivalent to actual knowledge in the context of section 23(1) of the *Criminal Code*. For example, in *Duong* (1998), the accused was charged with being an accessory after the fact to a murder allegedly committed by Lam. Both television and newspaper reports had linked Lam to two homicides. Lam told Duong that he was "in trouble for murder" and needed shelter. Duong allowed Lam to hide in his apartment for about two weeks before the latter was discovered by the police. Duong knew of the media reports but did not ask Lam any questions about them. He told the police that Lam "just came to me and told me he was in trouble for it but I didn't want to know anything because I knew I would be in trouble for helping him hide, so I didn't want to know anymore." The Ontario Court of Appeal ruled that wilful blindness on the part of the accused would be sufficient *mens rea* for conviction of the offence of being an accessory after the fact.[6] As Justice Doherty noted,

> Wilful blindness refers to a state of mind which is aptly described as "deliberate ignorance."... Actual suspicion, combined with a conscious decision not to make inquiries which could confirm that suspicion, is equated in the eyes of the criminal law with actual knowledge. Both are subjective and both are sufficiently blameworthy to justify the imposition of criminal liability.

The punishment for being an accessory after the fact is set out in section 463 of the *Code*; it is the same as the punishment for an attempt to commit an offence.

THE IMPACT OF SECTION 23.1 OF THE CRIMINAL CODE

Section 23.1 of the *Criminal Code* (which came into force in April 1984) stipulates that an accused person may become a party to a criminal offence, even if the person who actually commits it cannot be convicted of that offence:

> For greater certainty, sections 21 to 23 apply in respect of an accused notwithstanding the fact that the person whom the accused aids, abets, counsels or procures or receives, comforts or assists cannot be convicted of the offence.

A child under the age of 12 years may not be found criminally responsible for his or her actions (section 13 of the *Criminal Code*). Section 23.1 ensures that, should an adult employ a child under the age of 12 years to commit an offence, such as theft, the adult will be found to be a party to the offence regardless of the fact that the child may not be prosecuted. However, section 23.1 is general in its application and is not limited to the case where the principal offender is a young child. For example, in the case of *S. (F.J.)* (1997), the accused had been charged with being an accessory after the fact to murder. Her brother was tried separately in Youth Court for having committed the murder but was acquitted. It was argued on behalf of the accused that she could not be convicted as an accessory after the fact if the alleged principal had been acquitted. However, the Nova Scotia Court of Appeal ruled that, in light of section 23.1 of the *Code*, the accused should nevertheless be convicted of the offence. It is important to bear in mind that the trial judge in the accused's case had found, strictly on the basis of the evidence presented at the accused's trial, that the accused's brother had, in fact, committed murder and that the accused had deliberately tried to cover it up.

In delivering the judgment of the Court of Appeal, Justice Jones noted that section 23.1 had made a significant change to the old common law concerning the liability of accessories:

> It would appear that the provisions of the *Code* were intended to treat parties to offences in the same manner, i.e. that accessories before the fact, aiders and abettors and accessories after the fact would be treated as principals. This is confirmed by s. 23.1 of the *Code*. It is clear from that section and s. 592 of the *Code* it is not necessary to convict a principal in order to convict an accessory.[7] While the language does not refer to the acquittal of the principal, in my

---

[6] *Duong* was ultimately convicted of being an accessory after the fact to manslaughter because, after a successful appeal, Lam was found guilty of manslaughter rather than murder (*Duong* (2001)).

[7] S. 592 provides: "Any one who is charged with being an accessory after the fact to any offence may be indicted, whether or not the principal or any other party to the offence has been indicted or convicted or is or is not amenable to justice."

view the words "whether or not the principal" is convicted, are broad enough to encompass the acquittal of the principal. Those provisions have changed the common law.

This remarkably expansive interpretation of section 23.1 was later endorsed by the Supreme Court of Canada [*S. (F.J.)* (1998)].

INCHOATE OFFENCES

The final section of this chapter concerns an extremely important topic, namely, the various **inchoate offences** (incomplete or preventive offences) that are defined in the *Criminal Code*. The rationale for such offences is fairly obvious in that they permit the police to intervene and prevent the commission of potentially serious crimes. As the Ontario Court of Appeal stated in the case of *Chan* (2003), "[S]trictly inchoate crimes are a unique class of criminal offences in the sense that they criminalize acts that precede harmful conduct but do not necessarily inflict harmful consequences in and of themselves." However, the Canadian courts have nevertheless emphasized that individuals must not be punished for their malevolent intentions alone: indeed, it is clear that the Crown must prove some overt act on the part of the accused person to justify conviction of an inchoate offence. The inchoate offences to be considered in this chapter are (1) counselling, (2) attempt, and (3) conspiracy.

1. COUNSELLING AN OFFENCE THAT IS NOT COMMITTED

Earlier in this chapter, we discussed the criminal liability of individuals who counsel the commission of offences that are ultimately perpetrated; this liability is governed by section 22 of the *Code*. However, section 464 deals with the situation where an individual "counsels" another person to commit an offence that is not ultimately perpetrated:

> Except where otherwise expressly provided by law, the following provisions apply in respect of persons who counsel other persons to commit offences, namely,
>
> (a) every one who counsels another person to commit an indictable offence is, if the offence is not committed, guilty of an indictable offence and is liable to the same punishment to which a person who attempts to commit that offence is liable; and

> (b) every one who counsels another person to commit an offence punishable on summary conviction is, if the offence is not committed, guilty of an offence punishable on summary conviction.

It should be remembered that section 22(3) states that, for the purposes of the *Criminal Code*, the word "counsel" includes "procure, solicit or incite." In the *Hamilton* case (2005), Justice Fish, in delivering the majority judgment of the Supreme Court of Canada, provided definitions of these terms:

> In their relevant senses, the *Canadian Oxford Dictionary* (2nd ed. 2004) defines "counsel" as "advise" or "recommend (a course of action)"; "procure", as "bring about"; "solicit", as "ask repeatedly or earnestly for or seek or invite", or "make a request or petition to (a person)"; and "incite", as "urge". "Procure" has been held judicially to include "instigate" and "persuade." . .

In the *Sharpe* case (2001), Chief Justice McLachlin on behalf of the majority of the Supreme Court of Canada emphasized that, although the word "counsel" "can mean simply to advise," in the "criminal law it has been given the stronger meaning of actively inducing." In the *Hamilton* case (2005), Justice Fish of the Supreme Court of Canada reiterated this meaning of the word "counsel," noting that "the *actus reus* for counselling will be established where the materials or statements made or transmitted by the accused *actively induce* or *advocate*—and do not merely *describe*—the commission of an offence."

However, it is not necessary for the Crown to prove that anyone was actually influenced by the accused's counselling behaviour. This proposition is well illustrated by the case of *McLeod and Georgia Straight Publishing Co.* (1970). In this case, the publishing company and its editor-in-chief were charged with counselling the commission of an indictable offence that was not committed—namely, the cultivation of marijuana (contrary to the provisions of section 6 of the (now repealed) *Narcotic Control Act*).[8] Under the heading "Plant Your Seeds," an issue of the *Georgia Straight* magazine contained an article that furnished detailed instructions concerning the planting, fertilization, cultivation, and harvesting of the marijuana plant. A woman who had purchased

---

[8] See now section 7 of the *Controlled Drugs and Substances Act*, S.C. 1996, c. 19.

a copy of the magazine appeared as a witness at the trial and admitted she was not influenced by the counselling contained in the article concerned. However, the provincial court judge convicted both McLeod and the publishing company, stating that "if the person bought the paper and the only fair inference is that it was on public sale at the corner of Georgia and Granville Street and if the person bought the paper and read it, they were in fact being counselled to grow marijuana." The defendants appealed to the British Columbia Court of Appeal, which affirmed the company's conviction but set aside McLeod's conviction on the basis that there was "insufficient evidence" to convict him. Justice Maclean made the following significant observations:

> Defence counsel has suggested that "counselling" is not complete unless the person to whom the communication is directed has been influenced by the communication. I cannot accept this submission as in my view there is no justification for assigning such a limited meaning to the word "counselling."... In my view, the purchaser of this newspaper was counselled to cultivate marijuana.

Just as it is no defence that the person who was counselled was not, in fact, influenced by the accused's efforts to persuade him or her to commit an offence, it is likewise not open to an accused person to assert that he or she should not be convicted of counselling an offence because the accused later repented and renounced his or her previous actions. Since counselling is, by definition, an inchoate offence, the courts have taken the view that the offence has been irrevocably committed just as soon as the accused has attempted to persuade another person to commit a crime. This principle was strongly articulated in the *Gonzague* case (1983), which involved a charge of procuring the commission of the offence of first degree murder (which was, fortunately, not committed). The accused had incited another individual to murder a business rival. However, when this individual (wearing a body pack recorder provided by the police) later approached Gonzague, the accused told him to forget about the matter and to keep the $200 that he had previously paid him in advance. It was suggested that Gonzague had renounced his previous intention of procuring the murder of his rival and that this renunciation should provide him with a valid defence. This suggestion was unequivocally rejected. In the words of Justice Martin, who delivered the judgment of the Ontario Court of Appeal:

> The offence of procuring under s. [464] is complete when the solicitation or incitement occurs even though it is immediately rejected by the person solicited, or even though the person solicited merely pretends assent and has no intention of committing the offence. There is no authority in either the Canadian or Commonwealth decision(s) in support of the view that renunciation of the criminal purpose constitutes a defence to a charge of "counselling, procuring or inciting" under s. [464]....

The Supreme Court of Canada has ruled that the *mens rea* required for conviction of counselling is either an intention that the offence actually be committed by the person who is counselled or extreme recklessness with respect to this outcome. In the case of *Hamilton* (2005), the accused had sold computer files and documents to other individuals, using the Internet to do so. These files contained instructions for bomb making, house breaking, and a program that generated credit card numbers that might be used for fraudulent purposes. Hamilton was charged with counselling the commission of four offences that were not in fact committed: namely, making explosive substances with intent, doing anything with intent to cause an explosion, break and enter with intent, and fraud. At his trial, Hamilton admitted that he had read a computer-generated list of the files concerned but denied that he had actually read the contents of those files. Although he had generated some credit card numbers, he had never used them and there had been no complaints from the bank concerning their misuse. The trial judge acquitted Hamilton of all charges because, in her view, he never intended that these offences should be committed. The Alberta Court of Appeal upheld the acquittals. The Crown subsequently appealed to the Supreme Court of Canada. The pivotal issue before the Supreme Court concerned the *mens rea* elements that must be proved for conviction of the offence of counselling.

In delivering the judgment of the majority of the Supreme Court in *Hamilton* (2005), Justice Fish articulated the *mens rea* requirements for the offence of counselling under section 464 of the *Criminal Code*:

> ... [T]he *mens rea* consists in nothing less than an accompanying *intent or conscious disregard of the substantial and unjustified risk inherent in the counselling:* that is, it must be shown that the accused either intended that the offence counselled be committed, or knowingly counselled the commission of the

offence while aware of the unjustified risk that the offence counselled was in fact likely to be committed as a result of the accused's conduct. [emphasis in original]

Prior to the *Hamilton* case (2005), it had been assumed that only the actual intent that the counselled offence be committed would constitute sufficient *mens rea* for a conviction under section 464. However, the Supreme Court of Canada now appears to have added extreme recklessness as an alternative form of *mens rea* that will be sufficient for conviction of counselling an offence that was not, in fact, committed. Indeed, Justice Fish indicated that, if recklessness is to be relied on as satisfying the *mens rea* requirements, the Crown must prove that the accused person was subjectively aware of, and consciously disregarded, the "*substantial* and unjustified risk inherent in the counselling." It would appear that consciously disregarding a mere *possibility* that the offence may be committed would not satisfy the standard of recklessness developed by Justice Fish. There must be awareness on the part of the accused that there is a *substantial* risk that the offence will be committed. Justice Fish emphasized that the standard of recklessness required for conviction under section 464 is a high one. He expressly rejected the contention that a less rigorous standard should be adopted in order to combat the potential misuse of the Internet for criminal purposes:

> ... I would resist any temptation to depart in this case from that relatively demanding standard. The Internet provides fertile ground for sowing the seeds of unlawful conduct on a borderless scale. And, at the hearing of the appeal, Crown counsel expressed with eloquence and conviction the urgent need for an appropriate prophylactic response.
>
> In my view, however, this task must be left to Parliament. Even if they were minded to do so, courts cannot contain the inherent dangers of cyberspace crime by expanding or transforming offences, such as counselling, that were conceived to meet a different and unrelated need. Any attempt to do so may well do more harm than good, inadvertently catching morally innocent conduct and unduly limiting harmless access to information.

The Supreme Court of Canada affirmed Hamilton's acquittal on the charges of counselling the commission of the crimes of making explosive substances with intent, doing anything with intent to cause an explosion, and break and enter with intent: in the view of the majority of the justices, the trial judge had correctly found that Hamilton lacked the

necessary *mens rea* for conviction of the offence of counselling. However, the Court ordered a new trial on the charge of counselling the offence of fraud. The majority of the Supreme Court concluded that the trial judge should have found that Hamilton did have the necessary *mens rea* for conviction of counselling the commission of fraud. Hamilton had sent an e-mail "teaser" to various individuals in which he advertised software that could generate "valid working credit card numbers." As Justice Fish stated in his judgment,

> ... [A]s regards the credit card number generator, the trial judge concluded that the documents offered for sale—and sold—by Mr. Hamilton "actively promote or encourage the actions described in them."... [S]he found that the documents "are likely to incite and are 'with a view to' inciting the offence."...
>
> Nothing in the evidence suggests that Mr. Hamilton intended these documents to be read in a different manner or that they be used for a different purpose. Moreover, the trial judge expressly found that Mr. Hamilton had "subjective knowledge that the use of false credit card numbers is illegal."...
>
> ... [Hamilton] sought to make "a quick buck" by encouraging the intended recipients of his Internet solicitation to purchase a device that generated credit card numbers easily put to fraudulent use.

The trial judge's conclusion that Mr. Hamilton did not intend to induce the recipients to use those numbers is incompatible with the plain meaning of the "teaser" e-mail and with her other findings of fact, including her finding that Mr. Hamilton well understood that use of the generated numbers was illegal.

2. ATTEMPT

Section 24 of the *Code* and Attempt

The rationale underlying the law of **criminal attempt** is undoubtedly the wisdom of preventing crimes before they are committed. It would be absurd if a police officer were required to wait until a robber actually mugged a victim before the officer could intervene and make an arrest. Similarly, it is necessary to punish an individual who has made a serious attempt to commit a crime because it is highly likely that, if the failed attempt is not sanctioned in some way, the accused will keep trying until he or she is successful. However, the problem that one immediately encounters is that it is certainly not an easy task to decide when the accused person has travelled far enough along the road toward completion of an offence to justify the intervention of the police and an ultimate conviction of the crime of attempt.

The general provision concerning criminal attempts is set out in section 24 of the *Criminal Code*:

(1) Every one who, having an intent to commit an offence, does or omits to do anything for the purpose of carrying out his intention is guilty of an attempt to commit the offence whether or not it was possible under the circumstances to commit the offence.

(2) The question whether an act or omission by a person who has an intent to commit an offence is or is not mere preparation to commit the offence, and too remote to constitute an attempt to commit the offence, is a question of law.

The various punishments for criminal attempts are set out in the *Criminal Code*. Essentially, the maximum penalties are as follows:

- Life imprisonment, if the accused is convicted of attempted murder. There is a mandatory minimum prison term where a firearm is used in the commission of the offence (section 239).[9]
- Imprisonment up to a maximum term of 14 years, if the accused is convicted of attempting to commit an indictable offence that carries a maximum sentence of life imprisonment (section 463 (a)).
- For an attempt to commit any other indictable offence, imprisonment up to one-half of the longest term that might have been imposed if the accused person had successfully completed the offence (section 463(b)). For example, if the accused is found guilty of attempted theft of property worth more than $5000, the maximum penalty would be a prison term of five years since this constitutes one-half of the maximum punishment for the offence of theft over $5000 (10 years).
- For an attempt to commit a summary conviction offence, the same maximum sentence that might be imposed if the accused had successfully completed the offence (section 463(c)). The maximum penalty

for a summary conviction offence is normally a fine of $2000 and/or imprisonment for six months (section 787(1)).

- For offences that may be tried either on indictment or by summary conviction procedures, the maximum penalty will depend on the form of trial that is ultimately selected (section 463(d)). Where the accused is tried on indictment and convicted of such an offence, the maximum penalty is one-half of the maximum sentence of imprisonment that might have been imposed if the accused had been convicted of the completed offence. Where the accused is convicted of an attempt by means of summary conviction procedures, the maximum penalty is the same as that which might be imposed upon conviction of the completed summary conviction offence.

The *Mens Rea* Relating to Criminal Attempt

Since the major objective of the criminal law relating to attempts is unequivocally preventive in nature, it is scarcely surprising that the courts have emphasized the *mens rea* requirements of criminal attempts. As Justice Laidlaw of the Ontario Court of Appeal commented in the *Cline* case (1956),

Criminal intention alone is insufficient to establish a criminal attempt. There must be *mens rea* and also an *actus reus*. But it is to be observed that whereas in most crimes it is the *actus reus* which the law endeavours to prevent, and the *mens rea* is only a necessary element of the offence, in a criminal attempt the *mens rea* is of primary importance and the *actus reus* is the necessary element.

Significantly, section 24(1) of the *Code* clearly requires proof of "an intent to commit an offence" as a prerequisite for conviction of any criminal attempt. This requirement of an actual intent to commit an offence undoubtedly implies that the *mens rea* for an attempt may be quite different from that required for conviction of the completed offence. This situation would arise where the *mens rea* for the completed offence falls short of an intention to commit it. Take, for example, the offence of unlawfully causing bodily harm, contrary to section 269 of the *Code*. In the *DeSousa* case (1992), the Supreme Court of Canada ruled that the accused may be convicted of the complete offence of unlawfully causing bodily harm without having the actual intention to cause bodily harm. However, in the case of a charge of *attempt* to

---

[9] For a use of a "restricted or prohibited" firearm, the mandatory minimum sentence is five years for a first offence and seven years for a second offence. In "any other case where a firearm is used in the commission of the offence," the mandatory prison term is four years. If any type of firearm is "used in the commission of the offence and the offence is committed for the benefit of, at the direction of, or in association with, a criminal organization," the mandatory minimum prison sentence is five years for a first offence and seven for a second offence.

unlawfully cause bodily harm, the Crown would be required to prove the intention to cause bodily harm before it could obtain a conviction against the accused. Indeed, this was precisely the conclusion of the Quebec Court of Appeal when it considered this situation in the case of *Colburne* (1991). As Justice Lebel pointed out,

> Even if in certain respects one may find it illogical that the incomplete offence [or attempt] requires a degree of *mens rea* greater than that required for the completed offence, to do otherwise is to transform the attempt into a purely relational offence whose constituent elements would strictly depend on the underlying offence. It exists by itself, although it requires the identification of the underlying offence that the author of the attempt was pursuing. Its distinctive element, in respect of the identification of its mental element, is found precisely in this desire to commit the underlying offence, which corresponds to the notion of specific intent. Section 24(1) makes an attempt a question of intent, of desire of a result and not only, for example, of negligence or gross imprudence, even if that would be sufficient to find the presence of the guilty mind required for the completed offence.

The Supreme Court of Canada emphasized the need for the Crown to prove an actual intent to commit the completed offence in the case of *Ancio* (1984). The accused was charged with attempted murder, and the Crown argued that he could be convicted of this offence if he had the necessary *mens rea* to commit murder in any of the ways for which provision is made in the *Criminal Code*. As mentioned in Chapter 4, an accused person may be convicted of murder even though he or she lacks the actual intent to kill the victim. For example, an accused person may be convicted of murder, under section 229(a)(ii) of the *Criminal Code*, if he or she causes the death of a human being in the situation where the accused "means to cause him bodily harm that he knows is likely to cause his death, and is reckless whether death ensues or not." Undoubtedly, section 229(a)(ii) provides that the completed offence of murder may be committed by "reckless" defendants who deliberately inflict injuries that they know are likely to cause death. In *Ancio* (1984), the Supreme Court unequivocally ruled that, even though it is possible to be convicted of murder without an actual intent to kill, this is not the case for the crime of attempted murder: for conviction of an attempt to commit murder, nothing less than an actual intent to kill will suffice. In the words of Justice McIntyre,

A reading of s. 24 of the *Code* and its predecessors since the enactment of the first *Code* in 1892 confirms that the intent to commit the desired offence is a basic element of the offence of attempt. Indeed, because the crime of attempt may be complete without the commission of any other offence and even without the performance of any act unlawful in itself, it is abundantly clear that the criminal element of the offence of attempt may lie solely in the intent....

The completed offence of murder involves a killing. The intention to commit the complete offence of murder must therefore include an intention to kill. I find it impossible to conclude that a person may intend to commit the unintentional killings described in ss. [229 and 230] of the *Code*. I am then of the view that the *mens rea* for an attempted murder cannot be less than the specific intent to kill.

Justice McIntyre also addressed the issue of whether it is illogical to require a higher degree of *mens rea* for the offence of attempted murder than for the completed offence of murder. He stated that

[t]he intent to kill is the highest intent in murder and there is no reason in logic why an attempt to murder, aimed at the completion of the full crime of murder, should have any lesser intent. If there is any illogic in this matter, it is in the statutory characterization of unintentional killing as murder.

Earlier in this chapter, it was noted that, in the *Hamilton* case (2005), the Supreme Court of Canada modified the preexisting *mens rea* requirements for the crime of counselling an offence that is not committed. Prior to this case, the law had been that only an actual intent that the counselled offence be committed was sufficient for conviction of this inchoate crime. However, the Court expanded the scope of the *mens rea* requirements for counselling by adding extreme recklessness as a state of mind that would justify conviction of an accused person. It would, perhaps, be logical for the Supreme Court to apply this new approach to the crime of attempt, thereby effecting a significant change in the law. However, it remains to be seen if this development will take actually place in the years ahead.

The case of *Coleville* (1988) illustrates the proposition that the *mens rea* for an attempt may be inferred from the surrounding circumstances. The accused was charged with the attempted theft of a car. He was observed attempting to break into the car on the passenger door side. He and his companion fled when they saw that they had been spotted. They were later apprehended by the police and were found to be in possession of a number of items that are frequently used to break into cars as well as to remove and replace starting mechanisms. The trial judge acquitted the accused on the basis that the evidence did not permit him to ascertain with certainty whether it was the victim's vehicle or its contents that the accused intended to steal. The Crown appealed, and the Quebec Court of Appeal ultimately allowed the appeal and entered a conviction against the accused. Justice Chevalier said that

> [t]he specific intent of a person found attempting to open a vehicle, while he has in his possession a "slim Jim" or a clothes-hanger is perhaps not totally certain. However, if one finds that in addition he has a tool which can be used to rip out the starting mechanism for the motor ("puller"), for which the intruder does not have the key, and a complete replacement mechanism for the one removed, I consider that one can logically conclude that the purpose of the operation was not to carry out some little search inside the area commonly called the glove compartment. It is only normal to think that it is the automobile and not its hypothetical contents that the intruder was attempting to steal. Even more so, when there is nothing in the evidence indicating that there were some suitable objects within the respondent's view which might have attracted his attention and stimulated his covetous desire.

The *Actus Reus* Requirements Relating to Criminal Attempts

In the case of *Root* (2008), the Ontario Court of Appeal emphasized the rather elusive nature of the *actus reus* elements of criminal attempts:

> In every case of an attempt to commit an offence, the *mens rea* of the substantive offence will be present and complete. In every attempt, what is incomplete is the *actus reus* of the substantive offence. But incompleteness of the *actus reus* of the substantive offence will not bar a conviction of attempt, provided the *actus reus* is present in an incomplete, but more than preparatory way.

Providing a general definition of the *actus reus* requirements of criminal attempts is an extraordinarily difficult task since such requirements must necessarily vary in relation to the different types of criminal offences that may be attempted. Historically, the courts have discussed the issue of the *actus reus* of an attempt in terms of whether the accused's conduct was too "remote" from the completed offence to justify the imposition of criminal

liability. The notorious and intractable problem underlying the law of criminal attempts is that of where to draw the line between acts that are sufficiently "proximate" to the completed offence so as to deserve the imposition of criminal liability upon the accused and acts that are too "remote" from the completed offence to justify any form of punishment. Significantly, section 24(2) of the *Code* provides that the question of whether an act or omission is to be considered "mere preparation to commit an offence, and [therefore] too remote to constitute an attempt to commit the offence," is to be treated as a "question of law" rather than of fact; in other words, in a jury trial, this question must be answered by the trial judge as a matter of legal interpretation rather than by the jury as an issue of fact.

The manner in which judges determine whether the *actus reus* requirements of the attempt have been established by the Crown must necessarily vary according to both the nature of the crime attempted and a number of circumstances peculiar to each individual case. There can be no universal test that will determine the *actus reus* requirements of all criminal attempts. This flexible approach is well illustrated by the leading Canadian case of *Cline* (1956). In delivering the judgment of the Ontario Court of Appeal in this case, Justice Laidlaw articulated a number of principles that have been widely applied by Canadian courts:

> The consummation of a crime usually comprises a set of acts which have their genesis in an idea to do a criminal act; the idea develops to a decision to do that act; a plan may be made for putting that decision into effect; the next step may be preparation only for carrying out the intention and plan; but when that preparation is in fact fully completed, the next step in the series of acts done by the accused for the purpose and with the intention of committing the crime as planned cannot, in my opinion, be regarded as remote in its connection with that crime. The connection is in fact proximate.

Justice Laidlaw then proceeded to specify a number of basic requirements for proof of the *actus reus* elements of the crime of attempt:

> There must be *mens rea* and also an *actus reus* to constitute a criminal attempt, but the criminality of misconduct lies mainly in the intention of the accused.... It is not essential that the *actus reus* be a crime or a tort or even a moral wrong or social mischief.... The *actus reus* must be more than mere preparation to commit a crime. But ... when the

preparation to commit a crime is in fact fully complete and ended, the next step done by the accused for the purpose and with the intention of committing a specific crime constitutes an *actus reus* sufficient in law to establish a criminal attempt to commit that crime.

The factors in the *Cline* case illustrate the inherent difficulties involved in the task of determining whether the *actus reus* of attempt has been proved. Cline was charged with indecent assault on Peter C., who was 12 years old. Cline was convicted at trial and appealed to the Ontario Court of Appeal, which set aside the conviction of indecent assault and, instead, substituted one for attempt (see section 660 of the *Code*). Cline had approached Peter C., asking him to carry his suitcases for a "couple of dollars." In fact, Cline had no suitcases with him. Peter C. said "no" and went on his way. The boy testified that Cline had been wearing dark sunglasses that "almost covered his whole face," even though the encounter took place at night. If Cline's conduct had been an isolated act, it is doubtful that the Crown would have been able to establish that an attempt to commit an indecent assault had been committed.

However, evidence was introduced that clearly established that Cline had previously approached a number of other boys in similar circumstances; in at least one of these cases, Cline had actually performed an indecent act without the victim's consent. The

Court of Appeal ruled that this evidence was sufficient to establish the *mens rea* of the attempt to commit an indecent assault upon Peter C.: "[E]vidence of similar acts done by the accused before the offence with which he is charged, and also afterwards if such acts are not too remote in time, is admissible to establish a pattern of conduct from which the Court may properly find *mens rea*." The remaining question to be resolved was whether Cline's approach to Peter C. constituted "mere preparation" or whether it could be considered sufficiently "proximate" to the completed offence so as to justify conviction of an attempt; in other words, had the Crown established the *actus reus* of the attempt? In dealing with this issue, Justice Laidlaw stated,

> The appellant intended to commit the crime of indecent assault. He made a plan in detail to carry out his intention. The plan comprised a series of acts which form a clear-cut pattern of conduct, and the accused followed that pattern of conduct on all occasions or the occasion in question, and in precise accordance with that pattern of conduct, he chose a time and place where he might procure a victim necessary for the consummation of the crime. He went to that place at the chosen time. Before or after doing so he put on large sunglasses to disguise his identity. He then waited for the opportunity to pursue his planned conduct to the end. His preparation to commit the intended crime was fully complete. He was ready to embark on the course of committing the intended crime. It was necessary only to lure a victim to a secluded place.... The acts of the appellant from the first moment he approached Peter C. were not preparation. They were not too remote to constitute an attempt to commit the offence of indecent assault....

A significant example of the application of the flexible test articulated in the *Cline* case is furnished by the decision of the Supreme Court of Canada in *Deutsch* (1986). Deutsch was charged with attempting to procure women to have illicit sexual intercourse with other persons, contrary to the provisions of section 212(1)(a) of the *Code*. He interviewed three applicants for a secretary/sales assistant position with a franchise marketing business. During the course of the interviews, he indicated that a successful applicant would be expected to have sexual intercourse with clients if that was necessary to secure a contract for his company. He also suggested that a secretary/sales assistant could earn up to $100 000 per year from commission or bonuses in relation to the sale of

"When the preparation to commit a crime is in fact fully complete and ended, the next step done by the accused for the purpose and with the intention of committing a specific crime constitutes an actus reus sufficient in law to establish a criminal attempt to commit that crime" (Cline (1956)).

franchises. Deutsch did not actually make an offer of employment during the interviews. After they had heard what the job entailed, all three of the women said that they were not interested. A police officer also posed as an applicant. When she indicated that she was interested in the position despite the unusual requirements, Deutsch did not make an offer of employment to her but, rather, told her to think it over and let him know.

The critical issue in the *Deutsch* case was whether the acts and statements of the accused were sufficient to constitute the *actus reus* of an attempt to procure women to have illicit sexual intercourse. In short, had he gone beyond mere preparation? The trial judge ruled that the accused's actions were too remote from the commission of the full offence of procuring and that, therefore, they did not amount to an attempt. The judge apparently believed that, if the accused had actually made an offer of employment, he would have crossed the line between preparation and attempt. Deutsch was, therefore, acquitted at his trial. However, the Crown launched a successful appeal to the Ontario Court of Appeal, which ordered a new trial on the basis that the accused had indeed committed an attempt to procure. The Supreme Court of Canada upheld the Court of Appeal's decision in this respect. Justice Le Dain agreed with the proposition that it was not possible to formulate a "satisfactory general criterion" for drawing the line between mere preparation and attempt. Indeed, he suggested that this distinction should be left to "common sense judgment" in the context of individual cases and that, in his opinion,

> ... the distinction between preparation and attempt is essentially a qualitative one, involving the relationship between the nature and quality of the act in question and the nature of the complete offence, although consideration must necessarily be given, in making that qualitative distinction, to the relative proximity of the act in question to what would have been the completed offence, in terms of time, location and acts under the control of the accused remaining to be accomplished.

Justice Le Dain also stated that the accused's actions could constitute the *actus reus* of an attempt even if further acts were required on the part of the accused or a significant period of time might elapse before the offence could finally be completed. In the Deutsch case, Justice Le Dain believed that holding out the prospect of large rewards in the course of the interviews, during which the requirement of

sexual intercourse with clients was mentioned, could indeed constitute the *actus reus* of an attempt to procure the women involved. It could be considered "an important step" in the commission of the offence:

> Before an offer of employment could be made in such circumstances an applicant would have to seek the position, despite its special requirement. Thus such inducement or persuasion would be the decisive act in the procuring. There would be little else that the appellant would be required to do towards the completion of the offence other than to make the formal offer of employment.

Similarly, in *Gladstone* (1996), the two accused men were charged with attempting to sell herring spawn on kelp, which had not been not caught under the authority of the licence that was required by the terms of the *Pacific Herring Regulations*, SOR/84-324. The accused were members of the Heiltsuk Band, and they shipped 4200 pounds (1900 kg) of herring spawn on kelp from Bella Bella to Richmond, a suburb of Vancouver. The accused entered a fish store in Vancouver and asked the owner if he was "interested" in herring spawn on kelp. The owner declined and the accused, who had been placed under surveillance, were arrested by fisheries officers. Their entire supply of herring spawn on kelp was later seized. The accused claimed that the requirement for a licence to sell herring spawn on kelp infringed their Aboriginal right to fish. The case proceeded all the way to the Supreme Court, which ordered a new trial on the question of whether the fisheries regulations were valid. However, the Court did advert to the important issue of whether the Crown had established the necessary *actus reus* requirement for the charge of attempting to sell the herring spawn on kelp.

Chief Justice Lamer held that the accused had gone beyond mere preparation and had, in fact, attempted to sell the herring spawn on kelp:

> In this case the facts as found by the trial judge clearly demonstrate the appellants attempted to sell herring spawn on kelp to Mr. Hirose. The appellants arranged for the shipment of the herring spawn on kelp to Vancouver, they took a sample of the herring spawn on kelp to Mr. Hirose's store and they specifically asked Mr. Hirose if he was "interested" in herring spawn on kelp. The appellants' actions have sufficient proximity to the acts necessary to complete the offence of selling herring spawn on kelp to move those actions beyond mere preparation to actual attempt.

Finally, in the more recent case of *Boudreau* (2005), the Nova Scotia Court of Appeal furnished a striking example of the application of the principle that, once an accused person has finished his or her preparations, the next step taken toward completion of the offence that he or she desires to commit constitutes the *actus reus* of a criminal attempt. Boudreau had recently separated from his wife and arrived at her house in a rage. He was carrying a rifle and told her that he wanted to know what she was "putting him through." He pointed the rifle at his wife with "one hand in the trigger area." On three occasions, Boudreau's wife gestured to him to calm down. Each time this happened, Boudreau told his wife to "back up." However, she eventually escaped. Boudreau followed her to a house across the street and tried unsuccessfully to kick in the door. He told a number of neighbours that he intended to kill his spouse. For some 10 minutes, he remained on the veranda, playing with his gun (it was not clear whether he was trying to load or unload it). He was then arrested and was subsequently charged and convicted of attempted murder. Boudreau appealed against his conviction on the basis that the trial judge had erred when he concluded that Boudreau's actions went beyond mere preparation and constituted the *actus reus* of attempted murder. However, the Nova Scotia Court of Appeal dismissed Boudreau's appeal. The Court agreed with the trial judge's finding that the Crown had proved beyond a reasonable doubt that Boudreau intended to kill his wife. However, the main issue to be decided was whether the *actus reus* of attempted murder had been established. On this matter, Chief Justice MacDonald stated that

> ... the trial judge had evidence of the appellant doing the following acts:
>
> - either before entering Ms. Boudreau's kitchen or on Ruby Swaine's veranda, loading the gun with three bullets,
> - carrying the gun from his car to the victim's home with "one hand in the trigger area",
> - pointing the gun at his victim on at least three occasions,
> - following his victim across the street to Ms. Swaine's home,
> - attempting to kick Ms. Swaine's door open.

These facts provided the trial judge with ample justification to conclude that the *actus reus* had been established. In reaching this conclusion, I am mindful that the appellant's actions did not progress beyond pointing the gun. In other words, the trial judge found no reliable evidence to conclude that the appellant tried to fire a shot. Yet, there need not necessarily be an attempt to shoot in order to sustain a conviction for attempted murder. Again, there need be only one step following preparation to establish the *actus reus*.

Clearly, in the view of the chief justice, it was not necessary for the Crown to prove that Boudreau had actually attempted to shoot his wife in order to obtain a conviction for attempted murder.

Attempting the Impossible

It will be remembered that section 24(1) of the *Code* provides that an accused person may be convicted of an attempt to commit an offence "whether or not it was possible under the circumstances to commit the offence." This provision may seem to be a little strange at first sight. However, Canadian courts have generally encountered few difficulties in applying it in practice. The judicial approach, in this matter, is well illustrated by the leading case of *Scott* (1964). In this case, the accused was charged with attempting to steal "cash valued at less than $50." The facts were that Scott put his hand in the back pocket of a man called Dodd. Scott was apprehended by Dodd and turned over to the police. There was a wallet in Dodd's pocket but it contained no cash. The accused was convicted of attempted theft, and his subsequent appeal to the Alberta Court of Appeal was dismissed. Justice Macdonald, in delivering the majority judgment, stated that

> [t]here can be no doubt about the appellant's attempt to steal from the pocket of Dodd. The difficulty arises from the fact that he was charged with attempting to steal money, while there is nothing in the evidence to show that Dodd had any money in his pocket.
>
> In the present case, the appellant pickpocket could not know what was in the pocket of Dodd. I think, however, it is a self-evident fact that a pickpocket is desirous of stealing money. A pickpocket could not be convicted of stealing money unless the money was there, but it does seem that an attempt to steal money stands on an entirely different footing.
>
> It seems to me that the proper and reasonable inference to be made under the circumstances that existed was that the appellant had the intent to steal money from the pocket of Dodd. The evidence established that the appellant did an act towards the accomplishment of that objective.

Similarly, in *Kerster* (2003), the accused was convicted of attempting to obtain for consideration (payment) the sexual services of a person whom he believed to be under the age of 18 years (contrary to section 212(4) of the *Criminal Code*). Kerster had exchanged e-mail messages with a Vancouver police officer who used a false name. The accused expressed an interest in paying for the sexual services of a young person under the age of 18. The police officer made arrangements for Kerster to meet with a woman who posed as the mother of an 11-year-old child. The woman and Kerster then went to a hotel room where she said the child would be waiting. However, the only occupant of the room was a member of the Vancouver Police Vice Squad and he immediately arrested Kerster. The child with whom Kerster believed he was going to have sexual relations never existed. Kerster was convicted at trial and his appeal was later dismissed by the British Columbia Court of Appeal. Kerster unsuccessfully contended that he could not be convicted of an attempt if the person whose sexual services he sought to procure never even existed. However, this contention was rejected. Chief Justice Finch, in delivering the judgment of the Court of Appeal, agreed with the analysis of the trial judge, who had stated the following:

> I am satisfied beyond a reasonable doubt that the accused performed steps beyond mere preparation to carry out his intent here. He embarked on negotiations to pay for the sexual services of a person under 18 in his e-mail correspondence. He specified the services he wished her to perform, and produced money to pay for these. He then accompanied the "mother" of the girl to meet her. In my view, it matters not whether the hotel room contained an 11 year old girl, an adult police officer posing as a young girl, or no girl at all. His actions were unambiguous and constituted legally sufficient steps going beyond mere preparation to commit the offence set out in s. 212(4).

In *United States v. Dynar* (1997), the Supreme Court of Canada undertook an extensive analysis of the so-called question of "**impossibility**" in the law of criminal attempts and reaffirmed the view that section 24(1) of the *Code* must be given a literal interpretation insofar as it clearly precludes an accused person from raising impossibility as a defence to a charge of attempt. *Dynar* (1997) involved an extradition request by the United States of America. Dynar had been the subject of a failed "sting" operation

conducted by the Federal Bureau of Investigation in the United States, and the United States government now sought to extradite Dynar from Canada on charges of attempting to launder money and conspiracy to launder money. Dynar could not be extradited unless it could be established that his conduct would have amounted to a criminal attempt or criminal conspiracy if it had taken place entirely in Canada.

The two relevant money laundering offences under Canadian criminal law arose under section 462.31(1) of the *Criminal Code* and section 19.2(1) of the (now repealed) *Narcotic Control Act*. At the time that the case first arose, the offences of money laundering under these two statutes required that the Crown prove that the accused laundered money "*knowing*" that it had been obtained by the commission of a designated offence. In fact, the monies involved in the Dynar sting operation were not the proceeds of crime at all, but rather monies belonging to the United States government. This meant that Dynar could not have committed the (completed) money laundering offences because one cannot know something that is not true.[10] However, the critical question was whether he could instead be convicted of *attempting* and/or *conspiring* to commit these offences. The Supreme Court of Canada ultimately rejected Dynar's argument that, since it would have been impossible for him to have committed the completed money laundering offences, he had, therefore, not committed any offences known to Canadian law. In light of the Court's ruling that Dynar could potentially have been convicted of both an attempt and a conspiracy to commit the money laundering offences, he was ordered to be extradited to stand trial in the United States.

Justices Cory and Iacobucci stated that "sufficient evidence was produced to show that Mr. Dynar intended to commit the money-laundering offences, and that he took steps more than merely preparatory in order to realize his intention." They pointed out that this was "enough to establish that he attempted to launder money contrary to s. 24(1) of the *Criminal Code*." The Supreme Court essentially held that the issue of impossibility was, by virtue of the wording of

---

[10] Section 462.31(1) of the *Criminal Code* has now been amended so that it is an offence for a person to launder money "knowing *or believing that* all or a part of that property or of those proceeds was obtained or derived directly or indirectly as a result of (a designated offence)." [emphasis added]

section 24(1), totally irrelevant to the determination of whether an accused person is guilty of a criminal attempt. Indeed, Justices Cory and Iacobucci firmly noted that so-called "impossible" attempts "are no less menacing than other attempts":

> After all, the only difference between an attempt to do the possible and an attempt to do the impossible is chance. A person who enters a bedroom and stabs a corpse thinking he is stabbing a living person has the same intention as a person who enters a bedroom and stabs someone who is alive. In the former instance, by some chance, the intended victim expired in his sleep perhaps only moments before the would-be assassin acted. It is difficult to see why this circumstance, of which the tardy killer has no knowledge and over which he has no control, should in any way mitigate his culpability. Next time, the victim might be alive. Similarly, even if Mr. Dynar could not actually have laundered the proceeds of crime this time around, there is hardly any guarantee that his next customer might not be someone other than an agent of the United States Government.

It was clear that Dynar had attempted to engage in activities that, if they had been completed, would have fallen within the definition of crimes that were duly established under the *Criminal Code* and the (now repealed) *Narcotic Control Act*. However, it is noteworthy that the Supreme Court of Canada took the opportunity to make it clear that an accused person who attempts to do *something that does not, in fact, amount to a crime* cannot be found guilty of an attempt under section 24(1)—even if the accused fervently believes that he or she is involved in activity that is criminal. Putting it more simply, there can be no criminal liability for attempting to commit an **"imaginary crime."** As Justices Cory and Iacobucci noted in their judgment, there is a critical distinction between "a failed attempt to do something that is a crime and an imaginary crime":

> It is one thing to attempt to steal a wallet, believing such thievery to be a crime, and quite another to bring sugar into Canada, believing the importation of sugar to be a crime. In the former case, the would-be thief has the *mens rea* associated with thievery. In the latter case, the would-be smuggler has no *mens rea* known to law. Because s. 24(1) clearly provides that it is an element of the offence of attempt to have "an intent to commit an offence," the latter sort of attempt is not a crime.

The Supreme Court of Canada emphasized that the major purpose of the law of criminal attempts is to discourage individuals from committing subsequent offences. However, this purpose would not be served by punishing attempts to commit so-called "imaginary crimes." As Justices Cory and Iacobucci aptly pointed out,

> ... [O]ne who attempts something that is not a crime or even one who actually does something that is not a crime, believing that what he has done or has attempted to do is a crime, has not displayed any propensity to commit crimes in the future, unless perhaps he has betrayed a vague willingness to break the law. Probably all he has shown is that he might be inclined to do the same sort of thing in the future; and from a societal point of view, that is not a very worrisome prospect, because by hypothesis what he attempted to do is perfectly legal.

In the *Williams* case (2003), the Supreme Court of Canada held that the accused should be convicted of attempted aggravated assault in the situation where he had engaged in unprotected sexual intercourse without disclosing his HIV-positive status. Subsequently, his female partner was also diagnosed as HIV-positive. It was agreed that she would never have engaged in unprotected intercourse with Williams had she known of his HIV-positive condition. Williams commenced his relationship with the complainant in June 1991. However, he did not learn of his HIV status until November 15, 1991, when he was informed that he had tested positive. Therefore, it was perfectly possible that Williams' partner was already infected at the time that he first learned of his condition. In these circumstances, the Crown could not prove that the accused actually endangered the life of the complainant with simultaneous knowledge that he was HIV-positive. Putting it another way, the Crown could not establish that the necessary *mens rea* coincided with the *actus reus* of the completed offence of aggravated assault. In fact, it was quite likely that the complainant was already infected when Williams discovered that he was HIV-positive and, if this were the case, then it would have been impossible for the accused to deliberately risk the infection of the complainant at a time when he was in full knowledge of his dangerous condition. However, although the Crown could not prove the completed offence of aggravated assault, the Supreme Court ruled that Williams should nevertheless be found guilty of attempted aggravated assault. In this respect, Justice Binnie stated that

> [f]ailure to prove endangerment of life was fatal to the prosecution in this case of aggravated assault but it is not fatal to a conviction for *attempted* aggravated

assault. Clearly, the respondent took more than preparatory steps. He did everything he could to achieve the infection of the complainant by repeated acts of intercourse for approximately one year between November 15, 1991 and November 1992 when the relationship ended….

Here the *actus reus* of aggravated assault "is present in an incomplete but more-than-merely preparatory way."… The respondent therefore stands properly convicted of attempted aggravated assault.[11]

3. CONSPIRACY

The General Principles and Section 423

As is the case with the crimes of counselling and attempt, the *raison d'être* of the offence of **conspiracy** is the prevention of crime. As Justices Cory and Iacobucci noted in their judgment in the Supreme Court of Canada's decision in the United *States v. Dynar* case (1997),

… [T]he rationale for punishing conspirators coincides with the rationale for punishing persons for attempted crimes. Not only is the offence itself seen to be harmful to society, but it is clearly in society's best interests to make it possible for law enforcement officials to intervene before the harm occurs that would be occasioned by a successful conspiracy or, if the conspiracy is incapable of completion, by a subsequent and more successful conspiracy to commit a similar offence.

Police authorities generally regard the offence of conspiracy as an absolutely vital weapon for fighting organized crime, and certainly a considerable number of convictions of individuals involved in organized crime are obtained primarily as a result of proving conspiracies through "wiretap" evidence. However, conspiracy is an offence that is viewed with extreme suspicion by civil libertarians, owing to its vague parameters. Furthermore, the power to charge

an accused person with conspiracy is believed to place an unfair advantage in the hands of the Crown; indeed, the offence is sometimes referred to as "the darling in the prosecutor's nursery." Some of the trepidation experienced by civil libertarians when analyzing the nature of conspiracy is reflected in the following passage from Justice Dickson's judgment, in the Supreme Court of Canada's decision in the case of *Cotroni and Papalia* (1979):

Conspiracy is an inchoate or preliminary crime, dating from the time of Edward I, but much refined in the Court of Star Chamber in the 17th Century. Notwithstanding its antiquity, the law of conspiracy is still uncertain. It can, however, be said that the indictment for conspiracy is a formidable weapon in the armory of the prosecutor. According to the cases, it permits a vague definition of the offence, broader standards of admissibility of evidence apply; it may provide the solution to prosecutorial problems as to situs and jurisdiction…. But the very looseness generally allowed for specifying the offence, for receiving proof, and generally in the conduct of the trial, imposes upon a trial Judge an added duty to ensure against the possibility of improper transference of guilt from one accused to another. There is, I have no doubt, a subconscious tendency upon the part of jurors in a conspiracy case to regard all co-conspirators alike and ignore the fact that guilt is something individual and personal.

The *Criminal Code* provision dealing with conspiracy is 465, which in part states:

(1) Except where otherwise expressly provided by law, the following provisions apply in respect of conspiracy:

    (a) every one who conspires with any one to commit murder or to cause another person to be murdered, whether in Canada or not, is guilty of an indictable offence and liable to a maximum term of imprisonment for life;

    (b) every one who conspires with any one to prosecute a person for an alleged offence, knowing that he did not commit that offence, is guilty of an indictable offence and liable

        (i) to imprisonment for a term not exceeding ten years, if the alleged offence is one for which, on conviction, that person would be liable to be sentenced to imprisonment for life or for a term not exceeding fourteen years, or

---

[11] It should be noted that Justice Binnie argued that the *mens rea* for an attempt had been established by the Crown: "The crime of attempt, as with any offence, requires the Crown to establish that the accused intended to commit the crime in question…. The requisite intent is established here for the period after November 15, 1991. The respondent, knowing at that time that he was HIV-positive, engaged in unprotected sex with the complainant intending her thereby to be exposed to the lethal consequences of HIV. The evidence showed that he had been fully counselled by two doctors and a nurse on all relevant aspects of the potential result of unprotected sex." Some might argue that Justice Binnie was really referring to extreme recklessness on the part of the accused rather than an actual intent to expose the victim to infection with HIV.

(ii) to imprisonment for a term not exceeding five years, if the alleged offence is one for which, on conviction, that person would be liable to imprisonment for less than fourteen years;

(c) every one who conspires with any one to commit an indictable offence not provided for in paragraph (a) or (b) is guilty of an indictable offence and liable to the same punishment as that to which an accused who is guilty of that offence would, on conviction, be liable; and

(d) every one who conspires with any one to commit an offence punishable on summary conviction is guilty of an offence punishable on summary conviction.

It will be noted that, in general, the penalties for conspiracy are considerably harsher than is the case for criminal attempts. Indeed, the penalties for conspiracy in relation to an indictable offence are normally identical to those imposed where the complete offence has actually been committed; however, in the case of criminal attempts, the penalties for attempting to commit indictable offences are (normally) only one-half of those that may be imposed for committing the complete offence (section 463 of the *Code*). In *United States v. Dynar* (1997), the Supreme Court of Canada indicated why Parliament has treated conspiracy as constituting such a serious threat to social order. Indeed, Justices Cory and Iacobucci stated that

[t]he crime has a long and malevolent history. Conspirators have plotted to overthrow monarchs from biblical times through the time of the Plantaganets and Tudors. Guy Fawkes conspired with others to blow up the parliament buildings. Today conspirators plot with others to carry out terrorist acts, to commit murders or to import forbidden drugs. Society is properly concerned with conspiracies since two or more persons working together can achieve evil results that would be impossible for an individual working alone. For example, it usually takes two or more conspirators to manufacture and secrete explosives or to arrange for the purchase, importation and sale of heroin. The very fact that several persons in combination agree to do something has for many years been considered to constitute "a menace to society."... In fact, the scale of injury that might be caused to the fabric of society can be far greater when two or more persons conspire to a crime than when an individual sets out alone to do an unlawful act.

The function of the *Criminal Code* provisions concerning conspiracy is, therefore, to prevent conspirators from putting their unlawful plans into execution, i.e., to intervene and punish those involved before any serious harm is caused to society. Furthermore, according to Justices Cory and Iacobucci, the severe penalties are necessary to deter the accused persons from repeating their conduct in the future. Curiously, the *Code* does not provide any statutory definition of the elements of conspiracy. As a consequence, Canadian courts have adopted the traditional common law requirements formulated by the English courts. For example, Justice Taschereau, in delivering the judgment of the majority of the Supreme Court of Canada in the case of *O'Brien* (1954) adopted the following definition of conspiracy, which had been fashioned by Justice Willes in the old English case of *Mulcahy* (1868):

A conspiracy consists not merely in the intention of two or more, but in the agreement of two or more to do an unlawful act, or to do a lawful act by unlawful means. So long as such a design rests in intention only, it is not indictable. When two agree to carry it into effect, the very plot is an action itself, and the act of each of the parties ... punishable if for a criminal object.

The *actus reus* of conspiracy is the agreement; the requisite *mens rea* is to be found in the objective of the agreement. The *actus reus* is complete as soon as agreement is reached between the parties. It therefore does not matter that no steps are subsequently taken in order to carry out the objective of the agreement; the parties are guilty of conspiracy just as soon as the agreement is reached with the necessary *mens rea*. As Justices Cory and Iacobucci noted in the decision of the Supreme Court of Canada in the *United States v. Dynar case* (1997), "there must be an intention to agree, the completion of an agreement, and a common design."

For the purpose of analysis, it may be useful to analyze the offence of conspiracy in terms of three separate elements:

- an agreement for a common purpose;
- an agreement between at least two persons; and
- an agreement to commit a crime.

Element 1: Agreement for a Common Purpose

The necessity of establishing the element of an agreement for a common purpose is well illustrated by the leading Canadian case of *Cotroni and Papalia* (1979). As Justice Dickson of the Supreme Court of Canada suggested, "the facts of the case are bizarre." Cotroni and Papalia were tried in Toronto on a charge that they, together with two men named Swartz and Violi, "unlawfully did conspire together each with the other and with persons unknown to have possession of $300 000, more or less, knowing that the said $300 000 was obtained by the commission in Canada of the indictable offence of extortion." The Crown contended that Swartz and Papalia extracted some $300 000 from Bader and from Rosen (a friend of Bader in Toronto). The money was paid in response to Swartz's story that Bader would be killed if he did not come up with the cash. Swartz indicated that the threats to Bader's life emanated from Montreal. Both Bader and Rosen believed Swartz's story implicitly. Approximately one year later, two residents of Montreal, Cotroni and Violi, came to believe that their names had been used in order to extort the $300 000 from Bader. They therefore telephoned Papalia and demanded the **extortion** money for themselves. Papalia indicated that he had received only $40 000 and suggested that they "beat up" Swartz to obtain the rest. Violi told Papalia that this information "[is] gonna save your life."

It was eventually agreed that Violi would come to Toronto to relieve Swartz of the money. The planned meeting in Toronto never took place. Cotroni, Papalia, Swartz, and Violi were all convicted of conspiracy. They appealed to the Ontario Court of Appeal. The appeals of Swartz and Papalia were dismissed, but the appeals of Cotroni and Violi were allowed. The Crown appealed Cotroni's acquittal (Violi having died in the interim period) to the Supreme Court of Canada, and Papalia appealed against the dismissal of his appeal.

The Supreme Court of Canada upheld the judgment of the Court of Appeal and dismissed the appeals of both the Crown and Papalia. Justice Dickson pointed out that there was no evidence of any "common agreement" or "common object" among Cotroni, Violi, Papalia, and Swartz. In his view, the evidence established the existence of two separate conspiracies. The first conspiracy involved Papalia and Swartz; its purpose was to have possession of the extorted money. The second conspiracy involved Cotroni and Violi and, possibly, Papalia; its purpose was to obtain, and subsequently to have possession of, a portion of the same money. Justice Dickson also pointed out that the second conspiracy

took place solely within Quebec, and therefore the Province of Ontario had no jurisdiction in relation to it. Justice Dickson proceeded to conclude that "this is not the conspiracy described in the indictment." He ruled that Papalia was properly convicted of the conspiracy with Swartz. However, he determined that "the only evidence against Cotroni is in respect of a conspiracy not covered by the indictment."

Justice Dickson's judgment casts considerable light on the requirement that there be an agreement for a common purpose:

> The word "conspire" derives from two Latin words, "con" and "spirare," meaning "to breathe together." To conspire is to agree. *The essence of criminal conspiracy is proof of agreement*. On a charge of conspiracy the agreement itself is the gist of the offence.... The *actus reus* is the fact of agreement.... The agreement reached by the co-conspirators may contemplate a number of acts or offences. Any number of persons may be privy to it. Additional persons may join the ongoing scheme while others may drop out. So long as there is a continuing overall, dominant plan there may be changes in methods of operation, personnel, or victims, without bringing the conspiracy to an end. *The important inquiry is not as to the acts done in pursuance of the agreement, but whether there was, in fact, a common agreement to which the acts are referable and to which all of the alleged offenders were privy....* There must be evidence that the alleged conspirators acted in concert in pursuit of a common goal.... [I]n order to have a conspiracy, one must have agreement between the co-conspirators. There was simply no evidence of agreement between the four alleged conspirators. There was not the common purpose of a single enterprise, but rather the several purposes of two separate adventures. It is true that, in the most general of terms, it might be said that each of these adventures had a common object, money, with Swartz and Papalia in possession of extorted funds, and Cotroni and Violi desirous of relieving them of those funds, but there was no general agreement. A common desire to have money cannot create a conspiracy in the absence of a meeting of minds. The facts here show two competing and mutually exclusive objects. Counsel suggested the analogy of four hungry dogs, fighting over a bone.... [emphasis added]

The courts have held that, although there must be a "common object" or "common agreement" in order to establish a conspiracy, it is not necessary for the Crown to establish that there is any direct communication between the co-conspirators. For this reason, it is possible to impose criminal liability for

Cartoon by Greg Holoboff

The Cotroni and Palpalia case: for a conspiracy to exist, there must be a meeting of the minds and a common objective.

participation in so-called "chain" and "wheel" conspiracies. In a "chain" conspiracy, defendant A is in contact with defendant B, B with C, C with D, and so on. In a "wheel" conspiracy, one or more defendants communicate with each of the other conspirators, thus serving as the "hub" of the conspiracy. However, Canadian courts have been vigilant to ensure that the Crown does not roll up what are, in fact, several separate conspiracies into one overall conspiracy. For example, in *Longworth, Freeman, Newton and Wolfe* (1982), the Ontario Court of Appeal ruled that a drug dealer who purchases a relatively small quantity of drugs for the purpose of resale to his own customers does not, as a consequence of this simple purchase, thereby become a party to an overall conspiracy that has the distribution of drugs as its object and to which the distributor, his supplier, and all the distributor's customers are parties. In this particular case, the Crown had, inappropriately, attempted to establish the existence of a wheel conspiracy, with the distributor allegedly being the hub of the conspiracy. In delivering the judgment of the Court of Appeal, Justice Martin said,

> I agree that it is not necessary to show that parties to a conspiracy were in direct communication with each other, or even that they were aware of the identity of the alleged co-conspirators. Moreover, it is not necessary to show that each conspirator was aware of all the details of the common scheme, but it must be shown that each of the conspirators were aware of the general nature of the common design and intended to adhere to it....
>
> ... I cannot think that a retailer who purchases from a distributor a relatively small quantity of marijuana for resale to his customers thereby becomes a party to an overall conspiracy having for its object the distribution of marijuana (which might involve millions of dollars worth) and to which the distributor, his supplier and all the distributor's

customers are parties. It seems to me that if the mere purchaser thereby becomes a party to such an overall conspiracy, there is no logical reason why he does not equally become a party to a conspiracy to import where he knows that the marijuana is of foreign origin.... I do not think that because the evidence permits an inference that the "retailer" (Newton) must have known that he was not the only customer of the distributor (Wolfe), and that the distributor in all likelihood had a supplier, without more, that fact makes him a party to an over-all conspiracy such as is here alleged.... *There must be evidence beyond reasonable doubt that the alleged conspirators acted in concert in pursuit of a common goal.* [emphasis added]

In the *Longman, Freeman, Newton and Wolfe* case, the court evidently entertained a reasonable doubt as to whether the various accused parties had agreed to a common objective that involved the widespread distribution of illegal drugs. Therefore, it was not possible to find them guilty of participating in a broad conspiracy to traffic in drugs. However, where large quantities of drugs are sold, the court may well conclude that the parties involved in such large-scale transactions do indeed intend to participate in a broad conspiracy to distribute drugs; in other words, they form a common objective that goes far beyond the confines of the simple sale of the drugs by one party to another. Take, for example, the case of *Chaulk and DiCristo* (1991), in which the accused had been charged with conspiracy to traffic in a narcotic drug (namely, cannabis resin). Chaulk had picked up at least one package containing cannabis resin from an Air Cargo Depot in the Wabush–Labrador city area. He had also sent at least two packages containing $9000 each to DiCristo in Montreal. Defence counsel raised the argument that a single transaction, involving the sale of a drug, could not support the conclusion that Chaulk and DiCristo formed the mutual objective to traffic in that drug. However, this contention was rejected at their trial and they were convicted. Their appeal to the Newfoundland Court of Appeal was subsequently dismissed. As Justice Marshall noted,

> Whether or not a single transaction forms the basis of a common design to traffic will depend upon whether the compact pursuant to which the transaction was undertaken is found to transcend beyond a mere agreement of purchase and sale between the dealer and buyer to one establishing an intention by both parties for resale. The scope to be attributed to such an agreement depends upon the individual circumstances.

Clearly, a critically important circumstance in this respect is the quantity of drugs involved. In the case of *Chaulk and DiCristo* (1991), the amount of drugs contained in the package was quite inconsistent with the possession for the purpose of purely personal use and, therefore, the inference could be drawn that it was intended for resale. On this basis, the Court of Appeal concluded that "the scope of the agreement of sale and purchase extends beyond transaction between the appellants and extends it to a conspiracy to traffic in the prohibited substance."

Where accused persons are alleged to have joined a *preexisting conspiracy*, they may not be convicted of the crime of conspiracy unless the Crown can prove that they *adopted the criminal plan as their own and consented to participate in carrying it out*. Merely knowing about the existence of a conspiracy does not render one criminally liable. Take, for example, the case of *Lamontagne* (1999). A criminal gang in Quebec City possessed two stolen trailers and sought to sell them to a criminal gang in Montreal. The accused was an independent trucker who was contacted by an intermediary to bring his truck to a restaurant. The truck was driven away and was shortly thereafter returned to Lamontagne with a stolen trailer attached to it. Lamontagne was then arrested as he started to put gas into his vehicle. The accused was convicted of possession of the trailer (section 354(1) of the *Criminal Code*) on the basis that he was, at the very least, "wilfully blind" to the fact that it had been stolen. He was also convicted of conspiracy to commit theft and possession of stolen property. On his appeal to the Quebec Court of Appeal, the conviction for possession of stolen property was upheld but, significantly, the conviction for conspiracy was quashed.

In acquitting Lamontagne of conspiracy, the Court of Appeal emphasized that the accused learned of the existence of the stolen trailer only several days after the members of the two criminal gangs had formed their plan to transfer the trailer from one gang to the other. This, in itself, would not prevent Lamontagne from becoming party to the conspiracy, but he could do so only by adopting the unlawful object (dealing in stolen property) as his own and by consenting to take part in its implementation. In the view of the Court of Appeal, the Crown could not prove these essential elements of the offence of conspiracy in the particular circumstances of this case. As Justice Dussault pointed out,

> It was not sufficient for the Crown to prove that the appellant was wilfully blind as to the unlawful provenance of his load, in order to prove that the appellant voluntarily participated in the conspiracy. The Crown had to prove beyond a reasonable doubt that the appellant agreed with the other conspirators to commit the crime of possession of property obtained by crime and to participate in achieving it. In my view, the Crown did not prove this....

In the *O'Brien* case (1954), the Supreme Court of Canada ruled that, in addition to a common agreement or common intention, the Crown must prove that there was "an intention to put the common design into effect." In other words, if a party to an alleged agreement does not intend to carry out the common object, that party cannot be convicted of conspiracy. In the *O'Brien* case (1954), the accused was charged with having unlawfully conspired with Tulley to commit the indictable offence of kidnapping. Tulley was not charged and was called as a Crown witness at O'Brien's trial. Tulley testified that he had met with the accused on a number of occasions and that, for the sum of $500, he had agreed to assist O'Brien in the kidnapping of Mrs. Pritchard. Tulley also testified that he received $240 from O'Brien and that the accused had pointed out both the target and her residence to him. However, Tulley insisted that he "never had any intention of going through with this plan, but was just fooling the respondent, or hoaxing him." Tulley then indicated that he had both informed Pritchard of O'Brien's intentions and denounced the scheme to the police. O'Brien was convicted at his trial, but his appeal to the British Columbia Court of Appeal was successful and a new trial was ordered. The Crown appealed this ruling to the Supreme Court of Canada, which affirmed the decision of the Court of Appeal.

O'Brien's counsel contended that, if Tulley never intended to carry out the agreement to kidnap Pritchard, he could not have been a party to a conspiracy. Since there were no other parties involved, O'Brien must be acquitted because he could not conspire with himself. The Supreme Court of Canada essentially accepted this contention. In the words of Justice Taschereau, who delivered the judgment of the majority of the Court,

> It is, of course, essential that the conspirators have the intention to agree, and this agreement must be complete. There must also be a common design to do something unlawful, or something lawful by illegal means. Although it is not necessary that there should be an overt action in furtherance of the conspiracy, to complete the crime, I have no doubt that

there must exist an intention to put the common design into effect. A common design necessarily involves an intention. Both are synonymous. The intention cannot be anything else but the will to attain the object of the agreement. I cannot imagine several conspirators agreeing to defraud, to restrain trade, or to commit any indictable offence, without having the intention to reach the common goal....

In O'Brien's case, there was only one other potential co-conspirator (namely, Tulley), and once it was established that he did not have the intention to put the agreement into effect, it was clear that the accused could not be convicted of the offence charged because it takes at least two parties to hatch a conspiracy. However, as long as at least two parties to an alleged conspiracy do have the intention to carry out the agreement, it does not matter that various other alleged co-conspirators lack such intent. As Justice Lambert of the British Columbia Court of Appeal said in the case of *Miller* (1984),

> ... [T]he lack of intent of two of the co-conspirators, even if established, does not afford any defence to the other conspirators who have the requisite intent, unless the number of conspirators who have the requisite intent is reduced to one person. At that stage he cannot agree with himself and would be acquitted.

On the other hand, it is important to bear in mind that the courts will normally assume that an accused person who has entered into an agreement to commit an offence does, in fact, intend to carry it out. As the Supreme Court of Canada noted in the *Nova Scotia Pharmaceutical Society* case (1992),

> ... [T]he Crown must prove that the accused had the intention to enter into the agreement and had knowledge of the terms of that agreement. Once that is established, it would ordinarily be reasonable to draw the inference that the accused intended to carry out the terms in the agreement, unless there was evidence that the accused did not intend to carry out the terms of the agreement.

It should also be mentioned that it is possible to become a party to a conspiracy on the basis of *aiding and/or abetting* members of a conspiracy (section 21(1)(b) and (c) of the *Code*) or *counselling* other persons to join a conspiracy (section 22(1) of the *Code*). For example, in *Vucetic* (1998), the Ontario Court of Appeal ruled that an accused person may be convicted of conspiracy if he or she provides assistance or encouragement to members of an existing conspiracy—provided the Crown could prove that the accused "knew the object of the conspiracy" and that the assistance "was intended to assist the conspirators in attaining their unlawful criminal object." Similarly, in *Bérubé* (1999), the Quebec Court of Appeal held that it is "well-established in jurisprudence that one can be found guilty of conspiracy to commit an indictable offence by encouraging someone to become a member of the conspiracy."

Element 2: Agreement between at Least Two Persons

It is a common sense proposition that, since an agreement constitutes the essence of a conspiracy, there must be at least two parties. As the Supreme Court of Canada ruled in *O'Brien* (1954), an accused person cannot be convicted of conspiring with him- or herself. In Canadian criminal law, one of the consequences of this requirement is that a husband cannot be convicted of conspiracy with his wife and vice versa.

In the case of *Kowbel* (1953), the Supreme Court of Canada justified this rule on the basis that, historically, spouses have been treated, for the purpose of the law, as "one person." However, it is important to remember that this rule applies only in the situation where the husband and wife are the sole alleged co-conspirators. They can jointly or separately conspire with other individuals within one overall conspiracy and be convicted of the offence.

For example, in *Barbeau* (1996), the accused and her husband were charged, along with three men, of the offence of conspiracy to import cocaine. Both she and her husband could be convicted of this conspiracy if the Crown proved that each of them had intended to conspire with the three other men. However, Barbeau stated that all she had done was to give—and transcribe—messages by phone and fax because her husband's grasp of English was poor. She said that she had no knowledge of any conspiracy and that she thought the messages related to contraband cigarettes, not cocaine. Although there was no evidence that the accused had met or conspired with the other alleged co-conspirators or that she had agreed with anyone to join a conspiracy, the Crown took the position that she "knew that her husband was involved with others in a conspiracy to import cocaine and that she participated in it by her own acts in furtherance of the object of the conspiracy." Barbeau was convicted at her trial, but the

Quebec Court of Appeal subsequently set aside the conviction and ordered a new trial. The trial judge had instructed the members of the jury that they could find the accused guilty of conspiracy if she had been "wilfully blind" as to the existence and nature of the conspiracy that allegedly involved her husband. In so doing, the trial judge left the impression that the test for *wilful blindness* is an *objective* one—namely, would a *reasonable* person have asked questions in the particular set of circumstances facing the accused? In delivering the judgment of the Court of Appeal, Justice Rothman emphasized that wilful blindness is a form of *subjective*, not *objective*, *mens rea* and that, therefore, it was a serious error for the trial judge to have instructed the jury to consider what a "normal" person would have done in light of the knowledge that Barbeau had of the whole situation:

> The test was not whether the appellant "should" have known or should "normally" have known from the suspicious circumstances that her husband was probably involved in a conspiracy to import cocaine. The question was whether the circumstances were such that she, herself, was in fact, suspicious that this was the case but deliberately refrained from making inquiries so that she could remain in ignorance as to the truth.

Another implication of the "two parties" requirement is that, where an undercover police officer or **agent provocateur** makes an agreement with *only one other party*, there can be no conspiracy since, as the *O'Brien* case (1954) illustrates, the officer or *agent provocateur* will not have the intention to put the common design into effect. In the case of *Root* (2008), the Ontario Court of Appeal referred to a police officer operating in such circumstances as a "counterfeit conspirator"—"not someone with whom the [accused], for that matter anybody else, could conspire as a matter of law." Of course, it is possible that an accused person who is seeking to conspire with an undercover police officer could be convicted, instead, of counselling an offence.

Element 3: Agreement to Commit a Crime

Section 465 of the *Criminal Code* clearly stipulates that it is necessary for the Crown to prove that there was an agreement to commit a crime. More specifically, section 465(1) provides that it is an indictable offence to conspire to commit an indictable offence and a summary conviction offence to conspire to commit a summary conviction offence. However, it is not entirely clear whether it should be possible for the Crown to prosecute individuals for conspiracy to commit absolutely any summary conviction offence that may arise under either federal or provincial/ territorial legislation. Many provincial/territorial summary conviction offences might be considered very minor in nature and it might well be contended that it does not constitute sound policy to charge individuals with a conspiracy to commit a relatively trivial offence, such as jaywalking. On the other hand, section 465(1)(d) does make it clear that a conspiracy to commit a summary conviction offence is itself a summary conviction offence, carrying a relatively lenient maximum penalty.

In order to obtain a conviction of conspiracy, the Crown must prove that the parties intended to commit a crime that is known to Canadian criminal law. This is the same principle that was discussed earlier in this chapter in relation to the crime of attempt: one cannot either attempt or conspire to commit an imaginary crime. The Supreme Court of Canada firmly underscored this point in the *Dynar* case (1997). As Justices Cory and Iacobucci stated, planning to commit imaginary crimes falls outside the scope of the law: "conspiracy to commit such fanciful offences cannot give rise to criminal liability." However, if the accused do conspire to commit an offence known to the law, then it is irrelevant that, for some reason, it would have been impossible for them to have completed the offence. In this respect, the law of conspiracy is identical to the law of criminal attempts. As the Supreme Court of Canada ruled in the *United States v. Dynar* case (1997), the rationale for punishing those who conspire to commit a crime is to punish them *before* their combined efforts cause harm to society. Furthermore, according to Justices Cory and Iacobucci,

> ... [S]ince the offence of conspiracy only requires an intention to commit the substantive offence, and not the commission of the offence itself, it does not matter that, from an objective point of view, commission of the offence may be impossible. It is the subjective point of view that is important, and from a subjective perspective, conspirators who intend to commit an indictable offence intend to do everything necessary to satisfy the conditions of the offence. The fact that they cannot do so because an objective circumstance is not as they believe it to be does not in any way affect this intention. The intention of the conspirators remains the same, regardless

of the absence of the circumstance that would make the realization of that intention possible. It is only in retrospect that the impossibility of accomplishing the design becomes apparent.

It will be remembered that, in the *Dynar* case (1997), the accused would not have been able to complete the offence of money laundering because the funds that he believed were the fruits of crime were actually funds belonging to the United States government. Since the offence, at that time, required proof of *knowledge* that these funds were the proceeds of crime, Dynar could not be convicted of the completed offence of money laundering: he could not "know" something that was, in fact, false. However, as we have already seen, the Supreme Court had no difficulty in stating that Dynar could have been convicted of *attempting* to launder illicitly obtained money, and the very same logic was robustly applied to the offence of conspiracy to carry out this criminal intention.

Can There Be an Attempt to Conspire?

It is an interesting question as to whether Canadian criminal law recognizes the existence of an offence of attempting to conspire. In the case of *Déry* (2006), the Supreme Court of Canada unequivocally answered this question in the negative. Déry and Savard had discussed the possibility of stealing some liquor that was being temporarily stored outdoors in some trailers. Their conversations were unexpectedly intercepted in the course of an unrelated police investigation and, on the basis of these intercepted conversations, Déry and Savard were both charged with conspiracy to commit theft and conspiracy to possess stolen goods. The trial judge acquitted them of the conspiracy charges because it had not been established that they had formed a common intention to steal and possess the liquor. However, instead, the trial judge convicted Déry and Savard of *attempting* to conspire because, in his view, they had gone beyond mere preparation to commit a conspiracy. Déry appealed to the Quebec Court of Appeal, which upheld the convictions, but the Supreme Court of Canada unanimously allowed Déry's appeal and entered acquittals.

In delivering the judgment of the Supreme Court, Justice Fish emphasized that "attempting to conspire to commit a substance offence" had never previously been recognized in Canadian criminal law and that the Court had no intention of doing so at the present time. In the view of the Supreme Court:

By its very nature … an agreement to commit a crime in concert with others enhances the risk of its commission. Early intervention through the criminalization of conspiracy is therefore both principled and practical.

Likewise, the criminalization of attempt is warranted because its purpose is to prevent harm by punishing behaviour that demonstrates a substantial risk of harm. When applied to conspiracy, the justification for criminalizing attempt is lost, since an attempt to conspire amounts, at best, to a risk that a risk will materialize.

Finally, though Mr. Déry discussed a crime hoping eventually to commit it with others, neither he nor they committed, or even agreed to commit, the crimes they had discussed. The criminal law does not punish bad thoughts of this sort that were abandoned before an agreement was reached, or an attempt made, to act upon them.

STUDY QUESTIONS

1. Bucket, a uniformed police officer, is attempting to arrest Snapper for impaired driving. When Bucket informs Snapper of his intention to arrest him, Snapper starts to strike Bucket with his fists. Podder is a bystander who sees the attack by Snapper on Bucket, but does absolutely nothing to stop it. Podder does, however, yell, "Yippee!" three or four times before Bucket is able to restrain Snapper and to place handcuffs on Snapper's wrists. Snapper is convicted of assaulting a police officer in the execution of his duty (section 270(1)(a) of the *Criminal Code*). Could Podder also be convicted of this offence? Bucket will testify that he believes that Snapper understood Podder's use of the exclamation "Yippee!" to constitute a form of encouragement for Snapper to continue his attack on Bucket. Would it make a difference to your answer if Bucket had requested assistance from Podder in order to make the arrest of Snapper?

2. Magwitch, Merdle, and Murdstone make an agreement to kidnap Guppy (who is the heir to a vast fortune). The three men watch Guppy's movements for a couple of days and Magwitch (the ringleader) then pays Merdle and Murdstone $50 each "for services rendered." Murdstone then exposes the kidnapping plot to the police. He claims that he never really meant to take part in this plan, but went along with it

only as a means of "learning enough to protect Guppy." Magwitch, Merdle, and Murdstone are charged with conspiracy to kidnap Guppy. Are any (or all) of the co-accused guilty of the offence charged?

3. Perker and Fang decide to rob a store, which is owned by Tulkinghorn. Fang is known to be a very violent person. Perker acts as the lookout while Fang is in the store. However, Perker, who is becoming very fearful, decides to abandon the robbery and runs away before Fang has completed his task in the store. Meanwhile, Fang discovers that Tulkinghorn is surprisingly unwilling to part with the money in his cash register. Fang eventually strangles him and flees the scene, taking some $500 in cash with him. Fang is subsequently killed in a car accident as he tries to make good his escape. However, Perker is later arrested by the police and Crown counsel is wondering whether charges should be laid against him. What charges (if any) could reasonably be laid against Perker?

4. Nubbles and Rudge decide to rob the Tight Fist Bank. They make elaborate plans and purchase some firearms to assist them in their venture. On the appointed day, they drive to a street corner just one block away from the bank; they intend to observe the bank for a while and then undertake the robbery at the most appropriate moment. However, a police cruiser passes by and the two officers notice that Nubbles and Rudge look suspicious. The officers arrest the would-be bandits when they find two sawed-off shotguns and two masks on the back seat of the car. Nubbles and Rudge are subsequently charged with attempted robbery. Are they guilty of this offence?

5. Lancelot decides to steal a valuable diamond ring from Arthur. He goes to Arthur's house and tries to obtain entry by inserting a credit card into the lock on the front door. He is unable to open the door and returns to a bar, where he drowns his sorrows in whiskey. Guinevere, Lancelot's close friend, is disappointed when she discovers that he has failed to fulfill his criminal mission. She therefore travels to Arthur's house, where she manages to obtain entrance by using a set of skeleton keys. However, when she looks in the box in which Arthur usually keeps the ring, she discovers that it is empty. Arthur has taken the ring to a local jeweller for repairs. Merlin, who lives in the basement of Arthur's house, tells the police that he saw exactly what Lancelot and Guinevere had done and that he had heard them talk, on previous occasions, about stealing Arthur's ring. What charges (if any) could reasonably be laid against Lancelot and Guinevere?

6. Buccaneer believes that it is an offence to bring a certain type of computer chip into Canada without declaring it (and paying any duty). He arrives at an international airport in Canada, having concealed a large number of the tiny computer chips at the bottom of his suitcase. He attempts to pass through Canada Customs without declaring his hidden cargo. When his luggage is searched, the chips are discovered by a vigilant customs officer. However, the officer informs Buccaneer that, owing to the recent signing of a free trade agreement, this particular type of computer chip can now be imported into Canada without the need to pay any duty. Is Buccaneer guilty of a criminal offence? Would it make any difference to your answer if Buccaneer had agreed with his partner, Swallow, to smuggle the computer chips on a joint basis?

7. Pouch, Slug, and Toughey reach an agreement to rob a bank. They decide that Slug should obtain the necessary transportation and drive Pouch and Toughey to, and from, the bank. Slug enters an underground garage and breaks into a powerful sport-utility vehicle. Unfortunately, Haggage, the owner of the vehicle, sees what is happening and attempts to prevent Slug from driving away. Slug panics and runs over Haggage, killing him instantly. Slug is later arrested by the police, and he confesses that he planned to steal the vehicle in order to use it as a "getaway" vehicle in a bank robbery. Slug also tells the police about his agreement with Pouch and Toughey. Crown counsel intends to pursue a charge of second degree murder against Slug. What charges (if any) do you think should be laid against Pouch and Toughey?

8. Touchstone has informed a few of his friends that he wishes to hire someone to kill Oliver, who is Touchstone's business partner. The local police department is provided with the information that Touchstone is searching for a contract killer and Silvius, an undercover officer, is assigned the task of contacting Touchstone.

During a number of telephone calls and a couple of meetings in a bar, Silvius repeatedly offers to kill Oliver for $5000 but Touchstone is very wary and does not commit himself to any arrangement with Silvius. Eventually, Touchstone tells Silvius that "I accept your offer" and gives Silvius information that would help Silvius to identify Oliver and to learn various details about Oliver's everyday activities. However, before Silvius has time to reveal his true identity, Touchstone says that he has changed his mind and that he does not want Oliver killed after all. At this point, Silvius indicates that he is a police officer, informs Touchstone of his rights, and places Touchstone under arrest. Touchstone asserts that Silvius was "badgering" him (Touchstone) to accept an offer to kill Oliver and that he finally agreed to Silvius's proposition because he was feeling harassed by Silvius's repeated communications with him. Furthermore, he points to the fact that he quickly changed his mind and told Silvius that he had abandoned the idea of killing Oliver. Do you think that a charge of counselling an offence that is not committed (section 464 of the *Criminal Code*) would be successful at Touchstone's trial?

9. Blimber and Creakle decide to rob a local bank. They obtain some firearms, some masks, and a copy of the floor plan of the bank that they have chosen as their target. On the day appointed for the robbery, Blimber and Creakle persuade Squeers to drive them to the bank in a stolen vehicle. However, the vehicle breaks down about five blocks from the bank in question. Two police officers notice that Blimber, Creakle, and Squeers are behaving suspiciously and quickly ascertain that their vehicle has been reported stolen. After arresting Blimber, Creakle and Squeers, the officers discover the firearms, masks, and the copy of the floor plan of the bank. Upon further investigation, it is learned that the particular bank that Blimber and Creakle had selected for a robbery had been closed down a week before they were arrested by the police. Indeed, at the time of the arrest, the bank building was empty. Do you think that a charge of attempted robbery would succeed at the trial of Blimber, Creakle, and Squeers? (The charge would be laid under section 463 of the *Criminal Code*.)

10. Gradgrind and Krook meet in a bar. Gradgrind tells Krook that he has recently been released from prison and that he is looking for interesting work. Krook suggests that they kidnap Pardiggle, a wealthy stockbroker, and demand a ransom. Krook later invites Gradgrind to his apartment and introduces him to Frank and Margaretta Milvey, who were recently married. Krook, Gradgrind, and the Milveys develop a plan to kidnap Pardiggle at his residence. Krook gives Gradgrind the sum of $1000 for expenses that he may incur in carrying out his designated tasks in pursuit of the kidnapping plot. However, on the next day, police officers arrest Krook and the Milveys and reveal that Gradgrind is actually an undercover police officer. Crown counsel realizes that Gradgrind will testify that he never intended to carry out any part of the kidnapping plot and was merely pretending to agree with Krook and the Milveys in order to lay the basis for criminal charges to be laid against them. Do you think that charges of conspiracy to kidnap Pardiggle would be successful at the trial of Krook and the Milveys? (Note that the offence of kidnapping is defined in section 279(1) of the *Criminal Code*.)

FURTHER READING

Adams, D.M. 1998. The Problem of the Incomplete Attempt. 24 *Social Theory and Practice*: 317–344.

Alexander, L., and K.D. Kessler. 1997. *Mens Rea* and Inchoate Crimes. 87 *Journal of Criminal Law & Criminology*: 1138–1193.

Arenson, K.J. 2005. The Pitfalls in the Law of Attempt: A New Perspective. 69 *Journal of Criminal Law*: 146–167.

Christopher, R. 2004. Does Attempted Murder Deserve Greater Punishment than Murder? Moral Luck and the Duty to Prevent Harm. 18 *Notre Dame Journal of Law, Ethics and Public Policy*: 419–435.

Colvin, E., and S. Anand. 2007. *Principles of Criminal Law*. 3rd ed. Toronto: Thomson Carswell.

Crampton, S., and J.T. Kissick. 1993. Recent Developments in Conspiracy Law and Enforcement: New Risks and Opportunities. 38 *McGill Law Journal*: 569–619.

Culver, K. 1998. Analyzing Criminal Attempts: Critical Notice: *Criminal Attempts* by R.A. Duff. 11 *Canadian Journal of Law and Jurisprudence*: 441–456.

Davis, M. 1986. Why Attempts Deserve Less Punishment Than Complete Crimes. 5 *Law and Philosophy*: 1–32.

Ferguson, G. 2004. Failure to Disclose HIV Positive Status and Other Unresolved Issues in *Williams*. 20 *Criminal Reports (6th Series)*: 42–62.

Freedman, D. 2006. The New Law of Criminal Organizations in Canada. 85 *Canadian Bar Review*: 171–219.

Hoeber, P.R. 1986. The Abandonment Defense to Criminal Attempt and Other Problems of Temporal Individuation. 74 *California Law Review*: 377–427.

Katz, L. 2000. Why the Successful Assassin Is More Wicked Than the Unsuccessful One. 88 *California Law Review*: 791–812.

Law Reform Commission of Canada. 1985. Working Paper No. 45: *Criminal Law; Secondary Liability: Participation in Crime and Inchoate Offences*. Ottawa: L.R.C.C.

———. 1987. Report No. 31: *Recodifying Criminal Law*. 2nd ed. Ottawa: L.R.C.C. 45–49.

MacAlister, D., and S.N. Verdun-Jones. 2003. Unprotected Sexual Intercourse with Knowledge of HIV-Positive Results: Attempted Aggravated Assault or the Need for Legislative Reform? 13 *Criminal Reports (6th Series)*: 257–265.

Mackinnon, P. 1986. Attempting Murder Recklessly: The Significance of *R. v. Ancio*. 28 *Criminal Law Quarterly*: 121–128.

Manson, A. 1989. Recodifying Attempts, Parties and Abandoned Intentions. 14 *Queen's Law Journal*: 85–114.

Manson, A. 1997. Annotation: *United States v. Dynar (1997)*. *8 Criminal Reports (5th Series)*: 83–84.

Meehan, E.R. 1979. The Trying Problem of Criminal Attempt—Historical Perspectives. 14 *U.B.C. Law Review*: 137–161.

Meehan, E., and J. Currie. 2000. *The Law of Criminal Attempt —A Treatise*. 2nd ed. Toronto: Carswell.

Ohana, D. 2007. Desert and Punishment for Acts Preparatory to the Commission of a Crime. 20 *Canadian Journal of Law and Jurisprudence*: 113–142.

Roach, K. 2009. *Criminal Law*. 4th ed. Toronto: Irwin Law. Ch. 3.

Stewart, H. 2001. The Centrality of the Act Requirement for Criminal Attempts. 51 *University of Toronto Law Journal*: 399–424.

Stuart, D. 2007. *Canadian Criminal Law: A Treatise*. 5th ed. Toronto: Thomson Carswell. Chs. 9 & 10.

Stuart, D., R.J. Delisle, and S. Coughlan. 2009. *Learning Canadian Criminal Law*. 11th ed. Toronto: Thomson Carswell.

Verdun-Jones, S.N. 2007. *Canadian Criminal Cases: Selected Highlights*. 2nd ed. Toronto: Thomson Nelson. Ch. 8.

CHAPTER EIGHT

MENTAL IMPAIRMENT AND CRIMINAL RESPONSIBILITY: THE DEFENCES OF "NOT CRIMINALLY RESPONSIBLE ON ACCOUNT OF MENTAL DISORDER" (NCRMD) AND AUTOMATISM

OVERVIEW

This chapter examines the following:

1. how the criminal law deals with accused persons who are suffering from mental disorder;

2. the defence of "not criminally responsible on account of mental disorder" (NCRMD), which is set out in section 16 of the *Criminal Code*, and the distinction between the NCRMD defence and the issue of the accused person's fitness to stand trial;

3. the evolution of (what used to be known as) the insanity defence from the articulation of the so-called *M'Naghten* Rules in 1843 and the original *Criminal Code* formulation of the defence in 1892 right up to the present day;

4. the special verdict that, in most cases, results in the NCRMD accused person being subjected to restraints on his or her freedom (such restraints may include detention in a secure mental health facility or release into the community under close supervision);

5. the nature and scope of the NCRMD defence under section 16(1) of the *Criminal Code* and its interpretation by the courts;

6. the meaning of the terms "mental disorder" and "disease of the mind";

7. the meaning of the phrase "incapable of appreciating the nature and quality of the act or omission" and the word "wrong" in section 16(1) of the *Criminal Code*;

8. a number of important procedural issues that arise in the context of the NCRMD defence,

including the presumption that a defendant is not suffering from a mental disorder so as to be exempt from criminal responsibility and the requirement that the party who raises the defence prove it on the balance of probabilities (section 16(2) & (3) of the *Criminal Code*) as well as the power of the Crown to raise the NCRMD defence contrary to the wishes of the accused;

9. the roles played by review boards and courts in making decisions as to the disposition of not criminally responsible (NCR) accused persons;

10. the alternative dispositions that are available when an accused person has been found NCRMD: (a) custody order, (b) conditional discharge, and (c) absolute discharge;

11. the criteria that are applied when a review board or court makes a decision as to the disposition of a not criminally responsible accused person;

12. the defence of automatism and the situations in which the defence may be raised successfully;

13. the definition of automatism as a condition in which the accused person acts involuntarily as a consequence of severely impaired consciousness;

14. the principle that automatism caused by a "normal" condition, such as sleepwalking, entitles the accused person to an acquittal;

15. the principle that automatism triggered by an external event (such as a blow to the head) entitles the accused person to an acquittal;

16. the principle that automatism that is involuntarily induced by alcohol and/or drugs entitles the accused person to an acquittal;

17. the principle that automatism that is voluntarily induced by alcohol and/or other drugs does not entitle the accused person to an outright acquittal but only to the partial defence of intoxication;

18. the principle that automatism caused by a mental disorder ("disease of the mind") does not entitle the accused to an outright acquittal but rather to a finding that he or she is not criminally responsible on account of mental disorder (NCRMD) under section 16;

19. the difficulty of drawing a distinction between the defences of automatism and not criminally responsible on account of mental disorder as well as the very different consequences that follow from a successful assertion of these defences;

20. the ruling by the Supreme Court of Canada in the *Stone* case (1999) that there is a presumption that automatism has been induced by a mental disorder;

21. the situations in which the defence of automatism may not be raised because the accused was at fault in permitting him- or herself to become incapacitated;

22. the decision of the Supreme Court of Canada in the *Stone* case (1999) that the primary (persuasional) burden of proof is placed on the accused person if he or she raises (non-mental-disorder) automatism as a defence;

23. the principle that, for all defences, there is a secondary or evidentiary burden of proof that must be satisfied by the accused person if the defence is to be considered by the trier of fact (judge or jury); and

24. the decision of the Supreme Court of Canada in the *Fontaine* case (2004) that the secondary or evidentiary burden of proof will be discharged where there is some evidence that puts the defence "in play" and that "the defence will be in play whenever a properly instructed jury could reasonably, on account of that evidence, conclude in favour of the accused."

INTRODUCTION

This chapter examines the defences of *not criminally responsible on account of mental disorder* (NCRMD) and *automatism*. Both of these defences apply where an accused person has committed the act or omission that constitutes the basis for the criminal charge laid against him or her but is found not criminally responsible because of a severe impairment of mental capacity.

In the case of the NCRMD defence, it must be established that the accused person had a mental disorder that deprived him or her of the capacity to *appreciate* the **nature and quality of the act or omission** or to know that it was morally wrong. An accused person who has been found NCRMD is not acquitted of the charge but is held to be not criminally responsible for his or her actions and may potentially be held in custody in a psychiatric hospital or supervised in the community if it is considered that he or she poses a significant threat to the community.

The defence of automatism arises when an accused person acts involuntarily because of some form of temporary impairment of his or her mental faculties, such as clouded consciousness caused by a blow to the head. The defendant who successfully raises the defence of automatism gains an outright acquittal and may not be subjected to any restrictions on his or her liberty.

THE ISSUE OF FITNESS TO STAND TRIAL

Before proceeding to a discussion of the defences of NCRMD and automatism, it is necessary to distinguish them from the issue of the accused person's fitness to stand trial. The defences of NCRMD or automatism are concerned with the issue of criminal responsibility and are necessarily focused on the state of mind of the accused person at the time of the alleged offence. By way of contrast, the issue of fitness to stand trial is concerned exclusively with the state of mind of the accused person at the time of his or her trial and with the question of whether or not the accused person has the mental capacity to understand the nature and purpose of the trial proceedings and to communicate with his or her counsel.

Section 2 of the *Criminal Code* defines "unfit to stand trial" as being

... unable on account of mental disorder to conduct a defence at any stage of the proceedings before a verdict is rendered or to instruct counsel to do so, and, in particular, unable on account of mental disorder to

(a) understand the nature or object of the proceedings,

(b) understand the possible consequences of the proceedings, or

(c) communicate with counsel.

The courts have interpreted these criteria in a fairly narrow manner and, therefore, it is generally difficult to establish that an accused person is unfit to stand trial. As Justice Sopinka stated, in delivering the judgment of the Supreme Court of Canada in *Whittle* (1994), the *Criminal Code* test for unfitness to stand trial "requires limited cognitive capacity to understand the process and to communicate with counsel." Even if the accused person is experiencing delusions at the time of his or her trial, this does not necessarily mean that the court will find that he or she is unfit to stand trial. As the Ontario Court of Appeal held in the case of *Taylor* (1992), "the presence of delusions does not vitiate the accused's fitness to stand trial unless the delusion distorts the accused's rudimentary understanding of the judicial process" or prevents him or her from recounting to "his/her counsel the necessary facts relating to the offence in such a way that counsel can then properly present a defence."

Most mentally disordered accused persons will be found fit to stand trial because the limited cognitive capacity test consists of criteria that require only a minimal degree of ability to understand the nature and object of the court proceedings and to provide basic information to defence counsel. Indeed, in the case of *Jobb* (2008), Justice Smith, in delivering the judgment of the Saskatchewan Court of Appeal, emphasized the fact that the threshold for being found fit to stand trial is relatively low in Canada:

Many accused persons who are found not guilty by reason of a mental disorder are fit to stand trial. The fact that an accused is not criminally responsible within the meaning of s. 16 does not mean that he or she is unfit to stand trial. If the contrary were true there would be little purpose in providing for the plea authorized by s. 16. Most persons who suffered from the mental disorder defined in the section would be exempted from trial and would not get to plead until they had recovered subsequent to the date of the offence. [Italics in original]

The test for fitness to stand trial is quite different from the definition of mental disorder in s. 16. It is predicated on the existence of a mental disorder and focuses on the ability to instruct counsel and conduct a defence.... It requires limited cognitive capacity to understand the process and to communicate with counsel....

Accordingly, provided the accused possesses this limited capacity, it is not a prerequisite that he or she be capable of exercising analytical reasoning in making a choice to accept the advice of counsel or in coming to a decision that best serves her interests.

If an accused person is found unfit to stand trial, he or she may be kept in custody in a mental health hospital or may be supervised in the community until fitness to stand trial is restored.[1] In most cases, an accused person will become fit to stand trial after a relatively brief period of treatment.

THE DEFENCE OF NOT CRIMINALLY RESPONSIBLE ON ACCOUNT OF MENTAL DISORDER

As Justice McLachlin said in the Supreme Court of Canada's decision in the *Winko* case (1999),

In every society, there are those who commit criminal acts because of mental illness. The criminal law must find a way to deal with these people fairly, while protecting the public against further harms. The task is not an easy one.

In Canada, this difficult task is primarily undertaken through the application by the courts of the special defence of *not criminally responsible on account of mental disorder* (**NCRMD**). Since our system of criminal law is constructed on the premise that individuals should not be convicted of an offence unless they deliberately chose to do something wrong, the case of the mentally disordered offender clearly raises some fundamental questions about the appropriateness of applying the criminal law to persons who may not be capable of making real choices because of their mental illness. As Chief Justice Lamer of the Supreme Court of Canada said in the *Chaulk* case (1990),

The rationale underlying the [NCRMD] defence in Canada ... rests on the belief that persons suffering from insanity should not be subject to standard criminal culpability with its resulting punishment and stigmatization. This belief, in turn, flows from

the *principle that individuals are held responsible for the commission of criminal offences because they possess the capacity to distinguish between what is right and what is wrong.* [emphasis added]

However, as we shall soon see, the mere fact that an accused person was mentally disordered at the time of the alleged offence does not automatically excuse him or her from criminal responsibility. Indeed, only a relatively few mentally disordered persons meet the strict criteria for the successful application of the NCRMD defence.

The NCRMD defence is concerned with the state of mind of the accused person *at the time that the alleged offence was actually committed.* If the accused person concerned could not appreciate the nature or quality of the act or omission in question or did not realize it was wrong (in the sense that it would be morally condemned by reasonable members of society), he or she will be found not criminally responsible . Nevertheless, it is critical to bear in mind that the NCRMD defence is something of a misnomer. Indeed, it is not really a defence in the true sense of the word because, as section 672.1 of the *Criminal Code* clearly states, a verdict of NCRMD is not a finding that the accused "didn't do it" but rather a ruling that "the accused committed the act or made the omission that formed the basis of the offence with which the accused is charged but is not criminally responsible on account of mental disorder." Furthermore, although the defendant is found "not criminally responsible," he or she is not automatically entitled to walk out of the courtroom as a free man or woman; instead, the accused may well be subjected to restraints on his or her liberty (including the very real possibility of detention in a secure mental health facility). As Justice McLachlin stated in her judgment in the Supreme Court of Canada's decision in the *Winko* case (1999):

... The NCR accused is to be treated in a special way in a system tailored to meet the twin goals of protecting the public and treating the mentally ill offender fairly and appropriately. Under the new approach, the mentally ill offender occupies a special place in the criminal justice system; he or she is spared the full weight of criminal responsibility, but is subject to those restrictions necessary to protect the public.

THE *M'NAGHTEN* RULES

The foundations of the modern NCRMD defence in Canada were actually laid in the famous English case of *M'Naghten* (1843). In 1843, Daniel M'Naghten

---

[1] In those rare cases where an accused person is never likely to recover fitness and is not deemed a threat to public safety, a court may grant that person an absolute discharge.

shot and killed Edward Drummond (the secretary to Sir Robert Peel, the British prime minister of the day). M'Naghten shot at Drummond under the mistaken impression that he was Sir Robert Peel. M'Naghten believed that Peel and members of Peel's political party were responsible for a systematic campaign of persecution against him. M'Naghten was tried on a charge of murder and had the excellent fortune to be defended by the brilliant Queen's Counsel, Alexander Cockburn. At his trial, evidence was presented that M'Naghten was insane at the time of the shooting, and he was acquitted by the jury, who brought in a special verdict of insanity. It was generally felt that the test of insanity that had apparently been applied by the jury went considerably beyond the scope of the existing law. It had been argued that, even though M'Naghten's conduct had to a large extent appeared rational and even though he clearly knew what he was doing and was capable of telling right from wrong, he nevertheless was suffering from a form of insanity that deprived him of all "power of self control." The jury's verdict seemed to imply that, even though M'Naghten knew what he was doing and that it was wrong, he should be acquitted because his delusions of persecution caused him to lose his ability to control his actions.

M'Naghten was subsequently confined in hospital until his death in 1865. Although M'Naghten was kept in strict custody, there was a public outcry against his acquittal. Even Queen Victoria herself indicated that she definitely was "not amused." As a consequence of this negative public reaction, the House of Lords was asked a series of questions concerning the appropriate test of "insanity" that should be presented to a jury in future cases. Their Lordships' answers to the questions constitute what have become known as the *M'Naghten* Rules. The most important statement was as follows:

> We have to submit our opinion that the jurors ought to be told in all cases that every man is presumed to be sane and to possess a sufficient degree of reason to be responsible for his crimes until the contrary be proved to their satisfaction, and that to establish a defence on the ground of insanity it must be clearly proved that, *at the time of the committing of the act the party accused was labouring under such a defect of reason, from disease of the mind, as not to know the nature and quality of the act he was doing, or, if he did know it, that he did not know he was doing what was wrong.* [emphasis added]

It may well be conjectured that Their Lordships felt that M'Naghten should really have been convicted

of murder. After all, the somewhat narrow test of insanity they articulated would almost certainly not have been applicable to the specific facts of M'Naghten's case because M'Naghten did indeed appear to know what he was doing and that it was wrong to kill another human being. It is, therefore, one of the supreme ironies of legal history that the test of insanity, which is still applicable in England, Wales, and (in a modified version) in Canada, bears M'Naghten's name.

The debate over the appropriateness of relying on the *M'Naghten* Rules, as the basis for determining the criminal responsibility of mentally disordered accused persons, has raged for more than 165 years. The major criticism levelled against the Rules is that they focus almost exclusively on **cognitive** factors (that is, the accused's reasoning abilities) to the apparent exclusion of *emotional* and *volitional* factors. In particular, the Rules have been criticized for not taking into account the proposition that individuals may be perfectly aware of what they are doing and know that it is "morally wrong," but may, nevertheless, be utterly incapable of controlling their conduct.

THE MODERN NCRMD DEFENCE IN CANADA
Section 16 (1) of the *Criminal Code*

The basic elements of the *M'Naghten* Rules were incorporated into Canada's *Criminal Code* when it was first enacted in 1892. The present-day version of the rules is articulated in section 16(1) of the *Criminal Code*:

> No person is criminally responsible for an act committed or an omission made while suffering from a mental disorder that rendered the person incapable of appreciating the nature and quality of the act or omission or of knowing that it was wrong.

As the reader will immediately notice, this provision of the modern *Criminal Code* bears a close resemblance to the *M'Naghten* Rules of 1843. However, some significant differences must be taken into account. Perhaps the most noteworthy variation between the *M'Naghten* Rules and the version of section 16 originally enacted by the Canadian Parliament in 1892 is the use of the word "*appreciate*" as a substitute for the word "know" in the original phrase "know the nature and quality of the act." In addition, the Canadian Parliament referred to the issue of the accused's "*capacity*" to appreciate the nature and quality of an act or omission or to know that it was "wrong," whereas the *M'Naghten* Rules were concerned only with the accused's actual "knowledge" of these matters. These particular modifications to the *M'Naghten* Rules are still enshrined in today's version of section 16. It is reasonably clear that the Canadian Parliament, by making these modifications in 1892, sought to maintain the basic substance of the *M'Naghten* Rules while expanding their scope in certain critical respects. In 1991, Parliament amended section 16(1) by replacing the stigmatizing word "insane" with the term "*mental disorder*"; hence, it is now necessary to refer to the NCRMD defence rather than the insanity defence.

How have the Canadian courts interpreted the wording of the NCRMD defence that is now contained in section 16(1) of the *Code*?

The Meaning of "Mental Disorder" in Section 16(1) of the *Code*

Before defendants can successfully assert the NCRMD defence, they must first establish that, at the time of the alleged offence, they were experiencing a "**mental disorder.**" Section 2 of the *Criminal Code* states that "mental disorder" means "a disease of the mind."

The term "**disease of the mind**" was used in the *M'Naghten* Rules (1843) and has been extensively interpreted by the courts during the past 160 years. In the case of *Cooper* (1980), the Supreme Court of Canada adopted a remarkably expansive definition of "disease of the mind," as Justice Dickson said in his judgment:

> ... [I]n a legal sense "disease of the mind" embraces any illness, disorder or abnormal condition which impairs the human mind and its functioning, excluding, however, self-induced states caused by alcohol or drugs, as well as transitory mental states such as hysteria or concussion.

This broad definition covers almost any mental condition that a psychiatrist or psychologist would classify as a mental disorder, although it would exclude temporary states of intoxication caused by the voluntary ingestion of alcohol and/or other drugs as well as fleeting mental conditions caused by, for example, a blow to the head. However, it is extremely significant that Justice Dickson immediately added a qualifying statement to this definition: namely, that the NCRMD defence only comes into play if the disease is "of such intensity as to render the accused

incapable of appreciating the nature and quality of the violent act or of knowing that it is wrong." In other words, establishing that the accused person suffered from a "disease of the mind" is only the preliminary step toward advancing a successful NCRMD defence.

In the *Stone* case (1999), the Supreme Court of Canada emphasized the principle that "disease of the mind" is a legal, and not a strictly medical, term. Although expert medical evidence is necessarily of considerable relevance in determining whether a particular mental condition should be classified as a "disease of the mind," the ultimate decision on this issue must be made by the trial judge. This means that the trial judge may take into account issues of public policy, such as the need to protect the public. For example, an accused person may have a condition that may recur and pose a danger even though a psychiatrist or psychologist may not classify it as a mental disorder. Since an accused person who is found to be NCRMD may be detained in hospital or supervised in the community, the trial judge may find that, as a matter of law, the accused person had a "disease of the mind" in order to protect the public from a possible recurrence of dangerous behaviour. Courts in England and Canada have, for example, classified epilepsy as a "disease of the mind" even though traditionally it has not been regarded by mental health professionals as a mental disorder but rather as a physical condition that causes a temporary malfunctioning of the brain.

Since the designation of a particular mental condition as a "disease of the mind" constitutes a question of law, it is important to clarify the role of the trial judge in this process. In the *Stone* case (1999), Justice Bastarache, of the Supreme Court of Canada, stated that the trial judge is entrusted with the task of deciding "whether the condition the accused claims to have suffered from satisfies the legal test for disease of the mind." However, once the trial judge has made this legal determination, the question of whether the accused actually had a disease of the mind is a question of fact to be determined by the trier of fact (the members of the jury, if there is a jury trial, or the trial judge in all other cases). In other words, whether a particular condition, such as epilepsy, should be considered to be a "disease of mind" for the purpose of section 16(1) of the *Criminal Code* is a question of law that is determined exclusively by the trial judge. However, the issue of whether the accused actually had this condition at the time of the alleged offence is a question of fact that is left firmly in the hands of the trier of fact.

In practice, only accused persons who were experiencing a severe mental disorder at the time of the alleged offence are likely to be found NCRMD. In general, it must be established that the accused person had a mental disorder that manifested itself in the form of psychotic symptoms. According to the American Psychiatric Association's *Diagnostic and Statistical Manual of Mental Disorders, DSM-IV-TR*, (2000), the term "psychotic" has been defined in a variety of ways, none of which are entirely satisfactory. However, the *Manual* indicates that the term generally refers to a mental condition in which the individual experiences some or all of the following symptoms: "delusions," "prominent hallucinations," "disorganized speech," and "disorganized or catatonic behavior."[2] Individuals who have **psychosis** or a psychotic condition may find it very difficult to distinguish between what is real and what is unreal, and it is their loss of contact with reality that may render them incapable of appreciating the nature and quality of what they were doing or of knowing that it was wrong. A diagnosis of **schizophrenia** or some other type of psychotic disorder is, therefore, one of the most likely diagnoses to be made in relation to an NCRMD accused person. In this respect, it is important to note that an individual who has a **major depressive disorder** or **bipolar disorder** (formerly known as manic depression) may experience psychotic symptoms, and his or her condition may then be diagnosed as **schizoaffective disorder**, which is one of the "other psychotic disorders" listed in the *Diagnostic and Statistical Manual of Mental Disorders*.

Once it has been established that the accused person was experiencing a mental disorder ("disease of the mind"), the next step is to establish either (i) that the accused person lacked the capacity to appreciate the nature and quality of the act or omission that forms the basis of the charge against him or her or (ii) that the accused person lacked the capacity to know the act or omission was wrong. We shall now examine these two "arms" of the NCRMD defence.

---

[2] *Catatonic* means "in a state of inertia or apparent stupor often associated with schizophrenia and characterized by rigidity of the muscles" (*Encarta World English Dictionary*, 1999). Owing to the paralyzing nature of this condition, individuals with catatonic symptoms are highly unlikely to engage in acts of violence.

THE CAPACITY OF THE ACCUSED PERSON TO APPRECIATE THE NATURE AND QUALITY OF THE ACT OR OMISSION
The Meaning of "Appreciate" in Section 16(1)

It was indicated earlier that, when the *M'Naghten* Rules were incorporated into the 1892 *Criminal Code*, the word "**appreciate**" was substituted for "know" in the first "arm" of the mental disorder defence. This significant departure from the *M'Naghten* Rules was underscored in the case of *Barnier* (1980). In this case, the accused had shot and killed a woman in an office building and had subsequently taken his gun on the roof and demanded to speak to the prime minister of Canada. It was contended that the accused was experiencing severe delusions. However, at his trial for murder, there was a highly unusual development. All the psychiatrists were agreed that Barnier was incapable of *appreciating* the nature and quality of his act, but the Crown argued that, in law, the word "appreciate" means "know." The two Crown psychiatrists then changed their opinions. They testified that, if "appreciate" means no more than "know," then the accused knew what he was doing and that it was wrong.

The trial judge accepted the Crown's interpretation and Barnier was convicted of murder. The B.C. Court of Appeal allowed his appeal and substituted a verdict of not guilty by reason of insanity. In the view of the court, the trial judge had made a serious error in treating the word "appreciate" as being a mere synonym of the word "know." Although the Crown appealed this ruling, it was ultimately upheld by the Supreme Court of Canada. In delivering the unanimous decision of the Supreme Court, Justice Estey emphasized that Parliament had deliberately employed two different words in the critical portion of section 16(2), namely "appreciating" (the nature and quality of the act) and "knowing" (that the act is wrong). Therefore, it was obvious that Parliament intended these two words to be given different meanings; otherwise, the "Legislature would have employed one or the other only." In discussing the distinction between the two words, Justice Estey went on to say that

[t]he verb "know" has a positive connotation requiring a bare awareness, the act of receiving information without more. The act of appreciating, on the other hand, is a second stage in a mental process requiring the analysis of knowledge or experience in one manner or another. It is therefore clear

on the plain meaning of the section that Parliament intended that for a person to be insane within the statutory definition, he must be incapable first of appreciating in the analytical sense the nature and quality of the act or of knowing in the positive sense that his act was wrong....

The Supreme Court of Canada also had occasion to deal with the distinction between the words "know" and "appreciate" in *Cooper* (1980). In this case, the accused, a man with a long history of hospitalization for mental disorder, had strangled a female patient after a dance. There was medical evidence that, although Cooper may have been capable of intending bodily harm and of choking the young woman, he was not capable of intending to kill her. Nevertheless, he was convicted of murder at his trial and the Ontario Court of Appeal subsequently affirmed his conviction. However, the Supreme Court of Canada ultimately allowed his appeal and ordered a new trial. In delivering the judgment of the majority of the Supreme Court, Justice Dickson stated that the person who had drafted the original *Code* had made a deliberate change in language from the *M'Naghten* Rules by replacing "know" with "appreciate" in the first part of section 16(1). This change was made in order to "broaden the legal and medical considerations bearing upon the mental state of the accused and to make it clear that cognition was not to be the sole criterion." Indeed, Justice Dickson suggested that "emotional, as well as intellectual, awareness of the significance of the conduct is in issue." He went on to declare:

> With respect, I accept the view that the first branch of the test, in employing the word "appreciates," imports an additional requirement to mere knowledge of the physical quality of the act. *The requirement, unique to Canada, is that of perception, an ability to perceive the consequences, impact, and results of a physical act.* An accused may be aware of the physical character of his action (i.e. in choking) without necessarily having the capacity to appreciate that, in nature and quality, that act will result in the death of a human being. This is simply a restatement, specific to the defence of insanity, of the principle that *mens rea*, or intention as to the consequences of an act, is a requisite element in the commission of a crime. [emphasis added]

The Meaning of "Nature and Quality of the Act" in Section 16(1)

The Supreme Court of Canada has clearly stated that the phrase "nature and quality" of an act refers exclusively to the physical nature and quality of the act concerned. As Chief Justice Lamer said in the *Landry* case (1991), the "first branch of the s. 16(1) test protects an accused who, because of a disease of the mind, was incapable of appreciating the physical consequences of his act."

The Supreme Court's approach to this issue is perhaps best illustrated by the disturbing case of *Kjeldsen* (1981). The accused was charged with the brutal murder of a taxi driver. In the past, Kjeldsen had been found not guilty by reason of "insanity" on charges involving rape and attempted murder and had been detained in a psychiatric hospital. He was on a day pass from the hospital when he first raped, and then killed, the female taxi driver by shattering her skull with a large rock. All the medical witnesses agreed that Kjeldsen was "a dangerous psychopath with sexually deviant tendencies." The accused, however, was unsuccessful in his attempt to raise (what is now known as) the NCRMD defence. He was convicted at trial, and his subsequent appeals to both the Alberta Court of Appeal and the Supreme Court of Canada were rejected.

Although it was accepted that Kjeldsen had a form of mental disorder, there was some disagreement between the Crown and defence witnesses as to whether or not he was capable of appreciating the nature and quality of his violent actions. The expert witnesses for the defence sought to apply a broad test that would require that the accused have the capacity not only to foresee the physical consequences of his actions but also to predict and to understand the subjective or emotional reactions of his victim. In the view of the defence experts, a **psychopath** such as Kjeldsen was incapable of experiencing normal or appropriate feelings about the effects of his actions on other people: in short, he could not feel remorse or guilt and, therefore, could not appreciate the nature and quality of his conduct. However, the expert witnesses for the Crown assumed that section 16(1) referred solely to the accused's capacity to understand and foresee the *physical* consequences of his actions and that even a psychopath, such as Kjeldsen, would—in this more limited sense—be able to fully appreciate the nature and quality of his conduct. As Justice McIntyre stated, in delivering the judgment of the Supreme Court of Canada,

> To be capable of "appreciating" the nature and quality of his acts, an accused person must have the capacity to know what he is doing; in the case at bar, for example, to know that he was hitting the woman

on the head with a rock, with great force, and in addition he must have the capacity to estimate and understand the physical consequences which would flow from his act, in this case that he was causing physical injury which could result in death.

Justice McIntyre also expressly approved the following passage from the judgment of Justice Martin of the Ontario Court of Appeal in *Simpson* (1977):

> I do not think the exemption provided by ... [section16(1)] ... extends to one who has the necessary understanding of the nature, character and consequences of the act, but merely lacks appropriate feelings for the victim or lacks feelings of remorse or guilt for what he has done, even though such lack of feeling stems from "disease of the mind." *Appreciation of the nature and quality of the act does not import a requirement that the act be accompanied by appropriate feeling about the effect of the act on other people....* No doubt the absence of such feelings is a common characteristic of many persons who engage in repeated and serious criminal conduct. [emphasis added]

In rejecting Kjeldsen's appeal, the Supreme Court of Canada reached an eminently reasonable result in terms of public policy. After all, the Canadian public would scarcely tolerate a system of criminal justice that released back into the community dangerous individuals who have perpetrated violent crimes merely because they lacked the appropriate feelings for their victims or did not experience the appropriate pangs of remorse or guilt. Since Kjeldsen appreciated what he was doing and that it was wrong, the Court was fully justified in holding him accountable for his actions. Although Kjeldsen was diagnosed with a **personality disorder** (which the Supreme Court considered to be a "disease of the mind"), this condition undoubtedly failed to meet the criteria for an NCRMD verdict under section 16(1).

THE CAPACITY OF THE ACCUSED PERSON TO APPRECIATE THAT THE ACT OR OMISSION WAS WRONG

The Meaning of "Wrong" in Section 16(1)

The second "arm" of the NCRMD defence requires that the mental disorder that the accused person was experiencing rendered her or him incapable of knowing that the act or omission was "**wrong**." Parliament did not make clear whether the word "wrong" meant *morally* wrong or *legally* wrong.

The choice between these two alternatives may nevertheless prove to be the difference between a successful and an unsuccessful defence of NCRMD. Let us suppose that Dorrit kills Crummles, fully appreciating that he is killing the latter and realizing that it is a crime to do so. However, Dorrit (owing to a mental disorder) believes that he has been ordered by God or some other divine being to sacrifice Crummles in order to save the world from imminent destruction. There is no doubt that Dorrit appreciates the nature and quality of his act, so the first arm of the NCRMD defence does not apply to him. Furthermore, if "wrong" means *legally* wrong, then the second arm of the NCRMD defence does not apply to Dorrit either. However, if "wrong" means *morally* wrong, section 16(1) would be applicable because Dorrit believed that he was acting on the direct orders of the Almighty and was, therefore, acting in a manner that would be considered morally justified by his fellow citizens. In the *Chaulk* case

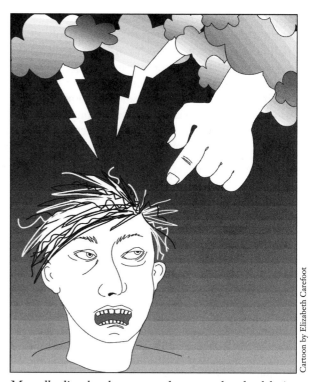

Mentally disordered persons, who are under the delusion that they are following a divine command, are entitled to be found not criminally responsible because they are incapable of knowing that their conduct would be considered "morally wrong" by the average member of Canadian society.

Cartoon by Elizabeth Carefoot

(1990), the Supreme Court of Canada finally settled this issue by ruling that "wrong" in section 16(1) means "wrong according to the ordinary moral standards of reasonable members of society."

Chief Justice Lamer, in delivering the majority judgment of the Supreme Court in the case of *Chaulk* (1990), stated that it would be unjust for the courts to find a mentally disordered accused person criminally responsible merely because he or she knew that his or her conduct was contrary to the law of the land. In his view,

> A person may well be aware that an act is contrary to law but, by reason of ... disease of the mind, is at the same time incapable of knowing that the act is morally wrong in the circumstances according to the moral standards of society. This would be the case, for example, if the person suffered from a disease of the mind to such a degree as to know that it is legally wrong to kill but ... kills "in the belief that it is in response to a divine order and therefore not morally wrong."...

Does the Supreme Court's ruling mean that those offenders who lack basic moral principles will now be acquitted as NCRMD? The answer is clearly in the negative. As the chief justice emphasized in his judgment, the Court's judgment provided absolutely no comfort to amoral offenders because, in order for an NCRMD defence to be successful, *the accused's incapacity to make moral distinctions must be causally related to his or her mental disorder.* Furthermore, the appropriate test is not whether the individual accused person believes his or her actions are morally justified but rather it is *whether he or she is capable of knowing that society at large regards the conduct as being morally wrong*; in other words, "the accused will not benefit from substituting his own moral code for that of society."

A straightforward illustration of the application of the Supreme Court's definition of "wrong" may be seen in the case of *Landry* (1991). The accused was charged with first degree murder and admitted that he had killed the victim. However, he advanced a defence of NCRMD. It was accepted that Landry had a severe psychosis that caused him to believe that he was God and that the victim was Satan. Landry was convinced that he had to kill "Satan" in order to fulfill his divine mission to rid the world of the forces of evil. Landry undoubtedly realized that murder was a crime but the Supreme Court of Canada ruled that he should be found NCRMD because his psychotic mental condition had rendered him incapable of

knowing that the **ordinary person** would regard the killing as being morally wrong.

A very significant application of the second "arm" of the NCRMD defence occurred in the case of *Oommen* (1994). The accused had killed a young woman by shooting her as she lay sleeping on a mattress in his apartment, and he was charged with **second degree murder**. It was generally agreed that there was no rational motive for the killing. The accused had for many years experienced "paranoid delusional psychosis." He came to believe that the members of a local union were involved in a conspiracy to kill him. Tragically, he formed the opinion that the young woman had been commissioned by his enemies to murder him in his own apartment and he became convinced that he had to destroy her before she had the opportunity to kill him. He, therefore, fired nine to thirteen shots at her from a semi-automatic weapon and she subsequently died. A psychiatrist testified that Oommen's mental disorder would not cause him to lose the intellectual capacity to distinguish between right and wrong in the abstract and to know that, in general, killing was wrong. However, his mental disorder would cause him to form an honest belief that the shooting of the young woman was justified under the particular circumstances (namely, that he honestly believed that she was going to kill him if he did not act first). The trial judge found that the killing was "caused, and indeed, compelled" by Oommen's mental condition and that "subjectively the accused did not believe his act to be wrong." However, the trial judge concluded that Oommen did have the "general capacity to know right from wrong" and ruled that he was not relieved from criminal responsibility under section 16(1).

Ultimately, a new trial was ordered in Oommen's case. The Supreme Court of Canada agreed with the Alberta Court of Appeal that the trial judge had misinterpreted section 16(1). In delivering the judgment of the Supreme Court, Justice McLachlin (as she then was) stated that "the focus must be on capacity to know that the act committed was wrong, and not merely on a general capacity to distinguish right from wrong." In Justice McLachlin's view, "[T]he issue is whether the accused possessed the capacity present in the ordinary person to know that the act in question was wrong according to the everyday standards of the reasonable person." She added that "the real question is whether the accused should be exempted from criminal responsibility because a mental disorder at the time of the act deprived him of the capacity for rational perception and hence rational choice about the rightness or wrongness of the act." In this sense, the trial judge had made a significant error in focusing on Oommen's general ability to distinguish right from wrong instead of concentrating on his capacity to know that the killing of the young woman was right or wrong in the circumstances as he honestly believed them to be. As Justice McLachlin commented, "[S]. 16(1) of the *Criminal Code* embraces not only the intellectual ability to know right from wrong, but the capacity to apply that knowledge to the situation at hand."

The Supreme Court of Canada dealt with the same issue some six years later. In the *Molodowic* case (2000), the accused was charged with second degree murder following the shooting death of his grandfather. There was no doubt that Molodowic had a serious mental disorder—paranoid schizophrenia— and was affected by visual and auditory hallucinations and delusions of persecution. In short, his mental disorder severely impaired his grasp of reality. The psychiatrists who were called to testify by the defence were agreed that Molodowic did appreciate the nature and quality of his act (namely, that he was killing his grandfather) and that he knew that this was a crime. However, they also expressed the opinion that Molodowic *did not know that his act was morally wrong*. Both of these psychiatrists testified to the effect that Molodowic's "act of shooting was consistent with his mental disorder having caused him to believe that only in so doing could he save himself from further torment." Significantly, the Crown did not call its own psychiatric experts to contradict this evidence.

Molodowic was convicted of murder by a jury, and his subsequent appeal to the Manitoba Court of Appeal was dismissed. However, on a further appeal to the Supreme Court of Canada, the conviction was set aside and a verdict of NCRMD was substituted. The Supreme Court ruled that the jury's verdict was unreasonable in light of the psychiatric testimony presented at the trial. In delivering the judgment of the Court, Justice Arbour stated that the evidence simply did not support the conclusion that, at the time of the shooting, Molodowic was sufficiently lucid to know that his acts were morally wrong. She went on to state that

> ... the totality of the psychiatric evidence did not give rise to the reasonable possibility that the appellant, who laboured under the effects of a severe mental disorder at the time he committed a homicide, and

whose moral judgment was impaired as a result, would have had a momentary reprieve from the effects of his disorder, at the critical time, sufficient to provide him with the moral insight necessary to engage his criminal responsibility....

> ... It is not necessarily easy for a jury to accept that, in lay person's terms, an accused who knows what he is doing and knows that it is a crime, could still genuinely believe that he would not be morally condemned by reasonable members of society for his conduct. In my view, the defence proved this to be the case and, on the evidence tendered at his trial, it was unreasonable to conclude otherwise.

However, it is important to remember that the mere fact that the accused had a severe mental disorder does not automatically lead to the conclusion that the accused lacked the capacity to know that his or her conduct would be considered morally wrong by ordinary members of society. In this respect, it is useful to compare the decisions of the Supreme Court of Canada in *Oommen* (1994) and *Molodowic* (2000) with the decision of the B.C. Court of Appeal in *W. (J.M.)* (1998). Here, the two accused were young persons who had been charged with hostage taking, kidnapping, and various weapons charges. They had hijacked a school bus that was transporting students from their school. Fortunately, the accused eventually surrendered to the police without anyone suffering physical injuries. Both of the youths were diagnosed as having a serious psychotic disorder—schizophrenia—and they laboured under a number of delusions that were generated by that mental condition. The hostage-taking scheme was originally conceived as a means of coercing the government into allocating the accused a portion of Baffin Island to establish their own state. This enclave was then to be used to accumulate a large cache of nuclear weapons with which they could threaten the rest of the world into implementing a new social order. The accused agreed that, if this ambitious plan failed, then they would use their hostages to negotiate a situation in which they would be held together in solitary confinement, "where they could meditate, expand their spirituality and power, as well as learning greater 'magic' and practice their music." The accused were convicted at their trial in Youth Court and appealed to the B.C. Court of Appeal.

The central issue was whether the accused fell within the second "arm" of the NCRMD test, articulated in section 16(1) of the *Criminal Code*—namely, did their mental disorder render them incapable of knowing that their plans and actions were wrong? The majority of the Court of Appeal affirmed the convictions, even though it was accepted that both of the accused suffered from a serious mental disorder. Chief Justice McEachern, speaking for the majority, took the view that this was not a case in which the accused lacked the capacity to understand society's values. They knew that the ordinary person would regard their actions as being morally wrong:

> The evidence ... does not establish that the accused were so driven by their delusions that they did not have the capacity to rationally choose which course to follow. *Rather the evidence supports the view that these young men believed that society's rules did not or should not apply to them.* The fact that they chose to proceed with their plan does not establish that they did not have the capacity rationally to assess their acts. [emphasis added]

THE PROBLEM OF IRRESISTIBLE IMPULSE

An accused person may well say, "I appreciated what I was doing and knew that I was doing something that was wrong; however, because I had a mental disorder, an irresistible impulse came over me and I couldn't help myself." Would such an accused person be entitled to claim the benefit of the NCRMD defence?

In Canada, it is perfectly clear that the so-called "irresistible impulse" defence is not recognized by the courts. If the accused does not meet the criteria of either of the two "arms" of the NCRMD defence set out in section 16(1), the question of irresistible impulse is absolutely irrelevant. Of course, as the Supreme Court of Canada noted in the *Borg* (1969) and *Abbey* (1982) cases, an irresistible impulse may be a "symptom or manifestation of a disease of the mind," but such a mental condition will not excuse the defendant under section 16(1) unless the other requirements of that provision are met.

Why have the courts taken such a firm stand on the issue of irresistible impulse as the basis for a defence of NCRMD? Perhaps they are understandably reluctant to open the door of the NCRMD defence to individuals who have only a personality disorder or who are classified as psychopaths and claim that they cannot help themselves. This attitude certainly seems to underlie the Supreme Court of Canada's leading decision in *Chartrand* (1976). In this case, the accused had been convicted of killing a police officer. His appeal to the Supreme Court was ultimately rejected. However, the Court's approach

Irresistible impulse? Assaulting another man even though two police officers are present.

to the issue of irresistible impulse is most interesting. It had been contended that the defendant had a psychopathic personality. The medical director of Montreal's *Institut Pinel*, Dr. Béliveau, stated that Chartrand was

> ... capable of distinguishing between right and wrong—he understands the nature of his actions, and so forth—but that does not mean that there is not an inner pathological process at work that can prompt him to exhibit a form of behaviour that is unacceptable, dangerous, violent and so on, as well as a psychotic process that would be clearly, if you will, obvious in another person.

However, the Supreme Court totally rejected this as a basis for a successful defence under section 16(1) of the *Code*. Indeed, Justice de Grandpré held that

> Chartrand was ... able to distinguish between right and wrong, and although he was ill, he was technically sane. What the witness adds on the subject of the inner pathological process cannot be taken into consideration under our criminal legislation, which does not recognize the diminished responsibility theory.

This decision clearly shut the door to the irresistible impulse claim as an independent basis for raising the NCRMD defence in Canada. The Supreme Court's approach clearly underlines the fact that section 16(1) has been interpreted in such a way as to focus upon *cognitive*, rather than volitional, factors in determining the issue of whether or not the accused person is NCRMD. It is always difficult to assess the validity of such claims. On the other hand, it may well be argued that there should be some kind of defence open to defendants who can make a plausible claim that they could not control their conduct because of their mental illness. In England and Wales, for example, such individuals may raise the defence of diminished responsibility in such circumstances. This defence operates only in relation to a charge of murder, however, and, if successful, leads to a conviction of manslaughter rather than an acquittal; in other words, it is only a *partial defence*. Whether some form of diminished responsibility defence should be made available in Canada is a matter that has been hotly debated for a number of years and, to date, Parliament has not been willing to introduce it into the *Criminal Code*.

Before leaving the matter of irresistible impulse, it might be useful to consider the possibility that the decision in the *Chaulk* case might open the door to some defendants' claiming that they suffered an irresistible impulse that caused them to lack the capacity to know that their conduct was wrong according to the ordinary standards of reasonable people. If a mentally disordered accused person can demonstrate that he or she was so overwhelmed by an irresistible impulse that he or she could not, with a reasonable degree of composure, think of the reasons that ordinary persons would view their conduct as right or wrong, such an accused person should be acquitted as being NCRMD. It remains to be seen whether the courts will be willing to view such a scenario as one in which the irresistible impulse is a symptom of a mental disorder that excuses the accused under the second arm of section 16(1).

MISCELLANEOUS PROCEDURAL ISSUES

THE POWER OF THE CROWN TO RAISE THE MENTAL DISORDER DEFENCE

Most people assume that the NCRMD defence is an issue raised exclusively by the accused person in order to avoid being found criminally responsible for his or her actions. However, in certain circumstances, the issue may be raised by the Crown—even in the face of staunch opposition by the accused person. In the *Swain* case (1991), the Supreme Court of Canada ruled that the Crown may only follow this course of action in two situations: (i) where the accused person puts his or her state of mind in issue at trial or (ii) after the jury or the judge has already concluded that the accused person committed the act or omission that formed the basis for the offence with which he or she is charged.

The Supreme Court considered that it was perfectly fair for the Crown to raise the defence of NCRMD where the accused deliberately puts his or her state of mind in issue. For example, if the accused claims that he or she was in a state of automatism at the time of the alleged offence, the Crown may reasonably assert that the accused's state of mind was the product of a mental disorder and that, instead of being granted an absolute acquittal, the accused should be found NCRMD and subjected to the possibility that restrictions will be placed on his or her liberty (for example, by being confined in a psychiatric facility). As Chief Justice Lamer said, "[T]he Crown's ability to raise evidence of [mental disorder] is not inconsistent with the accused's right to control the conduct of his or her defence because the very issue has been raised by the accused's conduct of his or her defence." Similarly, the Supreme Court took the view that the accused person's right to liberty and security of the person (guaranteed by section 7 of the *Charter*) would not be infringed if the Crown were permitted to raise the NCRMD defence *after* the accused person has had the opportunity to present his or her defence. Permitting the Crown to advance the NCRMD defence at the end of the trial ensures that there is no possibility that raising the issue of the mental disorder will prejudice the fact-finding process in those cases where the accused declines to put his or her state of mind in issue. For example, the accused may advance an alibi defence. If this defence is successful, then the jury or judge will grant the accused an absolute acquittal because he or she did not commit the act or omission with which he or she has been charged. Allowing the Crown to raise the NRCMD defence before the accused has presented this defence might well prejudice the accused's right to a fair trial. One possibility is that the members of the jury may reason that, if the accused is mentally disordered, then he or she is "just the sort of person" who would commit the offence that has been charged. Given the prejudice that is often shown against the mentally disordered, it is important to ensure that evidence of the accused's mental disorder does not taint the fact-finding process at the time that the jury is considering the question of innocence or guilt.

However, where the accused was clearly suffering from a serious mental disorder at the time of the alleged offence but imprudently refuses to permit his or her counsel to advance a defence of NCRMD, it may be necessary for the Crown to intervene. Indeed, in these circumstances, one might well argue that the Crown should raise the defence not only in fairness to the mentally disordered accused person but also in the public interest. For example, in the case of *Pietrangelo* (2008), the accused was convicted of aggravated assault and assault with a weapon following attacks on the mayor of Niagara Falls and his aide. At his trial, Pietrangelo represented himself and steadfastly refused to advance the NCRMD defence. The Crown had evidence that Pietrangelo had been suffering a major mental disorder at the time of the assaults, specifically a delusional disorder of the persecutory type (paranoid schizophrenia). The Crown had extensive information concerning Pietrangelo's mental disorder but, owing to a mistaken interpretation of the law, it did not introduce this evidence after the jury had found that Pietrangelo had committed the offences with which he was charged.

Pietrangelo appealed against his convictions to the Ontario Court of Appeal and, at this time, the Crown finally introduced evidence in support of a defence of NCRMD. The Ontario Court of Appeal set aside Pietrangelo's convictions and substituted a verdict of NCRMD. Justice Sharpe provided the following rationale in support of the Court of Appeal's decision:

> ... [T]he common law rule allowing the Crown to raise the issue of NCRMD is aimed not only at avoiding the unfair treatment of the accused but at maintaining the integrity of the criminal justice system itself. The accused is not the only person who has an interest in the outcome of the trial; society itself has an interest in ensuring that the system does not incorrectly label insane people as criminals....
>
> Entering an NCRMD finding on the evidence now before this court would, in my opinion, serve three important purposes deeply rooted in our law, all of which must be balanced with the appellant's interests and individual rights. Those purposes are: (1) maintaining the principle of fundamental justice that the criminal justice system not convict a person who was insane at the time he or she committed an offence; (2) protecting the public from presently dangerous persons requiring hospitalization; and (3) recognizing the public interest of having serious criminal charges resolved on the merits and with finality.

THE BURDEN AND STANDARD OF PROOF WHEN THE DEFENCE OF NCRMD IS RAISED

Normally, the Crown is placed under the burden of proving all the *actus reus* and *mens rea* elements of a

criminal offence in order to obtain a conviction. Furthermore, the standard of proof that must be met is "beyond a reasonable doubt." The NCRMD defence constitutes an exception to this general rule. Section 16(3) of the *Criminal Code* states that the party who raises the issue of the NCRMD defence must shoulder the burden of proving it. Furthermore, section 16(2) states that "every person is presumed not to suffer from a mental disorder so as to be exempt from criminal responsibility ... until the contrary is proved on the balance of probabilities." In other words, the party who raises the defence of NCRMD (either the accused or the Crown) must prove that it was more likely than not that the accused was NCRMD at the time of the offence.

In the *Chaulk* case (1990), the Supreme Court of Canada held that placing the burden of proving the defence of NCRMD on an accused person undoubtedly infringes the presumption of innocence that is guaranteed by section 11(d) of the *Charter*. However, the Supreme Court also ruled that section 16(2) and (3) constituted a reasonable limit on the presumption of innocence and, therefore, these provisions were saved by section 1 of the *Charter*. According to Chief Justice Lamer, Parliament was justified in enacting section 16(2) and (3) because, otherwise, the Crown would be saddled with the impossible burden of proving that the accused was not NCRMD and accused persons who were not really mentally disordered would wrongly escape criminal responsibility. Of particular importance to the Court was the fact that the Crown has no means of compelling an accused person to cooperate with an examination by a psychiatrist who will testify for the prosecution. If an accused person refuses to cooperate with a "Crown" psychiatrist, the prosecution could be placed in an impossible position if it were required to disprove that the accused was NCRMD at the time of the alleged offence. The defence may present testimony from a psychiatrist who has examined the accused firsthand, but the Crown would not be able to do so and this would place it at a considerable disadvantage before a judge and/or jury. Since the state of the accused's mind at the time of the alleged offence is something that is peculiarly within his or her knowledge, it is reasonable, in the view of the Supreme Court, to require him or her to present evidence on this matter and to prove that the requirements of section 16(1) are met before entering a verdict of NCRMD.

THE DISPOSITION OF NCRMD ACCUSED PERSONS

Prior to 1992, those accused persons who were found NCRMD were required to be kept "in strict custody" (in a psychiatric facility) for an indefinite period and could only be released by the provincial or territorial government concerned. However, in the *Swain* case (1991), the Supreme Court of Canada held that the automatic detention of every accused person who was found to be NCRMD violated sections 7 and 9 of the *Charter* and, therefore, the Court declared the relevant provision of the *Criminal Code* [section 614(2)] to be invalid. As a consequence, the Parliament of Canada was required to amend the *Criminal Code* and the new system for dealing with NCR accused came into effect in February 1992.

The new provisions of the *Criminal Code* required that **review boards** be established in each province and territory [section 672.38]. These tribunals have now taken over the primary responsibility for deciding whether an NCR accused should be detained and, if so, for how long.[3] When a review board makes such a decision, its membership will consist of a chair (who must be a judge or a person who is qualified for a judicial appointment), a psychiatrist, and one other person (whose background is unspecified but who may well be an individual with a background in social work or some other related field). In certain circumstances, the trial court may make a disposition of the NCR accused but most decisions about the fate of NCR accused will be made by the relevant review board. The dispositional alternatives available to the review board (or court) are

- an **absolute discharge**;
- a **conditional discharge**; or
- an order to hold the accused person in custody (in a psychiatric facility).

When a review board (or court) is choosing among these three alternatives, it must take into consideration "the need to protect the public from dangerous persons, the mental condition of the accused, the reintegration of the accused into society, and the other needs of the accused": in light of these considerations,

the review board (or court) must select the disposition that is 'the least onerous and least restrictive to the accused'" (section 672.54). Furthermore, if the review board (or court) is of the opinion that "the accused is not a significant threat to the safety of the public," then it must grant the accused an absolute discharge (section 672.54(a)).

How is a review board (or a court) supposed to make the choice among the three potential dispositions? In the *Winko* case (1999), the Supreme Court of Canada held that section 672.54(a) of the *Criminal Code* must be interpreted as meaning that, unless the review board (or court) is *satisfied* that the NCR accused person constitutes a "significant threat to the safety of the public," then it is required to order an absolute discharge. In delivering the judgment of the majority of the justices of the Supreme Court, Justice McLachlin stated:

> There is no presumption that the NCR accused poses a significant threat to the safety of the public. Restrictions on his or her liberty can only be justified if, at the time of the hearing, the evidence before the court or Review Board shows that the NCR accused actually constitutes such a threat. The court or Review Board cannot avoid coming to a decision on this issue by stating, for example, that it is uncertain or cannot decide whether the NCR accused poses a significant threat to the safety of the public. If it cannot come to a decision with any certainty, then it has not found that the NCR accused poses a significant threat to the safety of the public.

If the review board (or court) concludes that the NCR accused person does indeed pose a significant threat, then it has two choices: it may order that the accused be "discharged subject to the conditions the court or Review Board deems necessary" or "it may direct that the NCR accused be detained in custody in a hospital, again subject to appropriate conditions." Justice McLachlin made it very clear in her judgment in *Winko* that the threshold for justifying the imposition of restrictions on the liberty of the person who has been found NCR is very high:

> A "significant threat to the safety of the public" means a real risk of physical or psychological harm to members of the public that is serious in the sense of going beyond the merely trivial or annoying. *The conduct giving rise to the harm must be criminal in nature.* [emphasis added]

According to Justice McLachlin, "a minuscule risk of a grave harm will not suffice" and, "similarly, a high risk of trivial harm will not meet the threshold."

---

[3] Review Boards also have a general supervisory power over those individuals who are responsible for the treatment and rehabilitation of NCR accused persons. For example, a Board may require a hospital to prepare a new treatment plan for an NCR accused person (*Mazzei* (2006)).

Furthermore, she emphasized that there is no onus on the NCR accused person to prove that he or she is *not* dangerous—a task that would be extraordinarily difficult to accomplish. It is only if the evidence presented to the review board (or court) establishes that the NCR accused person constitutes a significant threat that restrictions may be placed on his or her liberty.

As noted above, section 672.54 of the *Criminal Code* provides that an important consideration in determining whether an NCR accused person constitutes a "significant threat to the safety of the public" is the "mental condition of the accused." In the case of *Wodajio* (2005), the Alberta Court of Appeal emphasized that "the 'significant threat' must relate to the appellant's mental condition or overall mental state at the time of the hearing" rather than at the time of the offence. As Justice Russell stated in delivering the judgment of the Court,

> The relative importance of the non criminally responsible accused's mental condition to the overall assessment of dangerousness depends on many variables, including the nature of the accused's mental disorder, available treatment, the accused's understanding of his mental condition, and willingness to conform to proposed treatment, and the accused's past and expected success or failure following treatment.

In two landmark cases, *Penetanguishene Mental Health Centre v. Ontario (Attorney General)* (2004) *and Pinet v. St. Thomas Psychiatric Hospital* (2004), the Supreme Court of Canada ruled that the statutory requirement—that the review board or court make a disposition that is "the least onerous and least restrictive to the accused"—applies not just to the choice among the three alternative dispositions (absolute discharge, conditional discharge, and custody order) but also to the conditions that form part of that disposition. In these two cases, the Court took the view that this requirement applied to the making of an order that the accused be detained in custody in a hospital. Both cases involved an NCR accused person who was required to be detained in a hospital in Ontario. Since the province of Ontario operates both maximum and medium security hospitals, the Supreme Court ruled that the NCR accused persons concerned were entitled to be placed in a medium—as opposed to a maximum—security hospital because, in these two cases, placement in a medium security facility represented the "least onerous and restrictive" disposition in light of the considerations that the review board

must take into account—namely, "the need to protect the public from dangerous persons, the mental condition of the accused, the reintegration of the accused back into society and the other needs of the accused" (section 652.54). As Justice Binnie stated in the judgment of the Supreme Court in *Penetanguishene Mental Health Centre v. Ontario (Attorney General)*,

> The "least restrictive regime", in ordinary language, would include not only the place or mode of detention but the conditions governing it.... The liberty interest of the NCR accused is not exhausted by the simple choice among absolute discharge, conditional discharge, or hospital detention on conditions. A variation in the conditions of a conditional discharge, or the conditions under which an NCR accused is detained in a mental hospital, can also have serious ramifications for his or her liberty interest....

The same logic would apply when a review board or court chooses to release an NCR accused person to the community under the terms of a conditional discharge. The package of conditions that is imposed on an NCR accused in the community must represent the "least onerous and restrictive" package in light of the statutory criteria that are articulated in section 672.54 of the *Criminal Code*.

It is noteworthy that, in the *Winko* case (1999), the Supreme Court of Canada also rejected a *Charter* challenge to the constitutional validity of section 672.54 of the *Criminal Code*—the provision that constitutes the heart of the new system for determining the disposition of those accused persons who have been found NCRMD. More specifically, the Court ruled that section 672.54 does not deprive an NCR accused person of his or her liberty or security of the person in a manner that infringes the fundamental principles of justice (section 7 of the *Charter*) because only those NCR accused persons who represent a significant threat to the public may be subjected to restrictions on their liberty after they have been absolved of criminal responsibility for their actions. In essence, before a decision is made about the disposition of an NCR accused, the review board or court must conduct an individualized risk assessment in order to determine whether that person is dangerous. Furthermore, where a conditional discharge or a hospital order is imposed, the review board will conduct periodic hearings to reassess the situation of the NCR accused and he or she also has the right to appeal to the Court of Appeal in his or her province or territory. The

Supreme Court of Canada also held that section 672.54 did not discriminate against the mentally disordered and, therefore, did not infringe section 15 of the *Charter*, which preserves the equality rights of Canadians. Indeed, Justice McLachlin pointed out that section 672.54 does not impose restrictions on the liberty of NCR accused simply because they have a mental disorder. Conditional discharges and custody orders are only imposed on those NCR accused who are judged to be *dangerous* in the sense that they pose a significant threat to the public in terms of their potential to commit criminal offences that are likely to cause either psychological or physical harm to others. In other words, the restrictions are not imposed because the NCR accused is mentally disordered but rather because he or she is considered dangerous. As Justice McLachlin suggests, "Parliament has signaled that the NCR accused is to be treated with the utmost dignity and afforded the utmost liberty compatible with his or her situation." In her view, the NCR accused is not to be punished but rather must "receive the disposition that is 'the least onerous and least restrictive' one compatible with his or her situation."

There is little doubt that the implementation of the new system for the disposition of NCR accused persons has rendered the NCRMD defence a considerably more attractive option for defendants in a criminal trial. Prior to 1992, NCR accused persons were automatically kept in custody for an indefinite period. However, the new regime

- provides courts and review boards with a set of flexible options;
- ensures that only those NCR accused persons who are proved to be dangerous are subjected to restrictions on their liberty; and
- provides access to the appeal courts for those NCR accused who wish to challenge any restrictions that may be placed on them by a review board or trial court.

Although the new system of dealing with NCR accused has already caused an increase in the number of successful NCRMD defences in Canada, it is important to bear in mind that they still constitute only a very small proportion of criminal cases. As our analysis of section 16 has demonstrated, it is only the most severely mentally disordered defendants who will be able to meet the strict criteria that Parliament has imposed as a prerequisite for raising the NCRMD defence successfully.

MENTAL DISORDER AS A PARTIAL DEFENCE

There are certain circumstances in which the mental disorder of the accused at the time of the alleged offence does not meet the strict criteria for a successful NCRMD defence under section 16(1) but may nevertheless be sufficient to reduce the severity of the charge laid against him or her. This situation arises where the mental disorder of the accused prevents him or her from forming the specific intent required for such offences as murder or robbery. For example, in the *Lechasseur* case (1977), the Quebec Court of Appeal held that, even though the accused had failed to prove that he was NCRMD, the members of the jury at his trial should have been informed that they should acquit the accused of murder and convict him of manslaughter if his mental disorder prevented him from forming the intent to kill. As Justice Casey said, "[E]vidence that falls short of what is required to establish the [NCRMD] defence may still be sufficiently strong to create a reasonable doubt as to the capacity of the accused to formulate the specific intent that the law requires."

Mental illness may also be relevant to the question of whether an accused person, who is charged with first degree murder, acted with the planning and deliberation that is required by section 231(2) of the *Criminal Code*. Indeed, mental disorder may prevent the accused from acting in a planned and deliberate manner and, if this is the case, then he or she should be acquitted of first degree murder and convicted instead of second degree murder. As Chief Justice Lamer of the Supreme Court of Canada stated in the case of *Jacquard* (1997),

> It is true that some factor, such as mental disorder, that is insufficient to negative the charge that the accused *intended* to kill, may nevertheless be sufficient to negative the elements of *planning and deliberation*. This is because one can intend to kill and yet be impulsive rather than considered in doing so. It requires less mental capacity simply to intend than it does to plan and deliberate. [emphasis in the original]

However, it is important to bear in mind that being mentally ill is not *necessarily* incompatible with a finding that the accused acted with deliberation and planning. As Justice Martin said, in delivering the judgment of the Ontario Court of Appeal in *Kirkby* (1985),

> Mental disorder may, of course, negative planning and deliberation, but if the murder is, in fact, both

planned and deliberate, the existence of mental disorder does not *per se* remove the murder from the category of first degree murder. Mental disorder may or may not negative the elements of planning and deliberation, depending on the nature of the mental disorder and the effects produced by it. The fact that the offender suffers from a mental disorder is not, however, *necessarily* incompatible with the commission by him of ... a "cold-blooded" murder.... I do not think that Parliament, by using the word "deliberate," imported a requirement that the offender's previous determination to kill the victim must be the result of reasonable or normal thinking or must be rationally motivated, provided the Crown has established that the killing was planned, and that the act of killing was considered and not the result of sudden impulse.

AUTOMATISM

DEFINITION OF AUTOMATISM

Automatism has been defined as "a state of impaired consciousness ... in which an individual, though capable of action, has no voluntary control over that action" (Justice Bastarache, on behalf of the majority of the Supreme Court of Canada in *Stone* (1999)). Provided the state of automatism did not arise because of a mental disorder or as a consequence of self-induced intoxication, then the individual affected by it is entitled to be acquitted of a criminal charge.

As Justice La Forest, of the Supreme Court of Canada, noted in the case of *Parks* (1992), the defence of automatism is directly relevant to the question of whether the Crown has established that the accused has committed the *actus reus* elements of a criminal offence:

> Automatism occupies a unique place in our criminal law system. Although spoken of as a "defence," it is conceptually a subset of the voluntariness requirement which in turn is part of the *actus reus* component of criminal liability.

It would be a mistake to confuse automatism with a state of complete unconsciousness. Indeed, as Justice Bastarache pointed out in the *Stone* case (1999), "medically speaking, unconscious means 'flat on the floor,' that is a comatose-type state": clearly a comatose individual is not capable of carrying out any actions at all—let alone a crime! Therefore, it is more accurate, Justice Bastarache said, to define automatism as being a form of "impaired consciousness, rather than unconsciousness." Perhaps it is most helpful to think of automatism as constituting a state of *severely clouded consciousness that prevents the accused from acting voluntarily*.

Conceptually, there are, at least, five separate categories of automatism: (i) automatism caused by such "normal" conditions as sleepwalking or hypnosis (which are not considered by the courts to be the result of mental disorder); (ii) automatism triggered by an external trauma, such as a blow to the head; (iii) automatism that is *involuntarily* induced by alcohol or other drugs; (iv) automatism that is voluntarily self-induced by the use of alcohol or other drugs; (v) automatism caused by a mental disorder (or a "disease of the mind"). However, only those conditions that fall within categories (i) to (iii) may lead to the acquittal of an accused person on the basis of the legal defence of automatism.

AUTOMATISM CAUSED BY SUCH "NORMAL" STATES AS SLEEPWALKING

A person who acts in a state of automatism that is associated with a "normal" condition, such as sleepwalking, is entitled to a complete acquittal of any criminal charge. The use of the adjective *normal* is intended to emphasize that these conditions are not the result of a mental disorder. The commission of criminal offences in such conditions is extremely rare; however, the important case of *Parks* (1992) demonstrates that, in certain circumstances, this category of automatism may result in an acquittal.

In *Parks* (1992), the evidence indicated that the accused had apparently fallen asleep and then driven some 23 kilometres to the home of his parents-in-law, where he stabbed and beat them both. His mother-in-law died from her injuries, while his father-in-law ultimately survived his serious injuries. A number of expert witnesses appeared for the defence and supported a defence based on sleepwalking; the Crown, however presented no expert evidence on this issue. Testimony was presented to the effect that Parks had enjoyed "excellent relations" with his parents-in-law prior to the incident in question and that several members of his family had been affected by sleep disorders, such as sleepwalking, adult enuresis (bed-wetting), nightmares, and sleeptalking.

Parks was acquitted at his trial on the basis that he was acting in a state of automatism at the time of the attacks on his parents-in-law. The Ontario Court of

Appeal affirmed his acquittal on an appeal by the Crown and underscored the view that sleepwalking is a normal condition. The Crown subsequently appealed to the Supreme Court of Canada, but the Supreme Court agreed with the Ontario Court of Appeal and dismissed the appeal. As Chief Justice Lamer pointed out, the medical evidence had been that "a person who is sleepwalking cannot think, reflect or perform voluntary acts." More specifically, there was expert testimony to the effect that "during the slow wave sleep stage the cortex, which is the part of the brain that controls thinking and voluntary movement, is essentially in coma" and that "when a person is sleepwalking, the movements he makes are controlled by other parts of the brain and are more or less reflexive." Since Parks was sleepwalking at the time of the attacks on his parents-in-law, he was not capable of acting voluntarily; therefore, he could not be convicted of a criminal offence.

AUTOMATISM TRIGGERED BY AN EXTERNAL TRAUMA

Perhaps the classic example of automatism is the situation in which an external blow to the head causes an episode of impaired consciousness, during which the accused engages in conduct that would otherwise be considered criminal. Even though a person who has suffered such a blow to the head may *appear* to be acting normally, he or she is nevertheless in a state of altered consciousness and is not able to control his or her conduct. Since the accused person, in these circumstances, acts in a state of impaired consciousness, it is clear that he or she will be unable to recall any of the events following the trauma to the head; therefore, an important element of the accused's condition is that he or she has amnesia.

In the case of *Bleta* (1965), for example, the accused and a man called Gafi were fighting in a Toronto street. In the course of the fracas, Bleta fell and hit his head on the pavement. Bleta regained his feet and followed Gafi, who had started to walk away. Bleta then drew a knife and fatally stabbed Gafi in the neck area. Two of the bystanders watching the fight, as well as a police officer, commented that Bleta appeared to be in a "dazed condition" at the time of the fatal blow. Bleta's counsel successfully contended that his client was acting unconsciously and with no voluntary control over his actions at the time of the stabbing. The Supreme Court of Canada implicitly accepted the legitimacy of the automatism defence, although it decided the *Bleta* case on other grounds.

AUTOMATISM INVOLUNTARILY INDUCED BY ALCOHOL OR OTHER DRUGS

Accused persons who, through no voluntary action on their part, become so severely impaired by alcohol or other drugs that they fall into a state of automatism are entitled to be acquitted of a criminal charge because they are incapable of acting voluntarily. For example, suppose that Fanny laces Lizzie's orange juice with vodka without the latter's knowledge. In these circumstances, if Lizzie lapses into a state of automatism, she must be acquitted of any criminal charge arising out of her activities while she was in such a condition. Similarly, in the case of *King* (1962), the accused visited a dentist in order to have two teeth extracted. For this purpose, he was injected with sodium pentothal, a quick-acting anesthetic. The accused claimed that he received no warning that he might subsequently become impaired by the drug and that he was not advised to refrain from driving a motor vehicle. King left the dentist's office, entered his car, and became unconscious while driving it. His car then crashed into a parked vehicle and he was charged with impaired driving. He was

Cartoon by Elizabeth Carefoot

Sleepwalking as the basis for a defence of automatism.

subsequently convicted at his trial; however, this conviction was set aside by the Ontario Court of Appeal. The Supreme Court of Canada affirmed the judgment of the Ontario Court of Appeal. Although the Supreme Court justices appeared to have different reasons for this decision, there was general agreement that an accused person should not be convicted of an offence if he or she did not act voluntarily. In the *King* case, it was clear that the accused's impairment was caused by a drug that had been administered by a dentist in the course of a recognized medical procedure and that the effect of the drug was apparently not made known to the accused.

It should be mentioned that the defence that was raised by the accused in the *King* case would be most unlikely to succeed before the courts of today. Hospitals, medical offices, and dentists' surgeries currently require a patient to sign a form prior to any medical procedure that requires the administration of an anesthetic that might impair consciousness. This form generally notifies patients that they must not drive a vehicle and should arrange for other transportation (e.g., relatives or a taxi) to pick them up after the procedure. Similarly, it is unlikely that accused persons who have taken prescription drugs would be able to successfully claim that they became impaired involuntarily because of lack of knowledge of the effects of the drugs in question. Indeed, in most parts of Canada, pharmacists routinely place a red warning label indicating that certain drugs should not be mixed with alcohol, or specifically warning patients that they should not operate machinery in the event of drowsiness. In short, in contemporary times, it would be very difficult for an individual to claim that he or she could not have foreseen that a drug or other intoxicating substance could cause impairment of consciousness. If there is *foresight of impairment* and the drug or substance is *taken of the individual's own accord*, then there is absolutely no basis for claiming that the accused acted involuntarily.

AUTOMATISM VOLUNTARILY SELF-INDUCED BY ALCOHOL OR OTHER DRUGS

The general rule of Canadian criminal law is that accused persons who have *voluntarily* ingested alcohol and/or other drugs and have, as a consequence, experienced a state of altered consciousness are *barred from raising the defence of automatism*. At best, they may be able to raise the *partial defence of intoxication* (discussed in Chapter 10) and, if successful, they will be convicted of a less serious offence rather than given an absolute acquittal. For example, a successful defence of intoxication will lead to the accused being acquitted of a charge of murder and convicted, instead, of the less serious offence of manslaughter.

Traditionally, the courts have assumed that those who *voluntarily* ingest intoxicating substances are *at fault* in so doing and are, therefore, not entitled to the absolute acquittal that follows a successful assertion of a defence of automatism. Such people would be considered to be at fault because it may be taken for granted that every citizen is fully aware that the consumption of intoxicating substances can lead to impairment and that this impairment might cause him or her to act in a way that might infringe the law. When individuals have ingested such substances of their own free will and with an awareness of the potential consequences of their conduct, then, naturally, the courts will consider that they have voluntarily chosen to run the risk that they might commit an offence of some kind.

However, an accused person may well say, "If I can establish that I was *acting involuntarily at the specific moment that I committed the conduct* in question, then convicting me of a criminal offence for what took place while I was in this state of automatism violates my rights under section 7 of the *Charter*." More specifically, the accused might contend that convicting him or her in such circumstances constitutes a deprivation of the "right to liberty and security of the person" in a manner that is not "in accordance with the principles of fundamental justice." Is this a valid constitutional argument against the traditional principle of criminal law that bars the accused from pleading automatism where he or she has voluntarily become intoxicated?

In the *Penno* case (1990), the Supreme Court of Canada was confronted with this constitutional argument in the context of a charge of being impaired while in care and control of a motor vehicle (section 253 of the *Code*). The accused contended that it was a violation of section 7 to convict him of this charge when he was in such an extreme state of intoxication that he had no awareness of even entering his vehicle. However, the Court firmly ruled that there was no violation of the *Charter* in these circumstances. The Court emphasized the fact that impaired driving offences are quite distinct from other "true crimes" that are to be found in the *Criminal Code* and that individuals accused of committing these serious offences should not be permitted to raise the defence of automatism. In effect, in order for people accused of an offence under section 253 to claim the benefit of the defence of automatism, it would have to be shown that they were intoxicated to such an extreme degree that they were not aware of what they were doing when they assumed care and control of, or started to drive, a motor vehicle. If such an argument were to lead to an acquittal, it would mean that the more intoxicated such accused persons were, the more likely they would be to gain a total acquittal on the basis of automatism! Obviously, this would fly in the face of the need to protect Canadians from the very real and immediate dangers posed to them by impaired drivers.

In rejecting the contention that highly intoxicated motorists can plead the defence of automatism, Justice Wilson pointed out, in her judgment in the *Penno* case (1990), that Parliament had made impairment an essential element of the *actus reus* of the offences contained in section 253 of the *Code* and there is no infringement of the *Charter* when the accused person, in such circumstances, is prevented from raising the defence of automatism. In her view,

> ... the mental element of the offence under [s. 253] includes the voluntary consumption of alcohol but the *actus reus* requires the voluntary consumption of alcohol to the point of impairment. The distinction appears to make sense in that alcohol consumption to the point of impairment could well negate the intent to have care or control of the motor vehicle and result in the absence of *mens rea* whereas simple consumption might not. The *actus reus* requires impairment by alcohol and not just the prior consumption of alcohol. By making the requirement of impairment an element of the *actus reus* rather than the *mens rea* of the offence, Parliament has avoided the vicious circle which would otherwise be inherent in the offence.

However, when the Supreme Court of Canada addressed a constitutional challenge to the traditional rule excluding self-induced intoxication from the scope of the automatism in a case that fell outside of the specific context of impaired driving charges, it adopted a totally different approach. Indeed, in *Daviault* (1994), a case involving a charge of sexual assault, the Court held that, if extreme—albeit voluntarily induced—intoxication produces a state of mind "akin to automatism or insanity," then the

accused is entitled to an outright acquittal. The Court held that it would indeed infringe section 7 of the *Charter* if severely impaired persons could be convicted of criminal offences despite the fact that they lacked even a minimal awareness of what they were doing. Justice Cory stated that the "fundamental principles of justice," enshrined in section 7 of the *Charter*, would be infringed in such circumstances because the Crown would not be able to establish the voluntariness component of the *actus reus* of the offence charged. Nevertheless, the impact of the *Daviault* case was remarkably short-lived. In 1995, Parliament decided to "trump" the *Daviault* decision by amending the *Criminal Code*. This move was felt to be necessary because many Canadians had expressed their shock at the implications of the Supreme Court's decision for the prosecution of those who, in a state of intoxication, commit violent acts against women and children.

Parliament added a new section, 33.1, in order to seriously blunt the impact of the *Daviault* case. The effect of the new provision was later summarized by Justice Bastarache, when he delivered the judgment of the majority of the Justices of the Supreme Court of Canada in *Daley* (2007):

> [Section 33.1] amends the *Code* so that those with a *Daviault* defence will be convicted of the same violent general intent offences they would have been convicted of before the Court's decision. This provision appears to amend the law such that extreme intoxication to the point of automatism or involuntariness is only available for offences that do not include as an element "an assault or any other interference or threat of interference by a person with the bodily integrity of another person."...

In light of section 33.1, those individuals who voluntarily induce a state of extreme intoxication are clearly precluded from raising the automatism defence if they should be charged with offences involving personal violence. Instead, section 33.1 limits these individuals to raising the *partial defence* of intoxication, which, as we shall see later, is only available in relation to a limited number of offences, known as "specific intent" offences.

Section 33.1, however, only applies to "*self-induced* intoxication." If intoxication is caused *involuntarily*, then the accused person may well advance a successful plea of automatism, resulting in an acquittal. The precise meaning of "*self-induced* intoxication" was considered by the Nova Scotia Court of Appeal in *Chaulk* (2007). The accused had broken into the victim's apartment and threatened him and his children with death. Chaulk also threw a computer and a television onto the floor. He removed all of his clothes and grabbed a female neighbour by the blouse. The police were called and Chaulk was arrested. He was "naked, sweating profusely and babbling, vacillating between compliant and combative." The police took Chaulk to the hospital, where the emergency room doctor was of the opinion that Chaulk's condition "was consistent with exposure to chemicals or stimulant-type drugs." Chaulk told another doctor that he had consumed a mixture of "acid, ecstasy and marijuana." However, he later repudiated this statement and claimed that he had not ingested any drugs or alcohol before attending a party, where he drank 8 bottles of beer, smoked a marijuana joint and consumed what he thought was a "wake-up" or caffeine pill. The trial judge ruled that Chaulk's intoxication was not self-induced and, therefore, section 33.1 did not apply to him. Chaulk successfully raised the defence of automatism/extreme intoxication (as defined in the *Daviault* case) and was acquitted on a number of criminal charges. However, the Crown appealed and the Nova Scotia Court of Appeal ordered a new trial. The appellate court ruled that the trial judge had applied an incorrect test in determining that Chaulk's condition was not self-induced and had failed to address the inconsistency in Chaulk's statements about the nature of the drugs and alcohol which he had consumed.

The Court of Appeal articulated the criteria that should be applied when a court is called upon to decide whether the accused person's state of automatism/extreme intoxication was "self-induced' within the meaning of section 33.1. In the words of Justice Bateman:

> I would ... express the test for self-induced intoxication as follows:
>
> (i) The accused voluntarily consumed a substance which;
>
> (ii) S/he knew or ought to have known was an intoxicant and;
>
> (iii) The risk of becoming intoxicated was or should have been within his/her contemplation.

The Court of Appeal also stated that, in order to establish that the accused person's state of intoxication was self-induced, the Crown does not have to prove that the accused person knew exactly what the substance was that he or she was taking nor that the accused person's purpose was to "experience its effects."

Unfortunately, there is considerable uncertainty as to whether or not section 33.1 of the *Criminal Code* is valid in light of the rights guaranteed by the *Charter*. To date, no appellate court has been called upon to decide this critical issue. However, at least three trial courts in Ontario have decided that section 33.1 infringes both sections 7 and 11(d) of the *Charter* and that it is not saved by the application of section 1.[4] On the other hand, different trial courts in British Columbia, the Northwest Territories, and Ontario have ruled that, although section 33.1 does indeed offend sections 7 and 11(d) of the *Charter*, it is nevertheless valid because it constitutes a "reasonable limit" under section 1 of the *Charter*.[5] The Supreme Court of Canada referred to section 33.1 in the *Daley* case (2007) but did not comment on the issue of its constitutionality in light of the *Charter*. This important issue is discussed in greater depth in Chapter 10.

AUTOMATISM DISTINGUISHED FROM AMNESIA

It is important to distinguish between *automatism* and *amnesia* (loss of memory). The defence of automatism is concerned with the question of whether accused persons acted voluntarily at the time of their alleged offences. The fact that they have no recollection of what happened does not necessarily mean that they acted involuntarily. For example, it is a common consequence of consuming alcohol that individuals may act *voluntarily and in a conscious, purposive manner* but still not have any memory of what happened at a certain point after they started to drink. Clearly, such people should not be absolved of criminal liability simply because they cannot remember the crimes that they committed while under the influence of alcohol that was consumed voluntarily.

Take, for example, the sad case of *Honish* (1991), in which the accused went to a motel and consumed a large quantity of antidepressant drugs and sleeping pills mixed with alcohol. His intention was to commit suicide. However, one hour later, he was driving his car and was involved in a serious accident; he went

---

[4] See *Dunn* (1999), *Jensen* (2000), and *Cedeno* (2005).
[5] See *Vickberg* (1998), *Brenton* (1999), and *Decaire* (1998).

through a yield sign and struck another vehicle, causing injuries to three of its occupants, including a small child. Honish drove through the intersection and came to a stop only when he struck a parked vehicle. He was charged with three counts of impaired driving causing bodily harm. However, Honish claimed that he had absolutely no recollection of what had happened between the time that he was lying down on his bed in the motel and the moment when he woke up in hospital after the accident. Was this state of amnesia relevant to Honish's criminal responsibility? A critical finding of fact made by the trial judge was that Honish was *not acting in a state of automatism* at the time of the accident. There were skid marks, indicating that Honish had attempted to take evasive action, and there was evidence that he had initially climbed out of his car and engaged in "sharp verbal exchanges" with one of the wounded passengers in the car that he had struck in the intersection. At that time, Honish also apologized for having hit the people in the other car and admitted he was drunk. The trial judge, therefore, held that Honish had not been in a state of automatism at the time of the accident, and this meant that his state of amnesia was irrelevant. The accused was convicted on all three counts and his appeals to both the Alberta Court of Appeal and the Supreme Court of Canada were rejected. (Incidentally, it is important to note that, even if the cocktail of drugs and alcohol ingested by Honish had indeed produced a genuine state of automatism, he would nevertheless still have been prevented from successfully raising a defence based on his extreme state of voluntarily induced intoxication: see the *Penno* case (1990) and section 33.1 of the *Criminal Code*, discussed in the previous section.)

AUTOMATISM CAUSED BY A MENTAL DISORDER

Where the accused's condition is caused by a mental disorder, he or she is not entitled to be acquitted by reason of the defence of automatism. Instead, the Court must treat the accused's defence as being that of "not criminally responsible on account of mental disorder" (NCRMD) in accordance with the provisions of section 16 of the *Code* (as was discussed earlier in this chapter).

The courts have drawn a sharp distinction between automatism, which leads to a complete acquittal of the accused, and the NCRMD defence, which leads to a special verdict, under section 672.34, that "the accused committed the act or made the omission but

is not criminally responsible on account of mental disorder." This distinction is critical because the special NCRMD verdict may result in the accused being kept in custody in a psychiatric facility or being released into the community under far-reaching conditions (section 672.54). In contrast, those defendants who are acquitted as a consequence of the successful assertion of a defence of automatism immediately leave the courtroom without any restrictions whatsoever on their future freedom of action. As Justice Bastarache, of the Supreme Court of Canada, aptly noted in the case of *Stone* (1999), "[T]he determination of whether mental disorder or non-mental disorder automatism should be left with the trier of fact must be taken very carefully since it will have serious ramifications for both the individual and society in general."

THE DEFINITION OF MENTAL DISORDER: PROBLEMS OF JUDICIAL INTERPRETATION

In the past, the courts have found it extremely difficult to decide whether certain types of mental condition (such as clouded consciousness associated with a sleepwalking episode or extreme psychological shock) should be placed within the category of "disease of the mind," thereby bringing the accused under the provisions of section 16 of the *Criminal Code*, or whether they should be classified as a form of automatism, thereby laying the basis for an unqualified acquittal should the accused person's defence prove to be successful at trial.

How have the courts attempted to resolve the question of whether the accused's condition does— or does not—constitute a "disease of the mind"? In the past, they relied on two major approaches. The first of these involved drawing a distinction between internal and external causes of a state of automatism. If a state of automatism is precipitated by an internal condition (such as epilepsy), then it must be classified as a "disease of the mind." On the other hand, if the state of automatism is induced by an external cause (such as a blow to the head or an injection of insulin), then it must be classified as non-mental-disorder automatism. The second approach, which is not necessarily inconsistent with the first, revolves around a determination as to whether the state of automatism is likely to recur—the so-called "continuing danger" theory. The courts took the view that, if a condition was ongoing in nature and likely to recur, it constituted sound social policy to classify it as a "disease of the mind": in this way, it would be possible to require that the accused person undergo the treatment that may be necessary to prevent a recurrence of the automatism.

However, in the *Stone* case (1999), the majority of the Supreme Court of Canada adopted the view that judges should not be restricted to the "internal cause" and "continuing danger" theories when they are required to determine whether a specific mental condition constitutes a "disease of the mind" for the purposes of section 16 of the *Criminal Code*. The Supreme Court ruled that judges should also take into account such questions of public policy as whether the alleged state of automatism may be easily feigned and whether acquittal of a defendant on the basis of a particular form of automatism, such as sleepwalking, would open the floodgates to a wave of similar defences in the future. In the *Stone* case, Justice Bastarache stated that the courts should embrace "a more holistic approach" when deciding whether a state of automatism should be categorized as a "disease of the mind." In his view,

> ... [T]he continuing danger factor should not be viewed as an alternative or mutually exclusive approach to the internal cause factor. Although different, both of these approaches are relevant in the disease of the mind inquiry. As such, in any given case, a trial judge may find one, the other or both of these approaches of assistance. To reflect this unified, holistic approach to the disease of the mind question, it is therefore more appropriate to refer to the internal cause factor and the continuing danger factor, rather than the internal cause theory and the continuing danger theory.

However, it is significant that, in the *Stone* case, the majority of the Supreme Court of Canada stated that there should be a *presumption that any state of automatism is the result of a mental disorder*. Justice Bastarache noted that "it will only be in rare cases that automatism is not caused by mental disorder." In his judgment, he suggests that there should be a "rule that trial judges start from the proposition that the condition the accused claims to have suffered from is a disease of the mind":

> [t]hey must then determine whether the evidence in the particular case takes the condition out of the disease of the mind category.

Undoubtedly, the *Stone* case signals an intention on the part of the Supreme Court to reduce the scope of the automatism defence in favour of an approach that results in a finding that the accused is NCRMD—a verdict that leaves the door open for the imposition of post-trial restrictions on the accused's liberty (e.g., the requirement of treatment).

An example of this new approach was manifested in the case of *Luedecke* (2008). The accused was charged with sexual assault of a stranger. Luedecke admitted having non-consensual sexual relations but asserted that he was unaware of what he was doing and was acting involuntarily at the time of the incident: specifically, he stated that he was in a state of sexomnia (engaging in sexual activity while asleep). A sleep disorder specialist, whose evidence was not challenged by the Crown, testified that Luedecke "was in a parasomniac state while engaging in sexual activity" with the victim. The expert stated that "parasomnia involves a sudden unexplained arousal from sleep" and "persons may carry out various physical activities while in a parasomniac state." The term, sexomnia, applies to "parasomnias during which an individual engages in some form of sexual activity." According to the expert, "a person who is experiencing a parasomniac episode acts without any volition, consciousness, or capacity to control his or her behaviour."

The trial judge found that Luedecke had acted involuntarily and that parasomnia was not a disease of the mind. He therefore acquitted Luedecke on the basis of non-mental-disorder automatism. The Crown appealed to the Ontario Court of Appeal, which ordered a new trial. The appellate court indicated that, in light of the decision of the Supreme Court of Canada in *Stone*, sexomnia should be considered a disease of the mind, thereby dictating that the accused should be found NCRMD and not given the benefit of an acquittal.

In delivering the judgment of the Court of Appeal, Justice Doherty set out the policy considerations that underlay the categorization of sexomnia as a mental disorder:

The respondent personifies one of the most difficult problems encountered in the criminal law. As a result of his parasomnia, he did a terrible thing, he sexually assaulted a defenceless, young victim. The reason for his conduct automatism brought on by parasomnia renders his actions non-culpable in the eyes of the criminal law. That very same explanation, however, makes his behaviour potentially dangerous and raises legitimate public safety concerns. An outright acquittal reflects the non-culpable nature of the conduct but does nothing to address the potential danger posed by the respondent's condition. The Canadian criminal law responds to the public safety concerns by treating almost all automatisms as the product of a mental disorder leading not to an acquittal but to an NCR-MD verdict. That verdict acknowledges that the accused committed the prohibited act but is not criminally culpable. An NCR-MD verdict also permits an individualized post-verdict dangerousness assessment of the accused leading to a disposition tailored to the specifics of the individual case. On a proper application of the principles developed in the Canadian case law, the respondent's automatism is properly characterized as a mental disorder and should have led to an NCR-MD verdict.

I would stress, however, that an NCR-MD verdict is not a medical diagnosis of the respondent. No one suggests that he is mentally ill. The criminal law uses the concept of mental disorder very differently than the medical profession…. A determination that an accused suffers from a mental disorder is more a reflection of the need for a further inquiry into the dangerousness of that accused than it is an assessment of his or her medical condition.

PSYCHOLOGICAL BLOW AUTOMATISM

Prior to the decision of the Supreme Court of Canada in *Stone* (1999), Canadian courts had recognized a form of automatism known as "psychological blow automatism." This version of the automatism defence strongly reflects the influence of the so-called "internal–external test." It is indisputable that a physical blow to the head must be considered an external factor and that, if it causes a state of unconsciousness, the accused is entitled to an absolute acquittal on the basis of automatism. However, what is the situation if the accused claims to have been in a state of dissociation (where the mind does not go with the body) as the consequence of a *psychological* blow? More specifically, should such a blow be considered an external or an internal factor?

Canadian courts have adopted the view that, if a psychological blow is alleged to have precipitated a state of automatism, then the question of whether this state should be considered as having been caused by a "disease of the mind" should be answered by determining whether an "average normal person" would have entered into a state of dissociation in the same circumstances. If the particular type of shock alleged would not cause an "average normal person" to enter into a state of automatism, then it may reasonably be concluded that the cause of the dissociation was something internal to the accused—that is to say, a

"disease of the mind." For example, in the *Rabey* case (1980), the accused had brutally assaulted a young woman with whom he was infatuated and claimed that he had entered a state of automatism after reading a letter in which she referred to him as a "nothing" and expressed an apparent sexual interest in another man. The Ontario Court of Appeal, with which the Supreme Court of Canada later agreed, held that being rejected by the object of one's affection is not the type of extreme shock that would cause the ordinary average person to enter into a state of automatism. Indeed, as Justice Martin stated in the Court of Appeal,

> The ordinary stresses and disappointments of life which are the common lot of mankind do not constitute an explanation for a malfunctioning of the mind which takes it out of the category of a "disease of the mind."… The dissociative state must be considered as having its source primarily in the respondent's psychological or emotional make-up.

However, Justice Martin also accepted the view that there may well be some "extraordinary external events" that would cause even the "average normal person" to enter into a dissociative state. Indeed, he listed a number of such situations—for example, where the defendant has witnessed the murder of, or a serious assault upon, a loved one. In sum, Justice Martin was prepared to permit an accused person who has suffered from a psychological blow to claim the benefit of the defence of automatism *if an "average normal" person might have become dissociated in the same circumstances.*

In the *Stone* case (1999), the Supreme Court of Canada reaffirmed the approach that it had approved in *Rabey* (1980). Stone was charged with the murder of his wife, whom he had stabbed 47 times. Stone stated that, while travelling with him by car, the victim had insulted and berated him over an extended period. He recounted that he had stopped the vehicle in a parking lot, where the alleged insults continued. According to Stone, the taunts made by his wife included some hurtful comments about his lack of sexual prowess. Stone stated that he had suddenly experienced a "whoosh" sensation that "washed over him from his feet to his head." When he was finally able to focus his eyes again, he found that he was standing over his wife's dead body and that he was holding a hunting knife in his hand. At his trial, Stone claimed that he had been in a "dissociative" state at the time of the killing and sought to rely on the defence of psychological blow automatism. The trial judge ruled that, if the accused really had been in a dissociative state, then it had been caused by a "disease of the mind" and the appropriate defence was that of NCRMD under section 16 of the *Criminal Code*. The jury ultimately rejected the NCRMD defence and convicted Stone of manslaughter (accepting the accused's alternative defence of provocation, as defined by section 215 of the *Code*).

The Supreme Court of Canada subsequently rejected Stone's appeal, ruling that, in the circumstances of this particular case, the trial judge had been perfectly correct to refuse to put a defence of psychological blow automatism to the jury. Justice Bastarache, speaking for the majority of the Court, stated that

> ... the internal cause factor and the continuing danger factor, as well as the other policy factors set out in this Court's decisions in *Rabey* and *Parks* all support the trial judge's finding that the condition the appellant alleges to have suffered from is a disease of the mind in the legal sense. In particular, the trigger in this case was not ... "extraordinary external events" that would amount to an extreme shock or psychological blow that would cause a normal person, in the circumstances of the accused, to suffer a dissociation in the absence of a disease of the mind.

Justice Bastarache emphasized that, where an accused person claims to have been suffering from psychological blow automatism, there must be evidence of "an *extremely shocking trigger*" because only such an overwhelmingly powerful event is likely to cause a "normal person" to react by "entering an automatistic state." In *Stone*, the accused could not point to such a severe trigger; rather, the circumstances of his case suggested that it was more appropriate for Stone to raise the partial defence of provocation (which reduces murder to manslaughter). It is also noteworthy that Justice Bastarache took the view that the "plausibility" of a claim of psychological blow automatism is significantly reduced if a single individual "is both the *trigger* of the alleged automatism and the *victim* of the automatistic violence" (as was the case with Stone's wife); indeed, such a claim should be "considered suspect." This is an important ruling insofar as it ensures that the psychological blow automatism defence may not be raised successfully in cases of alleged provocation. Finally, Justice Bastarache made some interesting observations about the applicability of the "continuing danger factor" in the context of a psychological blow automatism defence. He noted that the courts should really be focusing their attention on whether the alleged trigger of an automatistic episode is likely to recur:

> The greater the anticipated frequency of the trigger in the accused's life, the greater the risk posed to the public and, consequently, the more likely it is that the condition alleged by the accused is a disease of the mind.

All things considered, the combined effect of the *Rabey* and *Stone* cases will render it extremely difficult to successfully raise a defence of psychological blow automatism in the future. Only the most extreme forms of shock will be considered to constitute the kind of psychological blow that might cause an ordinary person to enter into a state of dissociation. In the absence of evidence of such an extreme assault on an individual's mind, the courts will hold that the only defence available to the accused is that of NCRMD under section 16 of the *Criminal Code*.

THE PROBLEM OF RECKLESSLY INDUCED AUTOMATISM

A critical question that must be addressed is whether accused persons who recklessly cause their own state of automatism should be entitled to an absolute acquittal. By using the word *recklessly* we mean to say that the accused persons concerned subjectively appreciate the fact that their conduct creates a risk of danger, but they deliberately choose to run that risk without any justification for doing so. We have seen that, in the case of intoxication as the result of the voluntary ingestion of alcohol or other drugs, special rules apply and that, in light of an amendment to the *Criminal Code* (section 33.1), defendants are precluded from raising the defence of automatism in such circumstances. What is the situation where individuals recklessly bring about a state of automatism by means other than alcohol and other drugs?

This issue was squarely raised in the English case of *Bailey* (1983), in which the accused was charged with wounding with intent or, alternatively, with unlawful wounding. His defence was that he had been acting in a state of automatism caused by a condition of hypoglycemia (low blood-sugar levels) that had arisen as a consequence of his failure to take sufficient food after an injection of insulin. The trial judge ruled that the defence of automatism was not open to the accused since his incapacity had been self-induced by his failure to eat properly, as was required after a dose of insulin. As a consequence, the accused was convicted of wounding with intent.

Upon Bailey's appeal, the Court of Appeal ruled that there had been a misdirection to the jury on the issue of self-induced incapacity. Indeed, Lord Justice Griffiths asserted that a defendant does not lose the benefit of the defence of automatism merely because his or her condition was self-induced: the defence would only be lost where the accused was reckless as to the risk that he or she would lapse into a state of automatism and engage in dangerous conduct. In the view of Lord Justice Griffiths, it was not common knowledge, even among diabetics, that a failure to eat food after taking an insulin injection may result in dangerous conduct. Of course, if a particular defendant did appreciate that such a failure may lead to dangerous conduct and, nevertheless, deliberately "ran that risk," then he or she would clearly have been reckless and would lose the benefit of the defence of automatism. However, in any given case, the Crown would have to establish the accused's subjective awareness of the inherent risks in his or her conduct before a conviction could be entered:

> In our judgment, *self-induced automatism, other than that due to intoxication from alcohol or drugs, may provide a defence to crimes of basic intent. The question in each case will be whether the prosecution has proved the necessary element of recklessness.* In cases of assault, if the accused knows that his actions or inaction are likely to make him aggressive, unpredictable or uncontrolled with the result that he may cause injury to others and he persists in the action or takes no remedial action when he knows it is required, it will be open to the jury to find that he was reckless. [emphasis added]

In other words, the Court of Appeal took the view that the answer to the question of whether a self-induced incapacity will disentitle an accused person from relying on the defence of automatism will (except in the case of intoxication from alcohol and/or drugs) *depend on the facts of each individual case* and, in particular, on whether the accused was reckless as to the risk of danger created by his or her conduct.

AUTOMATISM AND THE PRIMARY OR PERSUASIONAL BURDEN OF PROOF

A golden thread that runs through the fabric of Canadian criminal law is the presumption of innocence. Before an accused person may be found guilty of having committed a criminal offence, the *Crown must first prove all of the* mens rea *and* actus reus *elements of that offence*; furthermore, the Crown is required to prove its case *"beyond any reasonable doubt."* In other words, the **primary or persuasional burden of proof** is placed on the shoulders of the prosecution and the *standard of proof* that must be met is that of proof beyond a reasonable doubt.

Nevertheless, in the *Stone* case (1999), the Supreme Court of Canada (by a 5–4 majority) held that, where the defence of automatism has been raised, the primary—or persuasional—burden of proof must be placed on the accused: in other words, the accused has to prove his or her innocence—a requirement that constitutes a dramatic exception to the general rule that applies to the conduct of criminal trials in Canada. However, the **standard of proof** is not that of "beyond a reasonable doubt" but rather that of *"on the balance of probabilities"* (the same standard of proof that applies in civil trials in Canada). Put more simply, the accused must prove that it was more probable than not that, at the time of the alleged offence, he or she was in a state of automatism. As Justice Bastarache stated, on behalf of the majority in Stone, "[T]he legal burden in cases involving automatism must be on the defence to prove involuntariness on a balance of probabilities to the trier of fact."

Is it justifiable to require an accused person to prove the defence of automatism, rather than leaving it to the Crown to disprove it? Justice Bastarache reasoned that it is necessary for this exception to be made to the general rule. He took the view that genuine cases of automatism are "extremely rare" and the reality is that it is a condition that may be "easily feigned" by those who attempt to avoid all responsibility for their actions by merely saying, "I don't remember anything about it!" Furthermore, Justice Bastarache stated that most, if not all, of the necessary medical information concerning the alleged condition of automatism rests firmly in the control of the accused. Indeed, it would be impossible for the Crown to obtain necessary medical information if the accused should choose to be uncooperative with medical witnesses summoned by the Crown. Therefore, according to Justice Bastarache, it would be totally impractical to "saddle the Crown with the legal burden of proving voluntariness beyond a reasonable doubt." He noted that Parliament had already relieved the Crown of this very burden in relation to the defence of "not criminally responsible on account of mental disorder." Indeed, section 16 of the *Criminal Code* (subsections (2) and (3)) makes it clear that the burden of proof is on the accused to establish the mental disorder defence "on the balance of probabilities." Significantly, in *Stone*, Justice Bastarache fully admitted that placing the onus on the accused to prove the defence of automatism constitutes a violation of the presumption of innocence, guaranteed by section 11(d) of the *Charter*; however, he held that this nevertheless constitutes a "reasonable limitation" that is justified under section 1 of the *Charter*.

AUTOMATISM AND THE SECONDARY OR EVIDENTIARY BURDEN OF PROOF

It is important to bear in mind that every trial judge has the discretion to decide whether to permit a defence to be considered by the trier of fact at the end of a criminal trial. The trier of fact may be a jury or the trial judge, if sitting alone. In order to prevent entirely speculative defences from being placed before the trier of fact, the courts have developed the notion that accused persons must jump over an initial hurdle: this is known as the **secondary or evidentiary burden of proof.** Essentially, this means that defendants must be able to point to evidence that is sufficient to establish that there is "*an air of reality*" to their defence. For practically all of the defences that may be raised by an accused person in a criminal trial, the evidentiary burden of proof is met where the accused can satisfy the trial judge that there is *evidence that is capable of raising a reasonable doubt in the mind of the trier of fact*. If this relatively light burden is not met, then the defence will not be considered at the end of the trial when the judge or jury makes the decision as to whether the accused is innocent or guilty of the charges laid. However, if the evidentiary burden is met, then the defence is placed before the trier of fact and the onus is now placed on the prosecution to prove—beyond a reasonable doubt—every element of the *actus reus* and *mens rea* of the crime charged. It is critical to recognize that the decision as to whether the evidentiary burden of proof has been met is one that is made *exclusively by the trial judge as a matter of law* (hence, where there is a jury, the members of that body have no part to play in making this determination).

Where the defendant advances a defence of automatism, he or she is also required to meet the evidentiary burden of proof before it will be considered a "live issue" at the end of the trial. In order to meet the evidentiary burden of proof in a case of alleged automatism, it is clearly not enough for the

accused to merely claim that "I don't know what happened ... my mind went blank." Indeed, it is absolutely necessary that the accused point to *some expert psychiatric or psychological testimony* that lends support to the defence. Furthermore, it will generally be required that the accused point to some previous history of automatism or dissociative states. For example, in a case such as that of *Parks* (1992), the accused's defence of automatism was considered to be more credible in light of his (documented) history of previous sleepwalking episodes. In *Stone*, Justice Bastarache also noted that the accused will be more likely to satisfy the evidentiary burden of proof if there is corroborating evidence from bystanders that "reveals that the accused appeared uncharacteristically glassy-eyed, unresponsive and or distant immediately before, during or after the alleged involuntary act." Furthermore, Justice Bastarache suggested that a claim of automatism is more likely to be credible if there is no motive for the alleged offence: "a motiveless act will generally lend plausibility to an accused's claim of involuntariness."

In the case of *Fontaine* (2004), the accused was charged with first degree murder. He admitted killing the victim but claimed that he acted involuntarily as a consequence of a psychotic state that had been induced by longstanding abuse of marijuana. Fontaine was alleging that he was in a state of mental-disorder automatism and that he should be found NCRMD under section 16 of the *Criminal Code*. Section 16(2) places the primary burden of proof on the party who is claiming that the accused is NCRMD—in this case, Fontaine himself. Section 16(3) states that the standard of proof is "on the balance of probabilities." However, the critical issue that arose in this case was whether Fontaine had satisfied the secondary or evidentiary burden of proof. The nature of the secondary burden of proof is identical for both mental-disorder automatism and non-mental-disorder automatism: therefore, the decision by the Supreme Court of Canada in the *Fontaine* case is also relevant to cases of non-mental-disorder automatism.

At his trial, Fontaine gave evidence suggesting that he was acting involuntarily and his testimony was supported by the expert opinion of a defence psychiatrist. However, the trial judge refused to put the defence of mental-disorder automatism to the jury because there was disagreement between the Crown and defence experts and there were contradictions in Fontaine's own evidence. Fontaine was convicted but the Quebec Court of Appeal allowed his appeal and ordered a new trial because it ruled that the accused had satisfied the evidentiary burden of proof and was entitled to have his defence put to the jury at the end of the trial. The Supreme Court of Canada affirmed the decision of the Court of Appeal. Justice Fish stated:

> We are concerned with the evidential burden on a defence of mental disorder automatism and not with the "persuasive" burden on that defence.
>
> ... An "evidential burden" is not a burden of proof. It determines whether an issue should be left to the trier of fact, while the "persuasive burden" determines how the issue should be decided.
>
> ... These are fundamentally different questions. The first is a matter of law; the second, a question of fact. Accordingly, on a trial before judge and jury, the judge decides whether the evidential burden has been met. In answering that question, the judge does not evaluate the quality, weight or reliability of the evidence. The judge simply decides whether there is evidence upon which a properly instructed jury could reasonably decide the issue.

Justice Fish later quoted a passage from the decision of the Supreme Court of Canada in the case of *Cinous* (2002):

> The full question is whether there is evidence (some evidence, any evidence) upon which a properly instructed jury acting judicially could acquit. If there is any or some such evidence, then the air of reality hurdle is cleared. If there is no such evidence, then the air of reality hurdle is not cleared.

Justice Fish then suggested that, "in short, as regards all affirmative defences, I think it preferable to say that the evidential burden will be discharged where there is some evidence that puts the defence 'in play.'" He added that "the defence will be in play whenever a properly instructed jury could reasonably, on account of that evidence, conclude in favour of the accused." In the *Fontaine* case itself, Justice Fish concluded that the accused had met the evidentiary burden of proof because Fontaine had testified—in considerable detail—as to his state of mind at the time of the homicide and a psychiatrist had also testified that Fontaine "had a serious mental disorder akin to psychosis, which seriously distorted his perception of reality." The defence of mental-disorder automatism should, therefore, have been left to the members of the jury and they should

ultimately have been required to decide whether or not Fontaine had proved it on the balance of probabilities.

STUDY QUESTIONS

1. Gaspard is experiencing a severe form of schizophrenia. He acts under the delusion that Chuzzlewit, his neighbour, has a machine that generates death rays. One day, Gaspard comes to believe that Chuzzlewit is about to turn the death rays in his direction and, in order to preserve his own life, he must kill Chuzzlewit immediately. Gaspard breaks into Chuzzlewit's house and stabs him to death with a knife. When the police question Gaspard, it is clear that he realizes that he has killed Chuzzlewit but he insists that 'it was him or me and I had to get him before he wasted me with those death rays." Gaspard is charged with first degree murder. Would Gaspard be able to raise the defence of NCRMD with any degree of success at his trial?

2. Sikes brutally rapes Nancy, a young woman. In the course of the attack on his victim, he inflicts several severe injuries with a hunting knife that he used to force Nancy to have intercourse with him. Nancy, fortunately, recovers from her physical wounds, although she has been profoundly shocked by the whole appalling experience. Sikes is charged with aggravated sexual assault. His counsel raises the NCRMD defence. Chalmers, a psychiatrist for the defence, claims that Sikes is suffering from a "psychopathic" personality disorder. Sikes testifies that, because of his mental disorder, he simply could not control his violent impulses and that he could not possibly feel any sympathy for his victim. What likelihood is there that Sikes will be found NCRMD?

3. Duncan, a teller at a local bank, has killed Macbeth, the bank manager. Duncan has bipolar disorder and, at the time of the homicide, he was in a manic state and was experiencing delusions. Duncan believed that God had ordered him to destroy Macbeth because Macbeth was an agent of the devil. When he was arrested, Duncan told the police, "I suppose I shall be sent to prison for life." Would Duncan be found NCRMD?

4. Hamlet is charged with the first degree murder of Polonius. The circumstances are that Hamlet, who has a form of schizophrenia, killed Polonius

in the university laboratory where medical research was being conducted on animal subjects. Hamlet later stated that he killed Polonius because the latter was in charge of the laboratory and, as such, was responsible for the "torture of innocent animals." Hamlet also says that animals' lives are more important than those of human beings and that it was, therefore, his duty to destroy Polonius. Would Hamlet's mental disorder furnish him with any defence(s)?

5. Flintwich suddenly attacks his best friend, Smallweed. There is apparently no reason for the attack. When charged with assault causing bodily harm, Flintwich claims that he is a diabetic who was in a hypoglycemic state (as a consequence of taking his insulin injection without eating any meals). He says that he has never experienced such an episode before. Does Flintwich have any defence to the charge? Would it make any difference to your answer if Flintwich knew that he could become violent if he did not eat after taking his insulin injection?

6. Arabella is taking some powerful tranquilizers and is aware that she should not ingest alcohol while she is taking them. Unfortunately, she goes to a party and has a few glasses of wine. Subsequently, she leaves the party and enters her car. The police find her in a state of total unconsciousness, sitting in the driver's seat of her vehicle. Arabella later claims that she has absolutely no memory of leaving the party and was not conscious when she entered her car. However, the police wish to lay a charge of being in care or control of a motor vehicle while impaired (section 253 of the *Code*). Would such a charge be likely to succeed at trial? Would it make a difference to your answer if Arabella's physician had told her that it was safe for her to "drink in moderation" while she was taking the tranquilizers?

7. Defarge is walking toward his home when he sees a gang of armed robbers emerging from his local bank. The robbers brutally kill one of the customers, Micawber, who is standing outside the bank between the gang and their getaway car. Upon seeing this distressing scene, Defarge goes into a state of shock and attacks Slammer, one of the robbers, who is trying to give himself up to the police because he disapproves of the killing of Micawber by his colleagues. Slammer

is quite seriously wounded by this onslaught. After Defarge is taken to the police station, he claims that he does not remember anything about the attack on Slammer; all he remembers is the brutal killing by the other bank robbers. Does Defarge have any defence to a charge of assault causing bodily harm? Would it make any difference to your answer if Defarge was a "highly nervous" individual and was taking tranquilizers on a regular basis?

8. Tapley is taking a bus journey across the Prairie Provinces during a snowstorm. The weather conditions become so severe that he is required to stay overnight in a bus station. During the night, he sexually assaults a young woman, Louisa, who is a fellow passenger. Tapley is forcibly restrained by a security guard. He appears to be confused and unaware of his surroundings. When Tapley is later charged with sexual assault, he claims that he was asleep when the alleged offence occurred and that he has no memory of it. An expert witness is prepared to testify that Tapley suffers from sexomnia (engaging in sexual activity while asleep). What defence(s) might be available to Tapley? Would it (they) be likely to succeed at his trial? Would it make any difference if Tapley had a history of such attacks and was undergoing treatment at a sleep disorder clinic?

9. Prospero takes his four-year-old son, Ariel, for a walk in the local park. Once they enter the park, Prospero sits down in a chair and falls fast asleep. Ariel wanders away and is killed by a truck as he is trying to cross a busy road on the outskirts of the park. Prospero later states that he suffers from narcolepsy, which is a condition characterized by a frequent—and uncontrollable—desire to sleep. What charges might be laid against Prospero and, if such charges are laid, would he have any defence(s) available to him?

FURTHER READING

American Psychiatric Association. 2000. *Diagnostic and Statistical Manual of Mental Disorders*. 4th ed. Text Revision (DSM-IV-TR). Washington, DC: American Psychiatric Association.

Andoh, B. 1993. The *M'Naghten* Rules—The Story So Far. 61 *Medico-Legal Journal*: 93–103.

Barratt, E.S., and A.R. Felthous. 2003. Impulsive versus Premeditated Aggression: Implications for *Mens Rea* Decisions. 21 *Behavioral Sciences & the Law*: 619–630.

Becker-Blease, K., and J.J. Freyd. 2007. Dissociation and Memory for Perpetration Among Convicted Sex Offenders. 8 *Journal of Trauma & Dissociation*: 69–80.

Benedet, J. 2006. Annotation: *R. v. Luedecke*. 35 *Criminal Reports (6th Series)*: 206–207.

———. 2007. Annotation: *R. v. Chaulk*. 49 *Criminal Reports (6th Series)*: 173–174.

Berman, M.E., and L. Slaughter. 1998. Neurobiologic Correlates of Violence: Relevance to Criminal Responsibility. 17 *Behavioral Sciences & the Law*: 303–318.

Bloom, H., and R.D. Schneider. 2006. *Mental Disorder and the Law: A Primer for Legal and Mental Health Professionals*. Toronto: Irwin Law.

Bond, S. 1993. The Role of Crown Counsel in Post-verdict Disposition Hearings for Accused Found Not Criminally Responsible on Account of Mental Disorder. 2 *Dalhousie Journal of Legal Studies*: 292–309.

Bourget, D., and L. Whitehurst. 2007. Amnesia and Crime. 35 *Journal of the American Academy of Psychiatry and Law*: 469–480.

Brudner, A. 2000. Insane Automatism: A Proposal for Reform. 45 *McGill Law Journal*: 65–85.

Burt, L. 1993. The Mental Disorder Provisions: Community Residence and Dispositions under s. 672.54(c). 36 *Criminal Law Quarterly*: 40–48.

Carter, M. 1995. Non-Statutory Criminal Law and the *Charter*: The Application of the *Swain* Approach in *R. v. Daviault*. 59 *Saskatchewan Law Review*: 241–269.

Cartwright, R. 2004. Sleepwalking Violence: A Sleep Disorder, a Legal Dilemma, and a Psychological Challenge. 161 *American Journal of Psychiatry*: 1149–1158.

Carver, P., and C. Langlois-Klassen. 2006. The Role and Powers of Forensic Psychiatric Review Boards in Canada: Recent Developments. 14 *Health Law Journal*: 1–19.

Coles, E.M. 2000. Scientific Support for the Legal Concept of Automatism. 7 *Psychiatry, Psychology and Law*: 33–50.

Coles, E.M., and D. Jang. 1996. A Psychological Perspective on the Legal Concepts of "Volition" and "Intent." 4 *Journal of Law and Medicine*: 60–71.

Colvin, E., and S. Anand. 2007. *Principles of Criminal Law*. 3rd ed. Toronto: Thomson Carswell.

Crisanti, Arboleda-Florez, J., and H. Stuart. 2000. The Canadian Criminal Code Provisions for Mentally Disordered Offenders: A Survey of Experiences, Attitudes, and Knowledge. 45 *Canadian Journal of Psychiatry*: 816–821.

Davis, S. 1993. Changes to the *Criminal Code* Provisions for Mentally Disordered Offenders and Their Implications for Canadian Psychiatry. 38 *Canadian Journal of Psychiatry*: 122–126.

———. 1994. Fitness to Stand Trial in Canada in Light of the Recent *Criminal Code* Amendments. 17 *International Journal of Law and Psychiatry*: 319–329.

Delisle, R.J. 1999. Stone: Judicial Activism Gone Awry to Presume Guilt. 24 *Criminal Reports (5th Series)*: 91–96.

Denno, D.W. 2003. A Mind to Blame: New Views on Involuntary Acts. 21 *Behavioral Sciences & the Law*: 601–618.

Irshaad, E., W. Wilson, R. Marks, K.W. Peacock, and P. Fenwick. 2005. Violence, Sleepwalking and the Criminal Law: (1) The Medical Aspects. [2005] *The Criminal Law Review*: 601–613.

Fine, C., and J. Kennett. 2004. Mental Impairment, Moral Understanding and Criminal Responsibility: Psychopathy and the Purposes of Punishment. 27 *International Journal of Law and Psychiatry*: 425–443.

Friedman, S.H., D.R. Hrouda, C.E. Holden, S.G. Noffsinger, and P.J. Resnick. 2005. Murder Committed by Severely Mentally Ill Mothers: An Examination of Mothers Found Not Guilty by Reason of Insanity. 50 *Journal of Forensic Sciences*: 1466–1471.

Grant, I. 1997. Canada's New Mental Disorder Disposition Provisions: A Case Study of the British Columbia *Criminal Code* Review Board. 20 *International Journal of Law and Psychiatry*: 419–443.

Grant, I., and L. Spitz. 1993. Case Comment: *R. v. Parks*. 72 *Canadian Bar Review*: 224–237.

Grant, I., J.R.P. Ogloff, and K.S. Douglas. 2000. The British Columbia Review Panel: Factors Influencing Decision-Making. 23 *International Journal of Law and Psychiatry*: 173–194.

Hannan, B. 2005. Depression, Responsibility, and Criminal Defenses. 28 *International Journal of Law and Psychiatry*: 321–333.

Healy, P. 1991. *R. v. Chaulk:* Some Answers and Questions on Insanity. 2 *Criminal Reports (4th Series)*: 95–106.

Healy, P. 2000. Automatism Confined. 45 *McGill Law Journal*: 87–105.

Lalonde, J.K. 2001. Canadian and American Psychiatrists' Attitudes toward Dissociative Disorder Diagnoses. 46 *Canadian Journal of Psychiatry*: 407–412.

Laporte, L., B. Poulin, J. Marleau, R. Roy, and T. Webank. 2003. Filicidal Women: Jail or Psychiatric Ward. 48 *Canadian Journal of Psychiatry*: 94–98.

Lee, D.T. 2003. Community-Treated and Discharged Forensic Patients: An 11-Year Follow-Up. 26 *International Journal of Law and Psychiatry*: 289–300.

Leiper, J. 2009. Cracks in the Facade of Liberty: The Resort to *Habeas Corpus* to Enforce Part XX.1 of the Criminal Code. 55 *Criminal Law Quarterly*: 134–187.

Levy, N., and T. Bayne. 2004. A Will of One's Own: Consciousness, Control, and Character. 27 *International Journal of Law and Psychiatry*: 459–470.

Litwack, T.R. 2003. The Competency of Criminal Defendants to Refuse, for Delusional Reasons, a Viable Insanity Defense Recommended by Counsel. 21 *Behavioral Sciences & the Law*: 135–156.

Livingston, J.D., and S.N. Verdun-Jones. 2003. Sidebar Psychology: Discussing and Challenging the Defence of Psychological-Blow Automatism. 47 *Criminal Law Quarterly*: 79–110.

Livingston, J.D., D. Wilson, G. Tien, and L. Bond. 2003. A Follow-up Study of Persons Found Not Criminally Responsible on Account of Mental Disorder in British Columbia. 48 *Canadian Journal of Psychiatry*: 408–415.

Luther, G., & M. Mansfield. 2006. The Top Ten Issues in Law and Psychiatry. 69 *Saskatchewan Law Review*: 401–440.

Mackay, R.D., and B.J. Mitchell. 2006. Sleepwalking, Automatism and Insanity. [2006] *The Criminal Law Review*: 901–905.

Mackay, R.D., and M. Reuber. 2007. Epilepsy and the Defence of Insanity—Time for Change? [2007] *The Criminal Law Review*: 782–793.

McLeod, H.J., M.K. Byrne, and R. Aitken. 2004. Automatism and Dissociation: Disturbances of Consciousness and Volition from a Psychological Perspective. 27 *International Journal of Law and Psychiatry*: 471–487.

McSherry, B. 1993. Defining What Is a "Disease of the Mind": The Untenability of Current Legal Interpretations. 1 *Journal of Law and Medicine*: 76–90.

———. 1998. Getting Away with Murder? Dissociative States and Criminal Responsibility. 21 *International Journal of Law and Psychiatry*: 163–176.

———. 2003. Voluntariness, Intention, and the Defence of Mental Disorder: Toward a Rational Approach. 21 *Behavioral Sciences & the Law*: 581–600.

———. 2004. Criminal Responsibility, "Fleeting" States of Mental Impairment, and the Power of Self-Control. 27 *International Journal of Law and Psychiatry*: 445–457.

———. 2005. Men Behaving Badly: Current Issues in Provocation, Automatism, Mental Impairment and Criminal Responsibility. 12 *Psychiatry, Psychology and Law*: 15–22.

Morse, S.J. 1999. Craziness and Criminal Responsibility. 17 *Behavioral Sciences & the Law*: 147–164.

Moskowitz, A. 2004. Dissociation and Violence: A Review of Literature. 5 *Trauma, Violence and Abuse*: 21–46.

Newby, D., and R. Faltin. 2008. The Very Essentials of Fitness for Trial Assessment in Canada. 47 *Journal of Offender Rehabilitation*: 185–207.

O'Marra, A.J.C. 1993. *Hadfield to Swain*: The *Criminal Code* Amendments Dealing with the Mentally Disordered. 36 *Criminal Law Quarterly*: 49–107.

Patel, A.S. 2002. Landing in the Cuckoo's Nest: The Hospital Disposition of Guilty Mentally Ill Offenders: Lessons from the United Kingdom. 39 *Alberta Law Review*: 810–847.

Porter, S., A.R. Birt, J.C. Yuille, and H.F. Herve. 2001. Memory for Murder: A Psychological Perspective on Dissociative Amnesia in Legal Contexts. 24 *International Journal of Law and Psychiatry*: 23–42.

Pressman, M.R., M.W. Mahowald, C.H. Schenk, and M.C. Borneman. 2007. Alcohol-Induced Sleepwalking or Confusional Arousal as a Defense to Criminal Behavior: A Review of Scientific Evidence, Methods and Forensic Considerations. 16 *Journal of Sleep Research*: 198–212.

Roach, K. 2009. *Criminal Law*. 4th ed. Toronto: Irwin Law. Ch. 7.

Roberts, J.V., and S.N. Verdun-Jones. 2002. Directing Traffic at the Crossroads of Criminal Justice and Mental Health: Conditional Sentencing after the Judgment in Knoblauch. 39 *Alberta Law Review*: 788–809.

Schneider, R.D., and D. Nussbaum. 2007. Can the Bad Be Mad? 53 *Criminal Law Quarterly*: 206–226.

Schopp, R.F., and A.J. Slain. 2000. Psychopathy, Criminal Responsibility, and Civil Commitment as a Sexual Predator. 18 *Behavioral Sciences & the Law*: 247–274.

Schopp, R.F., R.L. Wiener, B.H. Bornstein, and S.L. Willborn. 2009. *Mental Disorder and Criminal Law Responsibility, Punishment and Competence*. New York: Springer.

Siever, L.J. 2008. Neurobiology of Aggression and Violence. 165 *American Journal of Psychiatry*: 429–442.

Smith, K. 2000. Section 33.1: Denial of the *Daviault* Defence Should be Held Constitutional. 28 *Criminal Reports (5th Series)*: 350–366.

Spitzer, C., H. Liss, M. Dudeck, S. Orlob, M. Gillner, A. Hamm, and H .J. Freyberger. 2003. Dissociative Experiences and Disorders in Forensic Inpatients. 26 *International Journal of Law and Psychiatry*: 281–288.

Spring, R.L. 1998. The Return to *Mens Rea*: Salvaging a Reasonable Perspective on Mental Disorder in Criminal Trials. 21 *International Journal of Law and Psychiatry*: 187–196.

Sreenivasan, S., et al. 2000. Neuropsychological and Diagnostic Differences between Recidivistically Violent Not Criminally Responsible and Mentally Ill Prisoners. 23 *International Journal of Law and Psychiatry*: 161–172.

Stuart, D. 2007. *Canadian Criminal Law: A Treatise*. 5th ed. Toronto: Thomson Carswell. Chs. 2& 6.

_____. 2004. *Fontaine*: Lowering the Bar for Evidentiary Burdens for Defences to be Put to Juries. 18 *Criminal Reports (6th Series)*: 238–240.

Stuart, D., R.J. Delisle, and S. Coughlan. 2009. *Learning Canadian Criminal Law*. 11th ed. Toronto: Thomson Carswell.

Swihart, G., J. Yuille, and S. Porter. 1999. The Role of State-Dependent Memory in "Red-Outs." 22 *International Journal of Law and Psychiatry*: 199–212.

Tollefson, A., and B. Starkman. 1993. *Mental Disorder in Criminal Proceedings*. Toronto: Carswell.

Trajanovic, N.N., M. Mangan, and C. Shapiro. 2007. Sexual Behaviour in Sleep: An Internet Survey. 42 *Social Psychiatry and Psychiatric Epidemiology*: 1024–1031.

Verdun-Jones, S.N. 1979. The Evolution of the Defences of Insanity and Automatism in Canada from 1843–1979: A Saga of Judicial Reluctance to Sever the Umbilical Cord to the Mother Country? 14 U.B.C. *Law Review*: 1–73.

———. 1989. Sentencing the Partly Mad and the Partly Bad: The Case of the Hospital Order in England and Wales. 12 *International Journal of Law and Psychiatry*: 1–27.

———. 1994. The Insanity Defence in Canada: Setting a New Course. 17 *International Journal of Law and Psychiatry*: 175–189.

———. 2000. Making the Mental Disorder Defence a More Attractive Option for Defendants in a Criminal Trial: Recent Legal Developments in Canada. In D. Eaves, J.R.P. Ogloff, and R. Roesch, eds. *Mental Disorder and the Criminal Code: Legal, Clinical and Research Perspectives*. Burnaby, BC: Mental Health, Law and Policy Institute. 39–75.

———. 2007. *Canadian Criminal Cases: Selected Highlights*. 2nd ed. Toronto: Thomson Nelson. Ch. 8.

Wigley, S. 2007. Automaticity, Consciousness and Moral Responsibility. 20 *Philosophical Psychology*: 209–225.

Wilkinson, J.S. 1997. The Possibility of Alcoholic Automatism: Some Empirical Evidence. 2 *Canadian Criminal Law Review*: 217–236.

Yeo, S.M.H. 1991. Recent Australian Pronouncements on the Ordinary Person Test in Provocation and Automatism. 33 *Criminal Law Quarterly*: 280–297.

Yeo, S. 2002. Clarifying Automatism. 25 *International Journal of Law and Psychiatry*: 445–458.

Zapf, P.A. 2001. Assessing Fitness to Stand Trial: The Utility of the Fitness Interview Test (Revised Edition). 46 *Canadian Journal of Psychiatry*: 426–432.

Zapf, P.A., and R. Roesch. 2001. A Comparison of the MacCAT-CA and the FIT for Making Determinations of Competency to Stand Trial. 24 *International Journal of Law and Psychiatry*: 81–92.

CHAPTER NINE

MISTAKE OF FACT, CONSENT, AND MISTAKE OF LAW AS DEFENCES TO A CRIMINAL CHARGE

OVERVIEW

This chapter examines the following:

1. the basic elements of the defences of mistake of fact, consent, and mistake of law; and the requirement that the accused meet the evidentiary burden of proof before a defence may be considered by the trier of fact;

2. the underlying rationale for the defence of mistake of fact: namely, that the accused lacks the necessary *mens rea* for the offence charged;

3. the general principle that a mistake of fact advanced as a defence to a criminal charge must be honest but need not be reasonable;

4. the exceptional requirement in section 273.2(b) of the *Criminal Code* that, where an accused person claims a mistaken belief in consent in response to a charge of sexual assault, it must be shown that "reasonable steps" were taken to ascertain the consent of the complainant;

5. the defence of consent to a criminal charge in the circumstances where the absence of consent is a vital element in the case that must be proved by the Crown;

6. the defence of consent in relation to cases of assault (section 265) and, in particular, to charges of assault arising in the context of professional sports;

7. the defence of consent in the context of a charge of sexual assault (sections 271, 272, 273, 273.1, and 273.2); and

8. the general principle that a mistake of law does not give rise to a valid defence to a criminal charge and the major exceptions to this principle: the defences of "officially induced error" and "colour of right."

INTRODUCTION

In Chapter 8, the special defences of NCRMD and automatism were considered. The remaining chapters in this book explore the other major defences that may be raised in a criminal trial in Canada. It is not possible to consider all of the various defences that may be asserted by a person who has been charged with a criminal offence, and those defences that are primarily procedural or technical in nature (such as **entrapment** or **double jeopardy**) have been omitted from the discussion: these latter defences are usually dealt with in works on criminal procedure. It should also be remembered that accused persons may choose to assert their constitutional rights under the *Charter* as a means of defending themselves against a criminal charge. Indeed, we have already examined a number of cases in which criminal charges were dismissed on constitutional grounds (for example, the *Morgentaler, Smolig and Scott* decision in 1988, which resulted in a declaration that section 287 of the *Criminal Code*, dealing with therapeutic abortions, was unconstitutional).

This chapter examines the defences of mistake of fact, consent, and mistake of law. Chapter 10 analyzes the defences of intoxication and provocation. Chapter 11 explores the defences of necessity and duress, while Chapter 12 examines the defences of self-defence and defence of property.

The defences of **mistake of fact** and consent are considered together in the present chapter because they are frequently (although not exclusively) raised in the context of trials involving charges of sexual assault. Mistake of law is generally not a valid basis for a defence to a criminal charge. However, this chapter examines a number of exceptions that the courts have recognized as a means of minimizing the degree of injustice that might otherwise be inflicted on accused persons should the general rule be applied in an excessively harsh and inflexible manner.

MISTAKE OF FACT

MISTAKE OF FACT: THE GENERAL NATURE OF THE DEFENCE

The lawyer for a defendant in a criminal trial may well say, "It's true that my client committed the *actus reus* of the offence but she was nevertheless operating under a serious mistake as to the real facts of the situation. In light of the facts as she honestly believed them to be, she had no reason to believe that she was committing a crime and, therefore, lacked the *mens rea* that the Crown must prove in order to obtain a conviction." Such an assertion may well lead to the acquittal of the client because, as the Quebec Court of Appeal stated in the case of *Charbonneau* (1992), "in offences requiring *mens rea*, honest mistake of fact on an essential factual element is, as a general rule, a defence to the charge."

Take, for example, the strange case of *Mailhot* (1996). The accused was charged with the offence of wilfully doing an indecent act "in a public place in the presence of one or more persons" (section 173(1)(a) of the *Criminal Code*). Mailhot had met a plainclothes police officer in a park and, after engaging in a conversation, the two men went to a spring. After drinking at the spring, the accused and the officer continued talking and, at one point, Mailhot twice asked the officer if he wanted to "see him." The officer did not answer. Mailhot then went to a tree, undressed, and started to masturbate. The officer then revealed his identity and arrested Mailhot. At his trial, the accused was convicted of wilfully doing an indecent act but, ultimately, the Quebec Court of Appeal set aside the conviction and entered an acquittal. An essential element of the *actus reus* of the offence is that the indecent act was committed in the presence of one or more persons *other than those persons who are engaged in the act itself*. Essentially, Mailhot argued that he mistakenly believed that the undercover officer wished to participate in a sexual act in the sense that he would at least watch the accused. On the facts as the accused honestly believed them to be, he would not be committing an offence because the only person present was a willing participant in the indecent act. In delivering the judgment of the Court of Appeal, Justice Chamberland said,

> In my view, the circumstances in which the events took place do not permit one to find guilty intent on the part of the appellant at the time that he undressed, caressed himself and masturbated. The meeting with the officer, the friendly conversation that they had, their stroll to the spring, the officer's silence when the appellant, twice, revealed his plans, all these elements contributed to leading the appellant to believe that the officer was interested in giving a sexual twist to their meeting. The appellant's mistake involved an essential element required for the existence of the crime prohibited by

s. 173(1)(a); the officer's conduct led him to honestly, but mistakenly, believe that the officer would participate in the act that he was preparing to commit, if only by looking at him and by getting emotional or sexual satisfaction from it. In my view, this belief eliminated the blameworthy state of mind which the appellant had to have in order to be guilty of breaching s. 173(1)(a) of the *Criminal Code*.

The *Mailhot* case (1996) illustrates the principle that the defence of mistake of fact is really an assertion that the Crown has failed to prove the necessary *mens rea* requirements of the offence charged. This principle may also be applied, for example, to the situation of an accused person who has been charged with sexual assault and who asserts the defence of honest, but mistaken, belief in consent. As Chief Justice Lamer stated, in delivering the judgment of the Supreme Court of Canada in the *Davis* case (1999), "[T]he defence of honest belief in consent is simply a denial of the *mens rea* of sexual assault."

> The actus reus of sexual assault requires a touching, of a sexual nature, without the consent of the complainant. The mens rea requires the accused to intend the touching and to know of, or to be reckless or wilfully blind as to the complainant's lack of consent.... In some circumstances, it is possible for the complainant not to consent to the sexual touching but for the accused to honestly but mistakenly believe that the complainant consented. In these circumstances, the actus reus of the offence is established, but the mens rea is not. [emphasis added]

MUST A MISTAKE OF FACT BE BOTH HONEST AND REASONABLE?

There is no doubt that a mistake of fact must be *honest* if it is to serve as a valid defence to a criminal charge. However, one may also ask whether the mistake of fact must also be *reasonable*—in the sense that it is the kind of mistake that might be entertained by a reasonable person in the same circumstances as those faced by the accused. As a matter of legal principle, the answer to this question must be an emphatic "no." In the case of *Rees* (1956), Justice Cartwright of the Supreme Court of Canada stated the issue in very clear terms:

> ... [T]he essential question is whether the belief entertained by the accused is an honest one and ... the existence or non-existence of reasonable grounds for such a belief is merely relevant evidence to be weighed by the tribunal of fact in determining such essential question.

A person who operates under the influence of a serious mistake of fact in relation to an essential element of the offence charged cannot be considered to have made a choice to do something wrong: for that reason, it would be unjust to convict him or her of a criminal offence. Even if the mistake is unreasonable, this does not alter the fact that the accused did not deliberately decide to do something wrong. However, as Justice Cartwright aptly pointed out, the reasonableness of a mistake of fact may well be a *relevant factor* in determining the credibility of the accused. In general, the more unreasonable a mistake of fact appears to be, the less likely it is that the judge or jury will believe that the accused is telling the truth. This principle is reflected in section 265(4) of the *Criminal Code* which applies to the offence of assault:[1]

> Where an accused alleges that he believed that the complainant consented to the conduct that is the subject-matter of the charge, a judge if satisfied that there is sufficient evidence and that, if believed by the jury, the evidence would constitute a defence, shall instruct the jury, when reviewing all the evidence relating to the determination of the honesty of the accused's belief, to consider the presence or absence of reasonable grounds for that belief.

Section 265(4) is clearly based upon the assumption that the more unreasonable the accused's belief as to consent, the less likely it is that the jury will believe that the accused held that belief honestly. However, this provision does not stipulate that a defence of mistaken belief as to consent will be successful only if the belief was reasonable. It merely requires that the trial judge instruct the members of the jury that they should take into account the reasonableness of the accused's alleged belief as a means of determining the accused's *credibility*. If the members of the jury have a reasonable doubt as to whether or not the accused's alleged belief was honest, then they must acquit him or her—even if they think that such a belief would never have been entertained by a reasonable person.

Although a mistake of fact does not have to be reasonable in order to serve as the basis for a successful defence, it is nevertheless important to bear in mind that the defence will be rejected where the Crown

---

[1] Where a *sexual* assault is concerned, the defence of mistaken belief in consent must be based on a finding that the accused person took reasonable steps to ascertain consent (s. 273.2(b)). This special provision is discussed in the next section of this chapter.

proves that the accused was reckless or wilfully blind. For example, section 264 of the *Criminal Code* defines the offence of criminal harassment and provides a defence to an accused person who honestly, but mistakenly, believes that the complainant is not being harassed: this situation may arise where the accused is following the complainant but honestly believes that the complainant is not aware of the accused's conduct. However, section 264 also states that this defence will fail if the accused acted "recklessly as to whether the other person is harassed." In other words, if the accused subjectively realized that there was a risk that the complainant knew that the accused was following him or her, then the defence of mistake of fact would not be available. It is significant that, although Parliament did not address this issue in section 264, the courts have held that the accused will also be denied the benefit of the defence of mistake of fact where he or she has been wilfully blind as to whether or not the complainant is being harassed.

The disturbing case of *Sansregret* (1985) dramatically illustrates the manner in which *wilful blindness* may prevent the accused from raising a successful defence of mistake of fact. The accused was charged with the rape of a woman with whom he had previously been living (today, the charge would be one of sexual assault). The background facts were that, in September 1982, Sansregret had broken into the victim's house during the very early hours of the morning. He was "raging" and terrorized the victim with a file-like weapon that he was carrying. The victim was terrified by Sansregret's conduct and, in order to calm him down, she held open the prospect of reconciliation and, eventually, they had sexual intercourse. She later reported the incident to the police, asserting that she had been raped; however, no action was taken, largely because the accused's probation officer intervened and asked her not to proceed with her complaint.

In October 1982, Sansregret once again broke into the victim's house in the very early hours of the morning. He was "furious and violent" and threatened her with a butcher knife. He struck the victim and threatened to kill her if the police came. At one point, he tied her hands behind her back. After an hour of enduring this terror, the victim tried to calm the accused down by holding out some hope of reconciliation. After some conversation, they engaged in sexual intercourse. The victim once again complained to the police and, on this occasion, a number of charges, including one of rape, were laid against the accused. Sansregret claimed that he had been operating under an honest mistake of fact as to the consent of the victim. The trial judge acquitted the accused of rape on the basis of this defence, even though she considered that the mistake was totally unreasonable:

> No rational person could have been under any honest mistake of fact. However, people have an uncanny ability to blind themselves to much that they don't want to see, and to believe in the existence of facts as they would wish them to be.

The learned trial judge also stated that

> I do not like the conclusion which this leads me to. There was no real consent. There was submission as the result of a very real and justifiable fear. No one in his right mind could have believed that the complainant's dramatic about-face stemmed from anything other than fear. But the accused did. He saw what he wanted to see, heard what he wanted to hear, believed what he wanted to believe.

The Crown appealed the acquittal and the Manitoba Court of Appeal allowed the appeal, entering a conviction. The accused appealed to the Supreme Court of Canada, which affirmed the judgment of the Court of Appeal, on the basis that Sansregret had been *wilfully blind* as to the issue of consent and was, therefore, not entitled to rely on the defence of honest mistake of fact. In delivering the judgment of the Court, Justice McIntyre stated that

> [h]aving wilfully blinded himself to the facts before him the fact that an accused may be enabled to preserve what could be called an honest belief, in the sense that he has no specific knowledge to the contrary, will not afford a defence because, where the accused becomes deliberately blind to the existing facts, he is fixed by law with actual knowledge and his belief in another state of facts is irrelevant.

It is clear that the Supreme Court's ruling was heavily influenced by the fact that the accused had engaged in similar conduct on one previous occasion and that he was aware of the complaint made to the police. In these particular circumstances, he clearly had been alerted to the likelihood that the victim was not giving a true consent to sexual activity with him. In other words, he deliberately closed his eyes to the obvious and, in these circumstances, he was treated as though he actually knew that there was no consent on the part of the complainant.

In the later case of *Esau* (1997), Justice McLachlin, of the Supreme Court of Canada, further elaborated on the concept of wilful blindness and the circumstances in which such a state of mind will preclude the accused from raising the defence of mistake of fact in the context of a sexual assault. Justice McLachlin asserted that

> [t]he term wilful blindness connotes a deliberate avoidance of the facts and circumstances. It is the legal equivalent of turning a blind eye, of not seeing or hearing what is there to see or hear. It is the making of an assumption that the complainant consents without determining whether, *as a matter of fact*, the complainant consents. Blindness as to the need to obtain consent can never be raised by an accused as a defence.... [emphasis in original]

It is significant that section 273.2(a)(ii) of the *Criminal Code* explicitly stipulates that an honest belief in consent may *not* be raised as a defence to a charge of sexual assault if "the accused's belief arose from the accused's recklessness or wilful blindness."

In sum, an honest mistake of fact as to a material element of the *actus reus* of the crime charged will constitute an effective defence even if the mistake was not one that would have been entertained by a reasonable person. On the other hand, if a defendant is either reckless or wilfully blind as to the element of the *actus reus* concerned, he or she will lose the benefit of the defence.

EXCEPTIONS TO THE GENERAL RULE THAT A MISTAKE OF FACT DOES NOT HAVE TO BE REASONABLE IN ORDER TO EXCUSE THE ACCUSED PERSON FROM CRIMINAL LIABILITY

As we have seen, the general rule is that a mistake of fact does not have to be reasonable for the accused to raise a successful defence to a criminal charge. However, Parliament has created a number of significant exceptions to this rule. One example of an offence that falls within this exceptional category is **bigamy.** Indeed, section 290(2)(a) of the *Criminal Code* stipulates that an accused person has a defence to a charge of bigamy if he or she believed "in good faith and *on reasonable grounds*" that his or her spouse was dead.

Perhaps one of the most important exceptions to the general rule concerns those who engage in sexual activity with children under the age of 16 and young persons under the age of 18. In general, it is no

defence to a charge of a sexual offence against a child under the age of 16 that the child consented to sexual activity with the accused (section 150.1(a)). Similarly, consent is no defence to a charge of sexual exploitation of a young person under 18 by abusing a position of trust or authority (section 153) nor is consent a defence to a charge of buying sexual services from a young person under 18 (section 212(4)). Since consent is no defence to these charges, clearly the accused person's knowledge of the age of the child or young person becomes a critical issue. However, the defence of mistaken belief as to age has been limited to those accused who *take all reasonable steps to ascertain the age* of the child or young person *before* engaging in sexual activity with them (section 150.1(4) & (5)).

Another very significant exception to the general rule concerns the defence of mistaken belief in consent where the accused is charged with sexual assault. As we have just seen, where children and young persons are concerned, consent may not be available as a defence to a charge involving a sexual offence. However, in relation to sexual offences involving adults, mistaken belief in consent will normally be a defence that is open to an accused person. Here again, under section 273.2(b) of the *Criminal Code*, Parliament has imposed a duty on those who wish to engage in sexual relations to take reasonable steps to ascertain that the other party is consenting to such activity.

How do these exceptional provisions operate in practice? Consider the issue of mistaken belief as to the *age* of a child or young person with whom the accused person has some form of sexual relationship. One example of an exceptional provision in this category is section 212(4) of the *Criminal Code*, which provides:

> Every person who, in any place, obtains for consideration, or communicates with anyone for the purpose of obtaining for consideration, the sexual services of a person who is under the age of eighteen years is guilty of an indictable offence and liable to imprisonment for a term not exceeding five years and to a minimum punishment of imprisonment for a term of six months.

If the accused raises a defence of mistaken belief that the **complainant** was over the age of 18, then section 150.1(5) strictly limits the scope of this defence:

> It is not a defence to a charge under section ... 212(4) that the accused believed that the complainant was eighteen years of age or more at the time the offence

is alleged to have been committed unless the accused took all reasonable steps to ascertain the age of the complainant.

This provision does not mean that the accused person must prove that he or she took all reasonable steps to ascertain that age of the complainant. Indeed, if the accused raises the defence of mistaken belief as to age, the Crown must prove beyond a reasonable doubt that the acccused did not take all such reasonable steps. As the Saskatchewan Court of Appeal ruled in the *Slater* case (2005), section 150.1(5) does not create a reverse onus clause and, in fact, "there is nothing in … [s. 150.1(4)] that expressly places any obligation on an accused to establish anything." In delivering the judgment of the Court, Justice Jackson quoted the following summary of the relevant case law:

> [W]here the defence of honest but mistaken belief in the complainant's age arises in circumstances where s. [150.1(5)] applies, the Crown must prove beyond a reasonable doubt that the accused did not take all reasonable steps to ascertain the complainant's age, or that he did not have an honest belief that her age was fourteen years or more. For the defence to succeed, it must point to evidence which gives rise to a reasonable doubt that the accused held the requisite belief, and in addition, evidence which gives rise to a reasonable doubt that the accused took all reasonable steps to ascertain the complainant's age.

In *Slater*, the accused was charged with six counts of obtaining the sexual services of someone under the age of 18 years. He had paid six young women, under the age of 18, to engage in sexual relations with him. Some of the victims told Slater that they were over 18, while others either said nothing or were not asked by the accused. One victim stated that she had told Slater she was 17. The trial judge convicted Slater of the offences, rejecting his defence of mistaken belief in consent because he had not taken all reasonable steps to ascertain the ages of the young women concerned. The Saskatchewan Court of Appeal affirmed the convictions and rejected Slater's appeal.

Justice Jackson identified the criteria that should be applied in determining whether the Crown had established that Slater had not taken all reasonable steps to ascertain the age of the six young women:

> In determining whether the Crown has proven beyond a reasonable doubt that Mr. Slater did not take all reasonable steps, the Court must determine

what steps would have been reasonable for the accused to take in the circumstances. Some *indicia* are:

   (a)   the complainant's physical appearance;

   (b)   the complainant's behaviour;

   (c)   the ages and appearances of those in whose company the complainant has been found;

   (d)   the relevant activities;

   (e)   the times, places and other circumstances in which the accused observed the complainant and the complainant's conduct.

Based on this list, Justice Jackson agreed with the trial judge that there was no evidence that Jackson had taken "all reasonable steps" to ascertain the age of the young women from whom he had purchased sexual services. Indeed, one of the young women had actually told him that she was 17, and Slater had taken no steps whatsoever toward establishing the age of four of the young women. As far as the one young woman who told Slater she was 18 was concerned, the trial judge had found that that, in all the circumstances, this did not constitute "all reasonable steps." On this matter, Justice Jackson concurred with the trial judge, stating that, "based on a consideration of all circumstances, this is a reasonable conclusion."

Undoubtedly, the reason for requiring an accused person to take "all reasonable steps" to ascertain the age of someone with whom he or she wishes to engage in sexual relations is to protect children (under 16) and young persons (under 18) from sexual exploitation. However, the rationale for restricting the defence of mistaken belief in consent where the accused engages in some form of sexual activity with an adult is based on the unique characteristics of the crime of sexual assault.

In the Supreme Court of Canada's decision in the *Park* case (1995), Justice L'Heureux-Dubé presents a convincing analysis of the reasons why the defence of mistake of fact raises unique problems when the accused is charged with sexual assault. She points out that, normally, accused persons raise the defence of mistake of fact when they can claim that they were under a fundamental misapprehension as to an element of the *actus reus* that is generally not in dispute. She gives the example of a defendant who shoots a man believing the latter is a deer. There would be no dispute as to the fact that the victim was killed by the accused's gunshot (the key element of the *actus reus* of an offence involving a homicide). The critical issue would then be whether the accused honestly believed that the victim was a deer. However, in cases of alleged sexual assault, a critical element of the *actus reus* is that there was an absence of consent on the part of the victim and there is frequently a fundamental dispute as to whether that particular element of the *actus reus* existed. As Justice L'Heureux-Dubé suggested,

> Assault differs importantly from most other *Code* offences in its interaction with the mistake of fact defence. Under most other offences, mistake of fact will primarily arise in contexts in which the *actus reus* of the offence is beyond dispute. Assaults raise a unique problem that the mental state of another person (i.e., consent or lack thereof) is an essential element that is relevant to both the *actus reus* and the *mens rea* of the offence—an element which almost invariably is materially in dispute.

Furthermore, Justice L'Heureux-Dubé made the critical point that, in trials involving charges of sexual assault, the courts face the difficulty that such assaults are not usually witnessed by anyone other than the accused and the complainant and that a conviction may be obtained without the need to prove "visible physical injury to the complainant." These factors render it more likely that there will be a dispute as to the issue of consent.

Justice L'Heureux-Dubé identified another critical reason why the defence of mistaken belief as to consent is so deeply problematic. In her view, there is a "clear communication gap between how most women *experience* consent, and how many men perceive consent." The learned justice notes that part of this gap is caused by "genuine, often gender-based, miscommunication between the parties" and another part is attributable to the "myths and stereotypes that many men hold about consent." Among these myths and stereotypes is the view that "coercive sexuality" is "normal." In light of the inherent danger of reinforcing such myths and stereotypes, the acquittal of accused persons who assert a totally unreasonable belief in consent represents a serious threat to the security of all women.

The unique difficulties created by advancing mistaken belief in consent as a defence to a charge of sexual assault constitute the main rationale for imposing the requirement that the accused take reasonable steps to ascertain consent. Therefore, section 273.2 of the *Criminal Code* (enacted in 1992) provides:

> It is not a defence to a charge under section 271, 272 or 273 that the accused believed that the complainant consented to the activity that forms the subject-matter of the charge, where
>
> (a) the accused's belief arose from the accused's
>
>   (i)   self-induced intoxication, or
>
>   (ii) recklessness or wilful blindness; or
>
> (b) *the accused did not take reasonable steps, in the circumstances known to the accused at the time, to ascertain that the complainant was consenting.* [emphasis added]

At the outset, it should be emphasized that section 273.2(b) differs in some important respects from section 150.1(4) and (5), which defines the defence of mistaken belief as to age. Section 273.2(b) reflects the modified objective test, which we encountered when we discussed objective *mens rea* in Chapter 5; more specifically, while the accused must take reasonable steps to ascertain consent, the court must judge the reasonableness of those steps in light of the *circumstances which were known to him or her at the time of the alleged offence.* The phrase "in the circumstances known to the accused," which clearly imports a subjective element into the defence of mistaken belief in consent, does not appear in section 150.1(4) and (5). Furthermore, while section 150.1(4) and (5) uses the phrase "*all* reasonable steps," section 273.2(b) contains only the words "reasonable steps."

How have the courts interpreted section 273.2(b)? In *Malcolm* (2000), the Manitoba Court of Appeal took the following view:

> Section 273.2(b) requires the court to apply a quasi-objective test to the situation. First, the circumstances known to the accused must be ascertained. Then, the issue which arises is, if a reasonable man was aware of the same circumstances, would he take further steps before proceeding with the sexual activity? If the answer is yes, and the accused has not taken further steps, then the accused is not entitled to the defence of honest belief in consent. If the answer is no, or even maybe, then the accused would not be required to take further steps and the defence will apply.

It is significant that the Ontario Court of Appeal ruled, in the *Darrach* case (1998), that section 273.2(b) of the *Criminal Code* does not infringe the fundamental principles of justice that are guaranteed by section 7 of the *Charter.* As Associate Chief Justice Morden stated, on behalf of the court, section 273.2(b) does not remove all of the elements of subjective fault that must generally be proved by the Crown in relation to "real crimes" and, in particular, those that carry a considerable degree of social stigma where the accused is convicted. Indeed, the court held that, although section 273.2(b) undoubtedly introduced an "objective component in the mental element of the offence," Parliament has modified this component by personalizing it "according to the subjective awareness of the accused at the time":

> ... The accused is to "take reasonable steps, *in the circumstances known to the accused at the time*, to ascertain that the complainant was consenting." In other words, the accused is not under an obligation to determine all the relevant circumstances—the issue is what he actually knew, not what he ought to have known.... [emphasis in original]
>
> ... [H]aving regard to the basic rationale underlying constitutionally mandated fault requirements that it is wrong to punish a person who is "morally innocent" ... it is difficult to contemplate that a man who has sexual intercourse with a woman who has not consented is morally innocent if he has not taken reasonable steps to ascertain that she was consenting.

The Ontario Court of Appeal also held that section 273.2(b) does not place the primary (or persuasional) burden of proof on the accused. In other words, the Crown must prove beyond a reasonable doubt that the accused did *not* take reasonable steps to ascertain whether the complainant gave consent in the circumstances known to the accused at the time of the alleged offence.[2]

What are "reasonable steps" in the context of a defence of honest mistake as to consent? It may well be the case that an individual who seeks to engage in sexual activity with another person should first seek explicit permission if the individuals concerned are strangers to each other. On the other hand, seeking advance permission might not be considered a practical requirement where the parties cohabit and have been routinely engaging in sexual activity with each other. As Justice Wood, of the British Columbia Court of Appeal, stated in the case of *G. (R.)* (1994),

> ... s. 273.2(b) clearly creates a proportionate relationship between what will be required in the way of reasonable steps by an accused to ascertain that the complainant was consenting and "the circumstances known to him" at the time. Those circumstances will be as many and as varied as the cases in which the issue can arise, and it seems to me that the section clearly contemplates that there may be cases in which they are such that nothing short of an unequivocal indication of consent from the complainant, at the time of the alleged offence, will suffice to meet the threshold test which it establishes as a prerequisite to a defence of honest but mistaken belief.

For example, in the case of *G. (R.)*, the accused and the complainant had been married but had later divorced. After the divorce, the accused asked his ex-wife to bring the children to visit him for the weekend. When the ex-wife arrived, the accused was intoxicated. He started to undo the buttons on the blouse of his ex-wife, who protested against this conduct. The accused became enraged and ordered her to leave the house. He then dragged her toward the door, while clutching her blouse. The ex-wife felt sick and lay down with the children on the floor. The accused apologized but then reclined beside his ex-wife and engaged in sexual intercourse with her. She did not protest, but she stated that she felt helpless and that she did want to cause her ex-husband to become angry again. When morning came, the accused woke up his ex-wife and again engaged in an act of sexual intercourse with her. The woman was afraid that the accused would become violent if she refused, so she said nothing. Later the ex-wife left and ultimately the accused was charged with sexual assault. The accused's defence of honest, but mistaken, belief in consent was rejected by the trial judge. The accused's conviction was upheld by the British Columbia Court of Appeal, which agreed with the trial judge, who had said that

> [t]he onus is on the accused, the confessed aggressor throughout the evening's events, to determine unequivocally that the woman is consenting. The onus is on him; not on her. He must make sure that she is consenting. It is not up to her to make sure that he knows that she is not consenting....
>
> I want to make it perfectly clear to this accused that what I am saying is this: That even though the woman never said no, the responsibility is his to make sure that he has an unequivocal consent, and I am satisfied in these circumstances he did not fulfil that onus in any subjective or objective manner and I find him guilty as charged.

---

[2] In 2000, the Supreme Court of Canada affirmed the decision of the Ontario Court of Appeal in *Darrach* but did not address the question of the constitutionality of s. 273.2 of the *Criminal Code*.

In this case, although the accused and the complainant had once been married to each other, they were now divorced and living apart at the time of the alleged sexual assault. Furthermore, the complainant had protested when the accused had tried to unfasten her blouse and, when he later became angry with her and physically assaulted her, she had become sick to her stomach. In these circumstances, nothing short of obtaining an unequivocal consent from the complainant would constitute taking "reasonable steps in the circumstances known to the accused at the time." Silence on the part of the complainant was clearly insufficient in this particular case.

Similarly, in *Cornejo* (2003), the accused and the complainant worked together. The complainant had made it clear to Cornejo that she did not want to engage in a sexual relationship with him. On the day of the incident that led to a charge of sexual assault, Cornejo and the complainant had both attended a company golf tournament. They did not talk to each other at the tournament. Both had been drinking heavily and left separately. After 12:30 a.m., Cornejo called the complainant at her apartment three times. He arrived at her apartment at 1:30 a.m. and found the door unlocked. The complainant was asleep on the couch. She testified that she "awoke to find Mr. Cornejo on top of her, naked and attempting to penetrate her." Both her jeans and her underwear had been removed. The complainant repeatedly asked what Cornejo was doing, explicitly stated that she did not want to engage in any sexual activity with him, and tried unsuccessfully to push him off her. Cornejo testified that, when he removed the complainant's jeans and underwear, she "lifted her pelvis." On the basis of this movement on the part of the complainant, Cornejo asserted that he honestly believed that she was consenting to sexual activity with him. The trial judge ruled that there was "an air of reality" to the defence of mistaken belief in consent and, in doing so, focused exclusively on the alleged pelvic movements. He instructed the jury to consider the defence and Cornejo was later acquitted of the charge of sexual assault. However, the Ontario Court of Appeal allowed the Crown's appeal against the acquittal and ordered a new trial. In delivering the judgment of the Court, Justice Abella held that the trial judge should not have permitted the jury to consider the defence of mistaken belief in consent because Cornejo had not satisfied the evidentiary or secondary burden of proof: the movements of the complainant's pelvis could not *per se* provide an "air

of reality" to the defence. The critical issue was whether there was any evidence that he had taken reasonable steps, in the circumstances known to him, to ascertain whether the complainant was consenting to sexual activity with him. In the words of Justice Abella,

> The only words Mr. Cornejo said the complainant expressed were "what the hell are you doing here", "no, not on the mouth", and "because I don't love you". Either in isolation or taken together, these are phrases of rejection. They are not ambiguous. It is hard to see how these statements could be interpreted as enticement entitling Mr. Cornejo to assume that he could proceed with his sexual activity.
>
> These were circumstances crying out for reasonable steps to ascertain consent. The complainant's prior rejections of his sexual advances, his apology to her in the past for his inappropriate sexual advances, her request to him that he hang up during the first two telephone calls so she could speak to her boyfriend, her ambiguous response to his third phone call, her failure to answer the door, his entering the apartment without permission and finding the complainant sleeping and shocked by his presence, all required that he take reasonable steps to clarify whether she was consenting to sexual activity. She never touched him, her eyes were closed, he knew she had been drinking that day, and every rejection by her that evening, even according to his own evidence, resulted in more aggressive sexual conduct on his part.
>
> Mr. Cornejo's counsel pointed to the following as reasonable steps taken to ascertain consent: he ran his fingers through her hair; he kissed her on the forehead; he kissed her on the mouth; the complainant lifted her pelvis when he removed her clothing.
>
> But this is a submission that permits Mr. Cornejo to transform his own acts into reflections of consent. In these circumstances, Mr. Cornejo ought to have taken steps before he engaged in any sexual activity to ascertain whether she was consenting.... In my view, no steps of any kind, let alone reasonable ones, were taken.
>
> On the basis of Mr. Cornejo's own evidence, the complainant said no and physically stopped him from kissing her on the mouth. This could not be interpreted as a reasonable step in ascertaining consent to sexual activity or as providing him with confidence that he had thus secured her consent to proceed further.
>
> Any reasonable person in Mr. Cornejo's position, who was aware of these same circumstances, would have taken further steps to ascertain consent before

proceeding with sexual activity. No reasonable person, on the other hand, when being told that someone was uninterested in being kissed because she did not love him, would assume that she would, in the alternative, be interested in having her clothes removed and engaging in sexual intercourse.

INTOXICATION AND THE DEFENCE OF HONEST MISTAKE OF FACT

May an accused person charged with sexual assault say, "I admit that my belief in consent was unreasonable but I was so drunk that I nevertheless honestly believed that the complainant consented to sexual relations"? The answer is definitely in the negative, since section 273.1(a) clearly states that a mistaken belief in consent that is the result of "self-induced intoxication" is not a valid defence.

The enactment of this provision in 1992 basically reflects the existing case law on the subject. For example, in *Moreau* (1986), the Ontario Court of Appeal had already ruled that, as a matter of sound legal policy, intoxication should only be a valid defence to a charge of an offence requiring proof of *specific* (as opposed to *general* or *basic*) intent. The offence of sexual assault requires proof only of *general* or *basic* intent and, for this reason, intoxication cannot be raised as a defence. Therefore, in the view of the court, a drunken (albeit honest) mistake as to the victim's consent cannot be considered a valid defence.

Section 273.1(a) only applies to sexual assaults, but the general principle articulated in the *Moreau* case still applies to other offences. An honest mistake of fact in relation to a crime of specific intent may be a defence even if the mistake was caused by intoxication, but a mistake of fact in relation to a crime of basic intent (such as assault or damage to property under section 430) is not a valid defence.

The general rules pertaining to intoxication as a defence are discussed in detail in Chapter 10.

WHEN CAN THE DEFENCE OF MISTAKE OF FACT BE CONSIDERED BY THE TRIER OF FACT?

The accused person in a criminal trial is not entitled to have *any* defence—no matter how speculative—placed before the trier of fact. Indeed, no defence may be considered by the trier of fact (either the jury or the trial judge sitting alone) until the accused has first satisfied the **evidentiary burden of proof**—a legal principle that was discussed in Chapter 8 in the context of the defence of automatism. The defence of honest mistake of fact is certainly no exception to this general principle. As the Supreme Court of Canada held in the *Esau* case (1997), "before a court should consider honest but mistaken belief or instruct a jury on it there must be some plausible evidence in support so as to give *an air of reality* to the defence" (emphasis added). It will be remembered from the discussion of the *Fontaine* case (2004) in Chapter 8 that Justice Fish of the Supreme Court of Canada defined the evidentiary burden of proof somewhat differently when he stated that, "[A]s regards all affirmative defences, I think it preferable to say that the evidential burden will be discharged where there is some evidence that puts the defence 'in play.'" He added that "the defence will be in play whenever a properly instructed jury could reasonably, on account of that evidence, conclude in favour of the accused." However, the cases dealing with mistake of fact as a defence primarily refer to the need to establish "an air of reality" as a prerequisite for satisfying the evidentiary burden of proof.

Of course, once the accused has satisfied the evidentiary burden of proof, the defence must be considered by the trier of fact. At the end of the trial, the onus then shifts to the Crown to prove *beyond a reasonable doubt* that the accused was not acting under an honest, but mistaken, belief as to one or more of the essential *actus reus* elements of the offence with which the accused has been charged; after all, the Crown is nearly always placed under the *persuasional burden of proof*. Conversely, if the trial judge should rule that the accused has failed to satisfy the evidentiary burden of proof, then the trier of fact will not even consider the defence when the time ultimately comes to decide the accused's guilt or innocence.

By way of example, let us examine how the evidentiary burden of proof is applied in the trial of an accused person who is charged with sexual assault and who advances a defence of mistaken belief in consent. In the Supreme Court of Canada's decision in *Davis* (1999), Chief Justice Lamer emphasized that it is clearly not sufficient for an accused person merely to assert that there was an honest mistake as to consent. Undoubtedly, there must be some plausible evidence to support any such contention. According to the Chief Justice, in order for the accused to satisfy the evidentiary burden of proof, "it must be possible for a reasonable trier of fact to conclude that the *actus reus* is made out but the *mens rea* is not." Only in these circumstances does the defence have "an air or reality" and, as Chief Justice Lamer put it, "[W]here there is no air of reality to the defence, it should not be considered, as no reasonable trier of fact could acquit on that basis."

In general, it will be very difficult for an accused person to convince a judge that there is an "air of reality" to the defence of honest, but mistaken, belief in consent. Indeed, in the case of *Ewanchuk* (1999), the Supreme Court of Canada noted that "cases involving a true misunderstanding between parties to a sexual encounter" arose only "infrequently." For example, in the case of *Despins* (2007), the accused had been charged with sexual assault. At his trial, he raised the defence of mistaken belief in consent and was acquitted by a jury. The Crown appealed this decision to the Saskatchewan Court of Appeal. The central issue in the appeal was whether the accused had met the evidentiary burden of proof. The trial judge had answered this question in the affirmative and instructed the jury to consider the defence. However, the Court of Appeal set aside the acquittal and ordered a new trial on the basis that there was no air of reality to the defence.

The facts in *Despins* were that the accused and the complainant, who had not known each other previously, had attended a party, where a considerable amount of alcohol had been consumed. The complainant and her boyfriend went to sleep on a single mattress. The complainant woke up to find that someone was having sexual intercourse with her. At first, she thought her boyfriend was having intercourse with her. However, it was actually Despins. When she realized her mistake, the complainant pushed Despins away. Despins claimed that he had no memory of how he came to be in bed with the complainant. However, he stated that he did remember that the complainant had kissed and caressed him before intercourse took place and that the sexual activity continued for several minutes before the complainant's boyfriend intervened.

The majority of the justices in the Court of Appeal considered the requirement, under section 273.2(b) of the *Criminal Code*, that the accused must have taken reasonable steps to ascertain the consent of the complainant if he or she wishes to advance a defence of mistaken belief in consent. The Court of Appeal ruled that there was insufficient evidence to give an air of reality to the defence in Despins' case. Indeed, there was no indication that Despins had taken any steps at all to ascertain consent. In the words of Justice Jackson:

… [T]here is no air of reality to the defence with respect to the time period before the accused had any recollection. As the accused has no knowledge of events up to the point he actually began to have sexual relations with the complainant, there is, of course, no evidence that he took reasonable steps to ascertain that she was consenting.

With respect to the later time period—after the accused gained memory—it cannot be divorced from the prior time period. It must be assessed in light of the fact that the accused has no recollection of what transpired that led him to remove his clothes and move to the bed of a woman he did not know—with whom he had had no prior exchanges, and who is lying asleep on a single mattress next to her boyfriend—and engage in sexual relations with her. The accused attempted to base his belief in consent by seeking signs of apparent responsiveness in eye contact and bodily movement *after* initiating and engaging in sexual contact with respect to which he either had no belief that the complainant had consented or the defence was otherwise barred.

If the accused's evidence could form the basis of mistaken consent, he did not take the reasonable steps required in the totality of the circumstances….

… [I]t is simply not enough for an accused to say that he thought the complainant was consenting where the circumstances include advances from an intoxicated stranger towards a sleeping complainant. The trial judge should not have left the defence of mistaken belief with the jury. It simply does not have a basis in the evidence or is barred by s. 273.2 of the *Criminal Code*.

HOW "HONEST" MUST A MISTAKE OF FACT BE?

Suppose that an accused person makes the following response to a criminal charge: "Owing to an honest mistake, I had no intention to commit the particular offence with which I am charged. It is true that, as a consequence of this mistake, I actually intended to commit a *different* offence. However, I should nevertheless be acquitted since I lacked the necessary *mens rea* in relation to the specific offence with which I am charged." Can such a defendant escape criminal liability?

The Yukon Court of Appeal addressed this issue in the somewhat bizarre case of *Ladue* (1965), in which the accused was charged with "indecently interfering with a dead human body" contrary to (what is now) section 182(b) of the *Criminal Code*. The accused either copulated or attempted to copulate with a dead woman. However, he claimed that because of intoxication, he did not realize that the woman was dead, and instead believed that she was only unconscious. In effect, Ladue claimed that he honestly believed that the woman was alive and, therefore, he clearly lacked the *mens rea* to commit the offence charged—namely, indecent interference with a dead human body. However, if the facts were as Ladue had actually believed them to be, it was clear that he possessed the *mens rea* for rape (an intent to have intercourse without consent). Ladue, therefore, committed the *actus reus* of the offence of indecent interference but had the *mens rea* for the offence of rape. In these circumstances, the court understandably rejected the defence of mistake of fact. Justice Davey asserted that

> ... it would be only in the most exceptional case where the offender might have any doubt whether a body was quick or dead, and in such a case he might defend himself by showing that he did not know the body was dead and that according to his understanding he was acting lawfully and innocently.
>
> That is what the appellant cannot show in this case, because if the woman was alive he was raping her.

Although the *Ladue* decision represents something of a departure from the principle that the Crown must prove that accused persons possessed the specific *mens rea* for the offence with which they are actually charged, the outcome of the case is not objectionable in terms of the principles of justice: after all, Ladue intended to commit a *more serious* offence than the one with which he was actually charged. What is the legal situation where an accused person commits the *actus reus* of a serious offence but, because of a mistake, only possesses the *mens rea* appropriate to a lesser offence? Does the reasoning in *Ladue* also apply here? The Canadian courts have dealt with this issue in the context of legislation relating to the illegal sale of drugs, and they have apparently expanded the reasoning employed in *Ladue*.

In *Kundeus* (1976), the accused had sold (what he allegedly believed to be) mescaline to an undercover police officer: in fact, the drug was LSD. Kundeus was charged with trafficking in LSD, which was a restricted drug under (what was then) the *Food and Drugs Act*. The penalty for this offence was a maximum of 18 months' imprisonment (upon summary conviction) and 10 years' imprisonment (upon conviction on indictment). In contrast, mescaline was not a controlled or restricted drug under the provisions of

The *Kundeus* case: Should he be convicted of attempting to sell mescaline or trafficking in LSD? Is his mistake of fact relevant to his culpability?

the *Food and Drugs Act*. However, it was an offence to sell mescaline under the *Food and Drugs Act* regulations. The penalty for this offence was a maximum of three months' imprisonment (for a first summary conviction), five months' imprisonment (for a secondary summary conviction), and a maximum of three years' imprisonment (for a conviction upon indictment). It is clear that the maximum penalty for the sale of LSD considerably exceeded that which could be imposed for the sale of mescaline. In essence, therefore, Kundeus alleged (in a statement that he gave to the police) that he believed he was committing the *actus reus* of the *less* serious offence (selling mescaline) but he actually committed the *actus reus* of the *more* serious offence (trafficking in LSD). Nevertheless, Kundeus was convicted of trafficking in LSD despite his alleged mistake of fact and the Supreme Court of Canada ultimately upheld his conviction.[3]

A similar case is that of *Futa* (1976), in which the accused was charged with being in possession of a narcotic (phencyclidine) for the purpose of trafficking contrary to the provisions of the (now

---

[3] Strictly speaking, the majority of the justices of the Supreme Court ruled that, since Kundeus did not testify or otherwise adduce evidence at his trial, he had not rebutted the presumption that he intended to sell LSD. However, the evidence of the undercover police officer who purchased the drug clearly established that Kundeus believed that he was selling mescaline. Indeed, when asked to supply "acid," Kundeus told the police officer that he was "all sold out" and offered to sell mescaline instead.

repealed) *Narcotic Control Act*. The maximum penalty for such an offence was life imprisonment. Futa, however, believed that he had MDA in his possession. MDA was a restricted drug under the provisions of the *Food and Drugs Act*, and the maximum penalties for conviction of the offence of possessing a restricted drug for the purpose of trafficking were 18 months' imprisonment (upon summary conviction) or 10 years' imprisonment (upon conviction by indictment). As in *Kundeus*, there was a considerable difference in the maximum penalties that could be imposed for illicit use of the two drugs in question. Futa believed that he was committing the lesser offence under the *Food and Drugs Act*, but he was, in fact, committing the *actus reus* of the more serious offence under the *Narcotic Control Act*. Unfortunately for Futa, the British Columbia Court of Appeal entered a conviction against him on the basis that his knowledge that he was dealing in a drug that was forbidden by the *Food and Drugs Act* was sufficient proof of the *mens rea* that must accompany the commission of the offence under the *Narcotic Control Act*. In other words, his mistake was not "innocent" in nature, and his general intention to deal in "forbidden drugs" was sufficient to deprive him of the benefit of the defence of honest mistake of fact.

It is questionable whether the approach adopted by the courts in *Kundeus* and *Futa* is either consistent with the doctrine of *mens rea* or desirable in terms of its results. It undoubtedly seems somewhat harsh to convict defendants of a more serious offence than the offence they were actually contemplating. Furthermore, there is absolutely no doubt that such an approach flouts the basic principles of the doctrine of *mens rea* in that the Crown is normally required to establish that the accused has the appropriate *mens rea* for the *specific offence(s) charged* before a conviction can be entered. In contrast, some people would argue that those who knowingly deal in illegal drugs should be made to accept the consequences of their actions; after all, their "honest" mistake of fact is tainted by their conscious involvement in an outlawed activity. Similarly, it might be contended that to permit a defence of honest mistake in such circumstances would "open the floodgates" to conveniently concocted defences; any individuals charged with the sale of a drug that attracts a high criminal penalty for its illicit use would automatically claim that they believed it was a drug that attracted a lesser penalty. It might well be difficult for the Crown to disprove that they really had such a belief.

CONSENT

THE GENERAL PRINCIPLES

Let us suppose that Fang visits his dentist, Pullem, in order to obtain treatment for an excruciating toothache. Pullem advises Fang that it is necessary to extract one of his teeth. The latter agrees to this proposition, and Pullem duly removes the offending tooth. One week later, Fang seeks to have Pullem charged with assault causing bodily harm and makes explicit reference to the fact that Pullem used a good deal of force in order to extract the tooth. Most readers will instinctively exclaim that, of course, Pullem is not guilty of an assault. However, what is the reason underlying this "common sense" view? Let us also suppose that Sleary asks Lizzie whether he can borrow the latter's expensive sports car. Lizzie answers in the affirmative and Sleary takes the car onto the highway where, within a few minutes, he loses control and crashes into a tree. The sports car is completely destroyed, although Sleary emerges relatively unscathed. However, Lizzie now charges Sleary with theft of the car. Is Sleary guilty of this offence? Once again, the "common sense" answer must be no. However, what is the rationale underlying this response?

In each of the cases hypothesized above, the accused individuals cannot be convicted of the offences charged because the *absence of consent* is a vital element in the case that must be proved by the Crown. Section 265 (assault) and section 322 (theft) clearly require that the Crown prove the absence of consent as an essential element of the *actus reus* of the particular offence charged. In a sense, therefore, the plea of "consent" is not really a special defence to a criminal charge; rather, it is an assertion that the Crown has not proved the *actus reus* of the offence charged.

In this chapter, we shall focus on the defence of consent in the context of a charge of assault and, in particular, a charge of sexual assault.

CONSENT AND ASSAULT UNDER SECTION 265

Section 265 of the *Criminal Code* provides, in part, as follows:

(1)   A person commits an assault when

   (a)   without the consent of another person, he applies force intentionally to that other person, directly or indirectly;

(b) he attempts or threatens, by an act or gesture, to apply force to another person, if he has, or causes that other person to believe upon reasonable grounds that he has, present ability to effect his purpose; or

(c) while openly wearing or carrying a weapon or an imitation thereof, he accosts or impedes another person or begs.

(2) This section applies to all forms of assault, including sexual assault, sexual assault with a weapon, threats to a third party or causing bodily harm and aggravated sexual assault.

(3) For the purposes of this section, no consent is obtained when the complainant submits or does not resist by reason of:

(a) the application of force to the complainant or to a person other than the complainant;

(b) threats or fear of the application of force to the complainant or to a person other than the complainant;

(c) fraud; or

(d) the exercise of authority.

It is clear from a close reading of section 265 that there are definite limitations to the defendant's plea of consent. Section 265(3) unequivocally states that consent obtained by the application of force or by threats or fear of the application of force or by fraud cannot be considered valid. Furthermore, section 265(3) states that no consent has been given where the complainant submits or does not resist because of the "exercise of authority" by the accused. Section 265(3) applies to all forms of assault, although much of the case law concerning this provision involves charges of sexual assault.

Although it is clear what is meant in section 265(3) by the application of force or threats or fear of the application of force, there is some uncertainty as to the meaning of fraud in the context of a charge of assault. This uncertainty will be examined later in this section. However, it appears that a consensus has emerged in relation to the interpretation of the phrase "exercise of authority." If an officer in the Canadian Forces were to order a subordinate to submit to sexual activity, it is perfectly clear there would be no consent since there has been an "exercise of authority." However, section 265(3) may also invalidate an apparent consent even where the accused does not have the right to issue commands or to compel obedience. For example, in the *Saint-Laurent* case (1993), the Quebec Court of Appeal suggested that section 265(3) would operate to negative any alleged consent given by patients to sexual activity with their treating psychiatrists because of the "overwhelming imbalance of power in the relationship between the parties." Similarly, in *Matheson* (1999), the accused was a psychologist who was charged with two counts of sexual assault in relation to sexual intercourse that had occurred with two of his patients. In delivering the judgment of the Ontario Court of Appeal, Justice Austin held that there was no real consent by the patients because of the power that Matheson had to influence their conduct:

> Whether or not the appellant had a right to command or to enforce obedience, he clearly had the power to influence the conduct and actions of others. He also, clearly, exercised that power for his own benefit and interest and against the interests of his patients X and Y.

Let us return to the question of the meaning of "fraud" in section 265(3) and examine the uncertainty that surrounds the interpretation by the courts of this provision. Section 265(3) stipulates that any consent obtained by fraud should not be considered a real consent and that an accused may not rely on it as a defence to a charge of assault. Until recently, the only type of fraud that was covered by this provision was fraud as to the actual nature of the act in question and fraud as to the identity of the accused. For example, if physicians engage in sexual activity with patients after having informed them that they are carrying out certain medical procedures, such fraud would render any consent totally invalid. Similarly, if the accused had impersonated the complainant's spouse (in a darkened room, for example), any ensuing consent to sexual activity would be vitiated as a direct consequence of the accused person's fraud. On the other hand, in *Petrozzi* (1987), the British Columbia Court of Appeal ruled that the accused's fraudulent behaviour in promising to pay a prostitute for her sexual services (when he had no intention of doing so) did not render her consent invalid under section 265(3) of the *Code*.

However, in the somewhat controversial case of *Cuerrier* (1998), the Supreme Court expanded the meaning of "fraud" in section 265(3)(c) to include dishonesty that exposes the complainant to a significant risk of serious bodily harm.

Cuerrier had been told by the public health authorities that he had tested positive for HIV. He was given explicit instructions to use a condom whenever he engaged in sexual intercourse and to inform his partner(s) that he was HIV-positive. Cuerrier angrily refused to accept this advice, complaining that he "would never be able to have a sex life" if he were to inform potential partners that he was HIV-positive. On numerous occasions, Cuerrier had unprotected sexual intercourse with two female complainants. He never informed them of his HIV-positive status. Both of the complainants testified that they would never have engaged in unprotected sexual intercourse with Cuerrier had they known that he was HIV-positive.

Cuerrier was charged with two counts of aggravated assault on the basis that his misrepresentation of his HIV status constituted fraud under section 265(3) and that, therefore, the complainants' apparent consent to intercourse with him was nullified. The trial judge ordered the jury to acquit the accused, stating that the only type of "fraud" that would operate to negative consent to sexual intercourse was fraud as to the nature and quality of the act itself or the identity of the accused. However, the trial judge stated that fraud as to one's HIV status did not come within these parameters. The British Columbia Court of Appeal upheld the trial judge's ruling, but the Supreme Court subsequently allowed an appeal by the Crown and ordered a new trial for Cuerrier.

Justice Cory, speaking for a majority of the Supreme Court, adopted the view that a person accused of concealing or failing to disclose that he or she is HIV-positive may be found to have committed a type of fraud that vitiates any apparent consent on the part of the victim to engage in sexual activity. According to Justice Cory,

> Persons knowing they are HIV-positive who engage in sexual intercourse without advising their partner of the disease may be found to fulfil the traditional requirements for fraud namely dishonesty and deprivation. That fraud may vitiate a partner's consent to engage in sexual intercourse.
>
> ... The actions of the accused must be assessed objectively to determine whether a reasonable person would find them to be dishonest. The dishonest act consists of deliberate deceit respecting HIV status or non-disclosure of that status.
>
> ... The second requirement of fraud is that the dishonesty result in deprivation, which may consist of actual harm or simply a risk of harm.... In my

view, the Crown will have to establish that the dishonest act (either falsehoods or failure to disclose) had the effect of exposing the person consenting to a *significant risk of serious bodily harm.* The risk of contracting AIDS as a result of engaging in unprotected intercourse would clearly meet that test. In this case the complainants were exposed to a significant risk of serious harm to their health. Indeed their very survival was placed in jeopardy. It is difficult to imagine a more significant risk or a more grievous bodily harm. [emphasis added]

Some commentators have expressed concern about the long-term implications of expanding the meaning of "fraud" in this manner. For example, it has been suggested that the criminal law should not be the method by means of which society deals with the problem of HIV transmission through unprotected sexual activity and that the decision in *Cuerrier* might actually undermine public health initiatives by deterring those individuals who are at high risk of contracting HIV from presenting themselves for testing because they might face possible criminal consequences if the test is positive. However, in this respect, Justice Cory argued that the "risk of infection and death of partners of HIV-positive individuals is a cruel and present reality" and that it is therefore necessary to protect those individuals in the most efficacious manner possible:

> If ever there was a place for the deterrence provided by criminal sanctions it is present in these circumstances. It may well have the desired effect of ensuring that there is disclosure of risk and that appropriate precautions are taken.
>
> ... It is unlikely that individuals would be deterred from seeking testing because of the possibility of criminal sanctions arising later. Those who seek testing basically seek treatment. It is unlikely that they will forego testing because of the possibility of facing criminal sanctions should they ignore the instructions of public health workers.

It is significant that Justice Cory stated that, when Parliament enacted the current section 265(3) in 1983, it intended to "provide a more flexible concept of fraud in assault and sexual assault cases." This may well mean that, in the future, decisions such as that made in the *Petrozzi* case (1987) may be re-evaluated, and falsely promising to pay prostitutes for their services, for example, may be considered a sound reason to invalidate consent on the basis of fraud: after all, no prostitute would consent to sexual activity if he or she knew that the client had no intention of paying for the services rendered. However, as a consequence of the decision of the Supreme Court of Canada in *Cuerrier* (1998), a considerable degree of uncertainty exists as to exactly how broadly Canadian courts will interpret fraud in the context of section 265(3).

SPECIAL PROVISIONS RELATING TO THE DEFENCE OF CONSENT IN RELATION TO A CHARGE OF SEXUAL ASSAULT

In 1992, the *Criminal Code* was amended in order to provide more specific directions to judges and juries who are required to determine whether the accused may raise a valid defence of consent when he or she is charged with sexual assault (under sections 271, 272, or 273). Indeed, section 273.1 of the *Code* states that, in general, consent in the context of a charge of sexual assault means *"the voluntary agreement of the complainant to engage in the sexual activity in question."* Without limiting the range of circumstances in which a judge or jury may find that consent has not in fact been obtained, section 273.1(2) states:

No consent is obtained for the purposes of sections 271, 272 and 273, where

    (a) the agreement is expressed by the words or conduct of a person other than the complainant;

    (b) the complainant is incapable of consenting to the activity;

    (c) the accused induces the complainant to engage in the activity by abusing a position of trust, power or authority;

    (d) the complainant expresses, by words or conduct, a lack of agreement to engage in the activity; or

    (e) the complainant, having consented to engage in sexual activity, expresses, by words or conduct, a lack of agreement to continue to engage in the activity.

When a defence of consent is raised in relation to a charge of sexual assault, the judge or jury must consider both section 265(3), which applies to assaults generally, and section 273.1, which pertains exclusively to sexual assaults. Section 273.1(2) clearly stipulates that no valid consent has been given where a third party purports to give consent to sexual activity on behalf of the complainant. For example, a defendant may not claim the defence of consent where the alleged consent was given by the husband of the complainant. Furthermore, this provision of the *Code* states that there can be no consent where the complainant "is incapable of consenting to the [sexual] activity"; for example, a complainant who is in a state of acute intoxication would be deemed incapable of giving a valid consent to sexual activity. Indeed, in the *Daigle* case (1998), the Supreme Court upheld the conviction of the accused where the complainant had been given a dose of PCP without her knowledge or consent. Justice L'Heureux-Dubé agreed with the reasoning of the Quebec Court of Appeal that "the evidence shows that [the complainant], then 15 years of age, who drank in one shot a glass of alcohol in which there was hidden the drug, was not capable of giving a valid consent."

Section 273.1(2) also provides that no consent has been obtained where the accused has induced the complainant to engage in sexual activity "by abusing a position of trust, power or authority." This provision would potentially cover, for example, such situations as those in which a university teacher engages in sexual activity with a student or a physician becomes physically involved with a patient. However, in order to obtain a conviction, the Crown would, of course, have to establish that the teacher or physician actually *abused* the position of trust in relation to the student and patient respectively. Interestingly, in the *Hogg* case (2000), the Ontario Court of Appeal held that, in certain circumstances, a drug dealer may be considered to be in a position of power or authority over an addicted client and that abuse of that position would invalidate any consent that may have been given to sexual activity. As Justice Finlayson said in delivering the judgment of the court,

> The protection of the vulnerable and the weak and the preservation of the right to freely choose to consent to sexual activity is clearly the aim of s. 273.1(2)(c).... I have no doubt that it could have application to the relationship between a drug dealer and an addicted client. However, the relationship is not one of an imbalance of power per se. This is not a case of a position of authority or trust, such as in the prototypic doctor/patient, teacher/student relationship, where vulnerability is inherent to the relationship itself. The trial judge should have instructed the jury that they must be satisfied that because the appellant was a supplier of illicit drugs to the complainant, that this relationship created a relationship of dependency that could be exploited by the appellant to vitiate the complainant's consent to engage in sexual activity....

Section 273.1(2) also stipulates that no consent is obtained where "the complainant expresses, by words or conduct, a lack of agreement to engage in the activity." This means that a sexual aggressor cannot raise the defence of consent merely because the complainant did not say "no"; if the complainant's *conduct* (e.g., pushing the accused away) expressed a refusal to engage in sexual activity, the accused will be disqualified from relying on the defence of consent. Finally, this provision of the *Code* expressly articulates the fundamental principle that individuals have the right to withdraw their consent to engage in sexual activity *at any time*, even if they initially gave a valid consent. If the accused refuses to cease such activity at any point after the complainant's consent has been withdrawn, he or she will be guilty of a sexual assault.

CAN AN INDIVIDUAL CONSENT TO THE INFLICTION OF BODILY HARM?

Section 14 of the *Criminal Code* provides that no one can consent to have death inflicted on him or her and that any consent that may have been given does not affect the criminal responsibility of a person who does inflict death in such circumstances. For this reason, a physician who carries out an act of voluntary euthanasia on a terminally ill patient is guilty of murder despite the fact that the patient, while competent to do so, has given an unequivocal consent to this course of action and, indeed, has persistently requested it because he or she is suffering from extreme pain. However, the *Criminal Code* does not deal explicitly with the question of whether an individual may consent to the infliction of a degree of bodily harm that falls short of death. Should individuals be able to give their consent to the infliction of bodily harm and turn what would otherwise be criminal assaults into lawful actions? In the *Jobidon* case (1991), the Supreme Court of Canada adopted the view that, unless there is some overriding social utility that may be identified in relation to the activity in question, consent should not be accepted as a defence to a charge of assault where the accused person intends to cause serious harm and such harm is, in fact, inflicted.

In *Jobidon*, the accused engaged in a fistfight with Haggart. The trial judge found that Jobidon and Haggart had agreed to a fight as a result of a prior altercation between them. Haggart died as a consequence of the blows meted out by Jobidon, and the latter was charged with manslaughter. The theory of the Crown was that Jobidon had committed the unlawful act of assault and, as a consequence, the victim had died; in these circumstances, the contention was that Jobidon was, therefore, guilty of "unlawful act" manslaughter. However, the trial judge found that there had been no assault, and hence no unlawful act. In his view, the victim had agreed to enter into a "fair fist fight," and Jobidon had not intended to exceed the scope of that consent (in the sense that he had no intention to inflict death or grievous bodily harm). In light of this view, the trial judge acquitted Jobidon, but the Crown appealed and the Ontario Court of Appeal substituted a verdict of guilty of manslaughter. The Court of Appeal took the view that, where the accused intends to cause bodily harm in a fist fight, the Crown is not required to prove the absence of consent.

Jobidon appealed to the Supreme Court of Canada, which dismissed his appeal. Speaking for the majority of the Court, Justice Gonthier said that *consent should not be a defence to a charge of assault whenever adults intentionally apply force that causes "serious hurt or non-trivial bodily harm to each other in the course of a fist fight or brawl."* According to Justice Gonthier, sound public policy dictates that such an approach be adopted: "Foremost among the policy considerations" is the "social uselessness of fist fights." It is just not in the public interest that adults intentionally cause harm to each other for no good reason. Such fights may lead to tragedy, as in the *Jobidon* case (1991) itself, or may result in an even greater brawl if bystanders become involved (which also happened in the *Jobidon* case (1991), when the brothers of the protagonists also become involved in a fist fight). Furthermore, if individuals are permitted to participate in consensual fist fights, they may eventually lose their inhibitions against using violence and may start to use their fists on their spouses or partners. Finally,

> [w]holly apart from deterrence, it is most unseemly from a moral point of view that the law would countenance, much less provide a backhanded sanction to the sort of interaction displayed by the facts of this appeal. *The sanctity of the human body should militate against the validity of consent to bodily harm inflicted in a fight.* [emphasis added]

The Supreme Court of Canada's decision in *Jobidon* (1991) does not mean that consent to the infliction of bodily harm will always be considered invalid. It states only that such consent will be invalid where there is no social utility to be gained from the activity in question. Therefore, for example, consent to "bodily harm" would be a defence where medical or surgical treatment was involved or where there was some socially redeeming value to be gained (as in the case of "rough" sports or games). Similarly, if individuals agree to perform stunts in a movie and, as part of that agreement, they consent to participate in "risky sparring or daredevil activities," their consent would be considered valid to a charge of assault, should they be injured in the course of these activities; the consent would be valid because those involved in making a movie are creating a "socially useful product."

The Supreme Court of Canada limited the application of its ruling to fist fights between adults. Indeed, Justice Gonthier stated that

> ... the phenomenon of the "ordinary" schoolyard scuffle, where boys or girls immaturely seek to resolve differences with their hands, will not come within the scope of the limitation. That has never been the policy of the law and I do not intend to disrupt the status quo. However, I would leave the question as to whether boys or girls under the age of 18 who truly intend to harm one another, and ultimately cause more than trivial bodily harm, would be afforded the protection of a defence of consent.

It is significant that, in the case of *W. (G.)* (1994), the Ontario Court of Appeal rejected the defence of consent that had been raised by the 16-year-old accused in relation to a charge of assault causing bodily harm. The charge was laid as a consequence of a consensual fist fight between the accused and another 16-year-old boy. The victim suffered serious injuries, including a broken nose and the loss of vision in one eye for several hours. The trial judge found that the accused "intended to do serious harm to the complainant" and convicted him of the charge. Following the suggestion made by Justice Gonthier in *Jobidon*, the Ontario Court of Appeal held that, where an accused intends to cause serious harm to his or her opponent, "the adolescence of the accused provides no policy reason for recognizing consent as a 'defence' to a charge of assault causing bodily harm." In the words of Justice Doherty, speaking on behalf of the Court of Appeal, "students must realize that acts of violence intended to do serious harm, which in fact cause bodily harm, will not be countenanced." On the other hand, in the case of *S.M.* (1995), the Ontario Court of Appeal held that consent *would* be a valid defence where the 16-year-old accused caused bodily

harm to another 16-year-old in what the accused believed was a consensual fight. In this case, the Court found that the accused did *not* intend to cause any bodily harm.

The *Jobidon* (1991) case does not imply that all consensual fist fights between adults necessarily constitute criminal assaults. Indeed, in the case of *Doherty* (2000), the New Brunswick Court of Appeal took the view that the critical issue in such cases is whether the adult combatants *intended* to inflict nontrivial bodily harm on each other. If there is no such intention, then the *consent* of the parties to exchange blows may be effective to absolve them of any criminal liability. On behalf of the court, Justice Drapeau stated that

> [e]ven in circumstances where serious harm is inflicted in the course of an altercation, the injured party's consent to the application of force to his or her person will preclude a finding of unlawful assault against the combatant who stands accused, unless the Crown establishes that such serious harm was intended by the latter's application of force. [emphasis added]

In the *Doherty* case (2002), the facts were that the accused was a bouncer at a strip club. He had expelled Gillan and his friend, Boyle, because they were drunk and engaging in "intolerable conduct." When Gillan later returned to the club and attempted to hit Doherty, the latter blocked the blow and delivered one punch to Gillan's jaw. Although Gillan later died from a head injury that occurred when he fell to the ground, the trial judge found that Doherty did not intend to cause Gillan any serious injury. The New Brunswick Court of Appeal ruled that Doherty should be acquitted of unlawful act manslaughter because Gillan had *consented to the infliction of force that was not intended to cause nontrivial bodily harm*. In the words of Justice Drapeau,

> There can be no serious challenge to the proposition that, once outside the club premises, Mr. Gillan was bellicose and intent on obtaining retribution for his expulsion by Mr. Doherty.... I am satisfied that Mr. Gillan's pre-altercation conduct and his physical attack on Mr. Doherty are *outward manifestations of his consent to the application of defensive force* by Mr. Doherty. [emphasis added]

According to the Court of Appeal, Gillan implicitly consented to the use of defensive force by the accused, on the understanding that the latter would not intentionally cause him serious bodily harm. If Gillan's consent was effective in law, then Doherty did not commit an unlawful assault when he punched

Gillan on the jaw. Clearly, in these circumstances, Doherty could not be found guilty of unlawful act manslaughter.

In the important case of *Paice* (2005), the Supreme Court of Canada emphasized that *Jobidon* (1991) had decided that consent to a fist fight would only be nullified when (i) the accused person *intended* to cause serious bodily harm and (ii) when such harm was in fact inflicted on the victim. In *Paice*, Justice Charron clearly rejected the assertion, for example, that a mere intention to cause serious bodily harm would on its own nullify consent to a fist fight:

> ... [T]he intention to cause serious bodily harm alone cannot serve to negate the other person's consent to the application of force if, in fact, no bodily harm is caused. The activity, a consensual application of force that causes no serious bodily harm, would fall within the scope of the consent and not in any way fall with the *Code* definition of assault.

However, it is unfortunate that the *Jobidon* case left many questions unanswered. For example, does the sport of boxing have "social utility" when the argument might be made (although not without considerable opposition) that it supports the values of violence and involves the deliberate infliction of blows that may be extremely dangerous? If it does not have such social utility, presumably participation in boxing amounts to assaultive behaviour. Similarly, the question arises as to what extent an individual may consent to non-essential "surgical" procedures that inflict bodily harm. Presumably, one can consent to body-piercing or tattooing because they may have some social utility in terms of giving individuals choices in the area of fashion or enhancing their psychological well-being, but exactly how far may one go in terms of submitting to so-called cosmetic procedures that may conceivably involve the risk of serious injury? All of these issues must, no doubt, be dealt with by the courts on a case-by-case basis.

In the case of *Welch* (1995), the Ontario Court of Appeal adopted the view that, on grounds of public policy, an individual cannot consent to the deliberate infliction of non-trivial bodily harm even if that individual claims that such harm occurred in the course of consensual sexual activity. In *Welch* (1995), the accused was charged with sexual assault causing bodily harm. According to the complainant, the accused had prevented her from leaving his condominium and then had pushed her onto a bed and tied her hands and legs. She also stated that, although she protested throughout, the accused then attempted a number of acts of sexual intercourse, beat her with a belt, and inserted an object into her rectum. The complainant suffered extensive bruising to her breast, abdomen, arm, leg, and buttocks as well as bleeding from her rectum for several days.

The accused claimed that the complainant had unequivocally consented to, and had actually encouraged, what he called "rough sex." The trial judge ruled that, even if the complainant had consented to this type of injury, consent was no defence to a charge of sexual assault causing bodily harm. Welch was subsequently convicted by a jury, and the central issue in his appeal to the Ontario Court of Appeal was whether the trial judge had erred in refusing to place the defence of consent before the jury. Speaking on behalf of the court, Justice Griffiths stated:

> In my view ... the message delivered by the majority in *Jobidon* is that the victim cannot consent to the infliction of bodily harm upon himself or herself, as defined in section 267(2) of the *Code*, *unless the accused is acting in the course of a generally approved social purpose when inflicting the harm*. Specifically, the majority in *Jobidon* recognized that consent may be a defence to certain activities such as rough sporting activities, medical treatment, social interventions, and "daredevil activities" performed by stuntmen, "in the creation of a socially (valuable) cultural product." Acts of sexual violence, however, were conspicuously not included among these exceptions. [emphasis added]

According to the Court of Appeal, the facts in *Welch* (1995) revealed a course of "sadistic sexual activity" involving bondage and the deliberate infliction of harm on the body and rectum of the complainant. Even if the complainant had consented to this activity, her consent could not have detracted from the "inherently degrading and dehumanizing nature of the conduct." In such circumstances, the "personal interests of the individuals involved must yield to the more compelling societal interests which are challenged by such behaviour." As Justice Griffiths put it, it is arguable that society has the right to "enforce one fundamental residual moral value," namely, that "hurting people is wrong and this is so whether the victim consents or not, or whether the purpose is to fulfil a sexual need or to satisfy some other desire."

The problem with the *Welch* case (1995) is that it raises the spectre of state interference with consensual sexual activity that takes place in private. The facts in *Welch* (1995) raise serious questions about whether the complainant ever did consent to what can only be termed brutal treatment. However, there may be some situations in which truly consenting adults, for example, may wish to engage in sexual activity that includes the deliberate infliction of some degree of bodily harm in order to enhance sexual pleasure. Take, for example, the practice of flagellation, which may well cause "non-trivial" bruising on the bodies of the recipient(s). Should the courts use the argument of public policy to invalidate the consent of such adults and turn their sexually oriented activities, which do not harm anyone else, into criminal acts?

CONSENT TO THE INFLICTION OF BODILY HARM IN THE CONTEXT OF SPORTING ACTIVITY

The issue of consent to what would otherwise be an assault is frequently raised in the somewhat controversial arena of contact sports. It is indisputable that the very nature of such games as hockey or football requires the intentional application of force to one's opponents. Therefore, it may generally be said that individuals who voluntarily participate in such sports should be deemed to have given **implied consent** to the infliction of a certain degree of force upon their bodies. However, the question will always arise as to exactly where the law should draw the line between legitimate bodily contact and the criminal application of force.

It is clear that the scope of implied consent to bodily contact in sports is not unlimited. In general, a participant in a contact sport may be considered to have consented only to the application of force that occurs within the bounds of fair play and that is reasonably incidental to the sport in question. It may safely be assumed that no hockey or football player would consent to the deliberate infliction of serious bodily harm or to the application of force that does not fall within the range of a player's reasonable expectations as to how the game in question should be played. On the other hand, injuries—often of a serious nature—may occur accidentally during the course of normal play, and the doctrine of implied consent will prevent such incidents from being dealt with as criminal offences.

Just how broad is the scope of implied consent in any given sport? In Canada, most of the cases that attempt to explore this issue have involved hockey

Is there implied consent to the application of force in contact sports?

games. For example, in the *Cey* case (1989), the Saskatchewan Court of Appeal ruled that there can be no implied consent to bodily harm that is *intentionally* inflicted. Furthermore, Justice Gerwing made the important point that "in sporting events ... the mere fact that a type of assault occurs with some frequency does not necessarily mean that it is not of such a severe nature that consent thereto is precluded." Justice Gerwing also stressed the importance of applying *objective criteria* in determining whether the implied consent of sport players to the application of force has been exceeded in any given case:

> Ordinarily consent, being a state of mind, is a wholly subjective matter to be determined accordingly, but when it comes to implied consent in the context of a team sport such as hockey, there cannot be as many different consents as there are players on the ice, and so the scope of the implied consent, having to be uniform, must be determined by reference to objective criteria.

These objective criteria include the setting of the game, the nature of the league in which it is played (e.g., is it amateur or professional?), the age of the players, the conditions under which the game is played (e.g., is protective equipment used?), the extent of the force used, the degree of risk of injury, and the probability of serious harm. In the particular circumstances of the *Cey* case (1989), Justice Gerwing focused on the inherent risk of injury and the severity of the injuries inflicted as being the central issues to be examined in determining the scope of any implied consent:

> Some forms of bodily contact carry with them such a high risk of injury and such a distinct probability of injury as to be beyond what, in fact, the players commonly consent to, or what, in law, they are capable of consenting to.

In the case of *McSorley* (2000), the court took the view that deliberately striking another player on the head with a hockey stick clearly fell outside the scope of any implied consent on the part of a professional hockey player in the National Hockey League (NHL). While a professional game was in progress, McSorley had pursued another player and struck him from behind. Swinging his hockey stick as though it were a baseball bat, McSorley hit his victim on the side of the head, causing the latter to suffer a *grand mal* seizure and a serious concussion. Undoubtedly, no player would ever consent to such a violent application of force, and there was no doubt that McSorley's conduct fell far outside the ordinary norms of conduct that apply in the professional sport of hockey. McSorley was convicted of assault with a weapon. The Provincial Court Judge was satisfied beyond a reasonable doubt that McSorley intended to hit his victim in the way that he did:

> He had an impulse to strike him in the head. His mindset, always tuned to aggression, permitted that. He slashed for the head. A child, swinging as at a Tee ball, would not miss. A housekeeper swinging a carpetbeater would not miss. An NHL player would never, ever miss. Brashear was struck as intended.

Similarly, in *Bertuzzi* (2004), the accused entered a plea of guilty to a charge of assault causing bodily harm. In the course of a professional game of hockey within the NHL, Bertuzzi skated behind the victim (Moore) and hit him on the right temple with a powerful and unprovoked punch. The victim collapsed on the ice and suffered severe spinal and neurological damage. Bertuzzi was granted a conditional

discharge. In passing sentence, Judge Weitzel stated that

> [t]he confronting of Moore initially may have been within the bounds of the game. To then have the pursuit literally down the ice and then to grab by the sweater in order to get that player to engage in something which it is clear he did not wish to consent to, clearly went beyond the reasonable limits of the game and is an aggravating factor.

The *Bertuzzi* case clearly demonstrates the principle that the doctrine of implied consent has no application when the accused person goes beyond the boundaries of the normal and reasonable expectations of fair play. The victim in this case would never have consented to being "mugged" from behind.

However, the *Leclerc* case (1991) illustrates the proposition that implied consent is not invalidated merely because there has been a serious injury in the course of sporting activity. Leclerc was charged with aggravated assault after he pushed his victim into the boards by striking him in the back or near the neck with his hockey stick. Unfortunately, owing to the speed at which Leclerc was travelling on the ice, his actions caused the victim to collide with the boards and, as a result, the latter was permanently paralyzed from the neck down. The trial judge found that Leclerc's application of force to the victim resulted from his "loss of balance and was part of [his] 'instinctive reflex action,' which had the object of minimizing the risk of bodily harm created by his high speed in close proximity to the boards." Leclerc was acquitted at his trial, and the Ontario Court of Appeal subsequently rejected an appeal by the Crown. Clearly, the outcome would have been very different if the accused had deliberately pushed his victim into the boards with intent to injure him.

Although the principles surrounding the issue of implied consent to the application of force in sporting activities are relatively straightforward, there is no doubt that trial courts have considerable discretion in applying them to the facts of individual cases.

MISTAKE OF LAW

THE GENERAL PRINCIPLE: MISTAKE OF LAW IS NOT A DEFENCE

Section 19 of the *Criminal Code* enshrines one of the most widely known principles of the criminal law: namely, that "ignorance of the law is no defence"; this ignorance is known as **mistake of law**. Indeed, as Chief Justice Lamer of the Supreme Court noted in the *Jorgensen* case (1995), "while mistakes of fact relevant to the commission of a criminal offence excuse an accused from criminal responsibility, mistakes regarding the law do not." For example, in *Klundert* (2008), the Ontario Court of Appeal ruled that the accused's mistaken belief that the *Income Tax Act*, R.S.C. 1985, c. 1 (5th Supp.), did not apply to him personally was no defence to a charge of tax evasion, contrary to section 239(1) of the Act: "… a person's mistaken belief that a statute is invalid *or is otherwise not applicable to that person's conduct* … is a mistake of law that is irrelevant to the existence of the fault requirement in s. 239(1)(d)."[4]

A dramatic example of the application of section 19 of the *Criminal Code* occurred in the case of *Forster* (1992), where the accused was a commissioned officer in the Canadian Armed Forces. She was ordered to report to a new posting. This would have involved moving to Ottawa from Edmonton, where her husband was stationed. Instead of obeying the order to report to her new posting in Ottawa, she attempted to submit her resignation from the Armed Forces.

Such an attempt was ineffective, since she did not follow the prescribed procedures under *Queen's Regulations* for accomplishing this end. She was later charged with being absent without leave, contrary to section 90 of the *National Defence Act*, R.S.C. 1985, c. N-5 and was convicted by a General Court-Martial in spite of her defence that she honestly believed that she had effectively resigned from the Armed Forces (i.e., an honest mistake of law). The Supreme Court later ordered a new trial on the basis that the General Court-Martial did not meet the requirements of section 11(d) of the *Charter* (specifically, that it be "an independent and impartial tribunal"). However, Chief Justice Lamer pointed out that Forster

> … was mistaken about the legal consequences of her actions, because of her failure to understand that she was under a continuing legal obligation to report for duty notwithstanding her purported resignation by letter from the forces. Thus, while she may not have intended to commit an offence under military law, this lack of intention flowed from her mistake as to the continuing legal obligation to report for duty which that regime imposed upon her until properly released from service in accordance with [*Queen's Regulations and Orders*].

Ignorance of the law is no excuse.

Cartoon by Elizabeth Carefoot

It is a principle of our criminal law that an honest but mistaken belief in respect of the legal consequences of one's deliberate actions does not furnish a defence to a criminal charge, even when the mistake cannot be attributed to the negligence of the accused…. This court recently reaffirmed … the principle that knowledge that one's actions are contrary to the law is not a component of the *mens rea* for an offence, and consequently does not operate as a defence.

Perhaps the most frequent justification advanced in support of this principle is that it is a practical necessity; indeed, it is contended that the Crown could never successfully shoulder the burden of proving, in every case, that defendants had actual knowledge of the particular law under which they are charged. Furthermore, it has been suggested that, if ignorance of the law were to be considered a legitimate defence, this would in effect place a premium on ignorance of the law—a situation that would scarcely be conducive to law-abiding behaviour. However, whatever the justification for section 19 may be, it is incontrovertible that its application may well prove to be extremely harsh in those circumstances where an individual is genuinely ignorant of the law.

The harshness inherent in the application of section 19 is well demonstrated in the case of *Molis* (1981). In this case, Molis was charged with trafficking in a restricted drug (MDMA) contrary to the provisions of section 48(1) of the *Food and Drugs Act*, R.S.C. 1985, c. F-27.[5] Molis operated a laboratory in which he manufactured a chemical substance known as MDMA (3,4-methylenedioxymethamphetamine).[6] At the time that he started manufacturing this substance (in August 1975), it was not illegal for him to do so. Unfortunately for Molis, MDMA was later added to

---

[4] Emphasis in the original.

[5] See now section 5 of the *Controlled Drugs and Substances Act*, S.C. 1996, c. 19.

[6] This drug is frequently referred to as "Ecstasy."

Schedule H of the Act and, at that time (June 1976), it became a restricted drug. This amendment to the schedule was brought into effect by a regulation that was duly published in the *Canada Gazette*. Molis, who was unaware of the regulation, continued to manufacture MDMA and was subsequently arrested and charged. The accused was convicted, and his appeals were dismissed by both the Ontario Court of Appeal and the Supreme Court of Canada. Molis contended that there was a significant distinction to be drawn between a mistake of law (that is to say, the wrong interpretation of the law) and ignorance of the existence of a particular penal provision. In the defendant's view, the provisions of section 19 of the *Criminal Code* applied only to ignorance of law in the sense of a mistake of law and not to the ignorance of the very existence of the law.[7] However, Justice Lamer, in delivering the judgment of the Supreme Court, rejected Molis's contention:

> Whatever may be the merit of such a distinction ... Parliament has by the clear and unequivocal language of s. 19 chosen not to make any distinction between ignorance of the existence of the law and that as to its meaning, scope or application.

Similarly, in *Custance* (2005), the accused had been released from a Remand Centre on bail. One of the conditions of his bail was that he reside at a particular address with his sponsor, Gaudet, and that he not move from that address without the permission of a judge. The address given by Gaudet turned out to be a storage room in an apartment building. In fact Gaudet did not have any keys to any suite in that building and, rather than returning to the Remand Centre or turning himself in to the police, Custance stayed for a few days in a vehicle in the parking lot before he returned to court for a hearing. Unfortunately, in the interim, the police had visited the apartment building in order to conduct a bail check and it was discovered that Custance was not living in the suite indicated on his bail order. Custance was charged with four counts of breach of recognizance under section 145(3) of the *Criminal Code* because he had failed to comply with the conditions of his release on bail. He was convicted on three counts by the trial judge and appealed to the Manitoba Court of Appeal, which affirmed his conviction. The Court of Appeal held that the Crown had proved the necessary *mens rea* for the offence: namely, that Custance had "knowingly or recklessly" breached the terms of his recognizance. In response to Custance's contention that he honestly believed that he could comply with the terms of his bail order by sleeping in his car, the Court held that this was a mistake of law and, as such, could not afford him a valid defence. In delivering the judgment of the Court, Justice Steel said,

> In this case, the accused appeared to rely on two mistakes. The first was that Mr. Gaudet had secured an apartment at the address specified. That was a reasonable mistake of fact. Mr. Gaudet gave the address in open court. There was no reason the accused should not have relied on that representation. On the evening he was released, the accused became aware of a possible problem, but still was hopeful that the problem could be resolved. However, once he arrived at the apartment, he was told that the keys to the apartment were not available and would not be available within the next little while. It was at this point that the second mistake occurred. Instead of giving himself up to the police as being unable to comply with his recognizance and waiting in custody for another residence to be obtained, he stayed in a car in the parking lot under the mistaken belief that such action would constitute compliance with his recognizance order. This was a mistake of law, and such a mistake, unlike mistake of fact, does not negative *mens rea*. By residing in his car in the parking lot all weekend (in an attempt to comply with the recognizance), the accused was mistaken about the legal consequences of his actions and was therefore operating under a mistake of law.

The Court of Appeal took the view that, as soon as Custance realized that it would be impossible for him to abide by the residence requirements, he should have turned himself in to the authorities:

> This is not a situation of a wrong suite number in the apartment building. This is a situation of no residence at all. The accused knew full well he was in trouble. His attempt to comply by remaining in the parking lot arose out of an understandable desire to avoid returning to the Remand Centre. Although technically still a breach of recognizance, the trial judge acknowledged the unique factual circumstances by way of a sentence of time served. While this court also has some sympathy for the position [in which] the accused found himself on that weekend, the interests of the justice system are not best served by allowing individuals to decide for themselves the legal parameters of compliance with the conditions of a recognizance.

---

[7] See now section 5 of the *Controlled Drugs and Substances Act*, S.C. 1996, c. 19.

In order to avoid the harshness of the application of section 19 in certain cases, the courts have shown considerable inventiveness in devising exceptions to the general rule articulated in section 19 of the *Code*. For example, in the case of *Ilczyszyn* (1988), the Ontario Court of Appeal ruled that a mistake as to the legal effect of the civil as opposed to the criminal law may constitute a defence to a criminal charge. The accused was charged with abduction of a child in contravention of the terms of a custody order (contrary to what is now section 282 of the *Code*). The accused knew of the existence of the custody order but believed, on the basis of legal advice, that it was no longer valid after she recommended habitation with the child's father. The accused's mistake was one of law; she knew the order existed but was mistaken as to its legal effect. The Ontario Court of Appeal nevertheless ruled that the accused had been correctly acquitted at trial. The court stated that

> [i]n most cases, the fact that an accused knew the terms of a custody order and in fact acted in contravention of its terms would be sufficient to persuade a trier of fact beyond a reasonable doubt that he or she intended to do so. However, in an unusual case such as the one before us, where the accused, although knowing of the terms of the order, truly believed on reasonable grounds that it was no longer in existence, there could be no intent to contravene a valid and subsisting order.

It is interesting that the British Columbia Court of Appeal made a similar decision in the case of *Hammerbeck* (1991). This would appear to suggest that Canadian courts are likely to recognize a general principle that a mistake as to the effect of the civil law will provide an effective defence to a criminal charge. The distinction between a mistake as to a matter of criminal law and a mistake as to a matter of civil law is, therefore, an important one to draw before applying section 19 of the *Code*. However, it is important to bear in mind that there must be reasonable grounds for a mistake as to the civil law before the courts will accept it as a valid defence to a criminal charge. For example, in the case of Finck (2003), the Ontario Court of Appeal affirmed the conviction of the accused on a charge under section 282(1)(a) of the *Criminal Code*—abducting a child contrary to the terms of a custody order. The Court of Appeal ruled that he had failed to establish that he had reasonable grounds for his belief that the custody order was no longer in effect. In delivering the judgment of the Court of Appeal, Justice Armstrong noted that

the *Ilczyszyn* case (1988) had established that "an objectively reasonable mistake of law might in unusual cases negate the *mens rea* of the offence of parental abduction under s. 282(1)(a) of the *Code*." However, Justice Armstrong stated that, as far as the case of *Finck* was concerned,

> ... there simply was no air of reality to the submission that the appellant "truly believed on reasonable grounds" that the custody order ... was "no longer in existence."

THE EVOLUTION OF A NEW DEFENCE OR "EXCUSE": OFFICIALLY INDUCED ERROR

There is little doubt that application of the rule that ignorance of the law is no excuse is becoming increasingly problematic in an age when Canadians are faced with a rapidly burgeoning mass of regulatory laws. Legislation at both the federal and the provincial/territorial levels has created a vast body of regulatory offences. What is particularly disturbing is that many of these offences are not contained in the provisions of a statute that is passed in Parliament or the provincial/territorial legislature and readily available to members of the public. Instead, they are incorporated into sets of detailed regulations that may be difficult to locate, and their existence may, indeed, be completely unknown to many of those persons affected by them.

Many statutes contain provisions that permit the appropriate minister(s) of the Crown to pass regulations into the law, and infringement of them may result in the accused being convicted of an offence. If we take a statute of the Province of British Columbia as a typical example, we may see that a significant number of regulations passed under the authority of section 209 of the British Columbia *Motor-Vehicle Act*, RSBC 1996, c. 318, deal with a host of detailed matters that it would be inappropriate to include within the *Motor-Vehicle Act* itself (for example, the detailed dimensions of permissible motor-vehicle equipment).[8]

It is clear that such regulations are considerably more inaccessible to the public than Acts of Parliament or the provincial/territorial legislatures. Therefore, it may well be contended that it is unfair to apply the principle that ignorance of the law is no

---

[8] There are currently 113 separate regulations issued under the Ontario *Highway Traffic Act*, R.S.O. 1990, c. H.8.

defence when the defendant is charged with an offence arising out of the alleged contravention of such a regulation. However, both the (federal) *Statutory Instruments Act*, R.S.C. 1985, c. S-22, section 11 and, for example, the (provincial) *Regulations Act*, R.S.B.C. 1996, c. 402, section 7, provide that, if a regulation is duly published in the *Canada Gazette* or the *British Columbia Gazette*, as the case may be, an accused person may be convicted for contravention of such a regulation in spite of the accused's complete ignorance of it. The only weakening of the general rule that precludes ignorance of the law as a defence arises when the regulation has not been published in the appropriate *Gazette*. In such a circumstance, both the *Statutory Instruments Act* and the *Regulations Act* provide that the accused person may not be convicted unless it is proved that, at the time of the alleged offence, reasonable steps were taken to bring the substance of the regulation to the attention of the public in general or, at least, of the persons most likely to be affected by it.

Given the fact that Canadians are faced with a vast array of offences, many of which are "buried" in hard-to-find regulations, should there be any general exceptions to the principle that ignorance of the law is no excuse? It appears that Canadian courts are, indeed, prepared to recognize such an exception, although it is very circumscribed in its nature and application. This new defence is based on the notion of **"officially induced error."** More specifically, if accused persons rely on an interpretation of the law made by a public official whose duty it is to provide citizens with advice, then it has been argued that they should be absolved from criminal responsibility if the official's advice proves to be incorrect.

The Ontario Court of Appeal unequivocally recognized the existence of the defence of "officially induced error" in the gruesome case of *Cancoil Thermal Corp. and Parkinson* (1986). In this case, there had been an accident at a factory that produced heat transfer coils. An employee had lost the tips of six of his fingers when both of his hands came into contact with a moving blade that was part of the machine with which he was working. The machine in question had originally been equipped with a guard that would have prevented this type of accident, had the guard been in place. Unfortunately for the employee, the guard had been removed on the initiative of both the supervisor and the general manager of the factory. These individuals believed the guard created a hazard since its presence made it more

difficult for the operator of the machine to clear away pieces of scrap metal. In addition, it was felt that there was an alternative safety device, namely a foot pedal that had to be depressed before the blade could be started. As it turned out, while the employee was removing pieces of scrap metal from the machine, he accidentally hit the pedal and, as a consequence, was injured. The accused were charged with a number of offences arising under the *Ontario Occupational Health and Safety Act*, R.S.O. 1980, c. 321.

The trial judge acquitted the accused on the basis of a technical interpretation of the statute. The Crown appealed the acquittal, and the Ontario Court of Appeal agreed that the trial judge's interpretation of the statute was in error. However, the accused raised the defence of "officially induced error" (for the first time) before the Court of Appeal. It was suggested that, two months before the accident, an inspector from the Occupational Health and Safety Division had been informed that the guard had been removed from the machine in question and that he had commented that "it was safe to remove the particular piece of metal in question and that with the machine being operated according to instructions that it was safe to do so."

The Court of Appeal ordered that a new trial be held to deal with this issue. Most significantly, the Court ruled that Canadian criminal law did, indeed, recognize the existence of the defence of "officially induced error." Justice Lacourcière held that it

> ... is available as a defence to an alleged violation of a regulatory statute where an accused has reasonably relied upon the erroneous legal opinion or advice of an official who is responsible for the administration or enforcement of the particular law. In order for the accused to successfully raise this defence, he must show that he relied on the erroneous legal opinion of the official and that his reliance was reasonable. The reasonableness will depend upon several factors including the efforts he made to ascertain the proper law, the complexity or obscurity of the law, the position of the official who gave the advice, and the clarity, definitiveness and reasonableness of the advice given.

It will be most interesting to see exactly how the defence of "officially induced error" will evolve in the years ahead. It has now been recognized as a valid defence by the Supreme Court of Canada and has been applied by a number of provincial appellate courts. In the case of *Jorgensen* (1995), Chief Justice Lamer was the first member of the Supreme Court of Canada to express the view that the defence of officially induced error should be accepted as part of Canadian criminal law. He noted that "the complexity of contemporary regulation makes the assumption that a responsible citizen will have a comprehensive knowledge of the law unreasonable." In his opinion, the very phenomenon of extensive **regulation** "is one motive for creating a limited exception to the rule" that ignorance of the law is no excuse.

Although Chief Justice Lamer stated his belief that the defence of officially induced error would arise most frequently in the context of regulatory offences, he also indicated that the defence could equally well apply to the realm of "true crimes." For example, in the *Jorgensen* case (1995), the accused had been charged with a number of counts of knowingly selling obscene material (contrary to section 163(2)(a) of the *Criminal Code*). The accused operated a video store and was charged after undercover police officers purchased eight videotapes. All of these tapes had been approved by the Ontario Film Review Board. Nevertheless, the trial court ruled that three of the tapes were obscene, and the accused was convicted. The Supreme Court entered acquittals on behalf of the accused on the ground that he had not "knowingly" sold obscene material. The Crown had not established that the accused "knew of the presence of the ingredients of the subject-matter which as a matter of law rendered the exploitation of sex undue" and, therefore, obscene.

Chief Justice Lamer, speaking for himself alone, took the view that the accused could have been acquitted on the basis of the officially induced error that arose from the board's approval of the films in question. The chief justice's summary of the nature and scope of the defence carries a considerable degree of weight since it was later endorsed by a unanimous Supreme Court of Canada in the case of *Lévis (Ville) v. Tétreault* (2006). According to Chief Justice Lamer,

> ... [O]fficially induced error functions as an excuse rather than a full defence. It can only be raised after the Crown has proven all the elements of the offence. In order for an accused to rely on this excuse, she must show, after establishing she made an error of law, that she considered her legal position, consulted an appropriate official, obtained reasonable advice and relied on that advice in her actions. . . .

Chief Justice Lamer went on to state that, since officially induced error should be seen as an "excuse"

rather than a "justification," it should not lead to a conventional acquittal, but rather to a stay of proceedings by the trial court:

> ... [T]he accused has done nothing to entitle him to an acquittal, but the state has done something which disentitles it to a conviction ... the successful application of an officially induced error of law argument will lead to a judicial stay of proceedings rather than an acquittal. Consequently, as a stay can only be entered in the clearest of cases, an officially induced error of law argument will only be successful in the clearest of cases.

It is particularly noteworthy that, in the decision of the Supreme Court of Canada in *Lévis (Ville) v. Tétreault* (2006), the Court unequivocally expressed agreement with Chief Justice Lamer's analysis, although it did not apply the defence of officially induced error in the particular circumstances of this case.[9] In delivering the judgment of the Court, Justice LeBel stated that the "analytical framework" articulated by Chief Justice Lamer in *Jorgensen* "has become established" in Canadian criminal law:

> Provincial appellate courts have followed this approach to consider and apply the defence of officially induced error.... It should be noted ... that it is necessary to establish the objective reasonableness not only of the advice, but also of the reliance on the advice.... Various factors will be taken into consideration in the course of this assessment, including the efforts made by the accused to obtain information, the clarity or obscurity of the law, the position and role of the official who gave the information or opinion, and the clarity, definitiveness and reasonableness of the information or opinion.... It is not sufficient in such cases to conduct a purely subjective analysis of the reasonableness of the information. This aspect of the question must be considered from the perspective of a reasonable person in a situation similar to that of the accused.

Neither the company (2629-4470 Québec Inc.) nor the individual (Tétreault) accused in the *Lévis* case had received any advice from any officials about their obligations to renew, and pay, for the company's vehicle registration and Tétreault's driver's licence respectively. Since they had not received any official interpretation of the relevant legislation, the defence of officially induced error was clearly not applicable in this particular case. The accused relied on

---

[9] The facts of the *Lévis* case were discussed in Chapter 6.

the argument that they had expected to receive renewal notices in the mail, but had failed to do so. However, as Justice LeBel aptly commented in his judgment, "[P]assive ignorance is not a valid defence in criminal law."

MISTAKE OF LAW AND "COLOUR OF RIGHT"

Officially induced error may provide a defence to a criminal charge in a limited number of circumstances. However, there is one general exception to the legal doctrine that ignorance of the law is no excuse. This exception is encompassed by the important principle that a mistake of law may constitute a valid defence where it operates to negative the specific intent required by the definition of an offence. For example, in defining theft, section 322(1) provides that the offence is committed only when the accused takes or converts property to his or her use fraudulently and without **colour of right**. The latter phrase refers to the legal principle that accused persons may not be convicted of theft if they honestly believe that they have a legal right to the property in question. In other words, accused persons may be acquitted where they act under an honest mistake of law as to whether or not they have a legal right to such property. In essence, a person who is operating "under colour of right" is mistaken as to a matter concerning his or her private property rights, and the relevant provisions of the *Code* reflect the view that it would be unduly harsh to convict such a person of a criminal offence.

A typical example of the "colour of right" defence is provided by the English case of *Skivington* (1967), in which the defendant demanded wages that he believed were owing to him and his wife. He compelled his employer's agent to hand over two wage packets at knifepoint. Skivington was acquitted of robbery because he had an honest belief that he had a legal right to the wage packets. Since robbery basically involves theft with violence, Skivington had to be acquitted of this charge once it was established that the specific intent required for theft (namely, that the accused acted without "colour of right") was negatived by his honest mistake of law.

This case may usefully be compared with the Canadian decision in *Hemmerly* (1976), in which the accused was charged with robbery after taking some money from his victim at gunpoint. Hemmerly contended that he had acted under "colour of right" because he claimed that the victim owed him money as a result of a prior transaction for the sale of illegal drugs. Hemmerly's conviction of robbery was upheld by the Ontario Court of Appeal because he knew very well that he would have no claim in *law* to funds arising from the illicit sale of drugs. Justice Martin went on to say that, "even if the appellant believed that he had a moral claim to the money (which I am far from holding), a belief in a moral claim could not constitute a colour of right." In other words, Hemmerly was not operating under an honest mistake as to his *legal* rights at the time he committed the robbery.

Similarly, in *Manuel* (2008), the B.C. Court of Appeal emphasized that the colour of right defence is only available to an individual who *honestly* believes that he or she has a *legal right* to the property in question. In this case, the accused were members of a First Nation who participated in a roadblock, which prevented motorists from entering or exiting from a resort. As a consequence, they were charged with intimidation, contrary to section 423(1)(g) of the *Criminal Code*. The accused asserted the defence that they acted under colour of right because they believed, "based on historical documents and their knowledge of the traditional way of life of their people," that their Nation had title to the land and that "their duty to the Creator to protect the land from damage, negated the *mens rea* for the offences." The federal government had rejected the First Nation's land claim in 1996 and the Nation had apparently taken no further action to assert its claim.

The trial judge rejected the defence of colour of right because the accused's belief was not based on a *honest* mistake as to their *legal* rights. The accused appealed their convictions but their appeals were rejected by the B.C. Court of Appeal. In delivering the judgment of the appellate court, Justice Levin stated that

> [t]he issue in this case was whether the appellants' beliefs that title to the land gave rise to a legal right to block Sun Peaks Road were *honest* in light of their knowledge that the legal rights claimed by them were unadjudicated and unconfirmed in law (taking into account all of Canadian law, including the aboriginal perspective, aboriginal legal systems, and Canadian common law and criminal law), and conflicted with established common law property rights. It was not a matter of choosing one system of law over another, or of rejecting the appellants' beliefs because aboriginal title had not been established. The question was whether there was any reasonable doubt that the appellants honestly believed they had the legal right to block Sun Peaks Road in light of the uncertainty and conflict of legal rights.

To the knowledge of the appellants, the process of reconciling their people's beliefs in their title to the land with the assertion of Crown sovereignty was neither resolved nor ongoing at the time of the blockade.

When the honesty of the appellants' beliefs in their people's title to the land is tested, as it was by the trial judge, in the context of their evidence and all of the relevant facts and laws of which they were aware, it becomes clear that there was no error in the trial judge's conclusion that they did not honestly believe they had the legal right to block Sun Peaks Road and that both the *actus reus* and the *mens rea* for the offences with which they were charged were proved beyond a reasonable doubt.

It is important to bear in mind that the defence of acting "under colour of right" applies despite the fact that a court may subsequently find that the accused persons concerned did not have the legal right they thought they did. This principle is clearly demonstrated by the case of *Lilly* (1983), in which the accused was a real estate broker who had been charged with the theft of $26 000 that had been deposited in trust with his company in connection with various real estate transactions. It was alleged that the accused had misappropriated the funds in question because he took them out of the trust account *before* the various transactions had been completed. Lilly contended, *inter alia*, that he honestly believed that he had a right to take out his commission from the trust account just as soon as the offers to purchase the various properties had been accepted by the vendors. Despite this contention, the accused was convicted at his trial. The judge directed the jury that, insofar as the issue of "colour of right" was concerned, the real question was when did the commission become payable to the accused's company. He also told the jury that it was "up to you to determine if the company, through the accused, had the right to transfer the commission from the trust account" at the time that such transfer was, in fact, made. In effect, the judge was inviting the jury to decide the validity of Lilly's legal claim rather than the question of whether he honestly believed that he had such a right. Ultimately, the Supreme Court allowed the accused's appeal and ordered a new trial. Justice Lamer, speaking for the Court, held that

> [t]he fate of the accused's defence of colour of right was not dependent upon the jury determining when the commissions were payable. That question was indeed important as relevant to whether the moneys were his or those of his clients. The fact that they

still be the property of the client was a prerequisite to his having to raise a defence to the taking or conversion. Rather, the accused's defence was dependent upon whether they, the jury, were satisfied beyond a reasonable doubt that he, the accused, had not, at the time of the transfers, an honest belief that he had the right to that money, and not, as they were told, dependent on what they, the jurors, thought his rights were.

A similar situation arose in the case of *Dorosh* (2004), where the accused had been convicted of theft of a trailer under the value of $5000. Dorosh had purchased a van with a steam cleaning unit designed for carpet cleaning. The payment consisted of cash and of other items, including a cargo trailer. Dorosh rapidly concluded that, contrary to the vendor's oral representations, the steam cleaning unit did not work and required expensive repairs. Dorosh could not locate the vendor and contacted his lawyer because he had become suspicious of the deal. As a consequence of information received from his lawyer, Dorosh honestly—but mistakenly—believed that there were "liens against the van,"[10] and, in light of this belief and the problems with the steam cleaning unit, he assumed that the "deal was dead." It is significant that the document of sale had stated that the van was "free and clear of all debts." Dorosh, therefore, retrieved the trailer and sold it about a month later. He was then charged with theft of the trailer. The trial judge rejected Dorosh's defence that he acted with "colour of right." The judge treated Dorosh's defence as though the critical issue was whether Dorosh actually had a valid claim in civil law rather than whether he honestly believed he had such a claim. The Saskatchewan Court of Appeal subsequently set aside Dorosh's conviction of theft and ordered a new trial because his defence of colour of right had not been given appropriate consideration. In delivering the judgment of the Court of Appeal, Chief Justice Bayda stated that

> [a] colour of right can have its basis in either a mistake of civil law (a colour of right provides an exception to s. 19 of the *Code* ...) or in a mistake in a state of facts. The mistake in each case must give rise to either an

---

[10] A lien is a legal charge or encumbrance against a specific asset that secures the payment of a debt or the performance of some other obligation. The asset constitutes the security for the money or any other obligation that is owed by the property owner and must generally be paid before the asset is sold. In *Dorosh* (2004), the accused believed that there was a legal charge or encumbrance on the van, which he had purchased.

honest belief in a proprietary or possessory right to the thing which is the subject matter of the alleged theft or an honest belief in the state of facts which if it actually existed would at law justify or excuse the act done....

The judge appears to have acknowledged that the defendant had a belief he had a claim to the trailer. But, instead of asking himself: Did the defendant have an honest belief in his claim even though the claim may be unfounded in law and in fact?, the judge, in effect, asked himself the question: Was the defendant's claim unfounded in law? The judge then proceeded to answer the latter question in the negative and on that premise concluded the defendant had no colour of right.

The defence of "colour of right" is not limited to mistakes about ownership of private property. Indeed, section 429(2) of the *Criminal Code* expressly furnishes a defence of acting "with colour of right" in the context of Part XI of the *Code*, which deals with such offences as *mischief* (destroying, damaging, obstructing, or interfering with the use of property) and *arson*. In *Watson* (1999), the accused, an environmental activist, was charged with two counts of mischief causing actual danger to life and one count of mischief (section 430). By various methods, the accused attempted to prevent a Cuban trawler from fishing for (what he believed was) cod. Watson contended that he honestly believed that he had the right to intervene in light of the provisions of the *World Charter for Nature* (an international convention originally signed in 1982). The trial judge ruled that Watson did not, in fact, have the legal right to intervene as he did. However, the judge did instruct the jury that the defence of "colour of right" was available to the accused:

> ... [T]here can be "colour of right" where an accused honestly, but incorrectly believes that he had a legal right to do something that would otherwise be a crime because he was specifically legally authorized in the particular circumstances facing him to do it.
>
> ... Now, in this case, Mr. Watson says that, he was justified in the circumstances here, in obstructing, interrupting or interfering with the *Rio Las Casas* because he honestly believed he was authorized to do so by the *World Charter of* [*sic*] *Nature*. Now, I am telling you that, in principle, this could constitute a defence of "colour of right."

Significantly, the Newfoundland Court of Appeal agreed with this statement of the law, indicating that "colour of right is an honest belief in a state of facts or civil law, which, if it existed, would negate the *mens rea* of an offence."

STUDY QUESTIONS

1. Perker strikes Snubbin and steals his wallet. Snubbin is seriously injured. Perker is charged with robbery, but he claims that he was only recovering a gambling debt that Snubbin owed him and refused to pay. Does Perker have any defence(s)?

2. Cordelia visits her dentist, Dr. Frankenstein, because she has a toothache. Frankenstein tells Cordelia that he will have to fill the tooth because parts of it are decaying. While Frankenstein goes to see another patient in an adjoining room, Cordelia tells Miranda, the dental nurse, that under no circumstances can she have an injection of novocaine because she is highly allergic to it. Miranda enters this information in Cordelia's file but forgets to tell Frankenstein. While Miranda is attending another patient, Frankenstein returns to the room in which Cordelia is waiting. He tells her to open her mouth and Cordelia does so (at the same time, she closes her eyes). Frankenstein says he is going to freeze Cordelia's tooth at the same time as he starts to inject her gum with novocaine. Cordelia makes a loud noise in protest but, by the time Frankenstein withdraws the needle, it is too late. Cordelia suffers a painful reaction to the anesthetic and has to be treated in hospital. Cordelia is so angry about this incident that she goes to the police and asks them to consider charging Frankenstein with assault causing bodily harm. When interviewed, Frankenstein says that he honestly believed that Cordelia would consent to the injection and that it was not his fault that Miranda had forgotten to inform him of Cordelia's instructions. If Frankenstein were to be charged, would he have a defence?

3. Rosalind has an old handgun that has been in her family's possession for many years. She has always considered it to be an "antique collector's piece" and she has been told by Judith, a friend who is an RCMP officer, that she does not need to register it and that a licence is not necessary. In fact, the gun is not an "antique firearm" within the meaning of the definition set out in section 84(1) of the *Criminal Code*; therefore, both registration and licensing are required after all. One day, Rosalind's house is destroyed by fire. A police officer, who is investigating the

possibility of arson, finds the gun among the ashes and is thinking of charging Rosalind with the offence of unauthorized possession of a firearm contrary to section 91(3) of the *Criminal Code*. If she were charged, would Rosalind have any defence?

4. Cassio and Emilia have been living together for five years in a common law relationship. On a regular basis, they have engaged in consensual sexual activity with each other. They have not been in the habit of seeking explicit permission from each other before proceeding with such activity. On a certain night, Cassio attempts to initiate a sexual encounter with Emilia, but she says that she does not want to have any sexual relations with him because she is feeling sick. Cassio waits for some 30 minutes and then proceeds to engage in an act of sexual intercourse with Emilia, who says nothing and remains motionless. Emilia wishes to have Cassio charged with sexual assault. She tells the police that she had definitely not consented to the sexual activity with Cassio and that she remained silent merely because she was terrified of him losing his temper and subjecting her to physical violence. Cassio claims that, in light of his previous sexual relationship with his partner, he simply assumed that Emilia had changed her mind and was fully consenting to the act of intercourse. If Cassio were charged with sexual assault, would any defence(s) be available to him at his trial?

5. Orsino visits his local bar, where he meets Viola, who was previously unknown to him. After consuming a couple of drinks with Viola, Orsino invites her to come to his apartment. Viola accepts the invitation and she accompanies Orsino to his building. Once inside the apartment, Orsino and Viola engage in sexual activity. The next day, Viola travels to the local police station and accuses Orsino of having sexually assaulted her. She states that she had been drinking for some time before Orsino arrived in the bar and that she had no memory of what happened between the moment when Orsino entered the bar and the moment when she woke up next to him in his bed. Viola is adamant that she would never have willingly engaged in sexual activity with Orsino. Orsino tells the police that, although he realized Viola had been drinking, he assumed that she knew what she was doing

and that she had unequivocally told him that she wished to participate in sexual activity with him. If you were Crown counsel, would you charge Orsino with sexual assault? Do you think that Orsino would have any viable defence(s) to such a charge?

6. Cruncher and Slammer are professional hockey players who are playing on opposing teams. As Cruncher is carrying the puck, Slammer pushes him into the boards along the side of the hockey rink. An altercation develops between them and some punches are thrown. The referee whistles play dead, and after a brief period, the linesmen separate Cruncher and Slammer and lead them toward their respective penalty boxes. However, Cruncher breaks free from his accompanying linesman and skates up to Slammer and punches him in the eye—to the delight of the local fans. Cruncher is 6' 5" tall and weighs 280 lb. Slammer is 5' 8" tall and weighs 150 lb. The blow inflicted by Cruncher opens a deep cut underneath Slammer's eye and numerous stitches are required to close the wound. Cruncher is charged with assault causing bodily harm. Does Cruncher have any defence(s)?

7. Hippocrates is a medical practitioner who believes that boxing should be banned. In his view, those who participate in boxing are subjecting themselves to an unacceptably high risk of serious brain injury or even death. After a professional boxer dies as a consequence of head injuries inflicted in a fight, Hippocrates approaches Crown counsel and asks her to lay a charge of aggravated assault against the other protagonist in the fight. What arguments might he use to persuade Crown counsel to proceed with such a charge?

8. To what extent should implied consent be a defence to a criminal charge that arises in the context of the application of force during such contact sports as hockey and football? Should Crown counsel charge professional hockey players with assault if they engage in fights or inflict serious injuries on the ice? Should football players who deliberately set out to apply extreme force to an opponent be charged with an offence if the latter is seriously injured and unable to continue participating in the game in question? Should Crown counsel lay criminal charges against professional boxers who injure an opponent? If the object of professional boxing is to

knock out an opponent, could it be argued that no one has the right to consent to the deliberate infliction of serious bodily harm and that, therefore, implied consent should not be a defence to a charge of assault against a professional boxer?

9. Bardolph, a 30-year-old man, meets Imogen, a young woman, in a bar. She is drinking alcohol and Bardolph engages her in conversation for an hour or so. Bardolph asks Imogen to come back to his apartment, where they have consensual sexual intercourse. Next day, a police officer comes to the door and escorts Bardolph to the police station, where he is informed that he is being charged with sexual assault, contrary to section 271 of the *Criminal Code*. It turns out that Imogen was only 15 years old and had used a forged driving licence in order to obtain alcohol in the bar. Does Bardolph have any defence to the charge of sexual assault?

FURTHER READING

Archard, D. 1997. *Sexual Consent*. Boulder, CO: Westview Press.

Baxter, A. 2005. Hockey Violence: The Canadian *Criminal Code* and Professional Hockey. 31 *Manitoba Law Journal*: 281–299.

Benedet, J., and I. Grant. 2007. Hearing the Sexual Assault Complaints of Women with Mental Disabilities: Consent, Capacity, and Mistaken Belief. 52 *McGill Law Journal*: 243–289.

Bowland, A.L. 1994. Sexual Assault Trials and the Protection of "Bad Girls": The Battle between the Courts and Parliament. In J.V. Roberts and R.M. Mohr, eds. *Confronting Sexual Assault: A Decade of Legal and Social Change*. Toronto: University of Toronto Press. 241–267.

Boyle, C. 1994. The Judicial Construction of Sexual Assault Offences. In J.V. Roberts and R.M. Mohr, eds. *Confronting Sexual Assault: A Decade of Legal and Social Change*. Toronto: University of Toronto Press. 136–156.

Boyle, C., and S. de Groot. 2006. The Responsible Citizen in the City of Lévis: Due Diligence and Officially Induced Error. 36 *Criminal Reports (6th Series)*: 249–257.

Boyle, C., and M. MacCrimmon. 1998. The Constitutionality of Bill C-49: Analyzing Sexual Assault as if Equality Really Mattered. 41 *Criminal Law Quarterly*: 198–237.

Brett, N. 1998. Sexual Offences and Consent. 11 *Canadian Journal of Law & Jurisprudence*: 69–88.

Christie, T. 2000. Recalcitrant HIV-Positive Persons: The Problem of People Who Are Unwilling or Unable to Prevent the Transmission of Communicable Diseases. 20 *Health Law in Canada*: 53–57.

Colvin, E., and S. Anand. 2007. *Principles of Criminal Law*. 3rd ed., Toronto: Thomson Carswell.

Comiskey, M., and M. Sullivan. 2006. Avoidance, Deception and Mistake of Law: The *Mens Rea* of Tax Evasion. 51 *Criminal Law Quarterly*: 303–341.

Davies, C. 2006. Criminal Law and Assaults in Sport: An Australian and Canadian Perspective. 30 *Criminal Law Journal*: 151–158.

Fletcher, G.P. 1998. *Basic Concepts of Criminal Law*. New York: Oxford University Press. 130–132, 138–145.

Frank, D.J., T. Hardinge, and K. Wosick-Correa. 2009. The Global Dimensions of Rape-Law Reform: A Cross-National Study of Policy Outcomes. 74 *American Sociological Review*: 272–290.

Ginn, D. 2000. Can Failure to Disclose HIV Positivity to Sexual Partners Vitiate Consent? *R. v. Cuerrier*. 12 *Canadian Journal of Women & the Law*: 235–245.

Grant, I. 2008. The Boundaries of the Criminal Law: The Criminalization of the Non-disclosure of HIV. 31 *Dalhousie Law Journal*: 123–180.

Gray, C.B. 2008. The Colour of Law: Law Is Constituted from the Colour of Right. 49 *Les Cahiers de droit*: 393–412.

Greene, S.D. 1998. The Unconstitutionality of Section 43 of the *Criminal Code*: Children's Right to be Protected from Physical Assault: Parts 1& 2. 41 *Criminal Law Quarterly*: 288–317, 462–484.

Hatch, D.R. 1999. Culpability and Capitulation: Sexual Assault and Consent in the Wake of *R. v. Ewanchuk*. 43 *Criminal Law Quarterly*: 51–63.

Healy, P. 1993. Innocence and Defences. 19 *Criminal Reports (4th Series)*: 121–131.

Holland, W.H. 1998. *The Law of Theft and Related Offences*. Toronto: Carswell. 115–134.

Hughes, P. 1996. Women, Sexual Abuse by Professionals, and the Law: Changing Parameters. 21 *Queen's Law Journal*: 297–344.

Husa, A., and S. Thiele. 2002. In the Name of the Game: Hockey Violence and the Criminal Justice System. 45 *Criminal Law Quarterly*: 509–528.

Kastner, N.S. 1986. Mistake of Law and the Defence of Officially Induced Error. 28 *Criminal Law Quarterly*: 308–340.

Law Commission. 1994. *Criminal Law: Consent and Offences against the Person* (Consultation Paper no. 134). London: H.M.S.O.

Law Reform Commission of Canada. 1978. Report No. 10: *Sexual Offences*. Ottawa: Information Canada.

———. 1980. Working Paper No. 26: *Medical Treatment and Criminal Law*. Ottawa: Minister of Supply and Services Canada.

———. 1984. Working Paper No. 38: *Assault*. Ottawa: L.R.C.C.

———. 1986. Report No. 28: *Some Aspects of Medical Treatment and Criminal Law*. Ottawa: L.R.C.C.

———. 1987. Report No. 31: *Recodifying Criminal Law*. Rev. ed. Ottawa: L.R.C.C.

MacAlister, D., and S.N. Verdun-Jones. 2003. Unprotected Sexual Intercourse with Knowledge of HIV-Positive Results: Attempted Aggravated Assault or the Need for Legislative Reform? 13 *Criminal Reports (6th Series)*: 257–265.

Marin, A. 1995. When Is an "Honest but Mistaken Belief in Consent" NOT an "Honest but Mistaken Belief in Consent?" 37 *Criminal Law Quarterly*: 451–460.

Martin, R. 1993. Bill C-49: A Victory for Interest Group Politics. 42 *University of New Brunswick Law Journal*: 357–372.

McElman, M. 2000. A New Conception of Wilful Blindness: The Supreme Court of Canada's Decision in *R. v. Sansregret*. 9 *Dalhousie Journal of Legal Studies*: 324–343.

McGillivray, A. 1998. *R. v. Bauder*: Seductive Children, Safe Rapists, and Other Justice Tales. 25 *Manitoba Law Journal*: 359–383.

———. 2004. Child Physical Assault: Law, Equality and Intervention. 30 *Manitoba Law Journal*: 133–166.

McIntyre, S. 1994. Redefining Reformism: The Consultations that Shaped Bill C-49. In J.V. Roberts and R. Mohr, eds. *Confronting Sexual Assault: A Decade of Legal and Social Change*. Toronto: University of Toronto Press. 293–326.

Odem, M.E., and J. Clay-Warner, eds. 1998. *Confronting Rape and Sexual Assault*. Wilmington, DE: Scholarly Resources Inc.

Paciocco, D.M. 1999. *Getting Away with Murder: The Canadian Criminal Justice System*. Toronto: Irwin Law.

Patrick, J. 2006. Sexual Exploitation and the *Criminal Code*. 43 *Alberta Law Review*: 1057–1067.

Randall, M. 2008. Sexual Assault in Spousal Relationships, "Continuous Consent," and the Law: Honest but Mistaken Judicial Beliefs. 32 *Manitoba Law Journal*: 144–181.

Roach, K. 2009. *Criminal Law*. 4th ed. Toronto: Irwin Law.

Roberts, J.V. 1996. Sexual Assault in Canada: Recent Statistical Trends. 21 *Queen's Law Journal*: 395–422.

Roberts, J.V., and R. Mohr, eds. 1994. *Confronting Sexual Assault: A Decade of Legal and Social Change*. Toronto: University of Toronto Press.

Rolfes, B. 1998. The Golden Thread of Criminal Law—Moral Culpability and Sexual Assault. 61 *Saskatchewan Law Review*: 87–126.

Searles, P., and R.J. Berger. 1995. *Rape and Society: Readings on the Problem of Sexual Assault*. Boulder, CO: Westview Press.

Sheehy, E. 2000. From Women's Duty to Resist to Men's Duty to Ask: How Far Have We Come? 20 *Canadian Women Studies*: 98–104.

Somin, I. 2000. Revitalizing Consent. 23 *Harvard Journal of Law & Public Policy*: 753–806.

Stewart, H. 1998. Mistake of Law under the *Charter*. 40 *Criminal Law Quarterly*: 476–509.

———. 1999. *R. v. Darrach*: A Step Forward in the Constitutionalization of Fault. 4 *Canadian Criminal Law Review*: 9–23.

———. 2004. When Does Fraud Vitiate Consent? A Comment on *R. v. Williams*. 49 *Criminal Law Quarterly*: 144–165;

———. 2009. *Sexual Offences in Canadian Law*. Aurora, ON: Canada Law Book.

Stuart, D. 1993. Sexual Assault: Substantive Issues before and after Bill C-49. 35 *Criminal Law Quarterly*: 241–262.

———. 1999. *Ewanchuk:* Asserting "No Means No" at the Expense of Fault and Proportionality Principles. 22 *Criminal Reports (5th Series)*: 39–49.

———. 2002. *Cinous*: The Air of Reality Test Requires Weak Defences to Be Withdrawn from Juries. 49 *Criminal Reports (5th Series)*: 392–394.

———. 2007. *Canadian Criminal Law: A Treatise*. 5th ed. Toronto: Thomson Carswell. Chs. 4 & 8.

Stuart, D., R.J. Delisle, and S. Coughlan. 2009. *Learning Canadian Criminal Law*. 11th ed. Toronto: Thomson Carswell. Chs. 4 & 5.

Tang, K.L. 2000. Cultural Stereotypes and the Justice System: The Canadian Case of *R. v. Ewanchuk*. 44 *International Journal of Offender Therapy and Comparative Criminology*: 681–691.

Trotter, G.T. 2005. Annotation: *R. v. Bertuzzi*. 26 *Criminal Reports (6th Series)*: 72–73.

Vandervort, L. 1991. Consent and the Criminal Law. 28 *Osgoode Hall Law Journal*: 485–500.

———. 2004. Honest Beliefs, Credible Lies, and Culpable Awareness: Rhetoric, Inequality, and *Mens Rea* in Sexual Assault. 42 *Osgoode Hall Law Journal*: 625–660.

———. 2005. The Defence of Belief in Consent: Guidelines and Jury Instructions for Application of *Criminal Code* Section 265(4). 50 *Criminal Law Quarterly*: 441–452.

———. 2005. Sexual Assault: Availability of the Defence of Belief in Consent. 84 *Canadian Bar Review*: 89–105.

Verdun-Jones, S.N. 2007. *Canadian Criminal Cases: Selected Highlights*. 2nd ed. Toronto: Thomson Nelson. Ch. 9.

Way, M.C. 1993. Bill C-49 and the Politics of Constitutionalized Fault. 42 *University of New Brunswick Law Journal*: 327–334.

CHAPTER TEN

PROVOCATION AND INTOXICATION: PARTIAL DEFENCES TO A CRIMINAL CHARGE

OVERVIEW

This chapter examines the following:

1. two of the major defences that may be raised in response to criminal charges in Canada: provocation and intoxication;

2. the defence of provocation as a partial defence to a charge of murder, with particular attention to the requirements in section 232 of the *Criminal Code* that the alleged provocation must be such as would cause the "ordinary person" to lose the power of self-control and that the accused must act on the provocation "on the sudden and before there was time for his [or her] passion to cool";

3. the principle that, for the purposes of section 232, the "ordinary person" is deemed to possess a normal temperament and level of self control but that, in applying the "ordinary person" test, the court must take into account any personal characteristic of the accused or past relationship of the accused with the deceased that directly affects the gravity of the alleged wrongful act or insult;

4. the requirement stipulated in section 232 that, if the accused satisfies the "ordinary person" test, it must also be shown that he or she acted "on the sudden and before there was time for his [or her] passion to cool";

5. the requirement stipulated in section 232 that an accused person may not claim the benefit of the defence of provocation if the victim was "doing anything that he [or she] had a legal right to do";

6. the differing roles of the judge and jury in relation to the defence of provocation, and the situations in which accused persons may lose the benefit of the defence because their victims were doing what they had a "legal right to do";

7. the extent to which self-induced intoxication may be a partial defence to a criminal;

8. the three "*Beard* Rules" that have traditionally been applied by the courts in determining the nature and scope of the defence in Canada;

9. the traditional view of the courts that intoxication may be a valid defence if it negatives the *mens rea* for specific intent offences (such as murder and robbery) but that it is not available as a defence to a charge of a basic or general intent offence (such as manslaughter, assault, or damage to property);

10. the recognition by the Supreme Court of Canada in the *Daviault* case (1994) that intoxication that produces a mental state akin to automatism or mental disorder should be considered an absolute defence even in the case of a basic or general intent offence, such as sexual assault; and

11. the enactment by Parliament of section 33.1 of the *Criminal Code* in response to the *Daviault* case and the establishment of a statutory rule that even the most extreme forms of intoxication will not excuse an accused person who is charged with a basic or general intent offence that involves an element of assault or interference with personal integrity.

PROVOCATION AND INTOXICATION

The defences of provocation and intoxication differ from other defences, such as automatism and mistake of fact, insofar as they are only *partial* defences. In other words, successful defences of provocation and intoxication may reduce the severity of a criminal charge but will not lead to an absolute acquittal. An accused person who successfully pleads provocation will be convicted of manslaughter rather than murder. When an accused person successfully raises the defence of intoxication, he or she will be acquitted of a more serious offence, such as murder or robbery, and will usually be convicted instead of a lesser crime, such as manslaughter or assault respectively.

PROVOCATION

THE GENERAL NATURE OF THE DEFENCE AND SECTION 232

The defence of **provocation** may be raised only in relation to a charge of murder and, if successful, its sole effect is to ensure that the accused is convicted of manslaughter rather than murder. In essence, the defence of provocation represents an attempt by the criminal law to show a little mercy to those individuals who lose their power of self-control in the face of highly stressful circumstances. Significantly, the courts have emphasized that the defence of provocation is available to accused persons despite the fact that they *intended* to kill their victim. In the *Oickle* case (1984), for example, the Appeal Division of the Nova Scotia Supreme Court ordered a new trial, in part because the trial judge had not made it clear to the jury that provocation may reduce murder to manslaughter even if it was found that the accused had an intention to kill.

The defence of provocation is defined, in considerable detail, by section 232 of the *Criminal Code*. Therefore, Canadian judges have been somewhat circumscribed in their attempts to develop the law relating to provocation. The provisions of section 232 are as follows:

(1)   Culpable homicide that otherwise would be murder may be reduced to manslaughter if the person who committed it did so in the heat of passion caused by sudden provocation.

(2)   A wrongful act or an insult that is of such a nature as to be sufficient to deprive an ordinary person of the power of self-control is provocation enough for the purposes of this section if the accused acted upon it on the sudden and before there was time for his passion to cool.

(3)   For the purposes of this section the questions

   (a)   whether a particular wrongful act or insult amounted to provocation, and

   (b)   whether the accused was deprived of the power of self-control by the provocation that he alleges he received,

are questions of fact, but no one shall be deemed to have given provocation to another by doing anything that he had a legal right to do, or by doing anything that the accused incited him to do in order to provide the accused with an excuse for causing death or bodily harm to any human being.

(4)   Culpable homicide that otherwise would be murder is not necessarily manslaughter by reason only that it was committed by a person who was being arrested illegally, but the fact that the illegality of the arrest was known to the accused may be evidence of provocation for the purpose of this section.

Undoubtedly, the defence of provocation is not based solely on the assertion that the accused person lost self control as a consequence of overwhelming anger. This point was strongly emphasized by the Supreme Court of Canada in the case of *Parent* (2001). The accused had shot his estranged wife after she had made a remark that caused him to feel "a hot flush rising." He claimed that, because of this intense anger, he "didn't know what he was doing any more." The trial judge appeared to instruct the jury that intense anger could—on its own account—reduce the charge of murder to manslaughter. However, Chief Justice McLachlin decisively rejected this proposition. Indeed, she stated that, although anger may "play a role in reducing murder to manslaughter in connection with the defence of provocation," it cannot be advanced as a "stand-alone defence." More specifically, the chief justice asserted that anger may "form part of the defence of provocation [only] when all the requirements of that defence are met":

(1) a wrongful act or insult that would have caused an ordinary person to be deprived of his or her self-control; (2) which is sudden and unexpected; (3) which in fact caused the accused to act in anger; (4) before having recovered his or her normal control....

The great significance of the Supreme Court's decision in *Parent* was underlined by the judgment of the Alberta Court of Appeal in the subsequent case of *Walle* (2007). This case made it very clear that an accused person cannot claim that extreme anger *per se* prevented him or her from possessing the necessary *mens rea* for murder (as specified in section 229(a) of the *Criminal Code*). In the words of Justice Paperny of the Court of Appeal:

> After *Parent*, anger felt by an accused, short of provocation, cannot negative the intent to commit murder. It is an irrelevant factor under s. 229(a) and it is an error of law to consider it, whether alone or in combination with other factors.

THE PROVOCATION MUST BE SUFFICIENT TO DEPRIVE AN "ORDINARY PERSON" OF THE POWER OF SELF-CONTROL

Section 232(2) of the *Criminal Code* stipulates that the wrongful act or insult that ostensibly caused the accused to lose his or her temper must be of such a nature as to be sufficient to deprive an ordinary person of the power of self-control. It appears, on the face of it, that the courts are required to apply a strictly objective test, in which the personal susceptibilities and individual characteristics of the individual accused person must be ignored. However, recent court decisions indicate that the *objective* test must be modified to take into account relevant aspects of the accused person's particular background and characteristics. Indeed, Justice Cory, in delivering the judgment of the majority of the Supreme Court of Canada in the case of *Thibert* (1996), aptly pointed out that

> ... the objective aspect would at first reading appear to be contradictory for, as legal writers have noted, the "ordinary" person does not kill. Yet, I think that the objective element should be taken as an attempt to weigh in the balance those very human frailties which sometimes lead people to act irrationally and impulsively against the need to protect society by discouraging acts of homicidal violence.

Since Justice Cory referred to the need to balance recognition of "human frailties" against the need to protect the public, it is clear that the application of the "ordinary person" test leaves a certain amount of discretion to the courts. In his view,

> ... if the test is to be applied sensibly and with sensitivity, then the ordinary person must be taken to be of the same age, and sex, and must share with the accused

such other factors as would give the act or insult in question a particular significance. In other words, all the relevant background circumstances should be considered. In the context of other cases, it may properly be found that other factors should be considered. It is how such an "ordinary" person with those characteristics would react to the situation which confronted the accused that should be used as the basis for considering the objective element. [emphasis added]

This statement by Justice Cory plainly demonstrates that, in applying the "ordinary person" test, the jury must consider any particular characteristic of the accused person *provided only that such a characteristic directly affects the gravity of any taunt or insult that is relied on by the accused as the basis for a defence of provocation*. For example, it may be presumed that the impotence of an accused person should be taken into account, when applying the "ordinary person" test, if the victim taunted the accused with insults relating to this particular form of sexual dysfunction.

The only particular characteristics that should not be considered in applying the ordinary person test are those that relate to "temperament" and "power of self-control." As Chief Justice Dickson pointed out in the Supreme Court of Canada's decision in the *Hill* case (1986),

> ... there is widespread agreement that the ordinary or reasonable person has a normal temperament and level of self-control. It follows that the ordinary person is not exceptionally excitable, pugnacious or in a state of drunkenness.

If this were not so, a particularly bad-tempered accused person would have a definite advantage over a "normal" accused person when he or she seeks to raise the defence of provocation.

In the *Thibert* case (1996), the Supreme Court of Canada recognized that the objective test should include some consideration of the "background relationship between the deceased and the accused." As Justice Cory notes,

> ... the wrongful act or insult must be one which could, in light of the past history of the relationship between the accused and the deceased, deprive an ordinary person, of the same age, sex, and sharing with the accused such other factors as would give the act or insult in question a special significance, of the power of self-control.

For example, in the *Thibert* case, the accused's wife had, on a prior occasion, planned to leave him for the deceased, but he managed to dissuade her from doing so. He apparently hoped to secure a similar outcome when his wife left him on a second occasion. When Thibert was attempting to talk to his wife alone, the deceased took hold of the wife's shoulders "in a proprietary and possessive manner" and moved her around in front of him. The deceased simultaneously taunted Thibert to shoot him and ultimately the latter did inflict a fatal wound.

In approaching the question of whether there was some evidence capable of meeting the requirements of the objective test, the Supreme Court held that, in light of the past history that had passed between Thibert and the deceased, a jury might well find that the deceased's actions immediately before his death were "taunting and insulting." Justice Cory went on to state that

> [i]t might be found that under the same circumstances, an ordinary person who was a married man, faced with the breakup of his marriage, would have been provoked by the actions of the deceased so as to cause him to lose his power of self-control.

It is important to bear in mind that, in order to meet the requirements of the "ordinary person" test, the alleged provocation must have a direct relationship to the individual characteristic on which the accused relies. For example, a racist insult would be considered to be of such a nature as to deprive an "ordinary person" of the power of self-control only if that person in fact identifies himself or herself as a member of the racial group against which the insult is directed. However, in applying the "ordinary person" test, a court may be required to take into account the impact of the deceased person's words or behaviour on someone with the particular racial or ethnic background of the accused person. In the case of *Nahar* (2004), for example, the accused was a Sikh who had immigrated to Canada from Punjab, India. He was charged with second degree murder after he killed his wife. The accused raised the defence of provocation and contended that the trial judge should take into account the impact of the victim's behaviour on a married man who had been brought up in the Sikh culture. In particular, the accused asserted that his wife had failed to meet the expectations held in relation to a married woman in the Sikh community. The accused stated that his wife "was attracted to the company of other men and in time she began to associate with a group of young Sikh women who did not accept the conventional norms of their community that preclude married women

from smoking cigarettes, consuming alcohol, and consorting with men" and that "she was defiant and disrespectful, choosing to do as she pleased." The wife had moved into a separate dwelling, and the fatal encounter with the accused had occurred when the latter had visited her in her apartment A bitter argument had ensued and the wife had tried to push the accused out of her apartment, telling him that she did not wish to talk to him and that the accused could not prevent her from seeing other men if she so wished. At this point, the accused fatally stabbed his wife in the chest and neck. The trial judge rejected the defence of provocation and the British Columbia Court of Appeal affirmed his conviction. However, the Court of Appeal stated that

> ... the ordinary person must have been one who shared Mr. Nahar's cultural background so that the implications of his being a Sikh, and having been raised in the Sikh tradition, were to be taken into account in measuring the gravity of the insult which is said to have caused him to stab his wife.
>
> That being so, the question the trial judge was required to consider was not merely whether an ordinary married man would be severely distressed by the behaviour attributed to Ms. Nahar and her conduct just before she was stabbed. It was rather whether, having regard for the cause and duration of the couple's troubled relationship, an insult that carried the same emotional impact for an ordinary young married man of the same cultural background as it apparently carried for Mr. Nahar, would cause such a man to lose his power of self-control.

Nevertheless, the Court of Appeal ruled that the trial judge had not acted unreasonably when he concluded that the Crown had proved beyond a reasonable doubt that, even taking into account the accused person's particular cultural background, the ordinary person would not have lost the power of self-control in the same circumstances.

Taking cultural background into account in the application of the "ordinary person" test may be seen by many Canadians as being highly problematic. The *Canadian Charter of Rights and Freedoms* enshrines values supporting the equality of men and women. When they are called upon to apply the "ordinary person" test in relation to the defence of provocation, should Canadian courts take into account cultural and religious beliefs that may deny the equality of men and women, and that may countenance the use of punitive measures against women who do not conform to norms that might be viewed as being discriminatory against women? It is highly significant that, in the case of *Humaid* (2006), the Ontario Court of Appeal expressly left open the question as to whether or not cultural and religious beliefs should be considered in the "ordinary person" inquiry. The Court did not need to decide the issue because, in this particular case, there was no air of reality to the defence.

However, the Court of Appeal made a number of noteworthy comments on the relevance of cultural and religious beliefs in the context of a provocation defence. Humaid had been convicted of first degree murder following the brutal stabbing of his wife. The jury evidently believed that the killing was planned and deliberate and not the product of the spontaneous loss of control in response to sudden and unexpected provocation.

In delivering the judgment of the Court of Appeal, Justice Doherty addressed various elements of the accused's argument that his cultural and religious beliefs should be taken into account in applying the "ordinary person" test. Humaid had asserted that the last words uttered by his wife led him to believe that she had been sexually unfaithful to him. He then called an expert witness who presented evidence concerning the religion and culture that Humaid claimed to espouse. The expert stated that the

> culture was male dominated and placed great significance on the concept of family honour. Infidelity, particularly infidelity by a female member of a family, was considered a very serious violation of the family's honour and worthy of harsh punishment by the male members of the family.

The Court of Appeal ruled that, even if this expert evidence could properly be considered in the application of the "ordinary person" test (an issue that it declined to decide in this case), it was nevertheless irrelevant to Humaid's case because there was no evidence that Humaid himself actually subscribed to the beliefs described by the expert witness. Justice Doherty stated:

> Assuming that an accused's religious and cultural beliefs that are antithetical to fundamental Canadian values such as the equality of men and women can ever have a role to play at the "ordinary person" phase of the provocation inquiry, the expert evidence could not assist this appellant. There was no evidence that the appellant shared the religious and cultural beliefs ... [described by the expert witness].

The Court of Appeal also identified a second issue that was fatal to Humaid's claim of provocation:

namely, that there was no evidence that Humaid acted in the heat of passion in response to sudden provocation. Rather, Humaid appeared to be suggesting that his culture and religion would, in some way, lead him to believe that killing the victim was an appropriate response to her alleged infidelity. Justice Doherty explained this aspect of the case in the following manner:

> A provocation claim rests on the assertion that an accused in a state of extreme anger lost his ability to fully control his actions and acted while in that state. Provocation does not shield an accused who has not lost self-control, but has instead acted out of a sense of revenge or a culturally driven sense of the appropriate response to someone else's misconduct. An accused who acts out of a sense of retribution fuelled by a belief system that entitles a husband to punish his wife's perceived infidelity has not lost control, but has taken action that, according to his belief system, is a justified response to the situation....
>
> The thrust of [the expert witness's] ... evidence is not that ... men [sharing the cultural and religious beliefs described by the expert] will lose control and act in a rage when confronted with their wives' infidelities, but rather that their religious and cultural beliefs dictate that wives who are unfaithful deserve to suffer significant consequences. If an accused relies on religious and cultural beliefs like those described by ... [the expert witness] to support a provocation defence, the trial judge must carefully instruct the jury as to the distinction between a homicide committed by one who has lost control and a homicide committed by one whose cultural and religious beliefs lead him to believe that homicide is an appropriate response to the perceived misconduct of the victim. Only the former engages the defence of provocation. The latter provides a motive for murder.

Finally, the Court of Appeal duly noted that the *Humaid* case did not arise from a situation in which there had been a specific insult to the accused's religion and culture (for example, a racial or ethnic slur). In certain circumstances, it would be very appropriate to regard such insults as being likely to cause an ordinary person, with the accused's cultural and/or religious background, to lose the power of self-control within the meaning of section 232. However, there was no such insult in *Humaid*'s case.

THE RULE THAT THE ACCUSED MUST ACT IN THE HEAT OF THE MOMENT

Section 232(2) also provides that, in order for a defence of provocation to be successful, the accused must have acted upon the alleged provocation "on the sudden and before there was time for his passion to cool." In determining this issue, a *subjective* approach must be applied. In other words, the defence of provocation will not be successful merely because the accused establishes that the alleged provocation was sufficient to "deprive an ordinary person of the power of self-control." On the contrary, in order for the defence to be successful, it must also be established that *this particular defendant* was subjected to sudden provocation and acted in the heat of passion.

In relation to this element of the defence of provocation, juries must consider such subjective factors as, for example, the extent to which an accused person's state of intoxication caused him or her to lose the power of self-control. In the case of *Haight* (1976), for example, Justice Martin of the Ontario Court of Appeal said:

> Where there is evidence of provocation proper for the consideration of the jury, the jury is required to pass upon two questions:
>
> (1) whether there is a wrongful act or insult that is of such a nature as to be sufficient to deprive an ordinary person of the power of self-control, and
>
> (2) whether the accused was actually deprived of his power of self-control by the provocation.

The first question is to be decided in accordance with an objective standard, with reference to the ordinary person and without reference to any characteristics or condition peculiar to the accused. *The second question imports a subjective test in which it is proper and necessary for the jury in deciding whether or not the accused was actually deprived of his power of self-control to consider his particular characteristics and condition, for example, his condition with respect to drunkenness.* [emphasis added]

In light of the requirement that the accused act in response to **sudden provocation**, it is clear that the defence is not available to an accused person who initiates a fatal altercation with the victim. For example, in the case of *Salamon* (1959), the accused waited for the victim to return home and launched a bitter argument, which led to violence. After the fight was broken up by the victim's husband, the victim went into the bathroom to clean herself up. Salamon then entered the bathroom and called the victim "a dirty name." The victim answered in a similarly insulting manner and Salamon shot her. When he was charged with murder, Salamon claimed the benefit of the defence of provocation. However, the Supreme Court upheld his conviction of murder and pointed out that there was no suddenness in alleged provocation by the victim. In this respect, Justice Fauteux stated that

> [o]n this evidence, [the] appellant cannot justify or excuse his actions in saying that he was facing a situation characterized with suddenness, unexpectedness or lack of premonition. He had and kept the initiative of the situation in which he found himself. There was no sudden provocation on the part of Joyce Alexander causing sudden retaliation on his part.

The *Friesen* case (1995) provides an example of a situation in which it was determined by the courts that there had been time for the accused's passion to cool after sudden provocation. Friesen had killed a friend with a builder's nail gun after an alleged act of sexual provocation by the victim. Friesen claimed the defence of provocation when he was charged with first degree murder. However, the evidence established that, after the alleged provocation, the accused had left the victim and gone to the garage, where he connected a builder's nail gun to a compressor. Obviously, this took a fair amount of time to accomplish. He then returned to the house and shot the victim with "dozens of nails" from the gun. Significantly, at the time of the shooting, the victim was asleep. Friesen's conviction of murder was upheld by the Alberta Court of Appeal. In the view of the Court, no reasonable jury could have found that there had been provocation within the meaning of section 232. According to Justice Côté,

For a defence of provocation, the accused must have acted on the sudden and before there was time for passion to cool.

Cartoon by Elizabeth Carefoot

The accused took some time to go upstairs and out to the garage, to rig up the nail gun and all its power sources, and then to deploy them downstairs in the family room next to the victim. So it is very hard to think that that could be "on the sudden and before there was time for his passion to cool."...

The accused says that the victim was asleep when he shot him.... The victim knew all about nail guns, and that the accused had no proper use for one then and there. One cannot sneak up on a person awake, if one carries a nail gun trailing a long air hose charged by a compressor whose motor is running. Yet the accused says that he left the victim in a state of mental and physical sexual excitement. So if the accused's story about provocation was true, the victim went from such excitement to sleep before the shooting. That process would surely take time as well. So "there was time for his passion to cool."

THE MEANING OF "LEGAL RIGHT" IN SECTION 232(3)

Section 232(3) provides that "no one shall be deemed to have given provocation to another by doing anything that he had a legal right to do, or by doing anything that the accused incited him to do in order to provide the accused with an excuse for causing death or bodily harm to any human being." Although the basic intent of Parliament is clear in relation to this statutory provision, there is some question as to what is meant by "legal right" in this context. Canadian courts have, understandably, interpreted this phrase very restrictively. For example, in *Galgay* (1972), the accused was charged with the murder of his former girlfriend. There was evidence that the victim had caused Galgay to lose the power of self-control when she told him that she was going to leave him because he was "not going to be any good," he was "drinking all the time," and he was "stealing." The trial judge instructed the jury that the victim had a legal right to leave the accused and to tell him that she was going to leave him. Galgay was convicted of murder. However, the Ontario Court of Appeal ordered a new trial on the basis that the trial judge had misinterpreted what is now section 232(3). Justice Brooke asked the following question,

> What is the meaning of the term "legal right" in the provision of the section? Surely, it does not include all legal conduct not specifically prohibited by law. *The absence of a remedy against doing or saying something or the absence of a specific legal prohibition in that regard does not mean or imply that there is a legal right to so act.* There may be no legal remedy for an insult

said or done in private but that is not because of legal right. The section distinguishes legal right from wrongful act or insult and the proviso of the section ought not to be interpreted to license insult or wrongful act done or spoken under the cloak of legal right.

> One has a right to do and to say those things which one is specifically authorized by law to say or to do, such as a Sheriff proceeding to execute a warrant of the court. One has a right to do and to say those things which arise in the ordinary course of one's affairs and relationships. *But in neither case does the right extend to speaking or acting so as to insult the other person.* [emphasis added]

In the *Galgay* case (1972), the evidence was that the victim insulted the accused by denigrating his character. She certainly had every right to leave Galgay, but she did not, within the meaning of section 232(3), have the "legal right" to insult him. However, as the Nova Scotia Court of Appeal pointed out in the *Young* case (1993), merely terminating a relationship with someone cannot, on its own, be considered an "insult" or "wrongful act" that is capable of constituting provocation under section 232.

The approach adopted by the Ontario Court of Appeal in the *Galgay* case (1972) was later endorsed by the Supreme Court of Canada in *Thibert* (1996). As Justice Cory noted, in delivering the majority judgment in Thibert (1996),

> ... [T]he defence of provocation is open to someone who is "insulted." The words or act put forward as provocation need not be words or act [*sic*] which are specifically prohibited by the law.

One may well ask in what circumstances are the courts likely to find that the victim had a "legal right" to do what he or she did within the meaning of section 232(3)? A good example of such a situation is the case of *Louison* (1975), in which the accused was charged with the murder of a taxi driver who had picked him up. The victim had been brutally beaten to death with a hammer. It appears that the accused had pulled a knife on the victim and forced him into the trunk of the taxi. After keeping the victim in the trunk for a couple of hours, Louison decided to give him some air. The deceased hit the accused in the back with a hammer. However, Louison wrested the hammer away from the somewhat enfeebled victim and began to rain blows upon his head. When the body was discovered, the hammer was embedded in the victim's skull. Somewhat surprisingly, Louison advanced provocation as one of his defences. The accused was nevertheless convicted, and he appealed to the Saskatchewan Court of Appeal. One of the reasons given for rejecting Louison's appeal concerned the fact that the deceased had been acting in self-defence and, therefore, had a "legal right" to do what he did within the meaning of section 232(3). Chief Justice Culliton stated that

> [i]t seems to me that in a case of self-induced provocation s. [232] must be given a reasonable interpretation; for example—in an attempted rape, if the victim in resisting the assault should stick her finger in the eye of the assailant causing him injury and severe pain and he thereupon killed her, I think her act in this respect would be construed as something she had a legal right to do and would not be a wrongful act within s. [232]. Similarly, where the pilot of a plane is being held at gunpoint by a hijacker and if he should strike the hijacker with a fist or a wrench whereupon the hijacker shot him, I would not think such action would be considered a wrongful act within s. [232] of the *Criminal Code*.

Predictably, Louison's subsequent appeal to the Supreme Court was also rejected.

THE DIFFERING ROLES OF JUDGE AND JURY IN CANADA WHERE PROVOCATION IS RAISED

Section 232(3) provides that the determination of certain issues must remain within the exclusive realm of the jury. More specifically, the *Code* states that "whether a particular wrongful act or insult amounted to provocation" and "whether the accused was deprived of the power of self-control by the provocation that he alleges he received" are questions of fact. As such, the trial judge must leave such issues to the jury. However, the Supreme Court of Canada has, on a number of occasions, ruled that trial judges still have a duty to determine whether there is sufficient evidence of provocation to justify submitting the issue to the jury. As Justice Cory stated in delivering the majority judgment of the Supreme Court of Canada in *Thibert* (1996),

> Before the defence of provocation is left to the jury, the trial judge must be satisfied (a) that there is *some* evidence to suggest that the particular wrongful act or insult alleged by the accused would have caused an ordinary person to be deprived of self-control, and (b) that there is some evidence showing that the accused was actually deprived of his or her self-control by that act or insult. This threshold test can be readily met, so long as there is some evidence that the objective and

subjective elements may be satisfied. If there is, the defence must then be left with the jury.

In other words, trial judges are under a duty not to submit the issue of provocation to the jury unless they are satisfied that there is *some* evidence capable of raising a reasonable doubt in the mind of the jurors. However, the trial judge's role is not to weigh the sufficiency of such evidence; that is a matter entirely for the jury to decide. The trial judge's function in this respect is merely to make a *threshold* determination as to whether there is any evidence that could justify a reasonable jury coming to the conclusion that the accused person was subject to provocation as defined in section 232. In this respect, therefore, provocation is no different from any other criminal law defence. There is simply a requirement that the accused satisfy the *evidentiary burden of proof* before the defence may be considered by the trier of fact.

What is the duty of the trial judge when the accused person does not advance provocation as his or her primary defence in a murder trial? This situation may arise when the accused person is seeking to gain an outright acquittal by asserting that he or she acted in self-defence. Since provocation is only a *partial* defence to a charge of murder, it makes very good sense from the accused person's point of view to focus his or her trial strategy on claiming self-defence, which is, of course, a *complete* defence to a criminal charge. It is clear that, if there is sufficient evidence to give an air of reality to the defence, the trial judge is under a duty to instruct the jury to consider provocation—even if this is not the primary defence that is relied upon by the accused. This is exactly what happened in *Gill* (2009). In this case, the Ontario Court of Appeal held that, even if the accused person denies that one of the elements of provocation existed at the time of the homicide, the trial judge is nevertheless under a duty to put the defence to the jury if he or she concludes that, on the evidence presented, a reasonable jury might acquit the accused of murder and convict him or her instead of manslaughter.

Gill asserted that, while he was originally angered by the actions of the victim, fear subsequently replaced anger when the victim wielded a beer bottle and uttered challenging words. Gill, therefore, contended that, fearful as he was, he stabbed the victim in a reflex action of self-defence. At trial, Gill denied that he was affected by anger at the time of the stabbing. The trial judge put self-defence to the jury but declined to instruct them on the defence of provocation. The jury rejected the proposition that Gill acted in self-defence and convicted him of second degree murder.

Gill appealed against his conviction to the Ontario Court of Appeal, which ordered a new trial. The Court of Appeal ruled that the trial judge should have instructed the jury to consider the defence of provocation. In the words of the Court:

> … [P]articularly where a jury is invited to reject parts of a person's evidence that could be relevant to a proposed defence, it will be necessary for the trial judge to assess whether sufficient evidence will remain based on which a properly instructed jury acting reasonably could acquit if some or all the evidence relevant to a particular defence is rejected.…
>
> We agree that there will be some cases in which the appellant's disavowal of one of the elements of a defence will preclude the availability of the defence based on the air of reality threshold. However, this is not one of those cases. In challenging [Gill's] evidence that he was afraid at the time he stabbed [the victim], the Crown suggested, both in cross-examination and in his closing address to the jury, that the appellant's true emotion was anger. If the jury rejected the appellant's evidence that he was afraid, there was evidence capable of supporting an inference that he was angry. Similarly, there was evidence capable of supporting an inference that the appellant acted in the heat of passion or as a result of a loss of self-control. It was also open to the jury to conclude that the appellant was both frightened and angry.

The Court, therefore, concluded that, even though Gill had disavowed the notion that he was acting primarily under the influence of extreme anger, it would still have been possible for a reasonable jury to disregard this aspect of Gill's evidence and to find that there was provocation within the meaning of section 232. This case is a good example of the sheer complexity of the task facing a trial judge when the accused person advances more than one defence in response to a murder charge.

INTOXICATION

HISTORICAL OVERVIEW OF THE DEFENCE

Until 1996, the *Criminal Code* made no mention of the defence of intoxication. Prior to this date, the development of the defence of intoxication was exclusively a matter of common law; in other words, the nature of the defence was shaped by judges rather than by Parliament.

Historically, intoxication was treated by English courts as being an *aggravating* (rather than a *mitigating*) factor in a criminal prosecution. However, during the course of the nineteenth century, the English courts gradually started to relax their approach and fashioned a compromise, in which intoxication came to be regarded as a partial defence to most of the more serious criminal charges. It was considered a partial defence because it would operate to reduce the severity of the charge against the accused (e.g., from murder to manslaughter or from robbery to assault). Traditionally, the English courts took the view that intoxication should not be available as a *complete* defence to criminal charges. As we shall see, this view was based on the fundamental legal principle that intoxication *may* be a defence to a charge in which the Crown is required to prove *specific intent* in order to obtain a conviction (as in murder or robbery) but is *never* available where the offence concerned is considered to be one in which the Crown has to prove only *general or basic intent* (as in manslaughter or assault).

Until 1994, English and Canadian courts applied basically the same principles when dealing with the defence of intoxication. These principles were generally known as the **Beard** Rules, taking their name from the case in which they were first articulated. However, in the case of *Daviault* (1994), the majority of the justices of the Supreme Court broke away from the traditional approach to intoxication by declaring that there may be circumstances in which intoxication should be considered a *complete* defence after all. More specifically, they took the view that, if a defendant is charged with an offence of general (or basic) intent such as sexual assault, intoxication may be a valid defence if it is so extreme as to produce a "state akin to automatism or insanity." This, of course, represented a significant change in the law, because previously intoxication was considered to be an irrelevant factor whenever the accused was charged with an offence of general (or basic) intent.

In response to the *Daviault* case (1994), Parliament moved, for the first time, to pass legislation dealing with intoxication as a defence to a criminal charge, and section 33.1 was added to the *Criminal Code* (coming into force in 1996). Section 33.1 states that intoxication, however extreme it may be, will not be accepted as a defence to a charge of any general (or basic) intent offence that "includes as an element an assault or any other interference or threat of interference with the bodily integrity of another person."

In delivering the judgment of the majority of the justices of the Supreme Court of Canada in the leading case of *Daley* (2007), Justice Bastarache provided a succinct overview of the current status of intoxication as a defence to a criminal charge:

> Our case law suggests there are three legally relevant degrees of intoxication. First, there is what we might call *"mild"* *intoxication*. This is where there is alcohol-induced relaxation of both inhibitions and socially acceptable behaviour. This has never been accepted as a factor or excuse in determining whether the accused possessed the requisite *mens rea*. Second, there is what we might call *"advanced"* *intoxication*. This occurs where there is intoxication to the point where the accused lacks specific intent, to the extent of an impairment of the accused's foresight of the consequences of his or her act sufficient to raise a reasonable doubt about the requisite *mens rea*....
>
> A defence based on this level of intoxication applies only to specific intent offences....
>
> The third and final degree of legally relevant intoxication is *extreme intoxication akin to automatism*, which negates voluntariness and thus is a complete defence to criminal responsibility.... [S]uch a defence would be extremely rare, and by operation of s. 33.1 of the *Criminal Code*, limited to non-violent types of offences. [emphasis added]

In order to fully comprehend the somewhat complex nature of the law concerning the intoxication defence in Canada, it is necessary to examine it within an historical context. For this purpose, the analysis of the defence of intoxication will be undertaken in three sections: (1) the evolution of the *Beard* Rules from 1920 to the present day; (2) the decision of the Supreme Court of Canada in the landmark case of *Daviault* (1994); and (3) the enactment of section 33.1 of the *Criminal Code* and its aftermath.

The Evolution of the *Beard* Rules: 1920 to the Present Day

The classic authority concerning the defence of intoxication is the English case of *Beard* (1920) decided by the House of Lords. In this case, Lord Birkenhead articulated three rules that rapidly came to be regarded as the authoritative statement of the nature and limits of the intoxication defence. *As modified by subsequent judicial interpretations in Canada*, the three rules may be summarized in the following manner:

1. If intoxication induces a mental disorder ("disease of the mind") and renders the accused "not criminally responsible" within the meaning of section 16 of the *Criminal Code*, he or she must be acquitted as being "not criminally responsible on account of mental disorder" (NCRMD).

2. If intoxication prevents a defendant from forming the intent necessary for conviction of a crime of *specific* intent, he or she must be acquitted. However, intoxication can never be a defence to a charge of a crime of *general* (or *basic*) intent.

3. If intoxication falls short of preventing the accused from forming the intent necessary for conviction of a crime of *specific* intent, it does not constitute a valid defence (in particular, if the accused formed the necessary intent, it is irrelevant that the intoxication made it more difficult for him or her to control his or her actions).

The *Beard* Rules were enthusiastically endorsed by the Supreme Court of Canada in the case of *George* (1960) and their authority in Canada was later reaffirmed, without any qualification, in *Leary* (1977). The *George* case (1960) furnishes an excellent illustration of the application of the *Beard* Rules to a charge of robbery. The evidence indicated that the accused had visited the home of an 84-year-old man called Averis and demanded money from him. He then beat Averis severely with his bare fists, broke Averis's nose, and caused numerous other serious bodily injuries to the victim. He then stole the sum of $22. The victim indicated that George had threatened to kill him unless he gave him money. George's main defence was that he was in a severe state of intoxication at the time of the alleged offence. At his trial, the judge acquitted the accused on the following basis:

> You are being acquitted not because you didn't do it—there is no doubt in my mind that you did do it—you are being acquitted because I have found that you were so drunk on the night in question that you were unable to form an intent to do it.

The Crown appealed the accused's acquittal. The appeal was unsuccessful in the British Columbia Court of Appeal but was ultimately successful before the Supreme Court of Canada. Essentially, the Supreme Court affirmed the accused's acquittal on the charge of robbery. Since robbery is a **specific intent** offence, drunkenness may be a *partial* defence. Therefore, the Court judged that the accused had been properly acquitted. However, every charge of robbery necessarily includes a charge of assault (in essence, a robbery normally involves both an assault and a theft), and an accused person may always be convicted of any lesser offence that is considered to be included in the charge upon which he or she is tried. The Court pointed out that a simple assault is a crime of **general (or basic) intent**, and the *Beard* Rules dictate that drunkenness cannot be a valid defence to such a charge. Therefore, the Supreme Court entered a verdict of guilty of common assault against George.

Justice Ritchie offered an explanation for the distinction that the *Beard* Rules draw between **basic (or general)** and **specific intent** offences:

> In considering the question of *mens rea*, a distinction is to be drawn between "intention" as applied to acts done to achieve an immediate end on the one hand and acts done with a specific and ulterior motive and intention of furthering or achieving an illegal object on the other hand. Illegal acts of the former kind are done "intentionally" in the sense that they are not done by accident or through honest mistake, but acts of the latter kind are the product of preconception and are deliberate steps taken towards an illegal goal. The former acts may be purely physical products of momentary passion, whereas the latter involve the mental process of formulating a specific intent. A man, far advanced in drink, may intentionally strike his fellow in the former sense at a time when his mind is so befogged with liquor as to be unable to formulate a specific intent in the latter sense.

The various issues surrounding the NCRMD defence have already been addressed in Chapter 8; therefore, the application of the first *Beard* Rule will not be considered here. At this point, it will be sufficient to emphasize that the ingestion of alcohol and other drugs may, in certain circumstances, induce a serious mental disorder, including a **psychosis**. For example, the Manitoba Court of Appeal ruled in *Malcolm* (1989) that *delirium tremens* constitutes a "disease of the mind" for the purposes of section 16 of the *Code* and, in *Mailloux* (1985), the Ontario Court of Appeal endorsed the view that a cocaine-induced "toxic psychosis" could also be considered a "disease of the mind." More recently, in *Fontaine* (2004), the Supreme Court of Canada permitted a defence of NCRMD to be advanced by an accused person on the basis of an alleged cannabis-induced psychosis. However, these types of cases will be dealt with according to the provisions of section 16 of the *Criminal Code* rather than according to the legal rules governing the defence of intoxication. We shall now turn our attention to the application of the second and third *Beard* Rules.

THE CRITICAL DISTINCTION BETWEEN CRIMES OF SPECIFIC AND GENERAL (BASIC) INTENT

The initial question that must be answered before a court may apply the second and third *Beard* Rules is whether or not the crime charged is one of specific or general (basic) intent. If the crime is one of specific intent, intoxication may be a partial defence but, if the crime is one of general (basic) intent, then intoxication will not in any way absolve the accused of criminal responsibility for his or her actions. One of the most frequently quoted statements of the distinction between crimes of general (basic) and specific intent is contained in the judgment of Justice McIntyre of the Supreme Court in the case of *Bernard* (1988):

> *The general intent offence is one in which the only intent involved relates solely to the performance of the act in question with no further ulterior intent or purpose.* The minimal intent to apply force in the offence of common assault affords an example. *A specific intent offence is one which involves the performance of the actus reus, coupled with an intent or purpose going beyond the mere performance of the questioned act.* Striking a blow or administering poison with the intent to kill, or assault with intent to maim or wound, are examples of such offences. [emphasis added]

In the *Daley* case (2007), Justice Bastarache succinctly summarized this distinction by stating that "specific intent offences require the mind to focus on an objective further to the immediate one at hand, while general intent offences require only a conscious doing of the prohibited act."

Canadian courts have declared that the following offences may be considered to be crimes of **specific intent**:

- murder
- robbery
- breaking and entering with intent to commit an indictable offence
- theft
- assault with intent to resist arrest
- possession of a weapon for a purpose dangerous to the public peace
- touching a child for a sexual purpose
- attempting to commit an offence

On the other hand, the following offences have been declared to be crimes of **general or basic intent**:

- manslaughter
- assault
- assault causing bodily harm
- sexual assault
- mischief (damage to property)
- pointing a firearm
- impaired driving
- aggravated assault
- unlawfully causing bodily harm

The distinction between offences of specific and general (basic) intent has been criticized by many. Indeed, Chief Justice Dickson, in a dissenting judgment in the case of *Bernard* (1988), argued that the distinction should be abolished for the purpose of applying the defence of intoxication. In his view, the distinction serves as "an artificial device whereby evidence, otherwise relevant, is excluded from the jury's consideration." However, the call for the abolition of the distinction has been soundly rejected by the majority of the justices of the Supreme Court in both the *Bernard* (1988) and the *Daviault* (1994) cases.

In *Daviault* (1994), Justice Cory, with whom a majority of the justices of the Supreme Court of Canada agreed, curtly stated that "it is now well established by this court that there are two categories of offences … those requiring a specific intent and others which call for nothing more than general intent." However, in the earlier case of *Bernard* (1988), Justice McIntyre provided a more detailed rationale for maintaining the distinction in Canada:

> The distinction is not an artificial one nor does it rest upon any legal fiction. There is a world of difference between the man who in frustration or anger strikes out at his neighbour in a public house with no particular purpose or intent in mind, other than to perform the act of striking, and the man who strikes a similar blow with intent to cause death or injury. This difference is best illustrated by a consideration of the relationship between murder and manslaughter. He who kills intending to kill or cause bodily harm is guilty of murder, whereas he who has killed by the same act without such intent is convicted of manslaughter. The proof of the specific intent, that is, to kill or to cause bodily harm, is necessary in murder because the crime of murder is incomplete without it. No such intent is required, however, for the offence of manslaughter because it forms no part of the offence, manslaughter simply being an unlawful killing without the intent required for murder. The relevance of intoxication which could deprive an accused of the capacity to form the necessary specific intent in murder, and its irrelevance in the crime of manslaughter can readily be seen.

Whatever its merits and logical deficiencies may be, it seems that the pigeonholing of offences into crimes of either specific or general intent is deeply embedded in Canadian criminal law, and its existence will continue to have critical consequences for the manner in which the courts will apply the defence of intoxication.

APPLYING THE SECOND *BEARD* RULE TO CRIMES OF SPECIFIC INTENT

Once it has been established that the offence with which the accused has been charged is a crime of *specific* intent, the next matter to be considered is the nature of the circumstances in which intoxication may serve as a partial defence to such a charge. In formulating the second rule in the *Beard* case, Lord Birkenhead stated that

> … evidence of drunkenness which renders the accused incapable of forming the specific intent essential to constitute the crime should be taken into consideration with the other facts proved in order to determine whether or not he had this intent.

There is a major difficulty with the manner in which the second *Beard* Rule was articulated by Lord Birkenhead. The problem stems from his use of words that focus on the accused's *capacity* to form the specific intent required, rather than the accused's *actual intent* at the time of the alleged offence. Under the second *Beard* Rule, if the accused person's defence raises a reasonable doubt as to his or her capacity to form the specific intent that must be proved by the Crown, there is no question that the accused must be acquitted. However, it by no means follows that an accused person who was *capable* of forming such a specific intent did, *in fact*, form such intent. In light of all the circumstances of the case, there may very well be a reasonable doubt as to whether the accused actually formed the requisite specific intent. Unfortunately, a literal interpretation of the second *Beard* Rule would lead to a conviction of the accused person in such circumstances because the only ground for acquittal mentioned by Lord Birkenhead is the accused's *lack of capacity to form the intent*.

In the case of *Robinson* (1996), the Supreme Court of Canada held that the *Beard* rules, as written by Lord Birkenhead, violated both sections 7 and 11(d) of the *Charter* because they required a jury to convict an accused person even if they had a reasonable doubt about his or her actual intent. As Justice Bastarache pointed out in the later case of *Daley* (2007):

> An accused who was not so intoxicated as to lack capacity to form the intent may nevertheless not have exercised that capacity and formed the specific intent. The ultimate inquiry is always whether the accused possessed actual intent.

In *Robinson* (1996), Chief Justice Lamer clearly articulated the manner in which trial judges should instruct juries in relation to the second *Beard* Rule:

> ... [B]efore a trial judge is required by law to charge the jury on intoxication, he or she must be satisfied that the effect of the intoxication was such that its effect *might* have impaired the accused's foresight of consequences sufficient to raise a reasonable doubt. Once a judge is satisfied that this threshold is met, he or she must then make it clear to the jury that the issue before them is *whether the Crown has satisfied them beyond a reasonable doubt that the accused had the requisite intent*. In the case of murder the issue is whether the accused intended to kill or cause bodily harm with the foresight that the likely consequence was death. [emphasis added]

In *Lemky* (1996), a case involving a murder charge, the Supreme Court emphasized that, as with any other defence, the accused must satisfy the evidentiary burden of proof before the defence of intoxication may be considered by the trier of fact (whether it be judge or jury). As Justice McLachlin said,

> If the real question is whether the accused was prevented by drunkenness from actually foreseeing the consequences of his or her act, it follows that the threshold for putting the defence to the jury must be evidence sufficient to permit a reasonable inference that the accused did not in fact foresee those consequences. While capacity and intent may be related, it is possible to envisage cases where evidence which falls short of establishing that the accused lacked the capacity to form intent, may still leave the jury with a reasonable doubt that, when the offence was committed, the accused in fact foresaw the likelihood of death.

The correct application of the second *Beard* Rule, following its modification by the Supreme Court in

Robinson, was well illustrated by the case of *Daley* (2007). The accused was charged with the first degree murder of his common-law wife. After a night of drinking and partying, Daley returned home in the early hours of the morning to find that his house was locked. His neighbours heard him swearing and attempting to enter both the house and some vehicles that were parked outside. Daley's common-law wife was later found stabbed to death and Daley was discovered drunk in a bedroom.

At his trial, Daley claimed that, owing to his alcohol consumption, he had no memory of what happened after he returned to the house at 5 a.m. A pharmacologist testified for the defence and described the effects of alcohol on the "human body, brain functioning and behaviour." His testimony was that one may lose one's memory and experience impaired judgment owing to the ingestion of significant amounts of alcohol but he also said that one would "still be able to form ideas and carry out complex tasks," describing such a person as being in a state of "alcoholic amnesia." Daley was convicted by the jury of second degree murder. His appeal against conviction was rejected by the Saskatchewan Court of Appeal and he further appealed to the Supreme Court of Canada, which, by a 5–4 majority, dismissed Daley's appeal.

The crucial question raised in the appeal to the Supreme Court of Canada was whether or not the trial judge's instructions to the jury were correct. The trial judge had made it very clear to the jury that the critical issue in the trial was whether Daley had the intent to kill the victim. He told them that

> [i]ntoxication that causes a person to cast off restraint and to act in a manner which he would not act if sober is no excuse for committing an offence if he had the state of mind required to commit the offence. *Murder is not committed if Wayne Joseph Daley either lacked the intent to kill or the intent to cause bodily harm knowing it was likely to cause the death* of Teanda Manchur.
>
> To prove murder, *Crown counsel must prove beyond a reasonable doubt that Wayne Daley had the intent to kill or to cause bodily harm, knowing it was likely to cause death. To decide whether he had that intent you should take into account the evidence about his consumption of alcohol along with all the rest of the evidence which throws light on his state of mind* at the time the offence was allegedly committed. [emphasis added]

Justice Bastarache found that, viewed as a whole, the trial judge's instructions to the jury were appropriate in the circumstances. The jury were clearly instructed that they must acquit Daley of murder if they had a reasonable doubt whether he actually formed the intent to kill the victim (s. 229(a)(i)) or to inflict bodily harm with the foresight that the likely consequence was her death (s. 229(a)(ii)). In particular, the jury would have been very much aware that the critical issue was whether Daley's level of intoxication was so high that it prevented him from foreseeing the consequences of his actions.

Justice Bastarache rejected the suggestion that the trial judge had failed to instruct the jury as to the full implications of the expert witness's testimony. In effect, the expert witness had not clearly stated that Daley did not foresee the consequences of his actions, following his ingestion of alcohol. The expert had indicated that it is possible for an individual to lose his or her memory of events as a consequence of intoxication but he also stated that one might "still be able to form ideas and carry out complex tasks." According to Justice Bastarache, "[T]he link between loss of the capacity for judgment and evaluation of appropriateness and loss of the ability to foresee the consequences of one's actions was never clearly addressed" by the expert witness:

> It is questionable whether loss of the capacity to form judgments and judge the appropriateness of one's action equates with loss of the ability to foresee the consequences of one's actions.... [I]t is hard to accept that a person, here stabbing someone in the side, would not be able to realize such an action could kill. Expert evidence that the intoxication was such that one could not judge the appropriateness of one's actions can hardly be equated to evidence of intoxication sufficient to establish the incapacity alleged to have existed here.

Viewing the trial judge's instructions as a whole, and taking a "functional approach" to the task of deciding their adequacy, Justice Bastarache concluded that they were correct and that the jury were directed to consider the appropriate issue—namely, whether Daley foresaw the consequences of his actions when he stabbed his common-law wife.

APPLYING THE THIRD *BEARD* RULE

The third Rule, articulated by Lord Birkenhead in the *Beard* case (1920), reads as follows:

> ... [E]vidence of drunkenness falling short of a *proved incapacity* in the accused to *form the intent* necessary to constitute the crime, and merely establishing that

his mind was affected by drink so that he more readily gave way to some violent passion, does not rebut the presumption that a man intends the natural consequences of his acts. [emphasis added]

Basically, this Rule has been interpreted in modern times to mean that, if the accused cannot raise a reasonable doubt as to whether he or she formed the intent necessary for proof of the specific offence charged, intoxication is no defence. In particular, it is irrelevant that the accused claims that intoxication caused him or her to lose the power of self-control and engage in behaviour that he or she would not have committed if sober.

The original wording of the third *Beard* Rule raises many difficulties. For example, the use of the words "proved incapacity" might well suggest that the accused is under the burden of proving the defence of intoxication. In the case of *Malanik* (1952), the Supreme Court of Canada ruled that the word "proved" should be dropped from the Rule and it should be made clear to the jury that the accused only has to raise a reasonable doubt in order to be successful in advancing the defence. Another difficulty stems from the use of the word "incapacity." As we saw in the previous section, the Supreme Court of Canada ruled in *Robinson* (1996) that the real question is not whether the accused had the capacity to form the specific intent in question but whether he or she actually formed this intent. Finally, the third *Beard* Rule contains the phrase "does not rebut the presumption that a man intends the natural consequences of his acts." This is problematic because it might suggest to a jury that they should *presume* that every sane or sober person intends the natural consequences of his or her actions and that there is some onus on the accused to prove that intoxication prevented him or her from having such an intent. In both the *Seymour* (1996) and the *Robinson* (1996) cases, the Supreme Court of Canada took great pains to counter such an interpretation of this element of the third *Beard* Rule. For example, in *Robinson*, Chief Justice Lamer stated on behalf of the Court that he wished to "take the opportunity ... to hold that the presumption of intent to which *Beard* refers, should only be interpreted and referred to as a common sense and logical inference that the jury can but is not compelled to make." Similarly, in *Seymour*, Justice Cory stated on behalf of the Court that

> [c]ommon sense dictates that people are usually able to foresee the consequences of their actions.

Therefore, if a person acts in a manner which is likely to produce a certain result it generally will be reasonable to infer that the person foresaw the probable consequences of the act. In other words, if a person acted so as to produce certain predictable consequences, it may be inferred that the person intended those consequences.

However, different considerations will apply where there is evidence that the accused was intoxicated at the time of the offence. The common sense inference as to intention, which may be drawn from actions of the accused, is simply a method used to determine the accused's actual intent. That same common sense makes it readily apparent that evidence of intoxication will be a relevant factor in any consideration of that inference. It follows that the jury must be instructed to take into account the evidence of the accused's consumption of alcohol or drugs, along with all the other evidence which is relevant to the accused's intent, in determining whether, in all the circumstances, it would be appropriate to draw the permissible inference that the accused intended the natural consequences of his actions.

The question of the common sense inference, embedded in the third *Beard* Rule, also became an issue in the *Daley* case (2007; discussed above in connection with the second *Beard* Rule). It was argued on appeal that the trial judge had not made sufficient efforts to ensure that the jury was aware that they were not *required* to draw the common sense inference. However, Justice Bastarache, on behalf of the majority of the Supreme Court of Canada justices, rejected this assertion. He held that all a trial judge has to do, in these circumstances, is to *link the common sense inference to the evidence of intoxication*, as required by the *Seymour* case in the passage above. Justice Bastarache took the view that it is usually valuable for a jury to receive instructions about the common sense inference because this will assist them to understand the process by means of which they are to determine whether the accused person had the necessary *mens rea*. Justice Bastarache concluded his analysis of this aspect of the *Daley* case by stating that "I do not think the trial judge must take pains to tell the jury they are not bound to draw the inference where there is evidence of a significant degree of intoxication, as this is a matter of common sense." He then indicated his approval of comments made by Justice Huddart of the B.C. Court of Appeal in *Courtereille* (2001):

> [The common sense inference] does not die with the first drink. The collective common sense and

knowledge of life possessed by twelve jurors is of fundamental importance to the unique value of juries.... It is equally good sense and common experience that the effect of alcohol on thought processes is a continuum.... The more intoxicated a person becomes, the greater the likelihood that drink will result first in uninhibited conduct, and ultimately in unintended conduct. It is proper to remind the jury that they may use their common sense with respect to this, even if intoxication is advanced, provided the reminder includes the admonition that the inference is permissive and subject to a consideration of the evidence of intoxication.

The case of *Courville* (1982) dramatically illustrates the principle laid down in the third *Beard* Rule that, if accused persons do form the necessary intent to commit a specific intent offence, they are guilty despite the fact that they were intoxicated at the time. In this particular case, the accused was charged with robbery, but he claimed that he had been suffering from delusions induced by the consumption of drugs and alcohol. The gist of the defence was that the accused's conduct had been caused by "a loss of self-control or an irresistible impulse" that resulted from his state of intoxication. However, the evidence indicated that the accused was fully aware of what he was doing and had formed the specific intent necessary for proof of the crime of robbery. In these circumstances, the Ontario Court of Appeal ruled that Courville should be convicted of robbery despite his intoxication. The Supreme Court subsequently affirmed this decision in *Courville* (1985). The Supreme Court briefly stated that

> [l]oss of self-control or irresistible impulse caused by voluntarily induced intoxication is not a defence to a criminal charge in Canada.

THE DECISION OF THE SUPREME COURT OF CANADA IN THE *DAVIAULT* CASE (1994)

Before 1994, the orthodox approach to intoxication in Canadian courts was automatically to deny the benefit of the defence to *every* defendant charged with a crime of general (or basic) intent. However, in the *Daviault* case (1994), the Supreme Court decisively rejected this approach.

Daviault was charged with the sexual assault of a 65-year-old woman who was partially paralyzed and confined to a wheelchair. Daviault had apparently consumed some seven or eight beers during the day and then some 35 ounces of brandy on the evening of the alleged assault. He claimed that he did not remember anything between the time that he had a glass of brandy and the point where he woke up nude in the complainant's bed. In other words, he asserted that he had no recollection whatsoever of the events that constituted the alleged assault.

A pharmacologist, appearing on behalf of the defence, stated that, if Daviault had in fact consumed the amount of alcohol that he claimed, his blood alcohol level would have been in the region of 400 to 600 mg of alcohol per 100 mL of blood. In a normal person, this would cause death or coma. However, since Daviault was an alcoholic, he was less susceptible to the effect of alcohol and, in his case, this level of alcohol in the blood might cause him to suffer a "blackout" in which he might enter into a state of dissociation; in such a condition, he would have no awareness of what he was doing and, therefore, would have no memory of the events that occurred.

The trial judge acquitted the accused on the basis that there was a reasonable doubt as to whether he possessed the minimal intent necessary for conviction of the offence of sexual assault. However, the Quebec Court of Appeal substituted a conviction because, in its view, the trial judge had made a fundamental error in holding that intoxication can be a defence to a charge of a general intent offence such as sexual assault. In other words, the Quebec Court of Appeal reasserted the orthodox interpretation of the *Beard* Rules. However, Daviault appealed to the Supreme Court of Canada, claiming that this interpretation of the *Beard* Rules violated his rights under sections 7 and 11(d) of the *Charter*. The Supreme Court agreed and ordered a new trial.

Justice Cory indicated that the distinction between crimes of specific and general intent was so deeply entrenched in the fabric of Canadian criminal law that there was no question of abolishing it at this stage of our legal history. However, Justice Cory held that this did not mean that Canadian courts should continue to exclude the possibility of raising the defence of intoxication in cases involving charges of general (or basic) intent crimes; indeed, it was his view (shared by the majority of the Court) that, in certain circumstances, the *Charter* dictates that the accused should have the benefit of the defence of intoxication in relation to crimes of general intent. In essence, the majority of the Court adopted the view that a defence should be available to a person accused

Cartoon by Greg Holoboff

The Daviault case: extreme intoxication that produces a state akin to mental disorder or automatism should lead to an absolute acquittal.

of an offence of general intent if, owing to an *extreme degree of intoxication*, he or she was in a "state akin to automatism or insanity."

Justice Cory ruled that the principle that intoxication can never be a defence to a charge of a crime of general intent violated both the principles of fundamental justice guaranteed by section 7 of the *Charter* and the presumption of innocence enshrined in section 11(d) of the *Charter*. Indeed, he said that

[t]he mental aspect of an offence, or *mens rea*, has long been recognized as an integral part of crime. The concept is fundamental to our criminal law. The element may be minimal in general intent offences; none the less, it exists. In this case, the requisite mental element is simply an intention to commit the sexual assault, or recklessness as to whether the actions constitute an assault. The necessary mental element can ordinarily be inferred from the proof that the assault was committed by the accused. However, the substituted *mens rea* of an intention to become drunk cannot establish the *mens rea* to commit the assault.

Justice Cory rejected the view advanced by many Canadian judges that the voluntary consumption of alcohol is sufficient to constitute the *mens rea* necessary for conviction of the offence of sexual assault. The intent to become intoxicated cannot be substituted for the *mens rea* that the Crown must prove in relation to a charge of sexual assault. The so-called "substituted *mens rea*" rule effectively eliminates the minimal mental element required for proof of sexual assault and, in the view of Justice Cory, "*mens rea* for a crime is so well recognized that to eliminate that mental element, an integral part of the crime, would be to deprive an accused of fundamental justice."

On behalf of the majority of the Supreme Court, Justice Cory also ruled that the traditional *Beard* Rules infringed section 11(d) of the *Charter* because, under their provisions, it would be possible to convict an accused person of an offence even if there was a reasonable doubt as to one of the essential elements of the offence:

> For example, an accused in an extreme state of intoxication akin to automatism or mental illness would have to be found guilty although there was a reasonable doubt as to the voluntary nature of the act committed by the accused.... In my view, the mental element of voluntariness is a fundamental aspect of the crime which cannot be taken away by a judicially developed policy....
>
> The presumption of innocence requires that the Crown bear the burden of establishing all elements of a crime. These elements include the mental element of voluntariness.

Justice Cory also rejected the argument that the *Charter* is not violated by the traditional *Beard* Rules because the accused's voluntary decision to become intoxicated renders him or her "blameworthy." He stated that

> [v]oluntary intoxication is not yet a crime. Further, it is difficult to conclude that such behaviour should always constitute a fault to which criminal sanctions should apply. However, assuming that voluntary intoxication is reprehensible, it does not follow that its consequences in any given situation are either voluntary or predictable. Studies demonstrate that the consumption of alcohol is not the cause of the crime. A person intending to drink cannot be said to be intending to commit a sexual assault.

Having ruled that the defence of intoxication should be available to those who are charged with a crime of general intent, the Supreme Court of Canada made it clear in the *Daviault* (1994) case that it would be only in very rare and limited circumstances that such a defence would ever be successful. Why should this be so? According to Justice Cory,

> It must be remembered that those who are a "little" drunk can readily form the requisite mental element to commit the offence. The alcohol-induced relaxation of both inhibitions and socially acceptable behaviour has never been accepted as a factor or excuse in determining whether the accused possessed the requisite *mens rea*. Given the minimal nature of the mental element required for crimes of general intent, even those who are significantly drunk will usually be able to form the requisite *mens rea* and will be found to have acted voluntarily. In reality it is only those who can demonstrate that they were in such an extreme degree of intoxication that they were in a state akin to automatism or insanity that might expect to raise a reasonable doubt as to their ability to form the minimal mental element required for a general intent offence. Neither an insane person nor one in a state of automatism is capable of forming the minimal intent required for proof of a general intent offence. Similarly, as the words themselves imply, "drunkenness akin to insanity or automatism" describes a person so severely intoxicated that he is incapable of forming even the minimal intent required of a general intent offence. The phrase refers to a person so drunk that he is an automaton. As such he may be capable of voluntary acts such as moving his arms and legs but is quite incapable of forming the most basic or simple intent required to perform the act prohibited by a general intent offence.

In addition, the defence recognized in *Daviault* (1994) would be extremely difficult to establish in practice because the Supreme Court of Canada placed the **primary (or persuasional) burden of proof** on the shoulders of the accused. It is not enough, said Justice Cory, for the accused to raise a reasonable doubt as to whether he or she had the minimal intent required for proof of the general intent offence charged. Instead, the accused must establish *on the balance of probabilities* that he or she was in a state of extreme intoxication akin to automatism or insanity. No doubt the Supreme Court took this extraordinary step in order to ensure that the defence of intoxication would not be abused.

After the *Daviault* case (1994), the *Beard* Rules survived, but the second rule was considerably modified by the principle that the defence of intoxication should now be available, in very rare and limited circumstances, to a defendant charged with a crime of general (or basic) intent. Essentially, after *Daviault* (1994), the defence of intoxication will not be available to most defendants charged with a general intent crime because their state of intoxication would not be sufficiently serious to prevent them from forming the minimal intent required for proof of such offences. However, where the intoxication is so extreme as to produce a state akin to automatism or insanity, the accused will be entitled to an acquittal, provided he or she proves the requirements of the defence on the balance of probabilities.

THE ENACTMENT OF SECTION 33.1 OF THE *CRIMINAL CODE* AND ITS AFTERMATH

Although the majority of the justices of the Supreme Court apparently took considerable care in *Daviault* (1994) to indicate that it would only be in the rarest of cases that a defendant would be able to escape criminal liability for the commission of such general intent offences as sexual assault, their decision was subjected to a considerable degree of popular criticism. Much of this criticism stemmed from a deep-seated concern for the plight of sexual assault victims and a belief that the *Daviault* (1994) defence would permit violent men to avoid taking responsibility for sexual assaults that they committed while intoxicated.

In response to the robust criticism of the *Daviault* (1994) decision, Parliament amended the *Criminal Code* by adding a new section dealing explicitly with the issue of intoxication as a defence to a charge of a general intent offence.[1] Section 33.1, which came into effect in 1996, provides the following:

33.1 (1) It is not a defence to an offence referred to in subsection (3) that the accused, by reason of self-induced intoxication, lacked the general intent or the voluntariness required to commit the offence, where the accused departed markedly from the standard of care as described in subsection (2).

(2) For the purposes of this section, a person markedly departs from the standard of reasonable care generally recognized in Canadian society and is thereby criminally at fault where the person, while in a state of self-induced intoxication that renders the person unaware of, or incapable of consciously controlling, their behaviour, voluntarily or involuntarily interferes or threatens to interfere with the bodily integrity of another person.

(3) This section applies in respect of an offence under this Act or any other Act of Parliament that includes as an element an assault or any other interference or threat of interference by a person with the bodily integrity of another person.

Section 33.1 does not purport to be a comprehensive statutory treatment of the defence of intoxication. In fact, it deals only with *those offences of general intent that involve an element of assault or interference (or threat of interference) with the bodily integrity of another person.* This means that section 33.1 does not apply to those general (or basic) intent offences that do not involve violence or the threat of violence. For example, mischief (damage to property) under section 430 of the *Code* clearly falls outside the ambit of section 33.1 and will still be governed by the Supreme Court's decision in *Daviault* (1994). It is also particularly significant that Parliament did not address the issue of the intoxication defence in relation to specific intent offences, and it is clear that, for these offences, the courts will continue to apply the *Beard* Rules.

It should be emphasized that section 33.1 only applies to *self-induced* intoxication. As we saw in Chapter 8, an accused person who becomes intoxicated *involuntarily* is entitled to an absolute acquittal if he or she acts involuntarily in a state of automatism. It will no doubt be remembered that, in *Chaulk* (2007), the suggested criteria for finding that intoxication was self-induced were set out as follows:

- The accused voluntarily consumed a substance which;
- S/he knew or ought to have known was an intoxicant and;
- The risk of becoming intoxicated was or should have been within his/her contemplation.

Section 33.1 can essentially be viewed as a direct move by Parliament to overturn the Supreme Court's ruling in the *Daviault* (1994) case in those circumstances where the charge against the accused involves an offence *against the person* as opposed to an offence *against property*. However, the enactment of section 33.1 has, unfortunately, caused the law concerning intoxication to become undesirably complex. The present state of the law would appear to be as follows:

1. For crimes of **specific intent**, the second and third *Beard* Rules will continue to apply, and intoxication may be used as a defence where it prevents the accused from forming the specific intent that must be established by the Crown (e.g., intent to kill, intent to steal).
2. For crimes of **general (or basic) intent**, the situation is somewhat more complicated:

   (a) where the offence involves an element of assault or any other interference or threat of

---

[1] S.C. 1995, c. 32.

interference with the bodily integrity of a person (e.g., assault, manslaughter, sexual assault), self-induced intoxication can never be a valid defence no matter how severe it may have been at the time (section 33.1);

(b) where the offence does not involve an element of assault or any other interference or threat of interference with the bodily integrity of a person (e.g., damage to property), then, in those very *exceptional* cases where the intoxication is so extreme as to produce a state akin to automatism or insanity, the accused will have the benefit of an absolute defence (as required by the Supreme Court's ruling in *Daviault* (1994)).

A further difficulty with this statement of the existing law is that there are serious questions as to whether section 33.1 is valid under the *Charter*. It could well be argued that section 33.1 flatly contradicts the Supreme Court's unequivocal view, expressed in *Daviault* (1994), that it is a violation of sections 7 and 11(d) of the *Charter* to convict a person who lacks even a minimal degree of *mens rea* at the time that he or she commits a general intent offence, such as sexual assault. However, it could also be asserted that, even if section 33.1 does infringe an accused person's *Charter* rights, it should nevertheless be declared valid because it constitutes a reasonable limitation that is, in the words of section 1 of the *Charter*, "demonstrably justified in a free and democratic society."

The argument will no doubt be made that Bill C-72, which added section 33.1 to the *Criminal Code*, represents Parliament's first attempt to legislate in the area of intoxication and, insofar as Parliament represents the will of Canadians' elected representatives, the Supreme Court of Canada should give careful consideration to this legislation before deciding to strike it down as being invalid under the *Charter*. After all, the *Daviault* decision concerned the judge-made *Beard* Rules rather than legislation enacted by Parliament.

It is most likely that the real issue will be whether section 33.1 can be justified as a reasonable limitation under section 1 of the *Charter*. It would be difficult to imagine in light of what it said in *Daviault* that the Supreme Court would change its mind and hold that section 33.1 does not violate an accused's rights under sections 7 and 11(d) of the *Charter*. However, it is possible that the Court might reconsider whether section 33.1 of the *Code* can be saved under section 1 of the *Charter*.

In an unusual move, Parliament included in Bill C-72 a statement of the reasons for enacting section 33.1. This statement is contained in nine different "whereas" clauses that serve as a "preamble" to section 33.1. For example, four of these clauses read as follows:

> Whereas the Parliament of Canada is concerned about the incidence of violence in Canadian society;
>
> Whereas the Parliament of Canada recognizes that violence has a particularly disadvantaging impact on the equal participation of women and children in society and on the rights of women and children to security of the person and to the equal protection and benefit of the law as guaranteed by sections 7, 15 and 28 of the *Canadian Charter of Rights and Freedoms*;
>
> Whereas the Parliament of Canada recognizes that there is a close association between violence and intoxication and is concerned that self-induced intoxication may be used socially and legally to excuse violence, particularly violence against women and children...;
>
> Whereas the Parliament of Canada shares with Canadians the moral view that people who, while in a state of self-induced intoxication, violate the physical integrity of others are blameworthy in relation to their harmful conduct and should be held criminally accountable for it....

These clauses could well serve as the basis for the contention that Parliament's objective in enacting section 33.1 is, in the words of the test in the *Oakes* case (1986), related to "concerns which are pressing and substantial in a free and democratic society." Clearly, section 33.1 is directed toward the dangers posed to society by intoxication-related violence, and it is likely that dealing with this problem would be considered an objective that might justify overriding a defendant's *Charter* rights. However, there is a real question as to whether section 33.1 would meet the "proportionality" test. In answering this question, the Supreme Court of Canada would have to consider whether convicting an accused person who lacks even the minimal degree of *mens rea* for conviction of a general intent offence is a reasonable method of dealing with the problem of intoxication-related violence. It is interesting that, in this respect, it could be argued that Parliament should have moved to punish the act of becoming "drunk and dangerous" rather than to enact an amendment to the *Code* that results in convicting an accused of an offence for which he or she has no *mens rea*. Indeed, in the *Daviault* case (1994), Justice Cory stated on behalf of the majority of the Supreme Court of Canada that

> ... it is always open to Parliament to fashion a remedy which would make it a crime to commit a prohibited act while drunk.

Unfortunately, as we saw in Chapter 8, no appellate court has yet been called upon to decide the critical issue of the constitutionality of section 33.1. In *Daley* (2007), the Supreme Court of Canada referred to section 33.1 but it did not make any comment concerning the question of its constitutionality.[2] Ultimately, it is to be hoped that the critical question of the constitutionality of section 33.1 will finally be resolved by the Supreme Court of Canada whenever an appropriate case comes before it. At present, there are conflicting decisions at the trial level and this situation certainly generates uncertainty in the application of an important element in Canada's criminal law. Significantly, in the case of *Cedeno* (2005), a trial judge—Judge Duncan of the Ontario Court of Justice—expressed the opinion that

> ... the law in Ontario at this point appears to be that the section offends section 7 and 11(d) of the *Charter* and is not saved by section 1. It is therefore unconstitutional and of no force and effect.

MISCELLANEOUS ISSUES RELATING TO INTOXICATION AS A DEFENCE

The *Beard* Rules, the *Daviault* case, and section 33.1 of the *Code* do not address all of the issues that arise when the defence of intoxication is raised in a criminal trial. For example, they do not explicitly deal with the situation in which an accused person deliberately ingests alcohol and/or drugs in order to create a condition of mind in which it is easier for him or her to

commit a crime. Suppose such a person decides to kill someone and drinks a large amount of alcohol for "liquid courage." This individual then proceeds to slaughter the victim while under the influence of alcohol. Can this person then claim the benefit of the defence of intoxication on the basis that there is a reasonable doubt that he or she actually formed the intent to kill at the exact time when the victim was being dispatched? This precise issue was raised in *Gallagher* (1961), a case that originated in Northern Ireland and was ultimately taken to the House of Lords. On this particular matter, Lord Denning said,

> ... [I]f a man, whilst sane and sober, forms an intention to kill and makes preparation for it, knowing that it is a wrong thing to do, and then gets himself drunk so as to give himself ... courage to do the killing, and whilst drunk carries out his intention, he cannot rely on his self-induced drunkenness as a defence to a charge of murder, nor even as reducing it to manslaughter. He cannot say that he got himself in such a stupid state that he was incapable of an intent to kill. So, also, when he is a psychopath, he cannot by drinking rely on his self-induced defect of reason as a defence of insanity. The wickedness of his mind before he got drunk is enough to condemn him, coupled with the act which he intended to do and did do. The psychopath who goes out intending to kill, knowing it is wrong, and does kill, cannot escape the consequences by making himself drunk before doing it.

Another issue, which should be mentioned at this point, concerns the critical effect of intoxication in relation to a charge of first degree murder, which requires proof of "planning and deliberation" (see section 231(2) of the *Criminal Code*). Evidence of intoxication may well raise a reasonable doubt as to whether the accused "planned" the murder or committed it with due "deliberation." In other words, even though a jury may be satisfied beyond a reasonable doubt that the accused did form the requisite specific intent to commit murder (thereby rejecting the defence of intoxication), it may nevertheless entertain a reasonable doubt as to whether the accused's state of intoxication negatived the elements of "planning and deliberation" that are necessary for a conviction of first degree murder.

STUDY QUESTIONS

1. Pompey meets his friend Elbow in a bar. They start arguing about a sum of money that Elbow owes to Pompey. Suddenly, Pompey loses his

---

[2] As noted in Chapter 8, at least three trial courts in Ontario have decided that this provision infringes both sections 7 and 11(d) of the *Charter* and that it is not saved by the application of section 1. However, some trial courts in British Columbia, the Northwest Territories, and Ontario have ruled that, while section 33.1 does indeed offend sections 7 and 11(d) of the *Charter*, it is nevertheless valid because it constitutes a "reasonable limit" under section 1 of the *Charter*. In the case of *Jensen* (2005), the Ontario Court of Appeal declined to determine whether the trial judge had been correct to hold that section 33.1 was unconstitutional because the constitutional issue was "not relevant" to the "disposition of this appeal." However, the Court stated that "nothing in these reasons should be read as approving or disapproving of the trial judge's ruling on the constitutionality of s. 33.1."

temper and shouts at the top of his voice, "You're nothing but a slimy jailbird!" In response to this insult, Elbow rushes out of the bar and goes to his home, which is just a few blocks away. He retrieves a kitchen knife from his home and returns to the bar, where he stabs Pompey to death. Elbow had once been incarcerated in a federal correctional institution, but since his release 10 years ago, he has kept out of trouble with the law. With the exception of his wife and Pompey, no one in the local community knew that Elbow had once been an inmate of a prison. Does Elbow have a defence to a charge of murder?

2. Rosaline is married to Moth but she is having an affair with Costard, Moth's best friend. After Moth discovers the affair, he threatens Rosaline, who decides to leave him. About one month after Rosaline moves out, she and Costard are having a drink together in a public bar. Moth walks in and sees Rosaline and Costard. Moth tells Rosaline that she is a "faithless whore." Costard responds by telling Moth that Rosaline left him (Moth) because he was a "lousy lover." Moth then takes out a knife and stabs Costard to death. At his trial for murder, Moth asserts the defence of provocation. Is it likely that this defence would be successful?

3. Winkel is intoxicated and brutally assaults his best friend, Snodgrass. Winkel then steals Snodgrass's cellular phone. Winkel is charged with robbery. To what extent (if any) is Winkel's intoxication a defence to the charge of robbery?

4. Dracula takes a heavy dose of crystal meth (crystal methamphetamine) and becomes extremely violent. He kills his friend, Frankenstein. Dracula is charged with second degree murder but he claims that he cannot remember anything about the incident. Does Dracula have a defence to the charge laid against him?

5. Cheeryble is in the habit of simultaneously consuming both alcohol and (illicitly obtained) barbiturate drugs. One night, he smashes his way through a window in the living room of Betsey, an elderly woman. When Betsey comes to investigate the noise, she discovers Cheeryble standing in the middle of the room with a large stick in his hand. Cheeryble moves toward Betsey, who is terrified by this encounter and utters a piercing scream. Cheeryble hops out of the window and walks slowly down the street. Betsey calls the police, who have no difficulty in arresting Cheeryble on a neighbouring street corner. The Crown wishes to charge Cheeryble with breaking and entering, mischief (damaging property), and assault with a weapon. Cheeryble states that he has absolutely no memory of what happened at Betsey's residence. He states that his last memory was of being in a bar. A blood test reveals that Cheeryble has extraordinarily high levels of alcohol and barbiturates in his bloodstream. Does Cheeryble have any viable defence(s) to the potential charges that might be laid against him?

FURTHER READING

Anand, S. 2008. A Provocative Perspective on the Influence of Anger on the *Mens Rea* for Murder: The Alberta Court of Appeal's Interpretation of *Parent* in *Walle*. 54 *Criminal Law Quarterly*: 27–41.

Baker, B. 1998. Provocation as a Defence for Abused Women Who Kill. 11 *Canadian Journal of Law & Jurisprudence*: 193–211.

Benedet, J. 2007. Annotation: *R. v. Chaulk*. 49 *Criminal Reports (6th Series)*: 173–174.

Berger, B.L. 206. Emotions and the Veil of Voluntarism: The Loss of Judgment in Canadian Criminal Defences. 51 *McGill Law Journal*: 99–128.

Choi, J. 2003. The Viability of a "Cultural Defence" in Canada. 8 *Canadian Criminal Law Review*: 93–112.

Colvin, E., and S. Anand. 2007. *Principles of Criminal Law*. 3rd ed. Toronto: Thomson Carswell.

Coughlan, S.G. 2002. Duress, Necessity, Self-Defence and Provocation: Implications of Radical Change? 7 *Canadian Criminal Law Review*: 147–208.

Ferguson, G. 2006. Recent Developments in Canadian Criminal Law. 30 *Criminal Law Journal*: 103–105.

Garvey, S.P. 2009. Dealing with Wayward Desire. 3 *Criminal Law and Philosophy*: 1–17.

Gorman, W. 1999. Provocation: The Jealous Husband Defence. 42 *Criminal Law Quarterly*: 478–500.

Grant, I. 1995. The Limits of *Daviault*. 33 *Criminal Reports (4th Series)*: 277–282.

Healy, P. 1994. Intoxication in the Codification of Canadian Criminal Law. 73 *Canadian Bar Review*: 515–552.

Heller, K.J. 1998. Beyond the Reasonable Man? A Sympathetic but Critical Assessment of the Use of Subjective Standards of Reasonableness in Self-Defense and Provocation Cases. 26(1) *American Journal of Criminal Law:* 1-120.

Horder, J. 2005. Can the Law do without the Reasonable Person? 55 *University of Toronto Law Journal*: 253–269.

Husak, D.N. 1998. Partial Defences. 11 *Canadian Journal of Law & Jurisprudence*: 167–192.

Hyland, E.M. 1996–97. *R. v. Thibert:* Are There Any Ordinary People Left? 28 *Ottawa Law Review*: 145–170.

Klimchuk, D. 1994. Outrage, Self-control, and Culpability. 44 *University of Toronto Law Journal*: 441–468.

_____. 1996. Circumstances and Objectivity. 45 *Criminal Reports (4th Series)*: 24–32.

Klineberg, J. 2003. Anger and Intent for Murder: The Supreme Court Decision in R. v. Parent. 41 *Osgoode Hall Law Journal*: 37–73.

Levy, N. 2006. Autonomy and Addiction. 36 *Canadian Journal of Philosophy*: 427–448.

Lunny, A.M. 2003. Provocation and "Homosexual" Advance: Masculinized Subjects as Threat, Masculinized Subjects under Threat. 12 *Social & Legal Studies*: 311–333.

Morgan, J. 1997. Critique and Comment: Provocation Law and Facts: Dead Women Tell No Tales, Tales Are Told about Them. 21 *Melbourne University Law Review*: 237–276.

Mousourakis, G. 2007. Defending Victims of Domestic Abuse Who Kill: A Perspective. 48 *Cahiers de Droit*: 351–371.

_____. 2007. Reason, Passion and Self-Control: Understanding the Moral Basis of the Provocation Defence. 38 *Revue de Droit, Université de Sherbrooke*: 115–126.

Nelson, C.A. 2002. (En)raged or (En)gaged: The Implications of Racial Context to the Canadian Provocation Defence. 35 *University of Richmond Law Review*: 1007–1083.

Nicolson, D., and R. Sanghvi. 1993. Battered Women and Provocation: The Implications of *R. v. Ahluwalia*. [1993] *Criminal Law Review*: 728–738.

Onn, A. 1996. Self-Induced Intoxication: Balancing Principles of Justice and Responsibility (Intoxication as a Legal Defense: Recent Canadian Experience with Changes in Criminal Law). 23 *Contemporary Drug Problems*: 687–705.

Paciocco, D.M. 1995. Subjective and Objective Standards of Fault for Offences and Defences. 59 *Saskatchewan Law Review*: 271–310.

_____. 1999. *Getting Away with Murder: The Canadian Criminal Justice System*. Toronto: Irwin Law.

Plaxton, M.C. 2004. On Not Taking Provocation Too Seriously: A Partial Reply to Stephen Coughlan. 8 *Canadian Criminal Law Review*: 377–380.

Quigley, T. 1991. Battered Women and the Defence of Provocation. 55 *Saskatchewan Law Review*: 223–261.

_____. 1995. A Time for Parliament to Enact an Offence of Dangerous Incapacitation. 33 *Criminal Reports (4th Series)*: 283–288.

Reilly, A. 1997–1998. The Heart of the Matter: Emotion in Criminal Defences. 29 *Ottawa Law Review*: 117–151.

Roach, K.W. 1998. Editorial: Provocation and Mandatory Life Imprisonment. 41 *Criminal Law Quarterly*: 273–275.

Roach, K. 2009. *Criminal Law*. 4th ed. Toronto: Irwin Law.

Sahni, R. 1997. Crossing the Line: *R. v. Thibert* and the Defence of Provocation. 55 *University of Toronto Faculty Law Review*: 143–155.

Shaffer, M. 1996. *R. v. Daviault:* A Principled Approach to Drunkenness or a Lapse of Common Sense? 3 *Review of Constitutional Studies*: 311–329.

Smith, K. 2000. Section 33.1 of the *Criminal Code*: Denial of the *Daviault* Case Should Be Held Constitutional. 28 *Criminal Reports (5th)*: 350-366.

Stuart, D. 1995. Parliament Should Declare a New Responsibility for Drunkenness Based on Criminal Negligence. 33 *Criminal Reports (4th Series)*: 289–294.

_____. 2007. *Canadian Criminal Law: A Treatise.* 5th ed. Toronto: Thomson Carswell. Chs. 6 & 7.

Stuart, D., R.J. Delisle, and S. Coughlan. 2009. *Learning Canadian Criminal Law.* 11th ed. Toronto: Thomson Carswell. Chs. 6 & 7.

Trotter, G.T. 2002. Anger, Provocation, and the Intent for Murder (Case Comment). 47 *McGill Law Journal*: 669–690.

Tyson, D. 1999. "Asking for It": An Anatomy of Provocation. *The Australian Feminist Law Journal*: 66–85.

Verdun-Jones, S.N. 2000. "Making the Mental Disorder Defence a More Attractive Option for Defendants in a Criminal Trial: Recent Legal Developments in Canada." In D. Eaves, J.R.P. Ogloff, and R. Roesch, eds. *Mental Disorders and the Criminal Code: Legal Background and Contemporary Perspectives.* Burnaby, BC: Mental Health, Law, and Policy Institute, Simon Fraser University. 39–75.

———. 2007. *Canadian Criminal Cases: Selected Highlights.* 2nd ed. Toronto: Thomson Nelson. Ch. 10.

Wallace, T.J. 1999. Addiction as Defect of the Will: Some Philosophical Reflections. 18 *Law and Philosophy*: 621–654.

Watson, G. 1999. Excusing Addiction. 18 *Law and Philosophy*: 589–619.

Yeo, S.M.H. 1990. Recent Australian Pronouncements on the Ordinary Person Test in Provocation and Automatism. 33 *Criminal Law Quarterly*: 280–293.

CHAPTER ELEVEN

NECESSITY AND DURESS: TWO EXCUSES RECOGNIZED BY THE COURTS AS DEFENCES TO A CRIMINAL CHARGE

OVERVIEW

This chapter examines the following:

1. the defences of necessity and duress, which are considered to be "excuses" rather than justifications for acts that would otherwise be considered crimes;
2. the distinction between excuses and justifications;
3. the underlying rationale of the defences of necessity and duress—namely, "normative involuntariness";
4. the specific situations in which the defence of necessity may be raised as a defence to a criminal charge in Canada;
5. the principle that necessity may be a defence where the accused person claims that he or she had no choice but to break the law in order to avoid a greater evil;
6. the principle that necessity is a defence only in situations of "clear and imminent peril when compliance with the law is demonstrably impossible" and that the defence is not available where the accused person has a reasonable legal alternative;
7. the principle that the defence of necessity is available only where there is a degree of proportionality between the offence committed and the evil that it was designed to avoid;
8. the difficulties associated with applying the defence of necessity in relation to the more serious criminal offences in the *Criminal Code*;
9. the principle that duress may constitute an excuse where the accused person's freedom of choice is overwhelmed by a threat of violence from another person;
10. the nature and scope of the defence of duress both under section 17 of the *Criminal Code* and under the principles of the common law;
11. section 17 of the *Criminal Code*, which defines the circumstances in which duress may be raised by an accused person who actually committed the offence charged and states that an accused person may not raise the defence of duress if he or she committed one or more of 22 serious offences, ranging from murder to arson;
12. the invalidation of key elements of section 17 of the *Code* by the Supreme Court of Canada in the *Ruzic* case (2001);
13. the decision in *Ruzic* (2001), in which the Supreme Court of Canada held that the courts must now apply the elements of the common law defence of duress in all cases; the criteria for the common law defence of duress: (i) that there be a threat of death or serious bodily harm; (ii) that the threat does not have to be of immediate death or serious bodily harm, (iii) that the threats must be of such gravity that they might have caused a reasonable person to act in the same manner as the accused person; and (iv) that the accused must not have had an obvious safe avenue of escape; and
14. the fact that the Supreme Court did not declare the whole of section 17 to be invalid and that, for the present, the list of 22 offences for which duress may not be raised as a defence remains in effect.

THE DEFENCE OF NECESSITY

THE GENERAL PRINCIPLES

The defence of **necessity** arises where the accused can avoid some disaster or calamity only by breaking the law. In advancing the defence of necessity, the accused is basically asserting that the evil that he or she sought to avoid was greater than the evil inherent in the breaking of the law. In essence, the accused person asserts that he or she should be excused from criminal responsibility because the decision to break the law was dictated by necessity and was, therefore, not a free choice. The defence of necessity is not mentioned in the *Criminal Code*. However, as a common law defence, it has been preserved by section 8(3) of the *Code*.

THE RATIONALE FOR THE DEFENCE OF NECESSITY

In the Supreme Court of Canada's decision in *Perka* (1984), Justice Dickson drew a sharp distinction between "justifications" and "excuses." He considered that the defence of necessity constitutes an "excuse" rather than a "justification." Justice Dickson noted that a justification "challenges the wrongfulness of an action which technically constitutes a crime." For example, the police officer who shoots a hostage taker in order to save the life of an innocent victim is considered to have been fully justified in having used lethal force in these particular circumstances. On the other hand, according to Justice Dickson, an excuse "concedes the wrongfulness of the action but asserts that the circumstances under which it was done are such that it ought not to be attributed to the actor." For example, we certainly disapprove of the act of an accused person who engages in sexual activity with a child under the age of 16 years; however, we would excuse his or her behaviour—and withhold punishment—if the accused person had taken all reasonable steps to ascertain the age of the other party and honestly, albeit mistakenly, believed that he or she was over the age of 16.

In Justice Dickson's view, a valid claim of necessity should serve to "excuse" an accused person from responsibility on the basis that he or she *acted "involuntarily" from a "moral or normative" point of view*:

> The lost Alpinist who, on the point of freezing to death, breaks open an isolated mountain cabin is not literally behaving in an involuntary fashion. He has

control over his actions to the extent of being physically capable of abstaining from the act. Realistically, however, his act is not a "voluntary" one. His "choice" to break the law is no true choice at all; it is remorselessly compelled by normal human instincts.

Clearly, the availability of the defence of necessity reflects the willingness of the courts to recognize that it would not be just to punish individuals who, when faced with a dire emergency, chose to break the law rather than risk their own lives or the lives or safety of others: such a choice must be treated as being involuntary. According to Justice Dickson, a humane system of criminal law must be based on a "realistic assessment of human weakness" and should not punish those individuals who do not act voluntarily in the fullest sense of that word.

APPLYING THE DEFENCE OF NECESSITY IN RELATION TO LESS SERIOUS CRIMINAL OFFENCES

The assertion of a defence of necessity in a situation where the accused has been charged with the commission of a "less serious" offence generally does not create any formidable policy difficulties for the courts. Indeed, there have been a number of cases involving the alleged commission of various traffic offences in which the courts have been prepared to apply the defence of necessity. For example, in *Fry* (1977), the accused was acquitted of a charge of dangerous driving as the consequence of a successful assertion of the defence of necessity. The accused had been clocked at 117 km/h in a 50 km/h zone in the city of Regina, Saskatchewan. The accused claimed that he had been forced to travel at this speed because the vehicle behind him was tailgating at close quarters. According to the accused, the faster he went, the faster the vehicle behind him went. Judge Boyce acquitted the accused at his trial and stated that

> ... certainly, the accused here endangered the public but I do realize an extremity of circumstance can arise where a choice is made, that is, forced to be made. For example, as I mentioned possibly occurred here, to flee by speed an actual present danger thrust upon him, or to suffer its continuance with its fearsome potential. The way ahead was clear, in fact while I do not commend his judgment, his choice to my mind was not criminal. *He substituted a constructive danger to the public in place of the actual present danger to himself.* [emphasis added]

APPLYING THE DEFENCE OF NECESSITY IN RELATION TO MORE SERIOUS CRIMINAL OFFENCES

When the defence of necessity is raised in relation to "more serious" offences, such as murder, the courts are immediately faced with policy questions of extraordinary difficulty. Indeed, the courts have been extremely reluctant to permit the assertion of such a defence in relation to the most serious criminal offences.

A classic illustration of the traditional reluctance of the courts to recognize the defence of necessity in such circumstances is the somewhat macabre English case of *Dudley and Stephens* (1884). The accused were charged with the murder of a young cabin boy after they had been shipwrecked and were drifting without food or water on the open sea and without any apparent hope of immediate rescue. The defendants had killed the boy and then proceeded to eat his flesh and drink his blood. Had they not done so, it is highly unlikely that they would have survived long enough to have been rescued by a passing ship. The defendants' defence of necessity was rejected by the English court. Although the court indicated that it sympathized with the horrific situation in which the defendants found themselves, it was not prepared to acquit the accused on the basis of necessity. One of the major policy considerations that apparently influenced the court was the belief that the recognition of a defence of necessity in such circumstances would open the floodgates to wholesale misuse of the defence by unscrupulous criminals. In the words of Lord Chief Justice Coleridge,

> Who is to be the judge of this sort of necessity? By what measure is the comparative value of lives to be measured? Is it to be strength, or intellect, or what? It is plain that the principle leaves to him who is to profit by it to determine the necessity which would justify him in deliberately taking another's life to save his own. In this case the weakest, the youngest, the most unresisting, was chosen. Was it more necessary to kill him than one of the grown men? The answer must be "No."

Although the court sentenced the accused to death, it clearly anticipated that this sentence would never be carried out. In fact, the sentence was later commuted to six months' imprisonment with hard labour. The court appeared to believe that, in such cases as *Dudley and Stephens*, the firm letter of the law should be upheld but that it was the prerogative of the Queen to grant mercy. Lord Coleridge noted in this respect,

> There is no safe path for judges to tread but to ascertain the law to the best of their ability and to declare it according to their judgments; and if in any case the law appears to be too severe on individuals, to leave it to the Sovereign to exercise that prerogative of mercy which the Constitution has entrusted to the hands fittest to dispense it.

The first authoritative court decision in Canada that involved the assertion of the defence of necessity in relation to a serious criminal charge was the case of *Morgentaler* (1975), in which the accused, a physician, was charged with performing an illegal abortion. Under the provisions of section 287 of the *Criminal Code*, certain conditions had to be met and specified procedures followed before a medical practitioner could perform a therapeutic abortion. One of the provisions of this section required that such an operation had to be approved by the therapeutic abortion committee at an accredited or approved hospital. Of course, as we saw in Chapter 1, section 287 was declared unconstitutional by the Supreme Court in January 1988. However, the *Charter* had not been enacted at the time of the case that we are discussing. Dr. Morgentaler had performed an abortion in direct contravention of the requirements and procedures of section 287. One of the defences advanced by Dr. Morgentaler, at his trial, was that of necessity. The defendant presented evidence to the effect that he feared the pregnant woman would "do something foolish unless she was given immediate professional medical attention to relieve her condition and her anxiety." The jury acquitted Dr. Morgentaler. However, the Crown appealed to the Quebec Court of Appeal on the basis of a point of law. The Crown contended that there was no evidence upon which the jury could have acquitted the accused on the basis of necessity. The Court of Appeal substituted a verdict of guilty and, thus, overturned the jury's decision to acquit Dr. Morgentaler. The decision of the Quebec Court of Appeal was ultimately affirmed by the Supreme Court of Canada.

It is significant that the Supreme Court clearly hinted that the defence of necessity might be available as a common law defence in exceptional circumstances. However, the Court believed that, in this particular case, there was no evidence of the urgent necessity that might, in certain exceptional circumstances, justify the breaking of the criminal law. In this respect, Justice Dickson stated that, if the defence of necessity does exist, then

> ... it can go no further than to justify noncompliance in urgent situations of clear and imminent peril when compliance with the law is demonstrably impossible. No system of positive law can recognize any principle which would entitle a person to violate the law because in his view the law conflicted with some higher social value.

Dr. Morgentaler was subsequently prosecuted on a second charge of having performed an illegal abortion in the province of Quebec (see *Morgentaler* (1976)). Once again, he was acquitted by a jury and, once again, the Crown appealed. However, on this occasion, the Quebec Court of Appeal ruled that the Supreme Court of Canada had, in fact, recognized the existence of the defence of necessity in the previous *Morgentaler* decision (1975) and that there was some evidence upon the record that would entitle a jury to find that the defence had been proved. The Court of Appeal, therefore, declined to interfere with the jury's verdict. The second *Morgentaler* case (1976) was significant because it represented the first *successful* assertion of a necessity defence in relation to a serious criminal charge in Canada.

THE *PERKA* CASE

In 1984, the Supreme Court of Canada decided the case of *Perka*, in which it became clear that the Court was most concerned with setting strict limits upon the use of the defence of necessity. In *Perka* (1984), the accused were charged with importing and possession of narcotics for the purpose of trafficking. They had been arrested in Canadian waters in possession of a large quantity of cannabis. The accused asserted the defence of necessity, claiming that the load of drugs was originally supposed to have been unloaded in international waters off the coast of Alaska (in other words, the drugs were never intended for delivery in Canada). However, the accused contended that their vessel encountered a number of serious mechanical problems as well as poor weather and that, for the safety of the crew, they were obliged to enter Canadian waters in order to seek refuge and to make repairs. According to the accused, the vessel ran aground in a cove on the west coast of Vancouver Island and started to list; at this point, it was decided to start unloading the cannabis in order to prevent the vessel from capsizing. However, the police arrived, arrested the accused, and recovered 34 tonnes of cannabis. The trial judge put the defence of necessity to the jury, who acquitted the accused. However, the British Columbia Court of Appeal allowed the Crown's appeal and ordered a new trial. The Supreme Court affirmed this ruling.

In the Supreme Court, Justice Dickson conducted an exhaustive examination of the nature and scope of the defence of necessity. He restated his belief that the true rationale for the defence was based on the need to recognize that it is inappropriate to punish actions that are "*normatively involuntary.*" In the light of **normative involuntariness,** only those actions that can genuinely be regarded as being involuntary are entitled to the benefit of the "excuse" of necessity. The learned justice repeated his statement in the (first) *Morgentaler* case (1975) to the effect that the operation of the defence is limited to those cases where the accused has broken the law in "situations of clear and imminent peril when compliance with the law is demonstrably impossible." Only in these types of situations can the accused be considered to be acting involuntarily. He went on to say that "at a minimum, the situation must be so emergent and the peril must be so pressing that normal human instincts cry out for action and make a counsel of patience unreasonable."

For Justice Dickson, one of the most important factors in weighing the validity of a claim of necessity is the question of whether the accused had any *reasonable legal alternative to breaking the law*:

> The question to be asked is whether the agent had any real choice: could he have done otherwise? If there is a reasonable legal alternative to disobeying the law, then the decision to disobey becomes a voluntary one, impelled by some consideration beyond the dictates of "necessity" and human instincts.

Finally, Justice Dickson emphasized that a defendant claiming the defence of necessity should be able to show that there was some degree of "proportionality" between the offence committed and the evil that it was designed to avoid:

> No rational criminal justice system, no matter how humane or liberal, could excuse the infliction of a greater harm to allow the actor to avert a lesser evil. In such circumstances we expect the individual to bear the harm and refrain from acting illegally. If he cannot control himself we will not excuse him.

In the *Perka* case (1984), a new trial was ordered because the original trial judge had not directed the jury's attention to the question of whether any reasonable legal alternatives had been available to the accused. In the view of Justice Dickson, the trial judge had incorrectly left the jury with the impression that the only real issue was whether the accused had acted reasonably in heading for the shoreline, together with their cargo of drugs, rather than "facing death at sea." In Justice Dickson's view, this approach did not deal with the critical issue of "whether there existed any other reasonable responses to the peril that were not illegal." For example, a critical question in this respect would be whether the accused should have jettisoned the drugs before entering Canadian waters. Should this drastic course of action be considered a reasonable legal alternative to breaking the law? After all, with the drugs thrown overboard, the accused would have been able to enter Canadian waters without committing a criminal offence.

The question of the availability of reasonable legal alternatives was also central to the decision of the Ontario Court of Appeal in the case of *Carson* (2004). The accused and the complainant, who were both police officers, were engaged to be married and were

The Perka case (1984): did the accused have any "reasonable legal alternative" (such as throwing the drugs overboard before entering Canadian waters)?

living together in the complainant's house. Following an altercation, Carson picked up the complainant and carried her to her bedroom. According to Carson, he put the complainant on the bed and, since she was trying to fight him, "he held her down on the bed, lying on top of her, to calm her down and to keep her from hitting him." Carson claimed that he took this action because he was concerned that the complainant would injure herself should she continue to bang her head against the wall. Carson was convicted of assault and appealed to the Ontario Court of Appeal. He asserted that the trial judge had been wrong to reject the defence of necessity. However, the Court of Appeal dismissed the appeal against conviction. The Court stated that the defence of necessity was not available to the accused because he had other legal options available to him in order to ensure the complainant's safety:

> In this case, although the appellant may honestly have believed that he faced a situation of imminent peril, he did not testify that he believed he had no legal alternative open to him. Having regard to the objective component of the test, alternatives were open to the appellant: for example, he could simply have backed away from the complainant and waited to see if she stopped banging her head; alternatively, he could have attempted to place something behind the complainant's head to cushion the blows. Thus, even if the trial judge misapprehended the evidence with respect to the first element relating to the defence of necessity, a requisite component of the defence was not made out.

THE CASE OF ROBERT LATIMER

In *Latimer* (2001), the Supreme Court of Canada addressed the question of whether the defence of necessity may be raised in the context of a so-called "mercy killing." The facts of the case were undoubtedly tragic. Robert Latimer was charged with the first degree murder of his 12-year-old daughter, Tracy, whom he had killed by carbon monoxide poisoning. Tracy suffered from severe cerebral palsy and was a quadriplegic. Her disabilities were so severe that she had been bedridden for most of her life. She was described as having the mental capacity of a four-month-old infant and was totally dependent on others for her care. Tracy endured five or six seizures every day, and it was believed that she experienced a considerable degree of pain. Tracy was being spoon-fed and was losing weight because of a lack of essential nutrients. The option of inserting a feeding tube into the stomach had been presented to Tracy's parents. This device would have enhanced the process of providing nutrition and might have permitted more effective pain control. However, this option was rejected by the parents. Tracy had undergone surgery to correct some of her physical problems, but complications had developed that caused her considerable pain and further surgery was planned. However, Latimer had indicated that he regarded such surgical intervention as a form of mutilation. One month before this additional surgery was to occur, Tracy died. Just prior to her death, her father had declined an opportunity to place Tracy in a group home.

The circumstances of Tracy's death were that her father placed her in his pickup truck and inserted into the cab a hose that was connected to the exhaust pipe. Tracy succumbed to carbon monoxide poisoning. At first, Latimer asserted that she had died naturally in her sleep: however, he subsequently admitted to having killed her. Latimer was convicted of second degree murder, but the Supreme Court ultimately ordered a new trial because of certain irregularities in the conduct of Crown counsel prior to the trial. When Latimer was retried, his counsel tried to raise the defence of necessity, but the trial judge refused to place this defence before the jury because there was no air of reality to the defence:

> What Mr. Latimer saw as a situation that left him no other alternative but to end Tracy's life to alleviate her pain did not create a necessitous situation that the law defines as necessary to advance this defence for this particular crime. *There is no evidence that he had to do what he did to avoid a direct and immediate peril, or that there was no other reasonable course of action open to him.* [emphasis added]

The Supreme Court of Canada unanimously affirmed the decision of the trial judge to refuse to permit the jury to consider the defence of necessity. In its judgment, the Court referred to the decision in the *Perka* case (1984) and reaffirmed Justice Dickson's view that necessity may be raised as a defence only where there was genuine "involuntariness" on the part of the accused. The Court also agreed with Justice Dickson's ruling that the defence of necessity must be "strictly controlled and scrupulously limited" because there is a very real risk that this defence could become "a mask for anarchy."

In its ruling in *Latimer* (2001), the Supreme Court of Canada stated that

Perka outlined three elements that must be present for the defence of necessity. First, there is the requirement of imminent peril or danger. Second, the accused must have had no reasonable legal alternative to the course of action he or she undertook. Third, there must be proportionality between the harm inflicted and the harm avoided.

It is significant that the Supreme Court held that it is not sufficient for the accused person to assert that he or she subjectively believed that there was an "imminent peril" and that there was "no reasonable legal alternative." Applying the so-called "modified objective test," the Supreme Court stated that the defence of necessity is available only where the accused person's beliefs are reasonable in light of the particular circumstances facing the accused person and his or her perception of those circumstances:

> The accused person must, at the time of the act, honestly believe, on reasonable grounds, that he faces a situation of imminent peril that leaves no reasonable legal alternative open. There must be a reasonable basis for the accused's beliefs and actions, but it would be proper to take into account circumstances that legitimately affect the accused person's ability to evaluate his situation. The test cannot be a subjective one, and the accused who argues that he perceived imminent peril without an alternative would only succeed with the defence of necessity if his belief was reasonable given his circumstances and attributes.

How did the Supreme Court apply these principles to the case of Robert Latimer? The Court took the view that the trial judge had acted correctly when he had ruled that there was no air of reality to the defence of necessity. First, the Court held that there was no evidence of an "imminent peril" facing Latimer:

> Acute suffering can constitute imminent peril, but in this case there was nothing to her medical condition that placed Tracy in a dangerous situation where death was an alternative. Tracy was thought to be in pain before the surgery, and that pain was expected to continue, or increase, following the surgery. But that ongoing pain did not constitute an emergency in this case.... Tracy's proposed surgery did not pose an imminent threat to her life, nor did her medical condition. In fact, Tracy's health might have improved had the Latimers not rejected the option of relying on a feeding tube. Tracy's situation was not an emergency. The appellant can be reasonably expected to have understood that reality. There was no evidence of a legitimate psychological condition that rendered him unable to perceive that there was

no imminent peril. The appellant argued that, for him, further surgery did amount to imminent peril. It was not reasonable for the appellant to form this belief, particularly when better pain management was available.

Second, there was no air of reality to Latimer's assertion that he had no reasonable legal alternative to breaking the law. He could have done his best to maintain Tracy's life and to alleviate her pain as much as possible. According to the Supreme Court, Latimer could have achieved these goals by permitting the use of a feeding tube to improve her health and to reduce her pain through medication. Similarly, he could have accepted the offer of a place for Tracy in a group home. As the Court stated in its judgment,

> The appellant may well have thought the prospect of struggling on unbearably sad and demanding. It was a human response that this alternative was unappealing. But it was a reasonable legal alternative that the law requires a person to pursue before he can claim the defence of necessity. The appellant was aware of this alternative but rejected it.

Third, there was no evidence of proportionality in the sense that the harm that Latimer was seeking to avoid was proportionate to the harm that he inflicted. The Court commented that it is difficult to envisage any set of circumstances in which the requirement of proportionality could be met in the case of a homicide. However, even if it could be assumed that necessity could be available as a defence to a charge of murder, the accused would have to point to a harm that was of equal gravity to death. As the Court stated,

> The "harm avoided" in the appellant's situation was, compared to death, completely disproportionate. The harm inflicted in this case was ending a life; that harm was immeasurably more serious than the pain resulting from Tracy's operation which Mr. Latimer sought to avoid. Killing a person—in order to relieve the suffering produced by a medically manageable physical or mental condition—is not a proportionate response to the harm represented by the non–life-threatening suffering resulting from that condition.

In the case of *Nelson* (2007), the British Columbia Court of Appeal emphasized the need to ensure that the modified objective test is applied to the first two criteria articulated by the Supreme Court of Canada in the *Latimer* case. Nelson had a history of engaging in long fasts for the purpose of "spiritual cleansing." He went into the woods and after a 60-day fast broke into a house, consumed the homeowner's food, and wrapped himself up in the latter's blankets. The homeowner returned to find Nelson lying on the floor, apparently unconscious. The trial judge acquitted Nelson of the charge of breaking and entering a dwelling-house and committing mischief therein contrary to s. 348(1)(b) of the *Criminal Code*. The trial judge ruled that the defence of necessity applied because Nelson believed himself to be in a position of imminent peril because of his extreme hunger and state of hypothermia at the time of the break-in. However, the Court of Appeal set aside the acquittal and ordered a new trial because the trial judge had not applied the modified objective test to the particular circumstances in Nelson's case.

The Crown had contended that the situation in which Nelson had found himself was perfectly foreseeable and that, therefore, Nelson could have avoided it. The evidence was that Nelson had fasted on a number of previous occasions and that he knew that, at some point, he would lose control of himself; nevertheless, he decided to engage in another long fast. In the Court of Appeal, the Crown quoted the following passage from the Supreme Court of Canada's decision in *Latimer*: "Where the situation of peril clearly should have been foreseen and avoided, an accused person cannot reasonably claim any immediate peril."

The Crown also argued that Nelson had other legal alternatives open to him than breaking into someone else's home. For example, his original plan was to rummage through garbage cans. He could also have knocked on people's doors to ask for help or called 911. In this respect, the Court of Appeal stated that

> [i]t is the [Crown's] submission that while the trial judge made reference to other legal alternatives, the judge focused solely on [Nelson's] evidence and applied a subjective test, rather than a modified objective one.
>
> As [Crown] counsel put it, the trial judge erred in law by allowing his analysis to become unmoored from the objective underpinnings of the defence of necessity.

The Court of Appeal ruled that the trial judge had made a significant legal error by failing to ask whether Nelson's perception that he was in a situation of dire emergency and his belief that there were no legal alternatives open to him "had an objectively reasonable foundation." Therefore, a new trial was necessary.

OTHER LIMITS TO THE DEFENCE OF NECESSITY

The strange case of *Hendricks* (1988) illustrates two circumstances in which a defendant may lose the benefit of the defence of necessity. First, an accused person may not claim the benefit of the defence if his or her conduct goes beyond what is reasonably necessary to deal with an emergent situation. Second, the defence may not be raised successfully if the accused *voluntarily* created the emergent situation in circumstances in which a reasonable person would have foreseen the possibility that his or her conduct might result in the need to break the law; such an accused person would not meet the requirement that his or her actions are genuinely involuntary.

Hendricks was charged with having care or control of a motor vehicle at a time when his blood alcohol level was more than 80 mg of alcohol in 100 mL of blood. He had entered a car in order to have a sleep while waiting for his wife to collect him and take him home. He was sleeping on the front seat (on the passenger's side) and, because he felt cold, he turned on the ignition in order to heat the car. Unfortunately, the car was facing downhill and it started to move because it was in gear and the parking brake was not engaged. Hendricks climbed over into the driver's seat and took control of the vehicle in order to stop it. However, the accused continued to drive the car after the point at which he could have stopped it; in fact, he drove the car back to the street where it had originally been parked.

Hendricks was convicted at his trial in the Provincial Court. He then appealed his conviction to the Saskatchewan Court of Queen's Bench. However, Justice Noble dismissed Hendricks's appeal on the basis that even if necessity dictated that he take control of the vehicle in order to bring it to a halt, he had, by continuing to drive it back to the street where it had previously been parked, "gone beyond the point the necessity of the situation called for." Moreover, Justice Noble pointed out that Hendricks had "placed himself in this so-called position of necessity when he turned on the ignition." By entering a vehicle while intoxicated and by deliberately switching on the ignition, he was the author of his own misfortunes. Any reasonable person would have contemplated the possibility that turning on the ignition might have the effect of putting the vehicle in motion—particularly if no attempt is made to check whether the parking brake is engaged and whether the car is in gear.

The *Hendricks* case (1988), demonstrates that an accused person may lose the benefit of the defence of necessity if he or she may be considered the author of his or her own misfortunes. However, the critical issue in such cases is whether or not the accused person foresaw—or ought to have foreseen—that his or her actions would precipitate an emergency situation that would require the law to be broken. For example, in the case of *V. (C.W.)* (2004), the 17-year-old accused person was convicted of the offence of dangerous operation of a motor vehicle causing bodily harm. He had gone to a party with the purpose of retrieving a keg of beer, the ownership and possession of which he knew to be "hotly contested." The accused's vehicle was surrounded by a mob of some 20 to 40 persons and he was assaulted. The trial judge found that, "fearing for his safety," the accused "put his vehicle in reverse and attempted to escape. In doing so he hit two individuals, two other vehicles, and some trees." Fortunately, the injuries were minor. At his trial, the accused raised the defence of necessity. The trial judge found that the accused had met the requirements of the defence as they were articulated by the Supreme Court of Canada in *Perka* (1984). However, the trial judge held that an additional issue arose on the facts of this particular case:

> There is one other thing, and an important consideration is, did the accused know—and this is all important—that his presence on the Skinner property to retrieve a stolen keg of beer, which had previously been stolen by his friends, did he know that it might create a situation which might become explosive?

The trial judge rejected the defence of necessity because "the accused could not have proceeded to the Skinner property without some thought of a possibility of ensuing problems in retrieving the beer."

The Alberta Court of Appeal set aside the conviction and ordered a new trial. The majority of the justices held that the trial judge was entitled to take into account the issue of the accused person's contributory fault in determining whether or not he should be deprived of the defence of necessity. However, he had not made any specific finding as to whether or not the accused person had foreseen—or ought to have foreseen—the necessitous circumstances with which he was confronted. In delivering the judgment of the majority of the Court of Appeal, Justice Berger indicated that the governing principle in such cases had already been articulated by Justice Dickson in the Supreme Court of Canada's decision in *Perka* (1984):

In my view the better approach to the relationship of fault to the availability of necessity as a defence is based once again on the question of whether the actions sought to be excused were truly "involuntary". If the necessitous situation was clearly foreseeable to a reasonable observer, if the actor contemplated or ought to have contemplated that his actions would likely give rise to an emergency requiring the breaking of the law, then I doubt whether what confronted the accused was in the relevant sense an emergency. His response was in that sense not "involuntary". "Contributory fault" of this nature, but only of this nature, is a relevant consideration to the availability of the defence.

In a new trial, the pivotal issue would be whether or not the accused knew or ought to have known that going to the party to retrieve the keg of beer would be likely to create an emergency situation in which he would have no choice but to break the law in order to save himself from harm.

Finally, it will no doubt be remembered that an important element in Justice Dickson's judgment in the (first) *Morgentaler* case (1975) was his view that "no system of positive law can recognize any principle which would entitle a person to violate the law because in his view the law conflicted with some higher social value." This principle has been used by the courts to reject defences of necessity where accused persons have defied court orders because they believed that they were acting to preserve a "greater good" of some kind.

For example, in *MacMillan Bloedel v. Simpson* (1994), the accused were part of a group of protesters who attempted to block access to logging sites in the Clayoquot Sound area of Vancouver Island. They did so in violation of a series of British Columbia Supreme Court **injunctions** that were designed to prevent the obstruction of logging crews who wished to carry out their work in this area and the accused were, therefore, charged with contempt of court. One of the defences raised on behalf of the accused was that of necessity; in particular, it was asserted that clear-cut logging was so damaging to the environment that the accused were entitled to break the law. The trial judge refused to accept this defence and the accused were ultimately convicted of contempt. Their appeal to the British Columbia Court of Appeal was dismissed.

Speaking on behalf of the Court of Appeal, Chief Justice McEachern stated that the defence of necessity was not available for two reasons:

First, the defendants had alternatives to breaking the law, namely, they could have applied to the court to have the injunction set aside. None of them did that prior to being arrested. I do not believe this defence operates to excuse conduct which has been specifically enjoined. By granting the order, the court prohibited the very conduct which is alleged against the defendants. An application to the court, which could be heard on fairly short notice, would have determined whether the circumstances were sufficient to engage the defence of necessity.

Secondly, I do not believe the defence of necessity can ever operate to avoid a peril that is lawfuly [sic] *authorized by the law.* M. & B. had the legal right to log in the areas in question, and the defence cannot operate in such circumstances. [emphasis added]

THE DEFENCE OF DURESS

THE RATIONALE FOR THE DEFENCE

The defences of duress and necessity are closely intertwined. As we have seen, the defence of necessity may be raised where external circumstances (such as a violent storm at sea) create an emergent situation in which the accused person is forced to choose between risking a disaster and breaking the law. However, where the defence of **duress** is claimed, the accused is asserting that his or her power of choice has been overborne by a threat from another human being. The classic example of the application of the defence duress arises where the accused person is forced—at gunpoint—to break the law. Any humane system of criminal law would provide an excuse to an individual who is faced with the option of submitting to the threat and breaking the law or facing the prospect of death or grievous injury.

It is clear that the underlying rationale for both the defence of necessity and the defence of duress is identical—namely, that it is wrong to punish someone who has not acted in a truly voluntary manner. As Chief Justice Lamer stated, in the judgment of the Supreme Court of Canada in the case of *Hibbert* (1995):

In my view, the similarities between the two defences are so great that consistency and logic requires that they be understood as based on the same juristic principles. Indeed, to do otherwise would be to promote incoherence and anomaly in the criminal law. In the case of necessity, the Court has already considered the various alternative theoretical positions available (in *Perka*...), and has expounded a conceptualization of the defence of necessity as an excuse, based on the idea of normative involuntariness. In my opinion, the need for consistency and coherence in the law dictates that the common law defence of duress also be based on this juridical foundation. [emphasis added]

SECTION 17 AND THE STATUTORY DEFENCE OF DURESS

Although the defences of necessity and duress are based on the same rationale, there is certainly one significant difference between them. Whereas Parliament has chosen not to define the defence of necessity, it has done so in the case of duress. Section 17 of the *Criminal Code* provides as follows:

A person who commits an offence under compulsion by threats of immediate death or bodily harm from a person who is present when the offence is committed is excused for committing the offence if the person believes that the threats will be carried out and if the person is not a party to a conspiracy or association whereby the person is subject to compulsion, but this section does not apply where the offence that is committed is high treason or treason, murder, piracy, attempted murder, sexual assault, sexual assault with a weapon, threats to a third party or causing bodily harm, aggravated sexual assault, forcible abduction, hostage taking, robbery, assault with a weapon or causing bodily harm, aggravated assault, unlawfully causing bodily harm, arson or an offence under sections 280 to 283 (abduction and detention of young persons).

Section 17 undoubtedly imposes a number of strict limitations on the defence of duress:

- The threat made against the accused must be of *immediate* death or bodily harm.
- The threat must be uttered by a person who is *present* when the accused person commits the crime(s) in question.
- The defence may not be claimed where the accused person is a "party to a conspiracy or association whereby the person is subject to compulsion" (for example, membership of a criminal gang).
- The defence may not be raised in relation to 22 serious crimes (ranging from murder to sexual assault).

In the case of *Paquette* (1976), the Supreme Court of Canada ruled that section 17 applies only to those accused persons who "actually commit" a criminal offence—for example, by pulling the trigger in a

homicide or striking the victim in a case of assault. The provisions of section 17 do not cover those accused persons who become parties to a criminal offence by aiding and/or abetting or by virtue of common intention (for example, the "getaway driver" in a robbery case): according to the Supreme Court, such accused persons may instead rely on the common law defence of duress (the nature and scope of which will be discussed in the next section of this chapter).

Returning to section 17 of the *Criminal Code*, it is clear that two of the requirements of the statutory defence of duress may deny the benefit of the defence to an accused person who realistically has no choice but to break the law. More specifically, if a threat is made against the accused to inflict death or bodily harm *in the future* (as opposed to a threat of *immediate* death or bodily harm) or if the threat is made by a person who is not *physically present* at the time that the accused commits the crime in question, then the accused is precluded from raising the defence of duress. In the case of *Ruzic* (2001), the Supreme Court of Canada ruled that these particular *Criminal Code* requirements are invalid because they infringe the fundamental principles of justice guaranteed by section 7 of the *Charter*.

The facts of the *Ruzic* case provide a clear illustration of the injustice that might occur if the section 17 requirements of a threat of immediate death or bodily harm and the physical presence of the person making the threat are relied upon to deny an accused person the benefit of a defence of duress. In April 1994, Marijana Ruzic, a 21-year-old woman from Belgrade in the former Yugoslavia, arrived in Canada by air and was found to be in possession of heroin and a false passport. At her trial, she readily admitted the offences of unlawful importation of a narcotic and use of a false passport. However, she argued that she should not be convicted of these offences because she was acting under duress. She stated that, while she was in Belgrade, she had been systematically intimidated by a "warrior" (a member of a paramilitary group). An expert witness testified that, in 1994, law and order had effectively broken down in Belgrade and that the local citizens believed that the police could not be trusted to protect them from roaming paramilitary groups that engaged in criminal and "mafia-like activities." The "warrior" subjected Ms. Ruzic to a number of violent assaults (including burning her arm with a cigarette lighter and forcibly injecting her with a substance that was probably heroin). The "warrior" later ordered Ruzic to take three packages of heroin to a restaurant in Toronto. When Ruzic protested, the "warrior" threatened to harm her mother. She then flew to Toronto, via Athens, and entered Canada with the drugs strapped to her body. Ruzic testified that she did not seek the help of the police in Belgrade because she believed that they were corrupt and would not provide her with any assistance. Similarly, she stated that she did not seek help from Canadian authorities because was convinced that the only way she could protect her mother from harm was to carry out the "warrior's" instructions.

Since Ruzic actually committed the offences charged, she would be covered by the provisions of section 17. However, if the "immediacy" and "presence" requirements of section 17 were applied to Ruzic's situation, then she would not be able to claim the benefit of the defence of duress. After all, the threats were of harm that might be perpetrated against her mother in the future and they were made by a man who was thousands of kilometres away when Ruzic entered Canada with the drugs and the false passport. However, the trial judge ruled that these requirements were invalid because they infringed the *Charter*, and the jury was permitted to consider the common law defence of duress. Ruzic was acquitted by the jury, and both the Ontario Court of Appeal and the Supreme Court of Canada affirmed this acquittal.

Why did the Supreme Court of Canada agree with the trial judge that the "immediacy" and "presence" requirements of section 17 infringed the *Charter*? In delivering the judgment of the Court, Justice LeBel stated that, if these requirements had been applied to the case of Ruzic, she could have been convicted of serious criminal offences even though she had no realistic choice but to break the law. However, it is a fundamental principle of justice, guaranteed by section 7 of the *Charter*, that no accused person should be convicted of a crime if he or she was acting involuntarily:

> Although moral involuntariness does not negate the *actus reus* or *mens rea* of an offence, it is a principle which, similarly to physical involuntariness, deserves protection under s. 7 of the *Charter*. It is a principle of fundamental justice that only voluntary conduct—behaviour that is the product of a free will and controlled body, unhindered by external constraints—should attract the penalty and stigma of criminal liability. Depriving a person of liberty and

branding her with the stigma of criminal liability would infringe the principles of fundamental justice if the accused did not have any realistic choice. The ensuing deprivation of liberty and stigma would have been imposed in violation of the tenets of fundamental justice and would thus infringe s. 7 of the *Charter*.

Justice LeBel ruled that, since the "immediacy" and "presence" requirements of section 17 are no longer valid, Ruzic was entitled to rely on the more generous provisions of the common law defence of duress. As we shall see, the common law defence of duress encompasses threats of future harm and does not require the presence of the person uttering the threat at the scene of the crime: all that is necessary is that there be a threat of death or serious bodily harm and that the accused reasonably believe it will be carried out if he or she does not follow the orders of the person who is threatening him or her. Since Ruzic satisfied the requirements of the common law defence of duress, she was entitled to be acquitted.

In the *Ruzic* case (2001), the Supreme Court of Canada did not rule that every element of section 17 was invalid under the *Charter*. It did not strike down that part of section 17 that prevents an accused person from raising the defence of duress if he or she became subject to compulsion because of membership in a criminal gang. Furthermore, the Supreme Court expressly left open the question of whether it is an infringement of the *Charter* to deny the benefit of the defence of duress to an accused person who commits one of the 22 offences listed in section 17. This would be a difficult question to address because the offences listed in section 17 are so diverse. For example, it is probable that most Canadians would be reluctant to give the benefit of the defence of duress to a person who has committed murder. However, such reluctance might not be present in the case of an accused person who has committed the offence of arson under threat of death.

THE COMMON LAW DEFENCE OF DURESS

In the *Ruzic* case (2001), the trial judge told the jury that there were four main requirements of the common law defence of duress. The Supreme Court of Canada subsequently approved the trial judge's instructions to the jury. The four requirements are as follows:

- The accused person acted "solely as a result of threats of death, or serious bodily harm."

- "The threats were of such gravity or seriousness that the accused believed that the threats would be carried out."
- "The threats were of such gravity that they might well have caused a reasonable person placed in the same situation as the accused to act in the same manner as she did."
- "The accused must not have had an obvious safe avenue of escape."

The Threat(s) Must Be of Death or Serious Bodily Harm

The threat(s) must be of death or serious bodily harm against the accused or another person closely associated with the accused (for example, a child, parent, or spouse). Furthermore, the threat(s) may be of death or serious bodily harm either immediately or at some point in the future. However, in *Ruzic* (2001), Justice LeBel stated that, when an accused person raises the defence of duress, the trial judge should nevertheless instruct the jury that there is a "need for a close temporal connection between the threat and the harm threatened"; indeed, the longer the period between the threat and the harm threatened, the less likely it is that the accused may claim that he or she had no reasonable alternative but to break the law.

The Threats Were Sufficiently Serious That the Accused Believed They Would Be Carried Out

If the accused person does not believe that the threat(s) will be carried out, then there is no basis for raising the defence of duress because he or she would not be deprived of the power of choice. However, a threat does not have to be explicit in order to provide a basis for a successful defence of duress. This point was strongly affirmed by the Ontario Court of Appeal in the case of *Mena* (1987), in which Justice Martin stated that

> [t]he threat required to invoke duress may be express or implied.... [Mena] did not testify that Yee had expressly stated that he would shoot him unless he accompanied Yee but it would be open to the jury to find that Yee, by producing the gun, pointing it at [Mena] and telling him that he was to go with him, had conveyed a threat to [Mena] that if he did not go with Yee he would be shot. [Mena] testified that he believed Yee was going to shoot him.

The Threats Were of Such Gravity That a Reasonable Person Might Well Have Acted in the Same Manner as the Accused

The defence of duress may be raised only if the accused person acts with a reasonable degree of fortitude in the face of threats. The test is whether a reasonable person, in exactly the same situation as the accused, would have been likely to yield to the threats and to break the law. As Justice LeBel said in the *Ruzic* case (2001):

> The common law of duress ... recognizes that an accused in a situation of duress does not only enjoy rights, but also has obligations towards others and society. As a fellow human being, the accused remains subject to a basic duty to adjust his or her conduct to the importance and nature of the threat. The law includes a requirement of proportionality between the threat and the criminal act to be executed, measured on the objective-subjective standard of the reasonable person similarly situated. The accused should be expected to demonstrate some fortitude and to put up a normal resistance to the threat.

For example, a mother who is subjected to threats of violence to both herself and her children by an abusive male partner would not normally be expected to resist these threats, whereas a bouncer at a club might well be expected to resist threats made by a single unarmed male.

There Was No "Safe Avenue of Escape" Open to the Accused

A critical consideration when the defence of duress is raised is whether or not the accused could *reasonably* have been expected to take an alternative course of action. If such an alternative were available, then he or she would be expected to act on it and thereby avoid breaking the law. For example, if the opportunity to escape arises, the accused person must take it; otherwise, he or she will lose the right to claim the benefit of the defence of duress.

Indeed, in the case of *Keller* (1998), the Alberta Court of Appeal stated unequivocally that, where the accused person has a **safe avenue of escape** and fails to pursue it, the trial judge should not even allow the defence to go to the jury:

> Whether there was a safe avenue of escape is a question of fact for the jury.... However, if on the evidence most favourable to the accused, he had a safe means

of escaping the threatened harm without committing the offence, no reasonable jury could possibly acquit on the basis of the defence of duress. *There would be no air of reality to the defence and a trial judge would be obliged to keep the defence from the jury.* [emphasis added]

Why should a defendant who has a "safe avenue of escape" lose the benefit of the defence of duress? In the *Hibbert* case (1995), the Supreme Court of Canada answered this question by referring to the underlying rationale of the defence. In the words of Chief Justice Lamer, who delivered the judgment of the Court,

An accused person cannot rely on the common law defence of duress if he or she had an opportunity to safely extricate himself or herself from the situation of duress. The rationale for this rule is simply that in such circumstances the condition of "normative involuntariness" that provides the theoretical basis for both the defences of duress and necessity is absent—*if the accused had the chance to take action that would have allowed him or her to avoid committing an offence, it cannot be said that he or she had no real choice when deciding whether or not to break the law.* [emphasis added]

In *Hibbert* (1995), the Supreme Court of Canada also dealt with the critical question of whether the existence of a "safe avenue of escape" should be determined on an objective or a subjective basis. In approaching this question, Chief Justice Lamer took into account the views expressed by Justice Dickson when he was discussing the defence of necessity in the *Perka* case (1984). The chief justice restated his opinion that normative involuntariness constitutes the theoretical foundation for both the defences of duress and of necessity and came to the conclusion that courts should adopt an objective approach in determining whether the accused had a "safe avenue of escape." In his view,

... a degree of objectivity is inherent to excuses that are based on the notion of normative involuntariness, to the extent that this concept turns on the objective availability, or lack of availability, of true choice. Indeed, [Justice Dickson] clearly indicates that the operative standard for the defence of necessity is to be an objective one, based on whether "there is a *reasonable* legal alternative to disobeying the law."

However, Chief Justice Lamer hastened to add that, even though the "safe avenue of escape" issue was to be determined on an objective basis,

nevertheless the court must "take into account the particular circumstances of the accused, including his or her ability to perceive the existence of alternative courses of action." As the Alberta Court of Appeal stated in the *Keller* case (1998), "[T]he question is whether a reasonable person, with similar history, personal circumstances, abilities, capacities, and human frailties as the accused would, in the particular circumstances, reasonably believe there was no safe avenue of escape and that he had no choice but to yield to the coercion." It is noteworthy that the Alberta Court of Appeal also suggested that the accused must take reasonable steps to "discover his or her full range of options before deciding to engage in the wrongful conduct."

Naturally, a central consideration in determining whether there was a "safe avenue of escape" is the perceived availability of police protection for the accused. For example, in the *Keller* case (1998), the accused had been charged with trafficking in LSD. The accused argued that he had been threatened with death or bodily harm by a known drug dealer if he (Keller) did not comply with the instructions of the dealer. Over a period of four months, he retrieved at least 10 packages of drugs from the Calgary International Airport. Keller claimed that he had not sought the assistance of the police because he was frightened of the drug dealer and his

The defence of duress is not available when there is a safe avenue of escape.

friends, and Keller believed that the police were incapable of furnishing him with effective protection. The trial judge ruled that there was no air of reality to the accused's defence of duress and refused to put it to the jury. Keller was convicted and his subsequent appeal to the Alberta Court of Appeal was dismissed. The court pointed out that the conduct for which Keller had been charged occurred four months after he was allegedly threatened and that there had been no explicit threats in the interim. Furthermore, the court emphasized that Keller was "not abnormally vulnerable to threats of physical violence" and that he had "no reason to think that the police could not give him protection if he reported the situation." Furthermore, Keller had made absolutely no attempt to consider whether he had any legal alternatives open to him:

> He *did not attempt to contact the police, even anonymously, to see if they could provide protective options.* The appellant did not take reasonable steps, taking into account his history, personal circumstances, abilities, capacities, and human frailties, to discover his options. [emphasis added]

Similarly, in the *Valentini* case (1999), two of the accused were charged with importing and trafficking in narcotics and possession for the purpose of trafficking. They had attempted to smuggle 34 pounds (15 kg) of cocaine through customs at Pearson Airport in Toronto. They claimed that they had acted under duress—specifically, threats of violence from one of their co-accused. The trial judge instructed the jury that, in considering the question of whether the two accused had a "safe avenue of escape" open to them, they were entitled to take into account the fact that they had not sought the protection of the Canadian authorities upon their arrival at the airport after their flight from Aruba. The accused were convicted and their subsequent appeals to the Ontario Court of Appeal were dismissed. On behalf of the Court, Justice Rosenberg stated that

> ... the appellants could have sought the assistance of the authorities immediately upon entering the airport before they physically took possession of the contraband. The importing offence was at least not complete until that point.... The fact that neither appellant sought the assistance of the police or customs officials even after they had taken possession of the bags containing the drugs was compelling evidence that the reason for completing the importation was not the lack of a safe avenue of escape.

However, there may be circumstances in which it would be unreasonable to expect the accused person to seek the assistance of the police or other authorities. For example, in the *Ruzic* case (2001), the accused could not seek the protection of the police in Belgrade because, at the relevant time, law and order had apparently broken down and the local citizens could not trust the police to protect them from members of various violent paramilitary groups. Furthermore, Ruzic could not have been expected to seek the protection of the authorities in Toronto because the threats that had destroyed her power of choice were directed not toward her personally but toward her mother, who was thousands of kilometres away in Belgrade. As Justice LeBel noted,

> ... the law does not require an accused to seek the official protection of police in all cases. The requirement of objectivity must itself take into consideration the special circumstances where the accused found herself as well as her perception of them.

Finally, it is important to consider the impact of an accused person's prior involvement with a criminal organization when it is claimed that he or she acted under the shadow of threats made by that very organization. It has been held that the accused person may be denied the benefit of the defence of duress if he or she voluntarily joined or became involved with the criminal organization. Indeed, in the case of *Li* (2002), the Ontario Court of Appeal stated that the voluntary involvement of the accused person with a criminal organization must be taken into account when determining whether he or she had a safe avenue of escape. The facts in *Li* were that the three accused persons had been smuggled from China to Canada by a criminal organization known as the "Snakeheads." As a consequence, they all owed money to the Snakeheads. Tsang, a member of the Snakeheads organization, later approached the accused persons and asked them to participate in the kidnapping of three people. Tsang threatened the accused persons and their families with violence if they did not take part in the kidnapping and also told them that their debts to the Snakeheads would be written off should they participate. The accused persons forcibly abducted the victims from their apartment and took them to another location and held them there for 22 days. The victims were then rescued by the police, who had conducted a surprise raid on the premises. During the period of the victims' captivity, the accused had, for the most part, been left alone with their hostages. For all practical purposes, the accused persons were free to come and go as they pleased: indeed, each of the accused persons had run errands, such as purchasing food. Furthermore, they each had enjoyed the opportunity to make a telephone call to seek the assistance of the authorities, had they wished to do so.

The accused claimed the benefit of the defence of duress at their trial and based their claim on the threats made against them by Tsang, who was acting on behalf of the Snakeheads. However, they were nevertheless convicted on three counts of kidnapping and forcible confinement. The Ontario Court of Appeal dismissed their appeal against their convictions. The Court of Appeal agreed with the trial judge that there was no air of reality to the defence of duress because the accused had a safe avenue of escape open to them. In delivering the judgment of the Court, Justice Finlayson stated that

> [i]t is undisputed that these appellants knew they were purchasing the services of the Snakeheads before they left China. The appellant Liu even admitted that he previously used the Snakehead services to gain entry to the United States, and had returned to China before embarking on this effort at getting onto this continent. The appellant Chen testified that he knew the Snakeheads were "smugglers" and that their activity was illegal in China, but added that others use them and so it is perceived as legal. The appellant Li testified that he chose to use the Snakeheads to obtain passage to the United States, despite its high price. None claimed to be surprised on learning of the nature of the Snakeheads organization, nor did any of them claim to have laboured under some belief that it was a benign organization prior to availing themselves of its services.... *In evaluating the appellants' claim that they had no safe avenue of escape, it is important to take into account their voluntary decision to get involved with the Snakehead organization in the first place. The two concepts are interrelated by the authorities.* [emphasis added]

Justice Finlayson emphasized that, as far as the courts are concerned, it should be recognized that there is a "juxtaposition between a safe avenue of escape and the voluntary assumption of the risk in the first place." For example, when evaluating the accused persons' claim that seeking police protection would have been futile because they were in fear not only for their own lives but also the lives of their families in China, "the court should be reminded of their initiative in approaching the Snakeheads in the first place, and the fact that the threats of retaliation against them and their families was sweetened by the inducement of

retiring their debts to this organization." In the words of the Court of Appeal,

> There must be an air of reality to the defence of duress before the trial judge can permit it to be considered by the jury.... However, where as here the proposition put forward by the appellants is that they freely and without coercion placed themselves in the clutches of their alleged tormentors, it would be a mockery of justice to place the issue of the validity of the duress issue before the jury. We have a matter of policy here. The appellants made a deal with the devil and say that they had no alternative than to honour it. They ask this court to place their safety above the liberty and security of their innocent victims and thus encourage the Snakeheads to continue their campaign of extortion through the agency of persons similarly situated to the appellants.

It will, no doubt, be recalled that the statutory defence of duress, articulated in section 17 of the *Criminal Code*, indicates that the defence may only be claimed successfully if the accused person "is not a party to a conspiracy or association whereby the person is subject to compulsion." In this respect, there appears to be a considerable degree of convergence between the common law and statutory defences of duress. Significantly, the Supreme Court of Canada did not strike down this particular element of section 17 when it issued its decision in the *Ruzic* case (2001).

STUDY QUESTIONS

1. Wegg is taking part in a wilderness survival course with his friend Dedlock. The two men panic, lose their survival kits, and soon become lost. They wander around a forest for one day and one night without any food, except for the occasional berries that they can find on their way. Dedlock states that he is exhausted and wants to stay where he is. Wegg presses on alone and comes to a small log cabin. There is no one in the cabin and Wegg breaks down the door. He eats some food that he finds in the refrigerator and also drinks two or three beers. He then takes a truck that is standing outside, using the keys that he has found in the kitchen. He drives off at very high speed and, within a minute or two, reaches a town, where he asks for help. Dedlock is later rescued from the forest and soon recovers. The police are contemplating laying the following charges against Wegg: breaking and entering, theft, taking and driving a motor vehicle without

the owner's consent, and speeding. Would Wegg have any defence to these charges?

2. The *S.S. Lollipop* sinks in a terrible storm. There are not enough lifeboats and those that are operational are severely overloaded. One lifeboat is commanded by Captain Bligh, who escaped at the last minute from his sinking ship. The lifeboat is so overloaded and so much water is being taken on board that it is obvious the boat will sink within a few minutes. Bligh decrees that all male passengers over the age of 35 must leave the lifeboat and he commands that they be "put into the water." The other crew and passengers push the unfortunate "over 35" male passengers into the turbulent sea, where they are unable to hang on to the sides of the boat and they all perish. The remaining occupants of the lifeboat are later saved by a passing ship. Everyone is agreed that, if the unfortunate "over 35" males had not left the lifeboat, it is most probable that it would have sunk and everyone on board would have been killed. The Crown is thinking of charging Bligh with murder. Does he have any defence to any charges of murder that might be laid against him?

3. Polonius is a homeless person who has no money. It is a freezing night in the middle of winter, and he is cold and hungry. He is desperate for warmth, shelter, and food. However, since demand far outstrips supply, Polonius is turned away from the only two shelters available for an overnight stay. Polonius sees a restaurant that has been closed for the night. Polonius enters the restaurant by climbing in through a window. He eats some food, consumes one or two soft drinks, and turns on an electric heater to keep himself warm. The police discover Polonius in the restaurant and arrest him for breaking and entering with intent to commit theft. Polonius argues that he would have died from exposure and/or hunger if he had not entered the restaurant, eaten some food, and obtained warmth from the heater. Would Polonius be entitled to a defence of necessity?

4. Chuffey is a guard at a penitentiary. One of the inmates, a man called Murdstone, asks Chuffey to smuggle in some illegal drugs for the use of Murdstone and his cellmates, who are members of a well-known criminal gang. Chuffey initially refuses but Murdstone threatens to "arrange an accident" for Chuffey if he will not transport the drugs into the prison. Chuffey is terrified by the threat against him and, on Murdstone's instructions, goes to a local bar, where he is given a package by Buzfuz—a very large and intimidating gang member. Chuffey delivers the package to Murdstone but his actions are observed by another prison officer and he is arrested and charged with trafficking in heroin, contrary to section 5 of the *Controlled Drugs and Substances Act*, S.C. 1996, c. 19. Does Chuffey have any defence(s) to this charge?

5. Meagles witnesses a brutal killing that is perpetrated by Bounderby, a local mobster. Bounderby is charged with murder, and Meagles is subpoenaed by the Crown to give evidence at the trial. Before the trial takes place, Meagles receives a number of telephone calls from a man identifying himself as "the Avenging Angel." The gist of these calls is that, if Meagles does not have a convenient loss of memory at Bounderby's trial, Meagles's children will be killed. Meagles is too frightened to tell the police and gives false evidence at the trial. As a consequence, Bounderby is acquitted. Crown counsel decides to charge Meagles with perjury under section 131 of the *Code*. Are there any defences available to Meagles?

6. Hamlet is approached by Laertes and Claudius. Hamlet knows these men because he used to be part of the criminal gang to which they still belong. Hamlet severed his relationship with the gang one year previously. Laertes says to Hamlet, "Drive us to the Denmark Bank." When they reach the bank, Laertes orders Hamlet to remain outside in his van. Laertes and Claudius then enter the bank and remove all of the available cash from the tellers, who are terrified by Laertes' violent threats. As Laertes is leaving the bank, he fatally shoots the bank manager, who had disobeyed Laertes' command to remain still on the floor. Laertes and Claudius then enter Hamlet's vehicle in order to escape from the scene of the robbery. However, the police have surrounded the bank and eventually Laertes, Claudius, and Hamlet are taken into custody. Claudius and Hamlet both claim that they only acted as they did because of their overwhelming fear of Laertes, who has previously committed more than one murder. May Claudius and Hamlet claim the benefit of the defence of duress?

7. Cleopatra is a surgeon who has acquired a special expertise in the separation of conjoined twins. She

is asked to separate infant twins Hermione and Portia. Tragically, Portia lacks the necessary organs of her own to permit her to survive such an operation. The attending pediatricians tell Cleopatra that, unless she separates the twins, both of them will die because Portia's bodily needs will eventually overwhelm Hermione's vital organs. In short, Cleopatra is asked to choose between separating the twins and declining to intervene. If she separates them, Portia will immediately die but Hermione will almost certainly enjoy a normal life span. If she does not carry out the surgery, both Hermione and Portia will die in a matter of months. Cleopatra wishes to separate the twins but she is told that, if she does so, she could be charged with the murder of Portia. If this should happen, would Cleopatra have any defence(s) open to her?

FURTHER READING

Arnold, D.G. 2001. Coercion and Moral Responsibility. 38 *American Philosophical Quarterly*: 53–67.

Berger, B.L. 2002. A Choice among Values: Theoretical and Historical Perspectives on the Defence of Necessity. 39 *Alberta Law Review*: 848–863.

Berman, M.N. 2005. Lesser Evils and Justification: A Less Close Look. 24 *Law and Philosophy*: 681–709.

Brudner, A. 2009. Excusing Necessity and Terror: What Criminal Law Can Teach Constitutional Law. 3 *Criminal Law and Philosophy*: 147–166.

Buchanan, A., and G. Virgo. 1999. Duress and Mental Abnormality. [1999] *Criminal Law Review*: 517–531.

Chan, W., and A.P. Simester. 2005. Analysis. Duress, Necessity: How Many Defences? 16 *The King's College Law Journal*: 121–132.

Clarkson, C.M.V. 2004. Necessary Action: A New Defence. [2004] *Criminal Law Review*: 81–104.

Colvin, E., and S. Anand. 2007. *Principles of Criminal Law*. 3rd ed. Toronto: Carswell.

Coughlan, S.G. 2002. Duress, Necessity, Self-Defence and Provocation: Implications of Radical Change? 7 *Canadian Criminal Law Review*: 147–208.

Dickens, B. 1976. The *Morgentaler* Case: Criminal Process and Abortion Law. 14 *Osgoode Hall Law Journal*: 229–274.

Elliott, C. 2001. Comment: Murder and Necessity following the Siamese Twins Litigation. 65 *The Journal of Criminal Law*: 66–75.

Enns, R. 1999. *A Voice Unheard: The Latimer Case and People with Disabilities*. Halifax: Fernwood Publishing.

Fletcher, G.P. 1998. *Basic Concepts of Criminal Law*. New York: Oxford University Press. 130–132, 138–145.

Galloway, D. 1986. Necessity as a Justification: A Critique of *Perka*. 10 *Dalhousie Law Journal*: 158–172.

Gardner, S. 2005. Direct Action and the Defence of Necessity. [2005] *The Criminal Law Review*: 371–380.

Ghanayim, K. 2006. Excused Necessity: A Defence in the Criminal Code—A Comparative and Doctrinal Study. 11 *Canadian Criminal Law Review*: 53–96.

———. 2006. Excuse Necessity in Western Legal Philosophy. 19 *The Canadian Journal of Law & Jurisprudence*: 31–65.

Horder, J. 1998. Self-Defence, Necessity and Duress: Understanding the Relationship. 16 *Canadian Journal of Law & Jurisprudence*: 143–165.

———. 2004. *Excusing Crime*. Oxford: Oxford University Press.

Ibbetson, D. 2005. Duress Revisited. 64 *Cambridge Law Journal*: 530–532.

Klimchuk, D. 1998. Moral Innocence, Normative Involuntariness and Fundamental Justice. 18 *Criminal Reports (5th Series)*: 96–112.

Law Reform Commission of Canada. 1987. Report 31: *Recodifying Criminal Law*. Rev. ed. Ottawa: L.R.C.C.

Levy, S. 2003. The Lesser of two Evils: A Contextual View of the English Case of the Conjoined Twins. 22 *Medicine and Law*: 1–9.

McCauley, F. 1998. Necessity and Duress in Criminal Law: The Confluence of Two Great Tributaries. 33 *Irish Jurist*: 180–186.

Mewett, A.W. 1995. Editorial: A Jurisprudential Analysis of Duress. 38 *Criminal Law Quarterly*: 129–130.

Mitchell, G.C. 2001. No Joy in This for Anyone: Reflections on the Exercise of Prosecutorial Discretion in *R. v. Latimer*. 64 *Saskatchewan Law Review*: 491–510.

Morgan, E.M. 1984. The Defence of Necessity: Justification or Excuse? 42 *University of Toronto Faculty Law Review*: 165–183.

Morse, S. 1994. Causation, Compulsion, and Involuntariness. 22 *Bulletin of the American Academy of Psychiatry and the Law*: 159–180.

Ost, S. 2005. Euthanasia and the Defence of Necessity: Advocating a More Appropriate Legal Response. [2005] *Criminal Law Review*: 355–370.

Paciocco, D.M. 1999. *Getting Away with Murder: The Canadian Criminal Justice System*. Concord, ON: Irwin Law. 251–268.

Padfield, N. 1992. Duress, Necessity and the Law Commission. [1992] *Criminal Law Review*: 778–789.

Quigley, T. 1995. *R. v. Latimer*: Hard Cases Make Interesting Law. 41 *Criminal Reports (4th Series)*: 89–99.

Reed, A. 1996. Duress and Provocation as Excuse to Murder: Salutary Lesson from Recent Anglo-American Jurisprudence. 6 *Journal of Transnational Law & Policy*: 51–92.

———. 1997. The Need for a New Anglo-American Approach to Duress. 61 *Journal of Criminal Law*: 209–224.

Reilly, A., and R. Mikus. 1996. *R. v. Hibbert*: The Theoretical Foundations of Duress. 30 *U.B.C. Law Review*: 181–199.

Roach, K. 2009. *Criminal Law*. 4th ed. Toronto: Irwin Law. Ch. 8.

Rosenthal, P. 1989. Duress in the Criminal Law. 32 *Criminal Law Quarterly*: 199–226.

Schabas, P.B. 1985. Justification, Excuse and the Defence of Necessity: A Comment on *Perka v. The Queen*. 27 *Criminal Law Quarterly*: 278–287.

Schopp, R.F. 1998. *Justification Defenses and Just Convictions*. New York: Cambridge University Press.

Shaffer, M. 1998. Coerced into Crime: Battered Women and the Defence of Duress. 4 *Canadian Criminal Law Review*: 271–330.

———. 1998. Scrutinizing Duress: The Constitutional Validity of Section 17 of the Criminal Code. 40 *Criminal Law Quarterly*: 444–475.

Simons, K.W. 2005. Exploring the Intricacies of the Lesser Evils Defense. 24 *Law and Philosophy*: 645–679.

Smith, K.J.M. 1999. Duress and Steadfastness: In Pursuit of the Unintelligible. [1999] *Criminal Law Review*: 363–376.

Sneiderman, B. 2001. The Case of Robert Latimer: A Commentary on Crime and Punishment. 37 *Alberta Law Review*: 1017–1044.

———. 2001. Latimer in the Supreme Court: Necessity, Compassionate Homicide, and Mandatory Sentencing. 64 *Saskatchewan Law Review*: 511–544.

Strange, C. 2001. Mercy for Murderers? A Historical Perspective on the Royal Prerogative of Mercy. 34 *Saskatchewan Law Review*: 559–590.

Stuart, D. 2001. A Hard Case Makes for Too Harsh Law. 39 *Criminal Reports (5th Series)*: 58–64.

———. 2007. *Canadian Criminal Law: A Treatise*. 5th ed. Toronto: Thomson Carswell. Ch. 7.

Stuart, D., R.J. Delisle, and S. Coughlan. 2009. *Learning Canadian Criminal Law*. 11th ed. Toronto: Thomson Carswell. Ch. 7.

Trotter, G.T. 2003. Necessity and Death: Lessons from *Latimer* and the Case of the Conjoined Twins. 40 *Alberta Law Review*: 817–840.

Verdun-Jones, S.N. 2007. *Canadian Criminal Cases: Selected Highlights*. 2nd ed. Toronto: Thomson Nelson. Ch. 11.

Yeo, S.M.H. 1990. *Compulsion in the Criminal Law*. Sydney: The Law Book Company.

———. 1996. Voluntariness, Free Will and Duress. 70 *Australian Law Journal*: 304–312.

———. 2002. Challenging Moral Involuntariness as a Principle of Fundamental Justice. 28 *Queen's Law Journal*: 335–351.

———. 2002. Defining Duress. 46 *Criminal Law Quarterly*: 293–318.

Young, Diana. 2004. Excuses and Intelligibility in Criminal Law. 53 *University of New Brunswick Law Journal*: 79–110.

Young, R.E. 1999. Note and Comments: *R. v. Ruzic*. 42 *Criminal Law Quarterly*: 515–524.

CHAPTER TWELVE

SELF-DEFENCE AND DEFENCE OF PROPERTY

OVERVIEW

This chapter examines the following:

1. two of the major defences that may be raised in response to criminal charges in Canada: namely, self-defence and defence of property;
2. the situations in which private citizens may defend their persons or property against unlawful attack:
   (i) self-defence against an unprovoked assault, where the defendant did not intend to inflict death or grievous bodily harm (section 34(1)of the *Criminal Code*);
   (ii) self-defence where the defendant inflicts death or grievous bodily harm (section 34(2));
3. the use of force in order to prevent an assault (section 37);
4. the requirements in section 34(1) that the accused person be the victim of an unprovoked assault and that he or she use no more force than is necessary ("the requirement of proportionality");
5. the ruling of the courts that section 34(2) does *not* impose a requirement of proportionality and does *not* require that the accused person be the victim of an unprovoked assault;
6. the requirements in section 34(2) that the accused person act under a reasonable apprehension of death or grievous bodily harm and that he or she reasonably believed that there was no other way of preserving him- or herself from death or grievous bodily harm;
7. the rulings by the Supreme Court of Canada that section 34(2) may be raised by an accused person whether or not that person intended to cause death or grievous bodily harm and that, under

section 34(2), there is no requirement that the assault on the accused be imminent;
8. the ruling of the Supreme Court of Canada that evidence relating to the "battered wife syndrome" may be introduced in order to help members of the jury to determine whether or not a woman who kills an abusive partner meets the requirements stipulated by section 34(2);
9. that section 37 provides a defence to individuals who use force in order to prevent an assault either against the accused or anyone under his or her protection;
10. that section 40 of the *Criminal Code* provides a defence to an accused person who is in peaceable possession of a dwelling-house and who uses such force as is "necessary" to prevent someone from forcing his or her way into the dwelling-house;
11. that section 41(1) of the *Criminal Code* permits an accused person who is in peaceable possession of a dwelling-house or "real property" (land) to use "no more force than is necessary" to prevent a person from trespassing or to remove a trespasser; and
12. that section 41(2) provides that, if a trespasser actively resists the person in "peaceable possession" of the dwelling-house or real property, then the trespasser shall be deemed to be committing an unlawful and unprovoked assault and that the person in "peaceable possession" of the dwelling-house or real property may then raise the defence of self-defence under section 34 of the *Code*.

SELF-DEFENCE AND DEFENCE OF PROPERTY

THE STRUCTURE OF THE *CRIMINAL CODE* PROVISIONS

A number of provisions in the *Criminal Code* justify the use of force in **self-defence** (of the person or property). For example, sections 25 through 33 of the *Code* deal with the justified use of force by those individuals who are charged with the administration and enforcement of the law in Canada. Sections 34 through 42, in contrast, are concerned with delineating the circumstances in which a private citizen may defend person or property against unlawful attack. These sections are, unfortunately, quite complex in nature and it is clearly not possible to investigate all of them. This discussion will, therefore, be confined to an examination of the major sections of the *Code* that deal with the justifiable use of force by the private citizen.

SELF-DEFENCE AGAINST AN UNLAWFUL AND UNPROVOKED ASSAULT WHERE THE DEFENDANT DOES NOT INTEND TO INFLICT DEATH OR GRIEVOUS BODILY HARM

Section 34(1) of the *Criminal Code* provides the following:

> Every one who is unlawfully assaulted without having provoked the assault is justified in repelling force by force if the force he uses is not intended to cause death or grievous bodily harm and is no more than is necessary to enable him to defend himself.

It will be noted that this provision of the *Criminal Code* is applicable only where an **unprovoked assault** is committed on the defendant. (Section 36 of the *Code* provides a partial definition of provocation for this purpose, namely, "provocation includes ... provocation by blows, words or gestures.") Section 34(1) is also limited in its application to situations in which the defendant *did not intend to cause death or grievous bodily harm*. If the defendant did intend to inflict such a degree of injury upon an assailant, the appropriate defence would be formulated in terms of the provisions of section 34(2). Perhaps the most significant limitation to section 34(1), however, is the requirement that the force employed must be "no more than is necessary to enable [the accused] to defend himself." This restriction introduces the concept of the *proportionality* of force. To use an extreme example frequently quoted by academic writers, one may not "use a tank against a chariot." In other words, there must be a reasonable degree of proportionality between the force employed by the assailant and the force employed by the accused in self-defence.

The requirement of proportionality is well illustrated by the case of *Nelson* (1953), in which the accused was charged with manslaughter following a fight with the deceased victim. It appeared that the deceased had struck the accused with an open right hand, and the latter had responded with a blow that fractured the victim's jaw in several places. The victim fell and struck his head on the pavement, causing a brain hemorrhage that resulted in his death. Although the victim had been carrying an iron bar in his hand, he had not attempted to use it. The accused was convicted at his trial and appealed to the British Columbia Court of Appeal. By a majority decision, the court dismissed Nelson's appeal. Justice Sidney Smith summed up the situation in the following manner:

Cartoon by Elizabeth Carefoot

Under section 34(1), the force used by the accused must be proportionate to the force employed by the assailant. One cannot "use a tank against a chariot."

... [T]he accused was 29 years of age, 6 ft. in height and weighed 170 lbs., while the deceased was 59 years of age, 5 ft. 10 in. in height and weighed 130lbs....

It will be observed that a slap on the face was here answered with a blow of such force as to fracture the deceased's jaw in several places. With respect, I find it impossible on the evidence to say that this force was necessary for the purpose of self-defence, or that the appellant was under reasonable apprehension of death or grievous bodily harm....

Clearly, in the view of the Court of Appeal, the violent response of the accused was out of all proportion to the unprovoked "slap" perpetrated by the victim.

There is no doubt that Parliament intended to impose an *objective* test in section 34(1) of the *Code*. However, Canadian courts have tempered this requirement of objectivity by giving some limited recognition to certain subjective factors. For example, the courts have not insisted that individuals who are defending themselves against a violent attack must calculate the "necessary" degree of retaliatory force with mathematical precision. In the case of *Baxter* (1975), Justice Martin, in delivering the judgment of the Ontario Court of Appeal, stated that

[s]. 34(1) does not import a purely objective test. The doctrine of mistake of fact is applicable to s. 34(1) as well as s. 34(2). *An accused's belief that he was in imminent danger from an attack may be reasonable, although he may be mistaken in his belief.* Moreover, when deciding whether the force used by the accused was more than necessary in self-defence under both s. 34(1) and (2) the jury must bear in mind that a person defending himself against an attack, reasonably apprehended, cannot be expected to weigh to a nicety, the exact measure of necessary defensive action. [emphasis added]

In the *Doherty* case (2000), the New Brunswick Court of Appeal emphasized that an accused person may exercise the right to self-defence under section 34(1) of the *Code, even if he or she does not act out of fear for his or her own personal safety.* Doherty was a bouncer at a strip club and had expelled the victim from the premises. The victim and a companion became belligerent and banged and kicked on the club door. When Doherty responded by coming out of the premises, the victim attempted to hit him on the head. Doherty parried the blow and then punched the victim on the jaw. The victim fell to the ground and hit his head. He died a few hours later from a serious head injury. Doherty was convicted of manslaughter at his trial. The trial judge took the view that section 34(1) was not applicable because Doherty's blow to the jaw of the deceased was "not actuated by fear." He also ruled that Doherty's right of self-defence did not extend beyond merely "blocking" the punches thrown at him by the deceased. The Court of Appeal rejected both of these rulings by the trial judge and entered an acquittal. On behalf of the court, Justice Drapeau stated that

... [i]n the present case, the evidence is reasonably open to the interpretation that Mr. Doherty was unlawfully assaulted by Mr. Gillan without having provoked the assault, that, as found by the trial judge, the force used by Mr. Doherty was not intended to cause death or grievous bodily harm and, finally, that the force used by Mr. Doherty was no more than necessary to enable him to defend himself. That being the case, I conclude that the Crown has not proven that Mr. Doherty was unjustified in repelling force by force, as he did. It follows that s. 34(1) affords Mr. Doherty a complete defence to the charge.

In *Paice* (2005), the Supreme Court of Canada held that section 34(1) may not be raised by an accused person who was a party to a consensual fist fight because it would not be possible to establish that the accused person did not provoke the assault. In the words of Justice Charron:

... An accused can only rely on s. 34(1) if he was unlawfully assaulted "without having provoked the assault". Under s. 36 of the *Criminal Code*, provocation includes "provocation by blows, words or gestures". The defence of self-defence under s. 34(1) is expansive and allows a person to repel force by force as is necessary to enable him to defend himself without the necessity of the apprehension of death or grievous bodily harm. So long as the force used is not itself intended to cause death or grievous bodily harm, the conduct will be justified. Section 34(1) is only available where the accused is an innocent victim who has been assaulted without having provoked the assault. Where a person willingly engages in mutual combat, he cannot later say that he did not provoke the assault....

Finally, it is important to recognize that section 34(1) may be raised successfully even though the accused person *unintentionally* inflicts death or grievous bodily harm. For example, firing a warning shot with a gun may be considered a proportionate response to a violent assault. The fact that the bullet *accidentally* kills the victim does not deprive the accused person of the section 34(1) defence. This particular scenario occurred in the *Kandola* case (1993), where the B.C. Court of Appeal held that "it is important to note that it is the force itself, and not the consequence of the force used, which is justified if the limiting conditions of the statute are met." In other words, if the accused person's response to an assault is proportionate, the fatal consequences of that response are not relevant to the application of section 34(1).[1] However, as we shall see in the next section, an accused person is more likely to rely on section 34(2) whenever death or grievous bodily harm has occurred.

SELF-DEFENCE AGAINST AN UNLAWFUL ASSAULT WHERE THE ACCUSED EITHER INTENTIONALLY OR UNINTENTIONALLY INFLICTS DEATH OR GRIEVOUS BODILY HARM

Section 34(2) of the *Criminal Code* provides that

[e]very one who is unlawfully assaulted and who causes death or grievous bodily harm in repelling the assault is justified if

(a)   he causes it under reasonable apprehension of death or grievous bodily harm from the violence with which the assault was originally made or with which the assailant pursues his purposes, and

(b)   he believes, on reasonable grounds, that he cannot otherwise preserve himself from death or grievous bodily harm.

There are two fundamental differences between sections 34(1) and 34(2). First, as the Supreme Court of Canada noted in the *McIntosh* case (1995), section 34(2) applies even if the accused was the initial aggressor in the series of events that led to the use of extreme force in self-defence. Whereas section 34(1) includes the words "without having provoked the assault," section 34(2) does not. Second, section 34(2) does not require that the degree of force used by the defendant be "proportionate" to that inflicted by the assailant. In other words, the *Code* explicitly provides for the consideration of a number of *subjective* factors in the application of section 34(2). In the case of

---

[1] The Supreme Court of Canada endorsed this principle in *Kong* (2006).

Baxter (1975), Justice Martin of the Ontario Court of Appeal addressed this issue in the following manner:

Under s. 34(2) of the *Code* the ultimate question for the jury is not whether the accused was actually in danger of death or grievous bodily harm, and whether the causing of death or grievous bodily harm by him was in fact necessary to preserve himself from death or grievous bodily harm, but whether:

(1)   he caused death or grievous bodily harm under a *reasonable apprehension* of death or grievous bodily harm, and

(2)   he *believed on reasonable and probable grounds* that he could not otherwise preserve himself from death or grievous bodily harm....

The accused's subjective belief that he was in imminent danger of death or grievous bodily harm and that his action was necessary in self-defence was ... required to be based on reasonable grounds. In deciding whether the accused's belief was based upon reasonable grounds the jury would of necessity draw comparisons with what a reasonable person in the accused's situation might believe with respect to the extent and imminence of the danger by which he was threatened, and the force necessary to defend himself against the apprehended danger.

The need, under section 34(2), for the court to focus on the reasonableness of the accused's beliefs rather than on the objective proportionality of the force used in self-defence is clearly illustrated by the tragic case of *Berrigan* (1998). Here, the accused stabbed the deceased victim and claimed that he did so under the mistaken belief that the latter had been reaching into his pocket for a gun (in fact, the object in the deceased's pocket was a cellular phone). Since the victim was unarmed, there was clearly no objective proportionality between the degree of force threatened by the victim and the violent response of the accused. However, the B.C. Court of Appeal ruled that the accused person was nevertheless entitled to rely on the defence provided by section 34(2) because of his mistaken belief that his life was in danger. Justice Donald, on behalf of the Court, stated that it was "imperative" that "the jury be told that the appellant is entitled to rely on self-defence on a reasonable but mistaken belief because on his own evidence, his belief was mistaken." He went on to say that "the danger here is that the jury may have rejected self-defence on the basis that no actual assault occurred or was about to occur."

Although the courts have been quite flexible in their interpretation of section 34(2), it is still important to emphasize that, if defendants claim that they were operating under a misapprehension concerning the need to inflict death or grievous bodily harm in a self-defence situation, such a misapprehension must be based on *reasonable grounds*. This principle was strongly underscored by the Supreme Court of Canada in *Reilly* (1984). One of the issues in this case concerned the relevance of intoxication to a defence based on section 34(2). More specifically, can defendants who claim that they were mistaken as to the need for deadly force receive the benefit of the defence under section 34(2) if the mistake was induced by intoxication? The Supreme Court held that, since a defence under section 34(2) must be predicated on a belief in the need to use deadly force that is based on *reasonable grounds*, the accused's intoxication is irrelevant in the determination of the validity of the defendant's claim of self-defence. More specifically, Justice Ritchie stated that

> ... *although intoxication can be a factor in inducing honest mistake, it cannot induce a mistake which must be based on reasonable ... grounds*. The perspective of the reasonable man which the language of s. 34(2) places in issue here is the objective standard the law commonly adopts to measure a man's conduct. A reasonable man is a man in full possession of his faculties. In contrast, a drunken man is one whose ability to reason and to perceive are diminished by the alcohol he has consumed. [emphasis added]

Nevertheless, it is significant that in the case of *Nelson* (1992) the Ontario Court of Appeal ruled that, in applying the test of reasonableness in section 34(2), the courts should take account of any intellectual impairment that might affect the accused person's capacity to make decisions. In this particular case, the accused had suffered a serious head injury when he was a child. As Associate Chief Justice Morden stated,

> Where the accused has an intellectual impairment, not within his or her control, which relates to his or her ability to perceive and react to events—an impairment that clearly takes him or her out of the broad band of normal adult intellectual capacity—I think the deficit should be taken into account.

In some respects, the defence of self-defence resembles the defences of necessity and duress. Indeed, a common thread running through the requirements of each of the defences is the principle that the accused must take advantage of any less harmful course of action that one would expect a reasonable person to pursue in the same circumstances as the accused. Even though an accused person may fear for his or her life or physical safety, he or she is expected to accept any reasonable opportunity to escape from the situation rather than to inflict deadly force in self-defence. This point was emphasized by the Supreme Court of Canada in the case of *Cinous* (2002). Here, the accused was driving a van with two associates in order to carry out a theft of computers. Cinous contended that he believed that the two associates, who were located in the back of the van, intended to kill him. Cinous pulled into a service station and purchased some windshield washer fluid. He opened the back door of the van and, "seeing his opportunity," he shot one of the associates in the back of the head. The other associate fled from the scene. Cinous was convicted of murder at his trial and the conviction was ultimately affirmed by the Supreme Court. The Court held that there was no air of reality to Cinous's plea of self-defence because there was no evidence to suggest that he reasonably believed that he had no alternative but to kill his associate. As Chief Justice McLachlin and Justice Bastarache stated in their judgment,

> Section 34(2) does not require that an accused rule out a few courses of action other than killing. The requirement is that the accused have [*sic*] believed on reasonable grounds that there was no alternative course of action open to him at that time, so that he reasonably thought he was obliged to kill in order to preserve himself from death or grievous bodily harm. In this case, there is absolutely no evidence from which a jury could reasonably infer the reasonableness of a belief in the absence of alternatives. There is nothing in the evidence to explain why the accused did not wait in the service station rather than go back to the van. There is absolutely nothing to explain why he did not flee once he had left the van. Indeed, there is nothing to suggest the reasonableness of his conclusion that he needed to walk back to the van and shoot the victim.

On the other hand, it is significant that the courts have taken the view that one is not required to flee from one's home in order to avoid the need to employ force in self defence. Indeed, in the *Proulx* case (1998), the B.C. Court of Appeal stated that "the law is clear that flight from one's own home is not a reasonable option for self preservation, and that the defence of self-defence will still apply even if there is another way out of the house—the rationale is that one's home is already one's last line of defence against an assailant." It is significant that the court emphasized that an attack in one's home is the *only* circumstance in which there is never any duty laid upon the accused to consider the possibility of retreating from the assailant before using deadly force. In this respect, the court asserted that

> [t]he principle ... is simply that within one's home one need not retreat from an assailant before claiming the defence of self-defence. *But although retreat may be an irrelevant consideration when one is attacked at home, it does not follow that it is also irrelevant when one is attacked elsewhere.* [emphasis added]

Usually, section 34(2) will be raised by a defendant who has actually *intended* to inflict death or grievous bodily harm on another person. However, there may well be some situations in which the accused will be permitted to raise self-defence under section 34(2), even though the accused did not actually intend to kill or to cause grievous bodily harm. Take, for example, the case of *Pintar* (1996), in which the accused had been charged with two counts of second degree murder after fatally shooting two unarmed men who had previously broken into his home. At the time of the altercation, one of these men threatened Pintar with death, as he had done on numerous previous occasions. After a struggle took place over possession of the accused's gun, Pintar shot both of the intruders. At trial, the accused claimed that he had not intended to kill either of the victims; instead, he asserted that he had fired the rifle as *"an instinctive reaction to preserve my life."* The trial judge ruled that section 34(2) was available only to those defendants who intended to cause death or grievous bodily harm. Pintar was convicted of two counts of manslaughter. However, the Ontario Court of Appeal subsequently set aside the convictions and ordered a new trial on the basis, *inter alia*, that the trial judge had misdirected the jury as to the applicability of section 34(2) to the specific facts in Pintar's case. In delivering the judgment of the Court of Appeal, Justice Moldaver stated that

> [u]nlike s. 34(1) which speaks to the issue of intent, s. 34(2) does not. The plain wording of s. 34(2) reveals that the provision is triggered when a person who has been unlawfully assaulted *causes death or grievous bodily harm in repelling the assault.* On its face, this wording would certainly suggest that the applicability of s. 34(2) is dependent upon a finding

that the original assailant either died or suffered grievous bodily harm as a consequence of the responsive measures taken by the person assaulted. To go beyond that and hold that when the charge is murder, accused persons can only take advantage of s. 34(2) if they intend to kill or cause grievous bodily harm has the effect not only of adding words to the section which are simply not there, but also of creating an additional hurdle which they must overcome when the charge is murder. [emphasis in original]

Significantly, the Supreme Court of Canada reaffirmed this particular interpretation of section 34(2) of the *Code* in the more recent case of *Trombley* (1999).

An important issue that may arise when the accused person raises self-defence under section 34(2) is whether the danger that he or she apprehends must be "imminent." In most cases, accused persons who reasonably apprehend that they are likely to be subjected to death or grievous bodily harm will be facing either an ongoing or an imminent attack. However, what is the situation where the accused reasonably apprehends such a degree of violence but believes that the attack will take place at some time in the future? In the *Pétel* case (1994), the Supreme Court of Canada rejected the suggestion that section 34(2) is available only to an accused who is under actual attack or who is under imminent danger of such an assault. Chief Justice Lamer stated:

> There is ... *no formal requirement that the danger be imminent.* Imminence is only one of the factors which the jury should weigh in determining whether the accused had a reasonable apprehension of danger and a reasonable belief that she could not extricate herself otherwise than by killing the attacker. [emphasis added]

The facts in the *Pétel* case (1994) were that the accused was charged with the murder of the companion of her daughter's boyfriend (Edsell). Both Edsell and the deceased (Raymond) had been actively involved in drug trafficking. Edsell and the daughter moved into the accused's house, and Edsell started to use the premises as a base for his illicit activities. The accused stated that Edsell frequently threatened her and that he beat her daughter. Pétel was so upset by Edsell's presence in her household that she ultimately moved to another residence. However, her efforts proved to be in vain since Edsell continued to come to her house to traffic in drugs. On the day of the homicide (July 21, 1989), Edsell went to Pétel's residence with a revolver, some cocaine, and scales. He told Pétel to hide the gun and then forced her to weigh some cocaine. He then suggested that he would kill Pétel, her daughter, and her granddaughter. Soon afterward, Pétel's daughter arrived with Raymond. Pétel then consumed a small amount of drugs and went to retrieve the revolver she had hidden. Immediately, she fired the gun at Edsell, who fell down. Raymond lunged at Pétel and she shot him as well. Edsell survived his wounds, but Raymond later died.

At Pétel's trial, the judge instructed the jury that, in order for the accused to make a successful plea of self-defence under section 34(2), she must have been "unlawfully assaulted" and that the assault must have taken place on the very evening of the shooting. The accused was convicted, but her appeal to the Quebec Court of Appeal was successful, and a new trial was ordered. The Supreme Court of Canada rejected a subsequent appeal by the Crown. The Supreme Court ruled that the trial judge had been in serious error when he instructed the members of the jury that, in applying the requirements of section 34(2), they should consider only the threats made on the same evening as the shooting. As Chief Justice Lamer stated, the various threats made by Edsell during his cohabitation with Pétel were of particular relevance in the jury's determination of whether she had a reasonable apprehension of danger and reasonable belief in the need to kill Edsell and Raymond:

> The threats prior to July 21st form an integral part of the circumstances on which the perception of the accused might have been based. The judge's answer to this question might thus have led the jury to disregard the entire atmosphere of terror which the respondent said pervaded her house. It is clear that the way in which a reasonable person would have acted cannot be assessed without taking into account these crucial circumstances.

The Pétel case has been interpreted as having decided that it is not necessary, under section 34(2) of the *Criminal Code*, to establish that the accused person was, *in fact*, the victim of an "unlawful assault." It is sufficient if the accused person reasonably believed that he or she was in danger of being unlawfully assaulted. For example, in the decision of the Supreme Court of Canada in the *Cinous* case (2002), Chief Justice McLachlin and Justice Bastarache expressed the view that

> [i]n *Pétel*,... Lamer C.J. stated the three constitutive elements of self-defence under s. 34(2): "(1) the existence of an unlawful assault; (2) a reasonable apprehension of a risk of death or grievous bodily harm; and (3) a reasonable belief that it is not possible to preserve oneself from harm except by killing the adversary". All three of these elements must be established in order for the defence to succeed. The air of reality test must therefore be applied to each of the three elements. If any of these elements lacks an air of reality, the defence should not be put to the jury....

> Each of the three elements under s. 34(2) has both a subjective and an objective component. The accused's perception of the situation is the "subjective" part of the test. However, the accused's belief must also be reasonable on the basis of the situation he perceives. This is the objective part of the test. Section 34(2) makes the reasonableness requirement explicit in relation to the second and third conditions. *Pétel* held that the same standard applies to the first component of the defence, namely, the existence of an assault. With respect to each of the three elements, the approach is first to inquire about the subjective perceptions of the accused, and then to ask whether those perceptions were objectively reasonable in the circumstances.

As the Ontario Court of Appeal stated in the case of *LaKing* (2004), the question "is not whether the accused was unlawfully attacked, but whether he reasonably believed in the circumstances that he was being unlawfully attacked." Furthermore, it is not necessary for the accused to establish that there were violent acts or gestures prior to the accused's use of defensive force. Threatening words alone might constitute an assault for the purpose of section 34(2). Indeed, in *Young* (2008), Justice Smith of the B.C. Court of Appeal asserted that

> [a]s a general rule, threatening words standing alone without any associated threatening act or gesture cannot constitute an assault.... However, in cases of self-defence,... the words of threat must be considered in the context of the history of abuse and the reasonable perceptions of the accused.

Justice Smith applied this proposition to a case involving allegations by the accused of domestic violence on the part of the deceased victim:

> [Young] was entitled to have the trial judge instruct the jury that for purposes of s. 34(2), in addition to an attempt or threat by associated acts or gestures, an unlawful assault could consist of threatening words that would reasonably cause [Young] to think that she was about to be physically harmed unless she should do something to prevent it regardless of whether she

reasonably believed that an actual physical assault was in progress.

In the important case of *Lavallee* (1990), the Supreme Court of Canada ruled that, when a woman kills an abusive partner and raises the plea of self-defence under section 34(2) of the *Code*, the trial court may admit expert testimony concerning the so-called **battered wife syndrome**. Such testimony can assist the jury to answer the question of whether the accused believed on reasonable and probable grounds that she had to kill the accused in order to preserve herself from death or grievous bodily harm. In *Lavallee*, the accused had been in a battering relationship with a man (Rust) for several years. She had been to hospital several times with serious injuries caused by her partner's violence. She shot Rust in the back of the head as he was leaving her room and after he had physically assaulted her and threatened her with death. According to the accused, Rust had given her a gun and told her that he would kill her once all the guests had left the party that was taking place in their residence. Rust then said that, if Lavallee did not kill him first, he would kill her. The accused shot him after he had made this remark and turned away to leave the room.

At Lavallee's trial for murder, her counsel argued that Lavallee had acted in self-defence and, therefore, relied on the provisions of section 34(2). The trial judge permitted the defence to call a psychiatrist who testified with respect to the so-called battered wife syndrome. This evidence was introduced in order to establish that the accused reasonably apprehended death at the hands of Rust and that she reasonably believed that killing him was the only way of saving herself. The gist of the psychiatrist's opinion was that Lavallee "had been terrorized by Rust to the point of feeling trapped, vulnerable, worthless, and unable to escape the relationship despite the violence." In addition, he suggested that the continuing pattern of abuse by Rust placed the accused's life in danger. In this respect, he concluded that Lavallee's shooting of Rust should be viewed as "a final desperate act by a woman who sincerely believed that she would be killed that night." Lavallee was acquitted and the Supreme Court ultimately held that the trial judge had been correct to place the evidence of battered wife syndrome before the members of the jury.

Justice Wilson, speaking for the majority of the Supreme Court of Canada, noted that the relevant research literature has suggested that battered women experience clearly defined cycles of abuse. She emphasized that, in the case of a woman who has been subjected to such cycles of battering, "the mental state of the accused at the critical moment she pulls the trigger cannot be understood except in terms of the cumulative effect of months or years of brutality." Furthermore, the cyclical nature of abuse means that it becomes possible for the battered spouse to make accurate predictions as to the moment when her partner will commence his violent behaviour. Therefore, expert testimony is particularly relevant to the application of section 34(2) because it can point to the accused woman's "heightened sensitivity" to her spouse's acts and, thereby, clarify the question of whether she had a reasonable apprehension of death or grievous bodily harm.

The critical issue, according to Justice Wilson, is not "what an outsider would have reasonably perceived but what the accused reasonably perceived given her situation and experience." In this light, it is clear that defendants, such as Lavallee, do not have to experience an actual attack before resorting to self-defence under section 34(2). They do not have to wait "until the knife is uplifted, the gun pointed or the fist clenched before apprehension is deemed reasonable." As Justice Wilson remarked,

> ... the evidence showed that when [Lavallee] and Rust physically fought, [Lavallee] "invariably got the worst of it. I do not think it is an unwarranted generalization to say that due to their size, strength, socialization and lack of training, women are typically no match for men in hand-to-hand combat. The requirement ... that a battered woman wait until the physical assault is "underway" before her apprehensions can be validated in law would, in the words of an American court, be tantamount to sentencing her to "murder by instalment."

The *Lavallee* case is of considerable significance in the development of Canadian criminal law because it clearly recognizes that, when a woman raises the plea of self-defence in response to an attack by a male aggressor, she is not to be judged by the standards of the "reasonable man" but rather by the standards of the "reasonable woman" who finds herself in the same situation and shares the same experience as the accused. Expert testimony concerning battered wife syndrome is not introduced to establish a special defence based on the medical or psychological condition of the accused. On the contrary, it is taken into account as a means of establishing the *reasonableness*, under the terms of section 34(2), of the accused's beliefs and actions in light of her experience of chronic abuse at the hands of her partner.

In the *Malott* case (1998), the Supreme Court of Canada provided further guidance as to the relevance of expert testimony concerning the battered woman syndrome. The Court took the view that the trial judge should always inform the members of the jury exactly how this testimony may assist them in deciding whether the accused has acted in self-defence. More specifically, Justice Major suggested that the jury should be instructed that the battered woman syndrome evidence may assist them in understanding four separate questions:

1. *Why an abused woman might remain in an abusive relationship ...*

2. *The nature and extent of the violence that may exist in a battering relationship ...*

3. *The accused's ability to perceive danger from her abuser ...*

4. *Whether the accused believed on reasonable grounds that she could not otherwise preserve herself from death or grievous bodily harm.* [emphasis in original]

In the *Vaillancourt* case (1999), the Quebec Court of Appeal applied these principles to a tragic case in which the accused had shot her husband, to whom she had been married for 30 years, while he was sleeping in bed in the family home. The accused was subsequently charged with second degree murder. Evidence was presented at Vaillancourt's trial to the effect that her husband was "aggressive, irascible and violent" and that he had, in effect, treated his spouse like a "slave." There was "ample evidence" of "physical acts of violence, verbal and psychological violence" and "sexual violence," all of which had been directed against the accused by her husband. Vaillancourt wanted a divorce from her husband. However, he had frequently made death threats against her and Vaillancourt was terrified that her husband would find her, wherever she might go, and ultimately kill her. On the day of the shooting, the accused had tried to test her husband's reaction to a potential request for a divorce by recounting a newspaper story, in which a young woman had been strangled to death by her husband after asking him for a divorce. Vaillancourt's husband merely replied, "Good for him!" The accused testified that this incident caused her to believe that "my time is coming."

That night, Vaillancourt said that she could not sleep and, in a state of severe depression, she loaded a rifle with a view to committing suicide. However, she started to think of her children and grandchildren, and she recalled an incident in which her husband had sexually abused her grandchildren. Vaillancourt abandoned the plan to kill herself, walked into her husband's bedroom, and shot him to death.

Although evidence concerning the battered woman syndrome was presented at her trial, Vaillancourt was nevertheless convicted of murder by the jury. However, the Quebec Court of Appeal allowed her appeal and entered an acquittal because it considered that the jury's verdict had been "unreasonable" in light of the particular circumstances of the case. Justice Mailhot, speaking for the majority of the court, indicated that it would be preferable to substitute the phrase, "syndrome of women who are victims of violence," for "battered woman syndrome." In Justice Mailhot's view, use of this new terminology would represent an unequivocal recognition by the courts of the need to consider *psychological* violence as well as *physical* violence whenever an abused woman asserts self-defence under section 34(2).

According to Justice Mailhot,

The question to be asked is whether the accused could reasonably be considered in a position of self-defence taking into account that she was a person affected by *battered woman syndrome*. In other words, is it reasonable under the specific circumstances of the case that this person, who is suffering from this syndrome, would consider or believe herself to be in a position of self-defence. *For this analysis, it is necessary to place oneself in the situation of the accused and not in the position of a person who is suffering from the syndrome.* [emphasis added]

This statement by Justice Mailhot is important because it makes it perfectly clear that the central issue is the *reasonableness* of the defendant's fears and actions, given her particular circumstances. The "battered woman syndrome" evidence is *relevant* to the task of assisting the members of the jury to understand what the accused believed at the time that she used force; however, the accused is not required to establish that she has all of the symptoms of a "battered woman" in order to successfully raise the plea of self-defence successfully at her trial. In this respect, the *Vaillancourt* decision provides some degree of reassurance that abused women will not be "pathologized" if they seek to rely on section 34(2) of the *Code* in a situation where they have employed deadly force against their abusers.

As far as the unique circumstances of the *Vaillancourt* case are concerned, Justice Mailhot stated that

[i]t was clearly while thinking of her grandchildren that she came to the conclusion that she would be punishing herself in a useless and unjust manner by committing suicide because she would be indirectly punishing the grandchildren who would no longer benefit from the possibility of being protected by her once she was gone. So, Madame Vaillancourt clearly believed that she was protecting them, but was in no way able to protect herself from the real threat she felt in her mind of being killed unless she killed her husband and therefore considered herself in the legitimate position to take such an action to avoid being murdered by him.

In the *McConnell* case (1996), the Supreme Court of Canada injected an even greater dose of subjectivity into the interpretation of section 34(2) of the *Code*. McConnell and others had killed a fellow inmate in a penitentiary. The deceased was apparently a member of a group who had threatened the life of the accused. McConnell started to stockpile weapons (knuckle-dusters and a stick). When the victim walked by, McConnell approached him from behind and repeatedly hit him over the head with some knuckle-dusters, while another inmate stabbed the victim in the stomach. The victim died of his injuries, and McConnell was subsequently tried and convicted of manslaughter. The trial judge refused to place before the jury McConnell's plea of self defence under section 34(2), stating that McConnell did not believe that he was in imminent danger of death or serious bodily harm at the time of the fatal assault. The Supreme Court of Canada ultimately allowed McConnell's appeal against his conviction and ordered a new trial. Justice La Forest, in delivering the brief judgment of the Supreme Court, indicated that he and his colleagues agreed with the dissenting views expressed by Justice Conrad in the Alberta Court of Appeal's earlier decision to reject McConnell's appeal. Justice Conrad had asserted that, for the purposes of the application of section 34(2), an analogy should be drawn between the battered wife syndrome and the so-called "prison environment syndrome," a concept that was raised by an expert witness at McConnell's trial:

There was evidence from Dr. Weston about inmate behaviour and prison culture and the similarity in the environment to the battered wife syndrome. *There is evidence about the environment in which*

inmates had to "kill or be killed." Thus a person could believe he or she was being assaulted (a threat with present ability) without it being immediate. [emphasis added]

In ordering a new trial, the Supreme Court of Canada undoubtedly accepted McConnell's argument that section 34(2) should have been left to the jury because there was some evidence that he reasonably believed both that his life was in danger and that he had no alternative but to employ deadly force in self-defence. A similar approach was adopted by the Nova Scotia Court of Appeal in the case of *Chan* (2005). In this case, the Court of Appeal took the view that "evidence of the correctional officers concerning the culture of violence and the prevalence of weapons in the institution provide the necessary evidential basis" upon which a jury could conclude that the accused person "perceived himself to be exposed to a risk of death or grievous bodily harm, and that his apprehension was reasonable." Likewise, in *Raphael* (2009), the Saskatchewan Court of Appeal ordered a new trial in the case of an accused person who had been convicted of aggravated assault, following a fight with another inmate at the Regina Provincial Correctional Centre. Raphael had inflicted 14 shallow stab wounds on the other inmate, using a shank (an improvised dagger). Raphael's appeal against conviction was upheld because the trial judge had not applied section 34(2) correctly to the particular circumstances of Raphael's case. On behalf of the Court of Appeal, Justice Jackson held that

[t]he trial judge was required to consider the honesty of Mr. Raphael's belief that he could not preserve himself from harm other than by inflicting grievous bodily harm, having in mind the prison environment in which he found himself on that day. Similarly, in considering the reasonableness of his belief, he had to consider the situation of a reasonable person similarly situated to that of the accused, which included an objective consideration of the same prison environment.

Among the circumstances that should have been considered, according to Justice Jackson, were the facts that Raphael was a prisoner who was incarcerated in a part of the prison populated by a rival gang and that he had a broken hand at the time that he was assaulted by the other inmate. In addition, the fight took place within the confines of a six-foot-wide corridor and the only door that was open was the door to his own cell. Furthermore, the other prisoner had slammed shut a barrier gate, temporarily locking the prison guards on the other side of it. It was also relevant that, seven months previously, Raphael's throat had been slashed by a member of the rival gang, necessitating 14 stitches. All of these circumstances should have been taken into account in order to determine whether Raphael reasonably believed that using the shank was the only way in which he could preserve himself from death or grievous bodily harm.

The implications of the *McConnell*, *Chan*, and *Raphael* decisions are somewhat disturbing, since they appear to justify the use of a preemptive strike in a prison environment and/or to legitimate the stockpiling of weapons in anticipation of such an act of violence. Certainly, these decisions may prompt one to question not only whether the "law of the jungle" should rule in Canada's prisons but also whether the state is meeting its basic duty to provide safe and humane treatment to vulnerable and powerless inmates.

However, it does seem that this generous interpretation of section 34(2) has been limited to cases involving inmates living in the cauldron of a prison environment. It is significant that, in *Pilon* (2009), a case involving a homicide that took place at an Ottawa restaurant, a somewhat stricter approach was taken. Indeed, the Ontario Court of Appeal emphasized that, when a court is called upon to determine the reasonableness of an accused person's beliefs in the context of a claim of self defence under section 34(2), it should ignore the accused person's personal moral code or world-view. In this case, both Pilon and the deceased victim belonged to a "biker-gang subculture" and "neither was a stranger to the criminal activities, threats and intimidation associated with that lifestyle." Pilon had shot and killed the victim and was convicted by a jury of first degree murder. Upon his appeal against conviction to the Ontario Court of Appeal, Pilon contended that the trial judge made a serious error when she ruled that, since there was no air of reality to a claim of self defence under section 34(2), she would not permit the defence to be considered by the jury.

The trial judge had strongly dismissed Pilon's argument that "someone in Mr. Pilon's shoes, namely someone with a criminal record and with friends and associates in the criminal subculture, should not be expected to call on the police for assistance if his life has been or is being threatened, or if he is assaulted." She continued:

> The court is being asked to accept as being reasonable that such a person does whatever he considers appropriate—even if contrary to law—to protect

himself and react to any such threats or assaults. In this case, the proposition put forward by the Defence was that it was reasonable for Mr. Pilon to carry a loaded shotgun with him in his truck so that he would be ready to repel any attack by Marshall McKinnon [the deceased] or anyone hired as a hitman by Marshall McKinnon, and it should be considered reasonable for him to use it to ensure his future safety. The proposition was that, in the culture in which Mr. Pilon lived, this was an appropriate and reasonable response, and therefore this is the standard that the jury should apply.

The trial judge rejected Pilon's argument and noted that "the only way the defence *could* succeed is if the jury climbed into the skin of the respondent and accepted as reasonable a sociopathic view of appropriate dispute resolution." The Ontario Court of Appeal agreed with the trial judge and dismissed Pilon's appeal. In delivering the judgment of the Court, Justice Doherty articulated a forceful statement on the need to preserve the requirement of reasonableness of belief when applying section 34(2):

> I see a world of difference, however, between testing the reasonableness of an accused's apprehension and belief in the circumstances as the accused perceived them and testing the reasonableness of that apprehension and belief in light of the appellant's personal moral code or world view. It may well be, given the criminal sub-culture in which the appellant operated, that he lived by the motto "kill now or be killed later". In assessing the reasonableness of the appellant's conduct, however, the jury cannot accept that motto. To do so would be to effectively eliminate the "reasonableness" requirement from the defence of self-defence. Instead of reflecting community values and the community perception of when a killing is justified, the validity of the self-defence justification would lay entirely in the eye of the killer. A law of self-defence that justified what would otherwise be murder entirely on the basis of the accused's personal belief as to the need to kill to save himself would constitute a stunning devaluation of the rights to life and security of the person to which all members of the community are entitled.

THE USE OF FORCE IN ORDER TO PREVENT AN ASSAULT AGAINST THE ACCUSED OR ANYONE UNDER HIS OR HER PROTECTION

Section 37 of the *Criminal Code* provides the following:

(1) Every one is justified in using force to defend himself or anyone under his protection from

assault, if he uses no more force than is necessary to prevent the assault or repetition of it.

(2) Nothing in this section shall be deemed to justify the wilful infliction of any hurt or mischief that is excessive, having regard to the nature of the assault that the force used was intended to prevent.

To some extent, section 37 overlaps with section 34. However, section 37 does contain a noteworthy extension of section 34(1) insofar as a defence is made available not only where accused persons use force in order to defend themselves but also where such force is used to protect someone "under the protection" of the accused. In the case of *Webers* (1994), Justice O'Connor of the Ontario Court (General Division) held that

> ... the term "under his protection" is not limited to a formal guardianship relationship, such as a parent or guardian and child, or a teacher and student. In its broadest sense, it means anyone who requires protection which the accused may be able to provide.

In *Webers* (1994), the court ruled that a patient who was unlawfully subjected to the violent administration of an injection could be considered to be "under the protection" of a friend who had accompanied her to the hospital and that the latter was, therefore, entitled under section 37 to intervene to save her from the violent assault being perpetrated against her by both nurses and police officers. As is the case with section 34(1), section 37 requires that the force employed by the accused be "proportionate" to the threat posed by the assailant.

One of the problems that arises in the application of section 37 is that, except in the case of a defendant who takes action to protect someone under his or her protection, the provision would appear to duplicate—and even contradict—certain elements of both sections 34 and 35 of the *Criminal Code*. In the *McIntosh* case (1995), Chief Justice Lamer, on behalf of the majority of the members of the Supreme Court of Canada, noted that "Parliament's intention in enacting s. 37 is unclear." The Chief Justice pointed out that section 37 makes the defence of self-defence available where the force used by the accused is both necessary and proportionate. However, if section 37 is available to the initial aggressor in a confrontation (and the Court ruled that Parliament had not explicitly excluded this possibility), it "would appear to be in conflict with s. 35," which, as we shall

see shortly, places numerous restrictions on the use of self-defence by such an accused. In the words of Chief Justice Lamer,

> ... [I]t is difficult to understand why Parliament would enact the specific and detailed justifications in ss. 34 and 35, yet then make available a broad justification in s. 37 which appears to render ss. 34 and 35 redundant.

Judicial frustration with the poor drafting of the *Criminal Code* sections dealing with self-defence— and, in particular, section 37—has been expressed in a number of Canadian courts. For example, in delivering the judgment of the British Columbia Court of Appeal in *Grandin* (2001), Justice Finch referred to "the complex and confusing nature of the *Criminal Code* provisions on self-defence" and noted that

> ... the uncertain relationship between s. 37 and the other self-defence sections has also been particularly noted.... In the absence of any legislative remedy, courts have tried to find practical ways to explain the concept of self-defence to juries that are understandable and that conform to the *Code* provisions.

The potentially greater breadth of the defence under section 37 was illustrated by the case of *Mathisen* (2008). In this case, Mathisen's wife had admitted to having an affair and agreed that she would seek a divorce. However, the wife decided to remain temporarily in the matrimonial home. Mathisen came to believe that his wife was poisoning him and, following a fire which he claimed had been set by her, there was a confrontation. When his wife attempted to leave the house, Mathisen grabbed her by the arm. His wife hit him with her keys and grabbed his hair. Mathisen then wrestled his wife to the floor and landed on top of her, pinning her arms to the ground. Mathisen repeatedly demanded to know the "antidote to the poison." His wife continually denied that she had given him poison until she died while still being held down by Mathisen. It was not clear whether the death was the result of manual strangulation or, as Mathisen claimed, by the traumatic asphyxia caused by his laying on top of the victim and by the force of his knee on her chest. Mathisen weighed 380 pounds and his wife only 165 pounds.

Mathisen relied on two defences at his trial: self-defence and accident. The trial judge refused to allow the jury to consider self-defence under section 34(1). However, he did instruct the jury to consider section 37. The jury nevertheless convicted Mathisen of second degree murder. On his appeal to the Ontario

Court of Appeal, one of the issues raised was whether the trial judge should have let the jury consider self-defence under section 34(1). The Court of Appeal held that there was no air of reality to a defence under section 34(1) but that, in any event, Mathisen had not been prejudiced in any way because, in the particular circumstances of his case, section 37 clearly provided Mathisen with a much broader defence than was available to him under section 34(1).[2] In delivering the judgment of the Court of Appeal, Justice Laskin stated the following:

Self-defence under s. 34(1) has four elements:

- Mr. Mathisen reasonably believed that he was being unlawfully assaulted by Mrs. Mathisen;

- Mr. Mathisen did not provoke the assault by his words, blows or gestures;

- Mr. Mathisen did not intend to kill or seriously injure Mrs. Mathisen; and

- Mr. Mathisen did not use more force than necessary.

Section 37 provides a broader basis for self-defence than s. 34(1). To take advantage of s. 37, Mr. Mathisen need only show that he reasonably believed he was being assaulted and that the force he used to defend himself was not more than necessary to prevent the assault or the repetition of it. Unlike s. 34(1), Mr. Mathisen could rely on s. 37 even if he provoked the assault and even if he intended to kill or seriously injure his wife.

It may well be suggested that Parliament should take a second look at the self-defence provisions of the *Criminal Code* with a view to simplifying them and eliminating the apparent inconsistencies and contradictions that currently permeate them.

THE USE OF FORCE IN SELF-DEFENCE BY THE AGGRESSOR

Section 35 of the *Criminal Code* provides that

[e]very one who has without justification assaulted another but did not commence the assault with intent to cause death or grievous bodily harm, or has

without justification provoked an assault on himself by another, may justify the use of force subsequent to the assault if:

(a) he uses the force:

(i) under reasonable apprehension of death or grievous bodily harm from the violence of the person whom he has assaulted or provoked, and

(ii) in the belief, on reasonable grounds, that it is necessary in order to preserve himself from death or grievous bodily harm;

(b) he did not, at any time before the necessity of preserving himself from death or grievous bodily harm arose, endeavour to cause death or grievous bodily harm; and

(c) he declined further conflict and quitted or retreated from it as far as it was feasible to do so before the necessity of preserving himself from death or grievous bodily harm arose.

This section is unnecessarily complex and has received relatively little judicial attention, apparently because it is not used with any degree of frequency. Certain of the requirements contained in section 34(2) reappear in section 35. For example, as the Manitoba Court of Appeal emphasized in the case of *Mousseau* (2007), an essential stipulation under section 35 is that "the accused is under reasonable apprehension of death or grievous bodily harm from the violence of the person whom he has assaulted or provoked." However, as a reading of section 35 quickly demonstrates, a number of strict requirements have been added as a prerequisite to the successful assertion of the defence of self-defence in the situation where the accused may be considered "the aggressor." In particular, section 35(c) imposes a duty on the accused to retreat whenever it is feasible to do so. In the *Tremblay* case (2006), the Quebec Court of Appeal indicated that section 35(c) would normally require that an armed person who is the aggressor in a confrontation with an unarmed victim should drop their weapon or otherwise indicate that they do not intend to use it before a court will consider that the duty to retreat has been fulfilled.

However, in light of the Supreme Court of Canada's decision in *McIntosh* (1995), it is most unlikely that an accused person will ever rely on section 35 where he or she has inflicted death or grievous bodily harm in self-defence. The *McIntosh* case, as we

[2] The Ontario Court of Appeal nevertheless ordered a new trial for Mathisen on the basis that the trial judge wrongly withheld the defence of accident from the jury, even though there was an air of reality to the defence, based on the evidence presented at the trial. The Court also upheld the trial judge's refusal to let the jury consider section 34(2) because there was no evidence that Mathisen reasonably believed that the only option available to him was to use extreme force.

have seen, decided that section 34(2) of the *Code* may be raised even where the accused was the initial aggressor. Since section 34(2) is far less restrictive for such an accused person than section 35, it is inevitable that he or she will rely on section 34(2) rather than section 35. Nevertheless, it is significant that Chief Justice Lamer recognized in the *McIntosh* case an element of "absurdity":

> One is struck ... by the fact that if s. 34(2) is available to an initial aggressor who has killed or committed grievous bodily harm, then that accused may be in a better position to raise self-defence than an initial aggressor whose assault was less serious. This is because the less serious aggressor could not take advantage of the broader defence in s. 34(2), as that provision is only available to an accused who "causes death or bodily harm." Section 34(1) would not be available since it is explicitly limited to those who have not provoked an assault. Therefore, the less serious aggressor could only have recourse to s. 35, which imposes a retreat requirement. It is, in my opinion, anomalous that an accused who commits the most serious act has the broadest defence.

DEFENCE OF PROPERTY

Sections 38 to 42 of the *Criminal Code* make provision for the justified use of force in relation to the defence of property. It will be noted that sections 38 and 39 deal with "movable property," whereas sections 40 to 42 are concerned with the defence of "real property" and "dwelling-houses." The term "real property" essentially refers to property in buildings and land. Section 2 of the *Code* defines the term "dwelling-house" in a broad manner, and it is clear that the statutory definition includes apartments or even, as the Alberta Court of Appeal ruled in *Clark* (1983), rooms in a boarding house. Our discussion will primarily focus on sections 40 and 41 of the *Code*, particularly insofar as they interact with sections 34(1) and 34(2).

Sections 40 and 41 of the *Code* provide the following:

40. Every one who is in peaceable possession of a dwelling-house, and every one lawfully assisting him or acting under his authority, is justified in using as much force as is necessary to prevent any person from forcibly breaking into or forcibly entering the dwelling-house without lawful authority.

41.(1) Everyone who is in peaceable possession of a dwelling-house or real property and everyone lawfully assisting him or acting under his authority is justified in using force to prevent any person from trespassing on the dwelling-house or real property or to remove a trespasser therefrom, if he uses no more force than is necessary.

41.(2) A trespasser who resists an attempt by a person who is in peaceable possession of a dwelling-house or real property or a person lawfully assisting him or acting under his authority to prevent his entry or to remove him, shall be deemed to commit an assault without justification or provocation.[3]

In the case of *Gunning* (2005), the Supreme Court of Canada indicated that there are four elements to the defence articulated in section 41(1). In delivering the judgment of the Court, Justice Charron stated that

> [t]here are four elements to the defence raised by Mr. Gunning: (1) he must have been in possession of the dwelling-house; (2) his possession must have been peaceable; (3) Mr. Charlie must have been a trespasser; and (4) the force used to eject the trespasser must have been reasonable in all the circumstances.

The *Gunning* case concerned the fatal shooting of Chester Charlie, an uninvited person who came into Gunning's home during a party. Gunning asked Charlie to leave but the latter refused and assaulted Gunning, who picked up a loaded shotgun in order to "intimidate or scare" Charlie into departing from the premises. According to Gunning, the gun discharged accidentally and Charlie received a fatal wound to the neck. Gunning was charged with second degree murder and was convicted at his trial. Gunning's conviction was upheld by the British Columbia Court of Appeal but the Supreme Court of Canada later set aside the conviction and ordered a new trial. The Supreme Court held that the trial judge should have instructed the jury to consider the defence of property issue that arose under section 41(1). Gunning did not claim that he intentionally shot Charlie in self-defence. Instead, he asserted that the shooting was accidental. The Supreme Court noted that Gunning was in possession of his house, that the possession was peaceable, and that, after he had been asked to leave, Charlie was undoubtedly a trespasser. Only the

---

[3] **Trespass** is the unlawful interference with another's property, person, or rights.

fourth element of the defence of property under section 41(1) was in issue—namely, did Gunning use reasonable force in the circumstances of the case? The jury may well have concluded that it was reasonable for Gunning to retrieve a firearm for the sole purpose of scaring or intimidating Charlie into leaving Gunning's house. As Justice Charron indicated, "[A]ll of the events preceding the shooting had to be taken into account in determining whether Mr. Gunning had used reasonable force in his attempt to eject Mr. Charlie." At the new trial ordered by the Supreme Court, the trial judge would be required to instruct the jury to determine whether or not the accused had satisfied the four elements of the defence of property under section 41(1) of the *Criminal Code*.

The application of section 41(1) to a plea of defence of real property (land) is well illustrated by the decision in *George* (2000). In this case, the accused was part of a group of protestors who had occupied a provincial park and an adjacent Canadian Forces base. The protestors claimed that they had an Aboriginal treaty right to both the park and the military base. The accused drove a car at a group of police officers and was subsequently convicted of criminal negligence in the operation of a motor vehicle and assault with a weapon. On his appeal to the Ontario Court of Appeal, George asserted that the trial judge had erroneously failed to consider a potential defence under section 41(1). However, the appeal was dismissed. The Court ruled that there had been no **peaceable possession** of the land in question. Indeed, the police had clearly challenged the protestors in this respect, and the fact that the protestors had stockpiled rocks and sticks "made it clear that any

challenge to their occupation could result in violence." Furthermore, there was no evidence that the accused mistakenly believed that the protestors' possession of the property was peaceable. Undoubtedly, he knew that any interference by the police would be resisted. The Court also held that the defence under section 41(1) was not available because the force that he used was *not reasonable under the circumstances*:

> The appellant drove his car out of the parking lot and onto the grass shoulder of East Parkway Drive in such a manner that he struck a number of officers, seriously injuring one of them. At this time, the police were retreating from the park area. Their actions could not be construed as trespassing. *The force used against the police was not necessary, reasonable or proportionate.* [emphasis added]

It is important to emphasize that both sections 40 and 41(1) impose a requirement of proportionality when an individual uses force against a trespasser or would-be trespasser. This objective requirement was an important consideration in both the *Gunning* (2005) and the *George* (2000) cases discussed above. Similarly, in *Jamieson* (2002), the British Columbia Court of Appeal ruled that throwing acid over a trespasser who refuses to leave is, in no way, a proportionate response under section 41(1). As Justice Saunders stated:

> The learned trial judge found that the defence of self-defence had no air of reality. Even accepting that Patrick Jennings may have become a trespasser and that his behaviour was erratic from the consumption of prohibited chemicals, I, too, can see no air of reality to the argument that throwing acid at Patrick Jennings was in any way proportional to the circumstances, or in the words of s. 41(1), was no more force than was necessary.

The requirement of proportionality in section 41(1) does not necessarily mean that a property owner may never employ more than a minor degree of force in ejecting a trespasser. In *McKay* (2007), the accused had ordered an individual, Pashe, to leave his home, where a party had been held. Pashe later returned with a friend, who wished to retrieve his stereo equipment from the house. McKay said the friend could stay but not Pashe, who nevertheless refused to leave. McKay then threatened Pashe with a knife. However, Pashe disarmed McKay, who then went to another part of the house and returned with a paring knife in each hand. There was a struggle, in the course of which Pashe suffered a serious cut

Cartoon by Elizabeth Carefoot

Using reasonable force to eject a trespasser falls under section 41(1) of the Criminal Code.

across the face. McKay was charged with aggravated assault. The trial judge acquitted the accused on the basis that section 41(1) applied to the circumstances of this case. Pashe was clearly a trespasser. He had been unequivocally ordered to leave and given ample time to withdraw from McKay's house. In the view of the trial judge, there was a reasonable doubt whether McKay had used more force than was necessary and he held that he must give the accused the benefit of the doubt in the application of section 41(1).

The Manitoba Court of Appeal allowed the Crown's appeal against McKay's acquittal and entered a conviction of aggravated assault. On behalf of the Court, Justice Hamilton stated that "the defence of property alone will not justify the intentional use of a weapon against a trespasser or the intentional killing of a trespasser, and that such force will only be justifiable where the circumstances permit the accused to rely on self-defence principles." Significantly, the Supreme Court of Canada allowed McKay's appeal and ordered a new trial. The Supreme Court noted that the trial judge had not found that McKay had stabbed Pashe intentionally. It was possible that, during the struggle, Pashe had been cut accidentally. In a very important comment on the interpretation of section 41(1), Chief Justice McLachlin said:

> … We should not be taken as endorsing the Court of Appeal's analysis on the scope of the defence of property. By way of clarification, we should not be taken as endorsing the view that "defence of property alone will never justify the use of anything more than minor force being used against a trespasser" … or that, in all cases, 'the defence of property alone will not justify the intentional use of a weapon against a trespasser."

This statement clearly indicates that there may be certain circumstances in which it may be justifiable, under section 41(1), to use a significant degree of force, including threatening the trespasser with a weapon or even "using" a weapon.

What exactly is a trespasser? Essentially, a **trespasser**, in the context of these provisions of the *Code*, is someone who violates the rights of others by entering or remaining on their property without any authority to do so. The problem is that someone may be at some point invited onto another person's property either by the property owner or by an individual who is authorized to do so. For example, an individual may be given a specific invitation to attend

a party. Similarly, a person may enter a store on the basis that members of the public have an implicit invitation to do so. However, it is possible that an invitation to enter or remain on someone else's property can subsequently be withdrawn. If this occurs, can the "disinvited" guest become a trespasser and be ejected with the use of a reasonable degree of force? The answer is "yes," provided that the property owner gives the disinvited guest a reasonable amount of time in which to withdraw voluntarily.

These principles are illustrated by the case of *Keating* (1992). In this case, a youth had entered a shopping mall with a view to purchasing a jacket. However, he subsequently began to skateboard on the mall property even though there were signs that prohibited skateboarding in this area. The accused, who owned the mall, entered into a physical confrontation with the youth. The Appeal Division of the Nova Scotia Supreme Court held that the trial judge, who had convicted the accused of assault and threatening, had been wrong to ignore the accused person's plea under section 41(1) that he was entitled to remove a trespasser from his premises. The trial judge had taken the view that the youth was an "invitee" and, therefore, could not be treated as a trespasser. However, the Appeal Division ruled that the defence under section 41(1) should be considered and ordered a new trial. The fact that the youth was originally an invitee to the mall did not mean that he remained one indefinitely. In particular, he had been "invited" to enter the mall only for the purpose of shopping, not skateboarding. If the accused reasonably believed that the youth was trespassing at the time of the altercation, he was entitled to raise the defence under section 41(1).

Section 41(2) is particularly significant in that it provides that, should trespassers resist an attempt to remove them from a dwelling-house or real property (or an attempt to prevent their unlawful entry), they will be *deemed to commit an unjustified or unprovoked assault* upon the person who is in peaceable possession of the property. Section 41(2), therefore, may well have the effect of bringing section 34 of the *Code* into play for the benefit of the person in possession of the property concerned. However, it should be pointed out that the courts have interpreted section 41(2) somewhat restrictively. For example, in *Baxter* (1975), Justice Martin of the Ontario Court of Appeal stated that

> [t]he meaning of this subsection is not entirely clear. I am disposed to think that its effect is not to convert

mere passive resistance into an assault but merely to provide that if any force is used by the wrongdoer in resisting an attempt to prevent his entry or to remove him, such force is unlawful, and hence an assault. The amount of force that may be used to prevent or defend against any assault actually committed by the wrongdoer depends upon the ordinary principles of self-defence as set out in s. 34 of the *Code*.

STUDY QUESTIONS

1. Gradgrind invites Highball to a party, which is held in Gradgrind's apartment. Highball becomes quite obnoxious and insults Gradgrind's girl-friend, Tia Maria. Gradgrind tells Highball to leave the premises "forthwith," but despite repeated requests to remove himself, Highball refuses to do so. Gradgrind then attempts to throw his unwelcome guest out of the front door. Highball resists very strenuously and starts to punch Gradgrind in the face with a marked degree of force. Gradgrind grabs a metal bar and strikes Highball on the head until the latter "falls limp" and Gradgrind deposits the dazed Highball outside of his apartment in the corridor. Some other tenants spot Highball and take him to the Cocktail Hospital, where he is treated for concussion and lacerations of his scalp. He subsequently recovers without any permanent damage. If Gradgrind were to be charged for his role in this sordid affair, would he have any special defence(s) open to him?

2. Hermia has lived with Lysander for 10 years, during which he has, on various occasions, subjected her to physical assaults, some of which have caused serious injuries (such as extensive bruising to the body, a broken nose, and concussion). One night, Hermia returns home late from an evening meeting and Lysander becomes furious with her. He yells that he is "going to fix her once and for all." However, he is so drunk that he passes out on the couch. Hermia goes to the kitchen and picks up a large knife. She then returns to the room where Lysander is sleeping and stabs him to death. Would Hermia be able to raise a successful plea of self-defence if she were charged with murder or manslaughter?

3. Elbow is an inmate in a prison that has gained an unfortunate reputation for its brutal atmosphere. Most of the prisoners have been convicted of violent offences, and there is a widespread belief that, for inmates, one is only likely to survive if one acts on the maxim "kill or be killed." Pompey, a notoriously unpredictable and violent inmate, approaches Elbow and tells him that "his time is up." Elbow interprets this as a death threat and acquires a knife for self-protection. When Pompey is taking a shower, Elbow approaches him from behind and stabs him to death. When charged with first degree murder, Elbow claims that he was only acting in self-defence. Is Elbow likely to be successful in raising the defence of self-defence at his trial?

4. Creakle is drinking in a bar when he is accosted by a group of young men, who are evidently part of a gang. He refuses their demands for money and runs out into the parking lot. However, five or six of the gang members pursue him, threatening to beat him up. Creakle turns around and pulls out a knife, which he waves horizontally in the hope that his pursuers will stay away from him. Smike, one of the gang members, nevertheless moves toward Creakle and Smike's throat is cut. Smike dies within a few minutes. Creakle is charged with manslaughter. He strongly denies any intent to wound Smike. Would Creakle be able to successfully raise a defence of self-defence?

FURTHER READING

Beaman, L.G. 1998. Women's Defences: Contextualizing Dilemmas of Difference and Power. 9 *Women & Criminal Justice*: 87–115.

Boyle, C. 1990. The Battered Wife Syndrome and Self-Defence: *Lavallee v. R*. 9 *Canadian Journal of Family Law*: 171–179.

———. 1996. Annotation to *R. v. McConnell* (1996). 48 *Criminal Reports (4th Series)*: 200–203.

Castel, J.R. 1990. Discerning Justice for Battered Women Who Kill. 48 *University of Toronto Faculty Law Review*: 229–258.

Choi, J. 2003. The Viability of a "Cultural Defence" in Canada. 8 *Canadian Criminal Law Review*: 93–112.

Colvin, E., and S. Anand. 2007. *Principles of Criminal Law*. 3rd ed. Toronto: Carswell.

Coughlan, S.G. 2002. Duress, Necessity, Self-Defence and Provocation: Implications of Radical Change? 7 *Canadian Criminal Law Review*: 147–208.

Dimock, S. 2008. Reasonable Women in the Law. 11 *Critical Review of International Social and Political Philosophy*: 153–175.

Dressler, J. 2006. Battered Women and Sleeping Abusers: Some Reflections. 3 *Ohio State Journal of Criminal Law*: 457–471.

Dutton, D.G. 2006. *Rethinking Domestic Violence*. Vancouver: U.B.C. Press.

Dutton, M.A., and L.A. Goodman. 1994. Posttraumatic Stress Disorder among Battered Women: Analysis of Legal Implications. 12(3) *Behavioral Sciences & the Law*: 215–234.

Ferguson, G. 2000. Self-Defence: Selecting the Applicable Provisions. 5 *Canadian Criminal Law Review*: 179–219.

Finkelstein, C.O. 1999. On the Obligation of the State to Extend a Right of Self-Defense to Its Citizens. 147 *University of Pennsylvania Law Review*: 1361–1402.

Heller, K.J. 1998. Beyond the Reasonable Man? A Sympathetic but Critical Assessment of the Use of Subjective Standards of Reasonableness in Self-Defense and Provocation Cases. 26(1) *American Journal of Criminal Law*: 1–120.

Hubble, G. 1997. Feminism and the Battered Woman: The Limits of Self-Defence in the Context of Domestic Violence. 9 *Current Issues in Criminal Justice*: 113–124 .

Huss, M.T., A.J. Tomkins, C.P. Garbin, R.F. Schopp, and A. Kilian. 2006. Battered Women Who Kill Their Abusers: An Examination of Commonsense Notions, Cognitions, and Judgments. 21 *Journal of Interpersonal Violence*: 1063–1080.

Kahan, D.M., and D. Braman. 2008. The Self-defensive Cognition of Self-Defence. 45 *American Criminal Law Review*: 1–65.

Kathol, T. 1993. Defence of Property in the *Criminal Code*. 35 *Criminal Law Quarterly*: 453–479.

Kazan, P. 1997. Reasonableness, Gender Difference, and Self-Defense Law. 24 *Manitoba Law Journal*: 549–575.

Klimchuk, D. 1996. Circumstances and Objectivity. 45 *Criminal Reports (4th Series)*: 24–32.

Kutz, C. 2000. Self-Defense and Political Justification. 88 *California Law Review*: 751–778.

Law Reform Commission of Canada. 1987. Report No. 31: *Recodifying Criminal Law*. Rev. ed. Ottawa: L.R.C.C.

Mair, K.W. 2000. Experts and Ordinary Men: Locating *R. v. Lavallee*, Battered Woman Syndrome, and the "New" Psychiatric Expertise on Women within Canadian Legal History. 12 *Canadian Journal of Women & the Law*: 406–438.

Martinson, D. 1990. *Lavallee v. R.* The Supreme Court Addresses Gender Bias in the Courts. 24 *U.B.C. Law Review*: 381–396.

Martinson, D., et al. 1991. A Forum on *Lavallee v. R.*: Women and Self-Defence. 25 *U.B.C. Law Review*: 25–36.

Mousourakis, G. 2007. Defending Victims of Domestic Abuse Who Kill: A Perspective from English Law. 48 *Les Cahiers de Droit*: 351–371.

Paciocco, D.M. 1995. Subjective and Objective Standards of Fault for Offences and Defences. 59 *Saskatchewan Law Review*: 271–309.

Paciocco, D.M. 1999. *Getting Away with Murder: The Canadian Criminal Justice System*. Toronto: Irwin Law.

———. 2007. Applying the Law of Self-Defence. 12 *Canadian Criminal Law Review*: 25–94.

Parfett, J. 2001. Beyond Battered Women Syndrome Evidence: An Alternative Approach to the Use of Abuse Evidence in Spousal Homicide. 12 *Windsor Review of Legal & Social Issues*: 55–96.

Roach, K. 2009. *Criminal Law*. 4th ed. Toronto: Irwin Law.

Römkens, R. 2000. Ambiguous Responsibilities: Law and Conflicting Testimony on the Abused Woman Who Shot Her Sleeping Husband. 25 *Law & Social Inquiry*: 355–391.

Shaffer, M. 1997. The Battered Woman Syndrome Revisited: Some Complicating Thoughts Five Years after *R. v. Lavallee*. 47 *University of Toronto Law Journal*: 1–33.

Sheehy, E. 1994. Battered Woman Syndrome: Developments in Canadian Law after *R. v. Lavallee*. In J. Stubbs, ed. *Women, Male Violence and the Law*. Sydney: University of Sydney Institute of Criminology. 174–191.

———. 1995. *What Would a Women's Law of Self-Defence Look Like?* Ottawa: Status of Women Canada.

———. 2000. Review of the Self-Defence Review. 12 *Canadian Journal of Women & the Law*: 197–234.

———. 2001. Battered Women and Mandatory Minimum Sentences. 39 *Osgoode Hall Law Journal*: 529–554.

Simons, K.W. 2008. Self-Defense: Reasonable Beliefs or Reasonable Self-Control? 11 *New Criminal Law Review*: 51–90.

Stevens, D.J. 1999. Interviews with Women Convicted of Murder: Battered Women's Syndrome Revisited. 6 *International Review of Victimology*: 117–135.

Stewart, H. 2003. The Role of Reasonableness in Self-Defence. 16 *Canadian Journal of Law and Jurisprudence*: 317–336.

Stuart, D. 2002. *Cinous*: The Air of Reality Test Requires Weak Defences to Be Withdrawn from Juries. 49 *Criminal Reports (5th Series)*: 392–394.

———. 2007. *Canadian Criminal Law: A Treatise*. 5th ed. Toronto: Thomson Carswell. 494–517.

Stuart, D., R.J. Delisle, and S. Coughlan. 2009. *Learning Canadian Criminal Law*. 11th ed. Toronto: Thomson Carswell. Ch 7.

Stuesser, L. 1990. The "Defence" of "Battered Woman Syndrome" in Canada. 19 *Manitoba Law Journal*: 195–210.

Tang, K-L. 2003. Battered Woman Syndrome Testimony in Canada: Its Development and Lingering Issues. 47 *International Journal of Offender Therapy and Comparative Criminology*: 618–629.

Verdun-Jones, S.N. 2007. *Canadian Criminal Cases: Selected Highlights*. 2nd ed. Toronto: Thomson Nelson. Ch. 12.

Wong, C.M. 1999. Good Intentions, Troublesome Applications: The Cultural Defence and Other Uses of Cultural Evidence in Canada. 42 *Criminal Law Quarterly*: 367–396.

Yeo, S. 2000. Self-Defence in Homicide cases: Insights from Down Under. 5 *Canadian Criminal Law Review*: 263–275.

APPENDIX I

A BRIEF NOTE ON THE
CANADIAN CRIMINAL COURT SYSTEM

In order to assist the reader in acquiring a rudimentary understanding of the role of the courts mentioned in the text, this appendix offers a brief overview of the system of criminal courts in Canada. However, it should be emphasized that, at best, this overview paints a skeletal picture and the reader should be aware that there are numerous variations on the basic model as one moves from one province or territory to another.

All criminal cases enter the judicial system through the various *provincial or territorial courts*, where a provincially or territorially appointed judge sits without a jury.[1] However, although the majority of criminal cases are completed within the provincial courts, some cases must later move on to other courts for trial. All summary conviction offences are dealt with in the provincial or territorial courts, but whether an indictable offence will be tried there depends on the seriousness of the offence and, in some cases, on the choice of the accused person. Generally, the more serious criminal cases will not be tried in the provincial or territorial courts; instead, they are tried in the superior court of criminal jurisdiction of the various provinces and territories. Provincial and territorial court judges are appointed and paid by their respective provinces and territories. (In Ontario, the name for this level of court is the

Ontario Court of Justice; in Quebec, it is known as the *Court of Quebec*.) The provincial or territorial courts may be organized in different divisions, such as the Criminal Division, Youth Justice Court, Family Court, or Traffic Court. In recent years, there has been a trend toward the establishment of specialized provincial courts in certain urban jurisdictions; for example, Drug Treatment Courts in Toronto, Vancouver, Edmonton, Regina, Winnipeg, and Ottawa; Domestic Violence Courts in Ontario, Manitoba, Alberta, and the Yukon; a Community Court in Vancouver; and Mental Health Courts in Ottawa, Toronto, and Saint John, New Brunswick.

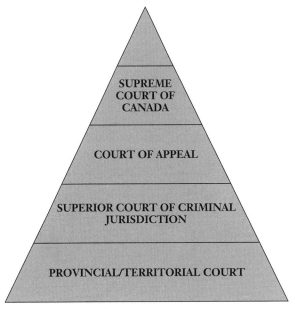

Hierarchy of Canadian criminal courts.

---

[1] In the Yukon and Northwest Territories, there are territorial courts. However, in Nunavut, the Nunavut Court of Justice combines the powers of the superior court of criminal jurisdiction with those of the territorial court. This permits the same judge to hear all criminal cases that arise in the territory. Such an approach is necessary given the fact that many communities in Nunavut are small and isolated: consequently, a judge has to travel to such communities in order to hear criminal cases.

In each province and territory, there is a *superior court of criminal jurisdiction*. The name of this court is not identical in each province. It is known as the *Supreme Court* in British Columbia, the Yukon and Northwest Territories, Nova Scotia, Prince Edward Island, and Newfoundland and Labrador; as the *Court of Queen's Bench* in Manitoba, Saskatchewan, Alberta, and New Brunswick; as the *Cour Supérieure* in Quebec; and as the *Nunavut Court of Justice* in Nunavut. In Ontario, this court is known as the *Superior Court of Justice*. Although the superior court has a broad jurisdiction to try criminal cases, in practice it tries only the more serious types of criminal offence. The superior court judge may try cases either sitting alone or with a jury. In certain circumstances, the superior court may hear appeals from the decisions of provincial courts in relation to summary conviction offences. Judges in the superior courts are appointed and paid by the federal government.

Above the superior court of criminal jurisdiction in the judicial hierarchy is an appeal court, known as the *Court of Appeal* (the *Appeal Division of the Supreme Court* in Prince Edward Island). The courts of appeal hear appeals directly from the decisions of the courts that have tried indictable offences and act as the second line of appeal in the case of summary conviction offences.

The highest tier in the hierarchy of courts in Canada is occupied by the *Supreme Court of Canada*,

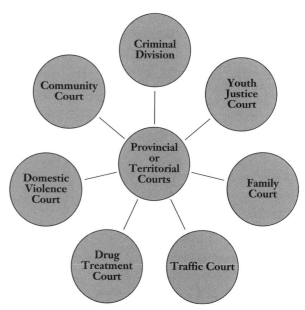

Organization of provincial and territorial courts. The specific divisions vary from one province/territory to another.

which hears appeals from the various provincial and territorial courts of appeal. The Supreme Court of Canada is the highest court in the land and is the final stage in the appeal process.

For further information, see Department of Justice Canada, *Canada's Court System* (2009): http://justice.gc.ca/eng/dept-min/pub/ccs-ajc/

APPENDIX II

A BRIEF GUIDE TO LAW REPORTS

Each case referred to in this book is accompanied by a formal, legal citation in the "Index of Cases." The citation of decided cases necessarily follows a rigid format, using standardized punctuation and abbreviations. In order to locate legal cases in a law library or to access them electronically, it is necessary to possess a basic understanding of the citation system that is used in connection with law reports. Reading cases in the original law reports will greatly enrich one's appreciation of the richness and complexity of the criminal law.

You should note that, in Canada, criminal cases involve an issue between the Crown and the accused. Hence, in Canada, the Queen (or "Regina," abbreviated as "R.") will always appear as one of the parties in a case name. For brevity in this text, "R. v." has been deleted from most case names. The case name is followed by the appropriate citation. Consider, for example, the citations below.

Case Name	Date	Volume	Series	Page	Court
(a) *R. v. Chalmers*	(2009)	243	C.C.C. (3d)	338	(Ont. C.A.)
(b) *R. v. Royz*	[2009]	1	S.C.R.	423	——

If the volumes of the series of law reports concerned are numbered sequentially, the date is given in round brackets (as in example (a)). However, square brackets are employed whenever the date itself is part of the volume reference (as in example (b)). In example (a), the reference is adequate without the date. If you went to a law library and attempted to look up the case cited in example (a), you would only need to locate volume 243 of the third series of *Canadian Criminal Cases*; the date is merely included as additional information. However, in example (b), the date is an essential component of the reference and is, in effect, part of the volume number. If you needed to look up the case cited in example (b), you would have to locate the first of those volumes of the *Supreme Court Reports* published in 2009. Finally, it should be noted that when the date is enclosed in round brackets, it refers to the year when the decision was actually rendered. When it is enclosed in square brackets, it refers to the year in which the decision was printed in the reporting series.

In academic works, it is customary to add the abbreviated name of the court in which the reported case was decided. You will notice that *R. v. Chalmers* was decided in the Ontario Court of Appeal (abbreviated as Ont. C.A.). However, it is not necessary to add (S.C.C.) after *R. v. Royz* because it was reported in the *Supreme Court Reports*, which only cover decisions of the Supreme Court of Canada.

There are numerous series of Canadian law reports. Some series are general in nature and may cover a broad range of legal issues (from criminal law to tax law), whereas others deal exclusively with a specific subject matter (such as criminal law or business law). As a consequence, some cases may actually be reported in four or five different series of law reports. Matters are somewhat complicated by the fact that there may be a number of different subseries within each series of law reports; for example, there are four separate subseries of *Canadian Criminal Cases*.

The following table provides information concerning the various series (and subseries) of law reports to which reference is made in this book.

Abbreviated Title	Title and Years Covered	Example of Citation
	CANADIAN LAW REPORTS	
C.C.C.	Canadian Criminal Cases, 1893–1962	*R. v. Chow Bew* (1955), 113 C.C.C. 377
[ ] C.C.C.	Canadian Criminal Cases, 1963–1970	*R. v. Taylor*, [1964] 1 C.C.C. 207
C.C.C.(2d)	Canadian Criminal Cases (2nd series), 1971–1982	*R. v. Haight* (1976), 30 C.C.C. (2d) 168
C.C.C.(3d)	Canadian Criminal Cases (3rd series), 1983–	*R. v. Swan* (2009), 244 C.C.C. (3d) 108
C.R.	Criminal Reports, 1950–1967	*R. v. Regan* (1954), C.R. 361
C.R.N.S.	Criminal Reports (new series), 1967–1970	*R. v. Peda* (1969), 7 C.R.N.S. 243
C.R. (3d)	Criminal Reports (3rd series), 1978–1990	*R. v. Conkie* (1978), 3 C.R. (3d) 317
C.R. (4th)	Criminal Reports (4th series), 1991–1996	*R. v. DeSousa* (1992), 15 C.R. (4th) 66
C.R. (5th)	Criminal Reports (5th series), 1997–2001	*R. v. Burk* (1999), 28 C.R. (5th) 149
C.R. (6th)	Criminal Reports (6th series), 2002–	*R. v. MacCormack* (2009), 64 C.R. (6th) 137
D.L.R.	Dominion Law Reports, 1912–1922	*R. v. Dalke* (1915), 27 D.L.R. 633
[ ] D.L.R.	Dominion Law Reports, 1932–1955	*R v. Marchello*, [1951] 4 D.L.R. 751
D.L.R.(2d)	Dominion Law Reports (2nd series), 1956–1968	*R. v. Howson* (1966), 55 D.L.R. (2d) 582
D.L.R.(3d)	Dominion Law Reports (3rd series), 1969–1983	*R. v. Henni* (1971), 18 D.L.R. (3d) 320
D.L.R. (4th)	Dominion Law Reports (4th series), 1984–	*R. v. Middleton* (2009), 306 D.L.R. (4th) 628
O.R.	Ontario Reports, 1882–1900 & 1931–1973	*R. v. Bleta*, [1964] 1 O.R. 485
O.R. (2d)	Ontario Reports (2nd series), 1973–1990	*R. v. Swain* (1986), 53 O.R. (2d) 609
O.R. (3d)	Ontario Reports (3rd series), 1991–	*R. v. Batisse* (2009), 93 O.R. (3d) 643
[ ] S.C.R.	Supreme Court Reports, 1923–1969	*R. v. George*, [1960] S.C.R. 871
[ ] S.C.R.	Supreme Court Reports, 1970–	*R. v. Royz*, [2009] 1 S.C.R. 423
[ ] W.W.R.	Western Weekly Reports, 1911–1950	*R. v. Anderson*, [1920] 1 W.W.R. 609
W.W.R.	Western Weekly Reports (new series), 1951–1970	*R. v. Roher* (1953), 10 W.W.R. 309
[ ] W.W.R.	Western Weekly Reports (current series), 1971–	*R. v. Briscoe*, [2009] 4 W.W.R. 430

For more detailed information, see Simon Fraser University Library, *How to Find Legal Cases,* at www.lib.sfu.ca/help/subject-guides/criminology/find-legal-cases.

APPENDIX III

USING THE INTERNET TO EXPAND YOUR KNOWLEDGE OF THE CRIMINAL LAW AND TO CONDUCT BASIC LEGAL RESEARCH

INTRODUCTION

The advent of the Internet has placed an immensely powerful research tool in the hands of those students who are able to gain access to its resources. Even if you do not have access through your own computer, you may readily obtain it through terminals in university or college computing laboratories or in your public library. By visiting relevant websites, you may gain further information about every legal topic discussed in this textbook, including the specific text of legislation (e.g., the *Criminal Code)* and cases decided in the courts (e.g., all recent Supreme Court of Canada decisions). This appendix is designed to provide you with some basic navigational guides to the exploration of those websites that may help you to expand your knowledge of criminal law in Canada.

GENERAL CANADIAN WEBSITES THAT CONTAIN LINKS TO A VARIETY OF LEGAL RESOURCES

If you are a relative newcomer to the legal resources available on the Internet, you should probably start with websites that gather together automatic links to a broad range of relevant resources (you merely click on the specific resources that are highlighted and you will immediately be connected to the relevant database).

Access to Justice Network

www.acjnet.org/nahome/default.aspx

It is suggested that one of your first visits should be to the Access to Justice Network. This extraordinarily useful website contains instant links to various sites providing information about Canadian law and justice

resource materials. In particular, it provides direct access to the text of legislation enacted by the Parliament of Canada and by the various provincial and territorial legislatures. The website also makes available the text of judicial decisions made by the Supreme Court of Canada and the Federal Court of Canada, as well as by the courts of the various provinces and territories. This website also contains links to the federal and provincial/territorial *Hansard* (which provides information about the proceedings of the Canadian Parliament and the provincial/territorial legislatures). It may be advisable to start with the introductory page, the *tour of ACJNet*, at www.acjnet.org/naabout/default.aspx.

Canadian Legal Information Institute (CANLII)

http://canlii.org/en/index.php

The website of the Canadian Legal Information Institute is exceptionally useful since it provides direct—and easy—access to both legislation and case law not only at the federal level but also at the provincial and territorial level. For example, the user of this site can find the list of databases and click on "Federal." Under the heading "Legislation," the user may then select "Statutes and Regulations," and then, under "Consolidated Statutes of Canada," click on the letter "C." The user may then select "Criminal Code" and gain access to the complete—and latest version of—the *Criminal Code*. The "Federal" database includes "Legislation," "Courts," "Boards and Tribunals," "Frequently Consulted Documents," and "External Links."

The "Courts" heading includes decisions of the Supreme Court of Canada. A similar database is available for each province and territory of Canada. The site also provides links to legal information institutes of a number of other countries (such as the Asian Australasian, British and Irish, and New Zealand Legal Information Institutes.).

SOQUIJ

La Société Québécoise d'Information Juridique

http://soquij.qc.ca/index.aspx

This site provides access to cases decided by courts in Quebec at http://www.jugements.qc.ca/.

The National Library of Canada—Canadian Information by Subject [34 Law]

www.collectionscanada.gc.ca/caninfo/ep034.htm

This is an extraordinarily valuable website. It enables you to click onto a variety of specific sites that provide a cornucopia of information about law. For example, there are links to various websites about the Constitution (342); Civil Rights (342.085); Criminal Law (345); Legislation (348); Law–Canada (349.71); Law–British Columbia (349.711), and Law–Ontario (349.713), and so forth.

Best Guide to Canadian Legal Research

http://legalresearch.org/

This site provides instant access to a broad range of legal research resources, both for Canada and for other jurisdictions (such as the United States, the United Kingdom, Australia, and the European Union), and for international law. It is extremely valuable as an introduction to legal research, particularly electronic research. It also provides direct links with other research tools.

LexUM (University of Montreal, Faculty of Law)

www.lexum.umontreal.ca/index_en.php

This website provides invaluable information about various legal resources relating to Canada (and specifically to Quebec). In particular, it provides access to judgments of the Supreme Court of Canada, dating back to 1948. The website describes LexUM as "a legal technology—offers *solutions and services* and conducts advanced research in order to identify the best uses of technology to provide efficient access to legal material."

Jurist Canada: The Legal Education Network

http://jurist.law.utoronto.ca

This website provides access to online articles about law and legal research as well as links to the specific websites of various Canadian law journals. It also enables you to search for legal subjects that have been discussed in online articles, and so on.

Duhaime.org

www.duhaime.org

This website provides access to a range of brief and straightforward articles on various legal topics. There is a separate heading for Criminal Law, which covers various topics dealt with in this textbook.

Canadian Bar Association: Legal Links

www.cba.org/CBA/links/Main/

The Canadian Bar Association's website includes a page that provides legal links to the official websites of all of the courts and governments of Canada.

Canadian Legal Resources

www.gahtan.com/cdnlaw/

This website provides links to a number of Canadian and U.S. legal resources available on the Internet and currently contains more than 1420 links. This site provides rapid access to decisions of the Supreme Court of the United States.

SPECIALIZED CANADIAN WEBSITES RELEVANT TO LAW

(PARTICULARLY CRIMINAL LAW)

There is a considerable number of specialized websites that will provide you with immensely valuable information and research tools that address specific legal topics. This appendix will provide you with an overview of some of these specialized sites, although it is important to remember that new sites are constantly being added, and existing sites are frequently modified (and, occasionally, eliminated).

Parliament of Canada

www.parl.gc.ca

This is an essential website for gaining an understanding of the contemporary functioning of the Parliament of Canada. For example, you may gain access to the text of bills that are currently being considered by the House of Commons and the Senate. In addition, you may read the daily debates in the chambers of the House of Commons and the Senate as well as reports of parliamentary committee proceedings by accessing online *Hansard*, which is the official publication of Parliament.

Government of Canada

http://canada.gc.ca/home.html

The Government of Canada Internet Site permits direct access to general information about Canada, its government, and various programs and services provided by the government.

Canada Gazette

www.gazette.gc.ca/index-eng.html

This is a new website (March 2009), providing access to the text of the *Canada Gazette*, which contains official information concerning regulations passed under the authority of federal statutes.

Department of Justice Canada

www.canada.justice.gc.ca

The Department of Justice plays a central role in the process of federal law reform (in particular, the *Criminal Code* and other criminal law statutes). It drafts legislation and assists in the process of developing policies that guide the operation of Canada's justice system. The website states that "[t]he Department monitors trends in criminal law, develops and implements options for criminal law reform and provides a centre of expertise for criminal law and procedure, criminal justice policy, sentencing and victims issues."

Connecting to this website will provide you with access to such valuable documents as *Canada's System of Justice; Canada's Court System;* and *Canada's Department of Justice*. The website also provides information concerning criminal law reform and, in particular, reform initiatives undertaken by the Department of Justice (for example, in 2009, "tougher laws targeting gangs and other forms of organized crime"—Bill C-14, *An Act to amend the Criminal Code* (organized crime and protection of justice system participants), which received Royal Assent on June 23rd, 2009). The website contains many useful links to the Parliament of Canada, federal and provincial court sites, and so forth.

The Supreme Court of Canada

www.scc-csc.gc.ca

This is the official website of the Supreme Court of Canada. It provides valuable background information about the Court and includes valuable links to related websites (including a link to all judgments of the Supreme Court of Canada from 1948 onward). You should check this site frequently in order to keep abreast of the very latest Supreme Court of Canada judgments.

The Federal Court of Canada

http://cas-ncr-nter03.cas-satj.gc.ca/portal/page/portal/fc_cf_en/Index

This is the official website of the Federal Court of Canada. Although the Federal Court does not directly adjudicate issues of criminal law, it does make decisions that affect, for example, the functioning of such federal organizations as the Correctional Service of Canada. The site provides access to judgments of the Court.

The Federal Court of Appeal

www.fca-caf.gc.ca/index_e.shtml

This is the official website of the Federal Court of Appeal, which hears appeals from the Federal Court of Canada (see above). The site provides information about the Court as well as access to its judgments.

Public Safety Canada

www.publicsafety.gc.ca/index-eng.aspx

According to this website, "Public Safety Canada (PS) was created in 2003 to ensure coordination across all federal departments and agencies responsible for national security and the safety of Canadians. From natural disasters to crime and terrorism, our mandate is to keep Canadians safe." This federal department plays a critical role in Canada's system of criminal justice since it provides "effective direction" to the following agencies: Royal Canadian Mounted Police (RCMP); Canadian Security Intelligence Service (CSIS); Correctional Service of Canada (CSC); National Parole Board (NPB); and Canada Border Services Agency. The site provides current information about the work of the department.

Statistics Canada (Information about Justice and Crime)

www.statcan.gc.ca/start-debut-eng.html

The website of Statistics Canada is an invaluable resource for statistical information about Canada's criminal justice system (e.g., crimes, victims, suspects, police, and courts).

See, for example, M. Dauvergne, *Crime Statistics in Canada* (2007):

www.statcan.gc.ca/pub/85-002-x/85-002-x2008007-eng.pdf

The Canadian Bar Association

www.cba.org/cba/

This website constitutes the information service of the Canadian Bar Association. It provides valuable updates about important legal developments in Canada. The site also contains a link that enables the user to search for articles in the *Canadian Bar Review*, one of Canada's leading law journals, at www.cba.org/cba_barreview/Search.aspx.

COURTS OF THE PROVINCES AND TERRITORIES

Many of the provincial and territorial courts in Canada have established their own websites. For example, you may find that the following sites contain useful information in relation to your own province or territory:

British Columbia

www.courts.gov.bc.ca/

Alberta

www.albertacourts.ab.ca/

Saskatchewan

www.sasklawcourts.ca/

Manitoba

www.manitobacourts.mb.ca/

Ontario

www.ontariocourts.on.ca/

Quebec

www.tribunaux.qc.ca/mjq_en/

Prince Edward Island

www.gov.pe.ca/courts/

Newfoundland and Labrador

www.court.nl.ca/

New Brunswick

www.gnb.ca/cour/index-e.asp

Northwest Territories

www.nwtcourts.ca/

Nunavut

www.nucj.ca/unifiedcourt.htm

Yukon

www.justice.gov.yk.ca/prog/cs/courts.html

LEGISLATURES OF THE PROVINCES AND TERRITORIES

By visiting the websites of the various provinces and territories, you may gain access to information about the regulatory legislation that constitutes a significant part of the "quasi-criminal law" discussed in the textbook.

British Columbia

www.leg.bc.ca/

Alberta

www.assembly.ab.ca/

Saskatchewan

www.legassembly.sk.ca/

Manitoba

www.gov.mb.ca/legislature/homepage.html

Ontario

www.ontla.on.ca/web/home.do

Quebec

www.assnat.qc.ca/

Nova Scotia

www.gov.ns.ca/legislature/

New Brunswick

www.gnb.ca/legis/index-e.asp

Prince Edward Island

www.assembly.pe.ca/index.php

Newfoundland and Labrador

www.assembly.nl.ca/

Northwest Territories

www.assembly.gov.nt.ca/_live/pages/wpPages/home.aspx

Nunavut

www.assembly.nu.ca/english/index.html

Yukon

www.legassembly.gov.yk.ca/

GOVERNMENTS OF THE PROVINCES AND TERRITORIES

Each province and territory in Canada maintains an official website. You may gain valuable information about governmental initiatives in the area of criminal justice by visiting the following sites:

British Columbia

www.gov.bc.ca/

Alberta

http://alberta.ca/home/

Saskatchewan

www.gov.sk.ca/

Manitoba

www.gov.mb.ca/index.html

Ontario

www.ontario.ca/en/residents/index.htm

Quebec

www.gouv.qc.ca/portail/quebec/pgs/commun/?lang=en

Nova Scotia

http://www.gov.ns.ca/

New Brunswick

www.gnb.ca/index-e.asp

Prince Edward Island

www.gov.pe.ca

Newfoundland and Labrador

www.gov.nl.ca/

Northwest Territories

www.gov.nt.ca/

Nunavut

www.gov.nu.ca/english/

Yukon

www.gov.yk.ca/

Note that, in most provinces and territories, the Department or Ministry of the Attorney General is responsible for the administration of criminal justice and it may be worthwhile to explore whether this department or ministry has its own website (see, for example, www.attorneygeneral.jus.gov.on.ca/ and www.gov.bc.ca/ag/index.html (British Columbia).

SIGNIFICANT WEBSITES RELATING TO THE LAW AND LEGAL INSTITUTIONS OF THE UNITED KINGDOM, AUSTRALIA, AND THE UNITED STATES

The criminal law of such countries as England and Wales, Australia, and the United States has exerted a fair degree of influence on the evolution of Canadian criminal law. It is, therefore, useful to keep abreast of developments in these jurisdictions, since many of the criminal law issues that are currently being addressed in Canada are also subject to legislative and judicial intervention in other countries. Undoubtedly, the experience of other jurisdictions constitutes a valuable resource for those readers who may wish to subject Canadian criminal law to a critical analysis and evaluation. The following is a very brief list of relevant websites:

THE UNITED KINGDOM

The United Kingdom Parliament

www.parliament.uk/

Government of the United Kingdom

www.direct.gov.uk/en/index.htm

The Incorporated Council of Law Reporting for England and Wales

www.lawreports.co.uk/#

House of Lords Judgments

www.publications.parliament.uk/pa/ld/ldjudgmt.htm

Her Majesty's Courts Service

www.hmcourts-service.gov.uk/

AUSTRALIA

Parliament of Australia

www.aph.gov.au

The High Court of Australia

www.hcourt.gov.au/

THE UNITED STATES OF AMERICA

The United States Senate

www.senate.gov/

The United States House of Representatives

www.house.gov/

The White House

www.whitehouse.gov/

The Supreme Court of the United States

www.supremecourtus.gov/

United States Sentencing Commission

www.ussc.gov/

The United States Justice Information Centre: NCJRS

www.ncjrs.org/

This impressive website, operated by the National Criminal Justice Reference Service (NCJRS), provides voluminous information about crime and criminal justice in the United States. There is a specific component of the site that is dedicated to the criminal courts at www.ncjrs.gov/App/Topics/Topic.aspx? TopicID=22.

INTERNATIONAL WEBSITES

The United Nations

www.un.org/en/

This is the official site of the United Nations and provides access to information about, *inter alia*, international law and human rights.

WEBSITES OF INTERNATIONAL COURTS

Although this textbook does not deal with the jurisdiction and functioning of international courts, you may wish to explore some of valuable websites that have been established by such courts. Some of the courts have no direct role in the development of international criminal law, while others clearly do.

There follows a short list of the websites of some of the most significant international tribunals.

The International Criminal Court

www2.icc-cpi.int/Menus/ICC/Home

According to this website, the International Criminal Court (ICC) is "the first ever permanent, treaty based, international criminal court established to promote the rule of law and ensure that the gravest international crimes do not go unpunished." The Court, which was finally established in 2002, is permanently situated at The Hague in the Netherlands. The Court tries individuals accused of committing genocide, war crimes, and crimes against humanity if existing national courts are unwilling or unable to do so.

International Criminal Tribunal for the Former Yugoslavia

www.icty.org/

This website provides access to the decisions made by the International Criminal tribunal in the trials of defendants charged with having committed war crimes in the former Yugoslavia. The Court is located at The Hague in the Netherlands.

International Criminal Tribunal for Rwanda

www.ictr.org/default.htm

The International Criminal Tribunal for Rwanda was established for the prosecution of persons responsible for genocide and other serious violations of international humanitarian law committed in Rwanda in 1994. It may also deal with the prosecution of Rwandan citizens who were responsible for genocide and other violations of international criminal law that were committed in neighbouring states in 1994. The tribunal is located in Arusha, United Republic of Tanzania.

The International Court of Justice

www.icj-cij.org/homepage/index.php?lang=en

This is the website for the International Court of Justice, which is located in The Hague, Netherlands. It is the principal judicial organ of the United Nations.

The European Court of Human Rights

www.echr.coe.int/echr/Homepage_EN

This is the official website of the European Court of Human Rights, which is located in Strasbourg. It provides access to information about the European

Convention on Human Rights, the nature and function of the Court, and the judgments and decisions of the Court.

Court of Justice of the European Communities

http://curia.europa.eu/jcms/jcms/j_6/

This is the official site of the European Court of Justice, which is the judicial organ of the European Community and is located in Luxembourg.

COMMERCIAL ELECTRONIC DATABASE SERVICES

There is a number of commercial electronic database services that provide immensely powerful legal research tools. You may research specific legal topics in these databases and obtain detailed information concerning the applicable legislation and case, as well as the relevant legal literature (law journal articles, etc.). These automated search tools are extremely effective and will save you a considerable amount of time and effort in your research endeavours. However, unless you obtain authorized access to these databases through a university or college library or similar institution, you will normally be required to establish an account with the service providers concerned, and charges will be levied for use of the relevant electronic research facilities.

BestCase

Canada Law Book

http://www.canadalawbook.ca/OnlinePublications.html

Contains Canadian law reports including, Canadian Criminal Cases, Dominion Law Reports, All-Canada Weekly Summaries and the Weekly Criminal Bulletin.

Criminal Spectrum

Canada Law Book

www.canadalawbook.ca/catalogue.cfm?DSP= Detail&ProductID=1247

This is a specialized service which focuses on Criminal Law. It provides access to case law (including *Canadian Criminal Cases*), legislation, commentary (including *Criminal Law Quarterly*), and a number of textbooks.

LawSource

Westlaw Canada

www.westlawecarswell.com/home/

This service provides access to a broad range of legal resources, including case law, legislation, law journals and reviews, *Canadian Encyclopedic Digest*, and *Index to Canadian Legal Literature*.

Criminal Source

Westlaw Canada

www.westlawecarswell.com/home/

This service specializes in Criminal Law. It includes access to case law (including the *Criminal Reports*), legislation, Carswell's *Criminal Law Digest*, annotations of criminal cases, *Canadian Criminal Law Review*, and legal textbooks.

Quicklaw

LexisNexis Canada

www.lexisnexis.ca/en/quicklaw/

QuickLaw was one of the first automated legal databases to be established in Canada. It provides access to Canadian court cases and tribunal decisions, legislation, commentary, journals, citators, and indexes.

LexisNexis Academic

LexisNexis (U.S.A.)

www.lexisnexis.com/about-us/#

This database provides access to information concerning a broad range of topics, including news, government, business, and law (derived from newspapers, journals, reports, and legal cases). The content is primarily focused on U.S. sources. Of particular importance is the access it provides to U.S. case law.

GLOSSARY

Abetting: Section 21(1) of the *Criminal Code* provides that an individual becomes a party to a criminal offence if he or she abets another person to actually commit that offence. In the context of section 21(1), abetting means instigating, procuring, or promoting a crime to be committed or encouraging another person to actually commit an offence.

Absolute and conditional discharge: When an accused person has been found NCRMD (see below), the court or board of review may order that the NCR accused person be held in custody in a psychiatric facility. However, the court or board of review may also grant an **absolute discharge**—an outright release with no restrictions on the liberty of the NCR accused person—or a **conditional discharge**—a release that is subject to various conditions, such as residence in a particular location and attendance for treatment.

Absolute liability: This form of liability may be imposed in relation to the less serious offences arising under regulatory legislation (either federal or provincial/territorial). The Crown may obtain a conviction for a violation of such legislation without having to prove *mens rea* on the part of the accused persons concerned. Furthermore, these accused persons are denied a defence even if they can prove that there was no negligence on their part. As a general rule, absolute liability may not be imposed where imprisonment is a potential penalty. Most regulatory offences impose strict, rather than absolute, liability (see **strict liability**).

Accessory: An individual who is involved in the commission of a crime in a secondary capacity.

Accessory after the fact: This term refers to a person who, knowing that an individual has been a party to a criminal offence, gives the latter comfort or assistance with the intention of enabling him or her to escape justice.

Accused: The accused is the person against whom a criminal charge has been laid.

Acquittal: An official discharge from prosecution, usually after a verdict of not guilty.

Active euthanasia: See **euthanasia**.

Actus reus: This term can only be understood in light of the concept of *mens rea*. **Mens rea** refers to the various mental elements (other than voluntariness) that are contained in the definition of a particular criminal offence. *Actus reus* refers to all the other elements of the offence that must be proved (including voluntariness) before an accused person may be convicted of the particular offence in question.

Agent provocateur: An individual (usually an undercover police officer or paid informer) who, for law enforcement purposes, associates with members of a group in order to incite them to commit an offence.

Aiding: Section 21(1) of the *Criminal Code* provides that an individual becomes a party to a criminal offence if he or she aids another person to actually commit that offence. "Aiding" means providing assistance with the intention of providing such assistance.

"Air-of-reality" test: See burden of proof.

Amnesia: The partial or total loss of memory. For the purposes of the Criminal Law, specific attention is paid to amnesia that occurs in connection with the commission of the *actus reus* of a criminal offence. *Retrograde amnesia* refers to memory deficits in relation to events that occurred *prior* to the incident in question. *Anterograde amnesia* refers to memory deficits in relation to the incident itself and to events following the incident. *Retrograde amnesia* is not relevant to an accused person's criminal responsibility. However, an accused person with *anterograde amnesia* may have been in a dissociative state at the time of the alleged crime and, therefore, may be entitled to the benefit of a defence of **automatism** or **NCRMD**.

A dissociative state refers to a "disruption in the usually integrated functions of consciousness, memory, identity, or perception" (see American Psychiatric Association's *Diagnostic and Statistical Manual of Mental Disorders*, 4th ed. Text Revision (2000)).

Appeal: A formal proceeding by means of which the Crown or the accused may request a review of a decision by a "higher court." For example, the provincial/territorial Court of Appeal is a higher court than the Superior Court of Criminal Jurisdiction or the Provincial Court, whereas the Supreme Court of Canada is, in turn, a higher court than the Court of Appeal.

Appellant: The party who appeals from the decision of a "lower court." In Canada, either the Crown (the prosecution) or the accused may appeal such a decision (in accordance with certain limitations defined in the *Criminal Code*).

Appreciate: Section 16(1) of the *Criminal Code* provides that an accused person must be found NCRMD if, at the time of the alleged offence, he or she was suffering from a mental disorder that rendered him or her "incapable of appreciating the nature and quality of the act or omission." In this context, "appreciate" means something more than simple awareness of one's conduct: the accused must have the capacity to "perceive the consequences, impact, and results of a physical act."

Assault: In criminal law, an assault arises when an individual applies force intentionally to another person or attempts or threatens to apply force to another person (section 265 of the *Criminal Code*).

Assisted suicide: It is an offence under section 241(b) of the *Criminal Code* to assist another person to commit suicide. The most common form of assisted suicide is the ingestion of a lethal dose of drugs provided by another person for this specific purpose.

Automatism: A state of impaired consciousness that renders a person incapable of controlling his or her behaviour while in that state. A person in such a state cannot be said to be acting voluntarily and, therefore, cannot be held criminally responsible for his or her conduct.

Battered wife syndrome: This is a condition that commonly appears among women who have been physically and/or mentally abused by an intimate partner over an extended period. It is also called *battered woman syndrome*. Among the major symptoms are intense fearfulness and feelings of helplessness. Where an accused person has killed or inflicted grievous bodily harm on her partner, she may raise the defence of **self-defence** (see below) under section 34(2) of the *Criminal Code*. Evidence of battered wife syndrome may be introduced in order to establish whether the accused person reasonably believed that her life was in danger and that she could only preserve herself by using deadly force. A more appropriate term is "abused woman syndrome" since this takes into account the significance of emotional or psychological abuse.

Beard **Rules:** These judge-made rules define the circumstances in which an accused person may successfully raise the defence of intoxication. The rules are as follows:

1. If intoxication induces a mental disorder and renders the accused "not criminally responsible" within the meaning of section 16 of the *Criminal Code*, he or she must be acquitted as being "not criminally responsible on account of mental disorder" (NCRMD).

2. If intoxication prevents a defendant from forming the intent necessary for conviction of a crime of specific intent, he or she must be acquitted. However, intoxication can never be a defence to a charge of a crime of *general* (or *basic*) intent.

3. If intoxication falls short of preventing the accused from forming the intent necessary for conviction of a crime of specific intent, it does not constitute a valid defence.

Bigamy: The offence of bigamy is committed when a person: goes through a form of marriage while still married to another person; goes through a form of marriage with another person knowing that this other person is still married to someone else; or goes through a form of marriage with more than one other person simultaneously (section 290 of the *Criminal Code*).

Bipolar disorder: A mental disorder that is characterized by alternating episodes of mania and depression. Mania may be defined as an abnormally elevated, expansive, or irritable mood. Bipolar disorder was previously known as manic-depressive disorder.

Blackmail: See **extortion**.

Bona **fide:** In good faith. That is to say, a party has acted without any dishonesty or fraud.

Burden of proof: This indicates which party is responsible for proving certain facts in a trial. Since the Crown is asserting, in a criminal trial, that the accused has committed an offence, the **primary or persuasional burden of proof** is normally on the Crown to establish that the accused did indeed commit the offence with which he or she has been charged. The **standard of proof** that must be met by the Crown is that of "*beyond a reasonable doubt.*" In the rare cases where the accused is placed under the burden of proof to establish a particular fact (e.g., that he or she was not criminally responsible because of mental disorder or was in a state of automatism), the standard of proof is "*on the balance of probabilities.*"

There is also a **secondary or evidentiary burden of proof** that refers primarily to the requirement that, before a defence (such as mistake of fact) may be put to the trier of fact, the trial judge must be satisfied that the accused has introduced sufficient evidence to give an "**air of reality**" to the defence. As the Supreme Court of Canada held, in the case of *Cinous* (2002): "[T]he full question is whether there is evidence (some evidence, any evidence) upon which a properly instructed jury acting judicially could acquit." If there is any or some such evidence, then the air of reality hurdle is cleared. If there is no such evidence, then the air of reality hurdle is not cleared." This burden of proof merely requires that the accused introduce some evidence capable of raising a reasonable doubt as to the issue in question. The burden placed on the accused in such circumstances is a light one and is primarily designed to prevent him or her from raising totally speculative defences that have no support in any of the evidence presented to the court. Once the defence is put to the trier of fact, the Crown must prove beyond a reasonable doubt that it does not apply (e.g., that the accused was not operating under a mistake of fact).

Bylaw: Legislation enacted by an inferior body that acts under delegated authority, such as the laws passed by a municipal council that have been granted authority under provincial government legislation.

Canadian Charter of Rights and Freedoms: The *Charter* is part of the Constitution of Canada. It was enacted by the *Constitution Act 1982* (UK) c. 11 and was proclaimed in force on April 17, 1982. The *Charter* guarantees certain rights and freedoms that are considered to be of great importance to Canadians. The *Charter* is one of the most important statutes in Canada since the courts may declare invalid any federal or provincial/territorial laws that infringe the rights or freedoms guaranteed by the *Charter*.

Care or control: Section 253 of the *Criminal Code* provides that it is an offence to have the "care or control" of a motor vehicle or vessel while one's ability to operate the vehicle or vessel is impaired by alcohol or another drug or while having a blood-alcohol level of more than 80 milligrams of alcohol in 100 millilitres of blood. In the *Toews* case (1985), the Supreme Court of Canada ruled that "acts of care or control" are "acts which involve some use of the car or its fittings and equipment, or some course of conduct associated with the vehicle which would involve a risk of putting the vehicle in motion so that it could become dangerous."

Careless driving: Careless driving or driving without due care and attention is an offence under provincial or territorial legislation. The offence may be proved by establishing that the accused person's driving conduct fell—even to a minor extent—below the standard of care expected of a reasonable driver acting prudently in the circumstances facing him or her.

Carelessness: Careless conduct is conduct that falls below the standard of care expected of a reasonable person acting prudently in the circumstances facing him or her.

Causation in fact: See **factual causation.**

Causation in law: See **legal causation.**

Circumstances: Circumstances always constitute an essential element of the *actus reus* of a criminal offence. The relevant or "material" circumstances that the Crown must prove are those that are contained in the definition of the offence. For example, when the accused person has been charged with sexual assault, a material circumstance that the Crown must prove is that there was no consent to sexual activity on the part of the complainant.

Circumstantial evidence: Evidence of a series of circumstances that may lead the trier of fact to draw an inference of guilt when no direct evidence is available (evidence is "direct" when a witness testifies as to what he or she actually observed by sight, hearing, etc.).

Civil law: This term must be distinguished from the concept of a civil law system (see below). The term "civil law" primarily refers to the body of laws that deals with the relationships between private citizens. For example, an individual citizen may bring a legal action for compensation on the basis that his or her neighbour's negligence has caused some degree of harm. The goal of the civil law action is solely to compensate the citizen for the loss caused by the neighbour. In contrast, the criminal law is primarily concerned with punishing a convicted person for the wrong done to the state by the latter's misconduct. The criminal law trial is a proceeding between the Crown and the accused, whereas the civil law action initiates a proceeding between private citizens.

Civil law system: This term (distinguished from Civil law, above) refers to a legal system based on the approach of Roman law and usually characterized by the existence of a comprehensive code. This system of law is predominant in continental Europe, Scotland, and (as far as the civil law is concerned) in the province of Quebec.

Code: A code is a collection or system of laws. In a civil law system, a code would ideally be a complete system of law, logically arranged according to basic principles and promulgated by the appropriate legislative authority. The origins of the civil law system are to be found in the collection of laws made by the Roman Emperor Justinian, and referred to as "The Code." In France, for example, the *Code Civil* (originally promulgated in 1804 and at one time known as the *Code Napoléon*) contains the civil law of that country.

Cognitive: Relating to a person's knowledge and reasoning abilities as opposed to the emotional factors that may influence his or her behaviour.

Colour of right: Accused persons who act under the influence of an honest, albeit mistaken, belief that they have a valid legal right are considered to be acting under colour of right. In certain circumstances, such persons may have a defence to a criminal charge. For example, they may have a valid defence to a charge of theft where they honestly believe that they have a valid right to the property in question, even though it subsequently turns out that this right is not recognized by a court of law.

Common intention: Section 21(2) of the *Criminal Code* provides that an individual may become a party to a crime committed by another person by virtue of having formed a common intention with that other person. Common intention exists where two or more individuals agree to commit a crime and to assist each other in carrying out that agreement. If one of these individuals subsequently commits another offence in the course of carrying out the common intention, then each of the other individuals concerned will be found to be a party to that other offence, provided he or she either knew or ought to have known that the commission of this other criminal offence "would be a probable consequence of carrying out the common purpose."

Common law: A term with at least two meanings. The term is used to denote a legal system inherited from England in which judges decide cases by applying the legal principles embodied in precedent cases decided in the past (see **precedent**). The doctrine of *stare decisis* requires courts to apply principles from those cases highest in their court hierarchy. In a related sense, common law also means the law common to all England. As cases were decided by courts in England, over time judges in various regions drew upon the rulings of those deciding cases elsewhere, eventually resulting in a common body of law. The common law system is predominant in England and Wales, the Canadian provinces and territories (with the exception of Quebec), the American states (with the exception of Louisiana), Australia, and New Zealand.

Complainant: One who makes a complaint to the authorities that he or she has been the victim of a criminal offence.

Conduct: A voluntary act or omission constituting the central feature of a criminal offence.

Consequences: The Crown usually has to prove that the accused person's conduct caused a certain consequence as an essential element of the *actus reus* of the criminal offence with which the accused person has been charged. However, there are a number of exceptions to this principle: for example, in order to obtain a conviction of the offence of perjury, the Crown does not have to prove that the accused person's lies were believed by anyone.

Conspiracy: An agreement by two or more persons to commit a crime.

Constitution Act, 1867: Canada's foundational constitutional document. It establishes Canada as a federal state, and it contains the provisions that delineate the spheres of responsibility for each of the two levels of government. It also contains provisions pertaining to the structure of Canada's court systems and a variety of provisions pertinent to the union of the former colonies into confederation.

Constitutional exemption: A potential remedy under the *Charter*. Instead of declaring a provision of the *Criminal Code* invalid, a court may rule that it is only unconstitutional in its application to a particular individual in exceptional circumstances. For example, in the *Latimer* case (2001), the accused was found guilty of second degree murder as a consequence of an act of so-called "mercy killing." Section 745 of the *Criminal Code* prescribes a mandatory sentence of life imprisonment (with no eligibility for parole for at least ten years) for second degree murder. The trial judge recognized that the Supreme

Court of Canada had ruled that section 745 does not constitute "cruel and unusual punishment," contrary to the requirements of section 12 of the *Charter*. However, he ruled that life imprisonment *in Latimer's very unusual circumstances* would be "grossly disproportionate" (hence, "cruel and unusual punishment," within the meaning of section 12 of the *Charter*) and he granted Latimer a constitutional exemption from the imposition of the mandatory sentence. Instead, Latimer was sentenced to one year in prison, followed by a one-year period of probation. The Saskatchewan Court of Appeal later ruled that Latimer was not entitled to a constitutional exemption and sentenced him to life imprisonment without eligibility for parole for 10 years. The Supreme Court of Canada upheld the decision of the Court of Appeal in *Latimer* (2001).

Contempt of court: Under section 9 of the *Criminal Code*, courts have the power to convict a person of criminal contempt of court. The term "criminal contempt" covers any wilful conduct on the part of the accused that tends to interfere with the proper administration of justice or to bring it into disrepute. It includes, but is not limited to, the deliberate defiance or disobedience of a court order in a public manner.

Controlled Drugs and Substances Act: The *Controlled Drugs and Substances Act*, S.C. 1996, c. 19 regulates "controlled drugs and substances," such as narcotics (including heroin and cocaine), cannabis, amphetamines, LSD, and barbiturates. Among the most important offences under this Act are possession, trafficking, possession for the purpose of trafficking, importing and exporting, and production of a controlled substance.

Counsel: In Canada, the term refers to the lawyer representing a party in a trial. In criminal cases, Crown counsel represents the Queen (that is to say, he or she is the prosecuting lawyer), whereas defence counsel represents the accused.

Counselling: Section 22(1) of the *Criminal Code* provides that a person who counsels an offence that is actually committed by another person becomes a party to that offence. Section 464 provides that an individual is guilty of the inchoate offence of counselling if he or she counsels another person to commit an offence that is not ultimately perpetrated. The *Code* states that "counsel" includes "procure, solicit or incite."

Crime: A crime consists of conduct that is prohibited because it is considered to have an "evil or injurious or undesirable effect upon the public" and a penalty that may be imposed when the prohibition is violated.

Crimes of specific and general (or basic) intent: According to Justice McIntyre in the case of *Bernard* (1988), a **specific intent offence** is "one which involves the performance of the *actus reus*, coupled with an intent or purpose going beyond the mere performance of the questioned act." Examples are murder (section 235 of the

Criminal Code); assault with intent to wound (section 244); and breaking and entering with intent to commit an indictable offence (section 349(1)(a)). According to Justice McIntyre, **a crime of general (or basic) intent** "is one in which the only intent involved relates solely to the performance of the act in question with no further ulterior intent or purpose." He noted that "the minimal intent to apply force in the offence of common assault affords an example." Another example is the crime of wilful destruction or damage of property (mischief) (see section 430). See also Justice Bastarache's summary of the distinction between specific intent and general (or basic) intent cases in *Daley* (2007): "[S]pecific intent offences require the mind to focus on an objective further to the immediate one at hand, while general intent offences require only a conscious doing of the prohibited act."

Criminal attempt: Section 24 of the *Criminal Code* provides that it is a crime to attempt to commit a criminal offence. In order to gain a conviction of criminal attempt, the Crown must prove that the accused actually intended to commit an offence and that he or she did or omitted to "do anything for the purpose of carrying out his (or her) intention." The accused must have gone beyond "mere preparation" to commit an offence and it is no defence that it would not have been possible to commit the offence in the circumstances.

Criminal Code: The *Criminal Code*, R.S.C. 1985, c. C-46 (first enacted by the Parliament of Canada in 1892) is the most important source of criminal law in Canada. This statute is divided into 28 parts and deals with both substantive criminal law and the procedural law relating to criminal matters.

Criminal law: That area of the law that delineates the rules and principles of culpability for acts and omissions deemed by the state to be crimes.

Criminal negligence: According to s. 219(1) of the *Criminal Code*, a person is criminally negligent if in "doing anything" or "in omitting to anything that it is his (or her) duty to do," he or she "shows wanton or reckless disregard for the lives or safety of other persons." This definition is applicable to the offences of causing death by criminal negligence; causing bodily harm by criminal negligence; and manslaughter by criminal negligence. These are offences that impose **objective *mens rea*** (see below).

Criminal procedure: This term refers to legislation that specifies the procedures to be followed in the prosecution of a criminal case and defines the nature and scope of the powers of criminal justice officials.

Dangerous driving: Section 249(1) of the *Criminal Code* creates the offence of dangerous driving. The Crown must prove that the accused's driving conduct constituted a marked departure from the standard of driving care expected of a reasonable driver acting prudently in the particular circumstances facing the accused. The *mens rea* of the offence is objective but the court must apply the **modified objective test** (see below). The accused must be acquitted if he or she raises a reasonable doubt whether a reasonable person, with the same knowledge of the circumstances, would have appreciated the risk created by the accused person's conduct. The *actus reus* of the offence consists of driving conduct that is dangerous in light of "all the circumstances including the nature, conditions and use of ... (the street, road, highway or other public place) ... at which the motor vehicle is being operated and the amount of traffic that at the time is or might reasonably be expected to be at that place."

De facto: In fact.

Defendant: In a criminal trial, the defendant is the person against whom a criminal charge has been laid and who is, therefore, placed in the position of defending himself or herself against such a charge.

Direct intention: This concept refers to the situation in which an accused person engages in conduct with the unequivocal desire to bring about the consequence(s) prohibited by the criminal law.

Disease of the mind: See **mental disorder**.

Double jeopardy: This refers to the ancient doctrine of the criminal law that accused persons may not be placed twice in jeopardy for the same incident. Therefore, if they are charged again in relation to this incident, they may plead their previous conviction or acquittal as a complete defence to the second charge. The special pleas in question are known as *autrefois convict* and *autrefois acquit*.

Dual offence: See **hybrid (or dual) offence**.

Due diligence: When an accused person is charged with an offence of **strict liability** (see below), he or she may raise the defence that he or she acted with due diligence. In order to gain an acquittal, the accused must prove this defence on the balance of probabilities. Generally, the accused must establish that he or she exercised all reasonable care and took reasonable steps to ensure that the standard of care required by the law was met.

Duress: The common law defence of duress may be raised where the accused person has committed an offence under the threat of death or serious bodily harm by another person. The accused person may be excused from criminal responsibility if he or she had no real choice but to break the law. In the *Ruzic* case (2001), the Supreme Court of Canada held that there are four main requirements of the common law defence of duress: (i) the accused person acted "solely as a result of threats of death, or serious bodily harm"; (ii) "the threats were of such gravity or seriousness that the accused believed that the threats would be carried out"; (iii) "the threats were of such gravity that they might well have caused a reasonable person placed in the same situation as the accused to act in the same manner as she did"; and (iv) "the accused must not have had an obvious safe avenue of escape."

Elevated standard of care: Where an individual is engaging in activities that are so inherently dangerous as to pose a serious risk to the safety of others, the *Criminal Code* may require him or her to meet an "elevated standard of care": this is the standard of care expected of a reasonable person who has acquired the necessary expertise and training to engage in such activities. Examples of situations in which the *Criminal Code* imposes such an elevated standard of care are possession of explosives, use and storage of firearms, and administration of surgical and medical treatment.

Entrapment: This occurs where law enforcement authorities (usually through the agency of undercover officers or paid informers) instigate others to commit criminal offences (primarily those offences involving the sale of illegal drugs) for the purpose of prosecuting them. Although the police are entitled to use undercover methods of investigation, they are not entitled to persuade an individual to commit an offence that he or she would not have committed but for their persistent pressure to do so. If entrapment of this type takes place, an accused person may be granted a stay of proceedings (a direction by the court that criminal proceedings be suspended).

Euthanasia: The literal meaning of euthanasia is "a good death." The word is derived from the Greek language (*eu* = "well or goodly" and *thanatos* = "death"). There are two major categories of euthanasia for the purposes of the criminal law. **Active euthanasia** is the deliberate use of a painless method of death in order to end the suffering of another person. This method may consist of the injection of a fatal amount of a drug by a physician in order to accelerate the death of a terminal patient. **Active euthanasia** is prohibited in Canada and the person who engages in this practice is guilty of murder. **Passive euthanasia** consists of withdrawing medical treatment with the clear understanding that taking this step will accelerate the onset of death from a pre-existing illness. While **active euthanasia** constitutes murder, **passive euthanasia** is not considered to be a crime, provided it is carried out with the *consent* of the individual concerned and that he or she is *competent* to make such a decision.

Evidentiary (or secondary) burden of proof: See **burden of proof.**

Extortion: A person commits the offence of extortion (section 346 of the *Criminal Code*) where he or she, without reasonable justification or excuse and with the intent of obtaining "anything" (e.g., money or property), induces or attempts to induce another person to "do anything or cause anything to be done" by means of "threats, accusations, menaces or violence." In popular terminology, this offence may sometimes be called blackmail.

Factual causation: According to the Supreme Court of Canada in *Nette* (2001), factual causation "is concerned with an inquiry about how the victim came to his or her

death, in a medical, mechanical, or physical sense, and with the contribution of the accused to that result."

Federal criminal law power: Under the *Constitution Act, 1867*, the Parliament of Canada has exclusive jurisdiction in the field of "criminal law and the procedures relating to criminal matters."

First degree murder: Section 231 of the *Criminal Code* indicates the circumstances in which murder will be considered first degree, as opposed to second degree, murder. In general, first degree murder is murder that is both **planned and deliberate** (see below). There are also certain exceptional circumstances in which a murder will automatically be classified as first degree murder, whether or not it is planned and deliberate (e.g., murder of a police officer or murder committed in the course of a sexual assault). The penalty for first degree murder is life imprisonment with no eligibility for parole for 25 years.

Foreseeability (of prohibited consequences): If the consequences of one's actions are foreseeable, it is relatively simple to conclude that there is a causal link between those actions and their consequences. The requirement of foreseeability in criminal law ensures that an accused person's responsibility for his or her actions is not unlimited: he or she may be punished only for prohibited consequences that could reasonably have been foreseen.

Fraud: S. 3 80 of the *Criminal Code* creates the general offence of fraud, which consists of the dishonest deprivation of another person's property. The Crown does not have to prove that the accused person's conduct caused any actual loss to the victim. It is enough that there was "prejudice or risk of prejudice to the economic interest of the victim."

Fraudulently: Section 322(1) of the *Criminal Code* provides that, in order to obtain a conviction for theft, the Crown must prove that the accused took another person's property "fraudulently." This means that the accused must take the property intentionally, under no mistake, and with knowledge that it belongs to someone else. Where the accused takes the property as a prank, the court may hold that he or she did not act fraudulently.

General (or basic) intent offence: According to Justice McIntyre, a crime of general (or basic) intent "is one in which the only intent involved relates solely to the performance of the act in question with no further ulterior intent or purpose." He noted that "the minimal intent to apply force in the offence of common assault affords an example." Another example is the crime of wilful destruction or damage of property (mischief) (see section 430). See also **crimes of specific** and **general (or basic) intent.**

"Halfway house" approach: See **strict liability.**

Hybrid (or dual) offence: An offence that may be prosecuted as an indictable or summary conviction offence, at the discretion of the Crown.

Imaginary crime: An accused person cannot be convicted of attempting to commit or conspiring to commit an imaginary crime. If the accused person attempts or conspires to do something that does not in fact constitute a crime, while nevertheless believing that what he or she has attempted or conspired to do is a crime, then he or she has attempted or conspired to commit an imaginary crime.

Implied consent: In certain circumstances, the existence of implied consent may be a defence to a charge of assault. Individuals who voluntarily participate in contact sports are automatically deemed to have given implied consent to the infliction of a certain degree of force upon their bodies. However, a participant in a contact sport may only be considered to have consented to the application of force that occurs within the bounds of fair play and that is reasonably incidental to the sport in question.

Impossibility: It is not a defence to a charge of criminal attempt or conspiracy that the offence that the accused was attempting or conspiring to commit would have been impossible in the circumstances. For example, it would not be a defence to a charge of criminal attempt that the accused attempted to steal money from a wallet that turned out to be empty.

Improper medical treatment: Improper medical treatment that is not administered in good faith may sever the chain of causation between the wounding of the victim and the victim's ultimate death: in such a case, the accused person would not be considered to have caused the death of the victim.

Inchoate offences: The criminal law does not punish individuals for thinking about committing a crime, but once they start on a course of conduct designed to achieve a criminal goal, they may, in certain circumstances, be convicted of an offence even though that goal is never achieved. These offences are known as inchoate because the accused persons concerned do not complete the crimes that they originally had in mind. The three inchoate offences recognized in Canadian criminal law are (i) attempt, (ii) conspiracy, and (iii) counselling an offence that is not committed.

Indictable offence: Indictable offences are, generally, the most serious criminal offences. Furthermore, those indictable offences that are considered to be particularly serious in nature may only be tried in the superior court of criminal jurisdiction. An indictment (from which the indictable offence takes its name) is a formal document that sets out the charge(s) against the accused and is signed by the attorney general or his or her agent.

Indirect intention: This concept refers to the situation in which an accused person does not desire to bring about the consequences prohibited by the criminal law but is nevertheless considered to have intended them.

Infanticide: According to section 233 of the *Criminal Code*, "A female person commits infanticide when by a wilful act or omission she causes the death of her newly-born child, if at the time of the act or omission she is not fully recovered from the effects of giving birth to the child and by reason thereof or of the effect of lactation consequent on the birth of the child her mind is then disturbed." In section 2 of the *Code*, a "newly-born child" is defined as "a person under the age of one year." The maximum sentence on conviction is five years' imprisonment.

Injunction: A court order prohibiting or requiring action.

Intention: According to Justice Dickson in the *Lewis* case (1979), intention means "the exercise of a free will to use particular means to produce a particular result."

Inter alia: Among others.

Intervening act: In certain circumstances, an intervening act may sever the chain of causation between the defendant's original wounding of the victim and the latter's subsequent death. Where this occurs, the defendant will not be held responsible for having committed a culpable homicide. However, even if there is an intervening act, the Crown may still obtain a conviction if it can show that the original wound inflicted by the accused was "operative" (or continuing to have some impact) at the time of the victim's death.

Intra: Within; inside.

Intra vires: Within the power of.

Legal causation: According to the Supreme Court of Canada in *Nette* (2001), legal causation "is concerned with the question of whether the accused person should be held responsible in law for the death that occurred." See also **factual causation**.

Major depressive disorder: According to the American Psychiatric Association's *Diagnostic and Statistical Manual of Mental Disorders*, 4th ed., Text Revision (2000), this mental disorder is "characterized by one or more Major Depressive Episodes (i.e., at least two weeks of depressed mood or loss of interest accompanied by at least four additional symptoms of depression)."

Manslaughter: Generally, this offence involves the commission of an unintentional homicide. The *mens rea* for the offence is generally objective in nature: either the Crown must establish that the accused's conduct amounted to a "marked and substantial departure from the standard of care expected of a reasonable person acting prudently" (manslaughter by criminal negligence) or that the accused killed the victim in the course of committing an offence (such as an assault) that a "reasonable person would have foreseen as being likely to cause non-trivial bodily harm" (**unlawful act manslaughter**). The successful use of the defence of provocation (section 232 of the *Code*) may result in an accused being convicted of manslaughter rather than murder, even though he or she intended to kill the victim; this is an exception to the general rule that manslaughter involves the commission of an unintentional homicide.

Marked departure test: When the *Criminal Code* imposes objective liability for such offences as dangerous driving or criminal negligence causing death or bodily harm, the Crown must prove that the accused person's conduct constituted a marked departure from the standard of care expected of a reasonable person acting prudently in the particular circumstances facing the accused person.

Mens rea: This concept refers to those mental elements (other than voluntariness) contained in the definition of any particular criminal offence that the Crown must prove before an accused person may be convicted of that offence.

Mental disorder: According to section 2 of the *Criminal Code*, this means "a disease of the mind." The Supreme Court of Canada approved the following definition in the *Rabey* case (1980): "Any malfunctioning of the mind having its source primarily in some subjective condition or weakness internal to the accused (whether fully understood or not) may be a 'disease of the mind' if it prevents the accused from knowing what he is doing, but transient disturbances of consciousness due to specific external factors do not fall within the concept of disease of the mind." Section 16 of the *Criminal Code* provides that an accused person will not be found criminally responsible if, as a consequence of a mental disorder, he or she lacks the capacity to appreciate the nature and quality of his or her conduct or to know that the average person would regard the conduct as morally wrong. See Chapter 8.

Mistake of fact: An accused person will generally be entitled to an acquittal if he or she operated under a mistaken belief as to one or more of the material circumstances surrounding the alleged crime. Where the accused person honestly believes in a state of facts, which, if they were true, would not constitute an offence, then he or she lacks the *mens rea* necessary for the crime with which he or she has been charged.

Mistake of law: Section 19 of the *Criminal Code* makes it clear that ignorance of the law is no defence to a criminal charge. Neither a mistaken interpretation of the law nor complete ignorance as to the existence of a particular law is a valid defence. However, the courts have ruled that section 19 only applies to mistakes concerning the criminal law: mistakes as to the civil law may give rise to a valid defence (e.g., a mistake as to whether a custody order is valid).

Modified objective test: The courts have ruled that certain offences, such as dangerous driving, criminal negligence causing death or bodily harm, and manslaughter, impose objective liability on an accused person. The Crown must prove that the accused person's conduct amounted to a marked departure from the standard of care expected of a reasonable person acting prudently. However, the Supreme Court of Canada has ruled that the test is not purely objective in the sense that the courts must take into account the particular circumstances facing the accused person and his or her perception of those circumstances. The modified objective test requires that the court ask whether a reasonable person, with the knowledge that the accused person had of the relevant circumstances, would have realized the risk that his or her conduct created and would have refrained from taking such a risk.

Motive: The reason for, or explanation of, a person's conduct. Generally, the *mens rea* requirements for conviction of criminal offences do not include any reference to the accused's motive. For example, a person may intend to kill another human being, and thereby commit the crime of murder, even though some people might consider that there is a laudable motive for killing the victim (e.g., "mercy killing").

Murder: This offence involves the commission of a homicide by a person who intends to kill his or her victim or who subjectively foresees that his or her conduct is likely to cause death. Section 229 of the *Criminal Code* indicates that murder is committed where (i) the accused intends to kill; (ii) the accused intends to inflict bodily harm that he or she knows is likely to cause death and is reckless whether death ensues or not; or (iii) the accused, for an unlawful object, does anything that he or she subjectively knows is likely to cause death and does thereby cause death notwithstanding that he or she wishes to achieve the unlawful object without causing death or bodily harm. (In this context, unlawful object refers to "the object of conduct, which, if prosecuted fully, would amount to a serious crime that is an indictable offence requiring *mens rea*.") There are two categories of this offence: **first degree murder** and **second degree murder.**

Nature and quality of the act or omission: Section 16(1) of the *Criminal Code* provides that an accused person must be found NCRMD if, at the time of the alleged offence, he or she had a mental disorder that rendered him or her "incapable of appreciating the nature and quality of the act or omission." "Nature and quality of the act or omission" refers exclusively to the *physical* nature and quality of the act or omission.

NCRMD: This is the common abbreviation of the verdict of "not criminally responsible on account of mental disorder" (section 672.34 of the *Criminal Code*). In order to be found NCRMD, the accused must prove that the criteria, established in section 16(1) of the *Code*, have been met. According to section 672.1 of the *Code*, a verdict of NCRMD "means that the accused committed the act or made the omission that formed the basis of the offence with which the accused is charged but is not criminally responsible on account of mental disorder."

Necessity: The common law defence of necessity arises where the accused can only avoid some imminent disaster or calamity by breaking the law. In advancing the defence of necessity, the accused is basically asserting that the evil that he or she sought to avoid was greater than the evil inherent in the breaking of the law. In essence, the accused person asserts that he or she should be excused from criminal responsibility because the decision to break the law was dictated by necessity and was, therefore, not a free choice. The defence will not be successful if the accused had a reasonable legal alternative to breaking the law.

Negligence: In criminal law, negligence is a form of objective *mens rea*. A person is negligent when his or her conduct falls below the standard of care expected of a reasonable person acting prudently. Negligence may be a sufficient form of *mens rea* to convict an accused person of certain *Criminal Code* offences, but only if that person's conduct amounts to a marked and substantial departure from the standard of care expected of a reasonable person facing the same circumstances as the accused. Only the most serious incidents of negligence will justify the accused's conviction of a true crime; such negligence may be called criminal (or penal) negligence.

Normative involuntariness: The rationale underlying the defences of **duress** and **necessity** is that the accused person had no real choice but to break the law. The Supreme Court of Canada has referred to this rationale as "normative involuntariness"—the notion that, in a moral sense, the accused person acted involuntarily.

***Oakes* test:**   The test, developed by the Supreme Court of Canada in the *Oakes* case (1986), in order to establish whether a limit placed on a *Charter* right or freedom can be justified under section 1 of the *Charter*. The test consists of two parts. The first requirement is that the objective of the impugned legislation imposing a limit on a right or freedom must be of "sufficient importance to warrant overriding a constitutionally protected right or freedom." In this respect, the legislative objective must "relate to concerns which are pressing and substantial in a free and democratic society before it can be characterized as sufficiently important." Second, the means chosen to implement the legislative objective must be "reasonable and demonstrably justified." This involves a "form of proportionality test": are the means chosen proportional to the objective that the legislation seeks to implement?

Objective *mens rea*:   Offences requiring proof of objective *mens rea* impose on the Crown the burden of establishing that a reasonable person would have appreciated the risk created by the accused's conduct and would have chosen not to take that risk. Objective *mens rea* is not concerned with what actually went on in the accused's mind at the time of the alleged offence, but rather with what the reasonable person would have known if placed in exactly the same circumstances as the accused. The fault of the accused lies in the failure to direct his or her mind to a risk the reasonable person would have appreciated.

Officially induced error: As a general rule, a mistake of law is not a valid defence to a criminal charge. However, a defence may be available in the case of "officially induced error." This defence may be raised successfully where the accused person has been charged with a violation of a regulatory statute and has reasonably relied on the erroneous legal opinion or legal advice of an official who is responsible for the administration or enforcement of the law in question.

Omission: The general principle in Canadian criminal law is that an accused person may not be convicted on the basis of a mere omission (a failure to act) unless he or she is under a prior (legal) duty to act.

Ordinary person: In order to establish the defence of **provocation**, it must be shown that the provocation was "of such a nature as to be sufficient to deprive an ordinary person of the power of self-control." In the *Thibert* case (1996), the Supreme Court of Canada held that "the ordinary person must be taken to be of the same age, and sex, and must share with the accused such other factors as would give the act or insult in question a particular significance."

Palliative care: Drug or other medical treatment designed to alleviate pain without curing the condition that causes the pain. The term is most commonly applied to the treatment administered to patients who have terminal illnesses.

Partial defence: Some defences operate to reduce the severity of the charge, of which the accused is ultimately convicted, instead of absolving the accused of all criminal responsibility whatsoever. For example, a successful plea of **provocation** merely reduces the charge of which the accused is convicted from one of **murder** to one of **manslaughter**. By way of contrast, if the accused successfully argues **self-defence** under section 34(2) of the *Criminal Code*, he or she is entitled to be absolved of all criminal responsibility; in this sense, self-defence is a complete defence.

Party to a criminal offence: There are a number of ways in which an individual may become a party to a criminal offence: (i) actually committing an offence; (ii) **aiding** and/or **abetting** an offence committed by another person; (iii) becoming a party to an offence by virtue of **common intention**; and (iv) **counselling** an offence that is actually committed by another person.

Passive euthanasia: See **euthanasia**.

Peaceable possession: In certain circumstances, sections 38 to 41 of the *Criminal Code* permit an individual who is in "peaceable possession" of property to use force in defence of that property. In this context, "peaceable possession" means possession "that is not seriously challenged by others."

Per se: In or of itself.

Person who actually commits an offence: Section 21(1) of the *Criminal Code* states that a person is a party to a criminal offence if he or she "actually commits it." This person is sometimes referred to as the **principal** or the perpetrator of the offence. He or she will nearly always be physically present at the scene of the crime but, in exceptional circumstances, may act through an innocent agent. For example, the accused person may have persuaded a small child to administer a fatal dose of poison to the victim. The accused person would be considered to have actually committed the offence of murder through an innocent agent (the child).

Personality disorder: A form of mental disorder in which the affected individual maintains a "good grip on reality" but whose behaviour and ways of thinking about his or her environment are considered as abnormal or deviant. In the context of criminal behaviour, the most relevant of these disorders is the antisocial personality disorder. According to the American Psychiatric Association's *Diagnostic and Statistical Manual of Mental Disorders*, 4th ed., Text Revision (2000), the essential feature of antisocial personality disorder is a "pervasive pattern of disregard for, and violation of, the rights of others that begins in childhood or early adolescence and continues into adulthood." Such conduct may bring an individual affected by this disorder into conflict with criminal justice authorities.

Persuasional or **primary burden of proof:** See **burden of proof**.

Planned and deliberate: Section 231(2) of the *Criminal Code* states that first degree murder is murder that is "planned and deliberate." This term means that the accused must act on a previously formulated plan and that his or her conduct must not be impulsive.

Precedent: A previous decision or judgment of a court that is referred to as an authority that should be followed by a judge in a similar factual situation.

Prima facie: At first sight; on the face of it. A *prima facie* case is literally one that will suffice until contradicted and overcome by other evidence.

Primary or **persuasional burden of proof:** See **burden of proof**.

Primary source of law: A main source of law, including statutes and case law in the Canadian legal system.

Principal: This refers to the person who "actually commits" a criminal offence as opposed to those individuals who become parties to the offence on some other basis (such as aiding and abetting).

Provocation: Section 232 of the *Criminal Code* provides that culpable homicide that would otherwise be murder may be reduced to manslaughter if the accused person who committed the homicide did so "in the heat of passion caused by sudden provocation." It must be established that there was a wrongful act or omission that would be sufficient to deprive "an ordinary person of the power of self-control" and that the accused person acted on the provocation "on the sudden and before there was time for his [or her] passion to cool."

Psychopath: An individual who shares many of the characteristics of those individuals who suffer from antisocial personality disorder. Although there is considerable debate as to the precise nature of psychopathy, psychopaths may be characterized by a lack of sound judgment, an inability to learn from previous experience, a lack of remorse or guilt for anything that they do in violation of the rights of others, and a lack of capacity to understand how others see them. However, a psychopath does not lose contact with reality in the sense that a person who has schizophrenia may do.

Psychosis: A mental disorder that is characterized by profound disturbances in a person's thoughts, emotions, and ability to perceive reality (e.g., schizophrenia).

Quasi: Seeming, not real, half-way, almost as if it were, analogous to.

Quasi-criminal law: Refers to regulatory offences as opposed to true crimes.

Re: In the matter of; with reference to.

Reasonable steps: Section 273.2 of the *Criminal Code* states that a person who is charged with sexual assault may not raise the defence of mistaken belief that the complainant consented to sexual activity unless the accused person can raise a reasonable doubt that he or she took "reasonable steps in the circumstances known to the accused at the time, to ascertain that the complainant was consenting." Reasonable steps are the steps that a reasonable person acting prudently would take in light of the specific knowledge of the surrounding circumstances that the accused person had at the time of the alleged offence.

Recklessness: This is a form of subjective *mens rea*. It arises where the accused subjectively knows that his or her conduct creates a risk that certain prohibited consequences will occur but nevertheless persists in that course of conduct when a reasonable person would not do so.

Regulation: Subordinate legislation, usually promulgated by a Cabinet minister under the authority of a statute granting the authority to create such legislation.

Regulatory offence: This is an offence arising under regulatory legislation (federal, provincial/territorial, or municipal). Such legislation deals with the regulation of inherently legitimate activities connected with commerce, trade, and industry or with such everyday matters as driving, hunting, fishing, and so forth. Regulatory offences are, generally, not considered to be serious in nature and usually result in the imposition of only a relatively minor penalty.

Respondent: Literally, this is the party who "responds" when an appeal is launched against the decision of a lower court by the other party to a criminal case (who is known, formally, as the appellant).

Review board: The special tribunal that has been established in each province (under Part XX.1 of the *Criminal Code*) in order to make or review decisions as to what should happen to those who have been found NCRMD ("not criminally responsible on account of mental disorder"). The dispositional alternatives available to the review board are an absolute discharge, a conditional discharge, or an order that the NCR accused person be held in custody in a psychiatric facility.

Safe avenue of escape: When an accused person raises the defence of duress, it must be established that he or she did not have an "obvious safe avenue of escape." If a reasonable person—with the same knowledge that the accused had of the surrounding circumstances—would have taken the opportunity to escape, then the defence would fail.

Schizoaffective disorder: A mental condition in which there are symptoms of both schizophrenia (see below) and an affective (or mood) disorder, such as depression or mania.

Schizophrenia: Refers to a group of severe mental disorders in which an individual may experience incoherence in thought and speech, hallucinations, delusions, and inappropriate emotional responses.

Secondary or **evidentiary burden of proof:** See **burden of proof.**

Second degree murder: Murder that is not first degree murder is second degree murder (section 231(7) of the *Criminal Code*). Where an individual is convicted of second degree murder, the automatic penalty is life imprisonment (section 745(c)). Section 745.4 of the *Code* provides that the trial judge may set a period of non-eligibility for parole ranging from a minimum of 10 years to a maximum of 25 years. If the accused has previously been convicted of culpable homicide, then the penalty is life imprisonment with no eligibility for parole for 25 years (section 745(b)).

Self-defence: The *Criminal Code* provides that, in certain circumstances, an individual may justifiably use force in self-defence. The most important provision that defines the defence of self-defence is section 34. Section 34(1) applies where the accused person was the victim of an unlawful and unprovoked assault and did not intend to inflict death or grievous bodily harm. Under section 34(1), the force used by the accused person must be proportionate to the force or threat of force used against him or her. Section 34(2) applies where the accused was the victim of an unlawful assault and inflicted death or grievous bodily harm. Under this provision, the defence of self-defence will be successful if the accused person acted "under reasonable apprehension of death or grievous bodily harm from the violence with which the assault was originally made or with which the assailant pursues his purposes" and if he or she "believes, on reasonable grounds, that he (or she) cannot otherwise preserve himself from death or grievous bodily harm."

Sources of criminal law: The primary sources of criminal law are (i) legislation and (ii) judicial decisions that either interpret such legislation or state the "**common law.**"

Specific intent offence: According to Justice McIntyre in the case of *Bernard* (1988), "one which involves the performance of the *actus reus*, coupled with an intent or purpose going beyond the mere performance of the questioned act." Examples are murder (section 235 of the *Criminal Code*); assault with intent to wound (section 244); and breaking and entering with intent to commit an indictable offence (section 349(1)(a)). See also **crimes of specific** and **general (or basic) intent**.

Standard of proof: See **burden of proof.**

Strict liability: In the context of criminal law, this form of liability may be imposed in relation to various regulatory offences arising under both federal and provincial/ territorial regulatory legislation. The Crown may obtain a conviction for a violation of such legislation without having to prove *mens rea* on the part of the accused. However, the accused may avoid liability by proving that he or she acted with "due diligence" in all the circumstances. Strict liability is sometimes referred to as the "half-way house solution" to the problem of finding an efficacious, yet fair, method of prosecuting regulatory offences.

Subjective *mens rea*: Offences that require proof of subjective mens rea impose on the Crown the burden of establishing that the accused intended the consequences of his or her conduct or that, knowing of the probable consequences of such conduct, the accused proceeded in reckless disregard of that risk, or that the accused was wilfully blind. Subjective mens rea is concerned with what actually went on in the accused's mind.

Substantial and integral cause: The special test of causation that applies exclusively to first degree murder under section 231(5) and (6) of the *Criminal Code*.

Substantive criminal law: This term refers to legislation that defines the nature of various criminal offences (such as murder, manslaughter, and theft) and specifies the various legal elements that must be present before a conviction can be entered against an accused person. The term also refers to legislation that defines the nature and scope of various defences (such as provocation, duress, and self-defence).

Sudden provocation: The defence of **provocation** may only be raised where the accused person responds to sudden provocation. If the accused person initiated the fatal altercation with the victim, the defence will fail.

Summary conviction offence: Generally, summary conviction offences are less serious in nature and may only be tried before a provincial court judge. These offences may be created by both federal and provincial/territorial legislation.

Transferred intent: Where A intends to strike B but misses and strikes C, he or she may be convicted of assault on the basis of the doctrine of transferred intent. A intends to commit the *actus reus* of assault but actually commits the *actus reus* of assault in a way other than he or she intended (that is, by striking the "wrong" victim). The *mens rea* for the *actus reus* of the assault that did not happen (the assault of B) is transferred to the *actus reus* of the assault that did occur (the assault of C). The doctrine applies to a number of offences (such as murder and the various types of assault in the *Criminal Code*), but it only operates within the confines of the same offence. For example, an intention to wound an animal cannot be transferred to the *actus reus* of assault of a human being, where the accused aims to strike a dog but instead strikes a person.

Trespass: The unlawful interference with another's property, person, or rights.

Trespasser: For the purposes of the criminal law, a trespasser is one who unlawfully enters another person's land, residence, or any other building. An individual who was originally invited to enter another person's property as a guest becomes a trespasser if, after having been requested to leave, does not do so within a reasonable period. Section 41 of the *Criminal Code* provides that a person in ***peaceable possession*** (see above) of a dwelling-house may use force to prevent a trespasser from entering the dwelling-house or to remove a trespasser from the dwelling-house provided he or she uses "no more force than is necessary." A trespasser who actively resists an attempt to prevent him or her from entering a dwelling-house or to remove him or her from a dwelling house will be deemed to "commit an assault without justification or provocation" and the occupier of the dwelling-house may be able to raise the defence of self defence under section 34(1) of the *Criminal Code*.

Trier of fact: The party responsible for deciding the facts in a trial. In the case of a jury trial, the members of the jury are the triers of fact and the judge is responsible for making decisions about the applicable law. Where the trial judge sits without a jury, then he or she is the trier of fact as well as the ultimate arbiter of the law.

True crimes: While **regulatory offences** are concerned with the regulation of inherently legitimate activities, true crimes are offences that represent a serious breach of community values and are considered to be both "wrong" and deserving of punishment. In general, true crimes consist of those offences contained in the *Criminal Code* as well as the serious offences contained in the *Controlled Drugs and Substances Act* (which is concerned with the punishment of those who are involved with the use of illegal drugs). The Law Reform Commission of Canada used a similar term to describe such offences, namely, real crimes.

Ultra vires: Beyond the powers of.

Unlawful act manslaughter: See **manslaughter**.

Unlawfully causing bodily harm: This offence is defined by section 269 of the *Criminal Code*. The *actus reus* consists of unlawful conduct by the accused person that causes bodily harm. The unlawful conduct must amount to an offence under either federal or provincial legislation. The *mens rea* is objective in nature: the Crown must prove that a reasonable person, facing the same circumstances as the accused, would have foreseen the risk of non-trivial bodily harm.

Unprovoked assault: When raising the defence of **self-defence** (see above), under section 34(1) of the *Criminal Code*, it must be established that the accused person was the victim of an unprovoked assault. Section 36 states that, for the purposes of section 34, provocation includes "provocation by blows, words or gestures."

Voluntariness: This concept refers to the basic requirement of the criminal law that an accused person's conduct be the product of his or her own free will. It is a fundamental requirement of the ***actus reus*** of an offence: where there is no voluntary action (e.g., because the accused is in a state of automatism), there is no ***actus reus*** and the accused must be acquitted. In addition, the issue of voluntariness may be particularly relevant to the establishment of certain defences. For example, the assertion that the accused was not able to make a genuinely free choice as to whether or not to break the law may constitute valid grounds for raising the defences of **duress** or **necessity** (here, the criminal law makes reference to **normative involuntariness** as the basis for recognizing these defences).

Wilful blindness: This form of ***subjective mens rea*** exists when an accused person is virtually certain that particular circumstances exist (for example, that goods are stolen) but deliberately "shuts his or her eyes" to these circumstances. The Crown must establish that the particular accused person had become subjectively aware of the need to make an inquiry as to the relevant circumstances but deliberately refrains from making the inquiry because he or she does not want to know the truth. Wilful blindness is treated as being equivalent to actual knowledge.

Wrong: Section 16(1) of the *Criminal Code* provides that an accused person must be found to be NCMD if, at the time of the alleged offence, he or she was suffering from a mental disorder that rendered him or her incapable of knowing that the act or omission in question was "wrong." In this context, "wrong" means morally wrong or "wrong according to the everyday standards of the reasonable person."

INDEX OF CASES

INDEX